Lecture Notes in Computer Scienc

Commenced Publication in 1973
Founding and Former Series Editors:
Gerhard Goos, Juris Hartmanis, and Jan van Leeuwen

Editorial Board

Khalid Saeed   Václav Snášel (Eds.)

Computer Information Systems and Industrial Management

13th IFIP TC8 International Conference, CISIM 2014
Ho Chi Minh City, Vietnam, November 5-7, 2014
Proceedings

 Springer

Volume Editors

Khalid Saeed
AGH University of Science and Technology
Faculty of Physics and Applied Computer Science
Mickiewicza 30, 30059 Krakow, Poland
E-mail: saeed@agh.edu.pl

Václav Snášel
VŠB-Technical University of Ostrava
Faculty of Electrical Engineering and Computer Science
17. listopadu 15, 70833 Ostrava-Poruba, Czech Republic
E-mail: vaclav.snasel@vsb.cz

ISSN 0302-9743   e-ISSN 1611-3349
ISBN 978-3-662-45236-3   e-ISBN 978-3-662-45237-0
DOI 10.1007/978-3-662-45237-0
Springer Heidelberg New York Dordrecht London

Library of Congress Control Number: 2014951535

LNCS Sublibrary: SL 3 – Information Systems and Application, incl. Internet/Web and HCI

Typesetting: Camera-ready by author, data conversion by Scientific Publishing Services, Chennai, India

Printed on acid-free paper

Springer is part of Springer Science+Business Media (www.springer.com)

Preface

CISIM 2014 was the 13th of a series of conferences dedicated to computer information systems and industrial management applications. The conference was supported by IFIP TC8 Information Systems. This year it was held during November 5–7, 2014, in Ho Chi Minh City, Vietnam, at Ton Duc Thang University.

Over 100 papers were submitted to CISIM by researchers and scientists from universities around the world. Each paper was assigned to three reviewers initially, and in case of conflicting decisions, another expert's review was sought for a number of papers. In total, about 300 reviews were collected from the reviewers for the submitted papers. Because of the strict restrictions of Springer's *Lecture Notes in Computer Science* series, the number of accepted papers was limited. Furthermore, a number of electronic discussions were held between the Program Committee (PC) chairs to decide about papers with conflicting reviews and to reach a consensus. After the discussions, the PC chairs decided to accept for publication in the proceedings book about 60% of the total submitted papers.

The main topics covered by the chapters in this book are biometrics, security systems, multimedia, classification and clustering with application, and industrial management. Besides these, the reader will find interesting papers on computer information systems as applied to wireless networks, computer graphics, and intelligent systems.

We are grateful to the three esteemed speakers for their keynote addresses. The authors of the keynote talks were Profs. Sushmita Mitra, (Machine Intelligence Unit, Indian Statistical Institute, Kolkata) Jaroslav Pokorný (Charles University, Prague, Czech Republic) and Ngoc Thanh Nguyen (Wroclaw University of Technology, Poland). We sincerely believe that the technical papers are well complemented by these keynote lectures covering state-of-the-art research challenges and solutions.

We would like to thank all the members of the PC, and the external reviewers for their dedicated effort in the paper selection process. We also thank the honorary chairs of the conference, Profs. Ryszard Tadeusiewicz, Danh Le Vinh, and Ivo Vondrák.

Special thanks are extended to the members of the Organizing Committee and the Springer team for their great efforts to make the conference another success. We are also grateful to Andrei Voronkov, whose EasyChair system eased the submission and selection process and greatly supported the compilation of the proceedings.

We hope that the reader's expectations will be met and that the participants enjoyed their stay in the beautiful city of Ho Chi Minh.

September 2014

Khalid Saeed
Václav Snášel

Message from the Host University

Welcome to the 14th International Conference on Computer Information Systems and Industrial Information Applications (CISIM 2014), held at Ton Duc Thang University, Vietnam! This conference aims at offering a forum for scientists, researchers, and managers from universities and companies to share their research findings and experiences in the field. In recognition of its special meaning and broad influence, we consider the organization of this conference as one of our strategic activities toward developing within three decades an applied research university.

Ton Duc Thang University (TDTU) has always described itself as a young yet aspiring and dynamically growing higher education institution in vibrant Ho Chi Minh City. It is steadily growing to meet the expanding demand for higher education as well as high-quality human resources in Vietnam. With fourteen faculties and around 25,000 students, the University is now ranked among the largest and fastest developing universities in Vietnam in all aspects.

On behalf of TDTU, the host institution of CISIM 2014, I would like to express my sincere appreciation to our great partners – VŠB-Technical University of Ostrava and the University of Science and Technology AGH – for their great effort in organizing this conference. I would also like to send my special thanks to conference committees, track chairs, reviewers, speakers, and authors around the world for their contributions to and interest in our event.

I believe that you will have an interesting and fruitful conference in Vietnam. I really look forward to welcoming all of you at our campus and hope that this conference will start a long term partnership between you and our university.

September 2014

Prof. Le Vinh Danh, Ph.D.
President
Ton Duc Thang University

Organization

Program Committee

Waleed Abdulla	University of Auckland, New Zealand
Raid Al-Tahir	The University of the West Indies St. Augustine, Trinidad and Tobago
Adrian Atanasiu	Bucharest University, Romania
Rahma Boucetta	National Engineering School of Gabes, Tunisia
Le Hoai Bac	University of Science, HCMC, Vietnam
Lam Thu Bui	Le Quy Don Technical University, Vietnam
Nabendu Chaki	Calcutta University, India
Rituparna Chaki	Calcutta University, India
Ryszard Choraś	ITTI Ltd., Poznan, Poland
Agostino Cortesi	Ca' Foscari University of Venice, Italy
Pierpaolo Degano	University of Pisa, Italy
Jan Devos	Ghent University, Belgium
Jiří Dvorský	VŠB-Technical University of Ostrava, Czech Republic
Pietro Ferrara	IBM T.J. Watson Research Center, USA
Raju Halder	Ca' Foscari University of Venice, Italy
Kaoru Hirota	Tokyo Institute of Technology, Japan
Wladyslaw Homenda	Warsaw University of Technology, Poland
Dong Hwa Kim	Hanbat National University, Korea
Ryszard Kozera	The University of Western Australia, Australia
Flaminia Luccio	Ca' Foscari University of Venice, Italy
Jan Martinovič	VŠB-Technical University of Ostrava, Czech Republic
Romuald Mosdorf	Technical University of Białystok, Poland
Debajyoti Mukhopadhyay	Maharashtra Institute of Technology, India
Yuko Murayama	Iwate University, Japan
Hien Thanh Nguyen	Ton Duc Thang University, Vietnam
Nobuyuki Nishiuchi	Tokyo Metropolitan University, Japan
Andrzej Pacut	Technical University of Warsaw, Poland
Jerzy Pejaś	West Pomeranian University of Technology in Szczecin, Poland
Piotr Porwik	University of Silesia, Poland
Jan Pries-Heje	Ghent University, Denmark
Tho Thanh Quan	Ho Chi Minh University of Technology, Vietnam
Isabel Ramos	University of Minho, Portugal

Khalid Saeed	AGH Kraków, Poland
Anirban Sarkar	National Institute of Technology, Durgapore, India
Kateřina Slaninová	VŠB-Technical University of Ostrava, Czech Republic
Krzysztof Ślot	Lodz University of Technology, Poland
Václav Snášel	VŠB-Technical University of Ostrava, Czech Republic
Andrea Torsello	Ca' Foscari University of Venice, Italy
Dao Trong Tran	Ton Duc Thang University, Vietnam
Nitin Upadhyay	BITS Pilani, India
Bay Dinh Vo	Ton Duc Thang University, Vietnam
Sławomir Wierzchoń	Polish Academy of Sciences, Warsaw, Poland
Michał Woźniak	Wroclaw University of Technology, Poland
Ivan Zelinka	VŠB-Technical University of Ostrava, Czech Republic

Additional Reviewers

Marcin Adamski	Białystok Technical University, Poland
Mohammed Chadli	Université de Picardie Jules Verne, France
Pavla Dráždilová	VŠB-Technical University of Ostrava, Czech Republic
Wu Jie	Hubei University of Technology, China
Jiří Koziorek	VŠB-Technical University of Ostrava, Czech Republic
Štěpán Kuchař	VŠB-Technical University of Ostrava, Czech Republic
Marek Penhaker	VŠB-Technical University of Ostrava, Czech Republic
Michal Pluháček	Tomas Bata University in Zlín, Czech Republic
Antonio Portero	VŠB-Technical University of Ostrava, Czech Republic
Mariusz Rybnik	Białystok Technical University, Poland
Miroslav Svítek	Czech Technical University, Czech Republic
Marek Ščerba	Transport Research Centre, Czech Republic
Roman Šenkeřík	Tomas Bata University in Zlín, Czech Republic
Svatopluk Štolfa	VŠB-Technical University of Ostrava, Czech Republic
Marek Tabędzki	Białystok Technical University, Poland
Katarzyna Wegrzyn-Wolska	ESIGETEL, France

Sponsoring Institutions

Ton Duc Thang University

Technical University of Ostrava

AGH University of Science and Technology

IT4Innovations
national
supercomputing
center

European Cooperation Center

Table of Contents

Biometrics and Biometrics Applications

Data Analysis and Information Retrieval

Industrial Management and Other Applications

Modelling and Optimization

Networking

Pattern Recognition and Image Processing

Various Aspects of Computer Security

Processing Collective Knowledge – Conflict Resolution and Integration Aspects

(Keynote Speech)

Ngoc Thanh Nguyen

Wroclaw University of Technology, Poland
ngoc-thanh.nguyen@pwr.edu.pl
Ton Duc Thang Univerisity, Vietnam

Abstract. In this talk we will present a framework for integrating knowledge of a collective and processing the inconsistency. The model for inconsistency of knowledge and knowledge integration using different structures like logical and ontological will also be presented and analyzed. We will show that inconsistency plays an important role in the quality of collective knowledge.

Keywords: Collective intelligence, collective knowledge, knowledge integration.

1   Collective Knowledge

Nowadays it happens very often that for making a decision we rely on knowledge originating from different and autonomous sources, for example, from experts or Internet. To make the use of this kind of knowledge, one has to integrate it. Taking into account the fact that very often the amount of knowledge is very large and its inconsistency, the integration process is a complex task. To make the process effective, a mechanism for inconsistency resolution is needed to be worked out.

A collective is understood as a set of some intelligent units which are autonomous in decision making. Each of them is assumed to have its own knowledge base and a mechanism for its processing. Collective intelligence, among others, deals with determining the knowledge of a collective which is consistent and complete in the sense that it should contain all elements not belonging to the knowledge of particular collective members, but can be inferred on the basis of knowledge of them. Methods for processing knowledge in collectives are more and more needed because of rapidly increasing of the number of autonomous sources of knowledge, for example in Internet. The knowledge originating from these sources is often inconsistent. For this process the methodologies for conflict resolution and knowledge integration seem to be very useful.

Collective knowledge on some subject is assigned to a collective which members have their own knowledge on this subject. Thus collective knowledge should be determined on the basis of the knowledge of its members. This process is called

K. Saeed and V. Snášel (Eds.): CISIM 2014, LNCS 8838, pp. 1–4, 2014.

the integration process. Taking into account the possibility of inconsistency of knowledge of the collective members one should take care of conflict resolution process during integration. Consensus methods have been proved to be very useful for determining collective knowledge [4], [5].

A general mathematical model based on distance spaces for analysis the dependence of collective members' knowledge on the knowledge of the collective has been proposed in [6], [9]. We have proved that in many cases the quality of collective knowledge is better than the quality of members' knowledge.

2   Inconsistency Aspect of Collective Knowledge

By a conflict situation we understand a set of data versions representing different opinions of collective members on some matter. Methods for conflict resolving depends on the structure of knowledge. In work [5] a general model for processing conflict has been proposed. This model is based on distance space of objects representing knowledge states of collective members. Next a set of inconsistency functions have been defined and analyzed. We have worked out several methods for:

- Conflict resolution in ontology integration on levels of instances, concepts and relationships between concepts [7], [8].
- Conflict resolution for logic structure of knowledge [5].
- Conflict resolution for relational structure of knowledge [5].

In works [6] and [9] we have proved that inconsistency can have an essential influence on the quality of collective knowledge. Concretely, the higher is the inconsistency degree the higher is the quality.

One of very important of collective knowledge is that it is not a normal "sum" of knowledge of its members, but often contains more knowledge. We have defined a function which for each collective assigns a value representing additional knowledge referring to the "sum" of knowledge of collective members.

3   Integration Computing

Integration is a process in which one of the following aspects should be realized:

- Several objects are merged to give a new element representing them.
- Several objects create a union acting as a whole.
- Determining a set of correspondences between on object and another one.

The first two aspects are most important and most popular [1], [2]. The third aspect refers mostly to ontology alignment [10]. In general, it is assumed that all objects to be included in an integration task have the same kind of structures. The kinds of structures mean for example logical, ontological, hierarchical, relational etc. For the first and the second aspects the following general criteria are the most popular [6]:

- All data included in the elements to be integrated should be in the result of integration. This condition guarantees the completeness, that is all information included in the component elements will appear in the integration result.
- All conflicts appearing among elements to be integrated should be solved. It often happens that referring to the same subject different elements contain inconsistent information. The integration result should not contain inconsistency, so the conflicts should be solved.
- The kind of structure of the integration result should be the same as of the given elements.

We have worked out methods for integrating knowledge for the following structures:

- Ontology integration and alignment on levels of instances, concepts and relationships between concepts [10], [12].
- Conflict resolution for logic structure of knowledge [5].
- Conflict resolution for relational structure of knowledge [5].

We have proposed a general framework for integration computing referring to determining collective intelligence [4]. We have shown that in general the knowledge of a collective is more proper than the knowledge of its members. This, in turn, proves that a collective is often more intelligent than single units. Some applications of integration computing methods in managing data warehouse federations and multi-agent systems have been worked out and analyzed [3], [11].

References

1. Duong, T.H., Nguyen, N.T., Jo, G.S.: Constructing and Mining: A Semantic-Based Academic Social Network. Journal of Intelligent & Fuzzy Systems 21(3), 197–207 (2010)
2. Duong, T.H., Nguyen, N.T., et al.: Comparative Analysis of Text Representation Methods Using Classification. Cybernetics and Systems 45(2), 146–164 (2014)
3. Maleszka, M., Mianowska, B., Nguyen, N.T.: A Method for Collaborative Recommendation Using Knowledge Integration Tools and Hierarchical Structure of User Profiles. Knowledge-Based Systems 47, 1–13 (2013)
4. Nguyen, N.T.: Consensus systems for conflict solving in distributed systems. In-formation Sciences 147(1-4), 91–122 (2002)
5. Nguyen, N.T.: Advanced Methods for Inconsistent Knowledge Management. Springer, London (2008)
6. Nguyen, N.T.: Processing Inconsistency of Knowledge in Determining Knowledge of a Collective. Cybernetics and Systems 40(8), 670–688 (2009)
7. Nguyen, N.T.: A Method for Ontology Conflict Resolution and Integration on Relation Level. Cybernetics and Systems 38(8), 781–797 (2007)
8. Nguyen, N.T.: Conflicts of Ontologies – Classification and Consensus-based Methods for Resolving. In: Gabrys, B., Howlett, R.J., Jain, L.C. (eds.) KES 2006. LNCS (LNAI), vol. 4252, pp. 267–274. Springer, Heidelberg (2006)
9. Nguyen, N.T.: Inconsistency of Knowledge and Collective Intelligence. Cybernetics and Systems 39(6), 542–562 (2008)

10. Pietranik, M., Nguyen, N.T.: A Multi-atrribute based Framework for Ontology Aligning. Neurocomputing (2014), doi:10.1016/j.neucom.2014.03.067
11. Sliwko, L., Nguyen, N.T.: Using Multi-agent Systems and Consensus Methods for Information Retrieval in Internet. International Journal of Intelligent Information and Database Systems 1(2), 181–198 (2007)
12. Truong, H.B., Duong, T.H., Nguyen, N.T.: A Hybrid Method for Fuzzy Ontology Integration. Cybernetics and Systems 44(2-3), 133–154 (2013)

How to Store and Process Big Data:
Are Today's Databases Sufficient?

Jaroslav Pokorný

Department of Software Engineering, Faculty of Mathematics and Physics
Charles University, Prague, Czech Republic
pokorny@ksi.mff.cuni.cz

Abstract. The development and extensive use of highly distributed and scalable systems to process Big Data is widely considered. New data management architectures, e.g. distributed file systems and NoSQL databases, are used in this context. On the other hand, features of Big Data like their complexity and data analytics demands indicate that these tools solve Big Data problems only partially. A development of so called NewSQL databases is highly relevant and even special category of Big Data Management Systems is considered. In this work we will shortly discuss these trends and evaluate some current approaches to Big Data management and processing, identify the current challenges, and suggest possible research directions.

Keywords: Big Data, NoSQL, NewSQL, Hadoop, SQL-on-Hadoop, ACID.

1 Introduction

Without doubts Big Data is a fashionable topic used by many people in different contexts and without precise semantics. In interview with Roberto V. Zicari[1], Jochen L. Leidner from R&D at Thompson Reuters says that buzzwords like "Big Data" do not by themselves solve any problem – they are not magic bullets. He offers some advice: to solve any problem, look at the input data, specify the desired output data, and think hard about whether and how you can compute the desired result – nothing but "good old" computer science. An excellent confirmation of this idea is offered in the book [8] describing methods, algorithms including their complexities, in context of very large amounts of data. Using today's other buzzwords the book provides a guide how to program so called Big Analytics.

Obviously, any efficient data processing system requires not only effective algorithms but also tools for storing and processing large datasets. We can use:

- traditional relational parallel database systems,
- distributed file systems and Hadoop technologies,

---

[1] http://www.odbms.org/blog/2013/11/big-data-analytics-at-thomson-reuters-interview-with-jochen-l-leidner/ (accessed 20 July 2014)

K. Saeed and V. Snášel (Eds.): CISIM 2014, LNCS 8838, pp. 5–10, 2014.

- NoSQL databases,
- new database architectures (e.g., Big Data Management Systems, NewSQL databases, NoSQL databases with ACID transactions).

The paper focuses on issues and challenges coming with use of these tools in context of processing Big Data. Its goal is also to show some alternatives in this area.

In Section 2 we mention shortly some basics concerning Big Data and Big Analytics. Section 3 presents an overview of technologies, platforms, and tools for Big Data storage and management. Finally, Section 4 summarizes the paper, tries to answer the question in its title, and offers some challenges.

2   Big Data and Big Analytics

There are many different (pseudo)definitions of Big Data. An attempt to compare them is offered in [12]. Usually we talk about the Big Data when the dataset size is beyond the ability of the current database tools to collect, process, retrieve, manage, and analyze the dataset.

Big Data are most often characterized by several V's which also pose problems for their storage and processing: *Volume*, *Velocity*, *Variety*, and *Veracity*. We can distinguish three areas concerning data management and processing of Big Data:

- storage and low-level file processing with simple database features,
- more sophisticated database processing with high-level query languages,
- so called Big Analytics working with big amounts of transaction data as extension of methods used usually in technology of data warehouses (DW).

What is Big Data analytics? Big Analytics is the process of examining large amounts of different data types, or Big Data, to uncover hidden patterns, unknown correlations and other useful information. In a Web context Big Analytics ca be charactrized in this way [1]: The crucial difference between Web search and Web data mining is that in the first case we know what we are looking for, while in the second we try to find something unusual that will be the answer to a (yet) unknown question.

The above rather simplified and vague Big Data characterization does not consider explicitly *complexity* occurring, e.g., in graph datasets and heterogeneous environments used for Big Analytics. Complexity together with big volume mostly requires a scalability of computer systems and algorithms used. In fact, just some well-known algorithms used to analyze data in DW may not scale and some techniques of their parallelization and distribution are needed. Big Analytics requires not only new database architectures but also new approaches to methods for data analysis. The latter means either reformulation of old data mining methods, or their new implementation, or even a development of completely new methods. A recent overview of Big Data issues is presented in [7].

3   Big Data Storage and Management

For storage and processing Big Data two features are preferred: scalability and high-speed access to massive volumes of information. We present some today's options in terms of their suitability for Big Analytics.

3.1   Relational DBMSs

Traditional relational DBMS both centralized or distributed is based on usage of SQL language and transactional properties guaranteeing ACID properties. ACID stands for atomicity, consistency, isolation and durability and is fundamental to database transaction processing. A significant part of the relational database technology usable for Big Data is called *Massively Parallel Analytic Databases* (MPAD). Unlike traditional DW, these DBMSs are capable of quickly proceed large amounts of mainly structured data with minimal data modeling required and can scale-out to accommodate multiple terabytes and sometimes petabytes of data. Interactive query capabilities are possible in MPAD. Possibilities of near real-time results to complex SQL queries are also at disposal.

3.2   Distributed File Systems and Hadoop Technologies

Distributed file systems considered here distinguish from traditional network file systems (e.g., in UNIX). They use, e.g., file partitioning and replications. The most famous is *Hadoop Distributed File System* (HDFS) [11].

Hadoop is a batch processing system based on the framework MapReduce [5] and HDFS. On the analytics side, MapReduce (M/R) emerged as the platform for all analytics needs of the enterprise. Because Hadoop clusters can scale to petabytes and even exabytes of data, enterprises no longer must rely on sample data sets but can process and analyze all relevant data.

Hadoop is the main part of well-known software architecture called *Hadoop stack*. A special attention belongs to the SQL-like language HiveQL. It is originally a part of infrastructure (DW application) Hive[2], which the first *SQL-on-Hadoop* solution is providing an SQL-like interface with the underlying MapReduce.

On the other hand, MapReduce is still very simple technique compared to those used in the area of distributed databases. Users require more complex, multi-stage applications (e.g. iterative graph algorithms and machine learning) and more interactive ad-hoc queries. Then faster data sharing across parallel jobs is needed.

Recently, there are other software tools providing a lot machine learning methods. They include, e.g., the engine Spark[3], distributed in-memory parallel computing framework. Spark is targeted for iterative and interactive algorithms, where Hadoop does not perform well. Its authors claim that it runs programs up to 100× faster than Hadoop MapReduce in memory or 10× faster on disk.

---

[2] http://hive.apache.org/ (accessed 20 July 2014)
[3] https://spark.apache.org/ (accessed 20 July 2014)

A lot of NoSQL databases are built on top of the Hadoop core, i.e. their performance depends on M/R jobs. For example, Big Analytics requires often iteration that is hardly achieved in NoSQL based on MapReduce. Consequently, some modifications like HaLoop framework [3] occur now which support iteration.

3.3   NoSQL Databases

NoSQL databases are a relatively new type of databases which were initiated by Web companies in early 2000s. Although some popular lists of them include all non-relational datastores such as XML databases, etc., mostly various key-value stores and graph databases represent this category now (see, e.g., [9, 6]). Beside their typical features like simplified data model, rather query driven database design, no support of integrity constraints, no standard query language, especially weakening ACID semantics is most relevant in context of Big Data processing.

NoSQL provide little or no support for OLTP as it is required for most enterprise applications. CAP theorem [5] has shown that a distributed computer system can only choose at most two out of three properties: Consistency, Availability and tolerance to Partitions. Then, considering P in a network, NoSQL databases support A or C. In practice, mostly A is preferred and the strict consistency is mostly relaxed to so-called *eventual consistency*. Eventual consistency guarantees only that, given a sufficient period of time during which there are no writes, all previous writes will propagate through the system so that all replicated copies of the data will be consistent. Eventual consistency has been widely adopted, becoming something of a default for NoSQL databases. However, there are some examples, where the consistency is tunable (e.g., in Cassandra[4]) or configurable (e.g., CP or AP in Oracle NoSQL database).

3.4   Big Data Management Systems

Some of NoSQL databases are a part of a more complex software architectures, e.g. Hadoop stack, or even so called *Big Data Management Systems* (BDMS). Unlike relational databases, where the user sees only SQL in the outermost DBMS layer for manipulating data, these systems allow to access the data through various means at different layers. Often the Hadoop stack is presented as the first generation of BDMS. ASTERIX [13, 2] uses different technologies than Hadoop stack: a special Hyracks data platform, an algebraic level Algebricks, HiveQL, but also a compatibility with Hadoop MapReduce. Typically, BDMS use a lot of other special high-level manipulations languages. Oracle sees BDMS as an architecture that seamlessly incorporates Hadoop, NoSQL and relational DW.

BDMS are often equipped by advance methods for data analytics. For example, Myria[5] is appropriate for actual statistical analysis. Some methods supporting similarity, preference, and uncertainty in data processing are becoming a part of basic algorithms used directly in DBMSs, e.g., fuzzy joins in ASTERIX. Today's BDMSs are evolving rather to completely remove the MapReduce layer.

---

[4] http://cassandra.apache.org/ (accessed 20 July 2014)

[5] http://myria.cs.washington.edu// (accessed 20 July 2014)

3.5   NewSQL Databases

In last years the development of data management shows that there are applications that want strong consistency. NewSQL is a subcategory of RDBMSs preserving SQL language and ACID properties, and moreover, the performance and scalability issues posed by traditional OLTP RDBMs. For example ClustrixDB[6], F1 [10], VoltDB[7], and MemSQL[8] belong here. These DBMSs achieve high performance and scalability by offering architectural redesigns that take better advantage of modern hardware platforms such as shared-nothing clusters of many-core machines with large or non-volatile in-memory storage. They allow real-time analytics and transaction processing at the same time.

3.6   NoSQL with ACID Transactions

Also many NoSQL designers are exploring a return to transactions with ACID properties as the preferred means of managing concurrency for a broad range of applications. Some observations show that CAP concerns only a part of the design space for distribution and scalability. When network partitions are rare it is not necessary to decide firmly between C and A, because it is usual adopting eventual consistency. Google's Spanner [4] belongs to this category. It is not a pure relational system implemented on top of a key-value store. Further, e.g., the FoundationDB Key-Value Store[9] is a distributed database with true ACID transactions, scalability, and fault tolerance. Such data stores offer also the SQL layer. Both examples also show that the data storage technology is decoupled from its data model.

4   Challenges and Conclusions

We can observe that there is a lot of possibilities how to store and process Big Data. Their use depends strongly on application, the data volume the application will access, the complexity of mining algorithms used, etc. A new feature is, that some of these systems have more different components that enable access and process data stored in various ways. Obviously, it requires an additional optimization and more complex decision making in the selection of the individual components.

A rather difficult challenge concerns role Big Analytics. So far, the mining process was controlled by the analyst or the data scientist. Dependent on the application scenario he/she determines the portion of data where/from the useful patterns can be extracted. A better approach would be the automatic mining process and to extract approximate, synthetic information on both the structure and the contents of large datasets. This seems to be the biggest challenge in Big Data.

---

[6] http://www.clustrix.com/ (accessed 20 July 2014)

[7] http://voltdb.com/ (accessed 20 July 2014)

[8] http://www.memsql.com/ (accessed 20 July 2014)

[9] https://foundationdb.com/ (accessed 20 July 2014)

Acknowledgments. This paper was supported by Czech Science Foundation (the grant No. P103/13/08195S).

References

1. Baeza-Yates, R.: Big Data or Right Data? In: Proc. of the 7th Alberto Mendelzon Int. Workshop on Foundations of Data Management, Puebla/Cholula, Mexico, May 21-23. CEUR-WS.org (2013)
2. Behm, A., Borkar, V.R., Carey, R.M., Grover, J., et al.: ASTERIX: Towards a Scalable, Semistructured Data Platform for Evolving-world Models. Distributed and Parallel Databases 29(3), 185–216 (2011)
3. Bu, Y., Howe, Y., Balazinska, M., Ernstm, M.D.: The HaLoop approach to large-scale iterative data analysis. The VLDB Journal 21(2), 169–190 (2012)
4. Corbett, J.C., Dean, J.C., Epstein, M., et al.: Spanner: Google's Globally-Distributed Database. In: Proc. of 10th USENIX Symposium on Operation Systems Design and Implementation (OSDI 2012), pp. 261–264 (2012)
5. Dean, D., Ghemawat, S.: MapReduce: Simplified Data Processing on Large Clus-ters. Communications the ACM 51(1), 107–113 (2008)
6. Hecht, R., Jablonski, S.: NoSQL evaluation: A use case oriented survey. In: CSC 2011 Proceedings of the 2011 International Conference on Cloud and Service Computing, pp. 336–341 (2011)
7. Kelly, J.: Big Data: Hadoop, Business Analytics and Beyond, Wikibon (2014), http://wikibon.org/wiki/v/Big_Data:_Hadoop,_Business_Analytics_and_Beyond (accessed July 20, 2014)
8. Leskovec, J., Rajaman, A., Ullman, J.D.: Mining of Massive Datasets. Cambridge University Press, Cambridge (2011)
9. Pokorny, J.: NoSQL Databases: a step to databases scalability in Web environ-ment. International Journal of Web Information Systems 9(1), 69–82 (2013)
10. Shute, J., Vingralek, R., Samwel, B., et al.: F1: A Distributed SQL Database That Scales. PVLDB 6(11), 1068–1079 (2013)
11. Shvachko, K., Kuang, H., Radia, S., Chansler, R.: The Hadoop Distributed File System. In: Proceedings of MSST2010, pp. 1–10. IEEE Press (2010)
12. Stuart, J., Barker, A.: Undefined By Data: A Survey of Big Data Definitions. CoRR, arXiv:1309.5821 (2013)
13. Vinayak, R., Borkar, V., Carey, M.-J., Li, C.: Big data platforms: what's next? ACM Cross Road 1, 44–49 (2012)

A New Contention Management Technique
for Obstruction Free Transactional Memory

Ammlan Ghosh, Anubhab Sahin, Anirban Silsarma, and Rituparna Chaki

University of Calcutta, Kolkata, India
{ammlan.ghosh,anirban.silsarma}@gmail.com,
anubhab.s@hotmail.com, rchaki@ieee.org

Abstract. Transactional Memory, one of the most viable alternatives to lock based concurrent systems, was explored by the researchers for practically implementing parallel processing. The goal was that threads will run parallel and improve system performance, but the effect of their execution will be linear. In STM, the non-blocking synchronization can be implemented by Wait-Freedom, Lock-Freedom or Obstruction-Freedom philosophy. Though Obstruction Free Transactional Memory (OFTM) provides the weakest progress guarantee, this paper concentrates upon OFTM because of its design flexibility and algorithmic simplifications. In this paper, the major challenges faced by two state of the art OFTMs viz. Dynamic Software Transactional Memory (DSTM) and Adaptive Software Transactional Memory (ASTM), have been addressed and an alternative arbitration strategy has been proposed that reduces the abort percentage both in case of Read-Write as well as Write-Write conflicts.

Keywords: Software Transactional Memory (STM), Obstruction-free Transactional Memory (OFTM), Contention Management, Concurrency.

1 Introduction

Developing systems with multiple threads that can execute concurrently is no more a notion, but a reality. And in the current era, it is more of a necessity to utilize the full capacity of multi-core processors. Improvement of performance within a single core becomes essential to utilize the computational power provided by chip level multiprocessing. Locking has been an in-vogue technique used by the programmers for writing parallel programs. Lock based synchronization, however, leads to a number of unwanted situations like occurrence of deadlocks, priority inversion of processes and complication of fine-grained locking.

Concept of transactional memory addresses these issues and provides a promising alternative to lock based synchronization. The idea is to allow concurrent execution of transactions maintaining atomicity, consistency and isolation (ACI property) of each, i.e. threads will run parallel and improve system performance, but the effect of their execution will appear linear. Unlike database transactions, transactional memory instructions are meant to be short span transactions that access a relatively smaller number of memory locations [1]. Transactional Memory systems can be purely hardware based (Hardware based Transactional Memory or HTM) [2], software-only

K. Saeed and V. Snášel (Eds.): CISIM 2014, LNCS 8838, pp. 11–22, 2014.

(Software Transactional Memory or STM) [3] or hybrid. Naturally, the level of flexibility in STM over modification and integration is maximum. In STM, the fundamental operations i.e. the processes of acquiring and releasing ownership of concurrent objects (shared memory locations) are done atomically by non-blocking synchronization techniques using design primitives LL/SC (Load Linked Store Conditional) [4] and CAS (Compare and Swap) [4,5,7]. The key advantages are low space complexity and reduced performance overhead. These atomic operations are widely supported by multi-core processors.

The non-blocking implementations of STM systems have been mostly designed on the basis of either Lock-Freedom or Obstruction-Freedom philosophy. An STM system is lock free if some transactions are guaranteed to commit in a finite number of steps [6]. Although Lock-Freedom often delivers exceptional results, there is a question mark over the correctness of semantics in these algorithms. An STM system is obstruction free if every transaction is guaranteed to commit in absence of contention. Obstruction freedom provides the weakest progress guarantee and also admits the possibility of livelocks. Still obstruction freedom has been the preferred choice of many as it substantially reduces the implementation complications i.e. codes are simple, flexible and depending upon the design, can considerably improve parallelism and scalability of a system with many cores.

In 2003, Herlihy et al. constructed one of the earliest obstruction-free STM systems called DSTM [10] to support dynamic sized data structures. Since then several OFTMs have been proposed including ASTM [11], RSTM [12] and NZTM [13], with considerable differences in their respective system designs. The researchers were mainly interested in improving the throughput and minimizing the computational overhead of transaction processing.

In this paper, some major challenges faced by two state of the art OFTMs viz. DSTM and ASTM, have been addressed and an alternative negotiation strategy has been proposed. Unlike the existing OFTM systems, the proposed method allows multiple Read-Only transactions to share data object concurrently along with Write transactions. When a Write transaction reaches its commit point it checks the maturity of the all active read-only transactions and decides which of them are allowed to be committed. The proposed algorithm also presents a new contention management policy to resolve conflicts between Write transactions. Section 2 describes some existing works, followed by section 3 which presents the proposed algorithm; section 4 evaluates the performance of the algorithm; finally we conclude and discuss future scope in section 5.

2   Background

The STM uses primitive atomic operations like and LL/SC (load-link and store-conditional) [4] and CAS (Compare and Swap) [5] for implementing read, write, commit and abort statements. Load-link and store-conditional are a pair of instructions used together in multithreading to achieve synchronization. Load-link returns the current value of a memory location and a subsequent store-conditional will store a new value if no updates are made in that location meanwhile. CAS is used to read from a particular memory location and to write back the modified value in the same location after ensuring that the location has not been altered in between. Of late a slightly sophisticated version viz. DCAS (Double-word Compare and Swap) [14] has been used in some STMs, which basically executes two CAS operations simultaneously. These primitive atomic operations are used to guarantee that consistency of the system is not hampered during an update. The common performance metrics for the various STM systems have been (i) Conflict Management, (ii) Transaction Granularity and (iii) Number of Basic Operations. In obstruction free environment, when a conflict occurs among two or more transactions (of which at least one is a Write transaction) over a particular resource, the management policy of the concerned system will determine which transaction(s) will progress and which will abort. This conflict management strategy of an OFTM is determined by the contention manager. The performance of an OFTM depends largely upon the efficiency of the contention manager [15]. Granularity is considered as the smallest data store memory unit that can be possessed by a transaction for its Read/Write operations.

The authors have discussed two well known OFTM implementations viz. DSTM [10] and ASTM [11] as the proposed methodology has been influenced by these implementations.

2.1 DSTM

Herlihy et al. proposed one of the earliest obstruction-free STM (OFTM) systems called DSTM [10] to support dynamic sized data structures. The highlight of this system was assurance of progress in practice with the introduction of a modular contention manager, thus removing the single biggest drawback of OFTM. In DSTM, the TM-Object (Figure 1) points to a locator object with three pointers: pointer 1 points to the descriptor of the most recent transaction that held the object; pointers 2 and 3 point to the old and new versions of the data object. When a transaction successfully commits, the new version of the data object is made permanent. On the other hand, when a transaction is aborted by other transaction, the old version of the data object is read by the aborting transaction before its execution. Concepts of early release and visible/invisible reads were also coined by the DSTM developers, which have been applied in various forms in the latter STM designs. The idea of early release is that a transaction may release an opened object before committing. This sometimes proves really beneficial in case of data structures like trees. The read visibility helps to avoid unnecessary contention between Read only transactions. In this scheme, each transaction maintains a separate Read-list of the objects that have been opened by Read only transactions. Before commit, a Write transaction checks the Read-list to resolve the contention. The read visibility yields a large performance benefit, especially in read-dominated work load, due to its easy read-object validation.

Herlihy et al. [10] proposed two basic contention managers viz. Aggressive Manager and Polite Manager. An Aggressive Manager directly aborts the conflicting transaction(s) whereas Polite Manager uses exponential back-off to acquire ownership of the TM-Object.

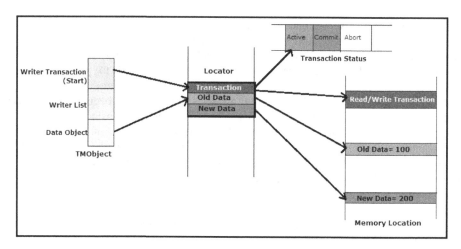

Fig. 1. Transactional Object (TM Object) structure in DSTM

2.2   ASTM

Adaptive Software Transactional Memory (ASTM) [11] used the structures of DSTM along with a modified conflict management scheme to overcome the loopholes of DSTM. ASTM offered adaptive methodology to adjust the workload. A transaction acquires an object in two ways. In eager acquire methodology a transaction acquires the objects at the beginning, where as in lazy acquire scheme a transaction acquires objects at commit time. Eager acquire method allows a transaction to detect contention earlier and helps to ensure consistency. Naturally eager-ASTM works better in write dominated workload while lazy-ASTM works better in read dominated workload. The flip side is that it increases the overhead of the system because of the adaptive nature of acquire methodology.

Initially ASTM did not introduce any new manager, but shortly ASTM-2 [16] was released with Adaptive Contention Management Policies. The Adaptive Contention Manager uses the idea of machine learning motivated by behaviorist psychology, i.e. from previous experience a manager decides how to take action in a particular environment so as to maximize transaction throughput. ASTM2 includes a number of contention managers viz. Karma Manager, Eruption Manager and Greedy Manager. Karma Manager gives absolute priority to the transaction that has done more work. Eruption Manager is based on the principle that the more number of transactions a particular transaction is blocking, the higher priority the blocker transaction should have. Finally Greedy Manager does not abort the conflicting transaction unless it has a lower priority or is currently waiting for another transaction; otherwise it aborts the running transaction.

For Write transactions (acquired state), the TM-Object points to a locator with similar structure as that of DSTM. But by default the TM-Object points to the data objects (unacquired state). So when a Read transaction follows a Write transaction, the former suffers indirection overhead, not only for acquiring the ownership of the TM-Object but also for the extra CAS for changing the direction of the pointer from locator to data. Analysis of this STM system over simulated test cases also verifies this finding; as expected, in workloads dominated by either read or write operations, ASTM gives excellent performance. But in case of a uniformly mixed set of Reads and Writes, the throughput degrades drastically.

The above STM systems use object granularity where there is no need to change the original object structure for converting a normal program to a transactional one. Object granularity also perfectly suits object oriented programming style.

Both in case of ASTM and DSTM, a transaction that opens n objects in write mode requires n CASes to acquire the objects and an additional CAS to commit which makes a total of $n+1$ CASes. But the cost might increase manifold in ASTM as the subsequent readers might perform up to n CASes to return the objects to unacquired state [6].

3   Proposed Scheme of Arbitration over a Resource between Two or More Competing Transactions

From the above inductive analysis we observe two major challenges common to both DSTM and ASTM:

(i)   Considerably high number of aborts, and
(ii)   The complexity involved in implementing modular contention management policy leads to a higher computational overhead

The frequent roll-backs of write transactions hamper the transactional processing greatly as normally write transactions execute longer than read-only transactions. The loss proves much costlier when a lengthy write transaction gets aborted by a much smaller write because of the rigidity of the concerned contention management policy. Also modular contention management schemes discussed above requires imparting intelligence in the software system such that based on the workload pattern the system can decide for itself which contention manager to use in a particular situation. Keeping these two major challenges in mind, this paper proposes a generic conflict management strategy aiming at reducing the abort percentage. The technique is based on the use of a single contention manager for all types of workload patterns. The proposed method uses lazy conflict detection scheme for both read-only as well as write transactions. In a bid to avoid spurious aborts for read-only transactions, a list of 'matured' read transactions (on the basis of their execution time) is maintained. When a write transaction tries to commit, it checks this list and backs-off to give a chance to these read-only transactions to commit. When a transaction detects conflicts, it either backs-off for certain time to give chance to the conflicting transactions or aborts conflicting transactions or aborts itself. The decision is taken after consulting the contention manager, in order to achieve synchronization in a non-blocking manner.

3.1   TM-Object Structure in Proposed OFTM

The proposed OFTM maintains the TM Object structure (Figure 2) similar to that of DSTM. Additionally, this TMObject has a pointer to the write transaction's Q_RdrLst, a list of qualified read-only transaction, on the basis of which a write transaction decides its back-off policy. Also for log file storage a descriptor is maintained by every transaction that stores the transaction metadata. The descriptor remains in the thread local storage (TLS) and is created right at the beginning, i.e. during thread initialization.

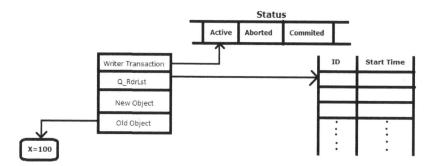

Fig. 2. TM Object structure in proposed OFTM

3.2   Nomenclature

It is presumed that transactions belonging to $\sum_{i=1}^{n} T^i_{R/W}$ and obtained from a Pseudo Random Number Generating Algorithm open the object 'O' for either reading or modifying (each write transaction acquires a different version).

The underlying assumption is that work done by a transaction is roughly an increasing linear function of its total execution time. The following is an exhaustive list of term definitions used to describe the functioning of the system.

t^{μ}_W: mean time taken by the CPU to finish a write transaction.

t^{μ}_R: mean commit time of a read-only transaction.

$\#T^s_W$: number of committed write transactions whose execution time is less than or equal to t^{μ}_W.

$\sum_{i=1}^{n} T^i_{R/W}$: set of all transactions that initiate and commit within time span 't'.

$\#T_W$: total number of committed write transactions.

t^i: total time for which a transaction $T^i_{R/W}$ has executed, as calculated at that particular time instant. $T^i_{R/W}$ may be in active/aborted/committed state.

RdrLst: all active read-only transactions are stored in this list.

$T^i_W.\mathbf{Q\_RdrLst} \subset \mathbf{RdrLst}$: Qualified Reader List is a 2-tuple {j, $Init^j_R$} list corresponding to write transaction T^i_W, which is the set of all active read-only transactions that started before T^i_W's *try_commit* point.

❖ **j**: Identity of the read-only transaction
❖ **$Init^j_R$**: timestamp at the initiation of T^j_R

Mtr_lvl^i_w: *maturity_level* of the ith write transaction; if any write transaction executes lesser than t^μ_w, then *maturity_level* of that transaction is considered as **LO**; if any write transaction executes longer than t^w_{max}, then *maturity_level* of that transaction is considered as **HI**,

❖ $t^w_{max} = t^\mu_w * \#T_w / \#T^s_w$

The values of t^μ_w and t^μ_R get modified every time a new write transaction or a new read-only transaction commits. *Maturity_level* is considered only for active write transactions.

3.3   Proposed Algorithm

For all transactions T^i_w that modified object O and has reached its *try_commit* point

If Found = TRUE

    If T^i_w.Q_RdrLst != Ø

        $t_b = t^\mu_R - Min(t^k) \; \forall \; T^k_R \in T^i_w$.Q_RdrLst

        T^i_w backs off for time t_b

        Commit all $T^k_R \in T^i_w$.Q_RdrLst that reach their respective *try_commit* points within this time period; remove them from RdrLst and T^i_w.Q_RdrLst

        Abort all $T^m_R \in T^i_w$.Q_RdrLst

    End if

    If Mtr_lvl^i_w = *LO*

        Check if there exists transaction, T^j_w which holds a version 'O$_j$'

        $\ni$ (Mtr_lvl^j_w = *HI*) && (O$_i$!= O$_j$)

        If Found = TRUE

            Complete execution of T^j_w and commit T^j_w

        End if

    End if

    Commit T^i_w

    Roll back all other write transactions holding O$_k$, $\ni$ O$_k$!= O$_i$ and free the corresponding memory locations

End if

3.4   Case Study

Normally it is observed that within a workload, even the longest read-only transaction executes for a shorter period than the smallest write transaction. But exceptions may happen especially in case of reads involving indirect addressing. In the proposed negotiation strategy, neither absolute free hand has been given to read-only transactions, nor occurrence of a conflict results in indiscriminate aborting of all reads under consideration. An intermediate approach has been adopted where only those read-only transactions that can finish execution within a stipulated time (t_b) are allowed to commit.

We have categorized the active Write transactions in terms of their total time of execution as maturity_level = *LO* and maturity_level = *HI*. Reverse ratio has been assumed while defining t^w_{max} because experimental results reveal that the number of committed write transactions which execute for less than 't^μ_w' time is considerably greater than #Tw/2.

3.4.1   Random Generation of Threads

We can visualize the system threads that use a particular object (say O) in the form of the following function,

$$i = \{(Rand(x) \ Mod \ \#T_n) + 1\}$$

This function gives a very good virtualization of random order acquisition of an object by different transactions (For e.g. T_i can be T_5, T_{33}, T_{17}, etc.).

But if all the threads are independent, i.e. they do not share any common object, each will commit on reaching its *try_commit* point without bothering the others. This, however is a trivial case and is very unlikely to happen in practical systems.

3.4.2   Checking Before Write Commit

Before a write transaction commits, the system basically performs the following: it checks if any read-only transaction(s) is holding an old version of the same object; next it verifies if the *maturity_level* of the *try_commit* write transaction is *LO*; if the outcome of this second check is affirmative, it performs the final check, i.e. if the transaction under consideration is forcing another write transaction with *maturity_level = HI* to roll back. From the outcome of this threefold checking, it effectively makes way for most read-only transactions (if not all) to commit and also saves any lengthy write transaction which would have been sacrificed otherwise. The value of back-off time t_b is environment dependent and might vary from one workload set to another. This is shown in the Figure 3a and 3b. Table 1 compares two well-known OFTMs i.e. DSTM and ASTM with the proposed one, by characterizing some important designing parameters.

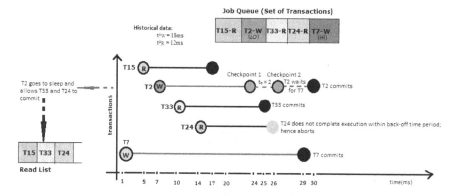

Fig. 3a. Case 1. T_2 waits for T_7 to commit

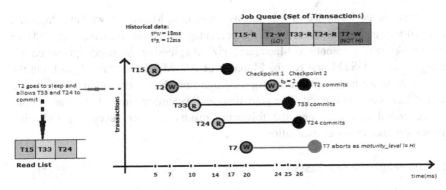

Fig. 3b. Case 2. T_2 forces T_7 to abort

3.5   Comparison of the Proposed OFTM with DSTM and ASTM

Table 1. Analysis of DSTM, ASTM and the proposed OFTM based on some designing parameters

Designing Parameters	DSTM	ASTM	PROPOSED OFTM
Synchronization	Obstruction Freedom	Obstruction Freedom	Obstruction Freedom
Granularity	Object Based	Object Based	Object Based
Conflict Detection	Eager	Lazy	Lazy
Update Strategy	Direct	Deferred	Deferred
Read Visibility	Invisible	Invisible	Visible
Data Organization	Keeps transactional data and object data in separate memory structures	Keeps transactional data and object data in separate memory structures	Keeps transactional data and object data in the same memory structure
Data Indirection	Two indirections	Two indirections	One indirection

4   Performance Evaluation

The efficiency and performance improvement of the proposed method over the existing OFTMs [10], [11] depends a lot upon the level of domination of reads in the set. This has been analyzed here in three different categories. However, towards the end of this section, it would be established that the proposed approach would guarantee at least equivalent throughput as compared to the existing approaches.

4.1   Metric of Evaluation

There are various parameters of evaluating the performance of an STM system. One fundamental approach is by measuring the percentage of committed transactions.

To compare the performance of the various Contention Managers, we have created a pool of fifty threads. With variation in the percentage of writes, we have executed two very well-known Contention Managers, viz. Aggressive Manager proposed by Herlihy et. al. in DSTM and Karma Manager of ASTM-2 in the thread pool. On the same test beds we have tested our proposed manager. Here contention over a single resource has been considered. The start time and execution time of the transactions were generated randomly and the following results were achieved.The following figures show the results of evaluation.

4.2   Performance Summary

The simulation results on the three different workload sets reveal that performance of the proposed algorithm is always better than performance of both these managers in case of read-write conflicts. This is because of the sensible back-off performed by the contention manager whenever there is a contention between a read transaction and a write transaction. Also it is found that performance of the proposed manager with respect to the others improves significantly with decrease in the domination of reads in the workload. From the graphs, it can be concluded that though the proposed manager performs slightly better than Karma manager, but it surpasses the commit percentage of Aggressive Manager by miles over all workloads.

By a non-weighted average across all the four test cases, our manager achieves a flat betterment of 36.85% over the performance of Aggressive Manager and 4.34% over that of Karma Manager.

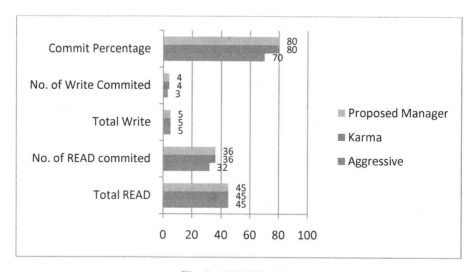

Fig. 4a. 10% Write Set

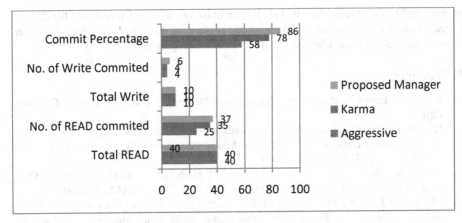

Fig. 4b. 20% Write Set

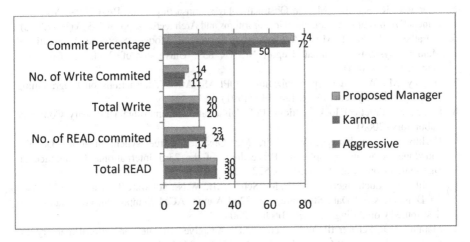

Fig. 4c. 40% Write Set

5   Conclusion and Future Scope

The proposed OFTM aims at reducing the number of aborts. It gives a fair amount of time period to the active read-only transactions so that they can complete execution and commit. In many cases it will not abort any of the read-only transactions. The novelty of this system lies in the fact that in case of write-write conflicts, it saves the matured writes, instead of aborting it. The system also performs clean-ups for all unsuccessful transactions and frees the corresponding memory locations. On the flip side, this STM system is not strictly non-blocking as putting T^i_w off to sleep is basically blocking it from completing its execution. In this regard we have made a trade-off between rigidity of non-blocking semantics and system throughput.

The authors plan to test the algorithm upon some more sophisticated benchmarks like Red Black tree and Hash Table. Once done, the performance of the proposed OFTM system shall be compared with the best known existing OFTMs. Considering the degree of reduction of computational overhead, a par performance or even 10% degradation in terms of throughput should be a satisfactory result for proposed OFTM.

References

1. Harris, T., Larus, J., Rajwar, R.: Transactional Memory, 2nd edn. Morgan & Claypool (2010)
2. Herlihy, M., Eliot, J., Moss, B.: Transactional memory: architectural support for lockfree data structures. In: ISCA 1993: Proc. 20th Annual International Symposium on Computer Architecture, pp. 289–300 (May 1993)
3. Shavit, N., Touitou, D.: Software transactional memory. In: ACM SIGACT-SIGOPS Symposium on Principles of Distributed Computing, pp. 204–213. ACM (August 1995)
4. Marathe, V.J., Scott, M.L.: Using LL/SC to simplify word-based software transactional memory (poster). In: PODC 2005: Proc. 24th ACM Symposium on Principles of Distributed Computing (July 2005)
5. Guerraoui, R., Kapalka, M.: On Obstruction-Free Transactions. In: SPAA 2008: Proc. 20th Annual Symposium on Parallelism in Algorithms and Architectures, pp. 304–313 (June 2008)
6. Marathe, V.J., Scott, M.L.: A Qualitative Survey of Modern Software Transactional Memory Systems. Technical Report Nr. TR 839. University of Rochester Computer Science Dept. (2004)
7. Herlihy, M.: Wait-free synchronization. TOPLAS: ACM Transactions on Programming Languages and Systems 13(1), 124–149 (1991)
8. Fraser, K.: Practical lock freedom, PhD Dissertation, Cambridge University Computer Laboratory (2003)
9. Herlihy, M., Luchangco, V., Moir, M.: Obstruction-free synchronization: Double-endedqueues as an example. In: Proceedings of the 23rd International Conference on Distributed Computing Systems, pp. 522–529 (2003)
10. Herlihy, M., Luchangco, V., Moir, M., Scherer III., W.N.: Software Transactional Memory for Dynamic-sized Data Structures. In: 22nd Annual ACM Symposium on Principles of Distributed Computing, pp. 92–101 (July 2003)
11. Marathe, V.J., Scherer III, W.N., Scott, M.L.: Adaptive software transactional memory. In: Fraigniaud, P. (ed.) DISC 2005. LNCS, vol. 3724, pp. 354–368. Springer, Heidelberg (2005)
12. Marathe, V.J., Spear, M.F., Heriot, C., Acharya, A., Eisenstat, D., Scherer III, W.N., Scott, M.L.: The Rochester software transactional memory runtime (2006), http://www.cs.rochester.edu/research/synchronization/rstm
13. Tabba, F., Wang, C., Goodman, J.R., Moir, M.: NZTM: non-blocking zero-indirection transactional memory. In: Proceedings of the 21st ACM Annual Symposium on Parallelism in Algorithms and Architectures (SPAA), pp. 204–213 (2009)
14. Attiya, H., Hillel, E.: The power of DCAS: highly-concurrent software transactional memory. In: Proceedings of the Twenty-sixth Annual ACM Symposium on Principles of Distributed Computing. ACM (2007)
15. Scherer III, W.N., Scott, M.L.: Advanced contention management for dynamic software transactional memory. In: PODC '05: Proceedings of the Twenty-Fourth Annual ACM Symposium on Principles of Distributed Computing, NY, USA, pp. 240–248 (2005)
16. Frank, J.C., Chun, R.: Adaptive Software Transactional Memory: A Dynamic Approach to Contention Management. In: PDPTA 2008: Proceedings of 14th International Conference on Parallel and Distributed Processing Techniques and Applications, Nevada, USA, pp. 40–46 (2008)

Evolutionary Algorithm for Decision Tree Induction

Dariusz Jankowski[1] and Konrad Jackowski[1,2]

[1] Wroclaw University of Technology, Department of Systems and Computer Networks,
Wybrzeże Wyspiańskiego 27, 50-370 Wrocław, Poland
[2] IT4Innovations, VSB – Technical University of Ostrava,
17. listopadu 15/2172, 708 33 Ostrava - Poruba, Czech Republic

Abstract. Decision trees are among the most popular classification algorithms
due to their knowledge representation in form of decision rules which are easy
for interpretation and analysis. Nonetheless, a majority of decision trees training
algorithms base on greedy top-down induction strategy which has the tendency
to develop too complex tree structures. Therefore, they are not able to effectively generalise knowledge gathered in learning set. In this paper we propose
EVO-Tree hybrid algorithm for decision tree induction. EVO-Tree utilizes evolutionary algorithm based training procedure which processes population of
possible tree structures decoded in the form of tree-like chromosomes. Training
process aims at minimizing objective functions with two components: misclassification rate and tree size. We test the predictive performance of EVO-Tree
using several public UCI data sets, and we compare the results with various
state-of-the-art classification algorithms.

Keywords: classification, decision tree induction, evolutionary algorithms.

1   Introduction

Decision tree (DT) has been widely used to build classification models, due to its
simple representation that resembles the human reasoning. There are many well-
known decision-tree algorithms: Quinlan's ID3 [1], C4.5 [2] and Breiman et al.'s
Classification and Regression Tree (CART) [3]. Decision trees have proved to be
valuable tools for classification tasks. They have various advantages: presenting an
interpretable output as a sequence of easy-to-understand tests, can handle numerical
and categorical data, hierarchical decomposition allows better use of available features. One of the main difficulties of inducing a recursive partitioning structure is
obtaining right sized tree (height and balance). Traditional top-down greedy strategy
for decision tree can create over-complex trees that do not generalise well from the
training data (overfitting problem). Several techniques have been suggested for obtaining right sized trees. The most popular of these is pruning. Since generating the
optimal model tree is a NP-complete problem traditional top-down greedy strategy for
decision trees may have a tendency to converge towards local optima rather than the
global optimum of the problem [4].

In this work, we propose use of the evolutionary algorithms (EAs) paradigm as
an alternate heuristic to generate model trees. EAs has been successfully applied to

K. Saeed and V. Snášel (Eds.): CISIM 2014, LNCS 8838, pp. 23–32, 2014.

decision tree induction, e.g. Papagelis and Kalles use genetic algorithm to directly evolve decision trees [5]. Worth mentioning is using by them a tree structure to represent decision trees instead of traditional binary strings representations.

In presented EVO-Tree algorithm we decide to use global metrics of tree quality, that is size and accuracy. Such approach reduce complexity of the final classifier by removal of sections of a classifier that may be based on erroneous data without reducing predictive accuracy. Also we can focus on what criteria an induced tree must satisfy rather than how to induce a tree (which impurity measure select, how prune, etc.). We test the predictive performance of our approach using public UCI data sets, and we compare the results with state-of-arts classification algorithms.

The paper is organized as follows. In section 2 the review of decision tree algorithm is presented. Section 3 describes principles of evolutionary algorithms. Section 4 shows how evolutionary algorithm can be used to inductively generate decision trees. In section 5 experimental results show the validity of the approach. In section 6 we conclude and prioritize the directions for further work.

2   Decision Tree

The tree is a structure build from elements called nodes and branches. Three types of nodes can be distinguish: a root, internal and terminal (leaf). The root and the internal nodes denote tests on the attributes and each branch represents the outcome of a test. Each leaf node holds a class label i.e. the final decision. The general algorithm for building decision tree has two phases: growth and pruning.

In the first phase a decision tree is built by selecting the best test attribute as the root of the decision tree. Based on the test the learning set is split into two subsets (two children nodes). Then, repeat recursively the procedure on each branch to induce the remaining levels of the decision tree until all instances in a leaf belong to the same class. Different algorithms use different metrics to determine the best way to generate the test in the node and split the records. The most common impurity measures (metrics) are: Gini Index, Information Gain, and Gain Ratio [6].

The second, pruning phase may be done only on the fully grown tree. The goal is to reduce the size of decision trees by removing "insignificant" nodes or even subtrees (sections of a nodes that may be based on noisy or erroneous data). A tree that is too large risks overfitting the training data and poorly generalizing to new samples.

3   Evolutionary Algorithm

The Evolutionary algorithm (EA) is search heuristic that mimics the process of natural biological evolution. The idea behind EA is the collective learning process within a population of individuals, each of which represents a search point in the space of potential solutions to a given problem. The first population of individuals is usually randomly initialized, and it evolves toward better and better regions of the search space by means of randomized processes of selection (which is deterministic in some algorithms), mutation, and crossover (also called recombination). The environment delivers quality information (fitness value) about the search points. In selection process the best individuals have a higher probability to reproduce more often than those of lower fitness. The recombination mechanism allows mixing information from two individuals and passing it to their offspring. Mutation causes small random changes in the individuals. After the evolution is completed, the fittest individual represents a "near-optimal" solution for the problem.

Most of decision tree induction algorithms relies on a greedy, top down, recursive partitioning strategy [7]. Such approach does not guarantee an globally optimal decision tree. One of the method to escape local minima in the search space is using randomized search techniques such as evolutionary algorithms. In [8] competitive co-evolution for DT induction is applied and a tree-encoding scheme is used. Works, that inheritance from the genetic algorithms conception, use fixed-length string representations (called "linear chromosomes") for coding individuals [9, 10]. The main disadvantage of such approach is hard implementation for nonbinary decision trees.

In [11, 12] authors finding with EA best combination of attributes for each split to induce oblique DTs. Such type of tree differs from traditional DTs but build an optimal oblique DT is also an NP-complete problem, what motivate authors to avoid greedy strategy.

Instead of evolve full decision trees EAs are sometimes using to improve specific components of decision tree classifier, for instance: tree pruning [13], calculating the cost of classification [14] or controlling parameters of trees [15].

4 The EVO-Tree Algorithm

EVO-Tree (EVOlutionary Algorithm for Decision Tree Induction) is a novel multi-objective evolutionary algorithm proposed to evolve binary decision trees for classification. In multi-objective EAs different objectives are aggregated and combined into one objective function using a fixed weight when more than one objective needs to be optimized. With such a weighted aggregation, one solution is obtaining in one run (see 4.3). Algorithm 1 shows the pseudocode of the EVO-Tree algorithm.

Algorithm 1. EVO-Tree pseudocode (adapted from [16])

```
1: Randomly generate initial population of trees
2: Compute the fitness value of each tree
3: repeat
4:   Select individuals based on fitness
5:   Apply crossover and mutation to selected individuals,
creating new trees
6:   Compute the fitness value of each new tree
7:   Update the current population (new individuals re-
place previous individuals)
8: until (stopping criteria)
```

4.1   Representation

The representation for the genotype–phenotype mapping is crucial element of a search space algorithm. We believe that tree-based representation for the candidate solution is the best one and natural. Each individual is stored in breadth-first order as an implicit data structure in two arrays (see Fig. 1). All nominal data and class labels are maps to an integer, so each component is a numeric (integer, real or null). Assuming that node has an index i, its left child can be found at indices $2i$ and the right child at $2i+1$ respectively (see Fig. 1). Terminal nodes assume null values and class number. The root has always index one. This method do not wastes space (even if the tree is not a complete binary tree) by using sparse matrices in Matlab environment. Advantages of such representation are more compact storage and better locality of reference in a context of memory utilization.

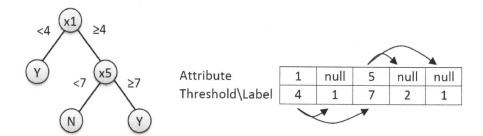

Fig. 1. Decision tree and corresponding structure

4.2   Initial Population

Trees are generated randomly. The growth of the trees is dictated by a parameter that indicates the maximum tree depth from root to leaf inclusive, but no less than 2 levels. Generation algorithm starts with a root node and two children. Next with probability P_{split} decides whether the children are split and another child nodes are created or the node becomes a terminal node (leaf). For the leaf node random class label is assigned. If the node is further expanded then algorithm randomly select attribute and split value. If selected attribute has k split values, it is replaced by $k-1$ calculated thresholds. First we sort all values of the attribute then with the following formula $\left(\frac{i^{th}+i^{th+1}}{2}\right)$ thresholds are set and one randomly selected. Advantage of such synthetic thresholds is protection against noisy or erroneous data. The default value of P_{split} is 0.7. Population size can be controlled by a *pop_size* parameter (details in chapter 5.1).

4.3   Fitness Evaluation

The goal of any classification system is best predictive accuracy for new unlabelled samples. For decision trees also size of the final tree is important. A tree that is too large risks overfitting the training data and poorly generalizing to new samples.

On the other hand a small tree might not capture important information about the sample space. To solve this problem in classical top-down induction algorithms various techniques for pruning decision trees were developed.

In our approach another solution is proposed. The fitness function (FF) is balanced between the number of correctly classified instances and size of the tree, with two extra parameters α_1, α_2 , to tune their relative weight:

$$FF = \alpha_1 f_1 + \alpha_2 f_2 \tag{1}$$

where

$$f_1 = 1 - \frac{Total\ no.of\ Samples\ Correctly\ Classified\ in\ Training\ Set}{Total\ no.of\ samples\ in\ Training\ Set} \tag{2}$$

$$f_2 = \frac{Tree_{current\_depth}}{Tree_{target\_depth}} \tag{3}$$

Parameters α_1, α_2 are the relative importance of the complexity term (default values are 0.99 and 0.01 respectively). There is no one optimal value of α_1, α_2 therefore tuning this parameters may lead to the improvement of the results. F_1 is the classification error estimated on the learning set. The growth of the trees is controlled by a parameter f_2 that penalizes the size of an individual (in depth of the tree) and allow to obtain the desired size of tree. The value of $Tree_{target\_depth}$ should be provided by the user by tuning it to the specific problem that is solved. This parameter was set to 21.

The fitness function is the function we want to optimize. Used Matlab toolbox tries to find the minimum of the fitness function so the best fitness value for a population is the smallest fitness value for any individual in the population.

4.4   Selection

During each generation the algorithm uses the current population to create the children that make up the next generation based on the fitness function. Some well-known selection methods are: tournament selection, roulette wheel selection, rank-based selection etc. Each individual can be selected more than once, in which case it spread its genes to more children. Stochastic uniform is default selection method in our algorithm. In this technique each parent corresponds to a section of the line of length proportional to its fitness value. The algorithm moves along the line in steps of equal size. At each step, the algorithm select a parent from the section it lands on. This prevents the EA from converging too fast which allows the algorithm to better search the solution space.

The elitism technique is also implemented. Three individuals with the best fitness values in the current generation are kept to the next generation. These individuals are called elite children.

4.5   Crossover

The algorithm creates crossover child by combining pairs of parents in the current population. First, two individuals are chosen by selection algorithm. From both trees random node is selected according to randomly selected number which can take values from 1 (root node) to n (total number of tree nodes). After identifying the sub-trees according to the randomly selected number in both parents, a new individual (offspring) is created by replacing sub-tree form first parent by the one from second parent. Figure 2 illustrates the crossover operation.

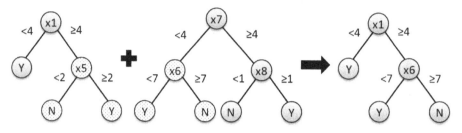

Fig. 2. Tree single point crossover

4.6   Mutation

Mutation options specify how the genetic algorithm makes small random changes in the individuals in the population to create mutation children. Mutation provides genetic diversity and enable the genetic algorithm to search a broader space. In our algorithm we implemented node condition mutation, which randomly change both attribute and split value of a randomly selected node (see Fig. 3). For terminal node class assignment is changed.

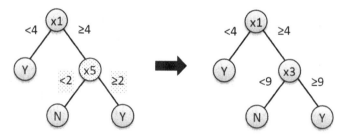

Fig. 3. Tree node mutation

4.7   Stopping Criteria

The algorithm terminates if the fitness of the best individual in the population does not improve during the fixed number of generations. This status indicates, that the algorithm has converged. Additionally, the maximum number of generations is specified, which allows limiting the computation time in case of a slow convergence. Default values one can find in chapter 5.1.

5   Experiments

In this section experimental validation of the proposed approach on real-life UCI datasets is described. Our main objectives was: effectiveness evaluation of EVO-Tree algorithm in comparative tests and identification of application domains.

5.1   Default Parameters

The parameters value are important and decide whether the algorithm will find a near-optimum solution and how efficiently. Choosing correctly the parameters is a time-consuming task. We decide to deterministic parameter control (user-specified). The default parameters of EVO-Tree used in the simulations were as follow: number of generations - 500, population size - 400, crossover/mutation probability - 0.6/0.4, selection method - stochastic uniform with elitism, stop criterion - 500 generations or 100 generations without improvement.

5.2   Datasets

There are two assumptions about data: first, there are no unknown or missing values and second, the classification of all instances is known. The datasets are briefly described in Table 1.

Table 1. Datasets specification

Dataset	Number of Instances	Number of Attributes	Number of Classes
abalone	210	7	28
ecoli	336	8	8
page-blocks	5473	10	5
winequality-red	1599	12	6
winequality-white	4898	12	7
breast tissue	106	10	6
seeds	210	7	3

5.3   Experimental Analysis and Results

All experiments were carried out in Matlab and KNIME framework using as a base classifiers implemented in Weka. The pool of compared classifiers consisted of 6 algorithms: EVO-Tree, Naive Bayes, Multilayer Perceptron, SVM, decision tree (C4.5), Random Tree. All experiments were carried out using 5x2 cross-validation and presented as averaged results (see Tab. 2). The advantage of this method is that all observations are used for both training and validation but never at the same time.

Additionally, we applied average ranks (AR) ranking method to resolve the issue which algorithm is the best on an unseen datasets. For each dataset we order the algorithms according to the measured accuracy and assign ranks (best algorithm has rank 1 and so on). The final ranking is obtained by averaging all values (see Tab. 3).

Table 2. Measured accuracy

Classifier	Breast tissue	Ecoli	Page blocks	Seeds	Segment	Wine q. red	Wine q. white	Abalone
EVO-Tree	0,621	0,810	0,955	0,901	0,908	0,566	0,530	0,248
J48	0,651	0,793	0,967	0,896	0,953	0,557	0,539	0,207
LibSVM	0,200	0,688	0,911	0,900	0,528	0,548	0,531	0,237
Multlayer Perceptron	0,243	0,540	0,268	0,324	0,193	0,267	0,187	0,042
Naive Bayes	0,636	0,843	0,898	0,909	0,802	0,519	0,444	0,232
Radom Tree	0,608	0,773	0,959	0,875	0,935	0,570	0,548	0,195

The abalone dataset requires a separate comment because it is very resistant to good performance under machine learning techniques. None of the supervised learning techniques that are presented here achieve good results. The reason is large number of classes and the highly overlapped data that does not split easily onto a particular class.

Table 3. Ranking generated for tested classifiers based on accuracy on all datasets

Classifier	Breast tissue	Ecoli	Page blocks	Seeds	Segment	Wine q. red	Wine q. white	Abalone	Avg. Rank
J48	1	3	1	4	1	3	2	4	2.38
EVO-Tree	3	2	3	2	3	2	4	1	2.50
Random Tree	4	4	2	5	2	1	1	5	3.00
Naive Bayes	2	1	5	1	4	5	5	3	3.25
LibSVM	6	5	4	3	5	4	3	2	4.00
Multilayer Perceptron	5	6	6	6	6	6	6	6	5.88

Our experiments seems to support the following conclusions:

- There is very little difference in the accuracy between the algorithms, however we can notice that all three decision tree-based algorithm in almost all cases outperformed other ones. We suppose that thus fact is caused by two factors:
  - First one can be found by analysis of tested benchmark datasets. According to Table 1 all of them consists of large number of attributes. Keeping in mind that decision trees algorithms has natural ability to select the most valuable features we suppose that high accuracy of them are caused by implicitly performed feature selection which eliminated irrelevant attributes.

— The second reason is, in our opinion, high relevancy of rule based model for particular datasets. It is known, that it is hard to find out optimal model for given decision problem as there are very few guidance on relation between the classifier model and characteristic of datasets. In our cases, decision tree based models appeared to be the most appropriate.

- Results for Abalone dataset has to be commented more profoundly, because J48 and Random tree gain surprisingly low accuracy tested on this dataset. We suppose that is caused by the fact that the dataset has is the most difficult ones. It consists of 28 classes and very few samples (only 210). Such a small number of samples caused the classical decision tree memorized the learning set loosing generalisation ability. Contrary to them, EVO-Tree get very high performance what, according to our assumptions, allows to draw conclusion that proposed algorithm effectively counteract overfitting.

- Overall high accuracy of EVO-Tree on Abalone dataset shows also high ability of this algorithm to deal with dataset described by few features comparing to large number of attributes. Apparently, EVO-Tree training procedure much more effectively extract useful information and create decision rules from such difficult datasets comparing to classical decision tree algorithms. We believe, that it proves effectiveness of application of EA which optimize the tree structure in a manner that allow to avoid falling into local minima, what is natural features of classical decision tree induction algorithms.

6   Conclusion and Future Work

In this article we describe and evaluate a novel evolutionary algorithm for decision tree induction. Because it is the first publication about the EVO-Tree, mostly we focus on description of the algorithm that evolve decision trees as alternative to greedy top-down approaches. Additionally, we present experimental results that prove usefulness of our algorithm. Proposed approach reduce tree size (measured by the number of decision rules) and classification error at the same time. While traditional decision trees induced in top-down greedy strategy require pruning to remove sections of the tree that provide little power to classify instances.

The presented system is constantly improved and currently we are working on adjusting the parameters of the algorithm, which can largely influence whether the algorithm will find a near-optimum solution. Another direction of our research is generating multivariate (oblique) decision trees. The main difference between multivariate and the traditional univariate decision trees is that the first one uses linear combinations of the features at each non-leaf node for testing (which divides the attribute space with hyperplanes). Oblique decision trees are usually much smaller and often more accurate. Furthermore, EVO-Tree can provide a groundwork for an online learning algorithm appropriate for processing data streams with ability to adapt the decision model to concept drift. The idea is to have a *window* and forgetting mechanism to maintain a relevant set of examples. Those are our first goals for the future work and we believe that above extensions improve significantly EVO-Tree algorithm.

Acknowledgement. This work was supported by the statutory funds of the Department of Systems and Computer Networks, Faculty of Electronics, Wroclaw University of Technology dedicated for Young Scientists (grant no. B30036/K0402).

This paper has been elaborated in the framework of the project Opportunity for young researchers, reg. no. cz.1.07/2.3.00/30.0016, supported by Operational Programme Education for Competitiveness and co-financed by the European Social Fund and the state budget of the Czech Republic.

References

1. Quinlan, J.: Learning efficient classification procedures and their application to chess end games. Mach. Learn (1983)
2. Quinlan, J.R.: C4.5: Programs for Machine Learning. Morgan Kaufmann (1993)
3. Breiman, L., Friedman, J.H., Olshen, R.A., Stone, C.J.: Classification and Regression Trees. Wadsworth (1984)
4. Hyafil, L., Rivest, R.L.: Constructing optimal binary decision trees is NP-complete. Inf. Process. Lett. 5, 15–17 (1976)
5. Papagelis, A., Kalles, D.: GATree: Genetically Evolved Decision Trees. In: IEEE Int. Conf. Tools with Artif. Intell., pp. 203–206 (2000)
6. Bramer, M.: Principles of Data Mining. Springer (2007)
7. Rokach, L., Maimon, O.: Data mining with decision trees: theory and applications. World Scientific Publishing Company (2008)
8. Aitkenhead, M.J.: A co-evolving decision tree classification method. Expert Syst. Appl. 34, 18–25 (2008)
9. Kennedy, H.C., Chinniah, C., Bradbeer, P., Morss, L.: The contruction and evaluation of decision trees: A comparison of evolutionary and concept learning methods. In: Corne, D.W. (ed.) AISB-WS 1997. LNCS, vol. 1305, pp. 147–161. Springer, Heidelberg (1997)
10. Bandar, Z., Al-Attar, H., McLean, D.: Genetic algorithm based multiple decision tree induction. In: ICONIP 1999. ANZIIS 1999 & ANNES 1999 & ACNN 1999. 6th International Conference on Neural Information Processing. Proceedings (Cat. No.99EX378), pp. 429–434. IEEE (1999)
11. Dumitrescu, D., András, J.: Generalized Decision Trees Built With Evolutionary Techniques. Stud. Informatics Control 14, 15 (2005)
12. Czajkowski, M., Kretowski, M.: Global induction of oblique model trees: An evolutionary approach. In: Rutkowski, L., Korytkowski, M., Scherer, R., Tadeusiewicz, R., Zadeh, L.A., Zurada, J.M. (eds.) ICAISC 2013, Part II. LNCS (LNAI), vol. 7895, pp. 1–11. Springer, Heidelberg (2013)
13. Chen, J., Wang, X., Zhai, J.: Pruning Decision Tree Using Genetic Algorithms. In: 2009 International Conference on Artificial Intelligence and Computational Intelligence, pp. 244–248. IEEE (2009)
14. Lomax, S., Vadera, S.: A survey of cost-sensitive decision tree induction algorithms. ACM Comput. Surv. 45, 1–35 (2013)
15. Bratu, C.V., Savin, C., Potolea, R.: A Hybrid Algorithm for Medical Diagnosis. In: EUROCON 2007 - The International Conference on Computer as a Tool, pp. 668–673. IEEE (2007)
16. Basgalupp, M.P., Carvalho, A., Barros, R.C., Freitas, A.: A Survey of Evolutionary Algorithms for Decision-Tree Induction. IEEE Trans. Syst. Man Cybern. Part C Appl. Rev. 1–10 (2011)

A New Method for Mining High Average Utility Itemsets

Tien Lu[1], Bay Vo[2,3], Hien T. Nguyen[3], and Tzung-Pei Hong[4]

[1] University of Sciences, Ho Chi Minh, Vietnam
[2] Divison of Data Science, Ton Duc Thang University, Ho Chi Minh, Vietnam
[3] Faculty of Information Technology, Ton Duc Thang University,
Ho Chi Minh, Vietnam
[4] Department of Computer Science and Information Engineering,
National University of Kaohsiung, Kaohsiung, Taiwan, ROC
lucaotien@gmail.com, tphong@nuk.edu.tw
{vodinhbay,hien}@tdt.edu.vn

Abstract. Data mining is one of exciting fields in recent years. Its purpose is to discover useful information and knowledge from large databases for business decisions and other areas. One engineering topic of data mining is utility mining which discovers high-utility itemsets. An itemset in traditional utility mining considers individual profits and quantities of items in transactions regardless of its length. The average-utility measure is then proposed. This measure is the total utility of an itemset divided by the number of items. Several mining algorithms were also proposed for mining high average-utility itemsets (HAUIs) from a transactional database. However, the number of generated candidates is very large since an itemset is not a HAUI, but itemsets generated from it and others can be HAUIs. Some effective approaches have been proposed to prune candidates and save time. This paper proposes a new method to mine HAUI from transaction databases. The advantage of this method is to reduce candidates efficiently by using HAUI-Tree. A new itemset structure is also developed to improve the speed of calculating the values of itemsets and optimize the memory usage.

Keywords: Utility mining, average utility, itemset mining.

1 Introduction

Pattern mining plays an important role in data mining. Frequent pattern mining is a task of searching for the associations and correlations among items in large transactional or relational datasets [2]. However, it considers only the occurrence of items, while the other factors such as price, profit are neglected. The significance of items is the same. The actual significance of an itemset thus cannot be easily recognized by using traditional approaches. Only frequency is thus not sufficient to identify highly profitable items. Chan proposed utility mining to solve this problem [10] or [7], his approach used a tree structure to mine high utility itemsets (HUIs) of which utility values are larger than or equal a predefined threshold. Many approaches

K. Saeed and V. Snášel (Eds.): CISIM 2014, LNCS 8838, pp. 33–42, 2014.

have been proposed for mining HUIs such as [9], [4]. However, utility mining is based on only the utility of itemset and does not consider their length while the longer length itemset is, the higher utility its value has. The average utility (au) measure was proposed by Hong in [3] where the author considered the length of itemset. However, due to the lack of "downward closure property", the cost of candidate generation for mining high utility itemsets is intolerable in terms of time and memory space. An itemset which is not a HAUI can combine with one or more other items to become HAUI. Therefore, the number of generated candidates is very large, which leads to a challenge for researchers. The solution of this problem is to reduce the number of candidates and the time for generating them. Using the average upper-bound value is one of solutions [3]. Some authors proposed structures to improve the generation steps. However, the speed was decreased trivially. Although the closure downward cannot be applied to HAUIs (high-average utility itemsets), HAUUBIs (high-average utility upper bound itemsets) have this feature. Thus, we utilize it to generate HAUIs effectively. We also proposed the HAUI-tree and a new structure for itemset to speed up calculation.

The rest of this paper is organized as follows. Section 2 presents some related researches in mining high utility itemsets and high average-utility itemsets. Section 3 presents the proposed algorithm. An illustrative example is described in section 4. Finally, section 5 includes experimental results and conclusions are in section 6.

2   Related Work

2.1   High Utility Itemset Mining

High Utility Itemsets (HUI) mining is different from Frequent Itemsets (FI) mining. FI mining regards to the appearance of itemsets in transactions, and does not consider other attributes of itemsets such as price and quantity. In HUI mining, the utility of item in a transaction is defined as multiplication of its quantity and its profit. The utility of itemset in a transaction is the sum of the utility of its items in that transaction. If the utility of itemset is greater than or equal to a predefined threshold, it is called a high utility itemset (HUI).

Liu proposed the two-phase algorithm for HUI mining. In the first phase, database is scanned and generated candidates are pruned by using the upper bound threshold. In next phase, database is scanned again, the actual utility value of remain candidates are calculated and the algorithm then gets HUI from candidates. The problem of this method is to reduce candidates and time for rescanning database.

Ahmed et al. pruned candidates by using HUC-Tree [1]. High utility itemsets are mined after scanning database two times. In 2011, Hong et al. proposed a new structure called the HUP-Tree [8] for mining high utility itemsets. First, the algorithm processes correlative utility values and creates 1-itemsets as candidates. Second, database is rescanned and the HUP-tree is generated. High utility itemsets can be obtained from HUP-tree.

2.2   High Average-Utility Itemset Mining

In high utility itemset mining, the utility of an itemset is the sum of the utilities of its items in all transactions including the itemset. The longer the length of itemset is, the larger its utility increases. Thus, using the same threshold for all itemsets is not fair. The average utility (au) was proposed in [3] where the measure also considered the number of all items in an itemset in addition to profits and quantities of items used in the original utility measure. The average utility of an itemset was defined as the summation of all utility values of its items in transactions divided by the number of its items. The downward-closure property used in utility mining is not directly applied to the average-utility mining. An itemset which is not a high-average utility itemset (HAUI) can be combined with one or more items to become a HAUI. This property leads to the larger number of generated candidates and slower.

To reduce candidates, most authors used the average utility upper-bound value (ub). In [3], Hong et al. used average utility upper-bound to prune generated candidates and create the set of itemsets having upper-bound value are greater than or equal threshold. The set of (r+1)-itemset is generated by combining r-itemsets and 1-itemsets which have high average utility upper-bound. However, some (r+1)-itemset was generated in many times. Furthermore, calculating values was not fast. So, in [6], Hong et al. improved the speed of calculation by using a structure which is the same as Index Table. Then, an algorithm was proposed in [5]. This algorithm, calculates values of itemsets and filters them were processed two times. However, this method requires much effort and time to computing values of itemsets.

3   Proposed Algorithm

In the high average utility itemsets mining algorithm proposed in [3], Hong et al. used the average utility upper-bound (ub) value to reduce the number of candidates by using items which have suitable ub. The ub values of these items are greater than or equal the threshold. A structure then used to speed up calculating was the Index Table proposed in [6]. This structure stored the position of the last item of current itemset in transactions to retrieve its values easily. In 2012, Hong et al. continued improving Hong's method using ub. They used ub to prune two times. Firstly, they removed unsuitable item and then calculated again without unsuitable item. However, this method took much time. Especially, downward closure properties can be applied for high average utility upper-bound itemsets. An itemset is the high average utility upper bound itemset, all its subitemsets is also the high average utility upper bound itemsets. This new method generated candidates faster and compared their average utility values with threshold to get HAUIs. This approach is similar to WIT-tree in [11] which is used for mining frequent itemsets.

3.1   Notations

Notation 1. $I=\{i_1, i_2, ..., i_n\}$ is a set of items, which may appear in transactions.
Notation 2. An itemset X is a subset of items, $X \subset I$. If $|X|=r$, the itemset X is called a r-itemset. For example, an itemset {AB} which contains 2 items is called a 2-itemset.

Notation 3. $T=\{t_1, t_2, ...,t_m\}$ is a set of m transactions in database.

Notation 4. $P=\{p_1, p_2, ..., p_n\}$ is a set of profits for items which may appear in transactions.

Notation 5. λ is predefined threshold.

Notation 6. ub_X is an average utility upper-bound value of an itemset X.

Notation 7. au_X is an average utility value of an itemset X.

Notation 8. T_X is a set of transactions which contain itemset X.

Notation 9. Pos_X is a set of correlative positions of the last item of itemset X in transactions which include it (T_x).

Notation 10. q_{ij} is the quantity of item i_i in transaction t_j.

Notation 11. The utility of item i_i in transaction t_j: $u_{ij}=q_{ij} \times p_i$.

Notation 12. $maxU_{t_j} = \max (u_{1j}, u_{2j}, u_{3j}, ..., u_{nj})$ is maximum utility of items in transaction t_j. So, $u_{ij} \le maxU_{t_j}$

Notation 13. The utility of itemset X in transaction t_j: $u_{Xj}=\sum_{i \in X} u_{ij} \times q_{ij} (t_j \in T_X)$.

Notation 14. The average utility of itemset X: $au_X = \dfrac{\sum_{t_j \in T_X} u_{Xj}}{|X|}$

Notation 15. The average utility upper-bound of itemset X:
$$ub_X=\sum_{t_j \in T_X} maxU_{t_j}$$

Notation 16. HAUUBI is a set of high average utility upper-bound itemsets.

Notation 17. HAUI is a set of high average utility itemsets.

3.2   The Downward Closure Properties of HAUUBI

Theorem 1: If itemset X is a high average utility upper bound itemset, then all its sub-itemsets are also the high average utility upper bound itemsets.

Proof: Let r-itemset X with $ub_X=\sum_{t_j \in T_X} maxU_{t_j}$ and (r+1)-itemset X' with X is sub-itemset of X' $(X \subset X')$. Thus, $|T_{X'}| \le |T_X|$ and $T_{X'} \subseteq T_X$. Furthermore, $ub_{X'}=\sum_{t_j \in T_{X'}} maxU_{t_j} \le ub_X = \sum_{t_k \in T_X} maxU_{t_k}$. If X' $\in$ HAUUBI or $ub_{X'} \ge \lambda$. Thus, $ub_X \ge \lambda$ or X $\in$ HAUUBI.

3.3   A New Structure of Itemset

To speed up calculating, we use some properties of an itemset as follow:

- List of items belong to itemset X.
- au_X: average utility of itemset X.
- ub_X: average utility upper bound of itemset X.
- T_X: a set of transactions including itemset X.
- Pos_X: a set of position of last item of itemset X in correlative transactions.
  $(|T_X|=|Pos_X|)$

3.4   Algorithm for Mining HAUI

Input: A set of transactions T, a set of profits of items P, predefined threshold λ (All items in transactions are ordered to generate candidates and calculate faster).

Output: High average utility itemsets.

Processes:

```
Prepare ()
{
   STEP 1: Initialize MaxU is a set of maxU of tⱼ (tⱼ ∈ T)
   STEP 2: Initialize L₁ is a set of 1-itemset generated from
items. Each itemset X includes auₓ, ubₓ, Tₓ, Posₓ
   STEP 3: For each transaction tᵢ in T, do the following
substeps:
o        Calculate maxUₜᵢ
o        Calculate auₓᵢ (X ∈ tᵢ, X ∈ L₁)
o        Add tᵢ to Tₓ, add the position of itemset X in tᵢ to
         Posₓ
o        Update auₓ, ubₓ of itemset X in L₁

   STEP 4: For each 1-itemset X in L₁ to choose itemsets, add to
HAUUBI₁ (1-itemsets have ub, which sastify predefined threshold)
and HAU₁(1-itemsets have au, which sastify predefined threshold)
   STEP 5: createHAUI(HAUUBI₁, nₕₐᵤᵤᵦᵢ₁)
}
```

The **createHAUI(L_r, n_{L_r})** (L_r: a set of itemsets, n_{L_r}: the quantity of itemsets in L_r)

```
createHAUI(Lᵣ , n)
{
    for i=1 to n-1 do
    {
        Initialize Lᵣ₊₁;
        for j=i+1 to n do
        {
            Itemset X = merge(Lᵣ[i], Lᵣ[j]);
            if(ubₓ > λ)
            {
                Add X to Lᵣ₊₁;
                if(auₓ> λ)     Add X to HAUI;
            }
        }
        createHAUI(Lᵣ₊₁ , nₗᵣ₊₁)
    }
}
```

3.5   Purposes of Using T_X and Pos_X

Let r-itemset $\{XI_j\}$ and $\{XI_j\}$ be two itemsets which have the same prefix X. We merge them to create (r+1)-itemset $\{XI_iI_j\}$ and calculate values of itemset $\{XI_iI_j\}$ by following formulas:

$$T_{\{XI_iI_j\}} = T_{\{XI_i\}} \cap T_{\{XI_j\}}$$

$$ub_{\{XI_iI_j\}} = ub_{\{XI_i\}} - \sum_{t_i \in T_{\{XI_i\}} - T_{\{XI_j\}}} maxU(t_i)$$

$$u_{\{XI_iI_j\}} = au_{\{XI_i\}} * r - \sum_{t_i \in T_{\{XI_i\}} - T_{\{XI_j\}}} u_{\{XI_i\}i} + \sum_{t_k \in T_{XI_j} \cap T_{XI_i}} u_{\{I_j\}t_k}$$

$$au_{\{XI_iI_j\}} = u_{\{XI_iI_j\}}/(r + 1)$$

4   Illustration

A set of transactions T and a set of profits of items P are shown in Table 1 and Table 2 below. The predefined threshold $\lambda=25$. This example is the same to example in [6].

Table 1. Transactions in database

TID	A	B	C	D	E	F
1	1	0	2	1	1	1
2	0	1	25	0	0	0
3	0	0	0	0	2	1
4	0	1	12	0	0	0
5	2	0	8	0	2	0
6	0	0	4	1	0	1
7	0	0	2	1	0	0
8	3	2	0	0	2	3
9	2	0	0	1	0	0
10	0	0	4	0	2	0

Table 2. Profits of Items

Item	Profit
A	3
B	10
C	1
D	6
E	5
F	2

Firstly, we calculate au, ub of 1-itemsets generated from input items. For example, the average-utility of 1-itemset {A} in transactions that belong to $T_{\{A\}}$ is calculated by $(1+2+3+2)*3/1=24$ in which the profits of item A is 3 and the quantities of 1-itemset A are 1, 2, 3, 2 in correlative transactions. $T_{\{A\}}=\{1,5,8,9\}$, $Pos_{\{A\}}=\{1,1,1,1\}$. The results are shown in Table 3, L_1 includes 1-itemsets X with properties au, ub, T_X, Pos_X and the mining process is based on L_1.

Table 3. Results after calculating values

TID	u_{Ak}	u_{Bk}	u_{Ck}	u_{Dk}	u_{Ek}	u_{Fk}	mu_k
1	3	0	2	6	5	2	6
2	0	10	25	0	0	0	25
3	0	0	0	0	10	2	10
4	0	10	12	0	0	0	12
5	6	0	8	0	10	0	10
6	0	0	4	6	0	2	6
7	0	0	2	6	0	0	6
8	9	20	0	0	10	6	20
9	6	0	0	6	0	0	6
10	0	0	4	0	10	0	10
ub	42	57	75	24	56	42	
au	24	40	57	24	45	12	

Table 4. List of 1-itemsets with properties in L_1

1-Itemset	au_X	ub_X	T_X	Pos_X
A	24	42	{1,5,8,9}	{1,1,1,1}
B	40	57	{2,4,8}	{1,1,2}
C	57	75	{1,2,4,5,6,7,10}	{2,2,2,2,1,1,1}
D	24	24	{1,6,7,9}	{3,2,2,2}
E	45	12	{1,3,5,8,10)	{4,1,3,3,2}
F	56	42	{1,3,6,8}	{5,2,3,4}

Table 5. HAUUB$_1$

1-Itemset	au_X	ub_X	T_X	Pos_X
A	24	42	{1,5,8,9}	{1,1,1,1}
B	40	57	{2,4,8}	{1,1,2}
C	57	75	{1,2,4,5,6,7,10}	{2,2,2,2,1,1,1}
E	45	56	{1,3,5,8,10)	{4,1,3,3,2}
F	56	42	{1,3,6,8}	{5,2,3,4}

Table 6. HAUI1

1-Itemset	au$_X$	ub$_X$	T$_X$	Pos$_X$
B	40	57	{2,4,8}	{1,1,2}
C	57	75	{1,2,4,5,6,7,10}	{2,2,2,2,1,1,1}
E	45	12	{1,3,5,8,10)	{4,1,3,3,2}

We obtain HAUI={{C},{B},{E}}

We illustrate the processing of the procedure createHAUI(L$_r$,n$_{Lr}$) procedure by using HAUI-tree as follows.

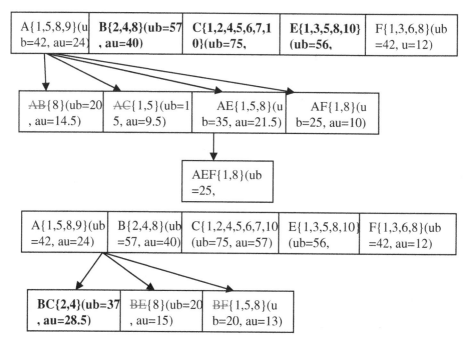

We get HAUI={{B},{C},{E},{BC}}

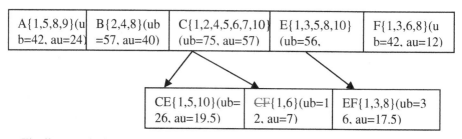

Finally, we obtain HAUI={{B},{C},{E},{BC}}.

5   Experiments

All algorithms were coded by C# 2010. The configuration of computer used for experimental evaluation is Intel core 2 dual with 2.20 GHz CPU, 2GB RAM and Windows 7 OS. Experimental databases have features as follow:

Table 7. Experimental databases

Database	#Trans	#Items
BMS-POS	515597	1657
Chess	3196	76

Table 8. The execution time of two algorithms along with different thresholds

Database	Threshold (%)	#HAUI	Execution time (minutes)	
			HAUI mining by UB and Index Table [6]	Proposed algorithm
BMS-POS	0.6	143	>180(unfinished)	1.11
	0.8	56	157	0.66
	1.0	34	62	0.55
	2.0	6	31	0.1
Chess	4.0	38	18.39	7.69
	5.0	1	2.45	1.22
	6.0	0	1.33	0.19

We compare our algorithm with the algorithm using ub and Index Table in [6]. Our algorithm is always faster than the algorithm using ub and Index Table. With BMS-POS database, when the threshold is very small, the algorithm in [6] run very slow. For example, with the threshold is 0.8, it takes 157 minutes while our algorithm takes 0.66 minutes. When we decrease the threshold to 0.6, the runtime is more than 180 minutes.

With HAUI-Tree, the generation of candidates is faster than other methods, because HAUI-Tree creates candidate for the next generations from the previous one. Besides, the other algorithms create candidates from scan each transaction. The quantity of transactions can be very large. So they is slower than HAUI-Tree. Furthermore, HAUI-Tree uses some properties of itemset to calculate utility values for the next generation quickly.

6   Conclusions and Future Work

This paper has presented a new method for mining high average utility itemsets from databases by using the HAUI-Tree algorithm and a new structure for itemset.

The proposed algorithm prunes and generates candidates fast and scans the database only once. Furthermore, the new structure for itemset improved the calculation and execution time. The proposed algorithm can be applied to large database (which include many items and transactions). Besides we are also interested in developing application for high utility average itemsets. In future, we will research efficient methods to find useful rules from high utility average itemsets.

References

1. Ahmed, C.F., Tanbeer, S.K., Jeong, B.S., Lee, Y.K.: HUC-Prune: An efficient candidate pruning technique to mine high utility patterns. Appl. Intell. 34, 181–198 (2009)
2. Han, J., Kamber, M.: Data mining: Concepts and Techniques, 2nd edn., p. 743. Morgan Kaufmann (2006)
3. Hong, T.P., Lee, C.H., Wang, S.L.: Effective utility mining with the measure of average utility. Expert Systems with Applications 38, 8259–8265 (2011)
4. Lan, G.C., Hong, T.P., Tseng, V.S.: Mining High Transaction-Weighted Utility Itemsets. In: Second International Conference on Computer Engineering and Applications (2010)
5. Lan, G.C., Hong, T.P., Tseng, V.S.: Efficiently mining high average-utility itemsets with an improved upper-bound strategy. International Journal of Information Technology & Decision Making, 1009–1030 (2012)
6. Lan, G.C., Hong, T.P., Tseng, V.S.: A Projection-Based Approach for Discovering High Average-Utility Itemsets. Journal of Information Science and Engineering 28, 193–209 (2012)
7. Lan, G.C., Hong, T.P., Lu, W.H.: An effective tree structure for mining high utility itemset. Expert Systems with Applications 38, 7419–7424 (2010)
8. Le, B., Nguyen, H., Cao, T.A., Vo, B.: A Novel Algorithm for Mining High Utility Itemsets. In: First Asian Conference on Intelligent Information and Database Systems (2009)
9. Liu, Y., Li, J., Liao, W.K., Shi, Y., Choudhary, A.: High Utility Itemsets Mining. International Journal of Information Technology & Decision Making 9(6), 905–934 (2010)
10. Liu, Y., Liao, W.-K., Choudhary, A.: A Two-Phase Algorithm for Fast Discovery of High Utility Itemsets. In: Ho, T.-B., Cheung, D., Liu, H. (eds.) PAKDD 2005. LNCS (LNAI), vol. 3518, pp. 689–695. Springer, Heidelberg (2005)
11. Vo, B., Coenen, F., Le, B.: A new method for mining Frequent Weighted Itemsets based on WIT-trees. Expert Systems with Applications 40, 1256–1264 (2013)

Spectral Clustering Based on Analysis of Eigenvector Properties

Małgorzata Lucińska[1] and Sławomir T. Wierzchoń[2]

[1] Kielce University of Technology, Kielce, Poland
[2] Institute of Computer Science Polish Academy of Sciences, Warsaw, Poland

Abstract. In this paper we propose a new method for choosing the number of clusters and the most appropriate eigenvectors, that allow to obtain the optimal clustering. To accomplish the task we suggest to examine carefully properties of adjacency matrix eigenvectors: their weak localization as well as the sign of their values. The algorithm has only one parameter — the number of mutual neighbors. We compare our method to several clustering solutions using different types of datasets. The experiments demonstrate that our method outperforms in most cases many other clustering algorithms.

Keywords: spectral clustering, nearest neighbor graph.

1 Introduction

Clustering is one of the most important research topics in both machine learning and data mining communities. It means an unsupervised classification of observed data into different subsets (clusters) such that the objects in each subset are similar while objects in different subsets are dissimilar one to another. Clustering has been applied in many research areas, like image segmentation [11], machine learning, and bioinformatics [13], to name a few.

A fundamental, and largely unsolved, problem in cluster analysis is the determination of the number of groups in a dataset. Numerous approaches to this problem have been suggested over the years (consult [2] for further details). The most common procedure is to use the number of clusters as a parameter of the clustering method and to select it from a maximum reliability criteria. The second approach uses statistical procedures (for example the sampling with respect to a reference distribution). Unfortunately, many of the methods require strong parametric assumptions, or to be computation-intensive, or both. Usually they include clustering algorithms as a preprocessing step.

Spectral clustering techniques [8], [16] belong to the most popular and efficient clustering methods. They use eigenvalues and eigenvectors of a suitably chosen matrix to partition the data. The matrix is an adjacency matrix (or a matrix derived from it) built on the basis of pairwise similarity of objects to be grouped. If it is clearly block diagonal, its eigenvalues and eigenvectors will relate back to the structural properties of the set [11]. In such a case the number of clusters is usually given by the value k, that maximizes the eigengap (difference between

K. Saeed and V. Snášel (Eds.): CISIM 2014, LNCS 8838, pp. 43–54, 2014.
© IFIP International Federation for Information Processing 2014

successive eigenvalues). Then the k principal eigenvectors are used for clustering the original data. However, an adjacency matrix generated from real-world data is virtually never block-diagonal, regardless of a similarity measure. In such situations an open issue of key importance in spectral clustering is choosing not only the proper number of groups but also the right eigenvectors, that reveal the structure of the data.

The SpecLoc2 algorithm, proposed in this paper, provides a solution for both the problems. We have developed an alternative approach to choosing the number of clusters and the most appropriate eigenvectors, which allow to obtain the optimal grouping. Our method is based only on spectral analysis of the adjacency matrix of the data points to be clustered. We have exploited carefully properties of adjacency matrix eigenvectors. The proposed algorithm constitutes an extension of the SpecLoc algorithm, our previous work [9]. The SpecLoc algorithm utilizes absolute values of weakly localized eigenvectors, which correspond to different clusters and reveal the structure of the data. Weak localization is characterized by slow decay of the component values away from its main existence subregion [3].

In the presented algorithm we use not only weak localization of eigenvectors, but also we take into consideration the sign of their values. The new method is more general than the original SpecLoc, and can be applied to much wider range of clustering problems, than the previous one. There is no need to search for parameters resulting in weak localization of eigenvectors. Practically all the spectra (within the area of spectral methods usefulness) allow to employ the new way of establishment of the cluster number.

We present an automated technique, which does not use any additional clustering processing, and verify our approach using well known real-world datasets. The performance of the SpecLoc2 algorithm is competitive to other solutions that require the number of clusters to be given as a parameter.

In section 2 the notation and related terms are presented. The next section describes some important properties of graph eigenvectors. Then, in section 4, we have presented the policy of selecting eigenvectors that reveal the structure of dataset. The main concepts used in the SpecLoc2 algorithm are explained in section 5. Section 6 includes the description of experiments and results obtained with the use of the SpecLoc2 algorithm. Finally, in section 7, the main conclusions are drawn.

2   Notation and Definitions

The set of data points to be clustered will be denoted by $\mathbf{X} = (\mathbf{x}_1, \mathbf{x}_2, ..., \mathbf{x}_n)$. For each pair of points i, j a similarity $s_{ij} \in [0, 1]$ is attached. The value $s_{ij} > 0$ implies the existence of the undirected edge $i \sim j$ in the graph G spanned over the set of vertices $\mathbf{X}$. The matrix $S = [s_{ij}]$ plays a role of the adjacency matrix for G.

Let $d_i = \sum s_{ij}$ denote the degree of node i and let D be the diagonal matrix with d_i's on its diagonal. In an undirected graph, the degree of a node is given by the number of its adjacent edges. It can also be defined as the sum of the weights of its adjacent edges.

The Laplacian matrix associated with graph G is the $n \times n$ matrix $L = D - S$. The normalized Laplacian, is defined as: $L_{sym} = D^{-1/2} L D^{-1/2}$. Its complement, $\mathbb{I} - L_{sym}$, is used in the NJW algorithm [12], which serves as a comparison with our solution in section 6.

The right eigenvector associated to the second smallest eigenvalue of the Laplacian matrix is called the Fiedler vector [2]. It carries significant structural information regarding the connectivity of the graph and forms the basis of spectral graph partitioning heuristics, see, e.g. [16] for a review. As the Fiedler vector has both positive and negative values, the signs of the values are used to partition the graph into two components: one associated with positive and the other with non-positive values. The original theorem proposed by Fiedler is presented in the next section.

3   Properties of Graph Eigenvectors

Fiedler has proved in [2] that if G is a connected graph and y is the eigenvector corresponding to the second eigenvalue of the Laplacian matrix L then one of the following two cases occurs:

- There is a single block B_0 in G which contains vertices with both positive and negative values of y. Each other block has either vertices with only positive, or only negative, or only zero y values.
- No block of G contains vertices with both positive and negative y values. Each block contains either vertices with only positive, or only negative, or only zero y values.

The eigenvector corresponding to the first (smallest) eigenvalue has only non-positive or only nonnegative values. This is the result of the fact that the sum of each row of the Laplacian equals zero. Thus, multiplying L by a constant vector x, we state that $Lx = 0 = 0 \cdot x$.

If we consider e.g. three infinitely far apart clusters, the adjacency matrix is block diagonal and consists of three blocks. Its eigenvalues and eigenvectors are the union of the eigenvalues and eigenvectors of its blocks (the latter padded appropriately with zeros) [12].

In [3] Filoche et al. study the behavior of eigenfunctions for a complex domain Ω with a bottleneck separating it into two subregions. In any partially separated subregion, an eigenfunction of Ω has only two possible choices: (1) either its amplitude is very small throughout this subregion, or (2) this eigenfunction mimics one of the subregion own eigenfunctions. The subregions are disjoint for a few dominant eigenfunctions. However, for the next eigenfunctions, initially disjoint subdomains begin to merge to form larger subregions. After reaching the critical point, completely new fully delocalized modes can appear.

Combining Fiedler's theorem with Filoche's observations one can generalize this theory to eigenvectors of graphs consisting of partially separated subgraphs. In the sequel by the graph eigenvectors we will understand eigenvectors of the graph adjacency matrix. In Figure 1 on the left, four principal eigenvectors of the adjacency matrix of a graph corresponding to two close and well separated sets of points are depicted. On the right we can see the two principal eigenvectors for the second subset only. Entries of the first and the second eigenvector (the left picture) are large only on one subset. They include the first eigenvectors of the two subsets, whereas the third eigenvector includes the second eigenvector of the second subset. The fourth eigenvector, with large entries for both subsets, emerges as a new mode consisting of eigenvectors of both subgraphs. The first three eigenvectors are weakly localized on one of the subset, contrary to the fourth one.

In a real situation, where the subgraphs are weakly separated, the picture is distorted and eigenvectors of the subgraphs mix with one another in the spectrum of the whole graph. For the clustering purposes the most appropriate are these eigenvectors that include the first or the second principal eigenvectors of its subgraphs. They mimic local eigenvectors of subgraphs of the whole graph and have one of the following form:

- eigenvectors with both large positive and negative values, and possibly near-zero entries, including the second eigenvectors of the subgraphs (Figure 1 left, the third eigenvector)
- eigenvectors with large entries for the relevant subgraph and near-zero values for the rest of vertices, including the first eigenvectors of the subgraphs (Figure 1 left, the first eigenvector) .

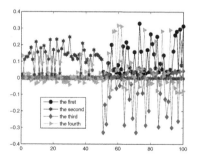 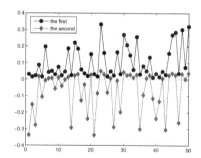

Fig. 1. The four principal eigenvectors of the adjacency matrix of the set consisting of two well separated groups (left) and two principal eigenvectors of the second subset of the set (right)

4   Preliminaries

Spectral clustering algorithms can be classified according to two approaches: recursive two-way spectral clustering algorithms (e.g. [6]) and direct K-way spectral clustering algorithms (e.g. [12]). The former finds the Fiedler eigenvector of the Laplacian matrix of a graph G and recursively partitions G until a K-way partition is found. The latter uses the first K eigenvectors and directly finds a partition using some heuristics. The K-way algorithms utilize K principal eigenvectors, however they do not take into consideration the special structure properties of the eigenvectors, using usually K-means algorithm for the final partitioning.

In the SpecLoc2 algorithm we have applied the approach that utilizes ideas used in both of the described above solutions. It is also an extension of our previous work, presented in [9]. Similarly to the SpecLoc algorithm we perform clustering on the basis of a few localized eigenvectors, but also increase the flexibility of the former solution by exploiting properties of other eigenvectors. We take into consideration not only absolute values of eigenvectors, but also the sign of an eigenvector entry.

In order to explain in an intuitive manner our policy we will analyze adjacency matrix eigenvectors of the well known dataset Iris [15]. It consists of three groups, the first one can be separated very easily whereas the second and third ones are very close to one another.

The adjacency matrix is constructed on the basis of the k-nearest neighbor graph. The way of constructing the k-nearest neighbor graph is described in section 5.

We compare eigenvectors of two different graphs obtained on the basis of two different numbers of the nearest neighbors for the Iris dataset. Figure 2 shows the first three principal eigenvectors of the Iris adjacency matrix in two cases. The figure on the left illustrates the situation, when a small k ($k = 5$) results in a very sparse adjacency matrix and its principal eigenvectors are weakly localized. Each of them mimics the first eigenvector of the appropriate subregion.

As the number of the nearest neighbors increases and the matrix becomes less sparse, weak localization of eigenvectors disappears. Figure 2 (right) shows the case when $k = 30$ and the adjacency matrix eigenvectors have completely different shapes. The second eigenvector remains still localized in the first cluster, which is well separated from the others. The first eigenvector is localized in the second and third cluster, whereas the sign of the third eigenvector allows to distinguish between the overlapping clusters. We can see that the third eigenvector structure falls in with the second case of the Fiedler's theorem. It mimics the structure of the second eigenvector of the subregion consisting of the overlapping clusters.

In order to partition sets with different structures we have to take into consideration not only weakly localized eigenvectors but also the ones that have both positive and negative values. Identifying both types of eigenvectors enables us also to establish the number of clusters. As some groups are indicated by weakly localized eigenvectors and the others by eigenvectors with both positive and

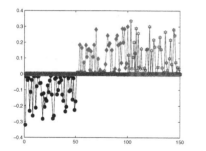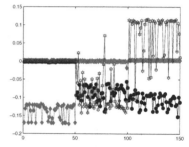

Fig. 2. The three principal eigenvectors of the adjacency matrix of the Iris dataset for $k=5$ (left) and $k=30$ (right)

negative values, the number of clusters equals the number of localized eigenvectors of one sign plus the clusters corresponding to the eigenvectors that have positive and negative values and include an eigenvector described in the second part of the Fiedler's theorem.

In real datasets, the challenging task is to identify weakly localized eigenvectors, each representing different cluster and to distinguish between vectors changing sign between two groups and within one group.

5   The SpecLoc2 Algorithm

The main steps of the SpecLoc2 algorithm are similar to these of the SpecLoc algorithm and they look in the following way:

The SpecLoc2 algorithm

```
Input: Data X, the number of nearest neighbors k
1. Form the adjacency matrix S.
2. Find c principal eigenvectors of S.
3. Calculate the eigenvector correlation matrix
4. Find uncorrelated weakly localized eigenvectors on the basis
   of the correlation matrix (eigenvector set WL).
5. Identify eigenvectors having positive values for one cluster
   and negative for others or vice versa (set PN).
6. Assign points to eigenvectors from the WL set
   and eigenvectors from the PN set.
```

The algorithm builds a graph, with points as vertices and similarities between points as edges. The weights of edges are calculated according to the Euclidean distance, using:

$$s_{ij} = \exp\left(-\frac{d_{ij}}{d_{max}}\right) \tag{1}$$

where d_{ij} is the Euclidean distance between objects i and j, and d_{max} is the maximum distance between any pair of objects from the dataset. On the basis of the metric we construct the k-nearest neighbor graph, connecting x_i to x_j if x_i is among the k-nearest neighbors of x_j. The algorithm uses the adjacency matrix because it is the simplest, nonnegative, and symmetric one. Its eigenvectors differ from L eigenvectors but they still obey assumptions of the Fiedler's theory. The vectors that take part in the partitioning are established on the basis of the pairwise correlation coefficients between each pair of c eigenvectors (c equals 20 in the algorithm, as we have assumed that the examined sets consist of maximum 20 clusters). The Pearson correlation coefficient between two eigenvectors v_i and v_j is defined as:

$$R_{ij} = \frac{\sum_{k=1}^{N}(v_{ik} - \overline{v_i})(v_{jk} - \overline{v_j})}{\sqrt{\sum_{k=1}^{N}(v_{ik} - \overline{v_i})^2}\sqrt{\sum_{k=1}^{N}(v_{jk} - \overline{v_j})^2}} \tag{2}$$

The coefficients R_{ij} range from -1 to 1. If two eigenvectors are linearly dependent, then the correlation between them will equal 1. The value of -1 indicates a perfect negative linear relationship between the vectors, and zero no linear relationship between the vectors. The correlation coefficient has been chosen as an efficient indicator whether two vectors have independent entries. If they are weakly localized in two different subregions their entries should differ from one another, so that they are linearly independent.

For the purpose of the algorithm we use absolute values of the eigenvector components in order to compute correlation coefficients. We have assumed that two eigenvectors are not localized in the same cluster if their correlation is smaller than 0.1 (the value has been established experimentally). Completely delocalized eigenvectors (with large, only nonpositive or only nonnegative values over the whole set) do not take part in calculation of the correlation coefficients, as they are not useful for partitioning purposes. We assume, that if the eigenvector median is higher than its standard deviation, the eigenvector is delocalized. The median is efficient location and dispersion measure for distributions revealed by delocalized eigenvectors.

Weakly localized eigenvectors, which are not correlated with any eigenvector related to higher eigenvalue, are written to the set WL and used for the final labeling of the data. Each eigenvector represents one cluster and each point is labeled according to the eigenvector with the highest entry for the point. Points assigned to the same eigenvector are further divided into two groups if the weakly localized eigenvector has both positive and negative values.

The next step of the SpecLoc2 algorithm is the identification of eigenvectors with relatively large both positive and negative values, which do not belong to the set WL. We have to distinguish between an eigenvector, that enables to separate two different clusters, and a vector that changes its sign within one group of vertices. According to the Fiedler's theorem the eigenvectors, we are interested in, occur after delocalized eigenvectors or eig envectors with only positive or only negative values in their region of localization. Because of the spectra perturbation the vector allowing to distinguish between two clusters sometimes will not appear as the second eigenvector in the complete spectrum, as it is the case for the Iris dataset, illustrated in Figure 2 right. Moreover, a few such vectors can exist. In order to find the right eigenvectors we check the vectors that appear after the localized ones or after a completely delocalized eigenvector (if it exists). We take into consideration only those that have the maximum values in that points, for which the already chosen eigenvectors are small (less than 0.1). Usually only one or two such eigenvectors are worth examination.

Next the assignment of points to the right partition is performed according to the procedure described below. For the purpose of partitioning two eigenvectors v and w are used. The first one is the vector with both positive and negative values from the set PN, whereas the second one serves for comparison. It is the closest to v vector in the set WL, related to a higher eigenvalue than v.

Partitioning on the basis of the Fiedler vectors

```
Input: A pair of vectors: the vector v and w
1. Find the sign of the maximum value vm of v absolute values
2. Set null values in v for all the points having opposite
   sign than the vm
3. Label each point x, having larger absolute value in v than in w
```

As each of the chosen weakly localized eigenvectors represents one cluster (or two if it changes its sign) and the vectors with positive and negative values divide unambiguously the set, we do not have to indicate the number of clusters manually or with the help of any other quality measure.

Computational complexity of the proposed algorithm is relatively small. First of all the adjacency matrix is sparse as we use the concept of k-nearest neighbors. Second the number of needed eigenvectors is relatively small, if we consider clusters of reasonable size only, i.e. if we require that the minimal cluster size exceeds 1 percent of the size of the whole data set. Moreover, in case of the adjacency matrix we seek for the principal eigenvectors, which are easier to find than eigenvectors corresponding to the smallest eigenvalues. In such the situation solving the eigenproblem even for a large dataset is not very time consuming. The other steps of the algorithm take time $O(n)$ each. So the solution is scalable.

6 Experiments

In this section we justify our approach by presenting a set of clustering experiments and comparing its performance to different solutions. The algorithms are evaluated on a several benchmark datasets, including both synthetic and real-world examples. They cover a wide range of difficulties that can be met during data segmentation. The algorithm was implemented in MATLAB.

In the first part of our experiments we would like to emphasize differences in the performance of the SpecLoc2 and the NJW [12] algorithms and show the dominance of our approach over the traditional solution. The NJW algorithm uses the similarity measure based on the Gaussian kernel function, defined as:

$$W_{ij} = \exp\left(-\frac{\|x_i - x_j\|^2}{2\sigma^2}\right) \tag{3}$$

where $\|x_i - x_j\|$ denotes the Euclidean distance between points x_i and x_j and σ kernel parameter. In order to compare the best achievements of the algorithms the values of the σ parameter were chosen manually, as described by Fischer et al. in [5]. For each dataset they have systematically scanned a wide range of σ and ran the clustering algorithm. We use their results in this comparison.

In this part of experiments we would like not only to compare the two approaches, but also show that the K-means algorithm, employed for the final partitioning in the NJW algorithm in many cases does not take into consideration some important information included in the eigenvector structure, contrary to our solution. We have modified the NJW algorithm by using the adjacency matrix built on the basis of the mutual k-nearest neighbor graph for the normalized Laplacian construction. Thanks to this both solutions use the same graph.

The algorithms are evaluated on the following benchmark datasets: 2RG (two rather high density rings and a Gaussian cluster with very low density), 4G (four Gaussian clusters each of different density in 3D), Iris, and Jain's toy problem [7]. Table 1 summarizes the partitioning results obtained by the SpecLoc2, NJW, and modified NJW algorithms.

Table 1. Comparison of classification errors for partitioning with the SpecLoc2, NJW, and modified NJW algorithms

Dataset	NJW	Modified NJW	SpecLoc2
2RG	6	6	3
4G	18	13	8
Iris	14	8	7
Jain	19	33	2

As can be seen the SpecLoc2 algorithm is the most flexible one and performs well independently on a dataset structure. Although both the SpecLoc2 and the NWJ algorithms use the same concept of eigenvector properties the second one often fails on real-world data or clusters with different densities. We will explain the reasons why such results are observed, with the help of the 4G set. The NJW algorithm uses the four principal eigenvectors in order to obtain correct partitions. The fourth eigenvector, representing the sparsest cluster, is quite distorted and causes wrong partitioning of some points. For the SpecLoc2 algorithm only the three principal vectors suffice for the correct partitioning (two uncorrelated localized eigenvectors and the vector with positive and negative values). In the other cases (e.g. the Wine dataset) the better performance of the SpecLoc2 algorithm lies in small differences between two eigenvectors entries, which do not influence K-means partitioning but are taken into account by the presented method.

We have also compared the performance of the SpecLoc2 algorithm to other methods, similarly as in [14]:

- NJW algorithm.
- Self-tune spectral clustering (SSC) algorithm [18], which computes automatically the scale and the number of groups and can handle multi-scale data.
- The KASP algorithm [17], fast approximate spectral clustering in which a distortion-minimizing local transformation is first applied to the data, based on local K-means clustering.
- The KWASP algorithm [19] that extends the Nyström method and improves the approximation of the eigensystem by introducing the probability density function as a natural weighting scheme.
- The Kernel-K-means-Ratio Assoc (KKRA) algorithm [1], that directly optimizes various weighted graph clustering objectives, such as the popular ratio cut, normalized cut, and ratio association.
- Fast Affinity Propagation clustering approach (FAP) [14] that simultaneously considers both local and global structure information contained in datasets.

In case of the NJW, SSC, and KKRA algorithms the adjacency matrix is computed as in [14].

We performed experiments on five UCI datasets, including Wine, Balance, Segments, Pendigits, and Optdigits [15]. The basic information of those real-world datasets are summarized in Table 2. Digits389 is a subset of the three classes 3, 8, 9 of the UCI handwritten digit recognition dataset from the UCI Machine Learning Repository– these three classes were chosen since distinguishing between sample handwritten digits from these classes visually is a difficult task.

Table 2. A summary of datasets

Dataset	Size	Dimensions	Classes
Wine	178	13	3
Balance	625	4	3
Segment	2310	18	7
Optdigits	1151	64	3
Pendigit-test	3498	16	10
Pendigit-train	7494	16	10

All the datasets are labeled, which enables evaluation of the clustering results against the labels using normalized mutual information (NMI) as a measure of division quality. We refer an interested reader to [10] for details regarding the measure.

The performance of the algorithms shows Table 3. We can see the superiority of the SpecLoc2 algorithm over the other tested solutions. The presented method is competitive to the other cases in terms of the quality of partitioning, measured with the help of the normalized mutual information.

Clustering results of our solution are stable, their do not depend on starting, randomly chosen settings, as those using K-means clustering. Moreover they are not very sensitive to the number of neighbors (the only parameter in our algorithm). In case of the Wine, Digits389, and Pendigit sets the NMI changes only by a few percent within a range of 10 subsequent number of neighbors. As the quality of partitioning for the Balance and Segment sets is not very high, the NMI remains stable for even much wider range of k values.

Table 3. Comparison of NMI for partitioning with different algorithms

Dataset	NJW	SSC	KKRA	KASP	KWASP	FAP	SpecLoc2
Wine	0.41587	0.43157	0.38027	0.40507	0.43447	0.44577	**0.8518**
Balance	0.14647	0.26267	0.21617	0.13057	0.18947	0.20467	**0.5278**
Segment	0.49407	0.56807	0.57117	0.56587	0.53117	0.64087	**0.6560**
Digits389	0.52647	0.60957	0.79357	0.76017	0.75417	0.90237	**0.9213**
Pendigit-test	0.68617	0.67997	0.69867	0.68967	0.68077	0.73627	**0.8239**
Pendigit-train	0	0	0.70357	0.70517	0.68167	0.75497	**0.8025**

Our approach shows the ability of discovering clusters that are difficult to distinguish. The SpecLoc2 algorithm has found the right number of clusters in case of the Wine, Optdigits, and Pendigit-train datasets, for Balance it has failed to detect one group and Pendigit-test has been divided into 11 clusters instead of 10. Only in case of the Segment dataset it was not able to find 3 groups.

We have compared the performance of the SpecLoc2 algorithm with our previous method the SpecLoc algorithm, which is also able to determine the number of clusters. In some cases, as for example for the Iris set, the results are the same for both solutions. However, in many cases the presented algorithm outperforms the older one either in terms of NMI or on account of the determined number of clusters. There are the cases, where the vectors with positive and negative values have great influence on partitioning. Moreover, the SpecLoc2 algorithm is less demanding, when it comes to tuning the parameter of nearest neighbors. It performs well in both localized and delocalized cases.

7 Conclusions

In this work, we have proposed a new approach for spectral clustering. Its goal is to make maximal use of information derived from the eigenvector structure in order to improve the quality of spectral partitioning and limit the number of parameters. We have analyzed the properties of eigenvectors and proposed methods for selecting the ones, that reveal the dataset structure in the best way.

Our algorithm is not only efficient, but also flexible to work with different cases that may occur in real-world datasets. We have used several UCI benchmark datasets to validate the advantage of our approach, by comparing to the classic and new clustering algorithms. Empirical results show that our method can find the true cluster assignment by using only one parameter, and it outperforms the other methods, even specifying more parameters.

References

1. Dhillon, I., Guan, Y., Kulis, B.: Weighted graph cuts without eigenvectors: a multilevel approach. IEEE Transactions on Pattern Analysis and Machine Intelligence 29(11), 1944–1957 (2007)
2. Fiedler, M.: A property of eigenvectors of nonnegative symmetric matrices and its application to graph theory. Czechoslovak Mathematical Journal 25, 619–633 (1975)
3. Filoche, M., Mayboroda, S.: Universal mechanism for Anderson and weak localization. Proc. of the National Academy of Sciences 109(37), 14761–14766 (2012)
4. Fridlyand, J., Dudoit, S.: A prediction-based resampling method to estimate the number of clusters in a dataset. Genome Biology 3, 7 (2002)
5. Fischer, I., Poland, J.: Amplifying the Block Matrix Structure for Spectral Clustering. Technical Report No. IDSIA-03-05, Telecommunications Lab, pp. 21–28 (2005)
6. Hagen, L., Kahng, A.: New spectral methods for ratio cut partitioning and clustering. IEEE Transactions on Computer-Aided Design 11, 1074–1088 (1992)
7. Jain, A., Law, M.: Data clustering: A user's dilemma. In: Pal, S.K., Bandyopadhyay, S., Biswas, S. (eds.) PReMI 2005. LNCS, vol. 3776, pp. 1–10. Springer, Heidelberg (2005)
8. Kannan, R., Vempala, S., Vetta, A.: On clusterings: good, bad and spectral. In: 41st Symposium on Foundations of Computer Science, FOCS (2000)
9. Lucińska, M.: A spectral clustering algorithm based on eigenvector localization. In: Rutkowski, L., Korytkowski, M., Scherer, R., Tadeusiewicz, R., Zadeh, L.A., Zurada, J.M. (eds.) ICAISC 2014, Part II. LNCS, vol. 8468, pp. 749–759. Springer, Heidelberg (2014)
10. Manning, C.D., Raghavan, P., Schtäuze, H.: Introduction to Information Retrieval. Cambridge University Press (2008)
11. Meila, M., Shi, J.: A random walks view of spectral segmentation. In: Proc. of 10th International Workshop on Artificial Intelligence and Statistics (2001)
12. Ng, A., Jordan, M., Weiss, Y.: On spectral clustering: Analysis and an algorithm. In: Dietterich, T.G., Becker, S., Ghahramani, Z. (eds.) Advances in Neural Information Processing Systems, vol. 14, pp. 849–856. MIT Press, Cambridge (2002)
13. Pentney, W., Meila, M.: Spectral clustering of biological sequence data. In: AAAI 2005, pp. 845–850 (2005)
14. Shang, F., Jiao, L.C., Shi, J., Wang, F., Gong, M.: Fast affinity propagation clustering: A multilevel approach. Pattern Recognition 45, 474–486 (2012)
15. http://mlearn.ics.uci.edu/MLRepository.html
16. von Luxburg, U.: A Tutorial on spectral clustering. Statistics and Computing 17(4), 395–416 (2007)
17. Yan, D., Huang, L., Jordan, M.: Fast approximate spectral clustering. In: Proceedings of the 15th ACM SIGKDD International Conference on Knowledge Discovery and Data Mining (KDD), pp. 907–916 (2009)
18. Zelnik-Manor, L., Perona, P.: Self-tuning spectral clustering. In: Proceedings of the Advances in Neural Information Processing Systems, vol. 17, pp. 1601–1608 (2005)
19. Zhang, K., Kwok, J.T.: Density-weighted Nyström method for computing large kernel eigen-systems. Neural Computation 21, 121–146 (2009)

Applying Recurrent Fuzzy Neural Network
to Predict the Runoff of Srepok River

Hieu Ngoc Duong[1], Quyen Ngoc Thi Nguyen[2], Long Ta Bui[3], Hien T. Nguyen[4],
and Václav Snášel[5]

[1] Faculty of Computer Science and Engineering, HCM University of Technology, Vietnam
[2] Tay Nguyen University, Vietnam
[3] Faculty of Environment and Natural Resources, HCM University of Technology, Vietnam
[4] Faculty of Information Technology, Ton Duc Thang University, Vietnam
[5] Department of Computer Science, VSB-Technical University of Ostrava, Czech Republic
dnhieu@cse.hcmut.edu.vn, ngocquyendhtn@yahoo.com.vn,
longbt62@hcmut.edu.vn, hien@tdt.edu.vn,
vaclav.snasel@vsb.cz

Abstract. Recurrent fuzzy neural network (RFNN) is proven to be a great method for modeling, characterizing and predicting many kinds of nonlinear hydrological time series data such as rainfall, water quality, and river runoff. In our study, we employed RFNN to find out the correlation between the climate data and the runoff of Srepok River in Vietnam and then to model and predict the runoff of Srepok River in the current, as well as in the future. In order to prove the advantage of RFNN, we compare RFNN with an environmental model called SWAT on the same dataset. We conduct experiments using the climate data and the daily river's runoff data that have been collected in 22 years, ranging from 1900 to 2011. The experiment results show that the relative error of RFNN is about 0.35 and the relative error of SWAT is 0.44. It means that RFNN outperforms SWAT. Moreover, the most important advantage of RFNN when comparing with SWAT is that RFNN does not need much data as SWAT does.

Keywords: Srepok, SWAT, Data Mining, RFNN, Runoff.

1 Introduction

The climate change is one of the greatest challenges for the mankind in the 21st century, affecting seriously to production, life, environment, as well as other fields of people in the world in generally and Vietnam in particularly. Therefore, all most of countries over the world have set a high priority to accommodate to climate change in the national development plan. In recognizing the serious causes of climate change, the Vietnamese Prime Minister, on December 02, 2008, approved the national target program accommodating to climate change. Two in eight important missions of the program are (i) to consider how the climate change effects to production and civilian and (ii) to determine solutions to accommodate to the climate change. To meet the call for attention in finding solutions for this emerging problem, in this paper, we propose an approach to predict the runoff of Srepok River in Vietnam in the futute.

K. Saeed and V. Snášel (Eds.): CISIM 2014, LNCS 8838, pp. 55–66, 2014.
© IFIP International Federation for Information Processing 2014

The Srepok River is located in the Central Highland of Vietnam. Its watershed has a plentiful lake system, districts evenly. Due to slope terrain, the water maintaining ability is not good and most of small streams of the river almost run out of water in the dry season and the water of several big lakes drop into a very low level. Together with the impact of climate change, the unusually change of the watershed of the Srepok River as observed recently has posed a challenging problem to water resource security of Vietnam. After monitoring the Srepok runoff in many years ranging from 1990 to 2011, we realize that the Srepok runoff has varied too strange that nobody can understand exactly what correct natural rules it holds, even for civilian. Naturally, the Srepok runoff varies with seasonal rule by year; it is low in dry season and high in wet season. But in a few years, the Srepok runoff decreases suddenly in dry season or increases suddenly in wet season and it is worth to warn because it impacts directly to people life in the Srepok basin. That raises the challenge is how to simulate and predict the Srepok runoff in order to help the managers and civilian adapt with its anomaly.

In the environment field, one often applies several kinds of environmental toolkit to model the impact of climate change to water resource, especially runoff of rivers. In [2] the authors used SWAT tool and Mike software to model the change of water resources and land resources. However, one of disadvantages of this method when adapting to the environments in Vietnam is that SWAT tool and Mike software require a lot kinds of data, ranging from climate, water resource to soil map data, but those of the environment and natural resources in Vietnam are not available.

In this paper, we propose a new method that applies data mining in order to model the correlation between the climate data and the Srepok runoff. And then the correlation is used to predict the Srepok runoff in the future. Among many effective models and algorithms available, we employ a hybrid of neural network and fuzzy theory to build a prediction toolkit. After developing the toolkit, we try to compare the result of two methods: SWAT and data mining. By the specific experiments, we conclude exactly the advantages of our approach and draw more researches for future work.

The rest of this paper is organized as follows. Section 2 presents the related work. Section 3 presents the dataset used in experiments. Section 4 introduces recurrent fuzzy neural network. In section 5, we present experiments. Some finding will be pointed out in Section 5. Finally, we draw conclusion and perspectives for future work.

2   Related Work

In this section, we present related work on river runoff predicting and especially employing artificial neural network. The authors in [8] identify the impact of climate change to hydrology of the Upper Nile River. They showed assessment of changes in water resources and the impacts of dam operation. The study was conducted with the hydrological data that are limited and therefore use the simple, reliable method, and simulate the impact of different change climate scenarios on hydrology and water resources in the river basin.

In 2007, Ibrahim Can [9] applied two different kinds of artificial neural network that are the feed forward neural network back propagation (FFBP) and Generalized Regression Neural Network (GRNN) in order to predict the Karasu River runoff. Besides, in 2009, a study of Lance E. Besaw et al. [10] also demonstrated the use of neural networks was effective for predicting driver runoff. Lance E. Besaw *et al.* pointed out that predictions based on hourly data more efficiently than using daily data because important relationships between climate and the runoff was lost as predicting by day. Also in other studies, Lekkas DF [11] confirmed a multilayer back-propagation network with almost all components used for hydrological applications. Also using neural networks for predicting, Saman Razavi *et al* [13] and Alireza Mardookhpour [14] confirmed neural network more effective than traditional methods. Neural networks are widely used for hydrologic prediction problem and were gradually replaced by the traditional prediction model, such as models of Transfer Function (TF) in the study by Demetris F. Lekkas [15].

In Viet Nam, 2007 Pham Thi Hoang Nhung, Quang Thuy Ha [3] studied how to use artificial neural network in predicting of the Hoa Binh runoff before 10 days. The authors analyzed artificial neural network to predict the runoff and applied genetic algorithm for learning neural network. Nguyen Thanh Son *et al.* [4] studied the effect of climate change to water resources of Nhue River basin. In the study the authors also indicated other methodologies as climate change scenarios or NAM models to study how important climate change is. They conducted the simulations of the climate change effects on water resources and had much valuable assessment.

Tran Thanh Xuan [5] studied the impacts of climate change on river runoff in and pointed out the factors that influence most to the river runoff. In [7], the author researched applications of artificial neural networks to predict rainfall and river runoff to prevent and restrict drought of the river basins in the Central Highland of Vietnam. In the study, the model proved very effective on predicting river runoff.

3   Data Set

In the Central Highland of Vietnam, there are several climate stations that gather automatically climate data. For our research, we gather 22 years data from 1990-2011 of the Srepok River. The data was collected daily. We stored the data collected each day in a record, each of which consists of nine fields capturing information of that day as follows: average of temperature, maximum of temperature, minimum of temperature, average of humid degree, minimum of humid degree, rain quantity, evaporation per day, the number of sunning hours, and runoff. In total we collected 7665 records.

After gathering and analyzing the Srepok runoff data and the climate data, we realize that are kinds of time series data and there are some hidden correlations between them. But, if we just only employ a few normal visualizing techniques to find out the correlation, it is hard to monitor by the analyzer. As a result, it also is difficult to conclude what happens with the Srepok runoff in the future when the climate is going to change little but continuously by time. So we propose a new method that employs data mining techniques to discover this correlation.

4   Proposed Method

There are many methods that can be used for predicting the time series data like the Srepok runoff data with accepted accuracy. We can use any regression methods to solve the issue such as linear regression, nonlinear regression, fuzzy system, artificial neural network, support vector machine, etc. Every method has some advantages and also disadvantages depending on the data with specific characteristics. However, it is not easy to state which method is better than other and the appropriate answer for the most suitable chosen method comes from analysis of experiment results. After evaluating the historical data of the Srepok runoff and the climate data we decided to employ a hybrid of artificial neural network and fuzzy system called recurrent fuzzy neural network (RFNN). RFNN works more effective than standard neural network [1, 6] when we compare these at two criterions (i) RFNN can estimate more complex relationship between dependent and independent variables and (ii) the convergence of RFNN is faster than standard neural network. Structure of RFNN is shown as Fig 1 and RFNN includes four layers as follows:

- Layer 1 is input layer that has N nodes, each of which corresponds with a parameter. In our data, input could be all parameters of the climate data.
- Layer 2 is called membership layer. Nodes in this layers will convert the crisp data in fuzzy data by applying membership functions such as Gauss function. Number of neural nodes in this layer is NxM where M is the number of fuzzy rules.
- Layer 3 is the layer of fuzzy rules. Each node in this layer plays the role of a fuzzy rule. Connecting between Layer 3 and Layer 4 presents for fuzzy conclusion.
- Layer 4 is the output layer including P nodes. In our model, P will be set to one and this is the driver runoff value.

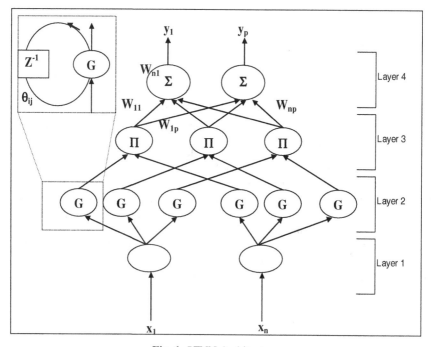

Fig. 1. *RFNN* Architecture

Model Process

We employ a popular algorithm that learns parameters m_{ij}, σ_{ij}, θ_{ij} and w_{jk} respectively. Let $u_i^{(k)}$ and $O_i^{(k)}$ be respectively the input and the output of the node ith in the layer k.

- Layer 1: $O_i^{(1)} = u_i^{(1)} = x_i(t)$ $\qquad i = 1 \div N$
- Layer 2: note that every node has 3 parameters, namely m_{ij}, σ_{ij} and θ_{ij} respectively.

$$O_{ij}^{(2)} = \exp\left[-\frac{\left(u_{ij}^{(2)} - m_{ij}\right)^2}{\left(\sigma_{ij}\right)}\right] \tag{1}$$

$i = 1 \div N$, $j = 1 \div M$, m_{ij} and σ_{ij} are the center and the variance of Gauss distribution function.

$$u_{ij}^{(2)}(t) = O_i^{(1)} + \theta_{ij} O_{ij}^{(2)}(t-1) \tag{2}$$

$i = 1 \div N$, $j = 1 \div M$, θ_{ij} denotes the weight of a recurrent node.

We easily realize that the input of the nodes in this layer has the factor $O_{ij}^{(2)}(t-1)$. This factor denotes the remaining information of the previous model. Therefore, after replacing $u_{ij}^{(2)}$ in (1) by (2), we get equation (3) as follows:

$$
\begin{aligned}
O_{ij}^{(2)} &= \exp\left[-\frac{\left[O_i^{(1)} + \theta_{ij} O_{ij}^{(2)}(t-1) - m_{ij}\right]^2}{\left(\sigma_{ij}\right)^2}\right] \\
&= \exp\left[-\frac{\left[x_i(t) + \theta_{ij} O_{ij}^{(2)}(t-1) - m_{ij}\right]^2}{\left(\sigma_{ij}\right)^2}\right]
\end{aligned}
\qquad i = 1 \div N, j = 1 \div M
\tag{3}
$$

- Layer 3: Each node in this layer corresponds with an AND expression. Each AND expression is defined as follows:

$$O_j^{(3)} = \prod_{i=1}^{N} O_{ij}^{(2)} = \prod_{i=1}^{N} \exp\left[-\frac{\left[x_i(t) + \theta_{ij} O_{ij}^{(2)}(t-1) - m_{ij}\right]^2}{\left(\sigma_{ij}\right)^2}\right] \quad where\ j = 1 \div M$$

- Layer 4: Nodes of this layer are responsible for converting fuzzy to crisp.

$$
\begin{aligned}
y_k &= O_k^{(4)} = \sum_{j=1}^{M} u_{jk}^{(4)} w_{jk} = \sum_{j=1}^{M} O_j^{(3)} w_{jk} \\
&= \sum_{j=1}^{M} w_{jk} \prod_{i=1}^{N} \exp\left[-\frac{\left[x_i(t) + \theta_{ij} O_{ij}^{(2)}(t-1) - m_{ij}\right]^2}{\left(\sigma_{ij}\right)^2}\right] \quad where\ k = 1 \div P
\end{aligned}
$$

After defining RFNN architecture, RFNN is learnt by back propagation algorithm. Each learning step spends much time to learn 85% of all data (18 years data). Then RFNN will be tested in 15% data and evaluated. If it gives prediction results correct, the learning step will be stopped; otherwise the learning is continuous.

Learning Algorithm

Back propagation algorithm is applied for learning RFNN that is the same with feed forward neural network (FFNN). The target of the applied algorithm is how to minimize the sum square error (SSE):

$$E = \frac{1}{2}\sum_t \left(y^{(d)}(t) - y(t)\right)^2 = \frac{1}{2}\sum_t \left(y^{(d)}(t) - O^{(4)}(t)\right)^2 , \text{ in which } y^{(d)}(t) \text{ is the real}$$

river runoff and $y(t) = O^{(4)}(t)$ is the calculated river runoff from RFNN at the tth tuple. In back propagation algorithm, the parameters are updated as follows:

$$W(t+1) = W(t) + \Delta W(t) = W(t) + \eta\left(-\frac{\partial E(t)}{\partial W}\right), \text{ in which } W \text{ is a parameter vector of the}$$

model and η is the learning rate.

Let $e(t) = y^{(d)}(t) - y(t)$, we have: $\dfrac{\partial E(t)}{\partial W} = -e(t)\dfrac{\partial y(t)}{\partial W} = -e(t)\dfrac{\partial O^{(4)}(t)}{\partial W}$

Therefore, m_{ij}, σ_{ij}, θ_{ij} and w_{jk} will be updated as:

$$w_{jk}(t+1) = w_{jk}(t) - \eta^w \frac{\partial E}{\partial w_{jk}} \quad ; \quad m_{ij}(t+1) = m_{ij}(t) - \eta^m \frac{\partial E}{\partial m_{ij}}$$

$$\sigma_{ij}(t+1) = \sigma_{ij}(t) - \eta^\sigma \frac{\partial E}{\partial \sigma_{ij}} \quad ; \quad \theta_{ij}(t+1) = \theta_{ij}(t) - \eta^\theta \frac{\partial E}{\partial \theta_{ij}}, \text{ in which}$$

$$\frac{\partial E}{\partial w_{jk}} = -e(t)O_j^{(3)}$$

$$\frac{\partial E}{\partial m_{ij}} = -e(t)\sum_{j=1}^{M} w_{jk}\frac{\partial O_j^{(3)}}{\partial m_{ij}}$$

$$= -e(t)\sum_{j=1}^{M} w_{jk}O_j^{(3)}\frac{2\left[x_i(t) + O_{ij}^{(2)}(t-1)\theta_{ij} - m_{ij}\right]}{\left(\sigma_{ij}\right)^2}$$

$$\frac{\partial E}{\partial \sigma_{ij}} = -e(t)\sum_{j=1}^{M} w_{jk}\frac{\partial O_j^{(3)}}{\partial \sigma_{ij}}$$

$$= -e(t)\sum_{j=1}^{M} w_{jk}O_j^{(3)}\frac{2\left[x_i(t) + O_{ij}^{(2)}(t-1)\theta_{ij} - m_{ij}\right]^2}{\left(\sigma_{ij}\right)^3}$$

$$\frac{\partial E}{\partial \theta_{ij}} = -e(t)\sum_{j=1}^{M} w_{jk}\frac{\partial O_j^{(3)}}{\partial \theta_{ij}}$$

$$-e(t)\sum_{j=1}^{M} w_{jk}\frac{-2\left[x_i(t)+O_{ij}^{(2)}(t-1)\theta_{ij}-m_{ij}\right]O_{ij}^{(2)}(t-1)}{\left(\sigma_{ij}\right)^2}$$

In summary, our learning model is a supervised learning model with t^{th} tuple $\{(X_t, y_t)\}$. $X_t = (x_1, x_2, \ldots, x_n)$ is a vector of the climate data and y_t is its corresponding the Srepok runoff at the same time. The work flow will be executed as follows:

- Step 1: Feed forward X_t through RFFN to get output as:

$$y_k = \sum_{j=1}^{M} w_{jk}\prod_{i=1}^{N}\exp\left[-\frac{\left[x_i(t)+\theta_{ij}O_{ij}^{(2)}(t-1)-m_{ij}\right]^2}{\left(\sigma_{ij}\right)^2}\right]$$

- Step 2: Calculating error between the real value and output of RFNN for s^{th} tuple. Let e(t) be the error value and e(t) = $y_k(t)$ - y(t), in which y_k (t) denotes the output value of RFNN and y(t) denotes the real value.

- Step 3: Updating $m_{ij}, \sigma_{ij}, \theta_{ij}$ and w_{jk} as the following expression:

$$w_{jk}(t+1) = w_{jk}(t)-\eta^w\frac{\partial E}{\partial w_{jk}} \quad ; \quad m_{ij}(t+1) = m_{ij}(t)-\eta^m\frac{\partial E}{\partial m_{ij}}$$

$$\sigma_{ij}(t+1) = \sigma_{ij}(t)-\eta^\sigma\frac{\partial E}{\partial \sigma_{ij}} \quad ; \quad \theta_{ij}(t+1) = \theta_{ij}(t)-\eta^\theta\frac{\partial E}{\partial \theta_{ij}}$$

Improving Learning Efficiency with Momentum Technique

There is a popular technique that can help the RFNN learning overcome local minima and speed up the RFNN learning: it is momentum technique. When applying the technique, updating of $m_{ij}, \sigma_{ij}, \theta_{ij}$ and w_{jk} are as the following expression:

$$w_{jk}(t+1) = w_{jk}(t)-\eta^w\frac{\partial E}{\partial w_{jk}}+\beta\times\Delta w_{jk}(t-1)$$

$$m_{ij}(t+1) = m_{ij}(t)-\eta^m\frac{\partial E}{\partial m_{ij}}+\beta\times\Delta m_{jk}(t-1)$$

$$\sigma_{ij}(t+1) = \sigma_{ij}(t)-\eta^\sigma\frac{\partial E}{\partial \sigma_{ij}}+\beta\times\Delta\sigma_{jk}(t-1)$$

$$\theta_{ij}(t+1) = \theta_{ij}(t)-\eta^\theta\frac{\partial E}{\partial \theta_{ij}}+\beta\times\Delta\theta_{jk}(t-1)$$

where β is momentum term.

5   Experiment

5.1   Experiments with SWAT Model

SWAT is a hydrologic quality model developed by United States Department of Agricultural-Agricultural Research Service (USDA-ARS). It is a continuous time model that operates on daily time duration. The objective of model is to predict the impact of management on water, sediment, agricultural chemical yields in a large basin. SWAT is regression model that simulates the relationship between input parameters and predicted parameters. For predicting river runoff, the input parameters are much complex including several major hydrology components such as: weather, erosion map, sedimentation map, soil temperature, plant map, pesticide use, etc [16]. SWAT model uses Nash – Sutcliffe Index (NSI) value and coefficient of determination (R^2) to assess the quality of simulating model. The simulating quality of model is assessed with four levels: $0.9 \leq NSI \leq 1$: good; $0.7 \leq NSI \leq 0.9$: quite; $0.5 \leq NSI \leq 0.7$: mean; $0.3 \leq NSI \leq 0.5$: weak.

As mentioning before, the input data is very important when applying SWAT to simulate river runoff. First of all, we must gather the input data of the Srepok runoff and the climate. Then, the input data are arranged with several different detail levels: 1) basin, sub-basin; 2) Hydrologic Response Units (HRUs); 3) space data: DEM, soil map, land use map; 4) climate data: max temperature, min temperature, rainfall, etc. Next, we process input data such as: land use map, soil map, topography, climatic conditions, etc that can be edited by ArcGis software. After that, SWAT model is applied to assess the impact of land use to the river runoff. In the end, we determine the relevant SWAT model to simulate the Srepok runoff.

Table 1. SWAT sensitive parameters and calibrated values

Parameter	Description of parameter	Calibrated value		
		Fitted value	Min value	Max value
CN2.	Initial SCS CN II value	-0.17	- 0.20	0.20
ALPHA_BF	Base Flow Alpha factor	0.17	0.00	1.00
GW_DELAY	Groundwater delay	160.20	30.00	450.00
GWQMN	Threshold water depth in the shallow aquifer for flow	1.26	0.00	2.00

Table 2. Model performance for the simulation of flow-out

Period	Time step	Value	
		R^2	NSI
Before calibration	Monthly	0.70	0.41
Calibration (2004-2008)	Monthly	0.75	0.68
Validation (2009-2011)		0.82	0.77

After simulating the Srepok runoff at a hydrological station called Buon Don, we carry out the calibration and validation of the model. Four parameters are chosen to calibrate the model including Curve Number (CN2), Base flow Alpha factor

(ALPHA_BF), Groundwater Delay (GW_DELAY), Threshold water depth in the shallow aquifer for flow (GWQMN). The calibration result is shown in Table 1. After that, we use calibrated result to run SWAT model again. Following that, we get the new values of NSI and R^2 that are higher than the first times. Table 2 shows the calibration of SWAT model in 2004-2008. The fit of the simulated and observed runoff is acceptable because NSI is 0.68 and R^2 is 0.75. Finally, we use the parameters found out from calibration to validate the model. In the result, the NSI value reached 0.77 and R^2 was 0.82 and in Fig 2 compares the different between the simulated and observed runoff in 2009-2011. Therefore, this study can state that SWAT model is suitable to simulate the Srepok river runoff.

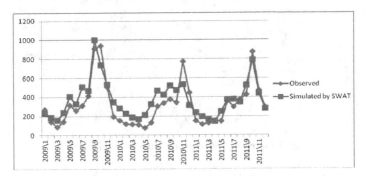

Fig. 2. Observed and simulated river runoff after validation

As mentioned-above, one of disadvantage of SWAT model is that SWAT must be provided enough and much data. Due to the lack of data, especially soil map data, in the current, we just only able to model the Srepok runoff to 2011. If provided enough and exactly input data, SWAT is potential to solve completely the raising problem.

5.2   Experiments with RFNN

In contrast with SWAT model, RFNN does not require much data but it has another disadvantage; RFNN is a black box for the analyzer. As mentioning in Section 4, in order to learn RFNN, the analyzer must input many parameters such as: learning rate, momentum, number of fuzzy rules. Unfortunately, it is hard to choose the relevant value for the parameters even the analyzer is an expert of RFNN researching. So for our experiment, we tried with several combinations of the parameters value and ran the algorithm 50 times, we found 5 combinations that give quite good result.

In Fig. 3 shows the simulated runoff by RFNN when we set the number of fuzzy rules is 10, learning rate is 0.001, momentum is 0.001 and epoch number is 200,000. We also use the data of Buon Don Station in 1900-2008 for learning and in 2009-2011 for testing. Fig. 4 compares the observed data with the simulated data modeling by SWAT and RFNN while Fig. 5 shows the relative error of two models. The relative error of RFNN is about 0.35 and if comparing with the relative error of SWAT is 0.44, we can see that RFNN outperforms SWAT. However, it is superficial and incorrect if concluding that RFNN is better than SWAT. If we assess the mathematical property of two models, both are regression models. SWAT is hydrological model based on data of climate, soil, and water resource, so if we have enough and exact data, SWAT will simulate the river runoff better RFNN even the analyzer can find the optimal parameters for RFNN. In our case, we would like to confirm again our problem is that we cannot gather enough data for SWAT model not only in the future but also in the current. As a result, the raising problem is how to predict the Srepok runoff is impossible if using SWAT, but with RFNN, it is possible. Fig. 6 shows the results of prediction in 2015-2018 with the previous RFNN model. In this case, the climate data is gotten from SEA-START[1].

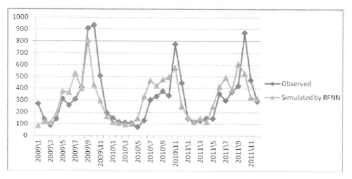

Fig. 3. Observed and simulated runoff with RFNN

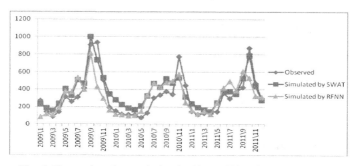

Fig. 4. Comparing observed, simulated runoff by SWAT and RFNN

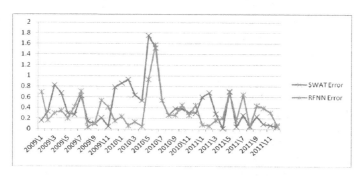

Fig. 5. Comparing related error between SWAT and RFNN

---

[1] http://startcc.iwlearn.org

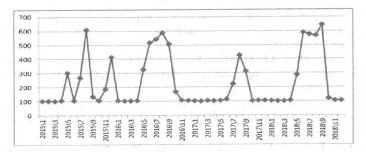

Fig. 6. The Srepok river runoff in 2015-2018 predited by RFNN

6   Conclusions

In this paper, we would like to introduce a new approach to simulate how climate changes influence to the Srepok runoff in Vietnam. Vietnam is an agricultural country, so water resources play a very important role in people life. Therefore, if the approach model can produce exactly data of the Srepok runoff in future, it will be so helpful for the national managers and the civilian. As mentioning in the experiment part, RFNN can predict quite exactly when comparing with the real data and the simulated data of SWAT model because the relative error of RFNN is quite low. Moreover, in Vietnam scenario, the most important advantage of RFNN when comparing with SWAT is that RFNN does not need much data as SWAT does. After analyzing the Srepok runoff we realize the data has seasonal varying. Therefore, in further research, we will try to highlight our time series data by applying chaos theory before employing RFNN.

References

1. Duong, H.N., Tran, Q.M., Dang, K.T.: Extendable Library of Basic Data Mining Algorithms. In: Proc. of the 11st Conference on Science & Technology, Ho Chi Minh City University of Technology (2009)
2. Nguyen, Q.T.N., Bui, L.T., Duong, H.N.: Assessment the impacts of land use and climate change on water discharge of Srepok river watershed. In: Proc. of the 34th Asian Conference on Remote Sensing, pp. 152–164 (2013)
3. Pham, N.T.H., Ha, H.T.: How to apply artificial neural network for predicting warter level of Hoa Binh Lake before 10 days. In: Proc of the 10th Conference of Selected Issues in Communication and Information Technology (2007)
4. Nguyen, S.T., Ngo, C.T., Van, H.T., Nguyen, N.Y.: Impact of climate change on water resource of NHUE River basin. In: 27th HaNoi National University Magazine of Science, pp. 218–226 (2011)
5. Tran, X.T., Hoang, T.M., Le, N.T., Luong, D.H.: Impact of climate change on river runoff. In: 8th Magazine of Science Presentation Selection, pp. 146–153 (2011)
6. Duong, H.N.: Using RFNN to Predict Price of Products in Market". In: Proc. of the 9st Conference on Science & Technology, HCM University of Technology (2006)

7. Nguyen, T.D.: Applying artificial neural network to predict rainfall and runoff to prevent and restrict drought in Viet Nam High Land basin rivers. Journal of Science and Engineering of Water Resource and Environment 22 (2008)

8. Kim, U., Kaluarachchi, J.J., Smakhtin, V.U.: Climate Change Impacts on Hydrology and Water Resources of the Upper Blue Nile River Basin, Ethiopia. In: IWMI Research Report, 126 (2008)

9. Can, I., Yerdelen, C., Kahyal, E.: Stochastic modeling of Karasu River (Turkey) using the methods of Artificial Neural Networks. In: Proc. of the AGU Hydrology Days, pp. 138–144 (2007)

10. Besaw, L.E., Rizzo, D.M., Bierman, P.R., Hackett, W.R.: Advances in ungauged stream flow prediction using artificial neural networks. Journal of Hydrology 386, 27–37 (2010)

11. Lekkas, D.F., Onof, C.: Improved flow forecasting using artificial neural networks. In: Proc. of 9th International Conference on Environmental and Technology, pp. 877–884 (2005)

12. Nazif, S., Karamouz, M., Zahmatkesh, Z.: Climate Change Impacts on Runoff Evaluation: A Case Study. In: World Environmental and Water Resources Congress, pp. 3350–3360 (2012)

13. Razavi, S., Araghinejad, S.: Reservoir Inflow Modeling Using Temporal Neural Networks with Forgetting Factor Approach, Water Resour Manage. International Journal of Water Resource Management 23, 39–55 (2009)

14. Mardookhpour, A.: Prediction of stream flow by utilizing artificial neural network in floodplain (Case study: Sepidroud watershed). International Journal of Forest, Soil and Erosion (2013)

15. Lekkas, D.F.: Development and Comparison of Data-Based Flow Forecasting Methods. PhD Thesis, Department of Civil and Environmental Engineering. Imperial College of Science, Technology and Medicine (2002)

16. Santhi, C., Arnold, J.G., Williams, J.R., Dugas, W.A., Srinivasan, R., Hauck, L.M.: Validation of the SWAT model on the large river basin with point and nonpoint sources. Journal of American Water Resources Association 37, 1169–1188 (2001)

17. Shudong, Z., Weiguang, L., Jun, N., Guangzhi, W., Lina, Z.: Combined Method of Chaotic Theory and Neural Networks for Quality Prediction. Journal of Northeast Agricultural University 17, 71–76 (2010)

Comparison of Chaos Driven PSO and Differential Evolution on the Selected PID Tuning Problem

Roman Senkerik[1], Michal Pluhacek[1], Ivan Zelinka[2], Donald Davendra[2], and Zuzana Kominkova Oplatkova[1]

[1]Tomas Bata University in Zlin , Faculty of Applied Informatics,
Nam T.G. Masaryka 5555, 760 01 Zlin, Czech Republic
[2]Technical University of Ostrava, Faculty of Electrical Engineering and
Computer Science, 17. listopadu 15,708 33 Ostrava-Poruba, Czech Republic
{senkerik,pluhacek,oplatkova,ivan.zelinka,
donald.davendra}@fai.utb.cz

Abstract. This paper presents results of the utilization of selected discrete chaotic map, which is Dissipative standard map, as pseudo-random number generator for the differential evolution (DE) optimization algorithm and Particle Swarm Optimization (PSO) algorithm in the task of PID controller design for the selected 4th order dynamical system. The results are compared with previously published results; both chaos driven heuristics with each other and finally the obtained results are compared with canonical PSO and DE versions, which do not utilize the chaos in the place of pseudo-random number generator.

Keywords: Differential Evolution, PSO, Deterministic chaos, PID tuning.

1 Introduction

These days the methods based on soft computing such as neural networks, evolutionary algorithms, fuzzy logic, and genetic programming are known as powerful tool for almost any difficult and complex optimization problem.

In the past decades, PID controllers became a fundamental part of many automatic systems. The successful design of PID controller was mostly based on deterministic methods involving complex mathematics [1, 2].

Recently, different soft-computing methods were used with promising results for solving the complex task of PID controller design [3]. These techniques [5-8] use random operations and typically use various kinds of pseudo-random number generators (PRNGs) that depend on the platform the algorithm is implemented. More recently it was shown that chaotic systems could be used as PRNGs for various stochastic methods with great results. Some of these chaos driven stochastic methods were tested on the task of PID controller design in [4]. In [3] it was shown that Particle Swarm optimization (PSO) algorithm is able to deal with the task of PID controller design with very good results. Following that in [9 - 12] the performance of chaos driven PSO algorithm was tested on this task with great results.

K. Saeed and V. Snášel (Eds.): CISIM 2014, LNCS 8838, pp. 67–76, 2014.

In this paper, the influence of promising discrete dissipative chaotic system to the performance of chaos driven heuristic algorithms, which is DE and PSO, are investigated and results are compared with previously published results of both canonical and chaos driven versions of evolutionary algorithm PSO [9 - 12] and with other techniques [3, 4] as well as with the canonical versions of DE (without chaotic pseudo-random number generator - CPRNG).

2   Motivation

Till now the chaos was observed in many of various systems (including evolutionary one) and in the last few years is also used to replace pseudo-number generators (PRGNs) in evolutionary algorithms (EAs).

This research is a continuation and extension of the previous successful initial application based experiments with chaos driven PSO and PID tuning task [9-12]. In this paper the DE/rand/1/bin strategy and PSO with inertial weight driven by Dissipative chaotic map (system) were utilized to solve the issue of evolutionary optimization of PID controller settings. Thus the idea was to utilize the hidden chaotic dynamics in pseudo random sequences given by chaotic Dissipative map system to help Differential evolution algorithm in searching for the best controller settings.

Recent research in chaos driven heuristics has been fueled with the predisposition that unlike stochastic approaches, a chaotic approach is able to bypass local optima stagnation. This one clause is of deep importance to evolutionary algorithms. A chaotic approach generally uses the chaotic map in the place of a pseudo random number generator [13]. This causes the heuristic to map unique regions, since the chaotic map iterates to new regions.

The primary aim of this work is to test, analyze and compare the implementation of different natural chaotic dynamics as the CPRNGs, thus to analyze and highlight the different influences to the system, which utilizes the selected CPRNG (including the evolutionary computational techniques).

3   PSO Algorithm

The PSO algorithm is inspired by the natural swarm behavior of animals (such as birds and fish). It was firstly introduced by Eberhart and Kennedy in 1995 [5]. Each particle in the population represents a possible solution of the optimization problem which is defined by the cost function (CF). In each iteration of the algorithm, a new location (combination of CF parameters) of the particle is calculated based on its previous location and velocity vector.

Within this research the PSO algorithm with global topology (GPSO) [14] was utilized. The CPRNG is used in the main GPSO formula (1), which determines a new "velocity", thus directly affects the position of each particle in the next iteration.

$$v_{ij}^{t+1} = w \cdot v_{ij}^t + c_1 \cdot Rand \cdot (pBest_{ij} - x_{ij}^t) + c_2 \cdot Rand \cdot (gBest_j - x_{ij}^t) \tag{1}$$

Where:

v_i^{t+1} - New velocity of the *ith* particle in iteration $t+1$.

w – Inertia weight value.

v_i^t - Current velocity of the *ith* particle in iteration t.

c_1, c_2 - Priority factors.

$pBest_i$ – Local (personal) best solution found by the *ith* particle.

$gBest$ - Best solution found in a population.

x_{ij}^t - Current position of the *ith* particle (component j of the dim. D) in iteration t.

$Rand$ – Pseudorandom number, interval $\langle 0, 1 \rangle$. CPRNG is applied only here.

The maximum velocity was limited to 0.2 times the range as it is usual. The new position of each particle is then given by (2), where x_i^{t+1} is the new particle position:

$$x_i^{t+1} = x_i^t + v_i^{t+1} \tag{2}$$

Finally the linear decreasing inertia weight [14, 15] strategy was used in this work. The inertia weight has two control parameters w_{start} and w_{end}. The values used in this study were $w_{start} = 0.9$ and $w_{end} = 0.4$.

4   Differential Evolution

DE is a population-based optimization method that works on real-number-coded individuals [8]. For each individual $\vec{x}_{i,G}$ in the current generation G, DE generates a new trial individual $\vec{x}'_{i,G}$ by adding the weighted difference between two randomly selected individuals $\vec{x}_{r1,G}$ and $\vec{x}_{r2,G}$ to a randomly selected third individual $\vec{x}_{r3,G}$. The resulting individual $\vec{x}'_{i,G}$ is crossed-over with the original individual $\vec{x}_{i,G}$. The fitness of the resulting individual, referred to as a perturbed vector $\vec{u}_{i,G+1}$, is then compared with the fitness of $\vec{x}_{i,G}$. If the fitness of $\vec{u}_{i,G+1}$ is greater than the fitness of $\vec{x}_{i,G}$, then $\vec{x}_{i,G}$ is replaced with $\vec{u}_{i,G+1}$; otherwise, $\vec{x}_{i,G}$ remains in the population as $\vec{x}_{i,G+1}$. DE is quite robust, fast, and effective, with global optimization ability. It does not require the objective function to be differentiable, and it works well even with noisy and time-dependent objective functions. Description of used DERand1Bin strategy is presented in (3). See [8], [16] and [17] for the description of all other strategies.

$$u_{i,G+1} = x_{r1,G} + F \cdot \left(x_{r2,G} - x_{r3,G} \right) \tag{3}$$

5   The Concept of CPRNG

The general idea of CPRNG is to replace the default PRNG with the chaotic system. As the chaotic system is a set of equations with a static start position, we created a random start position of the system, in order to have different start position for different experiments. This random position is initialized with the default PRNG, as a one-off randomizer. Once the start position of the chaotic system has been obtained, the system generates the next sequence using its current position.

Generally there exist many other approaches as to how to deal with the negative numbers as well as with the scaling of the wide range of the numbers given by the chaotic systems into the typical range 0 – 1:

- Finding of the maximum value of the pre-generated long discrete sequence and dividing of all the values in the sequence with such a maxval number.
- Shifting of all values to the positive numbers (avoiding of ABS command) and scaling.

5.1   Chaotic System for CPRNG

This section contains the description of discrete dissipative chaotic map, which was used as the CPRNG. The   direct output iterations of the chaotic map were used for the generation of the both integer numbers and real numbers scaled into the typical range for random function: <0 - 1>.

The Dissipative Standard map is a two-dimensional chaotic map. The parameters used in this work are $b = 0.6$ and $k = 8.8$ as suggested in [18]. The map equations are given in (4).

$$X_{n+1} = X_n + Y_{n+1} (\mathrm{mod}\, 2\pi)$$
$$Y_{n+1} = bY_n + k \sin X_n (\mathrm{mod}\, 2\pi)$$

$$(4)$$

The typical chaotic behavior of the utilized chaotic map, represented by the example of direct output for the variable x is depicted in Fig. 1.

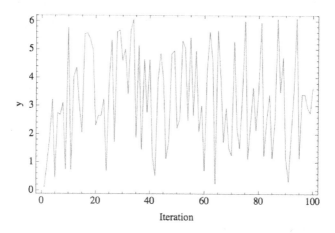

Fig. 1. Simulation of the chaotic behavior of Dissipative map (variable y – line-plot)

The illustrative histograms of the distribution of real numbers transferred into the range <0 - 1> generated by means of studied chaotic system is in Fig. 2.

Finally the Fig. 3 shows the example of dynamical sequencing during the generating of pseudo number numbers by means of studied CPRNG.

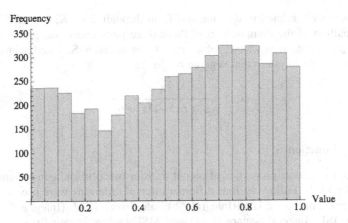

Fig. 2. Histogram of the distribution of real numbers transferred into the range <0 - 1> generated by means of the chaotic Dissipative standard map – 5000 samples

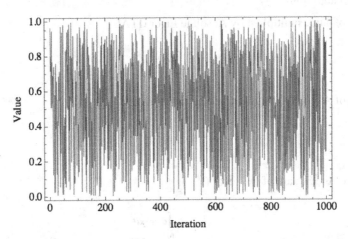

Fig. 3. Example of the chaotic dynamics: range <0 - 1> generated by means of the chaotic Dissipative standard map

6   Problem Design

6.1   PID Controller

The PID controller contains three unique parts; proportional, integral and derivative controller [1-4]. A simplified form in Laplace domain is given in (5).

$$G(s) = K\left(1 + \frac{1}{sT_i} + sT_d\right) \tag{5}$$

The PID form most suitable for analytical calculations is given in (6).

$$G(s) = k_p + \frac{k_i}{s} + k_d s \tag{6}$$

The parameters are related to the standard form through: $k_p = K$, $k_i = K/T_i$ and $k_d = KT_d$. Acquisition of the combination of these three parameters that gives the lowest value of the test criterions was the objective of this research. Selected controlled system was the 4th order system that is given by Eq. 7.

$$G(s) = \frac{1}{s^4 + 6s^3 + 11s^2 + 6s}$$ (7)

6.2   Cost Function

Test criterion measures properties of output transfer function and can indicate quality of regulation [1-4]. Following four different integral criterions were used for the test and comparison purposes: IAE (Integral Absolute Error), ITAE (Integral Time Absolute Error), ISE (Integral Square Error) and MSE (Mean Square Error). These test criterions (given by Eq. 8 – 11) were minimized within the cost functions for the enhanced PSO algorithm.

1. Integral of Time multiplied by Absolute Error (ITAE)

$$I_{ITAE} = \int_0^T t|e(t)|dt$$ (8)

2. Integral of Absolute Magnitude of the Error (IAE)

$$I_{IAE} = \int_0^T |e(t)|dt$$ (9)

3. Integral of the Square of the Error (ISE)

$$I_{ISE} = \int_0^T e^2(t)dt$$ (10)

4. Mean of the Square of the Error (MSE)

$$I_{MSE} = \frac{1}{n}\sum_{i=1}^n (e(t))^2$$ (11)

7   Results

In this section, the results obtained within experiments with ChaosDE and Chaos PSO algorithms are compared with each other and with previously published works [3, 4, 9 - 12]. Table 1 shows the typical used settings for the both ChaosDe and Canonical DE, whereas Table 2 contains the settings for both Chaos PSO and canonical PSO.

Table 1. DE settings

DE Parameter	Value
PopSize	20
F	0.8
CR	0.8
Generations	50
Max. CF Evaluations (CFE)	1000

Table 2. PSO settings

DE Parameter	Value
PopSize	20
v_{max}	0.2•Range
w_{start}	0.9
w_{end}	0.4
Priority factors c_1 and c_2	2
Iterations	50
Max. CF Evaluations (CFE)	1000

Table 3. Comparisons of results for other heuristics – 4th order system PID controller design

Criterion	ZN Step Response	Canonical DE	Chaos DE	Chaos SOMA	PSO	Chaos PSO
IAE	34.9413	12.3262	**12.3260**	12.3305	12.3738	12.3479
ITAE	137.5650	15.1935	**15.1919**	15.3846	16.4079	15.5334
ISE	17.8426	**6.40515**	**6.40515**	6.41026	6.40538	6.40516
MSE	0.089213	**0.032026**	**0.032026**	0.032027	0.032030	**0.032026**

Table 4. Statistical results of all 50 runs of Both Chaos heuristics versions

DE Version	Avg CF	Median CF	Max CF	Min CF	StdDev
		ITAE Criterion			
Chaos PSO Dissipative Map	12.4184	12.3959	12.6140	12.3479	0.072049
Chaos DE Dissipative Map	**12.3274**	**12.327**	**12.3314**	**12.3262**	**0.001216**
		IAE Criterion			
Chaos PSO Dissipative Map	17.6267	17.4012	21.5345	15.5334	1.594303
Chaos DE Dissipative Map	**15.2251**	**15.2127**	**15.3212**	**15.1919**	**0.033799**
		ISE Criterion			
Chaos PSO Dissipative Map	6.4059	6.4057	6.4083	6.40516	0.000841
Chaos DE Dissipative Map	**6.40516**	**6.40516**	**6.40517**	**6.40515**	**0.000025**
		MSE Criterion			
Chaos PSO Dissipative Map	0.03203	**0.03202**	0.03206	**0.03202**	$8 \cdot 10^{-6}$
Chaos DE Dissipative Map	**0.03202**	**0.03202**	**0.03202**	**0.03202**	$9 \cdot 10^{-9}$

Best results obtained for each method are given in Table 3. The statistical results of the experiments for all criterions are shown in Table 4, which represent the simple statistics for cost function (CF) values, e.g. average, median, maximum values, standard deviations and minimum values representing the best individual solution for all 50 repeated runs of canonical DE and ChaosDE. The bold values within the all Tables 3 and 4 depict the best obtained results.

Furthermore an example of the step responses of the system with PID controllers designed by means of Chaos DE is depicted in Fig 4.

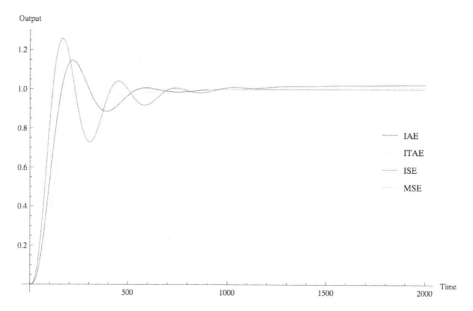

Fig. 4. Comparison of system responses – 4th order system; Chaos DE

8   Conclusion

In this paper the chaotic dissipative standard map was presented and investigated over their capability of enhancing the performance of DE and PSO algorithms in the task of PID controller design.

From the comparisons, it follows that through the utilization of chaotic systems; the best overall results were obtained and entirely different statistical characteristics of CPRNGs-based heuristic can be achieved. Thus the different influence to the system, which utilizes the selected CPRNG, can be chosen through the implementation of particular inner chaotic dynamics given by the particular chaotic system. When comparing both chaos driven heuristics, DE has outperformed PSO.

Promising results were presented, discussed and compared with other methods of PID controller design. More detail experiments are needed to prove or disprove these claims and explain the effect of the chaotic systems on the optimization and controller design.

Acknowledgements. This work was supported by Grant Agency of the Czech Republic - GACR P103/13/08195S, partially supported by Grants of SGS No. SP2014/159 and SP2014/170, VŠB - Technical University of Ostrava, Czech Republic, by the Development of human resources in research and development of latest soft computing methods and their application in practice project, reg. no. CZ.1.07/2.3.00/20.0072 funded by Operational Programme Education for Competitiveness, co-financed by ESF and state budget of the Czech Republic, further was supported by European Regional Development Fund under the project CEBIA-Tech No. CZ.1.05/2.1.00/03.0089 and by Internal Grant Agency of Tomas Bata University under the project No. IGA/FAI/2014/010.

References

1. Åström, K.J.: ControlSystem Design - Lecture Notes for ME 155A (2002),
   http://www.cds.caltech.edu/~murray/courses/cds101/fa02/
   caltech/astrom.html
2. Landau, I.D., Gianluca, Z.: Digital Control Systems. Communications and Control Engineering. Springer, London (2006)
3. Nagaraj, B., Subha, S., Rampriya, B.: Tuning Algorithms for PID Controller Using Soft Computing Techniques. International Journal of Computer Science and Network Security 8(4), 278–281 (2008)
4. Davendra, D., Zelinka, I., Senkerik, R.: Chaos driven evolutionary algorithms for the task of PID control. Computers & Mathematics with Applications 60(4), 1088–1104 (2010)
5. Kennedy, J., Eberhart, R.: Particle swarm optimization. In: IEEE International Conference on Neural Networks, pp. 1942–1948 (1995)
6. Dorigo, M., Di Caro, G.: Ant colony optimization: a new meta-heuristic. In: Proceedings of the 1999 Congress on Evolutionary Computation, CEC 1999 (1999)
7. Goldberg, D.E.: Genetic Algorithms in Search, Optimization, and Machine Learning. Addison-Wesley (1989)
8. Storn, R., Price, K.: Differential Evolution – A Simple and Efficient Heuristic for global Optimization over Continuous Spaces. Journal of Global Optimization 11(4), 341–359 (1997)
9. Pluhacek, M., Senkerik, R., Davendra, D., Zelinka, I.: Designing PID controller for DC motor system by means of enhanced PSO algorithm with discrete chaotic Lozi map. In: 26th European Conference on Modelling and Simulation, ECMS 2012, pp. 405–409 (2012)
10. Pluhacek, M., Senkerik, R., Davendra, D., Zelinka, I.: PID controller design for 4th order system by means of enhanced PSO algorithm with lozi chaotic map. Paper presented at the 18th International Conference on Soft Computing, MENDEL 2012, pp. 35–39 (2012)
11. Pluhacek, M., Senkerik, R., Davendra, D., Zelinka, I.: Designing PID Controller for DC Motor by Means of Enhanced PSO Algorithm with Dissipative Chaotic Map. In: Snášel, V., Abraham, A., Corchado, E.S. (eds.) SOCO Models in Industrial & Environmental Appl. AISC, vol. 188, pp. 475–483. Springer, Heidelberg (2013)
12. Pluhacek, M., Senkerik, R., Davendra, D., Zelinka, I.: Designing PID controller for 4th order system by means of enhanced PSO algorithm with discrete chaotic Dissipative standard map. In: EMSS 2012 24th European Modeling and Simulation Symposium, pp. 396–401 (2012)

13. Caponetto, R., Fortuna, L., Fazzino, S., Xibilia, M.G.: Chaotic sequences to improve the performance of evolutionary algorithms. IEEE Transactions on Evolutionary Computatio 7(3), 289–304 (2003)
14. Yuhui, S., Eberhart, R.: A modified particles warm optimizer. In: IEEE World Congress on Computational Intelligence, May 4-9, pp. 69–73 (1998)
15. Nickabadi, A., Ebadzadeh, M.M., Safabakhsh, R.: A novel particle swarm optimization algorithm with adaptive inertia weight. Applied Soft Computing 11(4), 3658–3670 (2011)
16. Price, K.V.: An Introduction to Differential Evolution. In: Corne, D., Dorigo, M., Glover, F. (eds.) New Ideas in Optimization, pp. 79–108. McGraw-Hill Ltd. (1999)
17. Price, K.V., Storn, R.M., Lampinen, J.A.: Differential Evolution - A Practical Approach to Global Optimization. Natural Computing Series. Springer, Heidelberg (2005)
18. Sprott, J.C.: Chaos and Time-Series Analysis. Oxford University Press (2003)

Improving Rule Selection from Robot Soccer Strategy with Substrategies

Václav Svatoň[1,2], Jan Martinovič[1,2], Kateřina Slaninová[1,2],
and Václav Snášel[1,2]

[1] Department of Computer Science, FEI, VŠB - Technical University of Ostrava,
17. listopadu 15, 708 33, Ostrava-Poruba, Czech Republic
[2] IT4Innovations, VŠB - Technical University of Ostrava,
17. listopadu 15, 708 33, Ostrava-Poruba, Czech Republic
{vaclav.svaton,jan.martinovic,katerina.slaninova,vaclav.snasel}@vsb.cz

Abstract. Robot Soccer is a very attractive platform in terms of research. It contains a number of challenges in the areas of robot control, artificial intelligence and image analysis. This article presents a method to improve the description of the strategy by creating substrategies in strategy and thus ensuring smoother implementation of actions defined by this strategy. In presented method we have extracted sequences of game situations from the log of a game played in our simulator, as they occurred during the game. Afterwards, these sequences were compared by methods for sequence comparison and thus we are able to visualize relations between the sequences of game situations and clusters of similar game situations in a graph. This output seems to be very helpful feedback for further strategy development.

Keywords: Robot Soccer, Strategy, Rule, Sequence.

1 Introduction

A complete set of options which are available to players in any game situation in order to achieve the objective is considered as a strategy in the game theory [1], [2]. The result of this strategy depends not only on the actions of the individual player but also on the actions of other players or elements of the game. The so-called pure strategy contains a list of all possible situations that may arise in the game. Any mapping or description of the space in which we know the geographic positions of the objects location can be considered for the strategy [3]. We have defined a finite set of rules that tell us how these objects can behave in a given situations. This principle can be applied to a number of areas from the real world and is generally called strategy planning [4]. We can use strategies to describe a space and objects in it, and to use the subsequent search for the optimal path or relocation of these objects in order to achieve our desired goals. The algorithms and approaches from this article may not serve only for use in the game of robot soccer.

The following sections contain an explanation of our robot soccer architecture, our view of strategies, rules and how we use them for mapping coordinates of the

K. Saeed and V. Snášel (Eds.): CISIM 2014, LNCS 8838, pp. 77–88, 2014.

real world. The article describes the main problem of the current approach to the selection of rules from strategy and in the following section we introduce a new method to improve this approach. Then, our method is practically applied to a robot soccer game created in our robot soccer simulator. The main section of the paper contains the results of experiments focused on the sequence extraction from the robot soccer game strategies and the overall comparison of the old and new method of rule selection from the strategy.

1.1   Robot Soccer Architecture

Our robot soccer library consists of a number of interconnected modules that contain the functionality required for prediction, image analysis and robot control. Such architecture brings many advantages, in particular the possibility to experiment with different methods used to select the best winning strategy, or even create a partially simulated game containing real and simulated robots. These modules falls into three main categories: Game information, Game and Log. Game information is a storage of information about the actual game state. It consists of our and the opponent's robots positions and directions and a ball position. Besides having information about actual game situation on the game field it is possible to fill this storage also with predicted information about the robots and the ball. Game part consists of the all necessary functionality for the calculations over strategies and tactics. Such type of calculations is performed every game step and the results are continuously actualized in the part Game information which is primarily used for the robots control.

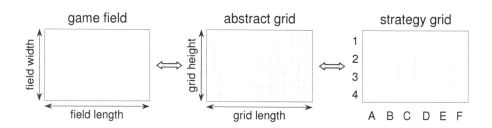

Fig. 1. Inner game field representation

In our work, the game is separated into logical and physical parts [5]. The logical part includes the strategy selection, calculation of robot movement and adaptation of rules to the opponents strategy. The physical part includes robot actual movement on the game field and recognition of the opponent movement. Due to this separation, the logical part is independent on the field size and the resolution of the camera (or physical engine of simulation) used in visual information system. In the logical part, the game is represented as an abstract grid with a very high resolution, which ensures a very precise position of the robots and the ball. However, this detailed representation of the game field is not suitable for the strategy description. Too many rules are required to describe a robot behavior. Therefore, a strategy grid is used which has a much lower resolution than an abstract grid. This simplification is sufficient, because it is unnecessary to know the robot's exact position in the scope of a strategy (see Fig. 1). Using the physical part based on the size of the game field and camera/engine resolution, we only need to transform the abstract grid into physical coordinates. The strategy, as we understand, is the quaternion $< X, Y, p, m >$ where

- $X \subset X^U$ where X is a selected set of game situations and X^U is the universe of all situations that may occur during the game
- $Y \subset Y^U$ where Y is a selected set of instructions to control the robots and Y^U is the universe of all possible instructions
- p is mapping $X \to Y$, each game situation is mapped to an instruction describing how to control our robots in this situation
- m is mapping $X^U \to X$, all possible situations that may occur during the game are mapped to a selected set of game situations
- $p(m(\overline{x}_u)) \in X^U$ where $\overline{x}_u \in X^U$: every real situation on the game field is assigned to a game situation from the strategy which also contains the instructions on where to move our robots

Strategy is a finite set of the rules that describes the current situation on the game field. Each rule can be easily expressed as the quaternion $< M, O, B, D >$, where M are the grid coordinates of our robots, O are the grid coordinates of opponent's robots, B are grid coordinates of the ball and D are grid coordinates of where our robots should move in the next step. The real situation on the game field is compared with the situations described by the strategy rules during the each game step. On the basis of a priori defined metrics, it is selected the most similar rule from the strategy, according to which are set the positions of the players on the game field in the following step. A detailed description of this metrics and the algorithm for the optimal rule selection can be found in [6].

The robot's behavior in the grid coordinates is then controlled by so called tactics [7]. The tactics contain functions for robot control such as turning the robot, shooting at goal or passing the ball. Therefore, in the terms of hierarchy, the strategy takes care of the placement of the robots in the grid coordinates while the tactics work with the physical coordinates and controls the robot inside the grid coordinate.

A 3D robot soccer simulator has been created using the above mentioned robot soccer architecture, see Figure 2. This simulator has been developed with Unity engine [8]. This engine has been selected for its support of physical engine PhysX [9]. Using already created physical engine eases simulator design very much. Especially, it allows us to avoid the necessity to create our own physics and all the problems connected with own solution of object collision on the game field. We can easily set material and weight of the robots, ball, and the game field using the Unity engine. The object collision is computed by the physical engine itself. The physical engine in Unity is non-deterministic, which means that the same simulation, launched repeatedly can return different results.

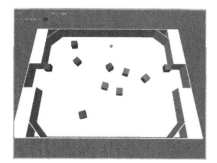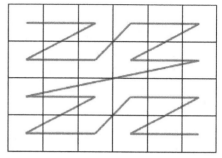

Fig. 2. (a) Robot Soccer Simulator ; (b) Grid 6x4 with Z-order curve

This non-deterministic behavior is a price for the fast physical engine, which is able to perform fast computations. Of course, there exist deterministic engines, but their main disadvantage is their slowness. However, we do not mind the non-determinism in our architecture. Just as in the real world, the robot soccer is a quickly changing dynamic system, and our proposed architecture must count with this non-determinism, and must be able to react to this. In other words, the team with better strategy should be able to win, regardless to minor differences in physical engine computation during the repeatedly launched simulation.

1.2 Rule Selection

Because the above mentioned robot soccer architecture is based on centralized control in every step of the game we have the access to the grid coordinates of each object on the game field. Therefore, in every step of the game we compare the current situation on the field with the situations described in the rules of the strategy. By comparing, it is meant computing the Euclidean distance between the real situation on the field and the situation described in the selected rule.

We have proposed a method to improve the rule selection from the strategy by using graph and space filling curves [11] in the article [6]. We have chosen a method named Z-order [12] for practical purposes. Z-order or Morton order is a function mapping the multi-dimensional space into the one-dimensional space while preserving the locality of data points. Due to its properties its suited for converting two-dimensional matrix representing the playing field into one-dimensional array of the coordinates of the individual robots. Figure 2 shows the final relocation of the robots located on the game field.

In the next step, an undirected connected graph with the edge evaluation is used. Let the graph be defined as a pair $G = < V, E >$ where V is a non-empty set of vertices and E is a set of two-element sets of vertices also called undirected edges. The set of vertices consists of the individual rules from the strategy in our case. The edges contain the evaluation which corresponds to a distance between the two neighboring vertices (rules). As a distance is considered a normalized value of Euclidean distance computed from two sorted sequences using the above mentioned Z-order applied to the neighbouring vertices which contain the robots grid coordinates.

To select the rule for the next step we just need to compare the real situation on the game field with the situations described by the selected neighbour rules and also with the currently selected rule (rule does not have to be necessarily changed in the each game step).

2   Problems with Current Approach

The method for the selection of the rules from the strategy, which was described in Section 1.2, has one fundamental disadvantage. All the rules which create one strategy are independent of each other. It means that every game step, each current situation on the field is compared with the all rules described in the strategy. Due to the optimisation of this method, space filling curves were used for robots ordering on the field and for the graph precomputing which is necessary for finding the similarity between these rules. This led to the effective optimisation of the rule selection, which achieve much better results than brute force approach for the rule selection. However, the examination of the log of played games showed that during the game, the most similar rule is always selected but without the connection to so-called game situation as was for example intended by the author of the strategy during its design.

Game situation is a subset of rules from the strategy, which should represent a specific intended set of subsequent actions. For example the first five rules from the strategy could represent the left wing offensive play, next five rules the right wing play, and after them followed by rules for the defensive play in the middle of the game field. This interpretation of rules can be intended during the design of a strategy, however due to the actual strategy definition, it is possible that the algorithm for finding the optimal rule selects the offensive rule in one step, and the defensive rule in the following step, thus completely neglecting intended game situations. See Figure 3 in section 4.

3   Substrategies

Our proposed solution of the problem described in Section 2 contains so-called substrategies. Substrategy can be understood as a representation of one specific game situation, for example right wing offensive play. Therefore, the whole strategy can include any number of rules. The algorithm for the most similar rule selection from the strategy was modified so that the rules included in the substrategy to which the current rule belongs are scanned first. For example, if the currently executed rule is from the substrategy which represents the right wing offensive play then we assume that in one game step (which lasts 20ms), the game situation does not change enough to be necessary to compare all the rules from the strategy. Therefore, we limit the rule selection to the same substrategy. Due to this approach, the time necessary for the rule selection is decreased and the succession of the rules in the same substrategy is preserved.

As a result of introduction of substrategies a question arose. When to change the substrategy and therefore change the game situation that is defined by this substrategy during the game. It is not sufficient to permanently scan the rules from the current substrategy. The current executed action, for example yet mentioned right wing offensive play, can be interrupted during the game before its end, for example due to the ball loss as a reason of the opponent's defenders activity. Therefore, the proposed method use threshold for determination, when the game situation on the field is so changed that the next game step will not be restricted only to the actual substrategy, but all the rules from the complete strategy will be scanned. Thus, this approach solves the transition from one substrategy to another and for example after the ball loss during the offensive play, the game is changed into the defensive substrategy. Section 3 is focused on description of the sequence extraction from the game log and therefore on the way how to transparently visualise the game progress from the rule selection point of view.

3.1   Game Profile

The proposed approach for game profile extraction proceeds from the original social network approach with a modification focused on robot soccer game. The modification is based on a definition of the "relationship" between played games. The original approach into the analysis of social networks deals with the assumption that the social network is a set of people (or groups of people) with social interactions among themselves [10]. Social interaction is commonly defined as an interaction between actors, such as communication, personal knowledge of each other, friendship and membership etc.

The modification extends the original approach of social network analysis by the perspective of the complex networks. This type of view differs from the original approach due to the description of the relations between nodes (in the presented context: played games). The relation between the games is defined by their common attributes, characterising by game situations extraxted from game log file.

The game profiles are extracted using the methods from process mining, especially the methods from log mining. Let us assume that an event log from the analysed system contains data related to rules selected from game strategy from played game.

Definition 1. (Base game profile, sequences)
Let $U = \{u_1, u_2, \ldots, u_n\}$, be a set of games, where n is a number of games u_i. Then, sequences of strategy rules $\sigma_{ij} = \langle e_{ij1}, e_{ij2}, \ldots e_{ijm_j} \rangle$, are sequences of strategy rules executed during a game u_i in the simulator, where $j = 1, 2, \ldots, p_i$ is number of that sequences, and m_j is a length of j-th sequence. Thus, a set $S_i = \{\sigma_{i1}, \sigma_{i2}, \ldots \sigma_{ip_i}\}$ is a set of all sequences executed during a game u_i in the system, and p_i is a number of that sequences.

Sequences σ_{ij} extracted with relation to certain game u_i are mapped to set of sequences $\sigma_l \in S$ without this relation to games: $\sigma_{ij} = \langle e_{ij1}, e_{ij2}, \ldots, e_{ijm_j} \rangle \rightarrow \sigma_l = \langle e_1, e_2, \ldots, e_{ml} \rangle$, where $e_{ij1} = e_1, e_{ij2} = e_2, \ldots, e_{ijm_j} = e_{ml}$.

Define matrix $B \in N^{|U| \times |S|}$ where

$$B_{ij} = \begin{cases} frequency\ of\ sequence\ \sigma_j \in S\ for\ game\ u_i & if\ \sigma_j\ \in S_i \\ 0 & else \end{cases}$$

A base game profile of the games $u_i \in U$ is a vector $b_i \in N^{|S|}$ represented by row i from matrix B.

Each such sequence extracted from the game log file was compared with other sequences, while the similar sequences were found. Thus, we are able to visualize them by graph of sequences, where the clusters of similar sequences are showed. The sequence comparison was done by The longest common substring method (LCS), The longest common subsequence method (LCSS) a The timewarped longest common subsequence (T-WLCS). The difference between the used methods and the way of their usage is described in more details in our previous article [13].

4 Experiments

The log of the played game was used for the extraction of the sequences. The log has been generated by the standard game which lasted 2 minutes between two strategies. The following experiments are focused only on the strategy of the left team which was created with the substrategies mentioned in Section 3. Strategy was created with several different game situations which are described in Table 1.

The log file consists of complete information about the game field situation for each game step. Besides the coordinates of the all robots and the ball, it also consists of information about the actual selected rule from the strategy for the left as well as the right side. Thus, the sequence is created by the sequence of the selected rules during the game for the left side team. The whole game lasted 2 minutes; one game step was performed every 20ms. Therefore, the final log file consisted of 6.000 records. It was necessary to decide which game situation will be the basic for the sequence determination. It was selected the situation holding the ball. The robot is holding the ball, when it touched the ball and after that it is inside the set border distance.

We have applied the algorithms for finding the similar sequences under the sequence collection, especially the LCS, LCSS, and T-WLCS method. The visualizations of the found similar sequence clusters are presented in Figures 3, 4, 5 and 6. Each node in the graph represents one sequence. Each sequence is labeled with a sequence number and number determining the possession of the ball (0 - none, 1 - our team, 2 - opponent's team). Each sequence contains a list of rules selected for the left team in every game step until the team possession of the ball has changed.

The Figure 3 shows clusters of sequences extracted from the log of the played game with our test strategy but without the implementation of subtrategies. Method T-WLCS achieved the best results of all three proposed methods used to find similar sequences. Upon a closer examination of extracted sequences, it is evident that during the game there was frequent switching of rules also independent of the intended game situation. Graph in Figure 3 shows number of sequences that are not part of any main cluster (137-1, 50-2, 12-2, 60-1, ...). These sequences contain rules from several different game situations. See Table 2 for sequence 137-1 and it's rules.

Figures 4, 5 and 6 show the clusters of extracted sequences from the log of the game which was created with rules divided into subcategories. For a real game, it was necessary to set the threshold determining when to scan all the rules from the strategy and therefore allow the transition between substrategies. This threshold is represented by the Euclidean distance (similarity) between the real situation on the game field and the rule from the strategy. Thresholds were chosen in values of 300, 400 and 500, because the average distance during the game varies from 100 to 700.

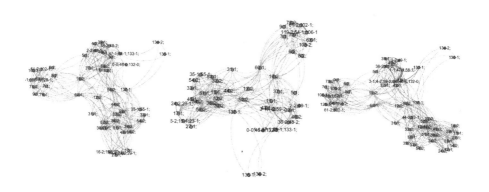

Fig. 3. Strategy without substrategies (a) LCS; (b) LCSS; (c) T-WLCS

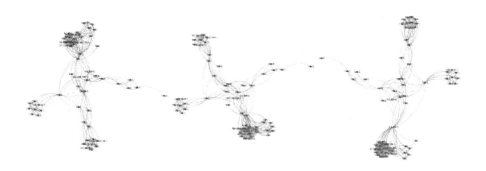

Fig. 4. Strategy with substrategies and threshold 300 (a) LCS; (b) LCSS; (c) T-WLCS

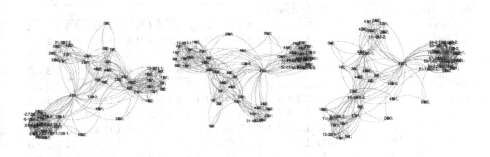

Fig. 5. Strategy with substrategies and threshold 400 (a) LCS; (b) LCSS; (c) T-WLCS

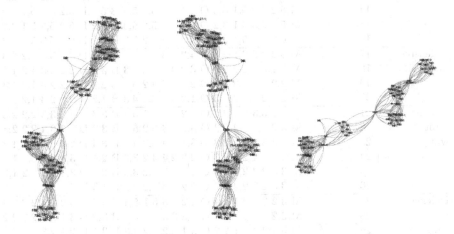

Fig. 6. Strategy with substrategies and threshold 500 (a) LCS; (b) LCSS; (c) T-WLCS

All the graphs on Figure 4, 5, and 6 show that lower thresholds are still causing frequent transitions between substrategies and therefore causing frequent switching between the game situations which are represented by these substrategies. With the increasing threshold value, the players remain in the selected game situation thus ensuring smoother progress of individual actions and therefore the overall smoother game. This is most noticeable from the graph in Figure 6. Extracted sequences are clearly divided into six main clusters which altogether represent all six game situations defined in the test strategy (see Table 1).

Sequence 53-2 (see Table 3) from the graph in Figure 6 is worth mentioning. This sequence is not part of the main sequence clusters because it contains the rules from several different substrategies. These rules are very similar to one another. These rules represent the starting position of every player at the start of the game because almost every game situation defined in the strategy starts

Table 1. Strategy

Substrategy	Rule num.	Rule description
Offensive	1	M 3,2 3,3 2,1 2,4 O 4,2 4,3 5,1 5,4 B 4,2 D 3,2 3,3 2,1 2,4
middle	2	M 4,2 4,3 2,2 2,3 O 4,2 4,3 5,1 5,4 B 4,2 D 5,2 5,3 2,2 3,3
	3	M 5,2 5,3 2,2 3,3 O 5,2 5,3 5,1 5,4 B 5,2 D 6,2 5,3 2,2 3,3
	4	M 6,2 5,3 2,2 3,3 O 5,2 5,3 5,1 5,4 B 6,2 D 6,2 5,3 2,2 3,3
Offensive	5	M 3,2 3,3 2,1 2,4 O 4,2 4,3 5,1 5,4 B 4,3 D 3,2 4,3 2,2 2,3
right	6	M 3,2 4,3 2,2 2,3 O 4,2 4,3 5,1 5,4 B 4,3 D 4,3 4,4 3,2 2,3
wing	7	M 4,3 4,4 3,2 2,3 O 4,2 4,4 5,2 5,3 B 4,4 D 4,3 5,4 4,2 2,3
	8	M 4,3 5,4 4,2 2,3 O 4,3 5,4 5,2 5,3 B 5,4 D 4,3 5,3 5,2 2,3
	9	M 4,3 5,3 5,2 2,3 O 4,3 5,3 5,2 5,3 B 5,3 D 4,3 6,3 5,2 2,3
	10	M 4,3 6,3 5,2 2,3 O 4,3 6,3 5,2 5,3 B 6,3 D 4,3 6,3 5,2 2,3
Offensive	11	M 3,2 3,3 2,1 2,4 O 4,2 4,3 5,1 5,4 B 3,2 D 3,2 3,3 3,1 2,3
left	12	M 3,2 3,3 3,1 2,3 O 4,1 4,2 5,1 5,3 B 3,1 D 4,2 3,2 4,1 3,3
wing	13	M 4,2 3,2 4,1 3,3 O 4,1 4,2 5,1 5,3 B 4,1 D 5,2 4,2 5,1 3,3
	14	M 5,2 4,2 5,1 3,3 O 4,1 5,2 5,1 5,3 B 5,1 D 5,2 4,3 5,1 3,2
	15	M 5,2 4,3 5,1 3,2 O 4,1 5,2 5,2 5,3 B 5,2 D 6,2 5,3 5,1 3,2
	16	M 6,2 5,3 5,1 3,2 O 4,2 5,2 6,2 5,3 B 6,2 D 6,2 5,3 5,1 3,2
Defensive	17	M 3,2 3,3 2,1 2,4 O 4,2 4,3 5,1 5,4 B 3,2 D 3,2 3,3 2,2 2,3
middle	18	M 3,2 3,3 2,2 2,3 O 3,2 3,3 4,1 5,3 B 3,2 D 2,2 2,3 1,2 1,3
	19	M 2,2 2,3 1,2 1,3 O 2,2 2,3 4,2 5,3 B 2,2 D 2,2 2,3 1,2 1,3
	20	M 2,2 2,3 1,2 1,3 O 1,2 2,3 3,2 4,3 B 1,2 D 2,2 2,3 1,2 1,3
Defensive	21	M 3,2 3,3 2,1 2,4 O 4,2 4,3 5,1 5,4 B 3,3 D 3,2 3,3 2,2 2,3
right	22	M 3,2 3,3 2,2 2,3 O 3,2 3,3 5,2 5,3 B 3,3 D 3,3 3,4 2,2 2,3
wing	23	M 3,3 3,4 2,2 2,3 O 3,3 3,4 5,2 4,3 B 3,4 D 2,3 2,4 2,2 1,3
	24	M 2,3 2,4 2,2 1,3 O 2,3 2,4 4,2 3,3 B 2,4 D 3,3 2,3 2,2 1,3
	25	M 3,3 2,3 2,2 1,3 O 2,2 2,3 4,2 3,3 B 2,3 D 3,3 2,3 2,2 1,3
	26	M 3,3 2,3 2,2 1,3 O 2,2 1,3 4,2 3,3 B 1,3 D 3,3 2,3 2,2 1,3
Defensive	27	M 3,2 3,3 2,1 2,4 O 4,2 4,3 5,1 5,4 B 4,2 D 3,2 3,3 2,2 2,3
left	28	M 3,2 3,3 2,2 2,3 O 4,2 3,3 5,2 5,3 B 3,2 D 3,1 3,3 2,1 2,2
wing	29	M 3,1 3,3 2,1 2,2 O 3,1 3,2 5,2 4,3 B 3,1 D 2,1 2,3 1,1 2,2
	30	M 2,1 2,3 1,1 2,2 O 2,1 2,2 4,2 3,3 B 2,1 D 2,2 1,3 1,2 2,3
	31	M 2,2 1,3 1,2 2,3 O 1,2 2,2 4,2 2,3 B 1,2 D 2,2 1,3 1,2 2,3

with the default positions of all players. Therefore the sequence was found that contains these seemingly different rules and thus represents the connection point between the clusters of sequences.

5 Conclusion and Future Work

Main part of the article discussed the strategies and the method for rule selection from strategies. Improvement of strategy using substrategies was presented. This method also allows the author to create a strategy, which will be performed during the game by such way, by which it was intended. Substrategies represent game situations such as left wing offence or right wing defence and ensures that

Table 2. Sequence 137-1 from Figure 3

137-1
2,2,2,2,2,2,2,2,2,2,28,28,22,22,22,22,22,22,22,22,22,22,22,22,22,22,2,12,12,12,12,12,12,12, 12,6,6,6,6,6,6,6,6,6,6,6,6,6,6,6,9,9,9,9,9,9,9,9,9,9,6,6,6,2,2,2,2,6,6,6

Table 3. Sequence 53-2 from Figure 6

53-2
29,29,29,29,29,29,29,29,29,29,29,29,29,29,29,29,29,29,29,29,29,29,29,29,29,29,29,29,29, 29,29,29,29,29,29,29,18,18,18,18,18,18,18,18,18,18,18,18,18,18,18,29,29,29,29,29,29,29,29, 29,29,29,29,29,29,29,29,29,29,29,29,29,29,29,29,29,29,29,29,29,29,29,29,29,29,29,29,29, 29,29,29,29,29,29,29,29,29,29,29,29,29,29,29,29,13,13,13,13,13,13,13,13,13,13,13,13,13, 13,13,13,13,1,1,1,1,1,1,1,1,1,1,1,1,1,1,1,1,1,1,1,1,1,1,1,1,1,1,1,1,1,2,2,2,2,2,2,2,2,2,2,2,2,2, 2,2,2,2,2,2,2,2,2,2,2,2,2,2,2,2,2,2,2,2,2,2,2,2,2,2,2,2,2,2,2,2,2,2,2,2,2,2,2,2,2,3,3,3,3,3,3,3,3,3,3,3,3

players will perform the strategy actions more continuously and in faster way then using the original approach.

An important task is to devise a way how to find an optimal threshold for substrategy selection. Such threshold does not restrict the players during the game and force them to perform still the same game situation or on the contrary not too lenient one to cause a frequent switching of rules from the various substrategies.

Generally speaking, games represent any situation in nature. Game theory can be applied for example for adversarial reasoning in security resource allocation and scheduling problems. Randomized policies mitigate a key vulnerability of human plans: predictability. We intend to use the presented method in the area of traffic prediction in the future work.

Acknowledgements. This work was supported by the European Regional Development Fund in the IT4Innovations Centre of Excellence project (CZ.1.05/1.1.00/02.0070) and the national budget of the Czech Republic via the Research and Development for Innovations Operational Programme, and supported by the project New creative teams in priorities of scientific research, reg. no. CZ.1.07/2.3.00/30.0055, supported by Operational Programme Education for Competitiveness and co-financed by the European Social Fund and the state budget of the Czech Republic, and co-financed by SGS, VSB Technical University of Ostrava, Czech Republic, under the grant No. SP2014/154 'Complex network analysis and prediction of network object behavior'. At this place we would like to thank the students of bachelors and masters studies at the VSB - Technical University of Ostrava who participated in the development and further improving of the simulator for robot soccer which has been used to create the above mentioned experiments.

References

1. Osborne, M.J.: An introduction to game theory. Oxford University Press, New York (2004)
2. Camerer, C.F.: Behavioral Game Theory: Experiments in Strategic Interaction. Princeton University Press (2003)
3. Ontañón, S., Mishra, K., Sugandh, N., Ram, A.: Case-based planning and execution for real-time strategy games. In: Weber, R.O., Richter, M.M. (eds.) ICCBR 2007. LNCS (LNAI), vol. 4626, pp. 164–178. Springer, Heidelberg (2007)
4. Kim, J.-H., Kim, D.-H., Kim, Y.-J., Seow, K.T.: Soccer Robotics. Springer Tracts in Advanced Robotics. Springer (2010)
5. Martinovič, J., Snášel, V., Ochodková, Z.L., Wu, J., Abraham, A.: Robot soccer - strategy description and game analysis. In: 24th European Conference on Modelling and Simulation, ECMS 2010, Kuala Lumpur, Malaysia (2010)
6. Snášel, V., Svatoň, V., Martinovič, J., Abraham, A.: Optimization of Rules Selection for Robot Soccer Strategies. International Journal of Advanced Robotic Systems (2014)
7. Klancar, G., Lepetic, M., Karba, R., Zupancic, B.: Robot Soccer Collision Modelling and Validation in Multi-Agent Simulator. Mathematical and Computer Modelling of Dynamical Systems: Methods, Tools and Applications in Engineering and Related Sciences 9, 137–150 (2003)
8. Unity Technologies, Unity @ONLINE, https://unity3d.com/
9. NVIDIA Corporation, PhysX @ONLINE, http://www.geforce.com/hardware/technology/physx
10. Newman, J.E.M.: Networks: An Introduction. Osford University Press (2010)
11. Sagan, H.: Space-filling curves. Springer (1994)
12. Morton, G.M.: A computer Oriented Geodetic Data Base and a New Technique in File Sequencing. Technical Report, IBM Ltd. Ottawa, Canada (1966)
13. Svatoň, V., Martinovič, J., Slaninová, K., Bureš, T.: Improving strategy in robot soccer game by sequence extraction. In: KES-2014, 18th International Conference on Knowledge-Based and Intelligent Information and Engineering Systems, Gdynia, Poland (2014)

Novel Ranking Methods Applied to Complex Membership Determination Problems

Loc Hoang Tran[1], Linh Hoang Tran[2], and Hoang Trang[3]

[1] University of Minnesota/Computer Science Department, Minneapolis, USA
tran0398@umn.edu
[2] Portland State University/ECE Department, Portland, USA
linht@pdx.edu
[3] Ho Chi Minh City University of Technology-VNU HCM
Ho Chi Minh City, Vietnam
hoangtrang@hcmut.edu.vn

Abstract. The biological motivated problem that we want to solve in this paper is to predict the new members of a partially known protein complex (i.e. complex membership determination). In this problem, we are given a core set of proteins (i.e. the queries) making up a protein complex. However, the biologist experts do not know whether this core set is complete or not. Our objective is to find more potential members of the protein complex by ranking proteins in protein-protein interaction network. One of the solutions to this problem is a network reliability based method. Due to high time complexity of this method, the random walk on graphs method has been proposed to solve this complex membership determination problem. However, the random walk on graphs method is not the current state of the art network-based method solving bioinformatics problem. In this paper, the novel un-normalized graph (p-) Laplacian based ranking method will be developed based on the un-normalized graph p-Laplacian operator definitions such as the curvature operator of graph (i.e. the un-normalized graph 1-Laplacian operator) and will be used to solve the complex membership determination problem. The results from experiments shows that the un-normalized graph p-Laplacian ranking methods are at least as good as the current state of the art network-based ranking method ($p=2$) but often lead to better ranking accuracy performance measures.

Keywords: Ranking, graph, p-Laplacian, protein complex, membership.

1 Introduction

Recent development in genome projects has shown that the pair of genes or group of genes sharing an edge (or hyper-edge) in the protein (hyper-) networks [1, 2] tends to have similar complex biological function. Therefore, in recent years, the considerable amount of research effort has gone into discovering the complete set of interacting proteins in an organism. Protein-protein interaction networks have become certainty in recent years thanks to high throughput methods such as yeast-two-hybrid [3, 4] and affinity purification with mass spectrometry [5, 6]. Corresponding to the readiness of

K. Saeed and V. Snášel (Eds.): CISIM 2014, LNCS 8838, pp. 89–99, 2014.
© IFIP International Federation for Information Processing 2014

protein networks, various graph analysis techniques have been proposed to mine these networks for protein function prediction [1, 2, 7, 8, 9, 10, 11] and complex/pathway membership determination [12, 13].

The biological motivated problem that we want to solve in this paper is to predict the new members of a partially known protein complex (i.e. complex membership determination). In this problem, we are given a core set of proteins (i.e. the queries) making up a protein complex. However, the biologist experts do not know whether this core set is complete or not. Our objective is to find more potential members of the protein complex by ranking proteins in protein-protein interaction network. Then the proteins with highest ranks (i.e. probability of membership in the partially known complex) will then be selected and checked by biologist experts to see if the extended genes in fact belong to the same complex/pathway.

One of the solutions to this problem is a network reliability based method proposed by [12]. This method finds the close proximity proteins. This method approximates the reliability between two nodes using Monte Carlo simulation. However, due to high time complexity of this method, the random walk on graphs method has been proposed to solve this complex membership determination problem [13]. The random walk method simulates a random walker that starts at a source node (i.e. the query or the member of the complex/pathway) and moves to other nodes through connecting edges. The random walker can also choose to teleport to the start node with a definite probability, the restart probability. The probability of finding the random walker at a certain node gives the similarity of that node to the starting node. To solve the complex membership determination problem, [13] simulates a random walker that starts from a set of nodes (i.e. the queries or the set of members of the complex/pathway) instead of a single node. Thus, given a set of proteins that are members of a partially known complex as the start set, the random walk on graphs method ranks the remaining proteins in the protein-protein interaction network with respect to their proximity to the queries' complex.

This ranking method [13] has also been employed by Google Company to exploit the global hyperlink structure of the Web and produce better rankings of search results [14]. Its idea [13] has also been employed in [1] to solve the protein function prediction problem (i.e. the classification problem). However, based on [1], the random walk on graphs method is not the best network-based method solving the classification bioinformatics problems such as protein function prediction [1, 11] and cancer classification [15]. To the best of my knowledge, the un-normalized graph (p-) Laplacian based semi-supervised learning method is considered the current state of the art network-based method solving protein function prediction problem [7, 11] and cancer classification problem [15]. However, the un-normalized graph (p-) Laplacian based ranking method has not yet been developed and obviously has not been applied to any practical applications. In this paper, the un-normalized graph (p-) Laplacian based ranking method will be developed based on the un-normalized graph p-Laplacian operator definitions such as the curvature operator of graph (i.e. the un-normalized graph 1-Laplacian operator). Finally, this proposed method will be used to solve the complex membership determination problem.

We will organize the paper as follows: Section 2 will introduce the preliminary notations and definitions used in this paper. Section 3 will introduce the definition of the gradient and divergence operators of graphs. Section 4 will introduce the definition of

Laplace operator of graphs and its properties. Section 5 will introduce the definition of the curvature operator of graphs and its properties. Section 6 will introduce the definition of the p-Laplace operator of graphs and its properties. Section 7 will show how to derive the algorithm of the un-normalized graph p-Laplacian based ranking method from regularization framework. In section 8, we will compare the accuracy performance measures of the un-normalized graph Laplacian based ranking algorithm and the un-normalized graph p-Laplacian based ranking algorithms. Section 9 will conclude this paper and the future direction of researches of other practical applications in bioinformatics utilizing discrete operator of graph will be discussed.

2 Preliminary Notations and Definitions

Given a graph $G=(V,E,W)$ where V is a set of vertices with $|V| = n$, $E \subseteq V * V$ is a set of edges and W is a $n * n$ similarity matrix with elements $w_{ij} > 0$ ($1 \leq i,j \leq n$).
  Also, please note that $w_{ij} = w_{ji}$.
  The degree function $d: V \rightarrow R^+$ is

$$d_i = \Sigma_{j \sim i} w_{ij}, \tag{1}$$

where $j \sim i$ is the set of vertices adjacent with i.
  Define $D = diag(d_1, d_2, ..., d_n)$.
  The inner product on the function space R^V is

$$< f,g >_V = \Sigma_{i \in V} f_i g_i \tag{2}$$

  Also define an inner product on the space of functions R^E on the edges

$$< F,G >_E = \Sigma_{(i,j) \in E} F_{ij} G_{ij} \tag{3}$$

  Here let $H(V) = (R^V, <.,.>_V)$ and $H(E) = (R^E, <.,.>_E)$ be the Hilbert space real-valued functions defined on the vertices of the graph G and the Hilbert space of real-valued functions defined in the edges of G respectively.

3 Gradient and Divergence Operators

We define the gradient operator $d: H(V) \rightarrow H(E)$ to be

$$(df)_{ij} = \sqrt{w_{ij}}(f_j - f_i), \tag{4}$$

where $f: V \rightarrow R$ be a function of $H(V)$.
  We define the divergence operator $div: H(E) \rightarrow H(V)$ to be

$$< df, F >_{H(E)} = < f, -divF >_{H(V)}, \tag{5}$$

where $f \in H(V), F \in H(E)$
  Next, we need to prove that

$$(divF)_j = \sum_{i \sim j} \sqrt{w_{ij}} (F_{ji} - F_{ij})$$

Proof:

$$< df, F >= \sum_{(i,j)\in E} df_{ij} F_{ij}$$

$$= \sum_{(i,j)\in E} \sqrt{w_{ij}}\,(f_j - f_i)F_{ij}$$

$$= \sum_{(i,j)\in E} \sqrt{w_{ij}}\,f_j F_{ij} - \sum_{(i,j)\in E} \sqrt{w_{ij}}\,f_i F_{ij}$$

$$= \sum_{k\in V}\sum_{i\sim k} \sqrt{w_{ik}}\,f_k F_{ik} - \sum_{k\in V}\sum_{j\sim k} \sqrt{w_{kj}}\,f_k F_{kj}$$

$$= \sum_{k\in V} f_k \left(\sum_{i\sim k} \sqrt{w_{ik}}\,F_{ik} - \sum_{i\sim k} \sqrt{w_{ki}}\,F_{ki}\right)$$

$$= \sum_{k\in V} f_k \sum_{i\sim k} \sqrt{w_{ik}}\,(F_{ik} - F_{ki})$$

Thus, we have

$$(divF)_j = \sum_{i\sim j} \sqrt{w_{ij}}\,(F_{ji} - F_{ij}) \tag{6}$$

4   Laplace Operator

We define the Laplace operator $\Delta: H(V) \to H(V)$ to be

$$\Delta f = -\frac{1}{2} div(df) \tag{7}$$

Next, we compute

$$(\Delta f)_j = \frac{1}{2}\sum_{i\sim j} \sqrt{w_{ij}}\,((df)_{ij} - (df)_{ji})$$

$$= \frac{1}{2}\sum_{i\sim j} \sqrt{w_{ij}}\,(\sqrt{w_{ij}}(f_j - f_i) - \sqrt{w_{ij}}(f_i - f_j))$$

$$= \sum_{i\sim j} w_{ij}\,(f_j - f_i)$$

$$= \sum_{i\sim j} w_{ij} f_j - \sum_{i\sim j} w_{ij} f_i$$

$$= d_j f_j - \sum_{i\sim j} w_{ij} f_i$$

Thus, we have

$$(\Delta f)_j = d_j f_j - \Sigma_{i\sim j} w_{ij} f_i \tag{8}$$

The graph Laplacian is a linear operator. Furthermore, the graph Laplacian is self-adjoint and positive semi-definite.

Let $S_2(f) = <\Delta f, f>$, we have the following **theorem 1**

$$D_f S_2 = 2\Delta f \tag{9}$$

The proof of the above theorem can be found from [15, 16].

5   Curvature Operator

We define the curvature operator $\kappa: H(V) \rightarrow H(V)$ to be

$$\kappa f = -\frac{1}{2} div(\frac{df}{\|df\|}) \tag{10}$$

Next, we compute

$$(\kappa f)_j = \frac{1}{2} \sum_{i\sim j} \sqrt{w_{ij}} \left((\frac{df}{\|df\|})_{ij} - (\frac{df}{\|df\|})_{ji} \right)$$

$$= \frac{1}{2} \sum_{i\sim j} \sqrt{w_{ij}} \left(\frac{1}{\|d_i f\|} \sqrt{w_{ij}}(f_j - f_i) - \frac{1}{\|d_j f\|} \sqrt{w_{ij}}(f_i - f_j) \right)$$

$$= \frac{1}{2} \sum_{i\sim j} w_{ij} \left(\frac{1}{\|d_i f\|} + \frac{1}{\|d_j f\|} \right)(f_j - f_i)$$

Thus, we have

$$(\kappa f)_j = \frac{1}{2}\Sigma_{i\sim j} w_{ij} \left(\frac{1}{\|d_i f\|} + \frac{1}{\|d_j f\|} \right)(f_j - f_i) \tag{11}$$

From the above formula, we have

$$d_i f = ((df)_{ij} : j\sim i)^T \tag{12}$$

The local variation of f at i is defined to be

$$\|d_i f\| = \sqrt{\Sigma_{j\sim i}(df)_{ij}^2} = \sqrt{\Sigma_{j\sim i} w_{ij}(f_j - f_i)^2} \tag{13}$$

To avoid the zero denominators in (11), the local variation of f at i is defined to be

$$\|d_i f\| = \sqrt{\Sigma_{j\sim i}(df)_{ij}^2 + \epsilon}, \tag{14}$$

where $\epsilon = 10^{-10}$.

The graph curvature is a non-linear operator.

Let $S_1(f) = \sum_i \|d_i f\|$, we have the following **theorem 2**

$$D_f S_1 = \kappa f \tag{15}$$

The proof of the above theorem can be found from [15, 16].

6   p-Laplace Operator

We define the p-Laplace operator $\Delta_p : H(V) \rightarrow H(V)$ to be

$$\Delta_p f = -\frac{1}{2} div(\|df\|^{p-2} df) \tag{16}$$

Clearly, $\Delta_1 = \kappa$ and $\Delta_2 = \Delta$. Next, we compute

$$\left(\Delta_p f\right)_j = \frac{1}{2} \sum_{i \sim j} \sqrt{w_{ij}} \left(\|df\|^{p-2} df_{ij} - \|df\|^{p-2} df_{ji} \right)$$

$$= \frac{1}{2} \sum_{i \sim j} \sqrt{w_{ij}} \left(\|d_i f\|^{p-2} \sqrt{w_{ij}} (f_j - f_i) - \|d_j f\|^{p-2} \sqrt{w_{ij}} (f_i - f_j) \right)$$

$$= \frac{1}{2} \sum_{i \sim j} w_{ij} \left(\|d_i f\|^{p-2} + \|d_j f\|^{p-2} \right)(f_j - f_i)$$

Thus, we have

$$\left(\Delta_p f\right)_j = \frac{1}{2} \sum_{i \sim j} w_{ij} \left(\|d_i f\|^{p-2} + \|d_j f\|^{p-2} \right)(f_j - f_i) \tag{17}$$

Let $S_p(f) = \frac{1}{p} \sum_i \|d_i f\|^p$, we have the following **theorem 3**

$$D_f S_p = p \Delta_p f \tag{18}$$

The proof of the above theorem can be found from [15, 16].

7   Discrete Regularization on Graphs and Protein Function Classification Problems

Given a protein network $G=(V,E)$. V is the set of all proteins in the network and E is the set of all possible interactions between these proteins. Let y denote the initial function in $H(V)$. y_i can be defined as follows

$$y_i = \begin{cases} 1 \; if \; protein \; i \; is \; the \; query \\ 0 \; if \; protein \; i \; is \; not \; the \; query \end{cases}$$

Our goal is to look for an estimated function f in $H(V)$ such that f is not only smooth on G but also close enough to an initial function y. Then each protein i is ranked as value of f_i. This concept can be formulated as the following optimization problem

$$argmin_{f \in H(V)}\{S_p(f) + \frac{\mu}{2}\|f - y\|^2\} \tag{19}$$

The first term in (19) is the smoothness term. The second term is the fitting term. A positive parameter μ captures the trade-off between these two competing terms.

7.1   2-smoothness

When $p=2$, the optimization problem (19) is

$$argmin_{f \in H(V)}\{\frac{1}{2}\Sigma_i\|d_i f\|^2 + \frac{\mu}{2}\|f - y\|^2\} \tag{20}$$

By theorem 1, we have

Theorem 4: The solution of (20) satisfies

$$\Delta f + \mu(f - y) = 0 \tag{21}$$

Since Δ is a linear operator, the closed form solution of (21) is

$$f = \mu(\Delta + \mu I)^{-1}y, \tag{22}$$

Where I is the identity operator and $\Delta = D - W$. (22) is the algorithm proposed by [1, 10].

7.2   1-smoothness

When $p=1$, the optimization problem (19) is

$$argmin_{f \in H(V)}\{\Sigma_i\|d_i f\| + \frac{\mu}{2}\|f - y\|^2\}, \tag{23}$$

By theorem 2, we have

Theorem 5: The solution of (23) satisfies

$$\kappa f + \mu(f - y) = 0, \tag{24}$$

The curvature κ is a non-linear operator; hence we do not have the closed form solution of equation (24). Thus, we have to construct iterative algorithm to obtain the solution. From (24), we have

$$\frac{1}{2}\Sigma_{i \sim j} w_{ij}\left(\frac{1}{\|d_i f\|} + \frac{1}{\|d_j f\|}\right)(f_j - f_i) + \mu(f_j - y_j) = 0 \tag{25}$$

Define the function $m: E \to R$ by

$$m_{ij} = \frac{1}{2}w_{ij}(\frac{1}{\|d_i f\|} + \frac{1}{\|d_j f\|}) \tag{26}$$

Then (25)

$$\sum_{i \sim j} m_{ij}(f_j - f_i) + \mu(f_j - y_j) = 0$$

can be transformed into

$$\left(\Sigma_{i\sim j} m_{ij} + \mu\right)f_j = \Sigma_{i\sim j} m_{ij} f_i + \mu y_j \tag{27}$$

Define the function $p\colon E \to R$ by

$$p_{ij} = \begin{cases} \dfrac{m_{ij}}{\Sigma_{i\sim j} m_{ij} + \mu} & if \; i \ne j \\[2mm] \dfrac{\mu}{\Sigma_{i\sim j} m_{ij} + \mu} & if \; i = j \end{cases} \tag{28}$$

Then

$$f_j = \Sigma_{i\sim j} p_{ij} f_i + p_{jj} y_j \tag{29}$$

Thus we can consider the iteration

$$f_j^{(t+1)} = \Sigma_{i\sim j} p_{ij}^{(t)} f_i^{(t)} + p_{jj}^{(t)} y_j \; \forall j \in V$$

to obtain the solution of (23).

7.3   p-smoothness

For any number p, the optimization problem (19) is

$$argmin_{f \in H(V)} \{ \tfrac{1}{p} \Sigma_i \| d_i f \|^p + \tfrac{\mu}{2} \| f - y \|^2 \}, \tag{30}$$

By theorem 3, we have

Theorem 6: The solution of (30) satisfies

$$\Delta_p f + \mu(f - y) = 0, \tag{31}$$

The *p-Laplace* operator is a non-linear operator; hence we do not have the closed form solution of equation (31). Thus, we have to construct iterative algorithm to obtain the solution. From (31), we have

$$\tfrac{1}{2} \Sigma_{i\sim j} w_{ij} \left(\| d_i f \|^{p-2} + \| d_j f \|^{p-2} \right) (f_j - f_i) + \mu(f_j - y_j) = 0 \tag{32}$$

Define the function $m\colon E \to R$ by

$$m_{ij} = \tfrac{1}{2} w_{ij} (\| d_i f \|^{p-2} + \| d_j f \|^{p-2}) \tag{33}$$

Then equation (32) which is

$$\sum_{i\sim j} m_{ij} (f_j - f_i) + \mu(f_j - y_j) = 0$$

can be transformed into

$$\left(\Sigma_{i\sim j} m_{ij} + \mu\right)f_j = \Sigma_{i\sim j} m_{ij} f_i + \mu y_j \tag{34}$$

Define the function $p\colon E \to R$ by

$$p_{ij} = \begin{cases} \dfrac{m_{ij}}{\Sigma_{i \sim j} m_{ij} + \mu} & if \ i \neq j \\[2mm] \dfrac{\mu}{\Sigma_{i \sim j} m_{ij} + \mu} & if \ i = j \end{cases} \tag{35}$$

Then

$$f_j = \Sigma_{i \sim j} p_{ij} f_i + p_{jj} y_j \tag{36}$$

Thus we can consider the iteration

$$f_j^{(t+1)} = \Sigma_{i \sim j} p_{ij}^{(t)} f_i^{(t)} + p_{jj}^{(t)} y_j \ \forall j \in V$$

to obtain the solution of (30).

8   Experiments and Results

Datasets
In this paper, we use the dataset available from [12, 13] and references therein. This dataset contains the probabilistic yeast network containing 3112 genes and 25113 undirected interactions (i.e. edges). This probabilistic yeast network is called ProNet. In order to evaluate the performance of the un-normalized graph p-Laplacian based ranking algorithms, we used three protein complexes from the MIPS databases. Table 1 shows the three protein complexes used in our experiments.

Table 1. Description of three protein complexes

Complex ID	Number of genes in complex	List of genes in the complex
1	3	ydr148c, yfl018c, yil125w
2	4	ybr126c, ydr074w, yml100w, ymr261c
4	3	ybr195c, yml102w, ypr018w

Experiments
In this section, we experiment with the above proposed un-normalized graph p-Laplacian ranking methods with p=1, 1.1, 1.2, 1.3, 1.4, 1.5, 1.6, 1.7, 1.8, 1.9 and the current state of the art method (i.e. the un-normalized graph Laplacian based ranking method p=2) in terms of accuracy performance measure. All experiments were implemented in Matlab 6.5 on virtual machine. The leave-one-out testing strategy is used to compute the accuracy performance measures of all methods used in this paper. For each of the complexes, one member gene is left out and the remaining genes are used as the core complex in the membership query. Effective ranking methods should report the left out gene in top k ranks. The parameter μ is set to 1. The accuracy performance measures of the above proposed methods and the current state of the art method is given in the following table 2.

Table 2. The comparison of accuracies of proposed methods with different p-values

Top k ranks		k=1	k=5	k=10	k=20
Accuracy Performance Measures (%)	p=1	10	60	90	100
	p=1.1	10	60	90	100
	p=1.2	20	70	100	100
	p=1.3	30	70	100	100
	p=1.4	30	80	100	100
	p=1.5	30	80	100	100
	p=1.6	30	80	100	100
	p=1.7	30	80	100	100
	p=1.8	40	80	100	100
	p=1.9	40	80	100	100
	p=2 (i.e. the current state of the art method)	40	70	100	100

The results from the above table shows that the un-normalized graph p-Laplacian ranking methods are at least as good as the current state of the art method ($p=2$) but often lead to better ranking accuracy performance measures.

9   Conclusions

We have developed the detailed regularization frameworks for the un-normalized graph p-Laplacian ranking methods applying to complex membership determination problem. Experiments show that the un-normalized graph p-Laplacian ranking methods are at least as good as the current state of the art method (i.e. $p=2$) but often lead to significant better ranking accuracy performance measures.

Moreover, these un-normalized graph p-Laplacian ranking methods can not only be used in complex membership determination problem but also in biomarker discovery problem in cancer classification. In specific, given a set of genes (i.e. the queries) involved in a specific disease (for e.g. leukemia), these methods can also be used to find more genes involved in the same disease by ranking genes in gene co-expression network (derived from gene expression data) or the protein-protein interaction network or the integrated network of them. The genes with the highest rank then will be selected and then checked by biologist experts to see if the extended genes in fact are involved in the same disease. This problem is called biomarker discovery in cancer classification.

Recently, to the best of my knowledge, the un-normalized directed graph p-Laplacian based ranking methods have not yet been developed and applied to any practical problems. This method is worth investigated because of its difficult nature and its close connection to partial differential equation on directed graph field.

References

1. Tran, L.: Application of three graph Laplacian based semi-supervised learning methods to protein function prediction problem. CoRR abs/1211.4289 (2012)
2. Tran, L.: Hypergraph and protein function prediction with gene ex-pression data CoRR abs/1212.0388 (2012)
3. Ito, T., Chiba, T., Ozawa, R., Yoshida, M., Hattori, M., Sakaki, Y.: A com-prehensive two-hybrid analysis to explore the yeast protein interac-tome. Proc. Natl. Acad. Sci. 98, 4569–4574 (2001)
4. Uetz, P., Cagney, G., Mansfield, T.A., Judson, R., Knight, J.R., Lockshon, D., Narayan, V., Srinivasan, M., Pochart, P.: A comprehensive analysis of protein-protein interactions in saccharomyces cerevisiae. Nature 403, 623–627 (2000)
5. Gavin, A.C., Bosche, M., Krause, R., Grandi, P., Marzioch, M., Bauer, A., Schultz, J., Rick, J.M., Michon, A.M., Cruciat, C.M.: Functional organization of the yeast proteome by systematic analysis of protein complexes. Nature 415, 141–147 (2002)
6. Ho, Y., Gruhler, A., Heilbut, A., Bader, G.D., Moore, L., Adams, S.L., Millar, A., Taylor, P., Bennett, K., Boutilier, K.: Systematic identification of protein complexes in saccharomyces cerevisiae by mass spectrometry. Nature 415, 180–183 (2002)
7. Tsuda K., Shin H.H., and Schoelkopf B. Fast protein classification with multiple networks. Bioinformatics (ECCB 2005) 21(suppl. 2), ii59–ii65 (2005)
8. Lanckriet, G.R.G., Deng, M., Cristianini, N., Jordan, M.I., Noble, W.S.: Kernel-based data fusion and its application to protein function prediction in yeast. In: Pacific Symposium on Biocomputing (PSB) (2004)
9. Letovsky, S., Kasif, S.: Predicting protein function from pro-tein/protein interaction data: a probabilistic approach Bioinformatics 19, i197–i204 (2003)
10. Tsuda, K., Noble, W.S.: Learning kernels from biological networks by maximizing entropy. Bioinformatics 20(S1), i326–i333 (2004)
11. Tran, L.: The un-normalized graph p-Laplacian based semi-supervised learning method and protein function prediction problem. In: The Fifth International Conference on Knowledge Systems and Engineer (2013)
12. Asthana, S., King, O.D., Gibbons, F.D., Roth, F.P.: Predicting protein complex member-ship using probabilistic network reliability. Genome Research 14, 1170–1175 (2004)
13. Can, T., Camoglu, O., Singh, A.K.: Analysis of protein-protein interaction networks using random walks. In: Proceedings of the 5th ACM SIGKDD Workshop on Data Mining in Bioinformatics, Chicago (August 2005)
14. Brin, S., Page, L.: The anatomy of a large-scale hypertextual Web search engine. Comput-er Networks and ISDN Systems 30, 107–117 (1998)
15. Tran, L., Tran, L.: Un-normalized graph p-Laplacian semi-supervised learning method applied to cancer classification problem. In: The Second International Conference on Intelligent and Automation Systems (2014)
16. Zhou, D., Schölkopf, B.: Discrete Regularization. In: Chapelle, O., Schölkopf, B., Zien, A. (eds.) Semi-Supervised Learning, pp. 221–232. MIT Press, Cambridge (2006)

Combination of Self Organizing Maps and Growing Neural Gas

Lukáš Vojáček[1,2], Pavla Dráždilová[2], and Jiří Dvorský[2]

[1] IT4Innovations, VŠB - Technical University of Ostrava,
17. listopadu 15/2172, 708 33 Ostrava, Czech Republic
[2] Department of Computer Science,
VŠB – Technical University of Ostrava, 17. listopadu 15/2172,
708 33 Ostrava, Czech Republic
{pavla.drazdilova,jiri.dvorsky,lukas.vojacek}@vsb.cz

Abstract. The paper deals with the high dimensional data clustering problem. One possible way to cluster this kind of data is based on Artificial Neural Networks (ANN) such as Growing Neural Gas (GNG) or Self Organizing Maps (SOM). The learning phase of ANN, which is time-consuming especially for large high-dimensional datasets, is the main drawback of this approach to data clustering. Parallel modification, Growing Neural Gas with pre-processing by Self Organizing Maps, and its implementation on the HPC cluster is presented in the paper. Some experimental results are also presented.

Keywords: self organizing maps, growing neural gas, high-dimensional dataset, high performance computing.

1 Introduction

Recently, the issue of high-dimensional data clustering has arisen together with the development of information and communication technologies which support growing opportunities to process large data collections. High-dimensional data collections are commonly available in areas like medicine, biology, information retrieval, web analyse, social network analyse, image processing, financial transaction analysis and many others.

Two main challenges should be solved to process high-dimensional data collections. One of the problems is the fast growth of computational complexity with respect to growing data dimensionality. The second one is specific similarity measurement in a high-dimensional space. Beyer et al. presented in [1] for any point in a high-dimensional space the expected distance, computed by the Euclidean distance to the closest and to the farthest point, shrinks with growing dimensionality. These two reasons reduce the effectiveness of clustering algorithms on the above-mentioned high-dimensional data collections in many actual applications.

The authors propose an effective data clustering algorithm which is based on *Growing Neural Gas* (GNG) [9] and *Self Organizing Maps* (SOM). The computational complexity is resolved by the parallel implementation of GNG with

K. Saeed and V. Snášel (Eds.): CISIM 2014, LNCS 8838, pp. 100–111, 2014.

pre-procesing by SOM. Some technical problems have to be resolved in order to effectively train such kind of neural network using an *High Performance Computing* (HPC) cluster with MPI. In our previous paper [14] we proposed a method of parallel implementation of GNG by using only MPI, but there were limitation to effective parallelization.

2 Artificial Neural Networks

In this section we will describe two type of neural network, the first is Self Organizing Maps and the second is Growing Neural Gas and then we present a combination of SOM and GNG.

2.1 Self Organizing Maps

Self Organizing Maps (SOMs), also known as Kohonen maps, were proposed by Teuvo Kohonen in 1982 [6]. SOM is a kind of artificial neural network that is trained by unsupervised learning. Using SOM, the input space of training samples can be represented in a lower-dimensional (often two-dimensional) space [7], called a *map*. Such a model is efficient in structure visualization due to its feature of topological preservation using a neighbourhood function.

SOM consists of two layers of neurons: an *input layer* that receives and transmits the input information, and an *output layer*, the map that represents the output characteristics. The output layer is commonly organized as a two-dimensional rectangular grid of nodes, where each node corresponds to one neuron. Both layers are feed-forward connected. Each neuron in the input layer is connected to each neuron in the output layer. A real number, or weight, is assigned to each of these connections.

2.2 Growing Neural Gas

The representation of Growing Neural Gas is an undirected graph which need not be connected. Generally, there are no restrictions to the topology. The graph is generated and continuously updated by competitive Hebbian Learning [8,10]. According to the pre-set conditions, new neurons are automatically added and connections between neurons are subject to time and can be removed. GNG can be used for vector quantization by finding the code-vectors in clusters [5], biologically influenced [12], image compression, disease diagnosis.

GNG works by modifying the graph, where the operations are the addition and removal of neurons and edges between neurons.

To understand the functioning of GNG, it is necessary to define the learning algorithm. The algorithm described by Algorithm 1 is based on the original algorithm [4] [5], but it is modified for better continuity in the SOM algorithm.

Remark. The notation used in the paper is briefly listed in Table 1.

Table 1. Notation used in the paper

Symbol	Description
M	Number of input vectors
n	Dimension of input vectors, number of input neurons, dimension of weight vectors in GNG output layer neurons
N	Current number of neurons in GNG output layer
N_{max}	Maximum allowed number of neurons in GNG output layer
n_i	i-th input neuron, $i = 1, 2, \ldots, n$
N_i	i-th output neuron, $i = 1, 2, \ldots, N$
e_{ij}	edge between neurons N_i and N_j for some $i, j = 1, \ldots, N$, where $i \neq j$.
E	set of all edges in GNG
G	undirected graph describing topology of GNG, $G(\{\mathsf{N}_1, \ldots, \mathsf{N}_N\}, \mathsf{E})$
T	Number of epochs
t	Current epoch, $t = 1, 2, \ldots, T$
X	Set of input vectors, $X \subset \mathbb{R}^n$
$\boldsymbol{x}(t)$	Current input vector in epoch t, arbitrarily selected vector from set X $\boldsymbol{x}(t) \in X$, $\boldsymbol{x}(t) = (x_1, x_2, \ldots, x_n)$
$\boldsymbol{w_k}(t)$	Weight vector of neuron N_k, $k = 1, 2, \ldots, N$ $\boldsymbol{w_k}(t) \in \mathbb{R}^n$, $\boldsymbol{w_k}(t) = (w_{k1}, w_{k1}, \ldots, w_{kn})$
N_{c_1}	The first Best Matching Unit (BMU_1), winner of learning competition
N_{c_2}	The second Best Matching Unit (BMU_2), second best matching neuron in learning competition
l_{c_1}	Learning factor of BMU_1
l_{nc_1}	Learning factor of BMU_1 neighbours
e_i	Local error of output neuron N_i, $i = 1, 2, \ldots, N$
B	Number of clusters (C)
C_i	ith cluster witch contains similar input vectors
m_i	Number of input vectors in cluster C_i
$\boldsymbol{Z}_i$	Centroid of cluster C_i
β	Neuron error reduction factor
γ	Interval of input patterns to add a new neuron
$\delta(C_i, C_j)$	Distance metric between C_i and C_j
a_{max}	Maximum edge age
BMU	Best match unit
$d(\boldsymbol{x}, \boldsymbol{y})$	Distance between two vectors
$epoch$	During training phase are all input data one time used
p, q	Natural numbers

Algorithm 1. Growing Neural Gas algorithm

1. Initialization of network. Two neurons N_1 and N_2 are created, $\mathsf{E} = \{\mathsf{e}_{12}\}$. Weight vectors $\boldsymbol{w_1}(t)$ and $\boldsymbol{w_2}(t)$ are initialized to random values $\boldsymbol{w}_{kj}(t) \in [0, 1]$ $\forall j = 1, \ldots, n$, $k = 1, 2$.
2. Select arbitrary unused input data vector.
3. Perform the one learning iteration.
4. Reduce error value e_i for all neurons N_i using factor β.
5. Returns to step 2, until all input data vectors have been used.
6. If $t < T$ return to step 2.

2.3   Combination of SOM and GNG

One of the problem with parallelization which we described in the previous paper [14] is that when adding a new neuron it is necessary to send, in the worst scenario, vectors of two BMU neurons, which takes a lot of time. In this chapter we will describe a method for parallelization of the GNG network, which is based on the distribution of dataset.

The basic idea is to pre-process the input data by SOM, as a result of which there are clusters of similar data. Subsequently, we created the same number of GNG network as clusters, and assigned each cluster to one GNG. Each GNG creates its own neural map and after the learning process is finished, the results are merged.

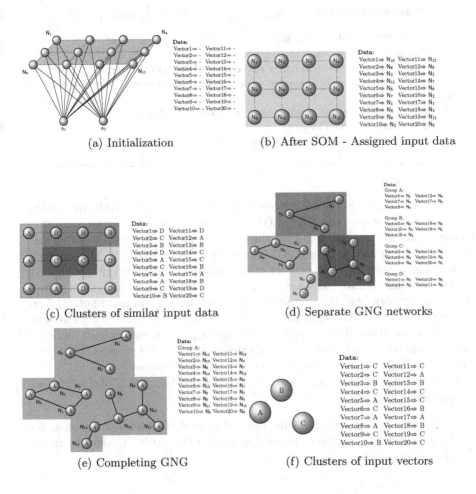

(a) Initialization

(b) After SOM - Assigned input data

(c) Clusters of similar input data

(d) Separate GNG networks

(e) Completing GNG

(f) Clusters of input vectors

Fig. 1. Combination of SOM and GNG

In general, the whole process is separated into a few phases, where the first phase contains the initialization of the SOM and running of the training process (Fig. 1(a)). In second phase each input vector assigned to one neuron (Fig. 1(b)). The main goal of the third phase is to create clusters of similar neurons (Fig. 1(c)). The clusters are created on the basis of Algorithm 2.

Algorithm 2. Algorithm of creating clusters by create spanning tree

1. Compute the dissimilarity for all $k = 1, \ldots, N$, between each neuron and its neighbors. It is possible to use:
   - Euclidean distance $d_e(\boldsymbol{w}_i, \boldsymbol{w}_j) = (\sum_{k=1}^{n} |\boldsymbol{w}_{ik} - \boldsymbol{w}_{jk}|^2)^{\frac{1}{2}}$,
   - Minkowski distance $d_m(\boldsymbol{w}_i, \boldsymbol{w}_j) = (\sum_{k=1}^{n} |\boldsymbol{w}_{ik} - \boldsymbol{w}_{jk}|^p)^{\frac{1}{p}}$, where $p \in R^+$,
   - cosine dissimilarity $d_c(\boldsymbol{w}_i, \boldsymbol{w}_j) = (1 - \frac{\boldsymbol{w}_i \cdot \boldsymbol{w}_j}{\|\boldsymbol{w}_i\| \|\boldsymbol{w}_j\|})$.
2. Sort dissimilarity from smallest to greatest.
3. Select smallest unused dissimilarity and an associated two neurons.
4. If selected neurons are not in connected component, then create connection between them.
5. If neither of the following conditions is met, return to step 3:
   - The number of the clusters.
   - Number (percentage) of input data in cluster.

This is the end of SOM pre-processing and from now on we will use a GNG network. Now the same number of GNG networks is created as the number of clusters from pre-processing and the clusters are assigned to networks. After running the training process on each GNG network we have learned GNG networks, each of which has a different number of neurons and connections (Fig. 1(d)). All the GNG networks have the same configurations. If the pre-processing is perfect the GNG networks can be completely separated, but to eliminate potential errors we merge all GNG networks into one GNG network, which we do likewise with the input data. After running the training process but without adding a new neuron; only connections between existing neurons are created (Fig. 1(e)). Connected GNG networks create clusters C_i of input vectors.

We implemented following indexes for determining the quality of clusters containing input vectors.

- Davies-Bouldin index [2] – This method is used to determine the distance between clusters and the cohesive. The smaller the resulting value, the better the quality of clusters.

$$S_i = \left(\frac{1}{m_i} \sum_{j=1}^{m_i} |\boldsymbol{x_j} - \boldsymbol{Z}_i|^q \right)^{1/q} \tag{1}$$

$$R_{ij} = \left(\sum_{k=1}^{B} |Z_{ik} - Z_{jk}|^p \right)^{1/p} \tag{2}$$

$$D_{ij} = \frac{S_j + S_i}{R_{ij}} \tag{3}$$

$$DB = \frac{1}{B} \sum_{i=1}^{B} \max_{i \neq j} (D_{ij}) \tag{4}$$

- Dunn index [3] – This method is used to determine the inter-cluster distance (the optimal is maximal) and intra-cluster distance (the optimal is minimal). The range of values are from 0 to 1, where values close to 0 means optimal clustering.

$$\delta(C_i, C_j) = \min_{x \in C_i, y \in C_j} d(x, y) \tag{5}$$

$$\Delta(C_i) = \max_{x, y \in C_i} d(x, y) \tag{6}$$

$$Dunn\ index = \min_{1 \leq i \leq m} \left(\min_{1 \leq j \leq m, j \neq i} \left(\frac{\delta(C_i, C_j)}{\max_{1 \leq k \leq m} \Delta(C_k)} \right) \right) \tag{7}$$

- Silhouette [11] – This method is aimed to evaluation object how well there are assigned to clusters. A range of values are from -1 to 1, where values close to 1 means optimal clustering. For each input vector is calculate silhouette Eq. (11) and then calculated average value Eq. (12).

$$a_i = \sum_{x_i, x_j \in C_k; x_i \neq x_j} \frac{d_*(x_i, x_j)}{m_k} \qquad \forall i = 1, \ldots M \tag{8}$$

$$d(x_i, C_j) = \frac{\sum_{x_k \in C_j; x_i \notin C_j} d_*(x_i, x_k)}{m_j} \tag{9}$$

$$b_i = \min_{C_j} d(x_i, C_j) \qquad \forall i = 1, \ldots M \tag{10}$$

$$s_i = \frac{b(i) - a(i)}{\max(a(i), b(i))} \qquad \forall i = 1, \ldots M \tag{11}$$

$$Silhouette = \frac{1}{M} \sum_{i=1}^{M} s_i \tag{12}$$

The entire description above can be summarized as follows: Help speeding up computation parallelization is shown in Fig. 2 where the top layer of parallelization (SOM) is something which the authors described in a previous paper [15].

The results of the SOM algorithm are collected in the process with rank 0, which creates a cluster of input data and assigns the individual processes. Each process (0 to m) creates a custom GNG network that is isolated and only works with assigned inputs. Subsequently, these neural networks were gathered in the process with rank 0, which performs an epoch over all input data.

Precipitated, obtained parallelization compared to using the GNG algorithm without hierarchy depends on the division of the input data into clusters. In the extreme case where all input data are only in one cluster, the hierarchical solution is less efficient than just the GNG algorithm because it still needs to count the extra time required for the SOM algorithm.

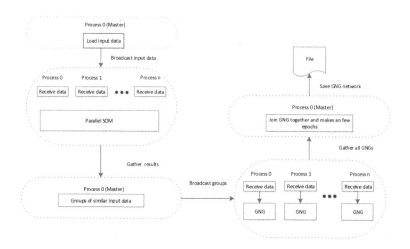

Fig. 2. Parallel Algorithm

3   Experiments

We will describe different datasets and we will provide experiments with datasets in this section.

3.1   Experimental Datasets and Hardware

Two datasets were used in the experiments. The first dataset was commonly used in Information Retrieval – *Medlars*. The second one was the test data for the elementary benchmark for clustering algorithms [13].

Medlars Dataset. The Medlars dataset consisted of 1,033 English abstracts from medical science[1]. The 8,707 distinct terms were extracted from the Medlars dataset. Each term represents a potential dimension in the input vector space. The term's level of significance (weight) in a particular document represents a

---

[1] The collection can be downloaded from `ftp://ftp.cs.cornell.edu/pub/smart`. The total size of the dataset is approximately 1.03 MB.

value of the component of the input vector. Finally, the input vector space has a dimension of 8,707, and 1,033 input vectors were extracted from the dataset.

Clustering Dataset. Three training data collections called TwoDiamonds, Lsun and Hepta from the Fundamental Clustering Problems Suite (FCPS) were used. A short description of the selected dataset used in our experiments is given in Table 2.

Table 2. Fundamental Clustering Problems Suite – selected datasets

Name	Cases	#Vars	#Clusters	Main Clustering Problem
Target	770	2	6	outlying clusters
Lsun	400	2	3	different variances in clusters
TwoDiamonds	800	2	2	touching clusters
Hepta	212	3	7	clearly separated clusters

Experimental Hardware. All the experiments were performed on a Windows HPC server 2008 with 6 computing nodes, where each node had 8 processors with 12 GB of memory. The processors in the nodes were Intel Xeon 2.27GHz. The topology with the connection between the head node and computing nodes can be found on the web[2] (topology number four). The Enterprise and Private Networks link speed was 1Gbps, the Application link speed was 20Gbps.

3.2 First Part of the Experiment

The first part of the experiments was oriented towards the comparison of algorithms under which is the calculated distance. The used datasets were *Medlars* and *Hepta*. All the experiments were carried out for 20 epochs; the random initial values of neuron weights in the first epoch were always set to the same values. The tests were performed for SOM with rectangular shape 10×10 neurons. The metrics used for determining the quality of clustering is Euclidean distance (in all the algorithms). The achieved quality of clustering is presented in Table 4.

3.3 Second Part of the Experiment

The second part of the experiments was oriented towards a comparison of the standard GNG algorithm and the parallel approach to this GNG learning algorithm with pre-processing by SOM. The *Medlars* dataset was used for the experiment. A parallel version of the learning algorithm was run using 9, 16, 25 and 36 MPI processes. The records with asterisk an (*) represents the results for only one process i.e. this is the original serial learning algorithm and there is no network communication and no SOM algorithm.

The GNG parameters are the same for all experiments and are as follows $\gamma = 200$, $e_w = 0.05$, $e_n = 0.006$, $\alpha = 0.5$, $\beta = 0.0005$, $a_{max} = 30$, M = 500, $\delta = 200$. The achieved computing time is presented in the Table 3.

---

[2] http://technet.microsoft.com/en-us/library/cc719008(v=ws.10).aspx

Table 3. Computing Time with Respect to Number of Cores, Standard GNG Algorithm, Dataset Medlars

Cores	SOM Dimension	Max # of vectors in one cluster	Computing Time [hh:mm:ss]	
			SOM	GNG
1*	–	1033	–	01:13:41
9	3×3	798	00:00:09	00:45:40
16	4×4	646	00:00:21	00:29:05
25	5×5	229	00:00:25	00:05:55
36	6×6	291	00:00:30	00:08:12

Table 4. Quality of Clustering

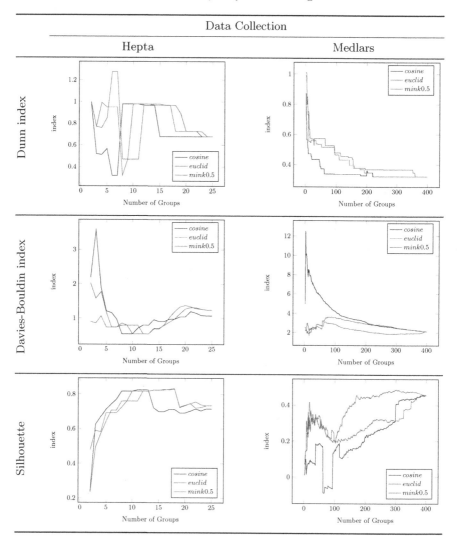

As we can see from Table 3, the computing time depends on the number of used core as well. In the latter case the experiment is to see that the time increased even though the reduction was expected. It is caused by the SOM algorithm, which has generated bigger cluster of input vectors for GNG.

Table 5. Graphical representations of data set layout and corresponding GNGs

	Data Collection		
	Target	Lsun	TwoDiamonds

3.4   Third Part of the Experiment

The third part of the experiments was oriented towards comparing the results obtained in the parallel (with preprocessing by SOM) and standard GNG algorithm. The Clustering dataset was used for the experiment. The parallel version of the learning algorithm was run using 16 MPI processes. The GNG parameters are the same as in the previous experiment.

The first row in the Table 5 shows a layout view of the input data, which are used for training GNG. The outputs of GNG algorithms (without using SOM) are in the second row, which are similar to the parallel version in the last row.

4   Conclusion

In this paper, the parallel implementation of the GNG neural network algorithm is presented. The achieved speed-up was very good and the results from the standard and parallel version of GNG are similar. Thus we can state that operation of the parallel version is optimal. However, the effectiveness of a parallel solution is dependent on the division by SOM. Any improper division may cause a reduction in the quality of the final solution.

In future work we intend to focus on sparse date, and use combinations of neural networks for improved results and improved acceleration.

Acknowledgment. This work was supported by the European Regional Development Fund in the IT4Innovations Centre of Excellence project (CZ.1.05/1.1.00/02.0070) and the national budget of the Czech Republic via the Research and Development for Innovations Operational Programme, and supported by the project New creative teams in priorities of scientific research, reg. no. CZ.1.07/2.3.00/30.0055, supported by Operational Programme Education for Competitiveness and co-financed by the European Social Fund and the state budget of the Czech Republic, and co-financed by SGS, VSB - Technical University of Ostrava, Czech Republic, under the grant No. SP2014/154 'Complex network analysis and prediction of network object behavior.

References

1. Beyer, K., Goldstein, J., Ramakrishnan, R., Shaft, U.: When is nearest neighbor meaningful? In: Beeri, C., Bruneman, P. (eds.) ICDT 1999. LNCS, vol. 1540, pp. 217–235. Springer, Heidelberg (1998)
2. Davies, D.L., Bouldin, D.W.: A cluster separation measure. IEEE Transactions on Pattern Analysis and Machine Intelligence PAMI-1(2), 224–227 (1979)
3. Dunn, J.C.: A fuzzy relative of the isodata process and its use in detecting compact well-separated clusters. Journal of Cybernetics 3(3), 32–57 (1973), http://dx.doi.org/10.1080/01969727308546046
4. Fritzke, B.: A growing neural gas network learns topologies. In: Advances in Neural Information Processing Systems 7, pp. 625–632. MIT Press (1995)

5. Holmström, J.: Growing Neural Gas Experiments with GNG, GNG with Utility and Supervised GNG. Master's thesis, Uppsala University (August 30, 2002)
6. Kohonen, T.: Self-Organization and Associative Memory, 3rd edn. Springer Series in Information Sciences, vol. 8. Springer, Heidelberg (1984, 1989)
7. Kohonen, T.: Self Organizing Maps, 3rd edn. Springer (2001)
8. Martinetz, T.: Competitive hebbian learning rule forms perfectly topology preserving maps. In: Gielen, S., Kappen, B. (eds.) ICANN 1993, pp. 427–434. Springer, London (1993), http://dx.doi.org/10.1007/978-1-4471-2063-6_104
9. Martinetz, T., Schulten, K.: A "neural-gas" network learns topologies. Artificial Neural Networks 1, 397–402 (1991), http://web.cs.swarthmore.edu/~meeden/DevelopmentalRobotics/fritzke95.pdf
10. Prudent, Y., Ennaji, A.: An incremental growing neural gas learns topologies. In: Proceedings. 2005 IEEE International Joint Conference on Neural Networks, IJCNN 2005, July 4-August, vol. 2, pp. 1211–1216 (2005)
11. Rousseeuw, P.J.: Silhouettes: A graphical aid to the interpretation and validation of cluster analysis. Journal of Computational and Applied Mathematics 20, 53–65 (1987), http://www.sciencedirect.com/science/article/pii/0377042787901257
12. Sledge, I., Keller, J.: Growing neural gas for temporal clustering. In: 19th International Conference on Pattern Recognition, ICPR 2008, pp. 1–4 (2008)
13. Ultsch, A.: Clustering with SOM: U*C. In: Proc. Workshop on Self-Organizing Maps, Paris, France, pp. 75–82 (2005)
14. Vojáček, L., Dvorský, J.: Growing neural gas – A parallel approach. In: Saeed, K., Chaki, R., Cortesi, A., Wierzchoń, S. (eds.) CISIM 2013. LNCS, vol. 8104, pp. 408–419. Springer, Heidelberg (2013)
15. Vojáček, L., Martinovič, J., Dvorský, J., Slaninová, K., Vondrák, I.: Parallel hybrid SOM learning on high dimensional sparse data. In: Chaki, N., Cortesi, A. (eds.) CISIM 2011. CCIS, vol. 245, pp. 239–246. Springer, Heidelberg (2011)

A Survey of Security and Privacy Issues for Biometrics Based Remote Authentication in Cloud

Tapalina Bhattasali[1], Khalid Saeed[2], Nabendu Chaki[1], and Rituparna Chaki[3]

[1] Department of Computer Science & Engineering, University of Calcutta, India
[2] Faculty of Computer Science, Bialystok University of Technology, Poland
[3] A. K. Choudhury School of IT, University of Calcutta, India
tapolinab@gmail.com, saeed@agh.edu.pl,
{nabendu,rchaki}@ieee.org

Abstract. Rapid development of smart technologies enables use of cloud service for large-scale data storage. Remote access of original data as well as biometric data from cloud storage enhances several challenges. It is inevitable to prevent unauthorized access of data stored in cloud. Biometrics authentication is more efficient than the known traditional authentication mechanisms. Authentication is a major security feature used to protect data privacy, whereas additional security features used to protect data may adversely affect it. There must be a balance between security and privacy during secure authentication design. Here a survey of security and privacy issues for biometrics based remote authentication in cloud is briefly presented and the research gaps are identified to attract more research on this domain in near future.

Keywords: Cloud Storage, Remote Authentication, Security, Privacy, Biometrics.

1 Introduction

Amount of digital content has been growing day by day with the exponential increase in number of devices connected to Internet. High volume data not only demand for huge storage space, but also looking for intelligent processing in a cost-effective manner. The popular choice in such cases is the cloud environment, which provides unlimited storage space, on demand service, parallel processing and rapid distribution of data. Cloud service provider provides a flexible way for users to access their data from anywhere and at any time. The flexibility of data usage however takes away control from the data owner. Thus the manner in which data are accessed, and by whom, is essentially under the control of cloud service provider. In such a scenario, the authentication of user is very important, so as to guarantee security of data and privacy of data source. Remote user authentication mechanism is useful in distributed domain to identify validity of remote users. There exist several techniques for remote authentication. Some of the essential requirements for enhancing quality of remote authentication in cloud are given below.

- Third party cloud service provider is not able to retrieve original data, or associated metadata stored in cloud.
- Ensure that an impostor cannot be impersonated as a legitimate user.

K. Saeed and V. Snášel (Eds.): CISIM 2014, LNCS 8838, pp. 112–121, 2014.

- System should be capable to respond to any incoming valid request.
- No intruder is allowed to modify original message.
- If timestamps are used, then it must be synchronized.
- System must optimize bandwidth usage in a cost effective manner.

Password-based authentication with smart card can be used to identify the validity of a remote user. Traditional identity-based authentication mechanisms are mainly based on password, which are very easy to break because of its simplicity. Cryptographic secret keys can also be used in remote authentication framework. Major drawback is that they are difficult to memorize, lost or even be stolen. As a result, it is very difficult to identify valid users accurately. As opposed to traditional password based remote user authentication, biometrics based authentication is increasingly popular because of its reliability [1] and efficiency to authenticate remote users. Cloud based remote authentication provides enhanced security by using biometrics traits [2] such as fingerprint verification, keystroke analysis, ECG analysis, iris analysis, facial analysis, handwritten signature verification etc. Each biometrics trait used in authentication has its own strengths and weaknesses. Biometrics based authentication may be unimodal having single biometrics trait or multimodal, combining multiple biometrics features. Cloud based biometrics technology has high potential market value and attracts interest of many researchers from all around the world.

Cloud framework and remote authentication technique have several challenges of their own. Preserving a balance between security and privacy is a major concern in remote framework of cloud. Privacy is the ability to decide what information should go where. Security acts as significant safeguard for privacy by protecting data. Security and privacy are often considered from two complementary angles. Despite a couple of surveys of biometrics authentication or remote authentication, a comprehensive survey of biometrics based remote authentication in cloud does not exist. The main objective of this paper is to study the balance between security and privacy in biometrics based remote authentication and point out the research gap in this domain. The contributions of this paper are as follows.

- To extensively survey some of the existing schemes that may be used for biometrics based remote authentication in cloud and determine general trends.
- To discuss open issues for future research area.

The rest of the paper contains the following. Section 2 gives a brief introduction of security challenges faced by biometrics techniques. Section 3 presents an extensive survey of some of the existing schemes in this area. Section 4 gives a comparative analysis of this study. Section 5 presents the open research issues in this area, and section 6 concludes the paper.

2   Security Challenges Faced by Biometrics Techniques

The biometrics features, although unique, face several threats in reality [3]. One of the most common threats involves spoofing, whereby users' biometrics templates can be misused. Impostor can produce fake biometrics during enrollment. Genuine templates can be replaced by impostor's template to gain unauthorized access. Spoofing attack involves replay of either raw data or biometrics features extracted from raw data to fool the system into believing an impostor as a real user. User's biometrics features may have extra noise and thus match with incorrect user template, causing false detection. Enhancement of interclass similarity or intra-class variability in the feature sets may cause high false detection rate. Impostors can easily enter into system because of increase in false acceptance rate (zero-effort attack). Data acquisition unit may fail to acquire biometrics trait of user due to limits of capturing technology or adverse environmental conditions. This may lead to failure-to-acquire (FTA) or failure-to-enroll (FTE) errors.

3   Literature Survey

This section provides a literature survey of some of the existing works. There are several works on cloud security and remote authentication. Here, we present a literature survey of existing works depending on the number of biometrics traits used and the additional security features for safeguarding the biometrics template.

3.1   Authentication Based on Singular Biometrics Features

Fingerprint based authentication [4] is the most popularly used technique in cloud environment because of its acceptability, uniqueness and immutability. Keystroke pattern analysis is another popular choice to authenticate users. Most important requirement of biometrics based remote authentication is liveliness detection, which is feasible by ECG based authentication. For this reason, a brief idea about some of the existing works on fingerprint, keystroke and ECG is presented here, where template data protection may not be major concern. During fingerprint verification, several image enhancement techniques [4] could be used such as histogram based, frequency transformation based, Gabor filter based enhancement. Gabor filter in wavelet domain improves accuracy level of fingerprint verification. Concept of Toeplitz matrix [5] is considered for fingerprint verification without information loss about fingerprint image. In [6], fingerprint search algorithm was proposed based on database clustering. It speeds up the search process and improves the retrieval accuracy. Fingerprint can be verified by using spectral minutiae representation [7] which can be either location based (SML) or orientation based (SMO). Both techniques have pros and cons in different scenarios. However, fusion of two techniques shows better result. Fingerprint verifier enables template protection scheme along with fixed length feature vectors. Work on keystroke analysis is vast in the literature [8]. Most of the user authentication techniques are based on measuring the distance between the user keystroke pattern and enrolled keystroke for fixed text or free text. Assessment of keystroke dynamics is based on the traditional statistical analysis or relatively newer pattern recognition techniques such as z-test, Bayesian classifiers, and neural network. Pattern matching may suffer from long search times. This issue can be solved by clustering user profiles. In [9], a combined standard deviation of keystroke duration and degree of disorder for keystroke latency along with disorder for keystroke duration is used for identification and authentication. In pressure-based user authentication system, the discrete time signal is transformed into the frequency domain. It is costly as it requires additional hardware to measure keystroke pressure. In a few cases, instability of typing patterns is reduced by introducing artificial rhythm concept. Keystroke recognition has been investigated for the virtual keyboard that used to interact with the hand held electronic devices, such as PDAs, and mobile phones. In ECG based authentication, correlation coefficient [10] between input image and feature vector stored in database is computed to check authentic person. Confusion matrix is generated to determine False Acceptance Rate (FAR) and False Rejection Rate (FRR). Gurkanet al. [11] proposed ECG authentication technique based on combining AC/DCT features, Mel-Frequency Cepstrum Coefficients (MFCC) features and QRS beat information of the Lead-I ECG signals. According to [12], authentication is possible by collecting ECG signal from fingertips. However, it may contain more noise compared to data collected directly from heart. In [13], feasibility of ECG is tested in a multi-biometric framework where it combines with fingerprint biometrics for individual authentication. Performance is evaluated using Equal Error Rate (EER), Receiver Operating Characteristics (ROC).

3.2   Authentication Systems with Encrypted Biometrics Features

Instead of storing original biometrics, transformed biometrics and transformation are stored in cloud database. Biometrics template protection [14] scheme can be categorized into two ways, (i) Biometric Cryptosystem, (ii) Feature Transformation. Biometric cryptosystem includes key binding (Fuzzy Vault), and key generation (Fuzzy Extractor). Features can be generally transformed either by biometric salting or biohashing and non-invertible transformation or cancellable biometrics template. For data protection, biometrics templates can be encrypted by chaotic encryption method [15], which makes the system more robust against attacks. It becomes dynamic by using the concept of one time biometrics. Blind protocol [16] could be used on any biometrics feature to reveal only identity without any additional information about the user. Real identity of the user is hidden to the server to provide better privacy by making the protocol completely blind. It is also secure under variety of attacks. In blind authentication, focus is on user's privacy, template protection, and trust issue. Cryptobiometric authentication protocol carries out authentication in fully automatic fuzzy vault [17], which aligns transformed template and query minutiae set of fingerprint without leaking data. Bio-capsule [18] is user-friendly technique adaptive to any environment. It provides security even if authentication server is compromised. It can be applied to several biometrics. This irreversible cryptographic hash function [19] is completely independent from any operating threshold. Non-invertible Gabor transform [20] is resistant to minor translation error and rotation distortion. In [20], user can be given number of cancellable biometric identifiers created from fingerprint image according to the requirement by issuing a new transformation key. The identifiers can be cancelled and replaced when compromised. User's biometrics can be verified using bio-hashing [19]. This scheme is efficient due to usage of one-way hash function and XOR operations. Remote user authentication use nonce or long pseudorandom numbers and timestamps for better security and strong mutual authentication between user and server. Sometimes accuracy level of biometrics can be enhanced by fusing it with multiple factors. Smartcard based authentication uses biometrics along with password and smart card. According to Li et al.'s two factor authentication scheme [21] , user tries to login to remote server by inserting smart card into card reader and input personal biometrics for verification. It fails to provide strong authentication. Fan et al. [22] proposed a three-factor authentication scheme by fusing password, smart card and biometrics. Yeh et al. [23] proposed an elliptic curve cryptography-based authentication scheme that is improved according to security requirements. However, it is seen from the comparative study of different multi-factor biometrics authentication schemes, that Huang et al.'s proposal [24] on generic framework based on three factor remote user authentication provides better results from the aspects of security and privacy. This type of authentication is flexible in nature. User's biometrics traits are kept secret from the server to enhance privacy and to avoid single point of failure.

4   Analysis

From the above study, it is observed that the following parameters are generally used as performance metrics for biometric systems.

- **True Acceptance Rate (TAR)** - Probability to correctly match input pattern to a matching template. It measures the percent of valid inputs which are correctly accepted.
- **True Rejection Rate (TRR)** - Probability to correctly detect non-matching input pattern to any template stored in the database. It measures the percent of invalid inputs which are correctly rejected.
- **False Acceptance Rate (FAR)** - Probability to incorrectly match input pattern to a non-matching template stored in the database. It measures the percent of invalid inputs which are incorrectly accepted. It is more dangerous than FRR.
- **False Rejection Rate (FRR)** - Probability to fail to detect a match between the input pattern and a matching template in the database. It measures the percent of valid inputs which are incorrectly rejected.
- **Receiver Operating Characteristic (ROC)** - ROC plot is a visual characterization of the trade-off between FAR and FRR.
- **Equal Error Rate or Crossover Error Rate (EER or CER)** - Rate at which both acceptance and rejection errors are equal. Value of EER can be easily obtained from ROC curve. Lowest EER represents high accuracy.
- **Accuracy** - Percentage of ratio of true detection (TAR+TRR) and overall detection (TAR+TRR+FAR+FRR).
- **Peak Signal to Noise Ratio (PSNR)**–It is a measure of peak error in decibels between two images. It is used as a quality measurement between original and reconstructed image.
- **Computation Time (CT)** –It estimates processing time involved in computation (e.g. enhancing the image).

Table 1 gives a quantitative analysis of few biometrics traits based on previously discussed performance metrics. It compares the estimated values of several existing works based on evaluation metrics and checks whether additional security features affect the performance of those works or not. It gives an idea about the security and privacy trade-off in biometric authentication level.

Table 1. Quantitative Analysis of Few Biometric Features

Topic	Additional Security Features	Evaluation Metrics	Estimated Values
Fingerprint verification with image enhancement [4]	No	Equal Error Rate (EER), Peak Signal to Noise Ratio (PSNR), Computation Time (CT)	9.345% EER 41.56db PSNR 0.894 sec CT
Fingerprint verification using spectral minutiae representation [7]	Yes Template Protection	Equal Error Rate (EER), Fused EER	6.4% EER for SML; 6.1 % EER for SMO; 4.8% EER for Fusion of SML and SMO
Continuous Dynamic Authentication for Identification [25]	No	False Acceptance Ratio (FAR), False Rejection Ratio (FRR)	20.25% FAR 4.18% FRR
Bio Password (keystroke fused with password) [26]	No	EER	3% EER
ECG based authentication by high frame rate system for imaging [27]	No	True Acceptance Rate (TAR), True Rejection Rate (TRR)	84.97% TAR 99.48% TRR
ECG based authentication using predefined signature and envelope vector sets [11]	No	TAR, TRR	97.25% TAR 99.91% TRR
Fingertips based ECG [12]	No	EER	9.1 % EER
ECG plus Fingerprint [13]	No	TAR	95% TAR
Crypto-biometric verification protocol for fingerprint [17]	Yes, Blind Authentication	Accuracy	84.45% Accuracy
Blind protocol [28] for fingerprint	Yes, Fuzzy Vault	Accuracy	96% for Accuracy
Bio-capsule [18] for iris	Yes, Feature Transformation	EER	0.029 EER
Bio salting[19]	Yes, Addition of Noise	EER	6.68% EER in worst case, 0.1% in best case
Non-invertible Gabor transform for fingerprint [20]	Yes, Cancellable Biometrics	FAR, FRR	0% FAR, 4.5% FRR

After analyzing major biometrics traits like fingerprint, keystroke and ECG, it can be said that accuracy level of fingerprint is better than keystroke and ECG. Keystroke is better than other two because of its simplicity and cost-effectiveness. ECG is better than other two because of its capacity to prove liveliness which is a major issue in biometric authentication. However, ECG suffers from several limitations. Time variation nature of ECG enhances interclass similarity of sample. Few random traces of abnormality can exist in a normal user, resulting into misclassification. Data acquisition is costly and it takes longer time. As ECG data acquisition needs to go through ethical approval, accuracy level is affected due to lack of data sample. Only fingerprint is capable to authenticate users accurately provided fingerprint scanner has very high resolution. However, this type of scanner is very costly and may not be affordable for all type of applications. So fingerprint verification can be fused with other factors to enhance accuracy level using low resolution fingerprint scanner. Keystroke dynamics gains its popularity among the behavioral biometric solutions for providing feasible authentication in distributed environment, because of its simple and natural way to enhance security. Keystroke biometrics is cheaper to implement in distributed framework than other biometrics. It has been studied that performance of keystroke based bio-password is better than vein pattern recognition [26] and is similar to fingerprint and voice recognition. Keystroke does not depend upon the location of the user as data can be collected from anywhere using Internet. It is a globally accepted mechanism which is easy to deploy and use. Keystroke analysis cannot be used alone because of its low permanence in data collectivity. Therefore, physiological trait fingerprint and behavioral trait keystroke analysis can be considered for remote authentication in cloud.

5   Open Issues

From the above analysis, several research gaps are identified and presented as open issues which need to be solved in near future for better performance.

5.1   Design of Effective Framework for Achieving Balance between Security and Privacy

At present, most of the remote authentication techniques are based on either biometrics traits such as iris, fingerprints, voice or the traditional authentication proof such as passwords. It is found through the analysis that remote user authentication schemes become useless if user-id is compromised. In the present social structure, it is very important to focus on balancing security and privacy while designing remote authentication schemes using individual biometrics features. Acceptable limit of security and privacy trade-off need to be determined. There is no privacy implementation without sufficient security. Privacy issues have different meanings in different cases and protection levels are provided according to state laws.

5.2   Design of Energy Efficient Multi-modal Biometrics based Authentication Scheme for Different State-of-the-Art Applications

At present, pervasive computing has given way to Internet of Things domain, where the application may demand recording of the user's each and every move, in order to assist in remote applications such as healthcare. However, these type of data are confidential to the user, and need to be protected from unauthorized access. Sensors used for sensing and data collectors used for sending information are rather low on energy and hence the authentication schemes involving them have to be highly energy efficient. The use of single biometrics features also fail to sufficiently safeguard the data, hence a fusion of different biometrics traits need to be used for effective protection [29].

5.3 Consideration of Psychological or Other Environmental Effects on Biometrics Features of an Individual for Better Authentication

As has been noticed earlier, keystrokes based authentication is an easy to implement technique. However, not much have been researched about the effect an individual might have on the typing pattern when he or she is either sick or depressed. There comes the effect of humidity, temperature, etc. to be considered with fingerprints.

5.4 Design of Cost-Effective Means to Record Biometrics Features

The devices available for recording the features need to be engineered so as to achieve energy efficiency and accuracy. As such, usage of any specialized device itself is often considered as an addditional overhead. This overhead can be justified only by improved efficiency in terms of biometrics feature extraction.

6 Conclusion

In today's world, use of third party cloud environment has become mandatory for the organizations handling huge amount of data cost-effectively. Securing data stored in cloud is a big challenge. Therefore, one of the most important challenges is to how to control access of data stored in cloud from remote location. Authentication is necessary step in security implementation for remote data access. It is studied that biometrics authentication is feasible solution in cloud. With growing popularity of biometrics features, database containing biometrics template and user details are also stored in cloud and vulnerable to various threats. Authentication mechanism has no significance without security. Similarly, complex security mechanism affects usability and accuracy of authentication. In this paper, we present a survey of security and privacy issues of biometrics based remote authentication in cloud after analyzing existing works from different angles. An insight into the open research issue is also presented.

The objective of this survey is to determine the challenges in biometrics based remote authentication in cloud; so that more effective user authentication could be proposed to resist attacks in remote environment besides identifying users accurately.

References

1. Tang, Q., Bringer, J., Chabanne, H., Pointcheval, D.: A Formal Study of the Privacy Concerns in Biometric-Based Remote Authentication Schemes. In: Chen, L., Mu, Y., Susilo, W. (eds.) ISPEC 2008. LNCS, vol. 4991, pp. 56–70. Springer, Heidelberg (2008)
2. Jain, A.K., Ross, A., Pankanti, S.: Biometrics: A Tool for Information Security. IEEE Transactions on Information Forensics and Security 1(2), 125–143 (2006)
3. Ignatenko, T., Willems, F.M.J.: Biometric Systems: Privacy and Secrecy Aspects. IEEE Transactions on Information Forensics and Security 4(4), 956–973 (2009)
4. Arora, K., Garg, P.: A Quantitative Survey of Various Fingerprint Enhancement Techniques. International Journal of Computer Applications 28(5), 24–28 (2011)
5. Surmacz, K., Saeed, K.: Robust Algorithm for Fingerprint Identification with a Simple Image Descriptor. In: Chaki, N., Cortesi, A. (eds.) CISIM 2011. CCIS, vol. 245, pp. 137–144. Springer, Heidelberg (2011)
6. Liu, M., Jiang, X., Kot, A.C.: Efficient Fingerprint Search based on Database Clustering. Elsevier Journal, Pattern Recognition 40(6), 1793–1803 (2007)
7. Xu, H., Veldhuis, R.N.J., Bazen, A.M., Kevenaar, T.A.M., Akkermans, T.A.H.M., Gokberk, B.: Fingerprint Verification using Spectral Minutiae Representations. IEEE Transactions on Information Forensics and Security 4(3), 397–409 (2009)
8. Karnan, M., Akila, M., Krishnaraj, N.: Biometric personal authentication using keystroke dynamics: A review. Elsevier Journal of Applied Soft Computing 11(2), 1565–1573 (2010)
9. Rudrapal, D., Das, S., Debbarma, S.: Improvisation of Biometrics Authentication and Identification through Keystrokes Pattern Analysis. In: Natarajan, R. (ed.) ICDCIT 2014. LNCS, vol. 8337, pp. 287–292. Springer, Heidelberg (2014)
10. Hegde, C., Prabhu, H.R., Sagar, D.S., Shenoy, P.D., Venugopal, K.R., Patnaik, L.M.: Human Authentication Based on ECG Waves Using Radon Transform. In: Kim, T.-H., Fang, W.-C., Khan, M.K., Arnett, K.P., Kang, H.-J., Ślęzak, D. (eds.) SecTech/DRBC 2010. CCIS, vol. 122, pp. 197–206. Springer, Heidelberg (2010)
11. Gurkan, H., Guz, U., Yarman, B.S.: Modeling of Electrocardiogram Signals using Predefined Signature and Envelope Vector Sets. EURASIP Journal on Advances in Signal Processing, Springer Open Journal, 1–12 (2007)
12. Da Silva, H.P., Lourenço, A., Fred, A.L.N., Raposo, N., De-Sousa, M.A.: Check Your Biosignals Here: A New Dataset for Off-The-Person ECG Biomet-rics. Elsevier Journal, Computer Methods and Programs in Biomedicine 113(2), 503–514 (2014)
13. Singha, Y.N., Singh, S.K., Gupta, P.: Fusion of Electrocardiogram with Unobtrusive Biometrics: An Efficient Individual Authentication System. Elsevier Journal, Pattern Recognition Letters 33(14), 1932–1941 (2012)
14. Isobe, Y., Ohki, T., Komatsu, N.: Security Performance Evaluation for Biometric Template Protection Techniques. International Journal of Biometrics 5(1), 53–72 (2013)
15. Gao, H., Zhang, Y., Liang, S., Li, D.: A New Chaotic Algorithm for Image Encryption. Elsevier Journal, Chaos, Solitons and Fractals 29(2), 393–399 (2006)
16. Nandakumar, K., Jain, A., Pankanti, S.: Fingerprint-based Fuzzy Vault: Implementation and Performance. IEEE Transactions on Information Forensics and Security 2(4), 744–757 (2007)
17. Upmanyu, M., Namboodiri, A.M., Srinathan, K., Jawahar, C.V.: Blind Authentication: A Secure Crypto-Biometric Verification Protocol. IEEE Transactions on Information Forensics and Security 5(2), 255–268 (2010)

18. Sui, Y., Zou, X., Du, E.Y., Li, F.: Design and Analysis of a Highly User-Friendly, Secure, Privacy-Preserving, and Revocable Authentication Method. IEEE Transactions on Computers 63(4), 902–916 (2014)
19. Jin, A.T.B., Ling, D.N.C., Goh, A.: Biohashing: Two Factor Authentication Featuring Fingerprint Data and Tokenised Random Number. Elsevier Journal, Pattern Recognition 37(11), 2245–2255 (2004)
20. Ratha, N.K., Chikkerur, S., Connell, J.H., Bolle, R.M.: Generating Cancelable Fingerprint Templates. IEEE Transactions on Pattern Analysis and Machine Intelligence 29(4), 561–572 (2007)
21. Li, C.T., Hwang, M.S.: An Efficient Biometrics based Remote User Authentication Scheme using Smart Cards. Elsevier Journal, Journal of Network and Computer Applications 33(1), 1–5 (2010)
22. Fan, C.I., Lin, Y.H.: Provably Secure Remote Truly Three-Factor Authentication Scheme with Privacy Protection on Biometrics. IEEE Transactions on Information Forensics and Security 4(4), 933–945 (2009)
23. Yeh, H.L., Chen, T.H., Hu, K.J., Shih, W.K.: Robust Elliptic Curve Cryptography-based Three Factor User Authentication Providing Privacy of Biometric Data. IET Information Security 7(3), 247–252 (2013)
24. Huang, X., Xiang, Y., Chonka, A., Zhou, J., Deng, R.H.: A Generic Framework for Three-Factor Authentication: Preserving Security and Privacy in Distributed Systems. IEEE Transactions on Parallel and Distributed Systems 22(8), 1390–1397 (2011)
25. Monaco, J.V., Bakelman, N., Cha, S., Tappert, C.C.: Developing A Keystroke Biometric System for Continual Authentication of Computer Users. In: Proceedings of European Intelligence and Security Informatics Conference, EISIC 2012, pp. 210–216 (2012)
26. Bio Password White Paper: Authentication Solutions through Keystroke Dynamics (2007), http://www.infosecurityproductsguide.com/technology/2007/Bio Password_Authentication_Solutions_WhitepaperFinal.pdf
27. Wang, S., Lee, W.N., Provost, J., Jianwen, L., Konofagou, E.E.: A Composite High-Frame-Rate System for Clinical Cardiovascular Imaging. IEEE Transaction on Ultrasonics, Ferroelectrics and Frequency Control 55(10), 2221–2233 (2008)
28. Moon, D., Chung, Y., Seo, C., Kim, S.Y., Kim, J.N.: A Practical Implementation of Fuzzy Fingerprint Vault for Smart Cards. Springer, Journal of Intelligent Manufacturing 25(2), 293–302 (2014)
29. Nagar, A., Nandakumar, K., Jain, A.K.: Multibiometric Cryptosystems Based on Feature-Level Fusion. IEEE Transactions on Information Forensics and Security 7(1), 255–268 (2012)

On the Comparison of the Keystroke Dynamics Databases

Piotr Panasiuk[1], Marcin Dąbrowski[2], Khalid Saeed[3,4],
and Katarzyna Bocheńska-Włostowska[5]

[1] DCC Labs, Warsaw, Poland
[2] University of Finance and Management in Bialystok, Elk Branch, Poland
[3] AGH University of Science and Technology
[4] Bialystok Technical University, Bialystok, Poland
[5] The Maria Sklodowska-Curie Warsaw Academy, Warsaw, Poland
piotr@panasiuk.org, marcin.dabrowski@poczta.fm,
saeed@agh.edu.pl, katarzyna.bochenska@uwmsc.pl

Abstract. This paper concerns about Keystroke Dynamics database quality which can vary depending on researchers' approach. Database classification has been presented and the most popular publicly available databases are introduced. Authors' database is presented and compared with the others. This paper introduces new database and compares the results of the same algorithms obtained on two almost identical databases. The results of comparison are discussed in terms of keystroke dynamics dataset quality. It has been proven that different methods can produce results of unanticipated kind.

Keywords: Keystroke dynamics, verification, behavioral biometrics, database acquisition, computer security.

1 Introduction

Biometrics is a field of science that focuses on measuring live beings in order to recognize the entity. Everyone is different. There are no two individuals who would be undistinguishable. There are two kinds of features that could be measured. The first one is basing on physical features of organism like fingerprint, retina scan, DNA, vein pattern and other resulting from how the organisms are built. This kind of biometric is called physical biometrics. The second group of biometrics is called behavioral because those features originate from how one do things. The most common biometrics in this group are voice, handwritten signature, gait and the subject of this paper – keystroke dynamics. This kind of biometrics is not related to genetics, so even twins with the same DNA would have different characteristics of writing, walking or typing on a computer keyboard.

Keystroke dynamics accounts to behavioral biometrics. It has been originated from the telegraph. Soon after the telegraph was invented, operators developed ability to recognize each other by a timing pattern of pressing dots and dashes of messages sent in Morse code. Keystroke dynamics seems to be perfect for securing personal com-

K. Saeed and V. Snášel (Eds.): CISIM 2014, LNCS 8838, pp. 122–129, 2014.
© IFIP International Federation for Information Processing 2014

puters due to similarity to the telegraph in sending electric signals [1]. Additionally each signal is supplied with the information of which key has been pressed or released and a timestamp of the event in milliseconds. This feature can be compared to the handwritten signature but written on the keyboard.

As an advantage, keystroke dynamics implementations does not require expensive hardware. Most researches have been conducted on simple PC with the most common keyboard. The greatest part of keystroke dynamics analysis is done by a software, which is the subject of this paper. Plain keyboard allows researchers to obtain such characteristics as press and release times of specific keys. There were few approaches to find some new characteristics to analyze. However those researches required specialized (often custom made) hardware such as pressure sensitive keyboards [2,3,4] or touchscreens [5,6,7] for analyzing field below finger during key press. There are also approaches basing on alternative text input methods like Swype on mobile phones [8].

2   Previous Approaches

Our teams' first documented research on keystroke dynamics is dated back on 2008 [9], where authors presented promising results with the use of simple classification techniques and analyzing only "dwell" and "flight" times. Every single user had to enter three different and independent samples (without any repetitive words), where two of them were 110 keystrokes each (used as reference) and last one had length of about 55 keystrokes (used for validation). Keys other than letters and "space" were ignored. These include: "shift", cursor keys, "delete", "backspace" and other non-alphanumeric keys. Algorithm was basing on 1-NN classifier and resulted with accuracy of 75.68% on a group of 37 individuals.

The purpose of the next approach [10] was to further analyze new methods. In this paper authors presented authentication experiments on one single-word phrase and two longer phrases in Polish and English languages respectively. In contrast to our teams' previous work, the letter or number represented by keystroke and position in phrase was taken into account this time. From that work one can deduct that acquiring and analyzing more samples from single user results in better classification accuracy. Also, longer phrase (28 keystrokes) allowed to obtain much better accuracy (90,83%) than the shorter one (9 keystrokes, 68,7%). These results were obtained for 21 and 23 users respectively.

The following experiments brought even greater accuracy by using improved k-NN algorithm [11]. An improvement was made by calculating weights for each flight and dwell time in training dataset. This was possible due to use of fixed-text phrase. Firstly the mean values and variances for each key in every peculiar user's sample were used to calculate the weights. For each key the mean set separations for users were then calculated using Fisher's discriminant. In the end the mean value from all separation factors for each key were calculated, and followed by normalization. Those results were used as weights for each time. This improvement increased the classification accuracy to 98.78% within 16 users.

Unfortunately, those results were calculated on different phrases with different amount of classes, so they are hardly comparable and their purpose is just informative how efficient keystroke dynamics authentication can be. The same issue appears when one wants to compare two different approaches presented by some researchers but their results have been processed on different databases collected in different way and at different conditions (supervision, classes, samples strength etc.). This paper is supposed to compare two almost identical databases and show if the results could be comparable.

3   Database Gathering

3.1   Database Classification

It has been shown that keystroke dynamics authentication results highly depend on the database quality [12,13]. Viable algorithms should deal with noisy samples: the ones with typos or random pauses in user typing. Among the databases the authors can distinguish ones collected in a supervised way, meaning every test subject was individually instructed by a supervisor before the start of the samples acquisition process. The supervisor can also make notes on how the subject types and what influences him. It guarantees samples of good quality. This type of database, however, usually does not reflect real world situations. Databases may have accounts duplicated, for example if the user forgets his password or just wants to have multiple accounts. When typing pattern is duplicated by some user, it could decrease the identification accuracy and in hybrid (rank-threshold) based verification methods it may increase the FRR. On the other hand FAR can be increased by typing with unnatural manner by a user.

Another factor is the purpose for which the database is gathered. Authentication requires user ID attached to keystroke data. Simulation of hacking requires the same text typed by many users. Passwords are usually short phrases often consisting additional characters like capital letters (that involve shift key), dots, semicolons, numbers and symbols. For identification, samples should be preferably longer, as this application is more complex.

There can be two additional approaches to keystroke data acquisition. The first is based on a fixed text. The second way is to use free-text authorization [13] to continuously monitor user's workstation while trying to authorize him/her. There are the following problems with free-text authorization: (i) how often user authentication algorithm should be run, (ii) more difficulty with data collection, (iii) more samples are needed for learning of the recognition algorithm. Additionally potential noise can be a unique feature that helps to recognize users, so removing it completely – without deeper analysis – would be a loss of valuable information.

3.2   Publicly Available Databases

Most of works were done basing on closed private datasets gathered for a specific research purpose only. This situation makes the results incomparable because amount of information carried by the sample is variable and depends on the length and used key sequences. Sample value depends on user proficiency in given language, occurrence of special characters, digits or case-sensitiveness. What is more each database and each experiment use different amount of users and different count of samples which also influences overall results. Although most of papers describe results calculated on closed databases, researchers' awareness is growing and more and more databases are released to the public. There are few databases available online currently. Below the most interesting ones are described.

The oldest database in this comparison has been built and released by Montalvao et al. [14]. Database has been stored in four archives. Sample data consist of press-press intervals only. Database A and B carry data of four fixed English phrases. Database C contains two fixed Portuguese words and database D keeps freely typed rows of text. Each data package was gathered in a different manner. For more details and knowledge about the database one can refer to:

http://www.biochaves.com/en/download.htm

One of the most interesting is the database built by Maxion et al. [15]. This database contains great quality samples as it has been gathered under supervised conditions. Collected samples contain lower-case, upper-case letters, digits and a special character. Samples were measured using external reference clock to get the time precision on the level impossible to get on common PC. The accuracy of the clock was +- 200 μs. There are 51 users registered in the database who left overall 400 samples each in 8 sessions. Maxion's database is available online for public use at:

http://www.cs.cmu.edu/~keystroke/

Database provided by Giot et al. [16] contains 133 users, 100 of which provided at least five sessions of samples. Session consisted of typing "greyc laboratory" twelve times on two different keyboards. It is stored in SQLite database file and contains both dwell and flight times. It is available online at:

http://www.ecole.ensicaen.fr/~rosenber/keystroke.html

Special attention deserves a database built by Allen [17], who additionally to press and release times made it possible to collect pressure force data while typing specific key. Amount of registered users is 104 which is quite a lot, however samples count left by users varies from 3 to 504 so many of them may occur unusable for some experiments. Each sample consists of three phrases. Database is available at:

http://jdadesign.net/2010/04/pressure-sensitive-
keystroke-dynamics-dataset/

One more database has been announced to become public in a short time. Idrus et al. [18] collected database of 110 individuals which 70 of them were located in France and 40 in Norway. What is additionally interesting subjects originated from 24 different countries. Every user left 20 samples under supervised conditions consisting of 5 phrases. Users located in France used keyboard with French layout and those located in Norway with Norwegian.

3.3 Authors' Database

Authors' dataset is based on Maxion's phrase ".tie5Roanl". In the opposite to Maxion's however data were gathered in unsupervised conditions and with the use of commonly available devices and technologies. The goal was to simulate real-life scenario. Authors wanted to verify how the results will change if the keystroke dynamics algorithm would be implemented in some web, browser-based application using JavaScript to gather key timing information. This question is valid since keyboard event timing may be affected by OS process queuing clock. While Maxion's database was built using arbitrary waveform generator [19] with accuracy of 200µs, in authors' database accuracy was limited to OS event clock precision, which is 15.625 ms (64 Hz) using MS Windows and 10 ms using most Linux distributions. Data gathering schema was similar to Maxion's. Each user taken under consideration in this study had to leave 400 samples in 8 sessions. The sample itself was identical to the one proposed by Maxion in his research and consisted of ".tie5Roanl" with Enter key at the end of the input. There are 45 users satisfying the condition of 400 valid samples. Database was gathered under unsupervised conditions, however collecting algorithm disallows corrections. In such case after making a mistake the sample was cleared and the user had to type it once again from the beginning.

4   Database Comparison in Practice

The goal of this experiment was to compare two similar databases collected under different conditions. In comparison we used algorithms provided by Maxion available online at: http://www.cs.cmu.edu/~keystroke/

Eight anomaly detection algorithms were chosen to examine gathered data. These include: Euclidean, Manhattan, Mahalanobis, Chebyshev, Canberra, Scaled Manhattan, k-NN and k-Means. Most of them were provided by Roy Maxion and Kevin Killourhy at: http://www.cs.cmu.edu/~keystroke/ksk-thesis/, while the others are authors' own implementation.

The experiment was conducted on two identically formed databases and with the same evaluation scripts. In order to keep the same amount of information the hold time of "Return" key had to be removed from Maxion's database. This was necessary because while author's mechanism was triggered by "Return" key press the release time was not stored in the database under some web browsers. Also count of identities in Maxion's database had to be trimmed because in author's database there are only 45 users satisfying the condition of 400 samples per user. This way the same amount of users can be found in both databases. Another unexpected issue was occurrences of zero values. In some cases two following key events were so close that they fell into the same operating system clock window. This resulted in zero distance between them. Because some metrics cannot handle zero values well (e.g. Canberra distance where division by zero may occur), we had to replace zero values with values near to zeros (in our case mean value of 10^{-7}). Both databases consisted of 45 users who typed phrase ".tie5Roanl" 400 times in 8 sessions. Figure 1 shows mean EER values.

Figure 2, however, presents the EER standard deviation.

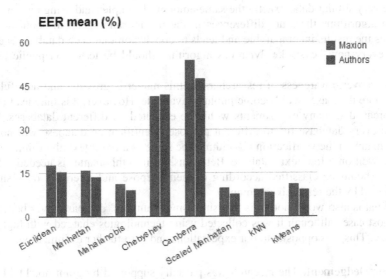

Fig. 1. Results of anomaly detectors on both databases. Mean EER values.

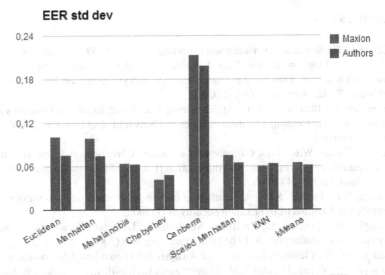

Fig. 2. Results of anomaly detectors on both databases. Standard deviation EER values.

5   Conclusions

The main goal of this paper was to verify if the same algorithm run on two theoreti-
cally identical databases, fulfilling the criteria of the same phrase, the same amount of
keystrokes and the same count of classes will provide the same results.

As one can see the results vary depending on which metric was used. However despite very similar data, exactly the same amount of samples and using the same evaluation algorithms there are differences in the results ranging up to about 30%. This makes the results incomparable and leads to conclusion that each database is different and every new keystroke dynamics algorithm should be tested on public reference one.

Moreover, awareness of researchers on this matter is growing and hopefully more and more databases will become publicly available. However, this may lead to another threat, that many experiments would be executed on different databases. What is more every database fits to different purpose. Identification database will not be the best match to the verification algorithm. The same as a fixed-text algorithm would not work well on a free-text database. Better insight into this matter is needed. The databases should be classified according to their purpose and reference ones should be preferred by the research community.

What is also worth noting is that surprisingly authors' database gives better results in most cases although it was collected using technologies charged with higher inaccuracy. This was opposite to our expectations and is to further examination.

Acknowledgement. The research was partially supported by grant no. 11.11.220.01, AGH University of Science and Technology in Krakow.

References

1. Checco, J.C.: Keystroke Dynamics and Corporate Security. WSTA Ticker (2003)
2. Dietz, P.H., Eidelson, B., Westhues, J., Bathiche, S.: A practical pressure sensitive computer keyboard. In: Proc. of the 22nd Annual ACM Symposium on User Interface Software and Technology, New York (2009)
3. Saevanee, H., Bhattarakosol, P.: Authenticating User Using Keystroke Dynamics and Finger Pressure. In: Consumer Communications and Networking Conference, Las Vegas, NV, pp. 1–2 (2009)
4. Loy, C.C., Lai, W.K., Lim, C.P.: Keystroke Patterns Classification Using the ARTMAP-FD Neural Network. In: Intelligent Information Hiding and Multimedia Signal Processing, Kaohsiung, pp. 61–64 (2007)
5. Clarke, N.L., Furnell, S.M.: Authenticating mobile phone users using keystroke analysis. International Journal of Information Security 6(1) (2006)
6. Campisi, P., Maiorana, E., Lo Bosco, M., Neri, A.: User authentication using keystroke dynamics for cellular phones. IET Signal Processing 3(4) (2009)
7. Karatzouni, S., Clarke, N.L.: Keystroke Analysis for Thumb-based Keyboards on Mobile Devices. In: Venter, H., Eloff, M., Labuschagne, L., Eloff, J., von Solms, R. (eds.) New Approaches for Security, Privacy and Trust in Complex Environments. IFIP, vol. 232, pp. 253–263. Springer, Boston (2007)
8. Trojahn, M., Ortmeier, F.: Toward Mobile Authentication with Keystroke Dynamics on Mobile Phones and Tablets. In: Advanced Information Networking and Applications Workshops (WAINA), pp. 697–702. IEEE (2013)
9. Rybnik, M., Tabedzki, M., Saeed, K.: A Keystroke Dynamics Based System for User Identification. In: 7th Computer Information Systems and Industrial Management Applications, CISIM 2008, pp. 225–230. IEEE (2008)

10. Rybnik, M., Panasiuk, P., Saeed, K.: User Authentication with Keystroke Dynamics Using Fixed Text. In: IEEE-ICBAKE 2009 International Conference on Biometrics and Kansei Engineering, Cieszyn, Poland, pp. 70–75 (2009)
11. Panasiuk, P., Saeed, K.: A Modified Algorithm for User Identification by His Typing on the Keyboard. In: Choraś, R.S. (ed.) Image Processing and Communications Challenges 2. AISC, vol. 84, pp. 113–120. Springer, Heidelberg (2010)
12. Killourhy, K.S., Maxion, R.A.: Comparing Anomaly-Detection Algorithms for Keystroke Dynamics. In: Dependable Systems & Networks, Lisbon, Portugal, pp. 125–134 (2009)
13. Panasiuk, P., Saeed, K.: Influence of Database Quality on the Results of Keystroke Dynamics Algorithms. In: Chaki, N., Cortesi, A. (eds.) CISIM 2011. CCIS, vol. 245, pp. 105–112. Springer, Heidelberg (2011)
14. Montalvao, J., Almeida, C.A.S., Freire, E.O.: Equalization of keystroke timing histograms for improved identification performance. In: International Telecommunications Symposium, pp. 560–565. IEEE (2006)
15. Killourhy, K.S., Maxion, R.A.: Comparing Anomaly-Detection Algorithms for Keystroke Dynamics. In: Dependable Systems & Networks, Lisbon, Portugal, pp. 125–134 (2009)
16. Giot, R., El-Abed, M., Rosenberger, C.: GREYC Keystroke: a Benchmark for Keystroke Dynamics Biometric Systems. In: IEEE Third International Conference on Biometrics: Theory, Applications and Systems (BTAS), Washington, DC, USA, pp. 28–30 (2009)
17. Allen, J.D.: An Analysis of Pressure-Based Keystroke Dynamics Algorithms, Master's thesis, Southern Methodist University, Dallas, TX, USA (2010)
18. Idrus, S.Z.S., Cherrier, E., Rosenberger, C., Bours, P.: Soft Biometrics Database: A Benchmark for Keystroke Dynamics Biometric Systems. In: International Conference of the Biometrics Special Interest Group (BIOSIG), pp. 1–8. IEEE (2013)
19. Killourhy, K.S., Maxion, R.A.: The Effect of Clock Resolution on Keystroke Dynamics. In: Lippmann, R., Kirda, E., Trachtenberg, A. (eds.) RAID 2008. LNCS, vol. 5230, pp. 331–350. Springer, Heidelberg (2008)

Influence of Eye Diseases on the Retina Pattern Recognition

Emil Saeed[1], Anna Bartocha[2], Piotr Wachulec[2], and Khalid Saeed[2,3]

[1] Department of Ophthalmology, Faculty of Medicine,
Medical University of Bialystok, Poland
[2] Faculty of Physics and Applied Computer Science,
AGH UST in Krakow, Poland
[3] Faculty of Computer Science, Bialystok University of Technology, Poland
{emilsaeed1986,bartochaanna,pioxan}@gmail.com, saeed@agh.edu.pl

Abstract. In this paper an algorithm to extract the retina characteristic points for a human eye with diseases is presented. The background of both medical and computer science matters is given. The cataract is described and discussed as a newly considered eye disease for retina pattern recognition. The processing of the retina with this disease is introduced for comparison with previous works. The structure of the applied method is illustrated in detail with examples. The procedure of minutiae extraction from the processed sick retina is given.

Keywords: Biometrics, Human identification, Identification of retina with anomalies, Retina diseases.

1 Introduction

The retina consists of many layers causing it to be of highly complicated structure. Optic disc is a location on the retina where the optic nerve exits the eye. It is also the entry point for the major blood vessels that supply the retina.

We use retina blood vessels to recognize people because human retina is unique [1]. Even identical twins do not share a similar pattern of the blood vessels network in the retina. However, serious retina diseases, may cause problems in its pattern identification. A detailed discussion of such diseases is given by authors in [2]. In this paper, however, a brief study is presented to show the influence of some retina diseases on its recognition. In this section we are listing them for the reader convenience.

Central Retinal Artery Occlusion, where a Part of the Artery may be Unseen

It is a disease where blood flow through retinal artery is blocked. The patient complains of sudden painless loss of vision. Cholesterol and calcific emboli may result in permanent obstruction. Sometimes the artery can recapitalize with time. Acute treatment of central and branch artery occlusions is aimed at dilating the arteriole to permit the embolus to pass more distally and limit the damage. Results are

K. Saeed and V. Snášel (Eds.): CISIM 2014, LNCS 8838, pp. 130–140, 2014.
© IFIP International Federation for Information Processing 2014

usually disappointing. Prolonged arterial occlusion results in severe, unrecoverable visual loss.

Central Retinal Vein Occlusion

This may result from abnormality of blood itself, an inflammation or an increased ocular pressure. The patient complains of sudden partial or complete loss of vision. Retinal laser treatment is given when it is necessary, some drugs can be taken such as rutoside, especially when we observe hemorrhages.

Retinal Detachment – which may Hide the Retinal Vessels

Patient notices the progressive development of a field defect, described as a 'shadow' or 'curtain'. It can be treated - surgically.

Sometimes, it is impossible to assess the retina because of the cataract (Fig. 2). Opacification of the lens of the eye (cataract) is the most common cause of treatable blindness in the world. The large majority of the cataracts occur in older subjects, as a result of cumulative exposure to environmental and other influences such as smoking, UV radiation and elevated blood sugar levels. A smaller number of cataracts is associated with specific ocular or systemic disease (for example hypocalcemia, infection, systemic drugs particularly steroids) and defined physicochemical mechanisms. Some are congenital and may be inherited. An opacity in the lens of the eye causes a painless loss of vision, glare and may change refractive error. Visual acuity is reduced.

A cataract appears black against the red reflex when the eye is examined with the direct ophthalmoscope. Slit lamp examination allows the cataract to be examined in detail, and the exact site of the opacity in the lens can be identified. It also can be treated – only surgically.

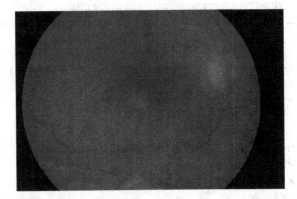

Fig. 1. Peripheral retinal detachment in eye with cataract

2   Retina Pattern Algorithm

I previous work [2] the authors presented their methodology giving the theory in a computer flowchart whilst the computer implementation was left to a future work. Here, in this paper, the pseudocode of the algorithm is given with some result examples.

Computer Program Pseudocode

```
AcquireData();
Image := LoadImage();

//Preprocessing
//ConvertToGrayscale
For I(x,y) in Image
    I(x,y) := (R(I(x,y)) + G(I(x,y)) + B(I(x,y)))/3

If(necessary)
{
    //NormalizeHistogram
    For I(x,y) in Image
        I(x,y) := 255 * (I(x,y)-Min(Image))/(Max(Image)-
Min(Image))

    //DenoiseImage (K-size median filter)
    For I(x,y) in Image
        Neighborhood := Epsilon(I(x,y),K)
        Neighborhood := Sort(Neighborhood)
        I(x,y) := Neighborhood[Neighborhood.Length/2]

    //EnhanceContrast
    LUT = GenerateContrastEnhancingToneCurve()
    For I(x,y) in Image
        I(x,y) := LUT[I(x,y)]
}
//CreateMask
Mask := new[Image.Width,Image.Height]
For I(x,y) in Image
    If(I(x,y)<Threshold)
        Mask[x,y] := 1
    Else
        Mask[x,y] := 0

//Vessel enhancement
GaussianMatchedFilter();
EntropyBinarization();
```

```
K3MThinning()
//ExtractMinutiae
For I(x,y) in Image
   If(I(x,y) = 1)
       VeinsCount := Sum(Epsilon(I(x,y),1)) - 1
       If(VeinsCount = 1)
          //Ending
       Else If(VeinsCount = 3)
          //Bifurcation
       Else If(VeinsCount = 4)
          //Crossing

FindOpticDisc(); //optional
FindFovea(); //optional
CreateFeatureVectors();

**
Legend:
Image - image of retina
I(x,y) - one pixel of image with coordinates x and y
R(I(x,y)) - pixel's red component value
G(I(x,y)) - pixel's green component value
B(I(x,y)) - pixel's blue component value
Min(Image)) - lowest value of pixel in the image
Max(Image)) - highest value of pixel in the image
Epsilon(I(x,y),K) - set of pixels which distance to
pixel I(x,y) is less or equal than K
   Sort(X) - sorting values in array X in ascending order
   GenerateContrastEnhancingToneCurve()        -        function
generates tone curve from image
   new[W,H] - creating new object of image with width W
and height H
   Threshold - certain threshold of binarization
   Sum(X) - sum of values in array X
```

The Algorithm Steps Involve Preprocessing, Mask Creation, Vessel Segmentation Patter Thinning, Minutiae Extraction and Feature Vector Creation

The image is first denoised contrast enhancement, conversion to greyscale and histogram normalization.

It is noticed that retinal vessel are the best visible on green color channel. Because of this fact, we can use only that layer for searching of minutiae.

The next step is vessel enhancement and segmentation with binarization. One of the approaches is using Gaussian Matched Filter [3] and then binarization (for example Local Entropy Thresholding [4][5]). Blood vessels usually have poor local contrast and edge detection algorithms results are not sufficient. In Gaussian Matched Filter method we receive grayscale image approximated by Gaussian shaped curve. The aim is to detect piecewise linear segments of blood vessels so we create 12 different mask filters and search for vessels in every 15 degrees. Fig. 2 shows the retina vessels after segmentation and enhancement.

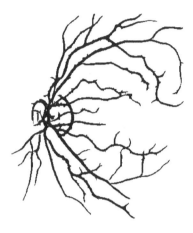

Fig. 2. Retina image after vessel segmentation and enhancement

Then the retina image is thinned. This operation allows to get the image skeleton. In our work K3M [6] is used and the thinning result is shown in Fig.3.

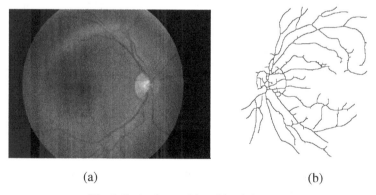

(a)   (b)

Fig. 3. Retina image (a) and its skeleton (b)

The next step to find bifurcations, crossings and end points of vessels. It can be done with the aid of masks. Examples of retina minutiae are shown in Fig. 4.

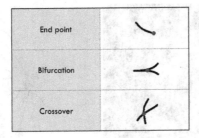

Fig. 4. Selected types of retina minutiae

This will help find the essential characteristic points for the whole retina pattern (Fig. 5). This way the feature vector is built on the basis of the feature points location [1,7].

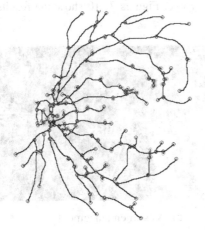

Fig. 5. Retina image after finding minutiae

The optic discs can also be located by identifying the area with the highest variation in intensity of adjacent pixels [7].

This feature vector will be used in classification process.

For classification, the algorithm follows Euclidean Distance or Manhattan Distance [2].

3   Experimental Results

The healthy retina gives the processing results shown in Fig 6.

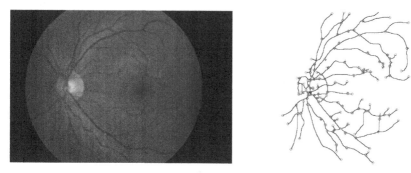

Fig. 6. Healthy retina – input images and results

Retina with one of the mentioned above diseases (section 1) or defects will furnish different images of its pattern. Therefore, the preprocessing steps will give results a little diverged from the healthy eye. Figures 7- 10 show the results of treating such cases.

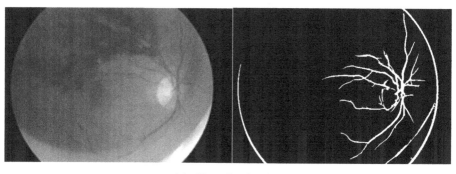

(a) Vessel enhancement

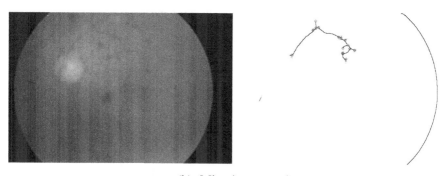

(b) Minutiae extraction

Fig. 7. Vein occlusion – input images and processing results. Vein occlusion makes veins ragged so algorithm removes huge part of them. It results in large losses of data (images b, c, d) which is required to confident recognition. In image (e) due to stain of blood we find a lot of false minutiae which makes recognition even harder.

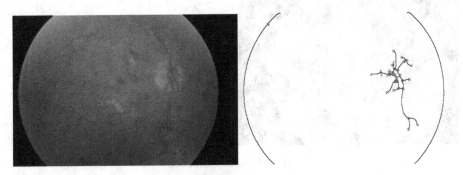

(c) Minutiae extraction

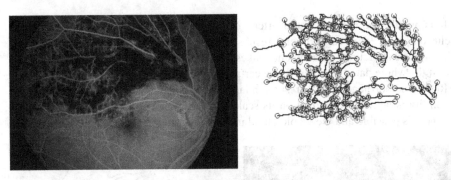

(d) Minutiae extraction

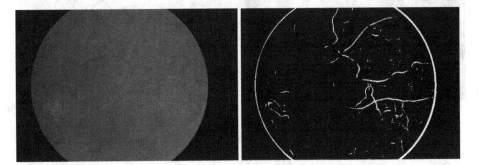

(e) Vessel enhancement

Fig. 7. (*continued*)

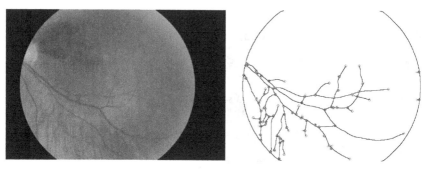

(f)   Minutiae extraction

Fig. 7. (*continued*)

It is worthy noticing that the artery occlusion creates same problems as vein occlusion [2]. A lot of ragged veins results in significant loss of data. From the other side, significant retinal detachment makes recognition impossible because we lose almost the whole data [2] except some certain cases.

Retinal hemorrhage (Fig. 8) results in large loss of data, so recognition success and possibility is heavily dependent on its scale and location. We have to remember that treatment is possible and the whole blood may disappear.

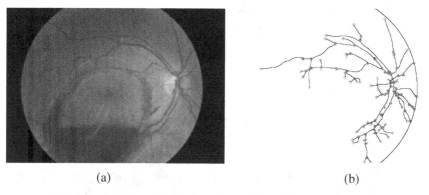

(a)   (b)

Fig. 8. Retinal hemorrhage – input image (a) and feature extract results (b)

Optic nerve (Fig. 9) head inflammation do not change pattern of the veins so recognition should be still possible.

Another eye disease is cataract (lens clouding), which shows completely different processing results (Fig. 10). It removes almost the whole data, making recognition impossible. Cataract surgery is very common nowadays, and it results in transparent vision, which makes recognition possible.

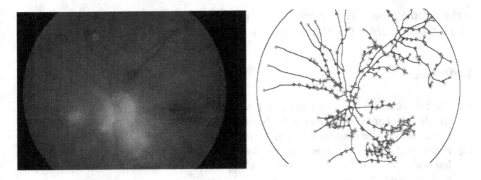

Fig. 9. Optic nerve head inflammation – input images and results

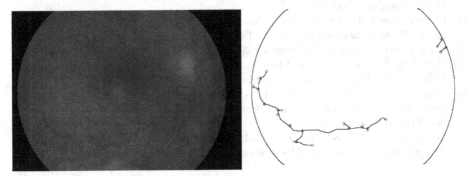

Fig. 10. Cataract – input images and results

4   Result Analysis and Conclusions

As we can see, there is a difference in features (quantitative and locally) between the healthy and diseased eye. Vein occlusion and artery occlusion often result in dashed veins after the usage of Gaussian Matched Filter. Current version of the algorithm cannot recover that state, and hence a large part of information is lost during the cleaning step (denoising and enhancement, …) which proceeds the thinning stage. Most of the eye diseases and particularly those which hit the retina would hide some parts of the retina would definitely cause data loss and makes recognition much harder and less confident.

On the other hand some diseases have only minimal influence like optic nerve head inflammation or retina detachment after successful treatment.

Authors are working on more cases and classification of new disease examples to prove the efficiency of the algorithm in treating general cases.

In the current state, the conclusion is that sick retina cannot guarantee good algorithm results and the successful recognition is therefore affected. However, this requires further research before giving the final definite decision on the sick retina identification results. This way we may at least exclude some of the diseases that would affect the results in a hundred percent.

Acknowledgement. The research was partially supported by grant no. WFiIS 11.11.220.01/Saeed, AGH University of Science and Technology in Krakow.

References

[1] Villalobos-Castaldi, M., Felipe-Riverón, E.M.: Fast Automatic Retinal Vessel Segmentation and Vascular Landmarks Extraction Method for Biometric Applications. In: IEEE International Conference on Biometrics, Identity and Security (2009)

[2] Bartocha, A., Saeed, E., Wachulec, P., Saeed, K.: Algorithm for Retina Recognition. In: International Conference on Applied Computation and Security Systems (ACSS), Proceeding on CD (2014)

[3] Chaudhuri, S., Chatterjee, S., Katz, N., Nelson, M., Goldbaum, M.: Detection of Blood Vessels in Retinal Images Using Two-Dimensional Matched Filters. IEEE Transactions of Medical Imaging 8(3) (1989)

[4] Chanwimaluang, T., Fan, G.: An Efficient Blood Vessel Detection Algorithm for Retinal Images Using Local Entropy Thresholding. In: Proceedings of the 2003 International Symposium on Circuits and Systems, vol. 5, pp. 21–24 (May 2003)

[5] HongQing, Z.: Segmentation of Blood Vessels in Retinal Images using 2-D Entropies of Gray Level-Gradient Co-occurrence Matrix. In: ICASSP 2004 (2004)

[6] Saeed, K., Rybnik, M., Tabedzki, M., Adamski, M.: K3M: A Universal algorithm for Image Skeletonization and Review of Thinning Techniques. Int. J. Appl. Math. Comput. Sci. 20(2), 317–335 (2010)

[7] Sinthanayothin, C., Boyce, J.F., Cook, H.L., Williamson, T.H.: Automated localisation of the optic disc, fovea, and retinal blood vessels from digital colour fundus images (1999)

Pupil and Iris Detection Algorithm for Near-Infrared Capture Devices

Adam Szczepański[1], Krzysztof Misztal[1], and Khalid Saeed[1,2]

[1] AGH University of Science and Technology
Faculty of Physics and Applied Computer Science
al. A. Mickiewicza 30, PL-30059 Kraków, Poland
[2] Faculty of Computer Science
Bialystok University of Technology,
Wiejska 45A, PL-15351 Bialystok, Poland
{Adam.Szczepanski,Krzysztof.Misztal,Khalid.Saeed}@fis.agh.edu.pl

Abstract. In this paper a simple and robust solution for the pupil and iris detection is presented. The procedure is based on simple operations, such as erosion, dilation, binarization, flood filling and Sobel filter and, with proper implementation, is effective. The novelty of the approach is the use of distances of black points from nearest white points to estimate and then adjust the position of the center and the radius of the pupil which is also used for iris detection. The obtained results are promising, the pupil is extracted properly and all the information necessary for human identification and verification can be extracted from the found parts of the iris. The paper, being both review and research, contains also a state of the art in the described topic.

Keywords: iris detection, pupil detection, gradient analysis, linear analysis.

1 Introduction

With the open borders and the ease of international travel human identification and verification is nowadays more important than ever before. On one hand it is essential for public safety, although on the other hand, people tend to dislike invasive methods of control. There are many biometric solutions that try to address this issue and all of them have their advantages and disadvantages. For example fingerprint images, which are commonly used as a biometric feature in modern identification documents, are easily obtainable although they are very vulnerable to identity theft. Also most of fingerprint scanners have to be touched which brings hygiene problems. For security reasons the iris image is the best option, although its acquisition is much more comfortable.

The iris, on the other hand, combines both high level of resistance for identity theft. It is hard to damage as the iris is an internal organ and is well protected by a highly transparent and sensitive membrane. It is different even between identical twins, does not change during the whole life and decays only a few

K. Saeed and V. Snášel (Eds.): CISIM 2014, LNCS 8838, pp. 141–150, 2014.

minutes after death. Also the physiological reaction of the iris towards the light and the natural movement of the pupil makes it impossible to replace the iris tissue with a photograph. The iris is also easy to acquire – the person needs just to look in the direction of the camera. This factors make the iris a reasonable choice of biometric feature both for identification and verification usages.

In this work the system of pupil and iris acquisition for such purposes is described. As this paper is both research and review, the first section of the paper contains a state of the art in described matter. Then the proposed solution is described along with the results of the tests of the algorithm. The last section contains conclusions and the description of future work.

2   State of the Art

While iris pattern is one of the most reliable biometric form of human identification, many methods have been developed for automatic iris recognition [1]. It is enough to mention following algorithms:

- the Gabor wavelet approach by Daugman [2],
- the Laplacian parameter approach by Wildes [3],
- zero-crossings of the wavelet transform at various resolution levels by Boles et al. [4],
- the Independent Component Analysis approach by Huang et al. [5],
- the texture analysis using multi-channel Gabor filtering and wavelet transform by Zhu et al. [6], and many others.

Iris segmentation and localization are one of the crucial steps in every of then. An iris-recognition algorithm first has to identify the approximately concentric circular outer boundaries of the iris and the pupil in a photo of an eye. One has often to deal with additional problems caused by the eyelids which can reduce the surface of the iris. In that case the mask template is also formed, which help to take into account bad pixel in iris feature generating and iris comparison.

Lets now look close on two of them [7].

John Daugman's algorithm uses the integro-differential operator for determining the localization of the circular iris and pupil in addition to the areas of the upper and lower eyelids. The operator is defined as follows:

$$\max_{r,x_0,y_0} \left| G_\sigma(r) * \frac{\partial}{\partial r} \oint_{r,x_0,y_0} \frac{I(x,y)}{2\pi r} ds \right|$$

where:

- $I(x,y)$ – image (containing the eye) pixel color,
- $G_\sigma(r)$ – the Gaussian smoothing function with scale (σ) is given by the following formula

$$G_\sigma(r) = \frac{1}{\sqrt{2\pi}\sigma} e^{-(r-r_0)^2/2\sigma^2}$$

- r – searching radius,
- s – contour given by circle with r, x_0, y_0 parameters.

The smoothed image is scanned for a circle that has the maximum gradient change that indicates an edge. To obtain a precise localization the operator, is applied iteratively. During this operation the smoothing function scale is changed to increase the accuracy. This not ends the algorithm, because we want to localize eyelids, which is done in similar way. The contours is changed from a circular into an arc.

The main drawback of this method lies on noise sensitivity. Thus it can failed on non-ideal environmental condition [8].

The second approach given by Wildes et al. algorithm perform localization and segmentation in two steps. Firstly the image is converted into edge-map - we extract information about the edge points in the image. One of the possible method to do this is thresholding the magnitude of the image intensity gradient:

$$|\nabla G_\sigma(x,y) * I(x,y)|,$$

where $\nabla = (\partial/\partial x, \partial/\partial y)$ and the G_σ is two-dimensional Gaussian with center (x_0, y_0) and standard derivation σ that smooth the image. We can alternatively use various other method in this step, ex. Sobel or Canny [9]. Second step allows us to select circles describing ex. pupil using voting procedure on parametric definitions of the iris boundary contours. which can be realized via Hough transforms [10].

By the knowledge that the eyelids are usually horizontally aligned Wildes [11] performing the preceding edge detection step with bias the derivatives in the horizontal direction for detecting the eyelids, and in the vertical direction for detecting the outer circular boundary of the iris. Consequently the eyelid edge map will corrupt the circular iris boundary edge map if all gradient data would be used. Taking only the vertical gradients for locating the iris boundary will reduce influence of the eyelids when performing circular Hough transform, and not all of the edge pixels defining the circle are required for successful localization.

However also in this case methods have same drawback. Since the Wildes' approach is based on intensive image processing, effects leading to alterations in the grey value distribution can influence the result negatively. Moreover Hough transform require high computation time (the complexity of fastest implementation is $O(N^3)$ in the number of considered (edge) points on the image [12]).

3 Proposed Algorithm

The algorithm was developed for the purpose of analysis of images captured by dedicated devices. The procedure is presented in Fig. 1.

The solution is split into four parts:

- Initial preprocessing
- Pupil acquisition
- Preprocessing for iris acquisition
- Iris acquisition

The second and third parts can be conducted simultaneously if multi-core solution is available.

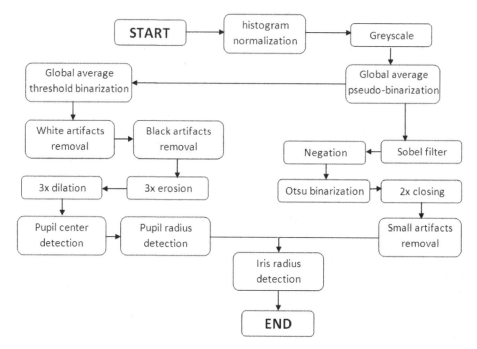

Fig. 1. Flowchart of the algorithm

3.1   Initial Preprocessing

Initial preprocessing consists of three basic steps which are conducted to normalize the data and reduce unnecessary information on the images. The first step is the normalization of histogram where the new value of pixel P(x,y) for each separate color channel of RGB palette is calculated using:

$$P(x,y) = 255 \cdot \frac{P(x,y) - minP}{maxP - minP}$$

Where $minP$ and $maxP$ are the maximum and minimum values of each channel. The second step is conversion of the image into gray scale by averaging the RGB values. The third step, which is called *global average pseudo-binarization* in Fig. 1 is conducted similarly to regular binarization with global average, however only the pixels which are above average are converted into white pixels, the pixels below or equal average are left unchanged. This step, as presented in Fig. 2, removes lighter fragments of the pictures, such as eyelids or parts of eyeballs, from further analysis. This step also improves the results of Sobel filter used in iris acquisition and alters the threshold of global binarization during pupil acquisition where only non-white pixels are analyzed.

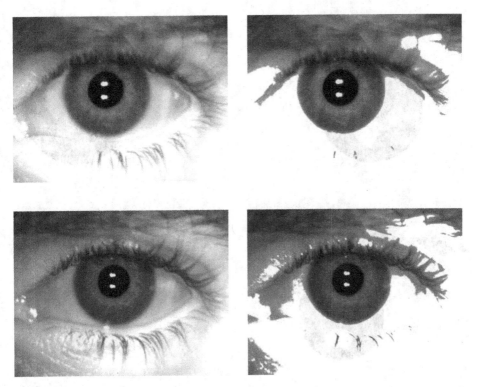

Fig. 2. Exemplary results of global average pseudo-binarization, on the left are original images and on the right are images after first step of proposed algorithm

3.2 Pupil Acquisition

This part of algorithm starts with binarization using 20% of global average as a threshold. The average is calculated using only non-white pixels of the image. Each pixel above this value is converted into black pixel and the rest are converted into white pixels. This operation, as presented in Fig. 3, leaves relatively good pupil shape with some minor artifacts. The white gaps inside the black shapes are filled using flooding algorithm and then all but the largest black shapes are converted into white ones using flooding algorithm again. The results of this operations are also presented in Fig. 3. Next the image is eroded three times and dilated three times to prepare it for pupil acquisition.

The first step of the acquisition is the calculation of the distances of every black pixel from the nearest white pixel. Then the coordinates of the initial center of the pupil are calculated by averaging the coordinates of the points with the longest distances. Having the initial central point, the radius of the pupil is acquired as described with pseudo-code below:

1. Calculate the rectangular borders of the shape
2. Calculate distances from the center point to the furthest left, right, top and bottom black pixel horizontally and vertically

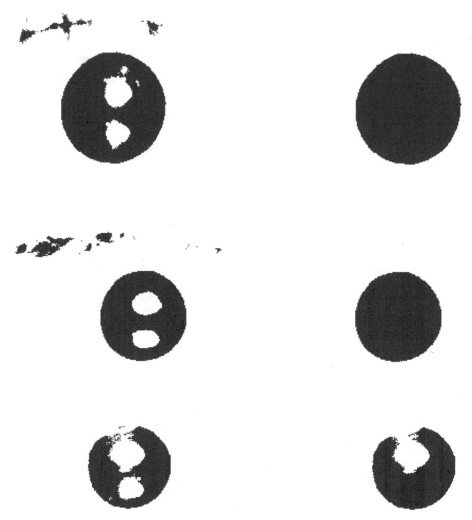

Fig. 3. Exemplary results of thresholding (left) and flooding algorithm (right)

3. Check which span is wider - between left and right pixel or between top and bottom
4. Calculate the radius as a half of the wider span
5. If it is not the first iteration of the loop and the radius is shorter than the radius calculated in the previous step - **end the procedure**
6. Calculate the difference between one of the distances of wider span and the radius and adjust the center point by this difference in the wider span direction (vertical or horizontal)
7. Calculate the distances of the moved center point from the borders of the shape in the shorter span direction

8. Choose the shorter distance. If it is left or bottom, the new value of center point in the shorter direction is the border point value in that direction + radius, else it is the border point value in that direction - radius

After this procedure the center and the radius of the pupil are acquired and can be used in the *Iris acquisition* step.

3.3   Preprocessing for Iris Acquisition

Separately from step two, the image is also prepared for iris acquisition. This step can be implemented simultaneously with previous step on multi-core systems. It begins with Sobel filtering and the negation of the filtering result. Then all the black pixels in the image are converted into white ones. This step eliminates the strong borders which separate the white and non-white regions of the image after Sobel filtering. Then the image is binariezed using Otsu algorithm. After binarization the closing operation is performed twice and the removal of artifacts is conducted using flooding algorithm. With this step all black shapes that consist the number of pixels lesser than 0.2% of total pixel count of the image are whitened.

The image is now prepared for iris acquisition using the pupil obtained in step 2.

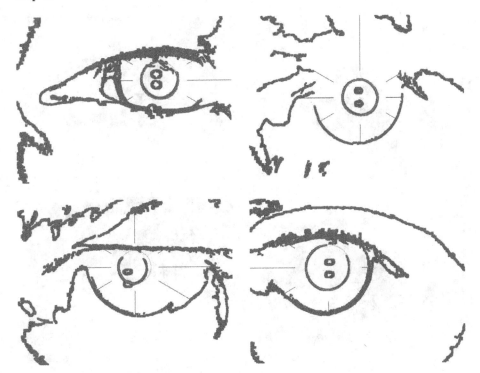

Fig. 4. Exemplary results of iris radius detection

3.4   Iris Acquisition

To acquire the iris, the eight lines are drawn from the center of the pupil. The lines start in the distance of 1.5×pupil radius from the center and are drawn horizontally to the left and right, vertically to the top and bottom and in the 30, 150, 210 and 330 degrees from the horizontal line. Each line ends when it meets the first black pixel or reaches the border of the image, as presented in Fig. 4. The distances between first found points and the center point are calculated and sorted. The median of these distances is used as the radius of the iris.

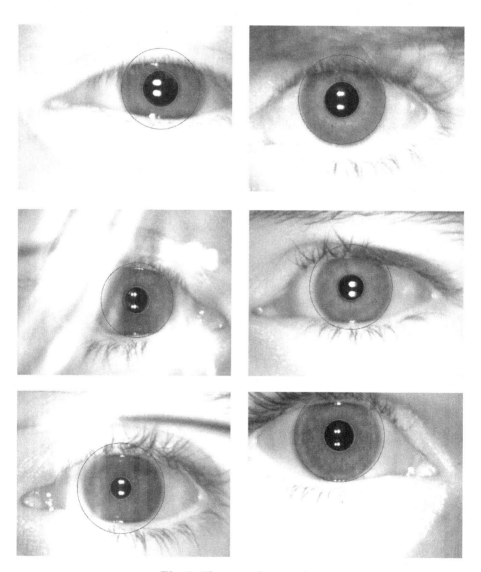

Fig. 5. The exemplary results

4   Results

The tests were conducted on 47 sample images from VeriEye SDK acquired using Retica Mobile-Eyes Ruggedized Dual Iris Capture Device. The images are compatible with **ANSI INCITS 379-2004** and **ISO/IEC 19794-6** standards. The database consists of pictures of both left and right eyes of 10 people. The number of samples of each person and each eye varies. The database was chosen due to the variety of iris positions and lighting conditions on the samples.

All the pupils were extracted correctly. In some cases the region of the found iris is larger than actual one although all the parts of the iris needed for human recognition and verification in each case were acquired. The exemplary results are presented in Fig. 5. In overall, the success rate of this initial tests was 100% although the authors are aware that more thorough tests are still required.

5   Conclusions and Future Work

As mentioned above, the results of the experiments are promising. The algorithm sometimes acquires redundant information, although the extra acquired iris neighborhood can be easily eliminated during a transformation of the iris into a rectangle. This neighborhood will transform into much lighter then the iris part of the strip and on this stage simple thresholding should be enough to address the issue.

Noticeable is that the algorithm handled correctly also the images which were overexposed.

The main disadvantage of the solution is the extensive use of dilation and erosion algorithms which, when poorly implemented, may be time-consuming. The authors recommend the use of calculation of distances to nearest white/black pixel in this process to reduce the computation time of the algorithm.

In their future work the authors will concentrate on the second part of the planned solution - the acquisition of characteristic features of the iris. The aforementioned transformation of the iris into a rectangle will be used for this purpose and any other necessary preprocessing will be conducted in this part of the system. Then the authors will work on the development of human identification and verification procedures to propose a complete solution.

Acknowledgement. The research of Krzysztof Misztal is supported by the National Centre of Science (Poland) [grant no. 2012/07/N/ST6/02192].

References

1. Masek, L., et al.: Recognition of human iris patterns for biometric identification. M. Thesis, The University of Western Australia 3 (2003)
2. Daugman, J.G.: High confidence visual recognition of persons by a test of statistical independence. IEEE Transactions on Pattern Analysis and Machine Intelligence 15, 1148–1161 (1993)

3. Wildes, R.P.: Iris recognition: an emerging biometric technology. Proceedings of the IEEE 85, 1348–1363 (1997)
4. Boles, W., Boashash, B.: A human identification technique using images of the iris and wavelet transform. IEEE Transactions on Signal Processing 46, 1185–1188 (1998)
5. Huang, Y.P., Luo, S.W., Chen, E.Y.: An efficient iris recognition system. In: Proceedings of 2002 International Conference on Machine Learning and Cybernetics, vol. 1, pp. 450–454. IEEE (2002)
6. Zhu, Y., Tan, T., Wang, Y.: Biometric personal identification based on iris patterns. In: Proceedings of 15th International Conference on Pattern Recognition, vol. 2, pp. 801–804. IEEE (2000)
7. Misztal, K., Saeed, E., Tabor, J., Saeed, K.: Iris Pattern Recognition with a New Mathematical Model to Its Rotation Detection, pp. 43–65. Springer, New York (2012)
8. Jillela, R., Ross, A.A.: Methods for iris segmentation. In: Handbook of Iris Recognition, pp. 239–279. Springer (2013)
9. Gonzalez, R.C., Woods, R.E.: Digital image processing (2002)
10. Illingworth, J., Kittler, J.: A survey of the hough transform. Computer Vision, Graphics, and Image Processing 44, 87–116 (1988)
11. Wildes, R.P., Asmuth, J.C., Green, G.L., Hsu, S.C., Kolczynski, R.J., Matey, J., McBride, S.E.: A system for automated iris recognition. In: Proceedings of the Second IEEE Workshop on Applications of Computer Vision, pp. 121–128. IEEE (1994)
12. Xie, Y., Ji, Q.: A new efficient ellipse detection method. In: Proceedings of 16th International Conference on Pattern Recognition, vol. 2, pp. 957–960. IEEE (2002)

Query Selectivity Estimation Based on Improved V-optimal Histogram by Introducing Information about Distribution of Boundaries of Range Query Conditions

Dariusz Rafal Augustyn

Silesian University of Technology, Institute of Informatics,
16 Akademicka St., 44-100 Gliwice, Poland
draugustyn@polsl.pl

Abstract. Selectivity estimation is a parameter used by a query optimizer for early estimation of the size of data that satisfies query condition. Selectivity is calculated using an estimator of distribution of attribute values of attribute involved in a processed query condition. Histograms built on attributes values from a database may be such representation of the distribution. The paper introduces a new query-distribution-aware V-optimal histogram which is useful in selectivity estimation for a range query. It takes into account either a 1-D distribution of attribute values or a 2-D distribution of boundaries of already processed queries. The advantages of qda-V-optimal histogram appears when it is applied for selectivity estimation of range query conditions that form so-called hot regions. To obtain the proposed error-optimal histogram we use dynamic programming method, Fuzzy C-Means clustering of a set of range boundaries.

Keywords: query selectivity estimation, data clustering, dynamic programming, distribution of range query conditions, V-optimal histogram.

1 Introduction

Processing a database query by DBMS (Database Management System) consists of two phases – a prepare phase and an execute one. During the prepare phase the optimal query execution plan is obtained. This is done by a query cost optimizer which needs to estimate selectivity values of query selection conditions. For a simple single-table selection condition the selectivity is the number of rows satisfying the condition divided by the number of all table rows. For a simple single-table range condition based on x attribute with a continuous domain, it may be obtained as follows:

$$sel(Q(a < x < b) = \int_a^b f(x)dx. \tag{1}$$

K. Saeed and V. Snášel (Eds.): CISIM 2014, LNCS 8838, pp. 151–164, 2014.

where x – a table attribute, a and b – range query condition boundaries, $f(x)$ – a probability density function (PDF) of x attribute. Commonly, to obtain the selectivity value the query optimizer requires a histogram as a non-parametric estimator of PDF.

Since years there are well-known approaches to represent a 1-dimensional distribution of attribute values (e.g. based on histograms: equi-width, equi-height, max-diff, V-optimal [11] or spline representation). Some research concentrates on problem of obtaining a space-efficient representation of multi-dimensional representation (e.g. based on cosine series [13], wavelet transform [7], Bayesian network [9], self-tuning histograms [6,12], kernel density estimator [10], and many others).

There are also some approaches which additionally use information about already processed queries ([8,6,12,1,2]). The proposed method uses it too, but it collects only information about the range conditions (values of boundaries), not about their real selectivity values obtained after a query execution (in opposite to the approaches presented in [8,6]).

The proposed method (designated for building a representation of 1 dimensional distribution of attribute values) introduces a new type of histogram i.e. qda-V-optimal one (**query-distribution-aware**). It takes into account information about a range query workload. Such proposed hybrid representation uses either a 1-D distribution of attribute or a 2-D distribution of query conditions. We assume that DBMS should collect information about range boundaries of recently processed query conditions in a limited-length buffer. A result of clustering of boundaries values allows to modify some boundaries of V-optimal histogram buckets what tends to obtain a qda-V-optimal one.

This method may allow to create a better distribution representation than [1,2], i.e. it is better adapted to a set of previously processed range queries. This results from taking into account full information about boundary pairs of processed query conditions (set of 2-D elements), in opposite to the approaches [1,2] where we use only 1-D include function describing aggregated information about all ranges of processed queries. This implies a little greater storage requirement, of course.

The main contributions of the paper are as follows:

- the qda-V-optimal histogram – a representation of distribution of attribute values that it is partially adapted to a query workload, i.e. the representation resolution also depends on distribution of condition boundaries of recently processed range queries,
- the method of obtaining of a qda-V-optimal histogram, i.e. improving a V-optimal histogram by obtaining new histogram bucket's boundaries through clustering values of range boundaries,
- the method of reduction of complexity of the procedure by rejection weak clusters.

2 Motivating Example – Description of the Proposed Method

2.1 Exemplary Attribute Values Distribution and its Representation

To illustrate the concept of the proposed method of distribution representation we need a sample distribution of x attribute. We may use here any x distribution (although a non-uniform one is rather expected).

In the example we assume the one which is based on superposition of $G = 4$ truncated Gaussian clusters with bounded support (limited to $[0\ 1]$), where parameters of used univariate normal distributions are shown in Tab. 1. PDF is defined as follows:

$$f(x) = \sum_{i=1}^{G} p_i\, \text{PDF}_{\text{TN}}(x, m_i, \sigma_i, 0, 1), \qquad (2)$$

where $\text{PDF}_{\text{TN}}(x, m_i, \sigma_i, l, r)$ is PDF of truncated normal distribution with a support based on interval $[l\ r]$:

$$\text{PDF}_{\text{TN}}(x, m_i, \sigma_i, l, r) = \frac{\frac{1}{\sigma_i}\phi\left(\frac{x-m_i}{\sigma_i}\right)}{\Phi\left(\frac{r-m_i}{\sigma_i}\right) - \Phi\left(\frac{l-m_i}{\sigma_i}\right)}, \qquad (3)$$

where ϕ is PDF of $N(0, 1)$ and Φ is cumulative density function (CDF) of $N(0, 1)$.

Table 1. Parameters of clusters used in the definition of exemplary PDF of x attribute

i – cluster number	1	2	3	2
p_i	0.25	0.25	0.3	0.2
m_i	0.2	0.8	0.6	0.7
σ_i	0.1	0.1	0.01	0.01

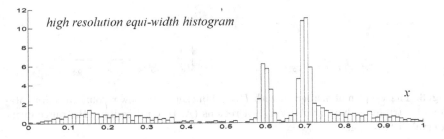

Fig. 1. High resolution representation of x attribute distribution – the equi-width histogram

The distribution consists of two narrow clusters ($i = 3, 4$; with relatively small σ_i) and two wide ones ($i = 1, 2$; with big σ_i). The high resolution empirical histogram with 100 intervals (built on 1000 samples) describing $f(x)$ is shown in Fig. 1.

Let us consider to use a V-optimal histogram [11] as a representation of the distribution. $B = 10$ is the assumed number of buckets in this histogram. Using the method of dynamic programming [11] we obtained such distribution of bucket boundaries (see Fig. 2) denoted by $b_{vo\,j}$ for $j = 1, \ldots, B + 1$ (where $b_{vo\,1} = 0$ and $b_{vo\,B+1} = b_{vo\,11} = 1$) that sum of variances of frequencies in buckets is the smallest. The frequencies are taken from the equi-width histogram (Fig. 1) with a relatively high resolution (with $10 \cdot B$ buckets). The result domain division is presented in Fig. 2 (dashed vertical lines). The result V-optimal histogram is shown in Fig. 3.

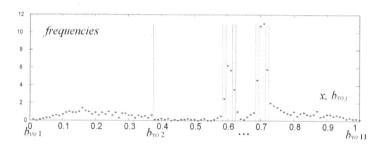

Fig. 2. $(b_{vo\,j})$ for $j = 1, \ldots, B + 1$ – found boundaries of V-optimal histogram

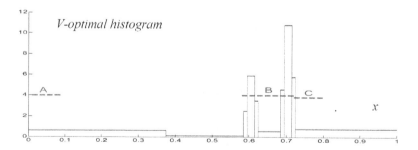

Fig. 3. The V-optimal histogram with $B = 10$ buckets – the low resolution representation of attribute value distribution. Hot regions (A, B, C) describing the range query interval distribution.

2.2 Exemplary of Distribution of Range Query Condition Bounds

In the proposed method we assume that we collect conditions of most recently executed queries.

Let us assume the situation from real world where a set of processed query conditions forms so-called hot regions.

In our example we used a superposition of distributions of hot regions A, B, C (Fig. 3), and the truncated 2D-uniform distribution.

Region **A** defines query boundaries based on the interval $[a, b] = [0.01, 0.09]$ i.e. we have a values located near 0.01 (and $0 \leq a \leq 1$) and we have b values located near 0.09 (and $a \leq b \leq 1$). Here, we assumed the following density functions for either left endpoints of intervals belonging to hot region A or right ones: $\mathrm{PDF}_{aA}(a) = \mathrm{PDF}_{TN}(a, m_{aA}, \sigma_{aA}, 0, 1) = \mathrm{PDF}_{TN}(a, 0.01, 0.0005, 0, 1)$ and $\mathrm{PDF}_{bA}(b|a) = \mathrm{PDF}_{TN}(b, m_{bA}, \sigma_{bA}, a, 1) = \mathrm{PDF}_{TN}(b, 0.09, 0.0001, a, 1)$. Those relatively small values of σ_{aA} and σ_{bA} (comparing to values of m_{aA} and m_{bA}) cause that all query ranges belonging to region A are almost the same. Thus, pairs (a, b) that belong to region A are described by:

$$\begin{aligned}
\mathrm{PDF}_A(a, b) &= \mathrm{PDF}_{aA}(a) \cdot \mathrm{PDF}_{bA}(b|a) = \\
&= \mathrm{PDF}_{TN}(a, m_{aA}, \sigma_{aA}, 0, 1) \cdot \mathrm{PDF}_{TN}(b, m_{bA}, \sigma_{bA}, a, 1) = \\
&= \mathrm{PDF}_{TN}(a, 0.01, 0.0005, 0, 1) \cdot \mathrm{PDF}_{TN}(b, 0.09, 0.0001, a, 1).
\end{aligned} \tag{4}$$

Analogously, we define regions B and C. Region **B** defines query boundaries based on the interval $[a, b] = [0.58, 0.72]$ i.e.:
$\mathrm{PDF}_{aB}(a) = \mathrm{PDF}_{TN}(a, m_{aB}, \sigma_{aB}, 0, 1) = \mathrm{PDF}_{TN}(a, 0.58, 0.0005, 0, 1)$ and
$\mathrm{PDF}_{bB}(b|a) = \mathrm{PDF}_{TN}(b, m_{bB}, \sigma_{bB}, a, 1) = \mathrm{PDF}_{TN}(b, 0.72, 0.0001, a, 1)$. Thus
$\mathrm{PDF}_B(a, b) = \mathrm{PDF}_{aB}(a) \cdot \mathrm{PDF}_{bB}(b|a)$.
Region **C** defines query boundaries based on the interval $[a, b] = [0.72, 0.8]$
i.e.: $\mathrm{PDF}_{aC}(a) = \mathrm{PDF}_{TN}(a, m_{aC}, \sigma_{aC}, 0, 1) = \mathrm{PDF}_{TN}(a, 0.72, 0.0005, 0, 1)$ and
$\mathrm{PDF}_{bC}(b|a) = \mathrm{PDF}_{TN}(b, m_{bC}, \sigma_{bC}, a, 1) = \mathrm{PDF}_{TN}(b, 0.8, 0.0001, a, 1)$. Thus
$\mathrm{PDF}_C(a, b) = \mathrm{PDF}_{aC}(a) \cdot \mathrm{PDF}_{bC}(b|a)$.
PDF of truncated 2D-unifrom distribution described as follows:

$$\mathrm{PDF}_{T2D-uniform}(a, b) = \begin{cases} 2 & \text{for } 0 \leq a \leq 1 \wedge 0 \leq b \leq 1 \wedge a \leq b \\ 0 & \text{otherwise} \end{cases} \tag{5}$$

is presented in Fig. 4b. The truncated 2D-uniform was used for introducing (into a result boundaries distribution) some events that not all pairs (a, b) come from hot regions, i.e. some of them are uniformly distributed in $[0\ 1]^2$ space (subject to $b \geq a$).

Finally the result distribution of query bounds is assumed as follows:

$$\begin{aligned}
\mathrm{PDF}_{ab}(a, b) &= 0.3 \cdot \mathrm{PDF}_A(a, b) + 0.3 \cdot \mathrm{PDF}_B(a, b) + \\
&\quad + 0.2 \cdot \mathrm{PDF}_C(a, b) + 0.2 \cdot \mathrm{PDF}_{T2D-uniform}(a, b).
\end{aligned} \tag{6}$$

$M = 20$ samples were generated according to the distribution given by eq. (6). The generated pairs (a_j, b_j) for $j = 1, \ldots, M$ are shown in Fig. 4a. They form a set named *Qset*. *Qset* is a collection of query boundaries from last M queries.

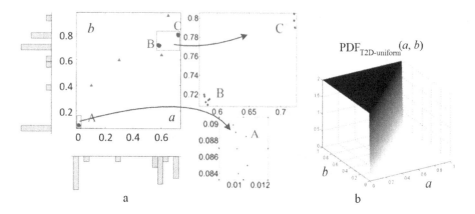

Fig. 4. a) $Qset$ – the set of sample query bounds – the exemplary set of pairs (a_j, b_j) for $j = 1, \ldots, M(M = 20)$, generated according to the $\text{PDF}_{ab}(a, b)$. b) Bivariate PDF of the truncated 2D uniform distribution (eq. (5)).

Those pairs that come from truncated 2-D uniform distribution are represented by 4 triangles in Fig. 4a.

In our method we recommend rather similar values of M and B, i.e. they should have the same order of magnitude (the size of metadata needed for describing range conditions should be rather similar to the size of metadata describing an attribute values distribution).

2.3   Verifying the Applicability of the Proposed Method

A verification step is performed before any essential activities of the proposed method. We create the 1-dimensional vector S which contains either a_j or b_j elements. S presented in Fig. 5, was built on all pairs (a_j, b_j) from $Qset$ (i.e. for $j = 1, \ldots, M$). In our example S consists of $2 \cdot M = 40$ elements.

Fig. 5. Distribution of values from S which consists of either a or b values from $Qset$

In this step of the proposed method, we check if elements of S do not represent the 1-D uniform distribution based on [0 1] interval. This is done by some well-known methods of nonparametric test for the equality of an empirical distribution and a reference one (e.g. we use chi-square test or Kolmogorov-Smirnov one). This is done to reject (at the assumed significance level) the null hypothesis that the data in S comes from the [0 1] uniform distribution. As we may expect, the exemplary set S shown in Fig. 5 is not a sample set coming from the uniform distribution (at 5% significance level). If S represented data from the uniform distribution then there would be no hot regions in $Qset$, so there would be no reason to improve a classic V-optimal histogram.

2.4 Using K-fold Cross Validation for Obtaining the Optimal Clusters of Boundaries of Range Query Condition

The proposed method introduces clustering of query bounds. The obtained set of centers of clusters will determine some new boundaries of buckets in a histogram which represents x distribution. Such histogram based on a V-optimal one will be named qda-V-optimal (query-distribution-aware).

To obtain the optimal number of clusters, denoted by C_{opt}, we use well-known K-fold cross validation method. To obtain C_{opt} we minimize a score function which is based on a mean relative selectivity error (described further by eq. (9) and (10)).

In our example, we assumed 5-fold cross validation. We divide $Qset$ into learning sets $Qset\_learn_k$ and test sets $Qset\_test_k$. There are $K = 5$ different either learning sets or test ones. Each $Qset\_learn_k$ has $(K-1)/K \cdot M = 16$ pairs of a and b. Each $Qset\_test_k$ has $1/K \cdot M = 4$ pairs. All sets $Qset\_learn_k$ and $Qset\_test_k$ satisfy the following constraint:

$$\forall_{k=1,...,K} \ Qset = Qset\_learn_k \cup Qset\_test_k. \tag{7}$$

To find the optimal C_{opt} by applying K-fold cross validation we use the score function values calculated for $Qset\_test_k$ (for $k = 1, \ldots, K$).

Let us define S_k ($S_k \subset S$) as a one-dimensional vector which contains either a values and b ones from $Qset\_learn_k$.

To obtain clusters in S_k we use the very well known method – FCM (Fuzzy C-Means) [4].

Clusters from S_k (which is based on $Qset\_learn_k$) will be used for finding a new set of bucket boundaries and construct a qda-V-optimal. The relevant $Qset\_test_k$ will be used for validate accuracy of this qda-V-optimal histogram the by calculations of selectivity estimation errors.

Steps of the method will be illustrated using S_1 – an exemplary S_k. Elements of vector S_1 are shown in Fig. 7 (values of S_1 are presented using vertical dashed lines).

2.5 Clustering Query Boundary Values from Learn Set and Rejecting Either Low Cardinality Clusters or Wide Ones

We assumed that the support of $f(x)$ is limited, i.e. $\min(x) = 0$ and $\max(x) = 1$ (Fig. 1), so this determines the first boundary of qda-V-optimal histogram and the last one. Thus, during the optimization we may only change positions of maximally $B - 1$ internal bucket boundaries of qda-V-optimal histogram. This determines the maximum of the number of clusters. Thus, C – the number of clusters – may vary, but it has to be less than the number of internal buckets in a standard V-optimal histogram, i.e. $2 \leq C \leq B - 1$.

We propose some constraints for cluster's properties. This allows to eliminate so-called weak clusters. We want to consider only:

- enough narrow clusters, i.e. such ones that 2· standard deviation of cluster element values is less than some assumed value – ϵ. In the example we assume $\epsilon = 1/B = 1/10$ (we use here $1/B$ – length of an equi-width histogram with B buckets and with domain $[0\ 1]$),
- only high cardinality clusters, i.e. such ones that the number of elements in a cluster is greater than $N_{min\_elem\_in\_cluster}$ – some assumed fraction of all S elements. In the example we assume $N_{min\_elem\_in\_cluster} = 10\%$ of $M = 0.1 \cdot 20 = 2$.

For any given C we may find C_{acc} – the number of accepted clusters ($C_{acc} \leq C$) – that satisfy the mentioned-above criteria.

In Fig. 6a, we present the result of clustering of the exemplary vector S_1, which elements come from $Qset\_learn_1$. We consider $C = 2, \ldots, B - 1 = 2, \ldots, 9$. In Fig. 6a we can see the properties of accepted clusters:

- **me** – center (median) value of an accepted cluster,
- **width** – width of a cluster (presented as a vertical interval with whiskers) with length given by 2· std of the cluster elements values,
- **card** – cardinality of a cluster.

According to the assumed constraints given by $(\epsilon, N_{min\_elem\_in\_cluster})) = (0.1, 2)$ we obtain the relevant numbers of accepted clusters as follows $C_{acc} = 1, 3, 3, 4, 4, 4, 4$ for given $C = 3, 4, \ldots, 9$ (Fig. 6a, 6b). For $C = 2$ there were no clusters that satisfy constraints for cluster's properties.

For decreasing values of C, cardinalities of clusters rather increase but the clusters also become wider. Dependency between $total\_card$ – the total sum of cardinalities of accepted clusters and C is presented in Fig. 6c. Dependency between $mean\_width$ – the mean width of accepted clusters and C is shown in Fig. 6d.

The described heuristic procedure of rejecting weak clusters allows to limit the number of considered C values. For small or big values of C there will be no accepted clusters, i.e. the relevant C_{acc} will equal 0 (too wide clusters or too low cardinality ones). In further steps we will only consider those C that satisfy $C_{acc}(C) > 0$. This advantage of the cluster rejection may be useful for high value of B (and high value of $C = 2, \ldots, B - 1$, respectively) because in real DBMSes we may expect such values of B (i.e. commonly hundreds).

2.6 Creating qda-V-Optimal Histogram – Rejecting Boundaries of V-Optimal Histogram That Are Close to Centers of Accepted Clusters

Let us deeply consider the case of S_1 clustering where the number of clusters $C = 6$ (so the relevant C_{acc} equals 4 (Fig. 6a, 6b)).

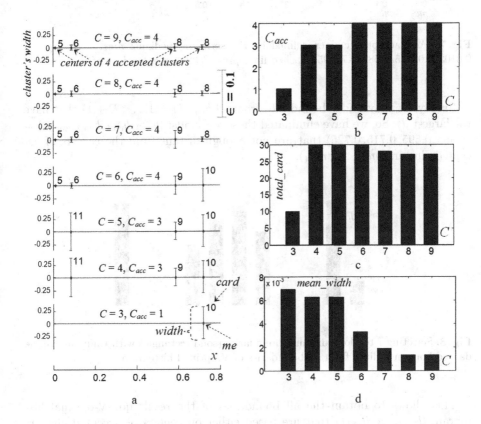

Fig. 6. a) Sets of accepted clusters for different values of C (the number of clusters used in FCM method). Dependency between C and: b) the number of accepted clusters, c) the total sum of cardinality of accepted clusters, d) the mean width of accepted clusters.

$C_{acc} = 4$ accepted centers of clusters (Fig. 7) become some of bounds of the required qda-V-optimal.

The rest of $B + 1 - C_{acc} = 11 - 4 = 7$ boundaries of the qda-V-optimal histogram will be selected from the $\{b_{vo\,j}\}$ i.e. boundaries of the V-optimal histogram (Fig. 2 and 3). We want to reject those that are placed near the centers of accepted clusters. To do this we may find the distance between a selected $b_{vo\,j}$ and the set centers of accepted clusters as follows:

$$d_j = \min_{i=1,\ldots,C_{acc}} |b_{vo\,j} - me_i|. \tag{8}$$

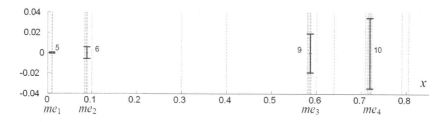

Fig. 7. Four accepted cluster defined by the series of medians: $me_1, \ldots, me_{Cacc} = 0.0103, 0.08875, 0.586, 0.71895$. Dashed lines present 32 element values of S_1.

Finally, we may find 7 boundaries from all $b_{vo\,j}$ $(j = 1, \ldots, B + 1)$ that have the largest d_j. So, we have eliminated those 4 bounds: $(b_{vo\,3}, b_{vo\,4}, b_{vo\,9}, b_{vo\,10}) = (0.585, 0.595, 0.715, 0.725)$ that are not enough distant from the centers of accepted clusters $(me_1, \ldots, me_4)$.

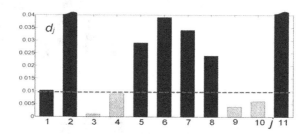

Fig. 8. Selecting 7 top long distance boundaries (solid rectangles with values above the dashed horizontal line) from all boundaries of V-optimal histogram

This allows to obtain the all boundaries of the result qda-V-optimal histogram $(b_{vo\,1}, \ldots, b_{vo\,11})$ that are based either on centers of accepted clusters $(me_1, \ldots, me_4)$ or selected boundaries from the V-optimal histogram, i.e. $b_{vo\,j}$ where $j = 1, 2, 5, 6, 7, 8, 11$.

Using frequencies from the high resolution equi-width histogram (Fig. 1) we may find values of the result qda-V-optimal histogram (Fig. 9a) which buckets are based on found boundaries $(b_{vo\,1}, \ldots, b_{vo\,11})$. This histogram will be scored by the mean relative selectivity estimation error in a next step of the proposed method.

Along $[0.01, 0.09]$ (hot region A) the qda-V-optimal histogram (Fig. 9) has 3 buckets while the standard V-optimal one (Fig. 3, 9b) has only one bucket. Thus, this qda-V-optimal histogram is better adapted to the query conditions belonging to the hot region A. (This improvement is at the expense of losing the accuracy of distribution representation in intervals not overlapped by hot query range regions).

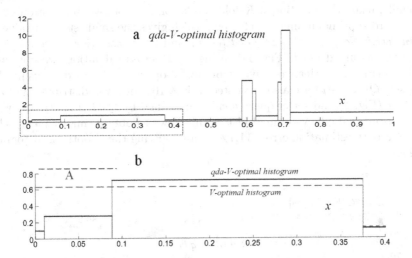

Fig. 9. a) The qda-V-optimal histogram (based on V-optimal one) built by clustering the values form S_1 (based on $Qset\_learn_1$) for the assumed number of cluster – $C = 6$ (and the relevant number of accepted clusters – $C_{acc} = 4$).
b) Zoomed part of the qda-V-optimal histogram (solid line) and the relevant V-optimal one (dashed line) for $x \in [0, 0.4]$. There are 3 buckets of the qda-Voptimal histogram in $x \in [0.01, 0.09]$ (hot region A).

2.7 Obtaining the Optimal Number of Clusters of Query Boundaries – Minimizing Mean Error of Selectivity Estimations Based on Qda-V-Optimal Histogram

Let us introduce the relative selectivity error as follows:

$$RelSelErr_H(a, b) = RelSelErr_H(Q(a < x < b)) = \frac{|\widehat{sel_H}(Q) - sel(Q)|}{sel(Q)} \cdot 100\%. \tag{9}$$

$\widehat{sel_H}$ denotes an approximated selectivity value based on some histogram H, where H is VO (V-optimal histogram) or $qdaVO$ (qda-V-optimal one). sel is an exact selectivity value (here calculated using a high resolution equi-width histogram, like this from Fig. 1).

Mean relative error of selectivity for some $Qset$ (some set of query conditions) and some histogram H is given as follows:

$$MeanRelSelErr_H(Q) = \text{maean}_{(a,b) \in Qset} \ RelSelErr_H(a, b). \tag{10}$$

Using the V-optimal histogram (Fig. 3) and the test set of query conditions $Qset\_test_1$, we obtained $MeanRelSelErr_{VO}(Qset\_test_1) \approx 38.3\%$. Using the qda-V-optimal histogram (Fig. 9a) and $Qset\_test_1$, we obtained $MeanRelSelErr_{qdaVO}(Qset\_test_1) \approx 11.9\%$ which is a better result than that obtained from the V-optimal histogram.

Finally, using the mentioned K-fold validation method, we may obtain C_{opt}, i.e. the error-optimal number of clusters, which gives the smallest mean value of $MeanRelErrSel_{qdaVO}$ over all $Qset\_learn_k$ and $Qset\_test_k$ (for $k = 1, \ldots, K$). For the assumed $Qset$ (Fig. 4a), using 5-fold cross validation, we obtained $C_{opt} = 6$ (Fig. 10). Mean relative errors for V-optimal (obtained by using the same sets $Qset\_test_k$) are also presented in Fig. 10. For given distribution of attribute x (Fig. 1) and set of query condition defined by $Qset$ (Fig. 4), applying the error-optimal qda-V-optimal histogram allows to obtain smaller mean relative selectivity estimation error (11.1%) than applying the V-optimal histogram (32.2%).

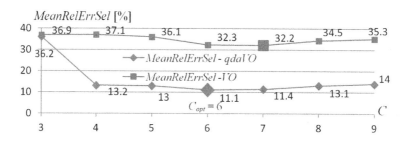

Fig. 10. K-fold cross validating the method of selectivity estimation using qda-V-optimal histogram for query condition given by $Qset$. Obtaining the optimal number of clusters ($C_{opt} = 6$) with the smallest mean relative selectivity ($\approx 11.1\%$).

For the exemplary distributions given in subsections 2.1 and 2.2, the qda-V-optimal histogram seems significantly better than the relevant V-optimal one.

3   The Algorithm of the Proposed Method

The proposed method is designated to obtain a qda-V-optimal histogram which may be applied for range query selectivity estimation.

The main goal is to find the error-optimal histogram for assumed B – an arbitrary given number of histogram buckets. To build a qda-V-optimal histogram we assume that we already have collected elements of $Qset$, i.e. M last processed range query conditions that operated on x attribute.

The proposed method should be invoked during execution of so-called update statistics command for x attribute.

The proposed method consists of the following steps:

1. Create a high resolution equi-width histogram (this is a temporary structure which is removed after finishing the method; the number of buckets of the equi-width histogram should be significantly greater than B).
2. Create a classic V-optimal histogram with B buckets using the equi-high histogram.

3. Check applicability of the proposed method, i.e. verify that elements from S (a set of values built on elements of $Qset$) do not come from uniform distribution (if so, than there are no hot regions of query conditions, so only the V-optimal histogram is returned as a result and the method is finished).

4. Using K-fold cross validation, obtain C_{opt} – the error-optimal number of clusters of query boundaries which determines the qda-V-optimal histogram (the equi-histogram histogram and the V-optimal one are used; elements form subset of S are clustered using FCM method; the constraints (small width or low cardinality) are applied for elimination weak clusters; those boundaries of the V-optimal histogram are used in the qda-V-optimal one, that they are enough distant from centers of accepted clusters).

5. Verify the superiority of the qda-V-optimal histogram over the V-optimal one for given $Qset$ (verifying that the qda-V-optimal histogram based on C_{opt} allows to calculate query selectivities for $Qset$ elements with less mean relative error than the V-optimal one; if so, the qda-V-optimal histogram is returned else the V-optimal one is).

4   Conclusions

The paper describes the method of query selectivity estimation based on improved V-optimal histograms. The proposed method additionally takes into account information about the query conditions of previously processed range queries. A proposed new qda-V-optimal histogram may allow to estimate the selectivities with small mean relative errors, especially when query conditions form so-called hot regions.

In future we may consider to introduce importance weights for conditions from the buffer (a newer condition is more important). We may also consider of applying a different policy of discarding elements from the full buffer (e.g. not to use LRU method (least recently used) but use hit ratios and LFU method (least frequently used)).

Further work may concentrate on a problem when a future query workload is not well represented by boundary samples already collected in a buffer, i.e. in last M query conditions. Some simple way to solve overlearning a qda-V-optimal histogram by no enough representative $Qset$ is to introduce some additional random samples (according to the truncated 2D-uniform distribution) to decrease too a large impact of a query distribution on the qda-V-optimal histogram construction.

The proposed method of obtaining a qda-V-optimal should be invoked during update statistics (not during on-line query processing) and it is not so time critical operation like a selectivity estimation. However, because of the complexity of the proposed algorithm, we consider using capabilities of GPGPU (General-Purpose computing on Graphics Processor Units) having in mind that parallel efficient GPU becomes useful in database processing (e.g. [5,3]).

References

1. Augustyn, D.R.: Query-condition-aware histograms in selectivity estimation method. In: Czachórski, T., Kozielski, S., Stańczyk, U. (eds.) Man-Machine Interactions 2. AISC, vol. 103, pp. 437–446. Springer, Heidelberg (2011), http://dx.doi.org/10.1007/978-3-642-23169-8_47, doi:10.1007/978-3-642-23169-8_47

2. Augustyn, D.R.: Query-condition-aware v-optimal histogram in range query selectivity estimation. Bulletin of the Polish Academy of Sciences. Technical Sciences 62(2), 287–303 (2014), http://dx.doi.org/10.2478/bpasts-2014-0029, doi:10.2478/bpasts-2014-0029

3. Augustyn, D.R., Zederowski, S.: Applying CUDA technology in DCT-based method of query selectivity estimation. In: Pechenizkiy, M., Wojciechowski, M. (eds.) New Trends in Databases & Inform. AISC, vol. 185, pp. 3–12. Springer, Heidelberg (2012)

4. Bezdek, J.C.: Pattern Recognition with Fuzzy Objective Function Algorithms. Kluwer Academic Publishers, Norwell (1981)

5. Breß, S., Beier, F., Rauhe, H., Sattler, K.U., Schallehn, E., Saake, G.: Efficient co-processor utilization in database query processing. Inf. Syst. 38(8), 1084–1096 (2013), http://dx.doi.org/10.1016/j.is.2013.05.004, doi:10.1016/j.is.2013.05.004

6. Bruno, N., Chaudhuri, S., Gravano, L.: Stholes: A multidimensional workload-aware histogram. SIGMOD Rec. 30(2), 211–222 (2001), http://doi.acm.org/10.1145/376284.375686, doi:10.1145/376284.375686

7. Chakrabarti, K., Garofalakis, M., Rastogi, R., Shim, K.: Approximate query processing using wavelets. The VLDB Journal 10(2-3), 199–223 (2001), http://dl.acm.org/citation.cfm?id=767141.767147

8. Chen, C.M., Roussopoulos, N.: Adaptive selectivity estimation using query feedback. SIGMOD Rec. 23(2), 161–172 (1994), http://doi.acm.org/10.1145/191843.191874,doi:10.1145/191843.191874

9. Getoor, L., Taskar, B., Koller, D.: Selectivity estimation using probabilistic models. SIGMOD Rec. 30(2), 461–472 (2001), http://doi.acm.org/10.1145/376284.375727, doi:10.1145/376284.375727

10. Gunopulos, D., Kollios, G., Tsotras, J., Domeniconi, C.: Selectivity estimators for multidimensional range queries over real attributes. The VLDB Journal 14(2), 137–154 (2005), http://dx.doi.org/10.1007/s00778-003-0090-4, doi:10.1007/s00778-003-0090-4

11. Jagadish, H.V., Poosala, V., Koudas, N., Sevcik, K., Muthukrishnan, S., Suel, T.: Optimal histograms with quality guarantees. In: VLDB, pp. 275–286 (1998)

12. Khachatryan, A., Müller, E., Böhm, K., Kopper, J.: Efficient selectivity estimation by histogram construction based on subspace clustering. In: Bayard Cushing, J., French, J., Bowers, S. (eds.) SSDBM 2011. LNCS, vol. 6809, pp. 351–368. Springer, Heidelberg (2011), http://dl.acm.org/citation.cfm?id=2032397.2032426

13. Yan, F., Hou, W.C., Jiang, Z., Luo, C., Zhu, Q.: Selectivity estimation of range queries based on data density approximation via cosine series. Data Knowl. Eng. 63(3), 855–878 (2007), http://dx.doi.org/10.1016/j.datak.2007.05.003, doi:10.1016/j.datak.2007.05.003

Dynamic Centrality for Directed Co-author Network with Context

Alisa Babskova[1], Jan Martinovič[1,2], Pavla Dráždilová[1], and Kateřina Slaninová[1,2]

[1] Faculty of Electrical Engineering, VŠB - Technical University of Ostrava,
17. listopadu 15/2172, 708 33 Ostrava, Czech Republic
[2] IT4Innovations, VŠB - Technical University of Ostrava,
17. listopadu 15/2172, 708 33 Ostrava, Czech Republic
{alisa.babskova.st,jan.martinovic,pavla.drazdilova,
katerina.slaninova}@vsb.cz

Abstract. Co-author network is a typical example of dynamic complex network, which evolves and changes over time. One of the ways how to capture and describe the dynamics of the network is determination of *Stationarity* for detected communities in the network. In the paper, we have proposed the modified *Stationarity*, which is focused only on co-authors of a given author and not on the whole community to which the author belongs. Therefore, this modified *Stationarity* is defined for each author in the network and is perceived as dynamic centrality. The relations in homogeneous co-author network are not only set by the number of common publications, but are given by a context to terms used by the author extracted from the article titles. This dynamic centrality calculates with the evaluation by context of directed edges in co-author network. Such modified *Stationarity* gives us information about stability or dynamics of the author's neighbourhood that influences her/him, or about the stability and dynamics of the author's neighbourhood, which the author influences in relation to context.

Keywords: Co-author Network, Directed Network, Context, Dynamic Networks, Stationarity.

1 Introduction

Co-author network of computer science bibliography (DBLP)[1] represents an example of dynamic complex network which can be analysed by various methods from the point of view focused on network evolution [2, 3]. It records not only the evolution of the whole network, but we are able to explore the evolution of author communities or selected individual authors during 34 years. It is also possible to investigate DBLP as a heterogeneous bibliographic network which contains multiple types of objects, such as authors, venues, topics and papers, as well as multiple types of edges denoting different relations among these objects. Several researchers [11, 2, 1] deal with analysis of complex networks evolution with the focus on the community analysis and their evolution in homogeneous networks [11] or heterogeneous networks [15]. Other articles [14] are focused on prediction of relations in heterogeneous bibliographic networks.

---

[1] Computer science bibliography (DBLP) website: http://dblp.uni-trier.de/

K. Saeed and V. Snášel (Eds.): CISIM 2014, LNCS 8838, pp. 165–174, 2014.

One of the methods for evolution analysis of co-author networks is evolutionary clustering for heterogeneous networks [6, 15]. Gupta et al. present an algorithm which performs such an agglomerative evolutionary clustering which is able to show variations in the clusters over time with a temporal smoothness approach. Network evolution can be also analysed on the centrality basis. For example in [8], authors study a model of network evolution where links are created or removed based on the centrality of the nodes incident to the links. Authors of article [7] propose a new centrality framework, called composite centrality (CC). The idea behind the CC-framework is that one first defines a set of characteristics of interest, and then chooses appropriate network (centrality) measures. Authors of paper [4] apply the combined approach of a topic modelling algorithm and a pathfinding algorithm to find whether authors tend to co-author with or cite researchers sharing the same research topics. In citation networks, which are directed and weighted, the authors of [9] present centrality for dynamic networks that measures the number of paths that exist over time in a network. They use this metric to rank nodes by how well connected they are over time to the rest of the network.

Our proposed method for stationarity calculation allows to evaluate stability of author's co-authors. The network is defined by the context. Therefore, the stationarity is also related to the stability of author's research domains. The obtained centrality is intended to be used for dynamic networks, in which the set of co-authors as well as the set of terms vary during time periods. The proposed approach allows us to define the evaluation of the directed edges within the co-authors network. We are able to evaluate the edges from the author towards his/her co-authors and otherwise. These weights are used for calculation of $Stationarity_{in/out}$, which tells us how the author is stable in relation to a set of co-authors and a set of used terms. Dynamic change centrality is defined in [5]. However, this centrality does not work with weighted graph. The change centrality of a node is a measure of the change of its connections over time, taking into account its adjacent nodes, the adjacent nodes of the latter and so on. The weight of changes of near and far neighbours depends on the choosing coefficients of the linear combination.

In this paper, a directed co-author network is constructed using context. Context is created by extracted terms which author used in titles of articles. Different sets of terms used by different authors then give the orientation and the weight in a new evaluation of relations in the co-author graph using the context. Therefore, a dynamics of evaluated directed network is determined not for the whole network or co-author communities, but for individual authors and their co-authors. Our proposed dynamic centrality describes the author influence into his/her neighbourhood ($Stationarity_{out}$) or the influence of his/her neighbourhood into the author ($Stationarity_{in}$).

This paper is organized as follows: The proposed approach of creation of context with a detailed description of the process which leads to a construction of new directed co-author network is presented in Section 2.2. Section 3 introduces principles of network's dynamic, dynamic evaluation of the neighbourhood of the selected author and our approach in the directed network created from DBLP and with the context. Experiments for directed co-author network with the context for finding dynamic centrality $Stationarity_{in/out}$ of selected author is presented in Section 4. A conclusions can be seen in Section 5.

2   Network with Context on the DBLP

This section describes the way how to create a homogeneous network of co-authors from the originally heterogeneous network DBLP. The evaluation of edges between the authors is represented by context based on the terms extracted from the article titles.

2.1   Digital Bibliography Library Project

DBLP (Digital Bibliography Library Project) is a computer science bibliography database hosted at University of Trier, in Germany. It was started at the end of 1993 and listed more than 2.3 million publications in May 2014. These articles were published in Journals such as VLDB, the IEEE and the ACM Transactions and Conference proceedings [10]. DBLP has been a credible resource for finding publications, its dataset has been widely investigated in a number of studies related to data mining and social networks to solve different tasks such as recommender systems, experts finding, name ambiguity, etc. Even though, DBLP dataset provides abundant information about author relationships, conferences, and scientific communities, it has a major limitation that is its records provide only the paper title without the abstract and index terms.

2.2   Author's Relationships with Context to Terms

We can create a one-mode graph from a bipartite graph [16], where the bipartite graph captures relations between to different types of groups (authors and their join publications). These author's relations would then be evaluated measuring the intensity of their shared activity. We have added context obtained from a data collection using term extraction [12] for the evaluation of relations.

Our method that we have used for more precise evaluation of the intensity of person's relations was to ascertain the context among authors and the terminology they used in article titles in DBLP.

We use terms for evaluation of the relation between co-authors. We extend standard evaluation of the relation, which is based on the number of the join publications or articles, by a factor that represent context between author and terms selected from the term set.

Term set is understood as a collection of all keywords, which are extracted from titles of articles. A detailed description of *term set* was published in [12].

Let A be a set of all authors in dataset. We define a single author A_i. For A_i, it is evaluated the strength of association with the other co-author. The strength of participation could be computed in a way that we go through all the author's publications while marking all the participated co-authors. Let set P be a set of all publications in DBLP and P_{A_i} be a set of all publications of author A_i.

The *Association* between the co-authors A_i and A_j can be defined by Jaccard coefficient that reflects mainly the proximity of both co-authors from number of their join publications:

$$Association(A_i, A_j) = \frac{|P_{A_i} \cap P_{A_j}|}{|P_{A_j}| + |P_{A_i}| - |P_{A_i} \cap P_{A_j}|} \tag{1}$$

If this method is applied to all the authors, we obtain weighted undirected graph of co-author network. This approach was inspired by [4].

If we define a set T as the set of all terms in the input text (titles of articles in DBLP) and T_{A_i} as the set of all the terms that could be found in titles of articles of author A_i, then t_k is the term belonging to the author A_i (t_k *in* T_{A_i}). Thus, we define (t_k *in* T_{A_i}) as the number of occurrences of term t_k in the input text T_{A_i}. This number is then approximated by the number of occurrences of term t_k in the all titles of articles (t_k *in* T). The higher value, the less relevant term t_k becomes. In addition, the result is approximated by T_{A_i}, because there is an assumption that T_{A_i}, which has a high cardinality, lower the importance of the individual terms, while low cardinality indicates that the author has only one subject matter. We can define the *relevance of author's terms* as:

$$R(A_i, t_k) = \frac{(t_k \; in \; T_{A_i})}{(t_k \; in \; T) + |T_{A_i}| - (t_k \; in \; T_{A_i})}. \tag{2}$$

And in normalized form:

$$R_{Norm}(A_i, t_k) = \frac{R(A_i, t_k)}{\max(R(A_i, t_1), \ldots, R(A_i, t_{|T_{A_i}|}))}. \tag{3}$$

The $ContextScore(A_i, A_j)$ of undirected edges is calculated by following Eq.4 for all terms in $(T_{A_i} \cup T_{A_j})$:

$$ContextScore(A_i, A_j) = ContextScore(A_j, A_i) = \tag{4}$$
$$= Association(A_i, A_j) \sum_{t_k \in (T_{A_i} \cup T_{A_j})} R_{Norm}(A_i, t_k) R_{Norm}(A_j, t_k)$$

These equations form an evaluation in undirected graphs, but do not describe sufficiently the situation in the co-author network. Relationships between co-authors are not equal in both directions. Due to this reason, we have created an evaluation for directed edges. The undirected relation weight includes relevancies of both authors in the evaluation of common relation (times *Association*). In directed graph, the relation weight includes only the relevance of one author (times *Association*) to define the influence (or power of the influence) of one author to another. Relevancy then represents the scope of his/her interest within the all terms.

Then the $ContextScoreD$ of directed edges is calculated by the next Eq. 5 for all terms in T_{A_i}:

$$ContextScoreD(A_i, A_j) = Association(A_i, A_j) \sum_{t_k \in T_{A_i}} R_{Norm}(A_i, t_k) \tag{5}$$

Similar situation is for the insufficient evaluation of edges due to time periods. A evaluation of edges in directed or undirected graphs depends on the time. Relationships between co-authors are not same in different time periods. So, we created an evaluation for edges in specified time periods. We calculate only with publications in the specified time period. The definition of the $Association(A_i, A_j)$ is extend to definition of the $Association(A_i, A_j, t_0, t_{max})$ where t_0 is the begin of the selected time period and the t_{max}

is the end of the selected time period and $P_{A_i}^{t_0,t_{max}}$ is the set of publications of author A_i in time period $< t_0, t_{max} >$.

$$Association(A_i, A_j, t_0, t_{max}) = \frac{|P_{A_i}^{t_0,t_{max}} \cap P_{A_j}^{t_0,t_{max}}|}{|P_{A_j}^{t_0,t_{max}}| + |P_{A_i}^{t_0,t_{max}}| - |P_{A_i}^{t_0,t_{max}} \cap P_{A_j}^{t_0,t_{max}}|} \qquad (6)$$

The *ContextScoreP* is calculated by the next Eq. 7 for selected time period and for terms used by author A_i in this time period $T_{A_i}^{t_0,t_{max}}$:

$$ContextScoreP(A_i, A_j, t_0, t_{max}) = \sum_{t_k \in T_{A_i}^{t_0,t_{max}}} ContextScoreP(A_i, A_j, t_k, t_0, t_{max}) \qquad (7)$$

3   Dynamic Network Analysis

Dynamic network analysis (DNA) varies from traditional social network analysis. DNA could be used for analysis of the non static information of nodes and edges of social network. DNA is a theory in which relations and strength of relations are dynamic in time and the change in the one part of the system is propagated through the whole system, and so on. DNA opens many possibilities to analyse and study the different parts of the social networks. It is possible study behaviour of individual communities, persons or the whole graph of the social network. We focus to analyse the behaviour of neighbourhood (exactly adjacent vertices) of selected author extracted from the network during a time period. The proposed approach which use dynamic metrics is inspired by work of Palla et al. [13].

The *AutoCorrelation* function $C(A_i, t_v, t)$ is used to quantify the relative overlap between two following neighbourhoods $N(A_i, t_v) = \{A_j; ContextScore(A_i, A_j, t_v) > 0\}$ of the same author A_i at t time steps apart:

$$C(A_i, t_v, t) = \frac{|N(A_i, t_v) \cap N(A_i, t_v + t)|}{|N(A_i, t_v) \cup N(A_i, t_v + t)|} \quad i = 1, \ldots, |A|, \qquad (8)$$

where $|N(A_i, t_v) \cap N(A_i, t_v + t)|$ is the number of common nodes (members) in $N(A_i, t_v)$ and $N(A_i, t_v + t)$, and $|N(A_i, t_v) \cup N(A_i, t_v + t)|$ is the number of nodes in the union of $N(A_i, t_v)$ and $N(A_i, t_v + t)$.

Palla et al. [13] evaluate communities in the network using *AutoCorrelation* function. However, we are interested in dynamics of individual nodes in the network and their neighbourhood rather then dynamics of different communities in the network. Therefore, we have defined *Stationarity* for $N(A_i, t_v)$, a set of the all neighbour nodes.

Provided that we consider for each moment an unitary relation weight $w(A_i, A_j, t_v) = 1$ then Eq. 8 can be modified to Eq. 9:

$$C(A_i, t_v, t) = \frac{|N(A_i, t_v) \cap N(A_i, t_v + t)|}{|N(A_i, t_v) \cup N(A_i, t_v + t)|} = \qquad (9)$$

$$= \frac{\sum_{A_j \in (N(A_i, t_v) \cup N(A_i, t_v + t))} w(A_i, A_j, t_v) w(A_i, A_j, t_v + t)}{\sum_{A_j \in (N(A_i, t_v) \cup N(A_i, t_v + t))} (\max(w(A_i, A_j, t_v), w(A_i, A_j, t_v + t)))^2}$$

Then consider, that the time axis is equidistantly divided into the years, for example $t_0 = 2000, t_1 = 2001, \ldots, t_{max} = 2014$ and t is 1 year. The *Stationarity* of neighbourhood of author A_i is defined as the average *AutoCorrelation* between subsequent states:

$$\zeta(A_i) = \frac{\sum_{t_v=t_0}^{t_{max}-1} C(A_i, t_v, t)}{t_{max} - 1 - t_0}, \tag{10}$$

where t_0 denotes the begin of the observation, t_{max} is the end of the observation and t is a step. Thus, $(1 - \zeta)$ represents the average ratio of members changed in the period [13].

Authors of the paper [13] found that the auto-correlation function decays faster for the larger communities, showing that the membership of the larger communities is changing at a higher rate. In contrast, they said that small communities change at a smaller rate with their composition being more or less static. The *Stationarity* was used to quantify static aspect of community evolution.

We extend our approach for the directed network with context which is created from terms. We look on the *Stationarity* of neighbourhood from directed point of view. The directed edges evaluated by $ContextScoreD(A_i, A_j)$ describe the influence power of author A_i into author A_j. AutoCorrelation is defined by a number of neighbours of the selected node. Due to this reason, the original definition would be $C_{in} = C_{out}$. However, this approach is not sufficient. Therefore, we have decided to eliminate a specific amount of edges by the following rules:

- determine $diff_{ij} = |ContextScoreD(A_i, A_j) - ContextScoreD(A_j, A_i)|$ for all $i, j = 1, \ldots, |A|$.
- create distribution of the differences $diff_{ij}$ and select the value $bound = 0.01$ as threshold.
- if $diff_{ij} < bound$ then same edges remain with $ContextScoreD(A_i, A_j)$ and $ContextScoreD(A_j, A_i)$ else delete weaker directed edge and stronger edge has a new weight $w(strongerEdge) - w(weakerEdge)$.

We have left the edges in both directions, if the authors influence each other by the nearly same power. If one of the authors influences the other *bound* more, the stronger edge has been left during the reduction.

Then we definite the AutoCorrelation in directed way by the Eq.11 The *AutoCorrelation* function $C_{in/out}(A_i, t_v, t)$ is used to quantify the relative overlap of directed weighted edges between two neighbourhoods $N_{in/out}(A_i, t_v) = \{A_j; ContextScore(A_{j/i}, A_{i/j}, t_v) > 0\}$ of the same author A_i at t time steps apart:

$$C_{in/out}(A_i, t_v, t) = \frac{|N_{in/out}(A_i, t_v) \cap N_{in/out}(A_i, t_v + t)|}{|N_{in/out}(A_i, t_v) \cup N_{in/out}(A_i, t_v + t)|} \quad i = 1, \ldots, |A|. \tag{11}$$

The *StationarityD* of neighbourhood of author A_i in directed graph is defined as the average *AutoCorrelation* between subsequent states:

$$\zeta_{in/out}(A_i) = \frac{\sum_{t_v=t_0}^{t_{max}-1} C_{in/out}(A_i, t_v, t)}{t_{max} - 1 - t_0}, \tag{12}$$

The more increases $C_{in}(A_i, t_0, t)$, the more dynamically is A_i influenced by its neighbourhood. If $\zeta_{in}(A_i) = 1$ then the influence of neighbourhood into A_i is more static in time. If $\zeta_{in}(A_i) < 1$ then the influence of neighbourhood is more dynamic.

The more increases $C_{out}(t)$, the more dynamic is the influence of A_i into its neighbourhood. If $\zeta_{out}(A_i) = 1$ then the influence of A_i into its neighbourhood is more static. If $\zeta_{out}(A_i) < 1$ then the influence of A_i into its neighbourhood is more dynamic.

4 Experiments

In general, *Stationarity* described in Section 3 determines the dynamics or the statics of the author's neighbourhood. We have generated weighted directed co-author graphs for each year from 1980 to 2014 in the experiments. The first phase of the experiments was focused on directed edges weighted by context $ContextScoreP(A_i, A_j, t_0, t_{max})$, see Eq. 7. Such obtained graphs contained two edges with opposite directions and with different evaluation between each two co-authors. As the edge evaluation is given by context, we can claim that the edge direction for each author express his/her influence to his/her co-authors (out) or the influence of his/her co-authors to him/her (in). Based on the consideration about the graph reduction and the reduction of less important edges due to obtaining a real image of the author's neighbourhood, we have defined $diff_{ij} = 0,01$ and have removed the edges according to the method described in Section 3. Then, we have calculated for selected authors $AutoCorrelation_{in/out}$, see Eq. 11 and $Stationarity_{in/out}$, see Eq. 12.

Based on the idea that the edge direction between the authors defines the influence of his/her publication activity to his/her co-authors, we have to explain the meaning of $Stationarity_{in}$ and $Stationarity_{out}$. $Sationarity_{in}$ in this case means the measure of stability or dynamics of the neighbourhood, which has the influence to the selected author. $Sationarity_{out}$ in this case means the measure of stability or dynamics of the neighbourhood, to which the selected author has the influence. Tab. 1 shows the values of $AutoCorrelation_{in}$ and $AutoCorrelation_{out}$ for the selected author A6. As we can see, the values did not much changed for the author A6 during the years 2008-2013. Moreover, the values of $AutoCorrelation_{in/out}$ are very close for each year. That means that neighbourhood N_{in} and N_{out} has changed in a relatively similar way in time. In addition, we can notice that the values of $AutoCorrelation_{in/out}$ were for the author A6 the lowest in years 2011 - 2012. This means that the author has changed the group of co-authors during this time period. Therefore, his/her neighbourhood seems to be more dynamical.

Table 1. $AutoCorrelation_{in/out}$ for selected author A6 and selected times

AutoCorrelation	2008-2009	2009-2010	2010-2011	2011-2012	2012-2013
C_{in}	0.24242	0.23333	0.22222	0.11363	0.22727
C_{out}	0.24137	0.20689	0.20454	0.09302	0.22727

We have concentrated on several selected authors during last years in the experiments. Table 2 and Table 3 show the selected authors and their $Stationarity_{out}$ and $Stationarity_{in}$ for different time periods. The values of $Stationarity_{out}$ and $Stationarity_{in}$ determine a neighbour stability of selected authors for particular time periods.

The selection of the authors was not random; we have selected the authors, whose publication activity is known for us, and for whom we also know their co-authors. We also have selected the authors with different publication activity. Due to this selection, we have ensured the suitable test data collection which we are able to intuitively assess and verify.

However, in our experiments, we do not use IDs nor author names, but we have done anonymisation by our own identification A1-A6.

We can see the values of $Stationarity_{in}$ and $Stationarity_{out}$ for the author A1 in Tab. 2 and Tab. 3. The values are absolutely identical, which in our evaluation means that the dynamics of the neighbourhood that influences the author A1 and the dynamics of the neighbourhood that the author A1 influences is the same. Since the values are small, we are talking about a relatively dynamic neighbourhood of the author A1. Very similar situation is for the author A2 with the difference that his/her neighbourhood is more stable then the neighbourhood of the author A1. Observing the author A3, see Tab. 3, we can find the gradual increase of the values of $Stationarity_{out}$. This can be interpreted as a possible stabilisation of the neighbourhood, to which has the author A3 influence. It can be possible to predict its better stabilisation in the future. Considering the neighbourhood, which has the influence to the author A3, we can see in Tab. 2 that $Staionarity_{in}$ stays nearly on the same value during the analysed time period. That means that the co-author community of the author A3 that influences him/her is permanently dynamic and do not stabilises.

Table 2. $Stationarity_{in}$ for selected authors and selected time period

Author	$\zeta_{in}2005 - 2010$	$\zeta_{in}2006 - 2011$	$\zeta_{in}2007 - 2012$	$\zeta_{in}2008 - 2013$
A1	0.17334	0.17123	0.16423	0.16728
A2	0.22614	0.23612	0.22833	0.21554
A3	0.24186	0.27344	0.27344	0.29395
A4	0	0	0.08	0.18
A5	0	0	0	0.033
A6	0.22051	0.21232	0.180505	0.20777

Table 3. $Stationarity_{out}$ for selected authors and selected time period

Author	$\zeta_{out}2005 - 2010$	$\zeta_{out}2006 - 2011$	$\zeta_{out}2007 - 2012$	$\zeta_{out}2008 - 2013$
A1	0.17334	0.17123	0.16423	0.16728
A2	0.21446	0.22445	0.22375	0.21554
A3	0.22282	0.24504	0.23852	0.24236
A4	0	0	0.08	0.18
A5	0	0	0	0.075
A6	0.19422	0.19068	0.16129	0.19462

5   Conclusion

In the paper, the authors proposed a modified method for determination of *Stationarity* in a directed network. As the edge evaluation by *ContextScoreD* means the knowledge scope, which one author can provide the other author, the *Stationarity_out* during the time corresponds with the influence power, which one author could have to the other co-authors. Contrary to the previous statement, *Stationarity_in* during the time corresponds with influence power from the other co-authors to the given author. Presented experiments show that the stability measure of the selected authors is low and the set of co-authors change in time. Moreover, the influence power of the author to his/her neighbourhood differs from the influence power from his/her neighbourhood to the author. We intent to focus on other types of weighted directed networks, in which is important to determine *Stationarity* of its members in the future.

Acknowledgments. This work was supported by the European Regional Development Fund in the IT4Innovations Centre of Excellence project (CZ.1.05/1.1.00/02.0070) and the national budget of the Czech Republic via the Research and Development for Innovations Operational Programme, by the project New creative teams in priorities of scientific research (reg. no. CZ.1.07/2.3.00/30.0055), supported by Operational Programme Education for Competitiveness, and co-financed by SGS, VSB - Technical University of Ostrava, Czech Republic, under the grant No. SP2014/154 Complex network analysis and prediction of network object behavior.

References

1. Backstrom, L.: Group formation in large social networks: membership, growth, and evolution, pp. 44–54. ACM Press (2006)
2. Barabâsi, A.-L., Jeong, H., Néda, Z., Ravasz, E., Schubert, A., Vicsek, T.: Evolution of the social network of scientific collaborations. Physica A: Statistical Mechanics and its Applications 311(3), 590–614 (2002)
3. Belykh, I., di Bernardo, M., Kurths, J., Porfiri, M.: Evolving dynamical networks. Physica D: Nonlinear Phenomena 267(Complete), 1–6 (2014)
4. Ding, Y.: Scientific collaboration and endorsement: Network analysis of coauthorship and citation networks. Journal of Informetrics 5(1), 187–203 (2011)
5. Federico, P., Pfeffer, J., Aigner, W., Miksch, S., Zenk, L.: Visual Analysis of Dynamic Networks Using Change Centrality, pp. 179–183. IEEE (2012)
6. Gupta, M., Aggarwal, C.C., Han, J., Sun, Y.: Evolutionary clustering and analysis of bibliographic networks. In: 2011 International Conference on Advances in Social Networks Analysis and Mining (ASONAM), pp. 63–70. IEEE (2011)
7. Joseph, A.C., Chen, G.: Composite centrality: A natural scale for complex evolving networks. Physica D: Nonlinear Phenomena 267, 58–67 (2014)
8. Koenig, M.D., Tessone, C.J.: Network evolution based on centrality. Physical Review E 84(5) (2011)
9. Lerman, K., Ghosh, R., Kang, J.H.: Centrality metric for dynamic networks. In: Proceedings of the Eighth Workshop on Mining and Learning with Graphs, pp. 70–77. ACM (2010)
10. Ley, M.: The DBLP computer science bibliography: Evolution, research issues, perspectives. In: Laender, A.H.F., Oliveira, A.L. (eds.) SPIRE 2002. LNCS, vol. 2476, pp. 1–10. Springer, Heidelberg (2002)

11. Y.-r. Lin. Facetnet: A framework for analyzing communities and their evolutions in dynamic networks. Social Networks, pp. 685–694 (2008)
12. Minks, S., Martinovic, J., Drázdilová, P., Slaninová, K.: Author cooperation based on terms of article titles from dblp. In: IHCI 2011 (2011)
13. Palla, G., Barabási, A.-L., Vicsek, T.: Quantifying social group evolution. Nature 446, 664–667 (2007)
14. Sun, Y., Barber, R., Gupta, M., Aggarwal, C.C., Han, J.: Co-author relationship prediction in heterogeneous bibliographic networks. In: 2011 International Conference on Advances in Social Networks Analysis and Mining (ASONAM), pp. 121–128. IEEE (2011)
15. Sun, Y., Tang, J., Han, J., Gupta, M., Zhao, B.: Community evolution detection in dynamic heterogeneous information networks. In: Proceedings of the Eighth Workshop on Mining and Learning with Graphs, MLG 2010, pp. 137–146. ACM, New York (2010)
16. Zweig, K.A., Kaufmann, M.: A systematic approach to the one-mode projection of bipartite graphs. Social Network Analysis and Mining 1(3), 187–218 (2011)

Towards a Conceptual Search
for Vietnamese Legal Text

Thinh D. Bui, Son T. Nguyen, and Quoc B. Ho

Faculty of Information Technology, University of Science, Ho Chi Minh City, Vietnam
{bdthinh,ntson,hbquoc}@fit.hcmus.edu.vn

Abstract. In this paper, a system of search engine is built based on documents of Vietnamese legal system. The key factor of this system is the ability of indexing documents in several aspects: not only on the whole text but also on logical structures and ontologies of Vietnamese legal documents. There are two important phases in the system; firstly, focusing on the recognition of the structure of Vietnamese legal text and the extraction of ontology of documents stored in the database of Vietnam Ministry of Justice; secondly, building an automated information retrieval system for the advanced search on demand of Vietnamese citizens. We study Vietnamese legal domain in both linguistic features and patterns of recognition. Experimental result on recognizing logical structures got of 64.37% on assumption annotation, 64.15% on provision annotation and 75.76% on sanction annotation in the $F_{\beta=1}$ score on the pre-built corpus of Vietnamese Enterprise Law articles. We also evaluated the precision of classifying ontology concepts and got 86.4 % in result on testing sample set of Vietnamese legal ontology. The goal is that a search engine is proposed with indexed logical and semantic properties based on works of the first phase.

Keywords: legal text processing, legal text mining, legal ontology, information retrieval.

1 Introduction

Legal texts are a kind of document with specific characteristics, which is different from other daily-used documents due to their length and complexity [1][2]. It is very important to be able to structure and extract information automatically from legal texts containing legal articles and cases in order to meet two clearly predefined goals [3]; firstly, supporting experts to establish complete and consistent laws and secondly deploying information systems which help citizens understand laws more effectively.

In syntactic aspect, our study of Vietnamese legal texts leads to a judgment that the law sentences and paragraphs have some specific structures [1][2]. In most cases, an article which is compound by one or many sentences can regularly be divided into two of three parts: the assumption part, the provision part, and the sanction part [4]. Recognizing the logical structures of legal articles is an

K. Saeed and V. Snášel (Eds.): CISIM 2014, LNCS 8838, pp. 175–185, 2014.
© IFIP International Federation for Information Processing 2014

important task to understand the meaning of legal domain and a preliminary step in problems such as translating a legal article into the logical form, legal text summarization, and question-answering in this domain [3]. In a legal article, the assumption part usually describes the subjects and cases in which the law can be applied, and the provision part tells mandatory regulations related to the subjects. The sanction part describes a forceful penalties in cases the subjects contravene the provision which is applied to them [4]. Therefore, the outputs of recognition of logical structures of legal text is very helpful to citizens who want to understand the law: what a legal article says, or which cases the law can be applied, or which subjects related to provision or sanction described in the legal article [1][2].

Moreover, since legal domain is highly entangled with common sense views on the nature of social events, roles, and actions, the task of building legal ontologies is essential to cover the understanding of these concepts and to help legal documents be machine readable. We presently aim to build a fulfilled Enterprise Law ontology on a schema as a subtree of LKIF core ontology schema [5][6].

In this paper, we present a conceptual search for Vietnamese legal text which use logical and semantic annotations. We also implement a system based on an open-source search engine and evaluate this system by Precison at k method [7].

The remains of this paper are organized as follows. Firstly, Section 2 present the related work on legal texts. Next, we describe the conceptual search and an information retrieval (IR) system implemented on a database of Vietnamese Enterprise legal documents in Section 3. Then, Section 4 presents some experiments on each phase of our system. Finally, conclusion and future work are presented in Section 5.

2   Related Works

According to our study of Vietnamese Law, Vietnamese legal documents have been composed carefully by experts, include a large amount of clear concepts and have some specific structures [4]. The language presented in these legal documents is Vietnamese written language which is used officially by the Vietnamese Government to ensure the seriousness, accuracy and consistency of these documents. As experts recommend, a law article regularly be analyzed into logical part annotations including the assumption part, the provision part, and the sanction part [4]. Our view on the recognition of logical structure of Vietnamese Law is closed to the latest research of authors in [1][2]. There might be some differences in the structure of legal documents of each nation but the background, motivation and target is the same.

In [1], the authors divided a law sentence into two parts: a requisite part and an effectuation part. These two parts again are composed of three parts: a topic part, an antecedent part, and a consequent part and there are 4 cases have been made from this composing. The authors presented how to model the task as a sequence learning problem. The model is experimented on an annotated corpus of Japanese national pension law sentences. Then, with the logical part annotations along with using natural language processing (NLP) techniques, the field of AI and Law – Legal Engineering can address a range of problems aiming to achieve a trustworthy electronic society [3].

While legal documents are always concerned with constraining and controlling social activities using documented norms, they are still lack of ontologies, in comparison with other domains such as medicine, engineering, or psychology [5]. In [5], the authors claimed that legal ontologies are about identifying concepts rather than recognizing any types of knowledge or reasoning roles. Any foundation ontology including notions about agent, actions, time, space ... should be constructed to be able to model and understand legal domain. Although there were some available foundation ontologies such as the CYC upper ontology and the IEEE-Standard Upper Ontology (SUO) but they are not sufficiently covering this domain []. The core ontologies about law can be mentioned such as FOLaw and followed by LRI-core [5][6]. In particular, the LRI core presents three layers of abstraction: the foundation ontology containing general concepts, the core-ontology containing typical concepts for law, and the specific domain-ontology (enterprise, criminal law as case studied)[5]. Next to LRI core, a legal core ontology called Legal Knowledge Interchange Format (LKIF) is developed in Estrella project, contains basic concepts for law with a considerable number of terms [6].

Until now, there are several approaches to ontology design and development mentioned in [8][6]: top-down approach, bottom-up approach and the hybrid approach called "middle-out". With the logical part annotations and ontology annotations along with using natural language processing techniques, the field of AI and Law can address a range of problems such as translating a legal rule into a logical form, question answering in legal domains, automated knowledge extraction from legal texts [3].

In Vietnam, it is still lack of legal domain ontology since the legal processing has not been started. The search engines on Vietnamese legal documents just simply treat legal documents as normal text. Based on our knowledge, it is the first research on semantic aspects of Vietnamese legal text.

3 A Conceptual Search for Vietnamese Legal Text

Our conceptual search for Vietnamese legal text is proposed based on results of two main tasks: structuring legal texts and building legal domain ontology. This search is deployed as an IR system. We firstly present the overall architecture of IR system in Section 3.1. Then, two main tasks would be presented in Section 3.2 and Section 3.3.

3.1 IR System Architecture

The architecture of proposed IR system has two isolated phases which are shown in Figure 1.

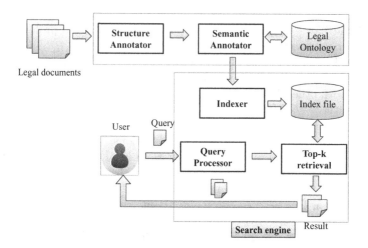

Fig. 1. IR System Architecture

In the first phase, there are two main components as follows:

(1) Structure annotator: is built in order to analyze the logical structures of Vietnamese Legal documents stored in law database of Vietnam Ministry of Justice.

(2) Semantic annotator: is consider as one component which takes responsibility for classifying the candidate terms and populating them into high level abstract concepts on our ontology schema, a subtree of LKIF core ontology schema [6][5]. An Enterprise Law ontology is gradually fulfilled and their instances would be matched backwards to documents to annotating them.

In the second phase, a search engine using Apache Lucene libraries [1] will be implemented based on the output of the previous phase. In particular, it would be a collection of annotated documents. An Indexer is used to index this collection and create index files on several fields: full content field, logical structure fields, and semantic concept fields.

The rest of the system is how the Query processor works on the input queries. Each query will be analyzed into a set of keywords (tokens). Next, proximity search method is used to increase the hits of relevant documents. Note that Top-k retrieval method with ranking score computed at Lucene matching model will be used also. A graphics interface is implemented to show out the results to user.

We should say that the core of this system is two main tasks in the first step that are describe below: (1) recognizing of logical structures of Vietnamese legal text; (2) building Vietnamese legal ontology based on LKIF core ontology.

---

[1] http://lucene.apache.org/

3.2   Recognition of Logical Structure of Vietnamese Legal Text

Our research on Vietnamese legal documents shows that only a few fundamental structures are used. Because legal texts are a kind of highly semantic and consistent document, we decide to apply a rule-based approach to recognize logical parts of text to annotate them based on regular expressions and linguistic features of Vietnamese legal documents.

The structure of legal documents in Vietnamese legal system can be described as follows: each document contains several chapters and each chapter includes at least one article. In some cases, a document contains only articles without any chapters. While analyzing legal articles which are the core of Vietnamese legal documents, we realize that an article is regularly divided into three types of logical part in different orders: the assumption part, the provision part, and the sanction part [4].

In the proposed approach, we study the sample patterns from Vietnam legal documents through analyzing their linguistic features. In particular, we use GATE framework [9] along with some NLP plugins such as ANNIE, VietNLP [2], Hash Gazetteer, and Java annotation patterns engine (JAPE). The input should be a Vietnamese legal text and it would be annotated with several annotation sets: chapter ($< chapter >$), article ($< article >$), assumption ($< a >$), provision ($< p >$), and sanction ($< s >$).

This annotating process is conducted based on the trigger sets which are transformed to hash gazetteers and the patterns written in JAPE transducer. One sample of patterns is presented in Table 1.

Table 1. A sample of pattern in regular expression

Pattern of Recognition
S1=
([<a> **ADV** VietToken* </a> *stopword* | " ,"])?
[<a> **AGENT** VietToken* </a>]
<p> **PROVISIONTRIGGER** VietToken* </p>
([<a> **ADV** VietToken* </a>])?

The trigger sets includes five kinds of tag as follows:

(1) *adv*: adverbs representing the situations of an assumption part.
(2) *agent*: nouns or noun phrases representing subjects and objects.
(3) *provisionPrefix*: verbs usually appearing in the beginning of a provision part.
(4) *provisionVerb*: main verbs usually appearing in a provision part.
(5) *sanctionVerb*: main verbs usually appearing in a sanction part.

---

[2] http://vlsp.vietlp.org:8080/demo/?page=resources

Note that mentioned-above *provisionTrigger* is composed of *provisionPrefix* and *provisionVerb*.

The output of these steps is an annotated text with logical structure annotation sets. Some annotated samples of article in Vietnamese and English are described in Table 2.

Table 2. Several samples of Vietnamese legal article (and in English)

Vietnamese	English
\<a\>Đối với Dự án trong Danh mục dự án đã công bố có từ 2 Nhà đầu tư trở lên cùng đăng ký thực hiện\</a\>, \<a\>Cơ quan nhà nước có thẩm quyền\</a\> \<p\> phải tổ chức đấu thầu rộng rãi trong nước hoặc quốc tế để lựa chọn Nhà đầu tư\</p\>.	\<a\> As concerned with the project in the publicized project directory which has been signed up to the development by at least 2 investors\</a\>, \<a\> authorized government offices \</a\> \<p\> have to give the bidding out the domestic or overseas public\</p\>.
\<a\>Tổ chức kinh tế hoạt động dưới danh nghĩa công ty nhà nước\</a\> mà \<a\>không có quyết định thành lập\</a\> thì \<s\>bị đình chỉ hoạt động và bị tịch thu tài sản nộp vào ngân sách nhà nước\</s\>.	\<a\>Business entity that operates under a state organization name \</a\> \<a\>without the establishment licenses \</a\> will \<s\> be suspended and all of its assets will be confiscated to contribute to the State Budget\</s\>.

3.3 Building Vietnamese Legal Ontology on LKIF Core Ontology Schema

The second task in the mentioned-above first phase is semantic annotating on legal concepts with corpus of Vietnamese Enterprise Law articles. This task is done by "middle-out" approach with four following steps: (1) ontology schema partial reuse; (2) chunk extraction; (3) candidate term selection; (4) term classification and population.

Firstly, we reuse a subtree of LKIF core-ontology schema[6] and do partial mapping to concepts in Vietnamese legal text, as described in Figure 2. The concepts at leaf nodes would be populated with terms. Then, the candidate terms which are extracted from the output of automatic linguistic analysis (chunking) will be selected to populated into classes of the ontology schema. This step is repeated to create a fulfilled ontology from Vietnamese Legal Text.

In the initial approach, noun chunks are chosen as candidate terms and we just use 5 concepts as main classes to classify terms. The rule to extract noun phrases is presented (in POS display) in Table 3.

Methods in [10] are used to select candidate terms by calculating phrases' N/NC value. The candidate ones will be classified into five main classes by a SVM classifier [3]: "Ca nhan" (*Personrole*), "Doanh nghiep" (*Enterpriserole*),

---

[3] http://www.csie.ntu.edu.tw/~cjlin/libsvmtools/

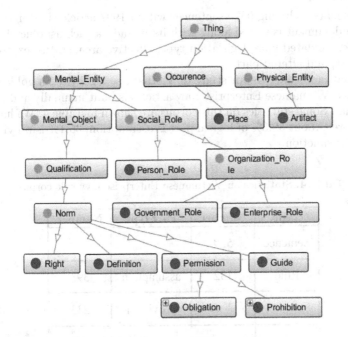

Fig. 2. Partial mapping from LKIF core ontology to Vietnamese Enterprise Law

Table 3. Pattern of Recognizing Noun Chunk

	Pattern of Recognition (in POS display)
Noun Chunk	(DETERMINER)*(NUMBER)*(ADJECTIVE)* <NOUN> (ADJECTIVE)* (ADVERB)*

"Nha nuoc" (*Governmentrole*), "Tai san" (*Artifact*), and "Noi chon" (*Place*). Finally, we will put legal terms into the ontology schema to form it gradually fulfilled.

4   Corpus and Evaluation Methods

This section presents our corpus for each task belongs to proposed framework and associated evaluation methods.

4.1   Vietnamese Legal Document Database and Training Corpus

We have implemented a semi-automated tool to collect and purge legal documents from Vietnam Ministry of Justice. A database of 83 Vietnamese Enterprise legal documents including 9379 sentences within 1997 articles is stored sustainably. Each document is stored along with its metadata such as: official number, issued date, validated date, legislation type, effective area, status, expired date, expired part, and altered part.

After that, according to our study of Vietnamese legal text, a golden corpus of annotated Vietnamese Enterprise Law articles is built manually and stored in XML format. Some statistics on this corpus are shown in Table 4. We have some remarks here. About 59.3% of logical part is assumption, 35.1% is provision and only 5.6% is sanction.

Table 4. Statistics on Vietnamese Enterprise Law rule corpus

Type	Number	Part type	Number
Sentence	529		
Rule	132	assumption	393
		provision	233
		sanction	37

4.2 The Task of Recognition of Logical Structure

We directly applied rule-based approach with our own recognition patterns to experiment the corpus. The results were evaluated using precision, recall and $F_{\beta=1}$ scores as follows [11]:

$$precision = \frac{\#correct\ parts}{\#predicted\ parts}$$

$$recall = \frac{\#correct\ parts}{\#actual\ parts}$$

$$F_{\beta=1} = 2 * \frac{precision * recall}{precision + recall}$$

A part is recognized correctly if and only if it has correct start word, correct end word and correct annotated type [1].

The result is shown in Table 5.

Table 5. Experiment result of rule-based approach

Annotation	Precision (%)	Recall (%)	$F_{\beta=1}$ (%)
assumption	67.13	61.83	64.37
provision	71.2	58.37	64.15
sanction	86.2	67.57	75.76

4.3 The Task of Ontology Instances Classification

On this task, there are 2733 noun chunks extracted from database of Vietnamese Enterprise Law and there are 299 candidate terms which are selected after that. In this experiment, we implemented SVM method with LIBSVM with a set of 5 linguistic features corresponding to each candidate term: character sequence, previous word, following word, previous part-of-speech, and following part-of-speech.

The training sample set and test sample set are built based on the above candidate terms with mentioned linguistic features. So, the size of training set reaches to 6500 samples. We also make a test set with 500 samples.

After training, the classifier achieved 86.4% in precision score with 432 correct samples over 500 test samples.

4.4 Evaluation on Information Retrieval System

We evaluated our IR system with the mentioned-above database. The range of criteria used for evaluation includes: on the whole document and on logical parts of the legal article.

In the first experiment, we used Precision at k method to identify the relative precision with proximity search function in Lucene framework to evaluate the system. The result is described in Table 6.

We have some remarks here about the correlation between Top k and word distance (in proximity search). The best precision is at case of $k = 30$ and $distance = 1$. In almost case, the precision goes down when distance increases. So, it is not effective with proximity search in Vietnamese legal texts. As table shows, when k increases to 30, the higher word distance lead to much worse precision.

In the second experiment, we performed searching on the whole document and on logical parts of the document with associated keywords. For example, a keywords set related to assumption will be used to evaluate system on two ranges of criteria: assumption and full-text. The result in Table 7 describes the percentage of relevant documents over all retrieval documents.

We should say that the result while searching on assumption part got lower precision than the result while searching on full-text. Note that we use a keywords

Table 6. Experiment result in case searching on the whole document

	Top k		
Word distance	K=10 (%)	K=20 (%)	K=30 (%)
1	56.00	**62.14**	**71.07**
2	54.00	59.93	70.00
3	60.00	57.75	59.69
4	**61.00**	58.10	59.05
5	**61.00**	57.18	59.64

Table 7. Experiment result in various range of criteria

		Keyword set		
		Assumption	*Provision*	*Sanction*
Range of criteria	*Assumption*	80%		
	Provision		63.33%	
	Sanction			64.67%
	Full-document	85%	62.22%	52%

set related to assumption here. The reason is the number of assumption is large but recognition of assumption part just got low precision.

5   Conclusion and Future Work

We presented a conceptual search for Vietnamese Legal text. This search is based on outputs of two main task: recognizing logical structures and building ontology of Vietnamese legal text. We implemented an information retrieval system using this conceptual search to work on documents stored in law database of Vietnam Ministry of Justice. With the input as a database of logical part annotated and semantic annotated legal documents, the system consists two phases that aim to retrieve most relevant documents; firstly, annotating logical parts and seman- tic concepts; secondly, using Lucene libraries to index on annotation fields and search with proximate range. Experiments on each individual phase showed that the task of recognizing can achieve positive result in $F_{\beta=1}$ score on Vietnamese legal article corpus and the classification model for Vietnamese Enterprise Law ontology got 86.4% in precision. The system is also evaluated by Precision at k method on other ranges of criteria. It is the baseline for future works on legal domain in Vietnam.

However, there are still some limitations in our research such as the small corpus and old methods utilized. Vietnamese legal ontology schema has been built but it is still lack of concepts. To get better result in further research, the corpus and ontology should be extended and state of the art methods should also be implemented. We also plan to extract verb phrases as candidate terms and expand the number of concepts in the ontology schema.

Acknowledgment. This work is supported by Vietnam National University, Ho Chi Minh City. We would like to thank Akira Shimazu and Nguyen Le Minh who has recommended this research topic to our research group at Information System department.

References

1. Bach, N.X., Nguyen, M.L., Shimazu, A.: Rre task: The task of recognition of requisite part and effectuation part in law sentences. Int. J. Comput. Proc. Oriental Lang. 23(2), 109–130 (2011)
2. Nguyen, M.L., Bach, N.X., Shimazu, A.: Supervised and semi-supervised sequence learning for recognition of requisite part and effectuation part in law sentences. In: FSMNLP, pp. 21–29 (2011)
3. Nakamura, M., Nobuoka, S., Shimazu, A.: Towards translation of legal sentences into logical forms. In: Satoh, K., Inokuchi, A., Nagao, K., Kawamura, T. (eds.) JSAI 2007. LNCS (LNAI), vol. 4914, pp. 349–362. Springer, Heidelberg (2008)
4. Duong, T.N., Viet, N.C., Nghi, P.H., Vinh, V.K., Thong, L.M., Dong, N.V., Huong, N.V.: General Theory of State and Law (2004)
5. Breuker, J.: The construction and use of ontologies of criminal law in the ecourt european project. In: Proceedings of Means of Electronic Communication in Court Administration, pp. 15–40 (2003)
6. Hoekstra, R., Breuker, J., Bello, M.D., Boer, A.: Lkif core: Principled ontology development for the legal domain. In: Law, Ontologies and the Semantic Web, pp. 21–52 (2009)
7. Manning, C.D., Raghavan, P., Schütze, H.: Introduction to information retrieval. Cambridge University Press (2008)
8. Francesconi, E., Montemagni, S., Peters, W., Tiscornia, D.: Integrating a bottom-up and top–down methodology for building semantic resources for the multilingual legal domain. In: Francesconi, E., Montemagni, S., Peters, W., Tiscornia, D. (eds.) Semantic Processing of Legal Texts. LNCS, vol. 6036, pp. 95–121. Springer, Heidelberg (2010)
9. Cunningham, H., Maynard, D., Bontcheva, K., Tablan, V.: A framework and graphical development environment for robust nlp tools and applications. In: ACL, pp. 168–175 (2002)
10. Frantzi, K.T., Ananiadou, S., Mima, H.: Automatic recognition of multi-word terms: the c-value/nc-value method. Int. J. on Digital Libraries 3(2), 115–130 (2000)
11. Goutte, C., Gaussier, É.: A probabilistic interpretation of precision, recall and F-score, with implication for evaluation. In: Losada, D.E., Fernández-Luna, J.M. (eds.) ECIR 2005. LNCS, vol. 3408, pp. 345–359. Springer, Heidelberg (2005)

A Vietnamese Question Answering System in Vietnam's Legal Documents

Huu-Thanh Duong and Bao-Quoc Ho

Faculty of Information Technology, University of Science, VNU-HCM
dhthanhqa@gmail.com, hbquoc@hcmus.edu.vn

Abstract. In this paper, we develop a Vietnamese Question Answering system to answer simple questions about provisions, processes, procedures, and sanctions in law on enterprises Vietnam. Research to build a Vietnamese Question Answering system is more difficult than English Question Answering system because of lack of Vietnamese processing resources and tools, or their results isn't high. We have utilized available Vietnamese resources, tools and modified some tools (such as Lucene) and algorithms, which worked well in English, applies in Vietnamese. From that, we have proposed a similarity-based model to build a Vietnamese Question Answering system in Vietnam's legal documents, namely vLawyer system. In experimental section, we achieved promising result, about 70% precision in legal documents, it proved that our approach is reasonable in legal document domain.

Keywords: Question Answering, QA, Legal Document, Law on Enterprises, Information Retrieval, IR, Natural Language Processing.

1 Introduction

Today, the development of the information technology has made people overwhelmed in huge documents in the internet. The internet contains lots of useful documents for users, but it has also no less dirty ones. So, to utilize useful documents quickly and effectively, it has to be necessary to develop a system to satisfy those demands. A Question Answering (QA) system is the answer for that. It isn't like the information retrieval (IR) system, only returning a list of documents related to keywords of user's query, QA gives a succinct and short answer for a query as user's natural language. QA becomes a subject which has attracted lots of research groups. It is a system inherited from the information retrieval system, it helps text mining becomes more effectively, quickly and practically. While the English QA achieved lots of remarkable results, the Vietnamese QA has still been under development because there are lots of difficulties in lack of resources and tools to process natural language such as Chunker, Named Entity Recognition (NER), etc. In this paper, we want to utilize some available tools in Vietnamese natural language processing such as VietTokenizer, jvnTagger, etc and other tools such as Lucene which is a very strong tool to support to build information retrieval systems. Besides, we have also utilized ideas of some algorithms

K. Saeed and V. Snášel (Eds.): CISIM 2014, LNCS 8838, pp. 186–197, 2014.
© IFIP International Federation for Information Processing 2014

applied in English effectively such as KEA (Keyphrase Extraction Algorithm) to identify the keyphrases, this algorithm is cross-language. With limited resources and tools, we hope to have a little contribution to build a Vietnamese QA system. In this system, we develop a Vietnamese QA system bases on Vietnam's legal documents, especially as law on enterprises 2005.

The remaining of this paper is organized as followed: in next section, we present some related works for our system. In section 3, we introduce to overview about legal documents. And in section 4, we present our built system, namely vLawyer, including the theoretical basis to build our system and system architecture. Finally, in section 5, we present a case study, give the conclusion and future works.

2   Related Works

While the IR system had more and more exact results, the QA system has not still impressed results yet, especially as Vietnamese. However, developing Vietnamese QA system has had first-step respected results. We will show some achievements in developing Vietnamese QA system as followed:

Vu Mai Tran, Vinh Duc Nguyen, Oanh Thi Tran, Uyen Thu Thi Pham, Thuy-Quang Ha [3] studied to build a Vietnamese QA system in travel domain by incorporating Snowball methodology and relational extraction using search engines. The system, firstly, extracted patterns and tuples into dataset. This system supported to answer simple questions about entities relationship. When it received a user's query, it would extract entities and look for related candidate relations. Then, it calculated similarities between query vector and all patterns of candidate relations to choose the best pattern. Finally, it built a query to database by using entity information (E) and relation (R) to get tuples contained relation R and entity E. According to authors, this system achieved 89.7% precision and 91.4% ability to give the answer when testing on traveling domain.

Mai-Vu Tran, Duc-Trong Le, Xuan-Tu Tran, Tien-Tung Nguyen [4] built a Vietnamese person named entity question answering model. It's a closed QA answering person factoid questions (such as Who, Whose, Whom). The question processing model used CRF mechine learning algorithm and two automatic answering strategies: indexed sentences database-based and Google search engine-based. If answers were not found in database, the question would be pushed into Google search engine. The system filtered candidate answer   collection based on their similarities with question and assigned a priotity number to the candidate answers. Finally, the system ranked the answers and sent to user for final validation in order to extract the exact answer. According to authors, the system obtains 74.63% precision and 87.9% ability to give the answer.

Dai Quoc Nguyen, Dat Quoc Nguyen, Son Bao Pham [5] proposed an ontoloy-based Vietnamese question answering system that allowed users to make a query in natural language. It included two components: question processing and answer retrieval. They built a set of relations in the ontology that included only two person relations. According to authors, results were relatively high, the Question Analysis module and the Answer Retrieval module achieve an accuracy of 95% and 70% respectively, 5% remaining errors are due to the lack of coverage of their Jape grammars in the pattern-matching module. However, the cost for building the database was high.

Dang-Tuan Nguyen and Ha Quy-Tinh Luong [9] built a system to search courses in Vietnam OpenCourseWare program, it allowed users to input question in vietnamese natural language. It, firstly, extracted terms from VOCW pages and stored in ontology-based knowledge. When it received user's query, the system would analysis question parser based on the set of defined syntax rules and build a query in SPAEQL to get data on VOCW ontology.

Dang Truong Son, Dao Tien Dung [11] built a Vietnamese QA system by mapping user's query with questions in a defined dataset as couples of question/answer which were extracted from the internet. With returned answers, authors hope that one of them will satisfy user's demand. According to authors, they extracted 90000 couples of question/answer from Yahoo Answer and also got 50 questions randomly for testing, they obtained higher results compared with answering results from Yahoo.

From these systems, we try to build a question answering system in a relatively popular and useful domain, namely legal documents, based on similarities between documents with using $tf \times idf$ weight and latent semantic indexing.

3 Vietnam's Legal Documents

In this section, we introduce overview of Vietnam's legal documents and a legal structure. According to Law No. 17/2008/QH12: "Legal documents are documents issued or jointly issued by state agencies in accordance with the authority, formats, sequence of steps and procedures prescribed in this Law or the Law on the Promulgation of Legal Documents of People's Councils and People's Committees, which includes common rules of conducts, which has compulsory effectiveness and the implementation of which is guaranteed by the Government to regulate social relations.". The system of legal documents includes (in order of legal priority):

- Constitution, laws and resolutions of the National Assembly.
- Ordinances and resolutions of the Standing Committee of the National Assembly.
- Orders and decisions of the State President.
- Decrees of the Government.
- Decisions of the Prime Minister.
- Resolutions of the Justices' Council of the Supreme People's Court and circulars of the Chief Justice of the Supreme People's Court.
- Circulars of the President of the Supreme People's Procuracy.
- Circulars of Ministers or Heads of Ministry-equivalent Agencies.
- Decisions of the State Auditor General.
- Joint resolutions of the Standing Committee of the National Assembly or the Government and the central offices of socio-political organizations.

- Joint circulars of the Chief Justice of the Supreme People's Court and the President of the Supreme People's Procuracy; those of Ministers or Heads of Ministry equivalent Agencies and the Chief Justice of the Supreme People's Court, the President of the Supreme People's Procuracy; those of Ministers or Heads of Ministry-equivalent Agencies.
- Legal documents of People's Councils and People's Committees.

A legal document content is divided by levels: chapters, sections, articles, clauses of an article, each clause can contain small sentences. When extracting legal documents from Ministry of Justice's website, the system also gets these documents and bases on this priority to assign a boost value to documents when indexing documents with Lucene. A legal structure includes: assumption, provision and sanction.

- Assumption designates situations (conditions and circumstances) which can occur in practice.
- Provision is subject's behaviors when it faces the situation which is mentioned in assumption section.
- Sanction gives penalities if the subject does not perform rightly what the provision section designated in the situation of the assumption section.

When extracting candidate passages, the system will get an article or a clause of the article or a sentence of the clause of the article, namely a legal.

4   vLawyer System

We named the system as vLawyer (Virtual Lawyer), this is a Vietnamese question answering system to answer simple questions about Vietnam's law on enterprises text. Questions can mention about provisions, processes, procedures and sanctions in law on enterprises. The system allows a question as natural language and the answer is an relevant article or a clause of the article or a sentence of the clause of the article.

4.1   Theoretical Basis

Document Preparation

A legal document must be concise, clear and conform. Thus, it's necessary to choose reliable sources to extract. We choose Vietnam Ministry of Justice's website to extract laws, decrees, circulars, decisions that are still validity or partially validity. All of documents were converted to lowcases and tokenized and tagged Pos by VietTokenizer and jvnTagger [16] respectively.

This corpus will be bigger and bigger during user's searching process. If the system doesn't find the answer in current corpus, it will push query to Google search engine to get more documents from Vietnam Ministry of Justice's website.

At present, we extracted about 113 documents, including laws, decrees, circulars, decisions related to law on enterprise.

Lucene Tool

Lucene [1] is a free and strong open-source information retrieval software library, developed by Dough Cutting. This library includes basic functions for indexing and searching. Lucene responses results quickly from a big set of files because Lucene searching bases on documents' index, but not simple to search on text directly. Lucene has chosen by lots of researchers because it's simple, effective and cross-language.

In Lucene, the unit of searching and indexing is documents. A document has lots of fields, each field is a couple of name/value. Indexing in Lucene is to create the document with one or lots of fields. To index the text, Lucene extracts the keywords and removes stopwords, keywords are created inverted index and stored into each segment for searching.

After indexing documents, we can search with Lucene based indexed results. Searching in Lucene bases on a list of keywords and logic operators (*AND, OR, NOT*). When searching, users must designate a field to search and make a query, Lucene uses this query to search results for user, based on ranking the similarity scores between documents and the query.

In this system, we use the set of documents extracted from Vietnam Ministry of Justice's website and they are tokenized by VietTokenizer and indexed by Lucene. When the system receives user's query, it will extract keyphrases/keywords and search relevant documents by using Lucene.

Term Weight

Three following weights are used the most in term weights:

- Term Frequency (*tf*): A number of times of a term appear in a document. It gives measure of importance of the term within the particular document.
- Document Frequency (*df*): A number of documents contain a term. It gives measure of distribution of the term in document collection.
- Collection Frequency (*cf*): The sum of term frequency of a term appears in all of documents of the collection.

tf×*idf* weight:

- Inverse Document Frequency (*idf*) is a measure of general importance of the term. We can use the following formular to calculate *idf*:

$$idf = \frac{N}{df_t}$$

where N is the number of documents in collection, df_t is document frequency of term t.

- $tf \times idf$ meanings: If the term appears lots of times within a document (*tf* is high), that term is able to be a keyword in that document. However, if that term also appears lots of times in various documents (*df* is also high), then it may be a common term (less meaningful) such as "và" ("and"), "hoặc" ("or"), ... When *idf* has responsible of descending the score of that term. This weight can be calculated as followed:

$$w(t, d) = \begin{cases} \left(1 + \log(tf_{t,d})\right)\log\dfrac{N}{df_t}, & if \ tf_{t,d} \geq 1 \\ 0, & if \ tf_{t,d} = 0 \end{cases}$$

Latent Semantic Indexing (LSI)
LSI is an approach to index automatically by mapping documents and terms into *LSI* space. The mapping way bases on a concept, namely Singular Value Decomposition (*SVD*). *SVD* is the way to reduce multi-dimension data, reduce a big data so that the remainder only focuses on necessary data   from original data. *LSI* solves two problems in vector space as synonymy and polysemy.

We perform to decompose term-document matrix into smaller matrixes. To do that, we use *SVD*: $C = U.S.V^T$ (where C namely a term-document matrix), where:

- U matrix is a matrix which each row is a vector of each term.
- V^T matrix is matrix which each column is a vector of each document.
- S matrix is a diagonal matrix with descending singular value, it gives importance of each dimension.

Reducing SVD: We only retain k singular value, the remainder values are assigned 0 $(k < min(M, N))$. When S matrix is $k{\times}k$, U matrix is $M{\times}k$, V^T matrix is $k{\times}N$, C_k matrix in *LSI* space is $M{\times}N$. We use *SVD* to calculate C_k matrix. Calculating similarities on C_k matrix will be more reliable result than on C matrix.

Noun Phrase and Verb Phrase
A Vietnamese noun phrase has overview of the structure as followed:
　　　　<previous sub-section> <center noun> <post sub-section>
Example: "mái tóc đẹp" (a beautiful hair), noun "tóc" (hair) is a center noun, "mái" is a previous sub-section, "đẹp" is post sub-section.

It notes that a noun phrase is able to be the lack of previous sub-section or post sub-section, but unable to be the lack of the center noun.

Based on this base and refer to [7], we chose the following patterns to extract Vietnamese noun phrases:

- *Noun + Noun.* Example: thủ_tướng chính_phủ (Prime Minister)
- *Noun + Noun + Noun.* Example: thống_đốc ngân_hàng nhà_nước (State Bank Governor)
- *Noun + Adjective.* Example: doanh_nghiệp lớn (a large enterprise)
- *Noun + Noun + Adjective.* Example: doanh_nghiệp tư_nhân lớn (a large private Enterprise)
- *Noun + Verb.* Example: giấy giới_thiệu (letter of recommendation)

- *Noun + Verb + Noun.* Example: dịch_vụ chứng_thực chữ_ký (signature authorization service)

The same as verb phrase, the overview of the structure as followed:

<previous sub-section> <center verb> <post sub-section>

In our using scope, we defined the following patterns to extract verb phrase:

- *Verb + Noun.* Example: đăng_ký doanh_nghiệp (enterprise registration)
- *Verb + Verb.* Example: thanh_toán chuyển_khoản (transfer payment)
- *Verb + Adjective.* Example: xử_lý nhanh (quick process)
- *Verb + Verb + Noun.* Example: đầu_tư phát_triển cơ_sở_hạ_tầng (invested in infrastructure development)

Besides, when extracting noun phrases and verb phrases, we also use the following rules:

- A phrase cannot start or end by stopwords, also contain special characters.
- A phrase has maximum length as 3.
- Using *idf* assigns score to the phrase to give the importance of the term in collection.

Based on documents were extracted on Vietnam Ministry of Justice's website, we extracted the set of 24771 two-terms phrases (both noun phrases and verb phrases) and 10360 three-terms phrases (both noun phrases and verb phrases).

Other Resources

In limited period of time, we also made two files manually so that the system gives results better:

- The set of synonymy terms in law text.
- An ontology about lines of business.

4.2   System Architecture

The vLawyer system includes two components:

- Question processing: in this one, the system will convert the question to lowcases and remove stopwords, special words in user query. It also tokenizes, assigns POS tagger to query and extracts keyphrases/keywords to build into Lucene query to search relevant documents.
- Answer selection: Based on documents searched above phase, we extract articles to calculate similarities with user's query and incorporate some heuristics to choose the best answer. If the system cannot give the answer from the current corpus, it will push the query to Google search engine to find more documents to supplement in current corpus.

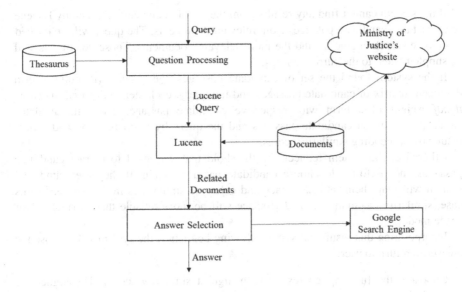

Fig. 1. System Architecture

Question Processing

The query will be converted to lowcases and tokenized by VietTokenizer, assigned POS Tag by jvnTagger and removed stopwords, special words and question words. Extracting keyphrases, they are noun phrases or verb phrases have:

- The higher is score, the better is keyphrases.
- Priority for two-words phrases. If a three-words phrase contains a two-words phrase, but the two-words phrase has a higher score than the three-words phrase, we choose the two-words phrase is keyphrases.

The remaining is keywords. Afterward, we get synonymy terms of extracted terms. We build into Lucene query to search relevant documents.

Answer Selection

We choose first top-ten documents which Lucene evaluates the best high score and perform to extract candidate passages in those documents. The candidate passage is able to be an article or a clause of the article or a small sentence of the clause of the article. They are extracted towards the following rules: When reading an article, the system calculates the similarity between the title of the article with the query, if the result is over a defined threshold, then it will extract the whole article as a candidate passage. Otherwise, it continues to read clauses 1, 2, ... of this article and each clause does the same as above to decide to choose that clause for candidate passage or not. If not, it will read smaller sentences of clause as a), b),... the process is the same as above. If it still does not choose any candidate passages, the article will be ignored and continue to read other articles. The process's performed like that until the end of the document.

If the system cannot find any results from the set of documents returned by Lucene or extract any candidate passages from relevant documents. The query will be pushed to Google search engine to find the more relevant documents. Those documents will be supplemented to the current corpus.

If the system found the set of candidate passages, the system will build a term document matrix of candidate passages and the query, each element of that matrix is *tf×idf* weight of a term with respective candidate passage. Then, it calculates similarities between candidate passages and the query by cosin function and orders results by descending similarity scores.

Otherwise, the system reduces the threshold that was used to extract candidate passages and performs to choose candidate passages again. If they are found, the system will map them into *LSI* space and calculate similarities in this space. In this case, similarity calculation is in *LSI* space will be more reliable than normal vector space model.

Incorporating this result and some following heuristics, the system will choose the answer to return to user:

- Choosing the first top-ten results with highest similarity scores. The higher the similarity score is between candidate passage and query, the more it is an answer.
- The more the candidate passage contains the keyphrases/ keywords of the query, the more it is the answer.
- If two candidate passages contain the same as a number of keyphrases/keywords, the system will choose the candidate passage of the shorter length.

From those, we build the following formula to choose answers:

$$Ans(Ca) = \alpha \times sim(Ca, Q) + (1 - \alpha) \times \frac{\sum score(K_i) \times num(Ca, K)}{len(Ca)}$$

Where *Ca*: the candidate passage; *Q*: the user query; *K*: the list of keyphrases or keywords extracted from the user's query; *sim(Ca, Q)*: the similarity score's between the candidate passage and user query; *num(Ca, K)*: A number terms of *K* which *Ca* contains; $\sum score(K_i)$: the sum of scores of terms of *K* which *Ca* contains.

We will choose first top-three results of *Ans(Ca_i)* score to give answers to user.

5 Experiment, Conclusion and Future Works

5.1 Experiment

We extracted about 113 documents, including laws, decrees, circulars, decisions. All of these documents were indexed by Lucene.

Based on these documents, we built the set of 24771 two-terms phrases (both noun phrases and verb phrases) and 10360 three-terms phrases (both noun phrases and verb phrases). They were used to extracted keyphrases or keywords of user's query.

We also build manually two resources: synonymy terms and ontology-based in law text.

To illuminate for our system model, we gives a following example: it assumes that user wants to query a question as: "Việc đăng ký thay đổi người đại diện theo pháp luật của công ty trách nhiệm hữu hạn, công ty cổ phần được pháp luật quy định như thế nào?" ("How to register the replacement of the legal representative of limited liability companies or joint-stock companies?")

This query will be converted into lowercase to tokenize and tag Pos as followed:

Q = "việc/N đăng_ký/V thay_đổi/V người/N đại_diện/V theo/V pháp_luật/N của/E công_ty_trách_nhiệm_hữu_hạn/N ,/, công_ty_cổ_phần/N được/V pháp_luật/N quy_định/V như_thế_nào/X"

Afterward, it will be removed stopwords, special words, question words to extract keyphrases and keywords. The result as followed:

- Noun phrase: người đại_diện,
- Verb phrase: đăng_ký thay_đổi
- Terms: pháp_luật, công_ty_trách_nhiệm_hữu_hạn, công_ty_cổ_phần

The system continue to get the synonymy terms of above terms and build a query and push to Lucene as followed:
("người đại_diện"~1 OR "chủ_sở_hữu"~) AND "đăng_ký thay_đổi"~1 AND "pháp_luật"~ AND ("công_ty tnhh"~1 OR "công_ty_trách_nhiệm_hữu_hạn"~) AND ("công_ty_cổ_phần"~ OR "công_ty cp"~1)

With the current corpus, Lucene searches 6 relevant documents, including (in order of descending scores):

- Decree No. 43/2010/NĐ-CP: Decree on Enterprise Registration, score = 0.43
- Circular No. 01/2013/TT-BKHĐT: Circular on Business Registration, score = 0.42
- Law No. 60/2005/QH11: Law on Enterprise 2005, score = 0.39
- Decree No. 102/2010/NĐ-CP: Decree Detailing a number of Articles of the Law on Enterprises, score = 0.26
- Decree No. 05/2013/NĐ-CP: Decree on amending and supplementing some Articles in the regulations on Administrative procedures stated in the decree No. 43/2010/NĐ-CP, score = 0.22
- Decree No. 59/2009/NĐ-CP: Decree on organization and operation of commercial Banks, score = 0.11

Then, the system will extract candidate passages from these documents, the system extracts 50 candidate passages. They will be calculated the similarity score with user query, the result as followed (in order of descending score):

- Article 43 of Decree No. 43/2010/NĐ-CP: "Registration of change of owner of single member limited liability company", score = 0.431
- Article 17 of circular No. 01/2013/TT-BKHĐT: "Dossier for change of legal repre-sentatives of limited liability companies and shareholding companies", score = 0.2321
- Article 18 of circular No. 01/2013/TT-BKHĐT: "Registration for change of the owner of an LLC1 because of the inheritance", score = 0.2229
- Article 38 of Decree No. 43/2010/NĐ-CP: "Registration of change of legal repre-sentative of limited liability company or shareholding company", score = 0.1991
- etc

The system will calculate other params in (*) and apply (*). As a result, it will give an answer to user as Article 17 of circular No. 01/2013/TT-BKHĐT and two reference answers: Article 18 of circular No. 01/2013/TT-BKHĐT and Article 43 of Decree No. 43/2010/NĐ-CP.

For testing, we got randomly 211 questions about law on enterprises and related law from reliable websites (such as Vietnam Ministry of Justice, vnexpress, ...) to test our system. We performed to match the result returned by our system and the answer of domain experts. We obtained the promising result, approximately 70% precision.

5.2   Conclusion and Future Works

In this paper, we presented an similarity-based approach for building the vLaywer system to answer questions about provisions, processes, procedures and sanctions in law on enterprises effectively. From [5][9], we also tried to build a ontology about lines of business manually. However, it's still small, so the results of some questions ,which related to establish lines of business, is not high. We will develop this in the future. Compare with [4][11] approaches, they also based on similarity between question and candidates or between question and other defined questions to choose answers for user's query, our obtained result is promising with the set of testing from internet randomly. With obtained results, it proved that our approach is reasonable.

We recognized if the set of synonymy terms and ontology in law text is larger, the result is higher. So, in the future, we will push more semantics into the system by developing ontology-based system and building synonymy corpus in legal documents automatically. Besides, we will broaden other laws and types of question.

References

1. Gospodnetíc, A., Hatcher, E.: Lucene in Action. Manning Publications Co. (2005)
2. Lê Thị Bích Ngọc, "Bài giảng: Pháp luật đại cương" , Posts and Telecommunications Institute of Technology, HCM city
3. Tran, V.M., Nguyen, V.D., Tran, O.T., Pham, U.T.T., Ha, T.-Q.: College of Technology, VNU Hanoi, VietNam: An Experimental Study of Vietnamese Question Answering System. In: 2009 International Conference on Asian Language Processing. (2009)
4. Tran, M.-V., Le, D.-T., Tran, X.-T., Nguyen, T.-T.: KTLab, University of Engineering And Technology: A Model of Vietnamese Person Named Entity Question Answering System. In: 26th Pacific Asia Conference on Language, Information and Computation, pp. 325–332.
5. Nguyen, D.Q., Nguyen, D.Q., Pham, S.B.: College of Technology Vietnam National University, Hanoi: A Vietnamese Question Answering System. In: International Conference on Knowledge and Systems Engineering (2009)
6. Phan, T.T., Nguyen, T.C., Huynh, T.N.T.: Question semantic analysis in vietnamese QA system. In: Nguyen, N.T., Katarzyniak, R., Chen, S.-M. (eds.) Advances in Intelligent Information and Database Systems. SCI, vol. 283, pp. 29–40. Springer, Heidelberg (2010)
7. Phú, D.: Research on application of frequent sets and association rules to semantic Vietnamese document classification. Science & Technology Development 9(2) (2006)

8. Son, D.T., Dung, D.T.: Apply A Mapping Question Approac. In: Building The Question Answering System For Vietnamese Language. Journal of Engineering Technology and Education, The, International Conference on Green Technology and Substainable Development (2013)
9. Nguyen, D.T., Luong, H.Q.-T.: Document Searching System based on Natural Language Query Processing for Vietnam Open Courseware Library. IJCSI International Journal of Computer Science Issues 6(2) (2009)
10. Nguyen, D.Q., Nguyen, D.Q., Pham, S.B.: A Knowledge-based QA System. In: Proc. Of KSE 2009, pp. 26–32. IEEE CS (2009)
11. Son, D.T., Dung, D.T.: Apply Mapping Question Approach in building the question answering system for Vietnamese language. Journal of Engineering Technology and Education – The 2012 International Conference on Green Technology and Substainable Development (2012)
12. Saruladha, K., Aghila, G., Raj, S.: A New Semantic Similarity Metric for Solving Sparse Data Problem in Ontology based Information Retrieval System, IJCSI International Journal of Computer Science Issues, Vol. 7(3(11)) (May 2010)
13. Yih, W.-T., Chang, M.-W., Meek, C., Pastusiak, A.: Question Answering Using Enhanced Lexical Semantic Models, Microsoft Research, Updated Version (July 29, 2013)
14. Vietnam Ministry of Justice's website,
    http://www.moj.gov.vn/Pages/home.aspx
15. Question Answering,
    http://en.wikipedia.org/wiki/Question_answering
16. VLSP Project, http://vlsp.vietlp.org:8080/demo/

An Inner-Enterprise Wiki System (IWkS) Integrated with an Expert Finding Mechanism for Lesson-Learned Knowledge Accumulation in Product Design

Ywen Huang[1], Zhua Jiang[1], Xde Xiang[2], Cneng He[2], Jfeng Liu[2], and Ying Huang[1]

[1] School of Mechanical Engineering, Shanghai Jiao Tong University, Shanghai, China
[2] Institute of Product Design, Shanghai Waigaoqiao Ship-building Company, Shanghai, China
{hywen2004,zhjiang}@sjtu.edu.cn

Abstract. In the process of product design, it is usually difficult for enterprises to timely and effectively accumulate lesson-learned knowledge, which should be revised several rounds by appropriate experts in a cooperative, multidisciplinary team to make sure of its accuracy and integrity. This study proposes a model of an inner-enterprise wiki system (IWkS) integrated with an expert finding framework to support the accumulation of lesson-learned knowledge in product design. By combining wiki' characteristics, the expert finding framework considers both users' expertise relevance, and social importance in IWkS. To validate our expert finding approach, some experiments are done in a famous ship-building company in China. Meanwhile, a working scenario of the IWkS integrated with an expert finding framework for knowledge accumulation is shown.

Keywords: Knowledge management, wiki, expert finding, product design.

1 Introduction

In recent years, more and more enterprises begin to realize that knowledge is extremely important [1], and management of knowledge resources is an essential way to enhance business efficiency and competitiveness [2]. Product design is a knowledge-intensive activity in manufacturing enterprises [3]. In the process of product design, engineers usually write lesson-learned documents for empirical knowledge sharing to others, and a lot of empirical knowledge is in the forms of lesson-learned documents (see Fig.1). As the task in product design is usually a cooperative, multidisciplinary team work, the lesson-learned knowledge is collaborative and combined with the individual intelligence of team members. So when an engineer creates a rough lesson-learned item, the enterprise wants it to be revised timely and correctly in several rounds to reach a high-quality level by appropriate experts. The aforementioned condition has become more feasible by the advent of Web 2.0 systems, such as wikis, which provides a mechanism for collective knowledge creation and sharing [4]. The characteristics of wikis, like openness, simplicity and ease of maintenance, have made them be adopted by enterprises [5]. However, the quality of the collectively created knowledge in wikis is usually not

K. Saeed and V. Snášel (Eds.): CISIM 2014, LNCS 8838, pp. 198–208, 2014.
© IFIP International Federation for Information Processing 2014

very high. An expert finding mechanism is therefore needed to actively select the most appropriate expert peers in the organization to improve the content and ensure the quality. In this paper we propose an inner-enterprise wiki system (IWkS) integrated with an expert finding mechanism to support lesson-learned knowledge accumulation in product design.

The expert finding technique has attracted attentions of many research groups in various contexts, such as organizations and online communities [6, 7]. Existing models mainly utilize three sources of expertise indicators to make expert recommendations: self-statement information [8], authored documents [6, 9], and social interaction history [10, 11]. Furthermore, very few studies focus on virtual communities, especially wikis, where information quality is often not so good as that in organizational knowledge repositories. In this research, a hybrid expert finding approach is proposed and integrated into an inner-enpterprise wiki, which evaluate users' expertise considers both contents of authored items (created or revised) and one's social importance within IWkS. Experiments have been conducted to assess and evaluate the effectiveness and usability of the proposed expert finding mechanism in the real world.

The rest of the paper is organized as follows. IWkS for knowledge accumulation is introduced in the next section. Section 3 presents a novel expert finding mechanism. Some experiments are done in Section 4 to validate our expert finding approach and a working scenario of the whole IWkS is shown in Section 5. Conclusions are then outlined in the last section.

2   IWkS for Lesson-Learned Knowledge Accumulation

2.1   Lesson-Learned Knowledge

In product design, lesson-learned knowledge represents the skill-related knowledge acquired from an engineer's past experience in performing design tasks. A lot of such knowledge is generated, which makes it possible for an engineer to reuse others'

Document ID	WD2012060302
Document Name	Structure modeling
Problem Description: In the structure modeling of ship H1115, the phenomena of interference among pipes and structures usually happen.	
Method Description: When doing structure design, distances among structure models should be controlled. Theoretically, as long as the distance between two structures is more than 20mm, it's OK for structure modeling. However, the production capacity of our company couldn't meet that requirement, and the distance should be larger than 50mm for structure manufacturing. So when designing structures and checking interferences among structures, we cannot just only obey to the standard files, we also have to know about the production capacity. What 'more, engineers of different majors should strengthen communication. When modeling, if space allows, the model spacing should be as large as possible.	
Author ID: Engineer024	Author Name: Cheng HE

Fig. 1. Content of a lesson-learned document

experience in accomplishing various tasks. In many enterprises without knowledge management tools, the lesson-learned knowledge is in the form of documents which are stored in the local network. Fig.1 shows content of a lesson-learned document on outfitting design of a ship-building company which is written by the design department, and each document has main parts: item title, problem description, method description, etc.

2.2   Mechanism of Knowledge Accumulation through IWkS

With a wiki system, the enterprise can have a better knowledge accumulation mechanism for engineers to create and accumulate lesson-learned knowledge. In Fig. 2, an overview of procedures of knowledge accumulation through IWkS is illustrated. After a new rough lesson-learned item is created and submitted into IWkS, or an existing item is revised, the item will be peer reviewed to assess its quality. Next, if quality of an item is inadequate, it is necessary to find the most appropriate engineer to improve the specific revise-to-be item, which is controlled by the expert finding mechanism. The details of the proposed expert finding approach are introduced later in Section 3.

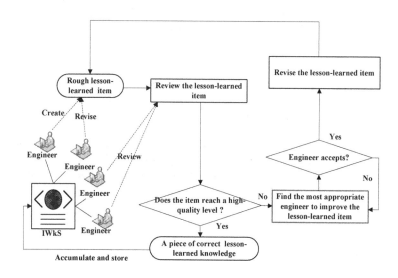

Fig. 2. An overview of knowledge accumulation through IWkS

As soon as a peer engineer, selected as an appropriate expert by the proposed algorithm, gives revisions to the lesson-learned item, it undergoes a re-assessment. The revision, review and expert finding processes can be repeated several times until the rough lesson-learned item has surpassed the quality threshold. Lesson-learned items, which reach a high-quality level, will be shared and reused among all the engineers in the future product design.

3   Expert Finding Approaches in IWkS

3.1   Framework for the Expert Finding Mechanism

In IWkS, there are many lesson-learned items in the domain of product design. Engineers are encouraged to create or give different revisions and comments on their familiar items to improve the quality of lesson-learned knowledge in IWkS. Whether an engineer can be selected as the potential appropriate expert on a certain topic depends not only on whether the engineer has relevant knowledge, but also on the social importance or authority in IWkS community.

Therefore, the expert rank $ExpertRank$ ($engr_i$, RI_k) of an engineer $engr_i$ for a certain rough lesson-learned item RI_k is defined as a combination of expertise relevance and social importance, which is shown in Formula (1).

$$ExpertRank\left(engr_i, RI_k\right) = a \cdot ER(engr_i, RI_k) + (1-a) \cdot SI(engr_i) \qquad (1)$$

Where ER ($engr_i$, RI_k) denotes expertise relevance score between an engineer's expertise and a rough lesson-learned item RI_k; SI ($engr_i$) denotes social importance score of the engineer $engr_i$, reflecting authority of the engineer within the IWkS community; and a [0, 1] is a coefficient of the linear combination strategy that combines expertise relevance and social importance into a single expert rank score. As shown in Fig.3, the framework of an expert finding mechanism in IWkS is proposed that attempts to detect experts from IWkS community, and has four main phases.

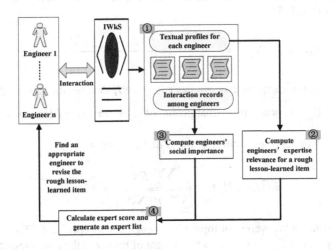

Fig. 3. The framework of expert finding mechanism

①Build textual profiles for each engineer and collect interaction records among engineers from IWkS. The textual profiles are used to extract expertise for each engineer. The interaction records among engineers are used to calculate engineers' social importance. ② Compute relevance between each engineer's expertise and a rough lesson-learned item. The details are introduced in Section 3.2. ③ Compute engineers' social importance. The details are elaborated in Section 3.3. ④ Compute expert rank score. In this phase, a hybrid method (see Formula 1) is used and a recommended expert list is generated.

3.2   Expertise Relevance Computation

Expertise Extraction. Each engineer' textual profile is built by merging all the items in IWkS that the engineer has previously created or revised. In general, specific text preprocessing is required before automated topic extraction. Once these pre-processes are finished, for a textual profile, some meaningless and superfluous words are filtered out, and some words are cut down to the root by a stemming algorithm[12]. Then each topic will receive a weight using a term weighting algorithm, which is based on the Term Frequency/Inverse Document Frequency (TF/IDF) method[13]. Once topics are ordered by weights, each engineer's expertise is denoted by a set of tuples (t, E_t), where t is the topic and E_t is its weight.

Relevance between Each Engineer' Expertise and a Rough Item. Once the topics of expertise are decided, the main issue is to calculate relevance score. Expertise relevance indicates whether an engineer in IWkS community has any level of expertise with regard to a rough lesson-learned item in product design. The rough item can also be represented as several topics and their weights (t, I_t) by using TF-IDF algorithm [13].

Then we can calculate an expertise relevance score between an engineer's expertise and a rough lesson-learned item by Formula (2), which is deployed to Formula (3), (4) and (5).

$$ER(engr_i, RI_k) = \frac{sim(EE_i, RI_k) \times \sum_{j \in C_{engr_i}} E_j \times T_j}{\left| C_{engr_i} \right|} \qquad (2)$$

Where EE_i *denotes* expertise of engineer $engr_i$; RI_k denotes the kth rough lesson-learned item; C_{engr_i} denotes the textual profile of engineer $engr_i$; j denotes the jth item in C_{engr_i}; $\left| C_{engr_i} \right|$ denotes the number of items in C_{engr_i} and $\left| C_{engr_i} \right| \geq 1$.

$$sim(EE_i, RI_k) = \frac{\sum_{t=1}^{m} E_t I_t}{\sqrt{\sum_{t=1}^{m} E_t^2 \sum_{t=1}^{m} I_t^2}} \qquad (3)$$

Where E_t denotes the weight of topic t in an engineer's expertise EE_i; m is the total number of topics in EE_i and I_t denotes the weight of topic t in the rough lesson-learned item RI_k.

$$E_j = 1 + \frac{n(positive\,evaluation) - n(negative\,evaluation)}{n(evaluation)} \qquad (4)$$

E_j is the evaluation result of lesson-learned item I_j, which is used as a factor to discriminate the quality of revisions made by the contributors. If someone thinks the revised lesson-learned item is low-quality level, he or she can give it a positive/neutral/negative evaluation, which is considered as plus, zero, and minus, respectively. n denotes the number of evaluations received and $n \geq 1$. To prevent the value of evaluation factor being lower than 0, we add one to the result.

$$T_j = e^{-\tau(t_{now} - t_j)} \tag{5}$$

The next factor considered is the time factor. It is reasonable to assume that the version of a revised item posted in the recent past is more important and up-to-date. The time weight of each version of item is calculated as Formula (5). Where t_{now} is the current date time; t_j is the date time of the item I_j being revised; τ is an adjustable parameter, which we set at 1/365 to avoid dropping too fast [14].

3.3   Engineers' Social Importance Computation

Social Network Construction. To determine an engineer's social importance in IWkS, firstly a social network should be constructed to represent interactions of engineers in the IWkS community. In IWkS, when an engineer initiates a lesson-learned thread by creating a new item on a certain topic, others may follow this thread and modify the item to get a new version. The engineer-item relationships are illustrated in Fig. 4(a). There are two sorts of vertices in the graph: engineer $engr_j$ and item thread I_k. The directed edge from an engineer to an item means that the item is initialized by the engineer. The directed edge from an item to an engineer means the same item is revised by the engineer. Engineer-engineer relationships are extracted through connecting engineers who participate in the same thread with directed edges from item creators to revisers: see Fig. 4(b). Social interactions are depicted in the engineer-engineer graph, which is used to infer an engineer's social importance in IWkS.

In the knowledge accumulation context of IWkS, according to social network theory, an engineer A will receive a vote of support from another engineer B whose initial rough item is revised by A. If several engineers give revisions to modify B's thread, the vote of support from B is evenly distributed to those engineers. Each element in the engineer-engineer relationship matrix U, can be calculated as Formula (6).

$$u_{ij} = \begin{cases} 0 & if\ (i, j) \notin E \\ 1\ /\ out\ (i) & if\ (i, j) \in E \end{cases} \tag{6}$$

Where $out\ (i)$ is engineer $engr_i$'s out-degree, i.e., the total number of engineers who have helped engineer $engr_i$ to revise the item. E is a set that consists of directed links from item thread creators to revisers. Each element u_{ij} represents the vote of support received for engineer $engr_j$ from engineer $engr_i$.

Take the engineer-engineer relationship graph in Fig. 4(b) as an example,

$$u_{ij} = \begin{bmatrix} 0 & 1/2 & 1/2 & 0 \\ 0 & 0 & 0 & 1 \\ 0 & 1/2 & 0 & 1/2 \\ 0 & 0 & 0 & 0 \end{bmatrix}.$$

(a)   (b)

Fig. 4. An engineer-item graph and an engineer-engineer relation graph

Social Importance Computation. The social importance score represents a user's authority in **an engineer-engineer relation graph**. PageRank algorithm is used to calculate social importance score, which is shown in Formula (7).

$$SI\left(engr_i\right) = d \cdot \sum_{j=1}^{N} SI\left(engr_j\right) \cdot u_{ji} + \left(1-d\right)\frac{1}{N} \tag{7}$$

Where d is a damping factor, it allows the recursive cycles to jump to a random engineer in IWkS. It is commonly set to 0.85 [11]. An iterative algorithm, like the power iteration method, can be used in the recursive computation. The initial value of social importance score $SI(i)$ can be given as $1/N$ [11]. The iteration ends when the social importance scores converge.

4   Experiments

Since the proposed expert finding mechanism integrated in IWkS is important for lesson-learned knowledge accumulation, it should be evaluated. So the experiment in this section is conducted to investigate (1) the performance influenced by changing the parameter a in Formula 1; and (2) the effectiveness of the proposed method.

4.1   Experimental Design

SWS is in a famous shipbuilding company in China. The engineers in the field of outfitting design are asked to use a traditional wiki system to share their lesson-learned knowledge. They are encouraged to give contributions and reviews for lesson-learned items. Moreover, technical consulting committee has manually identified the experts in the wiki community. Each quarter several distinguished engineers are selected to receive the Special Contribution Award for their enthusiasms and capability to improve the quality of the lesson-learned items. The historical identified expert lists can be naturally employed as the gold standard for the empirical evaluations. All the versions of items and interaction records among engineers in the wiki system from 2012 to the end of year 2013 are crawled, with approximately twenty eight projects.

Several information retrieval metrics are employed to evaluate our experimental results including precision (P), recall (R), macro-average F-measure (Ma), micro-average F-measure (Mi), Mean Reciprocal Rank (MPR), Mean Average Precision (MAP) and P@5 [11].

4.2 The Optimal Parameter Value

The first experiment is to determine the optimal parameter a in the linear combination strategy. We try different a to compute the final expert rank score in Formula (1). a is the parameter used to adjust the relative importance of expertise relevance score and social importance score. Fig. 5 shows the top-5 expert ranking results based on expert rank scores. For P@5 and MAP, the performance increases when a rises and peaks at $a = 0.7$, so the best performance is achieved by setting $a = 0.7$. The expertise relevance score is more important than the social importance score to derive the final expert rank score.

4.3 The Effectiveness of the Proposed Method

The second experiment is to evaluate the effectiveness of our expert finding approach by comparing with a baseline method, where only the content (textual profile)-based expertise relevance is considered to find the experts. And the parameter a value is set to its optimal value 0.7. The experimental results are shown in Fig. 6. The proposed approach significantly outperformed the content-based baseline method ($p < 0.001$). The proposed approach's F-measures (MacroF1 and MicroF1) are around 36%, while those of the baseline method are only about 12%.

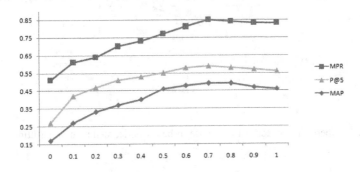

Fig. 5. Expert finding performance using different a

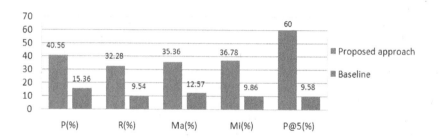

Fig. 6. Performance comparison between proposed approach and a baseline one

5   A Working Scenario of the Whole IWkS for Knowledge Accumulation

According to those considerations, we have designed an operational wiki system IWkS integrated with an expert finding mechanism for lesson-learned knowledge accumulation in outfitting design. The system framework including the knowledge accumulation fuction is realized by MediaWiki technique, and the expert finding mechanism is implemented by the method proposed in Section 3. As shown in Fig.7, when a rough lesson-learned item submitted into IWkS, by using our expert finding mechanism, the appropriate expert list will generate according to the expert rank. Then IWkS will send a system request to the top one expert to ask him or her give a revision on the item. The expert finding process can be executed by the system automatically. In some specific circumstances, the manager can use the "expert finding" button to find experts for certain items manually.

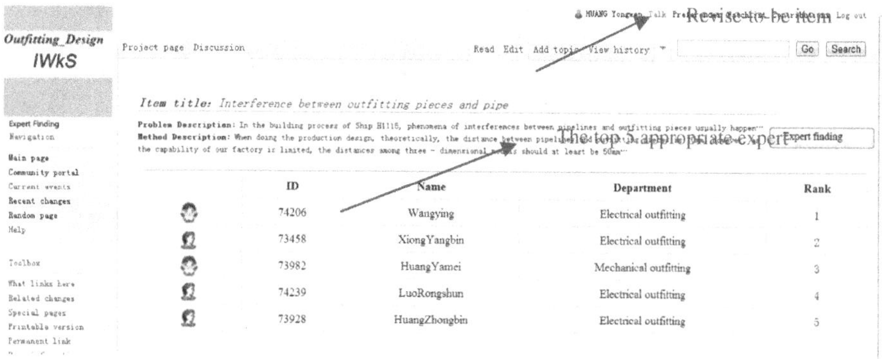

Fig. 7. Expert finding results for a revise-to-be lesson-learned item in outfitting design

6   Conclusions

This study proposes an inner-enterprise wiki system (IWkS) integrated with an expert finding mechanism to support the accumulation of lesson-learned knowledge in product design. By combining wiki' characteristics, the expert finding mechanism is a hybrid approach considering both users' expertise relevance, and social importance in IWkS. Experiments show that the proposed approach achieves better performance than the baseline one. The promising results may confirm the feasibility of our approach in helping engineers to better accumulate lesson-learned knowledge for an enterprise. The accumulated wiki web pages in IWkS can be viewed as a large high-quality level lesson-learned knowledge repository, which stores engineers' wisdom of product design for enterprises' knowledge reuse.

This research has several limitations. The current precision and recall is still not so high that continuous improvement has to be done. The proposed approach may not work if experts change their expertise domain (or specialize in small part of the domain) or get promoted. We would like to extend our work and design larger experiments to address these issues.

Acknowledgments. The research is supported by National Nature Science Foundation of China (No. 70971085, 71271133), Science and Technology commission of Shanghai (No. 13111104500), Shanghai Municipal Education Commission (13ZZ012), Research Fund for the Doctoral Program of Higher Education of China (No. 20100073110035). The authors would like to thank all the participants for their efforts in our experiments.

References

1. Carlucci, D., Schiuma, G.: Knowledge assets value creation map: assessing knowledge assets value drivers using AHP. Expert Systems with Applications 32(3), 814–821 (2007)
2. Taljaard, L., Smith, G.: Mapping the relationship between knowledge management and information architecture. In: 4th International Conference on Intellectual Capital, Knowledge Management and Organisational Learning, pp. 403–410 (2007)
3. Lu, Z., Zuhua, J., Hai-Tao, S.: Distributed knowledge sharing for collaborative product development. International Journal of Production Research 49(10), 2959–2976 (2011)
4. Lykourentzou, I., et al.: CorpWiki: A self-regulating wiki to promote corporate collective intelligence through expert peer matching. Information Sciences 180(1), 18–38 (2010)
5. Bughin, J., Manyika, J.: How businesses are using Web 2.0: A McKinsey global survey. McKinsey Quarterly Web Exclusive. McKinsey and Company (2007)
6. Zhao, H., Lu, W.: Using Document Weight Combining Method for Enterprise Expert Mining. In: International Conference on Wireless Communications, Networking and Mobile Computing, vol. 1-15, pp. 3721–3723, IEEE (2007)
7. Kumar, A., Ahmad, N.: ComEx miner: expert mining in virtual communities. International Journal of Advanced Computer Science and Applications 3(6), 54–65 (2012)
8. Yukawa, T., et al.: An expert recommendation system using concept-based relevance discernment. In: International Conference on Tools with Artificial Intelligence, pp. 257–264 (2001)

 9. Xuan, Z., et al.: An expert recommendation system of project reviewing based on the content-based model. Journal of Information and Computational Science 6(1), 1–7 (2009)
10. Davoodi, E., Kianmehr, K., Afsharchi, M.: A semantic social network-based expert recommender system. Applied Intelligence 39, 1–13 (2012)
11. Wang, G.A., et al.: ExpertRank: A topic-aware expert finding algorithm for online knowledge communities. Decision Support Systems 54(3), 1442–1451 (2013)
12. Porter, M.F.: An algorithm for suffix stripping. Program: Electronic Library and Information Systems 14(3), 130–137 (1980)
13. Salton, G., Buckley, C.: Term-weighting approaches in automatic text retrieval. Information Processing & Management 24(5), 513–523 (1988)
14. Liu, D., et al.: Integrating expert profile, reputation and link analysis for expert finding in question-answering websites. Information Processing and Management 49, 312–329 (2013)

Movie Recommendation Using OLAP and Multidimensional Data Model

Worapot Jakkhupan and Supasit Kajkamhaeng

Information and Communication Technology Programme, Faculty of Science,
Prince of Songkla University, Hat Yai Campus, Songkla 90112, Thailand
{worapot.j,supasit.k}@psu.ac.th

Abstract. This research proposes an adoption of data warehousing concepts to create a movie recommender system. The data warehouse is generated using ETL process in a desired star schema. The profiles of users and movies are created using multidimensional data model. The data are analyzed using OLAP, and the reports are generated using data mining and analysis tools. The recommended movies are selected using multi-criteria candidate selection. The movies which present the genres that match individual preference are recommended to the particular user. The multidimensional data model and OLAP provide high performance to discover the new knowledge in the big data.

Keywords: Movie recommender system, Data warehousing, MDX language, OLAP, Multidimensional data model.

1   Introduction

In the information overload era, it is very difficult for users to search for the interested information from the large amount of data. To facilitate users eliminating the useless data, recommender system (RS) has been developed. RS is a system that predicts the preferences of user from their previous interests, and offers them the pleasurable items that might meet user's satisfaction [1]. There are many successful examples of adopting the RS in the websites, for example, Amazon[1], Last.fm[2], and Movielens[3].

Nowadays, RS has been increasingly implemented in diverse areas [1, 2]. RS provides two important advantages. First, RS helps user to deal with big data presented in the internet by eliminating the information that user may not interest, and gives users the information that meets their interests. Second, RS helps business to gain more profits by increase an opportunity to offer their customers the items that related to the customers' preferences. RS uses various techniques, which suitable for the diverse purposes [3]. The well-known techniques are content-based RS [4], collaborative filtering RS [5], and hybrid RS [6].

---

[1] http://www.amazon.com
[2] http://www.last.fm
[3] http://www.movielens.org

K. Saeed and V. Snášel (Eds.): CISIM 2014, LNCS 8838, pp. 209–218, 2014.
© IFIP International Federation for Information Processing 2014

In the real world, movie RS should recommend users the new releases and top hits movies. Moreover, user prefers to see the movies based on personal taste, especially on the movie genres, thus, movie RS is a content-based [7]. Movie RS has to know which genres of movie that users prefer to see, called user profile, and the genre of each movie, called movie profile. If movie RS has sufficient user profile, it is possible to offer the movies that meet user preferences. Anyway, user behavior on rating the movies is unpredictable. Some users always rate the movies when they like, call positive rating, on the other hand, some users always rate the movies when they don't like, called negative rating. If user always obviously give positive rating, RS can recommend the items that similar with the previous items. On the other hand, if user always give negative rating, RS should select the opposite items with the previous items. The traditional content-based RS, if there is inadequate information, RS cannot find enough movies that similar to the target movie, on the other hand, if there are large amount of similar movies, RS requires high computational performance. Another solution for the content-based profiling is to use the data warehouse and multidimensional data model, which has been applied not only in the movie RS [8] but also in the various types of RS such as website [9, 10] and book [11].

This study proposes the adoption of data warehouse concepts to create the movie RS. The propose method was experimented on HetRec2011 MovieLens dataset[4]. The dataset is prepared using ETL to create data warehouse. OLAP aggregation is used to create user and movie profiles in the multidimensional data models. The recommended movies are selected using multi-criteria candidate selection. The details of the movies are gathered from IMDb movie database via data sharing API[5]. Finally, the result is shown to user using the web based mobile browser.

The rest of this paper is organized as follows. Sect. 2 introduces the overview of the recommender system. Sect. 3 describes the proposed method. Sect. 4 reveals the experimental results. Finally, discussion and conclusion are described in Sect. 5.

2   Background of Recommender System

2.1   Recommender System

Recommender system (RS) is the system that predict the preferences of user in which user would give to the items user had not yet considered. RS uses various techniques which suitable for the various types of data and purposes [3]. RS recommends the items to user using model built from the characteristics of an item, called content-based RS [4], or the social relationship between users, called collaborative filtering RS [5], or mix both techniques, called hybrid RS [6].

RS predicts user's preferences following three steps; extract user preferences from the data source, compute recommendation using appropriate techniques, and present the recommendation candidates to users. In the content-based and collaborative RS, system requires the similar matrix among users and items. The basic requirement of RS is shown in Fig. 1.

---

[4] http://www.grouplens.org/system/files/HetRec2011-movielens-2k.zip
[5] http://www.omdbapi.com/

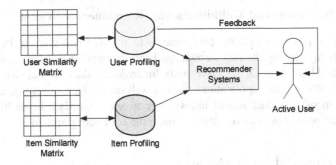

Fig. 1. Basic requirements of a recommender system

2.2   Content-Based Recommender System

The content-based RS predicts rating that user may give to the undesired items. There are two steps of content-based recommendation: finding the similar items using similarity function, after that, calculating the rating using rating prediction function.

Similarity Function. The similarity function is necessary in the collaborative filtering and content-based recommender system. There are two well-known and widely used similarity functions; Pearson Coefficient Correlation (PCC), and cosine similarity. The PCC is widely used to calculate the similarity between users in a collaborative filtering approach, and the cosine similarity is widely used to calculate the similarity between items in a content-based filtering approach. The cosine similarity equation is shown in Eq. 1.

$$\text{sim}(a, b) = \frac{\sum_{i=1}^{n} w_{a,i}, w_{b,i}}{\sqrt{\sum_{i=1}^{n} w_{a,i}^2} \sqrt{\sum_{i=1}^{n} w_{b,i}^2}} \tag{1}$$

where $\text{sim}(a, b)$ is the cosine similarity between item a and item b, $w_{a,i}$ is the weight of attribute a on item i, and $w_{b,i}$ is the weight of attribute b on item i.

Rating Prediction. Content-based recommender system recommends users the items that similar or related to their preferences in the past. This approach itself requires data of individual user, and the attribute of the item. Using this approach, there is a chance for new items to get recommended, and there is no population bias. The content-based recommender system estimates user's rating using Eq. 2.

$$PR_{u,i} = \frac{\sum_{j=1}^{n} \left(\text{sim}_{i,sj} \times r_{u,sj}\right)}{\sum_{j=1}^{n} \text{sim}_{u,sj}} \tag{2}$$

where $PR_{u,i}$ denotes the predicted rating of user u on item i, $\text{sim}_{i,sj}$ is the weight of attribute similarity between active item i and the selected item s, $r_{u,sj}$ is the rating of user u on selected item s, $\text{sim}_{u,sj}$ is the rating of user u on the selected item s, and n is the number of selected items that similar with item i.

2.3   Data Warehouse and Multidimensional Recommender System

Data warehouse provides extreme performance to manage and analyze big data in terms of explicitly finding the new knowledge from the large amount of massive data, including RS [12]. The OLAP and multidimensional data model are used to implement the RS in many applications such as web sites [11], movies [8], and books [10]. Multidimensional data model allows user to view the data in multi aspects. Moreover, data warehouse can be used to handle the cold-start problem [7].

3   Experimental Methodology

3.1   Architecture of the Proposed System

This research applies data warehouse into a movie recommender system. The architecture of the movie recommender system proposed in this research is drawn in Fig. 2. Firstly, the raw HetRec2011 MovieLens dataset are transformed to the desired data warehouse using ETL process. The data in data warehouse are analyzed using OLAP features, and the multidimensional data are created. The candidate movies are selected using multi-criteria selection method, and subsequently are presented to user.

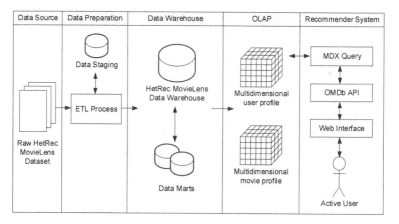

Fig. 2. Architecture of the proposed system

3.2   Data Preparation Using Extract-Transform-Load (ETL)

The HetRec2011 MovieLens dataset has collected the ratings of users on movies. In the HetRec2011-movielens-2k.zip, three data files were selected to generate the multidimensional data model. The movie_genres.dat, assigns 20,809 movies with 20 genres. The user_ratedmovies.dat provides 855,598 ratings of 2,113 users on 10,197 movies, which means 8,684 movies have never been rated. The allowed rating scores are 0.5, 1, 1.5, 2, 2.5, 3, 3.5, 4, 4.5, and 5, respectively. The movie.dat file gives the details of each movie, including imdbID, which is used to gather the details of movies from OMDb API. To integrate the data from these files and to generate the desired multidimensional data cube, this research used Pentaho Data Integration (PDI)[6] to operate the Extract-Transfer-Load (ETL) process. The multidimensional data cube is represented in ROLAP star schema stored in MySQL database as shown in Fig. 3.

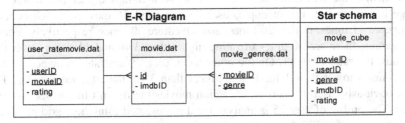

Fig. 3. ETL process using Pentaho Data Integration (PDI)

3.3   Multidimensional Data Analysis using OLAP

After generating the data warehouse using ETL process, the data in data warehouse are transformed into the desired multidimensional data cube. There are two data cube generated from OLAP; user profile and movie profile. The facts (or measurements) are acquired by count aggregation feature in OLAP. As shown in Fig. 4, the user profile consists of three dimensions: user, genre, and rating. Likewise, the movie profile consists of 3 dimensions: movie, genre, and rating. The advantage of multidimensional data is the data can be represented in multi aspect using slice or dice method. For example, R_{user}: {75, Action, 3.5} = 8 means user 75 has rated action genre with score 3.5 for 8 times. R_{movie}: {6874, {Action, Crime, Thriller}, 5} = 1,765 means movie 6874, contains 3 genres; action, crime and thriller, has been rated with score 5 for 1,750 times.

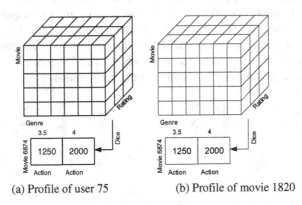

(a) Profile of user 75   (b) Profile of movie 1820

Fig. 4. Multidimensional data cube generated from movie data warehouse

Multidimensional User Profile. The average rating is used as a baseline score to define the behavior of users. For HetRec2011 dataset, the mean rating score is 2.5,

---

[6] http://www.pentaho.com/explore/pentaho-data-integration

therefore, if the average rating of user is higher than 2.5, it can infer that this user has positive rating behavior. For example, the average rating of user 75 is 3.46, therefore, user 75 prefers to give positive rating on the movies. To define the genres that user like or dislike, the frequency and the ratio between ratings higher and lower than average are compared. For example, user 75 has rated 56 movies, which contains action genre 41 times, thriller 26 times, and adventure 20 times, respectively. For the action genres, there are 30 times of rating higher than 3.46 and 11 times lower than 3.46, thus, the ratio is 30:11. On the other hand, user 75 has rated romance genre 4 times, 3 times lower than 3.46, 1 time higher than 3.46, thus, the ratio is 3:1. That means, obviously, user 75 likes to see action movies but doesn't like to see romance movies. The profile of user 75 is analyzed and represented using heat grid graph and bar chart as shown in Fig. 5.

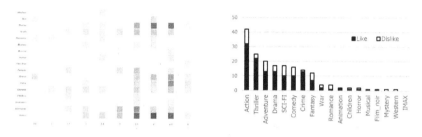

(a) Distribution of rating (positive behavior)   (b) Frequency and ratio of like and dislike

Fig. 5. Profile of user 75 using multidimensional data cube slice and dice

Multidimensional Movie Profile. There are three information used to create the movie profile; genres, rating score, and frequent of rating. Movie genres are explicitly defined in movie_genres.dat file. The global rating score and the frequent of rating are acquired from ratings.dat file. The multidimensional movie profile is created and is diced into a heat grid report as an example shown in Fig. 6. According to the profile of user 75, movie 6874 should be recommended to user 75 since it has high score on action and thriller, and movie 7361 should not be recommended.

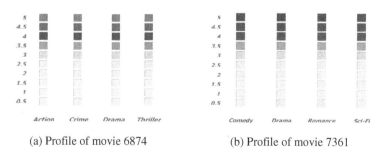

(a) Profile of movie 6874   (b) Profile of movie 7361

Fig. 6. Movies profiling using OLAP dice method

3.4   Multi-criteria Candidates Selection

To select the candidates for recommendation, the user profile and movie profile are considered. Firstly, RS selects the movies which user has never rated before. The selected movies are filtered by matching with the genres that match user preferred. Subsequently, the top-k movies are ordered by the frequent of global users view and rating. Finally, the candidate movies are ordered by newest release and are recommended to user.

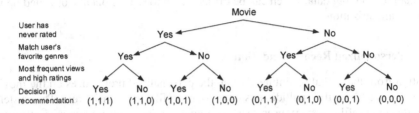

Fig. 7. Multi-criteria candidate selection for the movie recommendation

4   Experimental Results

4.1   Social Recommendation Using Frequent of Rating and Distribution of Score

The frequent rating is calculated using count aggregation feature of OLAP presented in pie graph, which reflects the interest of all users on each genre, but not reveals the positive or negative opinion. If the genre has high frequent of rating, it means users like to see the movies which present that genre. Likewise, the distribution of score reveals the trend of users given to each genre presented in heat grid graph. The high frequent and high score rating should be recommended to every user, especially new or anonymous user. Data warehouse and OLAP dice the large amount of data and reveal the report in multi-aspect as shown in Fig. 8.

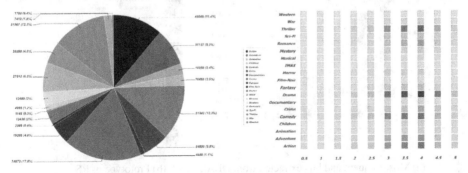

(a) Frequent of rating each genre   (b) Distribution of rating score grouped
                                                   by genres

Fig. 8. Global high frequent rating and high score rating generated from OLAP

The top-5 most frequent rated genres are drama, comedy, thriller, action, and adventure, respectively. This information reveals the concentrate of the genres users like to give rating. Likewise, the top-4 highest rating genres are drama, action, thriller, and comedy, respectively. This information reveals the genres of the movies that users prefer to see. Thus, According to the OLAP data analysis results, the movies that contain drama, action, thriller, and comedy should be recommended first for the new or anonymous user because those genres are most hits and most frequent view. The data aggregation feature provided by OLAP helps data analyst to generate the information from big data, which can be drilled down to see the details, or rolled up to see the summarization.

4.2   Personalized Recommendation

Addition from the global recommendation, the personalized preferences on the movie genres as stated in the multidimensional user profile are considered. The system generates the profile of every user, as an example, we have selected user 75 as a case study because user 75 has high frequent on movie rating, which adequate for the data analysis using OLAP. For example, according to Fig. 6a, user 75 has given high frequent and high rating on 3 genres; action, thriller, and drama. Thus, there are 7 sets (calculated from 2^n-1) of genres should be recommend to user 75 are M_{set} = [{action}, {action, thriller}, {action, drama}, {action, thriller, drama}, {thriller}, {thriller, drama}, {drama}]. According to the multidimensional movie profile, Fig. 9a reveals the list of movies that user 75 has never rated which have high score on action, thriller and drama extracted from movie profile using OLAP analyzer tool. The candidate movies are selected using multi-criteria and are presented to user 75 via web interface. The information of the movies are collected from IMDb using JSON API. The example screenshot of the movie recommendation prototype on mobile for user 75 is shown in Fig. 9b.

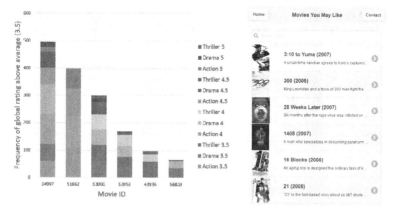

(a) Most frequent and hits extracted from OLAP   (b) Prototype of RS

Fig. 9. The movie recommendation for user 75 using OLAP analyzer

5   Discussion and Conclusion

In the content-based recommender system using cosine similarity and rating prediction, there are many factors affected the accuracy of the rating prediction. For example, since the average rating of user is high due to user's positive rating behavior, it has a high opportunity that the predicted rating might lower than average if only one genre that user does not like appears in the movie. Moreover, the calculation might not reliable if there is a lack of similarity items, and the calculation requires high computational performance if the data contain large amount of similar items. Therefore, this research adopts the data warehouse concept as an alternative technique to develop the movie recommender system. The proposed concept was experimented on the HetRec2011 MovieLens dataset. The raw data are transformed into star schema using ETL process, and subsequently the movie data warehouse is created. The multidimensional user and movie profiles are generated using OLAP aggregation tool. The data cube is slice and dice in order to generate the desired reports represented in the appropriate report types.

The multidimensional user profile reveals variety aspects of user, such as user rating behavior, and the distribution of like or dislike genres. The multidimensional movie profile with OLAP aggregation tool reveals the distribution of global rating, like or dislike from all users, and the frequent of rating on each genre. The most top hits and high frequent rating movies should be recommended to all users, especially new or anonymous user who the system has no previous record. Moreover, the personalized user preferences on movie genres are matched with the genres of each movie to select the movies using multi-criteria candidate selection method. Finally, after generating the movie recommendation list, the details of the recommended movies are acquired from IMDb web service API using JSON. The prototype of movie recommender system represent the results in web interface. The multidimensional data model and OLAP data analysis provide high performance to analyze the big amount of data, and to discover the new knowledge, which can be applied in the movie recommender system.

References

1. Bobadilla, J., Ortega, F., Hernando, A., Gutiérrez, A.: Recommender systems survey. Knowledge-Based Systems 46, 109–132 (2013)
2. Park, D.H., Kim, H.K., Choi, I.Y., Kim, J.K.: A literature review and classification of recommender systems research. Expert. Syst. Appl. 39, 10059–10072 (2012)
3. Adomavicius, G., Tuzhilin, A.: Toward the next generation of recommender systems: a survey of the state-of-the-art and possible extensions. IEEE T. Knowl. Data En. 17(6), 734–749 (2005)
4. Meteren, R., Someren, M.: Using content-based filtering for recommendation. In: Machine Learning in the New Information Age: MLnet/ECML 2000 Workshop, pp. 47–56 (2000)
5. Candillier, L., Meyer, F., Boullé, M.: Comparing state-of-the-art collaborative filtering systems. In: Perner, P. (ed.) MLDM 2007. LNCS (LNAI), vol. 4571, pp. 548–562. Springer, Heidelberg (2007)

6. Antonopoulus, N., Salter, J.: Cinema screen recommender agent: combining collaborative and content-based filtering. IEEE Intell. Syst. 21(1), 35–41 (2006)
7. Elsa, N., Franck, R., Oliver, T., Ronan, T.: Cold-Start Recommender System Problem Within a Multidimensional Data Warehouse. In: IEEE Seventh International Conference on Research Challenges in Information Science, pp. 1–8. IEEE press, New York (2013)
8. Miller, B.N., Albert, I., Lam, S.K., Konstan, J.A., Riedl, J.: MovieLens unplugged: experiences with an occasionally connected recommender system. In: 8th International Conference on Intelligent User Interfaces, pp. 263–266. ACM, New York (2003)
9. Gediminas, A., Alexander, T.: Extending Recommender Systems: A Multidimensional Approach. In: IJCAI Workshop on Intelligent Techniques for Web Personalization, Seattle, WA, USA, pp. 1–5 (2001)
10. Tiwari, R.G., Husain, M., Gupta, B., Agrawal, A.: Amalgamating Contextual Information into Recommender System. In: 3rd International Conference on Emerging Trends in Engineering and Technology, pp. 15–20. IEEE Press, New York (2010)
11. Thor, A., Rahm, E.: AWESOME – A Data Warehouse-based System for Adaptive Website Recommendations. In: 30th International Conference on Very Large Data Bases, pp. 384–395. VBLC Endowment (2004)
12. Krohn-Grimberghe, A., Nanopoulos, A., Schmidt-Thieme, L.: A Novel Multidimensional Framework for Evaluating Recommender Systems. In: ACM RecSys Workshop on User-Centric Evaluation of Recommender Systems and Their Interfaces, pp. 34–41. CEUR-WS.org (2010)

Decision Trees and Their Families in Imbalanced Pattern Recognition: Recognition with and without Rejection

Wladyslaw Homenda[1] and Wojciech Lesinski[2]

[1] Faculty of Mathematics and Information Science, Warsaw University of Technology
Plac Politechniki 1, 00-660 Warsaw, Poland
[2] Faculty of Mathematics and Computer Science, University of Bialystok
ul. Sosnowa 64, 15-887 Bialystok, Poland

Abstract. Decision trees are considered to be among the best classifiers. In this work we use decision trees and its families to the problem of imbalanced data recognition. Considered are aspects of recognition without rejection and with rejection: it is assumed that all recognized elements belong to desired classes in the first case and that some of them are outside of such classes and are not known at classifiers training stage. The facets of imbalanced data and recognition with rejection affect different real world problems. In this paper we discuss results of experiment of imbalanced data recognition on the case study of music notation symbols. Decision trees and three methods of joining decision trees (simple voting, bagging and random forest) are studied. These methods are used for recognition without and with rejection.

Keywords: pattern recognition, decision tree, bagging, random forest, optical music recognition, imbalanced data.

1 Introduction

A decision tree is a graph that uses a branching method to illustrate every possible outcome of a decision. It is powerful and popular tool for classification and prediction. Decision trees appeared in the literature in the context of sociological research in the sixties. In the field of machine learning decision trees appeared thanks to the work of Braiman and Quinlan. Currently they are regarded as one of the best classifiers' type. Decision trees connect the high speed of action with high efficiency [12].

A data set is called imbalanced if it contains many more samples from one class than from the rest of the classes. Data sets are unbalanced when at least one class is represented by only a small number of training examples (called the minority class) while other classes make up the majority. In this scenario, classifiers can have good accuracy on the majority class (or classes in multi-class problem) but very poor accuracy on the minority class(es) due to the influence that the larger majority class has on traditional training criteria. Most original classification algorithms pursue to minimize the error rate: the percentage of the

K. Saeed and V. Snášel (Eds.): CISIM 2014, LNCS 8838, pp. 219–230, 2014.

incorrect prediction of class labels. They ignore the difference between types of misclassification errors. In particular, they implicitly assume that all misclassification errors cost equally. For example, we will consider the two-class problem in which 99% of the objects belongs to the prevalent class. In this case, if we include all of the tested elements to this class, this will result in a very high, 99% efficiency.

Most of the publications concerning imbalanced data focus on the two-classes problem (e.g. [5] and [6]). Far less articles (inter alia [1], [16]) pertains to multi-class problems. In our study we focus attention on the multi-class issue. We have chosen the symbols of music notation as the example of this problem. Music notation recognition problem is imbalanced one because of three features: cardinality, shape and size. In this work, we mainly discuss class sizes with some attention given to other features, which also affect the classification effectiveness.

Automatic recognition and classification of music notation is a case of Optical Character Recognition. It may have many applications. This is primarily a music scores backup. Electronic processing of acquired information could be another application. With electronic record of music notation we can attempt to computerize music synthesis, we can also, by using the voice synthesizer, read this music score for the need of blind and visually impaired. Electronic music notation could also be used to verify the performances correctness of the musical composition, and to detect potential plagiarism. These applications lead to the conclusion that the optical recognition of music notation is an interesting and worthy research topic.

General methodology of optical music recognition has been already researched and described in [7] and [14]. We would like to highlight, that studied problem of imbalance of classes is an original contribution to the field of music symbols classification. The aim of our study is to investigate how decision trees and its families deal with imbalanced data. The research is based on actual opuses. Applied classification algorithms have been implemented in C++. Developed program works with both high and low-resolution images of musical symbols.

2   Theoretical Background

2.1   Decision Trees

A decision tree or a classification tree is a tree in which each internal (non-leaf) node is labeled with an input feature. The arcs coming from a node labeled with a feature are labeled with each of the possible values of the feature. Each leaf of the tree is labeled with a class or a probability distribution over the classes.

To classify an example, filter it down the tree, as follows. For each feature encountered in the tree, the arc corresponding to the value of the example for that feature is followed. When a leaf is reached, the classification corresponding to that leaf is returned.

Popular algorithms used for construction of decision trees have inductive nature using use top-down tree building scheme. In this scheme, building a tree starts from the root of the tree. Then, a feature for testing is chosen for this node and training set is divided to subsets according to values of this feature. For each value there is a corresponding branch leading to a subtree, which should be created on the basis of the proper testing subset. This process stops when a stop criterion is fulfilled and current subtree becomes a leaf. An example algorithm of tree construction is described in the next section.

Stop criterion shows when construction process needs to be brought to a standstill, that is when for some set of samples we need to make a leaf, not a node. An obvious stop criterion could be situation when:

- a sample set is empty,
- all samples are from the same class,
- attributes set is empty.

In practice criteria given above sometimes bring over-fitting to learning data. So then another stop criteria or mechanisms, such as pruning, is necessary to be applied in order to avoid the over-fitting problem.

Finally, classification of a given object is based on finding a path from the root to a leaf along branches of the tree. Choices of branches are done by assigning tests' results of the features corresponding to nodes. The leaf ending the path gives the class label for the object [4], [12].

2.2 ID3 Algorithm

ID3 (Iterative Dichotomiser 3) is an algorithm used to generate a decision tree. The algorithm was invented by Ross Quinlan [15]. This algorithm uses entropy as a test to divide training set. Entropy for a given set X split to classes $C_1, C_2...C_M$ is as follows:

$$entropy(X) = -\sum_{i=1}^{M} p_i(log(p_i)) \tag{1}$$

where $P = (p_1...p_M)$ are appearance probabilities of objects from $C_1, C_2, ..., C_M$ classes.

Average entropy in a given node v and for an attribute A_l is defined as follows:

$$avg\_entropy(X_v) = \sum_{i=1}^{k_l} \frac{|T_i|}{|X_v|} * entropy(T_i) \tag{2}$$

where $(T_1, T_2, ..., T_{k_l})$ is a division of the training subset X_v corresponding to the node v attribute A_l, T_i includes testing elements of the subset X_v, which have the value a_{li} of the attribute A_l, and k_l is the number of values of the attribute A_l.

The algorithm ID3 is based on information entropy and can be formulated as follows:

1. put the testing set in the root of the decision tree,
2. if for a given node of the tree all samples belong to the same class C_i, then the node becomes the leaf labelled by the class C_i,

3. if for a given node the attribute set is empty, then the node becomes the leaf labelled by the class C_i having majority in the testing subset in this node,
4. if for a given node the attribute set is not empty and samples in the testing set are not in the same class, then:

   - compute average entropy for each attribute,
   - choose an attribute with minimal entropy,
   - split the testing subset according to values of the chosen attribute,
   - for every set of the split: create the successor of the node and put the set in this node,
   - apply points 2, 3 and 4 for newly created nodes.

2.3   Families of Trees

Ensembles of classifier join computational capabilities of single classifiers and allow to build diverse models. In the case of conjunction methods, classifier is created with a number of other classifiers. Classifiers, which we use for connecting, we can call *weak classifiers*. Depending on the purpose, we may compose a model consisting of various single classifiers, but we may also manipulate with distinct parameters. There are also different ways of model construction. Two of those methods (simple voting and bagging) also may joined other classifiers, but in this work we use them for decision trees connecting.

Simple Voting. Simple voting is one of the simplest conjunction methods. We can use any weak classifiers in this method. Classifiers can be already trained, or they can be in the phase of training. The way of training is also not imposed. The only condition of start-up of this algorithm is having weak classifiers, which are statistically independent from each other. The sample $x \in X$ is tested by every weak classifier, then an answer is counted as a sum. The class which is indicated by largest number of weak classifiers, is chosen as the right one.

Bagging. Bagging, a name derived from "bootstrap aggregation", devised by Breiman [2], is one of the most intuitive and simplest ensemble algorithm providing good performance. It improve the stability, accuracy, reduces variance and avoid over-fitting of machine learning algorithms. Although it is usually applied to decision tree methods, it can be used with any type of method.

Bagging uses multiple versions of a training set, each created by drawing $n < N$ (where N is a number of elements of original training set) samples from training set D with replacement. Each of bootstrap data sets is used to train a different component classifier and the final classification decision is based on the vote of each component classifier. Traditionally the component classifiers are of the same general form - for example, all Hidden Markov models, or all neural networks, or all decisions trees - merely the final parameter values differ among them due to their different sets of training patterns.

Fig. 1. Example of music score

Random Forest. Random forest is a relatively new classifier proposed by Breiman in [3]. The method combines Breiman's [2] "bagging" idea and the random selection of features in order to construct a collection of decision trees with controlled variation.

Random forest is composed of some number of decision trees. Each tree is built as follow:

- Let the number of training objects be N, and the number of features in features vector be M.
- Training set for each tree is built by choosing n times with replacement from all N available training objects.
- Number $m << M$ is an amount of features on which to base the decision at that node. This features is randomly chosen for each node.
- Each tree is built to the largest extent possible. There is no pruning.

Each tree gives a classification, and we say the tree "votes" for that class. The forest chooses the classification having the most votes (over all the trees in the forest).

2.4 Classifiers Evaluation

To evaluate the classifiers in imbalanced data problem we starts from confusion matrix given i Table 1. The parameters given in the matrix are numbers of elements of a testing set which have the following meaning:

- TP - the number of elements of the considered class correctly classified to this class,
- FN - the number of elements of the considered class incorrectly classified to other classes,
- FP - the number of elements of other classes incorrectly classified to the considered class,

Table 1. Confiusion matrix for *two classes* problem

	Classification to the class	Classification to other classes
The class	True Positivse (TP)	False Negatives (FN)
Other classes	False Positives (FP)	True Negatives (TN)

– TN - the number of elements of other classes correctly classified to other classes (no matter, if correctly, or not).

In this study we consider multi class problem. Hence, parameters of *two classes problem* are turned to *one class contra all others*. Finally, three measures were used assess the quality of the classifier:

$$Sensitivity = \frac{TP}{TP + FN} \qquad (3)$$

$$Accuracy = \frac{TP + TN}{TP + FN + FP + TN} \qquad (4)$$

$$Precision = \frac{TP}{TP + FP} \qquad (5)$$

3   Experiment

3.1   Data Set

The recognized set of music notation symbols had about 27.000 objects in 20 classes and about 3000 foreign symbols, which not belong to the recognized classes. There were 12 classes defined as numerous and each of them had about 2.000 representatives. Cardinality of other eight classes was much lower and various in each of them (see Table 2). Part of the examined symbols was cut from chosen Fryderyk Chopin's compositions. Other part of the symbols' library comes from research projects [18] and [19]. Example of music score is on Figure 1.

Classes were divided into two groups: regular and rare classes. Regular classes include flat, sharp, natural, G and F clefs, piano, forte, mezzo-forte, quarter rest, eight rest, sixteenth rest and flagged stem. Irregular classes consist of accent, breve note, C clef, crescendo, diminuendo, fermata, tie and thirty-second rest. As mentioned, images sets coming from regular classes consisted of 2000 objects each. Sets of irregular classes are significantly smaller.

Set of foreign symbols includes various symbols from music scores, letters, digits and objects accidentally cuts from scores (unspecified parts of symbols and staves).

Table 2. Learning and testing sets for irregular classes

class	learning set	testing set
accent	30	65
breve	1	2
crescendo	55	100
diminuendo	51	97
fermata	35	46
clef C	100	178
tie	100	155
thirty-second rest	20	35

3.2   Features Vector

In this work experts features selection was used. Features selection based on previous works [9], [10] and [11]. Our features vector counted 50 elements. Features vector includes:

- maximal values and its positions and average values for projections, transitions and margins
- 3 regular moments
- 3 central moments
- 4 Zernike moments
- directions of 45, 90, 135 and 180 degrees
- field of symbol
- symbol's perimeter.

3.3   Recognition without Rejection

To evaluate the classifiers three measures was calculated: sensitivity, accuracy and precision. For this calculations our multi class problem was turned to m two class problems (*one class contra all others*). All measures was calculated for each class. In the end average measure was determined. In simple voting decision tree, k-Nearest Neighbor and classifier with Mahalanobis minimal distance were joined. In bagging 10 trees were constructed. In the case of random forest also 10 trees were joined and 5 features were drafted for splint in each node.

Accuracy. Accuracy shows influence of given class on whole testing set. The best accuracy was in small classes. Accuracy of all classifiers in breve note was 99.99 percent. For comparison sensitivity in this class was 0%! Other rare classes also had a good accuracy. It was between 99.89% and 99.99%. The worst accuracy was in natural and sharp classes. This classes had relatively poor sensitivity and had many elements in testing set. Related results were in rest group. Rest of regular classes were achieved better accuracy, but worse than rare ones. Results for all classes and all classifiers are shown on Figure 2.

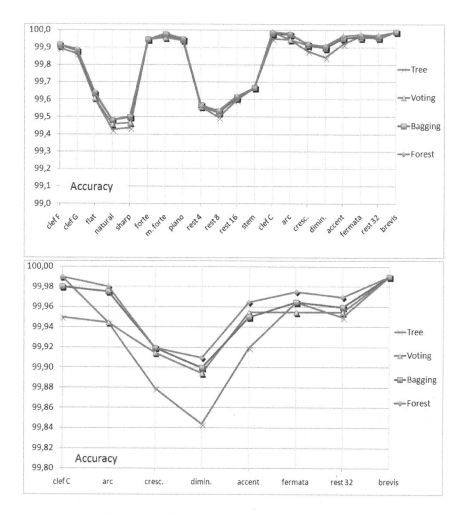

Fig. 2. Accuracy for all and rare classes

As same as in the case of sensitivity the best average accuracy was obtained by random forest classifier. A little worse average accuracy (98.48%) was reached by bagging. All classifiers had a very good values of accuracy. This measure does not show influence of rare classes. Therefore it seems improper measure for this problem.

Sensitivity. Sensitivity shows the recognition effectiveness in the given class. The highest value of this factor, 100%, was obtained in forte, mezzo-forte and piano classes. All regular classes reached a high values of this factor. Among the rare classes best sensitivity was achieved in C clef. The worst (0%) was in breve note class. This symbol was not recognized by any classifier. Results for all classes and all classifiers are shown on Figure 3.

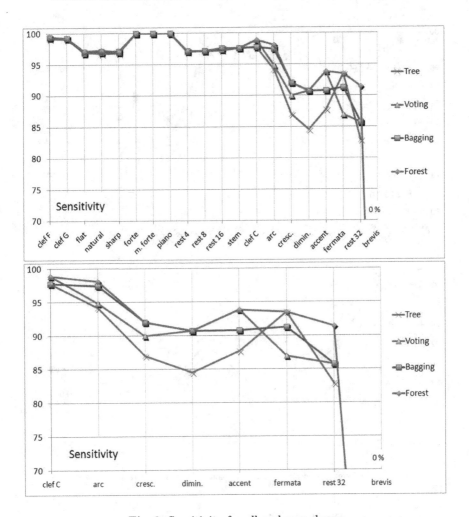

Fig. 3. Sensitivity for all and rare classes

Best average sensitivity was obtained by random forest classifier. It was 91.91%. Bagging, simple voting and decision tree also reached good performances. Breve note had big influence on this factor. If we calculate it without this class, it was obtained 96.74 for random forest classifier.

Precision. Precision shows how other classes influenced on given class. The highest values of this measure were in dynamics symbols classes and clefs classes. Precision for regular classes was better than for rare ones. The worst precision were in crescendo, diminuendo and thirty-second rest. For breve not this factor was undetermined, because TP and FP was equal 0 in this case. Results for all classes and all classifiers are shown on Figure 4.

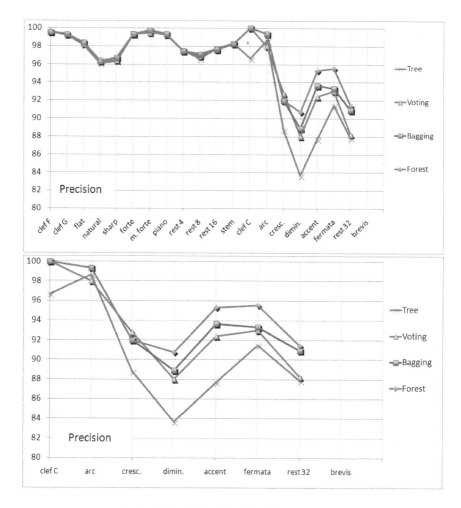

Fig. 4. Precision for all and rare classes

The best average precision was achieved by random forest classifier. It was 97.03 percent. Bagging had a little worse values of this factor (96.68%). Simple voting and decision tree also obtained a good results.

3.4   Recognition with Rejection

Pattern recognition problem not always has accurate symbols' extraction stage. Segmentation and extraction steps often produce many extraordinary undesirable symbols and ordinary garbage. We can call them *foreign symbols* in contrast to *native symbols* of recognized classes, c.f. [8]. In such a case a classification module, which assigns all extracted symbols to designed classes, will produce misclassification for every undesirable symbol and for every garbage symbol.

Improvements of classification require construction of such classifiers which could assign designed symbols to correct classes and reject undesirable and garbage symbols.

In our paper we treated undesirable and garbage symbols as representatives of one or more adding classes. In this case original set of classes M was increased by adding set of rejected classes M_R. The effectiveness of rejection was defined as the ratio of correct rejected symbols to the all symbols from rejected classes. In other words it was sensitivity of rejected classes.

In first experiment all rejected symbols were in one class. That was the worst way of rejection. In this case only 38 percent of symbols from undesired class was correctly rejected. Rest of this symbols were mistakenly classified to other class. Most of it was misclassified to the regular classes. Sensitivity for native classes was like in recognition without rejection, but precision was lower.

In next stage of tests the foreign class has been divided into smaller parts. The process of dividing was made by k-means clustering algorithm. Set of rejected symbols was split on 3, 5, 10 and 20 subclasses. In this way symbols were classified to 23, 25, 30 and 40 classes. The increasing the number of foreign classes caused rejection effectiveness increase. Sensitivity for rejected symbols (TP - correct rejected symbols, FN - incorrectly non rejected symbols) was 62% for 3 foreign classes, 81% for 5 foreign classes, 92% for 10 foreign classes and 94% for 20 foreign classes.

Unfortunately increase the number of foreign classes decreases the effectiveness of recognition of native classes. In the case of 20 foreign classes sensitivity of regular classes decreased by about 5 percent, for rare classes - from 10 to 15 percent.

4   Conclusions

In the paper was discussed the problem of imbalanced image recognition on the example of music notation symbols recognition. Authors present results of classification experiments performed with classifiers using decision trees on a dataset consisting of 27 000 elements of 20 classes.

Simple decision tree obtained efficiency equal 98%. The merger techniques gave slightly better results. This is particularly evident in the case of rare classes. Best results was obtained by random forest classifier. Decision trees and ensembles classifiers based on it were proved to be very effective. Tests for all measures gave good results. The study showed that the symbols of musical notation can be considered as imbalanced data.

Recognition with rejection was tested also. In this case rejected symbols were placed to one or more added classes. Rejection's effectiveness was better when rejected symbols were placed in a large number of classes. Unfortunately, in this case effectiveness of recognition of native symbols was worse.

Acknowledgement. The research is supported by the National Science Center, grant No 2012/07/B/ST6/01501, decision no UMO-2012/07/B/ST6/01501.

References

1. Abe, N., Zadrozny, B., Langford, J.: An Iterative Method for Multi-Class Cost-Sensitive Learning. In: Proc. ACM SIGKDD Int. Conf. Knowledge Discovery and Data Mining, pp. 3–11 (2004)
2. Breiman, L.: Bagging predictors. Machine Learning 26(2), 123–140 (1996)
3. Breiman, L.: Random Forests. Machine Learning 45, 5–32 (2001)
4. Duda, R.O., Hart, P.E., Stork, D.G.: Pattern Classification. John Wiley & Sons, Inc., New York (2001)
5. Garcia, V., Sanchez, J.S., Mollineda, R.A., Alejo, R., Sotoca, J.M.: The class imbalance problem in pattern recognition and learning. In: II Congreso Espanol de Informatica, pp. 283–291 (2007)
6. He, H., Garcia, E.A.: Learning from imbalanced data. IEEE Transactions on Knowledge and Data Engineering 21(9), 1263–1284 (2009)
7. Homenda, W.: Optical Music Recognition: the Case Study of Pattern Recognition. In: Computer Recognition Systems, pp. 835–842. Springer (2005)
8. Homenda, W., Luckner, M., Pedrycz, W.: Classification with rejection: concepts and formal evaluations. In: Andrzej, M.J. (ed.) Proceedings of KICSS 2013, pp. 161–172. Progress & Business Publishers, Krakow (2013)
9. Homenda, W., Lesinski, W.: Optical Music Recognition: Case of Pattern recognition with Undesirable and Garbage Symbols. In: Choras, R., et al. (eds.) Image Processing and Communications Challenges, pp. 120–127. Exit, Warsaw (2009)
10. Lesinski, W., Jastrzebska, A.: Optical Music Recognition as the Case of Imbalanced Pattern Recognition: a Study of Single Classifiers. In: Skulimowski, A.M.J. (ed.) Proceedings of KICSS 2013, pp. 267–278. Progress & Business Publishers, Krakow (2013)
11. Lesinski, W., Jastrzebska, A.: Optical Music Recognition as the Case of Imbalanced Pattern Recognition: A Study of Complex Classifiers. In: Swiątek, J., Grzech, A., Swiątek, P., Tomczak, J.M., et al. (eds.) Advances in Systems Science. Lesinski W., Jastrzebska A, vol. 240, pp. 325–335. Springer, Heidelberg (2014)
12. Koronacki, J., Cwik, J.: Statystyczne systemy uczace sie. Exit, Warszawa (2008) (in Polish)
13. Kuncheva, L.I.: Combining Pattern Classifiers. Methods and Algorithms. John Wiley & Sons (2004)
14. Rebelo, A., Fujinaga, I., Paszkiewicz, F., Marcal, A.R.S., Guedes, C., Cardoso, J.S.: Optical music recognition: state-of-the-art and open issues. International Journal of Multimedia Information Retrieval 1, 173–190 (2012)
15. Quinlan, J.R.: Induction of Decision Trees. Machine Learning 1, 81–106 (1986)
16. Zhou, Z.H., Liu, X.Y.: On Multi-Class Cost-Sensitive Learning. Computational Intelligence 26, 232–257 (2010)
17. http://www.stat.berkeley.edu/users/breiman/RandomForests/
18. Breaking accessibility barriers in information society. Braille Score - design and implementation of a computer program for processing music information for blind people, the research project no N R02 0019 06/2009 supported by by The National Center for Research and Development, Poland (2009-2012)
19. Cognitive maps with imperfect information as a tool of automatic data understanding. Ideas, methods, applications, the research project no 2011/01/B/ST6/06478 supported by the National Science Center, Poland (2011-2014)

An Approach for Integrating Multidimensional Database into Context-Aware Recommender System

Mai Nhat Vinh, Nguyen Nhat Duy, Ho Thi Hoang Vy, and Le Nguyen Hoai Nam

University of Science, Vietnam National University - Ho Chi Minh City
{1012531,1012561}@student.hcmus.edu.vn,
{hthvy,lnhnam}@fit.hcmus.edu.vn

Abstract. Recommender system (RS) suggests useful items to users. Most of existing techniques in RS focus on using a rating matrix of users and items without considering recommendation context. In this paper, we take advantage of multidimensional database to present context information in context-aware RS. Therefore, we exploit the ability of OLAP aggregate operations to estimate user ratings. We propose an approach to translate the concepts of content-based, collaborative filtering and context recommendation into OLAP aggregate operations and integrate them to rating estimation function. Furthermore, through OLAP aggregate operations, our rating estimation function tends to solve the cold-start problem in RS and the data sparsity problem in context-aware RS. We develop a context-aware tour RS with our approach. In this system, we survey related researches to identify context information and user, item information being suitable to tour RS. We evaluate the system by accuracy and performance.

Keywords: context-aware recommender system, rating estimation, multidimensional database, multidimensional data cube, OLAP operation.

1 Introduction

When we deal with huge amounts of information, we are confused about making decisions. A recommender System (RS) plays a role as an expert supporting us to solve the problem of overwhelming information easily and quickly. The recommender system has attracted much attention in information science because there are still many open issues yet to be resolved. Most of the researches on the recommender system often focus on algorithmic improvement or propose new techniques to suggest useful items to users. Recommender systems are software agents that elicit the interests and preferences of individual consumers and make recommendations accordingly [12]. They have the potential to support and improve the quality of the decisions of users while searching for and selecting items.

Three techniques for suggesting useful items in RS are collaborative filtering, content-based and hybrid [3][7]. They are mainly based on the user habits in the past or based on who have the same interests with them in the past to predict the preference that user would give to an item.

K. Saeed and V. Snášel (Eds.): CISIM 2014, LNCS 8838, pp. 231–242, 2014.
© IFIP International Federation for Information Processing 2014

The collaborative filtering technique uses the experience of a group of users to recommend items. It based on the assumption that users will give ratings to items implicitly or explicitly and users who have similar preferences in the past will have similar preferences in the future. The input of the system is only a matrix of user ratings on items. The output could be a (numerical) prediction indicating to what degree the current user will like or dislike a certain item or a top-N list of recommendation items. However, the weakness of this technique is that the system cannot provide a good recommendation if data is sparse. It means that the number of available ratings could be too small to compute a recommendation. The main reason for that problem is that users do not always provide ratings to items. Another problem is when new item or new user has just been entered to the system, the system has no its historical information to generate recommendation.

For content-based technique, the recommendation is based on the consideration of characteristics of the item that a user has preferred in the past. Consequently, users will not be able to get novel items which are completely different from the available items in the system. Especially, when a user has changed the current preferences, the system cannot give this user the best recommendation. Furthermore, a new user who has just been entered to the system has no its historical information for the system to generate recommendation.

Most of existing approaches have focused on problems suggesting related items for users without considering recommendation context. There are many researches on the CONTEXT definitions and one of general definitions is "conditions or circumstances which affect something" [1][4]. In personalized Recommender Systems, context information has been recognized as an important factor to be considered [1][2][3][4][5][6]. Therefore, Adomavicius et al. in [1] propose a multidimensional approach for presenting context information beside the information of users and items in RS in order to increase the quality and performance of recommendation. Concretely, this approach presents user, item and context information as dimension tables in data warehouse. Information about user ratings to an item in a specific context is stored in a fact table. Hence, when multidimensional database is built into multidimensional data cube from dimension tables and fact table in data warehouse, we take advantage of the benefits of OLAP operations on data cube with aggregate ability to compute user rating for an item on a specific context. The user rating computation for an item on a specific context in this approach presented by Adomavicius et al. in [4] is based on the content-based technique. For example, we may want to know how individual user "Mr.A" like a destination place "Nha Trang City", we need to compute R(Mr.A, Nha Trang) that is the predicted rating of "Mr.A" to "Nha Trang". Because beach is a feature of the "Nha Trang" destination, we can use the hierarchy that "beach"is higher level in destination place dimension to compute aggregate rating R(Mr.A, Beach). Concretely, R(Mr.A, Nha Trang) is computed by OLAP rollup operation on destination place dimension as following:

$$R(Mr.A, NhaTrang) = R(Mr.A, rollup\ NhaTrang) = AGGR_{x.feature=Beach} R(Mr.A, x) = R(Mr.A, Beach)$$

Inferentially, R(Mr.A, Beach) is considered as R(Mr.A, Nha Trang).

In [6], the authors propose a rating estimation function for user u to item i in a certain context c referred as r(u, i, c). That function in [6] is based on: (1) historical ratings of user u to all items being similar to item i referred as aggregate computation R(u, rollup i, c) like content-based concept or (2) historical rating of all users being similar to user u to item i referred as aggregate computation R(rollup u, i, c) like collaborative filtering concept.

However, we realize that:

- When a new user u_{new} is newly added to the system, if only using (1), the estimative rating of u_{new} for any items will have the result being equal to 0 because there is no information of purchase history of u_{new}. Or if only using (2) to estimate any user's rating for new item i_{new}, which is newly added to the system, the rating estimation function will also have the result being equal to 0 because there is no purchase history of any users for i_{new}. Therefore, we propose integrating (1), (2) in this approach to solve these problems. However, this integration is not enough when a new user and new item is added into the system, the recommender system could not estimate the rating of u_{new} for i_{new}. Hence, we propose component (3) to help to solve this problem, (3) is historical ratings of all users being similar to user u to all items being similar to item i referred as aggregate computation R(rollup u, rollup i, c). This integration should be translated into OLAP aggregate operations on multidimensional data cube of a multidimensional database.
- Furthermore, with the approach for presenting user, item and context information as dimension tables, how to design every dimensions including selecting dimension attributes to hierarchize a dimension.
- Applying context information to compute rating will increase the accuracy of recommendation but it also narrows down the set of data used in computing recommendation. This leads the case that there are few ratings for prediction. That is data sparsity problem in context-aware RS. Especially, if there are no ratings in context c, r(u, i, c) will be equal to 0.

In this paper, we propose an approach to solve three above problems when integrating multidimensional database to context-aware RS. We verify this solution by developing a context-aware tour recommender system.

2   The Approach

In our approach, user, item and contextual information are presented by a multidimensional data model with snowflake schema [10] as Figure 1. The aim is to take advantage of the aggregation and hierarchy with OLAP operation on multidimensional data cube in this model.

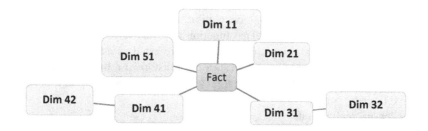

Fig. 1. Snowflake schema in multidimensional data model

In Figure 1, the fact table contains a measure presenting user rating with related dimensions. Each entity including context, user and item information will be presented by one dimension.

With the above model, we suggest a rating estimation function under OLAP aggregate operation on data cube of multidimensional database. Concretely, our rating estimation function for user u to item i in a specific context c referred as r(u,i,c) is as following:

$$r(u, i, c) = w_1 \times R(\text{rollup } u, i, c) + w_2 \times R(u, \text{rollup } i, c) \qquad (F1)$$

With r is prediction rating, R is available ratings in the system by user-supplied. Total of weights w_1 and w_2 must equal to 1.

As mentioned above, our rating estimation function will integrate (1) and (2). This integration is not only for solving the new user and new item problems but also for gaining better performance with fewer of the drawbacks of any individual one [18].Some of the combination methods that have been used such as Weighted, Switching, Mixed, Feature combination, Meta-level. Concretely, in this paper, we select the weighted method, which is shown in F1.Using weighted method, in our rating estimation function, the combination is linear, each element is assigned a weight and the weights can be adjustable according to user's feedbacks. Furthermore, these weights indicate the degree of each element in computing recommendation. Typically, if the weight of element R(rollup u, i, c) is higher than the weights of the others, that means that user u tends to get advices of the users who similar to user u. If the weight of element R(u, rollup i, c) is higher than the weights of the others, that means that user u tends to the items which user u liked in the past. For example, when a user wants to travel somewhere, he/she may consider asking guides from friends, relatives with basing on the features similar to destination places that he/she travelled before.

If our rating estimation function just integrates (1), (2), when a new user u_{new} and new item i_{new} is added into the system, the recommender system will not be able to estimate the rating of u_{new} for i_{new}, so r(u_{new}, i_{new}, c) is equal to 0. Because, when i_{new} is just added into the system, there is no rating of any users for i_{new}, so function R(rollup u_{new}, i_{new}, c) will be equal to 0. Similarly, when u_{new} is just added into the system, there is no rating of u_{new}, so function R(u_{new}, rollup i_{new}, c) will be equal to 0. Hence, we propose component (3) will help solve this problem. (3) is historical ratings of all users being similar to user u to all items being similar to item i referred as aggregate computation R(rollup u, rollup i, c). In this case, our rating estimation function is as following:

$$r(u, i, c) = R(\text{rollup } u, \text{rollup } i, c) \tag{F2}$$

Another important issue is how to design every dimensions including selecting dimension attributes to hierarchize each dimension. This depends on the considered dimensions in a certain domain. For example, in the tour recommender system, user dimension should be hierarchized by age or personality attribute because age or personality of users influence their selection of travel destination. Furthermore, the users who have the same age or the same personality often tend to like the same category of destination places. Therefore, user dimension may have two sub-dimensions as in Figure 2:

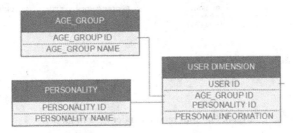

Fig. 2. Example of dimension design

When we roll up on the user dimension R(rollup u, i, c), we should consider rolling up on age or rolling up on personality or both. Our solution is to compute the average of all of them.

As mentioned above, considering user rating to items in a specific context may lead that prediction rating may be equal 0 if in the context which there is no rating or only a few rating. That is sparsity problem in context-aware RS. Hence, we propose to solve this problem by estimating rating in a context being similar to current context in this case. The similar context is the higher level of current context c and computed by rollup operation in context hierarchy. In this case, rating estimation function r(u,i,c) is described as following:

$$r'(u, i, c) = r(u, i, \text{rollup } c) \tag{F3}$$

3   Our Context-Aware Tour Recommender System

3.1   System Model

The proposed approach is applied to build a context-aware tour RS. The architecture of our tour RS is illustrated in Figure 3. It includes three modules:

- In the first module, the system will automatically get the tours from tourism websites then integrate and transfer them to data warehouse. This module is operated many times at regular intervals.

- The second module is the recommendation engine. Its input is context information from user. It is responsible for computing prediction rating by using the rating estimation function to generate a list of destination places that is the most suitable with the user. Then, the engine will search a list of tours in which the number of suitable destination places are maximal.
- The third module displays the recommendation to the user and receives user feedback.

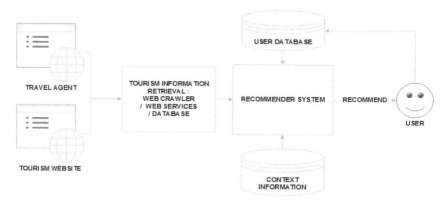

Fig. 3. Our tour recommender system model

3.2   Tour Context, User, Item Information

Based on [6][8][11][13][14][15], we summarize the criteria effecting to make decision of users who want to select some destination places to travel, then classify them into three groups: User, Item and Context to apply them into our context-aware tour RS. In Table 1, we illustrate some criteria that can be considered as context in tour context-aware RS.

Table 1. Criteria consideredas context

Context	Description	References
Time	**Season** :When should you travel to Japan? Eg: You should travel to Japan in Spring season because it got cherry-blossom in this season. **Festival** : When should you travel to Brazil ? Eg : You should travel to Brazil during Carnival time .	[15]
Goal	Which destinations should you travel for discovering Korea culture? Eg: You should find an area being well-known with the Kim Chi specialty	[8], [15]
Companion	If you travel with your lover where you should travel to? Eg: You and your lover may like a romantic scene at Themes river, London	[13], [15]

Table 1. *(Continued)*

Transport	By which transport you should travel to Pattaya island in Thailand? Eg: You ought to travel by boat to contemplate the coral	[15]
Weather	Which is the best weather to travel Honolulu? Eg: You should travel in summer time or when it's sunny	[15]
Distance	You are in USA. You want to travel to the beach. There are many choices for you such as Lanikai, Hawaii, Turquoise Bay, or Australia. They're all both exciting but you have to consider because it's a so far journey from USA to Australia.	[15]

In Table 2 and Table 3, we summarize criteria being attributes of user dimension and Destination dimension.

Table 2. Criteria considered as attributes for User dimension

Attribute	References	Is hierarchy attribute on the dimension?
Favorite	[6]	Yes
Age	[6], [8], [11], [13], [14]	Yes. This attribute highly effect to user 's decision mentioned in Table 1 in [8]
Sex	[6][8]	
Income	[8]	
Education level	[8]	

Table 3. Criteria considered as attributes for Destination dimension

Attribute	References	Is hierarchy attribute on the dimension?
Destination Category	[6], [13], [15], [16]	Yes
Region	[15]	Yes
Activity	[6], [13], [15], [16]	

3.3 Data Model

We had made the summary of important attributes that highly effects user decision. We identify a specific list of context dimensions and user, item dimension to apply to our context-aware tour RS as in Figure 4. Time context dimension should be separated into two dimensions which are season and festival as said in table 1. We differentiate festival from season dimension because we analyzed that the weather of the places depends on season so it will strong affect to user travel preferences and the festival dimension is either. In big festival occasions such as in Viet Nam, at Tet holiday, woman's day, Da Lat flower festival, etc…there are many special events than other occasion and users may be attracted. Therefore, in our system, we decide to include three contexts that are season (eg: summer, spring…), festival (eg: Tet holiday…) and companion because we couldn't collect enough data to the others context dimension.

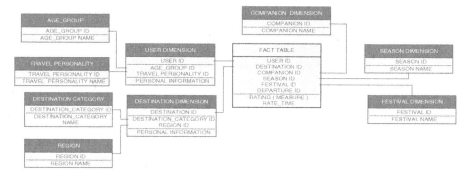

Fig. 4. Data model to build multidimensional cube of ratings

About rating data, we surveyed a number of participants by an online survey. At last, there are 5600 ratings were entered by 92 participants in two months from April 2014 to June 2014.The content of this survey includes two part: the first part with 8 questions about age and travel personality; the second part with 100 travel destinations belonging to 30 categories in 8 region, participants were required to provide the rating and answer the question related to context information as following: when and who you go with?. Overall, 89 participants responded to us and 5600 rating were collected. The collected data were transferred to multidimensional cube and ready for the estimation process.

4   Evaluation

4.1   Execution Time

We do experiment to measure the execution time of the system for estimating user rating. The execution time is taken in two data model of multidimensional database. For the first model, multidimensional database is presented by a relational data model in which context, user, item, rating are tables with foreign keys. For second model, multidimensional database is a multidimensional data cube which is built from relational data model of the first model.

The experiment is on HP 430 Core i5-2450M Sandy Bridge (2.5GHz up to 3.1GHz, 4GB 1333 MHz DDR3 SDRAM , 500GB), SQL server 2012. In relational data model, we use *System.Data.SqlClient* in .Net to execute queries to database engine in SQL server while in multidimensional data cube, *Microsoft.AnalysisServices.AdomdClient* is used for executing OLAP operation to data cube.

The result of the experiment is shown in Figure 5, when the number of rating records is less than 20000, the execution time in the relational data model is better than the execution time of the multidimensional data cube. However, when the number of rating records is more than 20000, the execution time of the multidimensional cube is far better than the execution time of the relational data model. Furthermore, when the number of rating records increases, the execution time in the relational data model increases quickly and reaches 109.932 milliseconds at 1 million rating records while the increase of the execution time of the multidimensional data cube is not considerable. The execution time of the multidimensional data cube is 7.414 milliseconds at 1 million rating records. The main reason is that when multidimensional database is presented by relational data model, rollup operation is executed by join operation on related tables, so the more the number of rating records, the more the execution time of rollup operation on it while multidimensional data cube specializes in supporting executing rollup operations

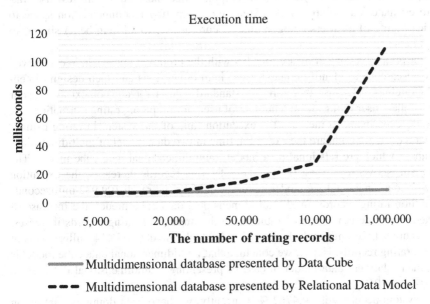

Fig. 5. The execution time of the system for estimating user rating

4.2   Accuracy

Using the metric in [17], the system accuracy was computed by counting the number of useful recommendations. Useful recommendations are collected by getting user feedback after receiving the recommendation. Concretely, the participants are required to enter context information then the system will predict a list of top 10 destination places being suitable to them. They then answer the number of recommended destination places satisfying their needs. There are 89 participants joined in the evaluation but till now, 21 responses out of 89 were collected. Currently, the system accuracy is 80.4762 %.

We also have used Mean Absolute Error (MAE) to compute the deviation between predicted ratings and actual ratings. Currently, just a few responses were collected from participants. However, we will continue doing the evaluation with more participants.

5   Conclusion

We desire to highlight the importance of context information in RS. Multidimensional database is one of suitable solution for presenting context information. Furthermore, multidimensional data cube model of multidimensional database facilitates OLAP aggregate operations. Therefore, we translated rating estimation function into OLAP aggregate operations on multidimensional data cube. Under OLAP aggregate operations, rating estimation function is the integration and overcoming of the existing technique in RS. About the data sparsity problem that means there are few user ratings to estimate, our solution is to extend the computing recommendation space to historical rating of all users being similar to current user to all item being similar to current item.

We developed a context aware tour RS with the proposed approach. We surveyed related researches to identify context, user, item dimensions and then design dimension hierarchies. Because there are not standard dataset for our context aware tour RS, we collect user ratings from a number of users for preparing rating estimation.

We do experiment to measure the execution time of the system in rating estimation. Moreover, we compare the execution time in two data model of multidimensional database which are relational data model, multidimensional data cube model. The comparison shows that when the number of rating records increases, the execution time with relational database model increases quickly and reach 109.932 milliseconds at 1 million rating records. With multidimensional data cube model, the increase of the execution time is not considerable when the number of rating records increases. The execution time with multidimensional data cube model is 7.414 milliseconds at 1million rating records. Hence, we conclude that multidimensional data cube model is better than relational data model in case of presenting multidimensional database in context-aware RS.

The system accuracy is 80.4762 %. Currently, we have been doing evaluation on higher number of users.

6   Future Work

Next time, we will focus on optimizing system performance by studying issues related to multidimensional data cube. Furthermore, we are trying to combine other methods to make clear the user preferences. Clearly, the more recommender systems understand user preferences, the better recommendations they can provide. Recommendation must base on user preferences. Therefore, understanding user preferences is very important but it's a really hard work. Modeling of user preferences needs their relevance feedback on the recommendations [9]. The relevance feedback may be collected either explicitly or implicitly. The explicit feedback indicates the rating user provided. However, it wastes user's effort, time, and cost because users have to stop their action to enter explicit rating, users don't like to give rating. So we can observer user behaviors such as time spent on viewing the items, number of accesses to an item, or the action click to view, like, shared, buy items... The implicit feedback can reduce the cost of rating items by saving the user's time, however there remains a computational cost in storing and processing the implicit rating data, this can be hidden from the user. Therefore, we can improve system performance and overcome the sparsity problem by combine them together. Moreover, we also integrate other techniques such as indexing, partition data on multidimensional database to improve the performance.

Acknowledgments. This research is supported by research funding from Advanced Program in Computer Science, University of Science, Vietnam National University - Ho Chi Minh City.

References

1. Adomavicius, G., Tuzhilin, A.: Multidimensional recommender systems: A data warehousing approach. In: Fiege, L., Mühl, G., Wilhelm, U.G. (eds.) WELCOM 2001. LNCS, vol. 2232, pp. 180–192. Springer, Heidelberg (2001)
2. Araque, F., Salguero, A., Abad, M.M.: Application of data warehouse and Decision Support System in soaring site recommendation. In: Information and Communication Technologies in Tourism, pp. 308–319 (2006)
3. Adomavicius, G., Tuzhilin, A.: Toward the Next Generation of Recommender systems: A Survey of the State-of-the-Art and Possible Extensions. IEEE Transactions on Knowledge and Data Engineering 17(6) (2005)
4. Adomavicius, G., Sankaranarayanan, R., Sen, S., Tuzhilin, A.: Incorporating Contextual Information in Recommender Systems Using a Multidimensional Approach. ACM Transactions on Information Systems (TOIS) 23(1), 103–145 (2005)
5. Adomavicius, G., Tuzhilin, A.: Context-Aware Recommender Systems. In: Recommender Systems Handbook. Springer (2011)
6. Rahman, M.M.: Contextual Recommender Systems Using a Multidimensional Approach. International Journal of Emerging Technology and Advanced Engineering 3(8) (August 2013)
7. Candillier, L., Jack, K., Fessant, F., Meyer, F.: State-of-the-Art Recommender Systems. In: Collaborative and Social Information Retrieval and Access: Techniques for Improved User Modeling, pp. 1–22. IGI global (2008)
8. Fang-Ming, H., Yu-Tzeng, L., Tu-Kuang, H.: Design and implementation of an intelligent recommendation system for tourist attractions: The integration of EBM model, Bayesian network and Google Maps. In: Fang-Ming, H., Yu-Tzeng, L., Tu-Kuang, H. (eds.) Expert Systems with Applications, vol. 39. Elsevier (2012)
9. Seo, Y.-W., Zhang, B.-T.: Learning User's Preferences by Analyzing Web-Browsing Behaviors. In: Proceedings of the 4th International Conference on Autonomous Agents, Barcelona, Spain, pp. 381–387 (2000)
10. Inmon, W.H.: Building the Data Warehouse. John Wiley (2002)

11. Schiaffino, S., Amandi, A.: Building an expert travel agent as a software agent. In: Expert Systems with Applications. Elsevier (2009)
12. Xiao, B.: E-commerce item recommendation agents: Use, characteristics, and impact. MIS Quarterly 31(1), 137–209 (2007)
13. Ananthapadmanaban, K.R., Srivatsa, S.K.: Personalization of user Profile: Creating user Profile Ontology for Tamilnadu Tourism. International Journal of Computer Applications (0975 – 8887) 23(8) (June 2011)
14. Hanlan, J., Fuller, D., Wilde, S.J.: The travel destination decision process and the relevance of segmentation studies to the marketing of regional tourism destinations in an Australian context. In: Center for Enterprise Development and Research Occasional P aper, no. 1, Centre for Regional Tourism Research, Southern Cross University, Coffs Harbour, NSW (2005)
15. Kabassi, K.: Personalizing recommendations for tourists. Telematics and Informatics 27, 51–66 (2010)
16. Agarwal, J., Sharma, N., Kumar, P., Parshav, V., Srivastava, A., Goudar, R.H.: Intelligent Search in E- Tourism ServicesUsing Recommendation System: Perfect Guidefor Tourist. In: 2013 7th International Conference on Intelligent Systems and Control (ISCO), India (2013)
17. Olmo, F.H., Gaudioso, E.: Evaluation of recommender systems: A new approach. Journal Expert Systems with Applications: An International 35(3) (October 2008)
18. Burke, R.: Hybrid Recommender Systems: Survey and Experiments (2009)

Vietnamese Sentence Similarity Based on Concepts

Hien T. Nguyen, Phuc H. Duong, and Vinh T. Vo

Faculty of Information Technology, Ton Duc Thang University, Vietnam
{hien,vothanhvinh}@tdt.edu.vn, huuphucduong@gmail.com

Abstract. We propose a novel method for measuring semantic similarity of two sentences. The originality of the method is the way that it explores the similarity of concepts referred to in the sentences using Wikipedia. The method also exploits Wiktionary to measure word-to-word similarity. The overall semantic similarity is a linear combination of word-to-word similarity, word-order similarity, and concept similarity. We build datasets consisting of 45 Vietnamese sentence pairs and then evaluate the method on these datasets. The results show that in the best cases, concept similarity help improving the performance of our method more than 15% point. The proposed method is language-independent and quite easy to employ. Therefore, one can readily adopt our method to measure semantic similarity for sentences written in other languages.

Keywords: Paraphrase Identification, Text Similarity, Semantic Similarity.

1   Introduction

We study the task of measuring semantic similarity of short texts, i.e., sentence, text segments or very short text snippets. With the development of natural language applications recently, this task has been playing an increasingly important role in plagiarism detection, question answering, machine translation, text summarization, information retrieval, etc. This is a challenging task. Considering the following two sentence pairs, two sentences in the first pair are more likely similarity in meaning even though not many words they contain are common; while all most all words in two sentences in the second pair are the same but their meanings are different.

- *"She has to pass the exam."* and *"She must get through the exam"*
- *"To gain admission to UCLA, you need to present an academic profile much stronger than represented by the minimum UC admission requirements below."*[1] and *"To gain admission to Berkeley, you need to present an academic profile much stronger than that represented by the minimum UC admission requirements"*[2]

Until now, there have been many methods proposed for measuring text similarity. Most of them use either knowledge-based or corpus-based word-to-word semantic

---

[1] www.admissions.ucla.edu/prospect/adm_fr/fracadrq.htm
[2] admissions.berkeley.edu/sites/default/files/docs/
Freshman_Flier.pdf

K. Saeed and V. Snášel (Eds.): CISIM 2014, LNCS 8838, pp. 243–253, 2014.
© IFIP International Federation for Information Processing 2014

similarity measures [1], in combination with syntactic information [4], [5], [13], [14] or string matching algorithm [2]. Some works exploited machine translation metrics [7], discourse information [6], or graph subsumption [12] for paraphrase identification. In summary, the work in literature did not exploit concepts, i.e. named entities and common concepts, including coreference and disambiguation, for measuring similarity of short texts. A concept we mean in this work is a named entity such as a person, a location, or an organization in particular, etc. or a common concept such as computer science or information technology.

We propose a novel method to compute semantic similarity between sentence pairs. We evaluate the method on a dataset consisting of Vietnamese sentences. The method explores concepts to determine how they contribute to the performance of measuring semantic similarity of sentences. It also exploits word-to-word similarity and word-order similarity as proposed by Li *et al.* in [4]. An intuition shows that exploring named entities (as well as concepts) and their features is potentially in improving the performance of semantic similarity of sentences, especially for those with the same meaning containing named entities but few words in common. For example, with these two sentences "*I am currently working at IBM*" and "*I am a developer at International Business Machines*", if we only compute the similarity based on words and word-order, the similarity score may not be high as it would be even though the entities *IBM* and *International Business Machines* are the same in the contexts of the two sentences.

One of the challenging problem when dealing with Vietnamese texts is that Vietnamese is a language with a deficient natural language processing support, such as no Vietnamese WordNet or corpus like Brown Corpus of American English for measuring semantic similarity between Vietnamese words. To overcome that limitation, we exploit Wikipedia[3] to recognize which concepts referred to in compared sentences exist in Wikipedia to expand the context of those sentences by different surface forms of the concepts and exploit Wiktionary[4] to estimate the similarity of words.

Wikipedia is a free online encyclopedia whose content is contributed by a large number of volunteer users. It consists of a large collection of articles, each of which defines and describes a concept. In reality, a concept may have several surface forms and one surface form may be used to refer to different concepts in different contexts. In Wikipedia, many-to-many correspondence between names and entities can be captured by utilizing *redirect pages* and *disambiguation pages*. A redirect page typically contains only a reference to an article. The title of a redirect page is an alternative surface form of the described entity or concept in that article. For example, from redirect pages of the United States, we extract alternative surface forms of the United States such as "US", "USA", "United States of America", etc. A disambiguation page is created for an ambiguous surface form which may use to denote two or more entities in Wikipedia. It consists of links to articles that define the different concepts having the same surface form. Wiktionary is a free-content multilingual dictionary, designed as the lexical companion to Wikipedia and opened for volunteers to edit all the contents. It provides the meaning of vocabulary, not includes the encyclopedic information – an advantage of Wikipedia.

---

[3] http://vi.wikipedia.org
[4] http://vi.wiktionary.org

The contributions of this paper is three-fold as follows: (i) we propose a novel method that based on concepts for measuring similarity of Vietnamese sentences, (ii) we build a dataset consisting of 45 Vietnamese sentence pairs, each of which was estimate by human subjects if it is paraphrase or not and evaluate our proposed method on this dataset. The method exploits Wiktionary to measure similarity of words, exploits Wikipedia to identify which concepts referred to in the compared sentences existing in Wikipedia for expanding the contexts of those sentences by different surface forms of the concepts. The originality of this work is the way that our method expands the contexts of compared sentences using Wikipedia.

The rest of this paper is organized as follows. Section 2 presents related work. Section 3 presents our proposed approach. Section 4 presents datasets, experiments and results. Finally, we draw conclusion in Section 5.

2   Related Work

There is much research on sentence similarity measurement. In [1], the authors proposed a method that estimates the semantic similarity between two short texts using both corpus-based and knowledge-based similarity measures of words. Given two short text segments, the method finds for each word in the first one the most similar matching word in the second one and then the similarity between those word pairs are included in the overall semantic similarity of the two text segments. In [2], the authors introduced a method that computes the text similarity by combining a corpus-based similarity measure of words and a modified version of the Longest Common Subsequence string matching algorithm. The method proposed in [9] uses word-to-word similarity derived from WordNet to identify paraphrase.

The methods proposed in [4], [5], [13], [14] measure text similarity based on semantic and syntactic information contained in the compared texts. In addition to using word-to-word similarity, the method in [4] presents the important role of word-order in improvement of sentence similarity measure, the method in [5] exploited adjectives and adverbs in two sentences, the method in [13] takes nouns and verbs in consideration, and the method in [14] exploited interdependent between word-to-word similarity and sentence similarity and computed both of them simultaneously by an iterative algorithm. In [12], the authors use graph subsumption (originally developed for recognizing entailment) with lexical, syntactic, synonymy and antonymy information to identify paraphrase.

The method proposed in [6] combines machine translation metrics and the ordered similarity between elementary discourse units (EDUs). An EDU are blocks of words playing an important role in sentence similarity. In [3], the authors proposed a method that takes advantage of web search results to extend context of short texts and in [8] the authors uses unfolding recursive auto-encoder method for measuring the similarity. In [11], instead of identifying the similarity, the authors propose a method detecting dissimilarities. The method proposed in [14] combines semantic and statistical information within short texts to compute the similarity. The method proposed in [13] takes advantage of corpus-based ontology to overcome the problem that evaluates the semantic similarity between irregular sentences.

In this paper, we propose a novel method that explores concepts to measure the similarity of sentences. In contrast with related methods, our method use Wiktionary instead of WordNet to measure the similarity of words. Moreover, it identifies which concepts referred to in the compared sentences existing in Wikipedia for expanding the contexts of those sentences by different surface forms of the concepts.

3   Proposed Method

We propose a novel method that computes overall semantic similarity of two sentences, let say S_1 and S_2, as follows:

$$Sim(S_1, S_2) = \alpha \times Sim_{word} + \beta \times Sim_{word-order} + \gamma \times Sim_{concept} \quad (1)$$

where Sim_{word}, $Sim_{word-order}$, $Sim_{concept}$ are sentence similarity measures based exclusively on word-to-word similarity, word-order similarity, and concept similarity respectively; $\alpha + \beta + \gamma = 1$; and the coefficients $\{\alpha, \beta, \gamma\}$ decide the contribution of word-to-word similarity, word-order similarity and concept similarity to the whole sentences. In following three sub-sections, we respectively present the similarity measures.

3.1   Model

Our method contains four main steps for computing semantic similarity between two sentences. The first step performs tokenizer. The second step calculates the similarity between sentences by using word-to-word similarity based on Wiktionary. The third computes similarity between sentences by using word-order similarity of the two sentences. The fourth step recognizes concepts in the two sentences using Wikipedia and expands the contexts of the sentences to compute the concept similarity; then the similarity between sentences is computed using the concept similarity. Finally, the overall sentence similarity score is derived by combining the word-to-word similarity, the word-order similarity and the concept similarity.

3.2   Sentence Similarity Based on Word Similarity

The essence of sentence similarity is word-to-word similarity. Thus, we propose to use the Text Overlap method to compute the word-to-word similarity between two words. To our knowledge, this is the most possible method for computing the word-to-word similarity based on Vietnamese Wiktionary. Text Overlap method was first introduced in 1986 by Michael Lesk [16]. The main idea of the method is based on the level of the intersection of gloss texts. The higher level of intersection is, the more similar two words are and otherwise.

We first have to split two input sentences into tokens, then, we will create semantic vectors base on those tokens. Now, we will go through all steps in word-to-word Similarity. Given two sentences S_1 and S_2, a joint word set is defined by $S = S_1 \cup S_2 = \{w_1; w_2; \dots; w_n\}$. The word set S contains all distinct words from the two sentences and includes all inflectional morphology words. For example, *word* and *words*, *thesis* and *theses* are considered as distinct words and must appear in *S*. For example, given the following sentences:

- S_1 = I am a developer at International Business Machines.
- S_2 = I am currently working at IBM.
- S = {I, am, a, developer, at, International, Business, Machines, currently, working, IBM}.

Because the word set *S* is derived from two sentences, we should use it as a standard semantic vector for comparing, denoted by *V*. The semantic vector of two sentences (V_1 and V_2) must have the same dimension of *V* and each value of an entry of the semantic vector (V_1 and V_2), denoted by s_i $(i = 1, 2, ..., m)$, is determined by word-to-word similarity method and should lie between [0,1]. Taking S_1 as an example:

- *Case 1*: if w_i appears in S_1, set s_i to 1.
- *Case 2*: if w_i not appears in S_1, word-to-word similarity method will be used to compute the similarity between w_i and each word in S_1. Thus, the word-to-word similarity score should be the highest number k. If k exceeds a standard threshold, then $s_i = k$, otherwise, set $s_i = 0$. Suppose that the highest number $k = 0.01$, the value of s_i should be 0, because 0.01 is closer to zero, and that's why we should have a standard threshold.

Unlike other text similarity methods, this approach keeps all function words, since these words contain syntactic information if the sentence is too short. Although they appear in the joint word set *S*, they can't affect the whole meaning of the sentence, as well as the semantic vectors, because we use a threshold to eliminate them. After we have two semantic vectors V_1 and V_2, the semantic similarity between two sentences is computed by cosine coefficient of those vectors:

$$Sim_{word} = \frac{V_1 \cdot V_2}{|V_1| \cdot |V_2|} \tag{2}$$

3.3   Sentence Similarity Based on Word Order Similarity

Before starting this section, we should look over the two example sentences below, they contain the same words in each sentence but differ from the position of two words *boy* and *girl* as follows:

- S_1 = A boy buys the girl a gift.
- S_2 = A girl buys the boy a gift.

We can see that if we only consider word-to-word similarity on that candidate pair, the similarity score will be maximum because all words in that pair are the same. The dissimilarity between S_1 and S_2 is caused by the different word-order. To resolve this problem, we form a joint word set *S*, each entry value denoted by w_i $(i = 1, 2, ..., m)$. S = {A, boy, buys, the, girl, a, gift}. We assign an index number for each word in S_1 and S_2. To compute the similarity score, a word-order vector R_i is formed for each sentence with the length equals to the size of S and each value of R_i is simply an index number in the sentence. Taking S_l as an example, for each word w_i in S, we will consider its position or the most similar between it and the others, look the cases as follows:

- *Case 1*: if w_i appears in S_l, entry value of this word in R_l is the index number from S_l.
- *Case 2*: if w_i doesn't appear in S_l, entry value of this word in R_l is zero.

For example of S_l and S_2, two word-order vectors R_l and R_2 should be:

- $R_1 = \{1, 2, 3, 4, 5, 6, 7\}$
- $R_2 = \{1, 5, 3, 4, 5, 2, 7\}$

Through this approach, we can see that R_1 and R_2 clearly show the basic structure of the sentence. Eventually, a measure for computing word-order similarity of the two input sentences is:

$$Sim_{word-order} = 1 - \frac{\|R_1 - R_2\|}{\|R_1 + R_2\|} \qquad (3)$$

3.4   Sentence Similarity Based on Concept Similarity

In order to improve the quality of assessment of similarity between two sentences, we determine the similarity between concepts occurring in sentences base on Wikipedia. To better understand the purpose of applying concept similarity, considering the following example with two sentences S_1 and S_2. If we only compute semantic similarity base on words and word-order, we can't detect two entities *Ho Chi Minh City* and *Sai Gon* are the same. As a result, it may lead to the similarity between two sentences not accurate.

- $S_1 = $ I am living in Sai Gon.
- $S_2 = $ I am living in Ho Chi Minh City.

We adopt the mention recognition of Huy *et al.* [19] to identify surface forms of Wikipedia concepts in a sentence. If an identified surface form has only one candidate concept, our method collects all of its surface forms - extracted from its title and its redirect page titles in Wikipedia. If an identified surface form is ambiguous, our method does not disambiguate it, but collects all surface forms of all of its candidate concepts based on the disambiguation page of the identified surface form in Wikipedia.

Given a pair of sentences, let SF_1 be a set of surface forms identified in the first sentence and SF_2 be a set of surface forms identified in the second sentence. The sentence similarity based on concept similarity is computed as follows:

$$Sim_{concept} = \frac{|SF_1 \cap SF_2|}{Min(|SF_1|, |SF_2|)} \qquad (4)$$

4   Dataset and Evaluation

4.1   Dataset

To evaluate the performance of our method, we build a dataset consisting of 45 pairs of sentences. Then the dataset is sent to different persons to estimate if each pair is paraphrase or not. If a pair is paraphrase, result will be 1, otherwise result will be 0. After collecting seven survey results, we analyze and create two datasets to serve the assessment process. The results show that there are 19 pairs getting the same agreement by 7 persons, 6 pairs getting the same agreement by 6 persons, 6 pairs getting the same agreement by 5 persons. In total 31 pairs get the same agreement by at least 5 persons. We give 7 persons a chance to discuss on these 31 pairs and get a dataset consisting of 31 sentence pairs with agreement by 7 persons, namely Dataset-1. We build Dataset-2 as follows: the assessments which have at least four number of 1 (the same agreement by at least 4 persons) will unify to 1, the others will be 0. It means that Dataset-2 consists of 45 pairs of sentences.

4.2   Evaluation

In the fields of science, engineering, industry, and statistics, "the accuracy of a measurement system is the degree of closeness of measurements of a quantity to that quantity's actual (true) value". In our case, we use a binary classification to measure of how well a test correctly identifies or excludes a condition. Let's take a look the problem we have: the output of computational process lies in [0;1], thus, which value of threshold τ give the similarity of two sentences is 1 or 0; and with that τ, how well the accuracy of the approach is. To solve the problem, we will initially set $\tau = 0.5$, each loop τ will increase a value $t = 0.01$, if the output of computational process is larger than τ, the similarity will be 1, otherwise, will be 0. The value of $accuracy$ calculated by applying the formula:

$$accuracy = \frac{TP+TN}{TP+FP+TN+FN} \tag{5}$$

where TP denotes true positive, TN denote true negative, FP denote false positive, FN denote false negative.

We evaluate our method on Dataset-1 and Dataset-2 respectively. Table 1 shows the results after running our method on Dataset-1. The column "τ" shows the τ values, The column "accuracy with concepts" shows overall sentence similarity of our method in the term of accuracy, and the column "accuracy without concepts" shows overall sentence similarity of our method in the case we do not use concept similarity. The results shown in Table 2 are explained as the same as doing for the results shown in Table 1.

As shown in Table 1, for Dataset-1, the accuracy is maximized at threshold $\{0.50 \text{ to } 0.55, 0.62, 0.63\}$ and minimized at $\{0.94, 0.95\}$. As shown in Table 2, for Dataset-2, the accuracy is maximized at threshold $\{0.50 \text{ to } 0.55, 0.62, 0.63\}$ and minimized at $\{0.94, 0.95\}$. Fig.1 and Fig 2 respectively show the curves comparing the performance of our method on Dataset-1 and Dataset-2 with and without using concept similarity.

We can see that, the higher threshold is, the smaller accuracy is, because the value of τ at low level is closer to people judgment. All in all, the results show that in the best cases, concept similarity help improving the performance of our method more than 15% point; which prove that concept similarity significantly contribute to the performance of our method.

Table 1. The overall accuray of our method on Datatset-1

τ	Accuracy with Concepts	Accuracy without Concepts	τ	Accuracy with Concepts	Accuracy without Concepts
0.50	93.55	77.42	0.73	64.52	38.71
0.51	93.55	77.42	0.74	64.52	38.71
0.52	93.55	77.42	0.75	64.52	38.71
0.53	93.55	77.42	0.76	64.52	38.71
0.54	93.55	77.42	0.77	64.52	38.71
0.55	93.55	77.42	0.78	61.29	38.71
0.56	90.32	74.19	0.79	54.84	35.48
0.57	90.32	74.19	0.80	48.39	35.48
0.58	90.32	74.19	0.81	41.94	35.48
0.59	90.32	74.19	0.82	41.94	35.48
0.60	90.32	70.97	0.83	38.71	35.48
0.61	90.32	70.97	0.84	38.71	35.48
0.62	93.55	70.97	0.85	38.71	32.26
0.63	93.55	67.74	0.86	38.71	29.03
0.64	90.32	64.52	0.87	35.48	29.03
0.65	87.1	64.52	0.88	32.26	29.03
0.66	83.87	58.06	0.89	32.26	29.03
0.67	83.87	58.06	0.90	32.26	25.81
0.68	80.65	58.06	0.91	29.03	25.81
0.69	80.65	51.61	0.92	29.03	22.58
0.70	77.42	45.16	0.93	29.03	22.58
0.71	74.19	45.16	0.94	25.81	22.58
0.72	67.74	41.94	0.95	25.81	22.58

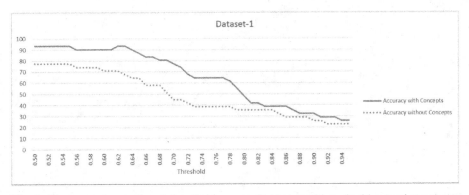

Fig. 1. The curves comparing the performance on Dataset-1 with and without using concept similarity

Table 2. The overall accuray of our method on Datatset-2

τ	Accuracy with Concepts	Accuracy without Concepts	τ	Accuracy with Concepts	Accuracy without Concepts
0.50	86.67	73.33	0.73	64.44	46.67
0.51	86.67	73.33	0.74	64.44	46.67
0.52	86.67	73.33	0.75	64.44	46.67
0.53	86.67	73.33	0.76	66.67	46.67
0.54	86.67	73.33	0.77	66.67	44.44
0.55	86.67	73.33	0.78	62.22	44.44
0.56	84.44	71.11	0.79	57.78	44.44
0.57	84.44	71.11	0.80	55.56	44.44
0.58	84.44	71.11	0.81	51.11	44.44
0.59	84.44	71.11	0.82	48.89	44.44
0.60	84.44	68.89	0.83	46.67	44.44
0.61	84.44	68.89	0.84	46.67	44.44
0.62	86.67	68.89	0.85	44.44	42.22
0.63	86.67	68.89	0.86	46.67	40.00
0.64	82.22	66.67	0.87	44.44	40
0.65	80	64.44	0.88	42.22	40
0.66	77.78	60	0.89	42.22	40
0.67	77.78	60	0.90	42.22	37.78
0.68	75.56	60	0.91	40	37.78
0.69	75.56	55.56	0.92	40	33.33
0.70	73.33	53.33	0.93	40	33.33
0.71	71.11	51.11	0.94	37.78	33.33
0.72	66.67	48.89	0.95	37.78	33.33

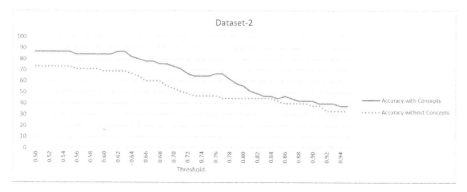

Fig. 2. The curves comparing the performance on Dataset-2 with and without using concept similarity

5   Conclusion

In this paper, we present a novel method for measuring semantic similarity of two sentences. The overall semantic similarity is a linear combination of word-to-word similarity, word-order similarity, and concept similarity. The method exploits Wiktionary to measure similarity of words, exploits Wikipedia to identify which concepts referred to in the compared sentences existing in Wikipedia for expanding the contexts of those sentences by different surface forms of the concepts in order to compute the concept similarity. We evaluate the method on the datasets consisting of Vietnamese sentence pairs. The results show that in the best cases, concept similarity help improving the performance of our method more than 15% point. The proposed method is language-independent and quite easy to employ. Therefore, one can readily adopt our method to measure semantic similarity for sentences written in other languages.

References

1. Mihalcea, R., Corley, C., Strapparava, C.: Corpus-based and knowledge-based measures of text semantic similarity. AAAI 6, 775–780 (2006)
2. Islam, A., Inkpen, D.: Semantic text similarity using corpus-based word similarity and string similarity. In: ACM Transactions on Knowledge Discovery from Data (TKDD) 2(2), Article 10 (2008)
3. Sahami, M., Heilman, T.D.: A web-based kernel function for measuring the similarity of short text snippets. In: Proceedings of the 15th International Conference on World Wide Web, pp. 377–386 (2006)
4. Li, Y., McLean, D., Bandar, Z.A., O'shea, J.D., Crockett, K.: Sentence similarity based on semantic nets and corpus statistics. IEEE Transactions on Knowledge and Data Engineering 18(8), 1138–1150 (2006)
5. Oliva, J., Serrano, J.I., del Castillo, M.D., Iglesias, Á.: SyMSS: A syntax-based measure for short-text semantic similarity. Data & Knowledge Engineering 70(4), 390–405 (2011)

6. Bach, N.X., Minh, N.L., Shimazu, A.: Exploiting discourse information to identify paraphrases. Expert Systems with Applications 41(6), 2832–2841 (2014)
7. Madnani, N., Tetreault, J., Chodorow, M.: Re-examining Machine Translation Metrics for Paraphrase Identification. In: Proceedings of 2012 Conference of the North American Chapter of the Association for Computational Linguistics (NAACL 2012), pp. 182–190 (2012)
8. Socher, R., Huang, E.H., Pennington, J., Ng, A.Y., Manning, C.D.: Dynamic Pooling and Unfolding Recursive Autoencoders for Paraphrase Detection. NIPS 24, 801–809 (2011)
9. Fernando, S., Stevenson, M.: A semantic similarity approach to paraphrase detection. In: Proceedings of the 11th Annual Research Colloquium of the UK Special Interest Group for Computational Linguistics, pp. 45–52 (2008)
10. Das, D., Smith, N.: Paraphrase identification as probabilistic quasi-synchronous recognition. In: Proceedings of the Joint Conference of the 47th Annual Meeting of the ACL and the 4th International Joint Conference on Natural Language Processing of the AFNLP, pp. 468–476 (2009)
11. Qiu, L., Kan, M.Y., Chua, T.S.: Paraphrase recognition via dissimilarity significance classification. In: Proceedings of the 2006 Conference on Empirical Methods in Natural Language Processing (EMNLP 2006), pp. 18–26 (2006)
12. Rus, V., McCarthy, P.M., Lintean, M.C., McNamara, D.S., Graesser, A.C.: Paraphrase identification with lexico-syntactic graph subsumption. In: FLAIRS 2008, pp. 201–206 (2008)
13. Lee, M.C.: A novel sentence similarity measure for semantic-based expert systems. Expert Systems with Applications 38(5), 6392–6399 (2011)
14. Wenyin, L., Quan, X., Feng, M., Qiu, B.: A short text modeling method combining semantic and statistical information. Information Sciences 180(20), 4031–4041 (2010)
15. Blacoe, W., Lapata, M.: A comparison of vector-based representations for semantic composition. In: Proceedings of the 2012 Joint Conference on Empirical Methods in Natural Language Processing and Computational Natural Language Learning, pp. 546–556 (2012)
16. Lesk, M.: Automatic sense disambiguation using machine readable dictionaries: how to tell a pine cone from an ice cream cone. In: Proceedings of the 5th Annual International Conference on Systems Documentation, pp. 24–26 (1986)
17. Tsatsaronis, G., Varlamis, I., Vazirgiannis, M.: Text relatedness based on a word thesaurus. Journal of Artificial Intelligence Research 37(1), 1–40 (2010)
18. Rubenstein, H., Goodenough, J.B.: Contextual correlates of synonymy. Communications of the ACM 8(10), 627–633 (1965)
19. Huynh, H.M., Nguyen, T.T., Cao, T.H.: Using coreference and surrounding contexts for entity linking. In: 2013 IEEE RIVF International Conference on Computing and Communication Technologies, Research, Innovation, and Vision for the Future (RIVF 2013), pp. 1–5 (2013)

Materialized View Construction Based on Clustering Technique

Santanu Roy[1], Ranak Ghosh[2], and Soumya Sen[2]

[1] Department of MCA, Future Institute of Engineering & Management Kolkata, India
[2] A.K.Choudhury School of Information Technology, University of Calcutta
{santanuroy84,ranakghoshmail,iamsoumyasen}@gmail.com

Abstract. Materialized view is important to any data intensive system where answering queries at runtime is subject of interest. Users are not aware about the presence of materialized views in the system but the presence of these results in fast access to data and therefore optimized execution of queries. Many techniques have evolved over the period to construct materialized views. However the survey work reveals a few attempts to construct materialized views based on attribute similarity measure by statistical similarity function and thereafter applying the clustering techniques. In this paper we have proposed materialized view construction methodology at first by analyzing the attribute similarity based on Jaccard Index then clustering methodology is applied using similarity based weighted connected graph. Further the clusters are validated to check the correctness of the materialized views.

Keywords: Materialized View, Clustering, Jaccard Index, Attribute Similarity Matrix, Weighted graphs.

1 Introduction

The motivation to create materialized view is to ensure the availability of frequently accessed data such that the query execution takes place faster. A key measure to quantify the merit of materialized view is to compute the hit ratio. It is defined as the ratio of hit to the materialized view divided by the total numbers of requests/queries to the database system. Hit means in this context, availability of data in the materialized views to successfully answer the queries. Over the time numbers of researches have been carried out to form the materialized views based on different methodologies. In this section we focus on some of the useful techniques to form materialized views. Materialized view formation is often employed in database system as well as data warehouse and OLAP systems.

Query rewriting [1] is way to optimize query execution in materialized views. Extended query rewriting algorithm [1] on join relation with foreign key, studied query system based on materialized views has been performed. However [1] work fine with small databases. Regarding query writing, group-by plays an important role both in database and data warehouse based applications. Group-by returns a modified, abstract view of the existing database. It is very much in data warehouse applications as

K. Saeed and V. Snášel (Eds.): CISIM 2014, LNCS 8838, pp. 254–265, 2014.
© IFIP International Federation for Information Processing 2014

it corresponds to roll-up operations. Group query based on Materialized View (GQMV) [2] accelerate the searching process making full use of the star schema and the materialized view technology, and combining the concerns of group bond and the technology of materialized view. Different traditional methodologies like genetic algorithm, simulated annealing are applied to form materialized views. M.Lee et. al. proposed an efficient solution towards speeding up query execution using genetic algorithm [3]. This genetic algorithm [3] based approach explores the maintenance-cost view selection problem in the context of OR view graphs. It performs better over the existing heuristic approaches. The problems with the greedy or heuristic approach fail are that, those fail to select good quality of materialized views in high dimensional data set. Simulated annealing based randomized view selection approach [4] select top-k views from multidimensional lattice which is useful in cube based data warehouse applications. Furthermore the simulated annealing approach has been upgraded further to incorporate parallel simulated annealing (PSA) to select views from an input Multiple View Processing Plan (MVPP) [5]. The extended scheme of parallelism [5] helps to work with multiple views and thousands of queries. As the numbers of queries grow into a system often the dynamic creation and modification of materialized views are high in demand. A dynamic cost model [6] was proposed based on threshold level incorporating the factors like view complexity, query access frequency, execution time and update frequency of the base table to select a subset of views from a large set of views to be materialized. Another work on dynamic materialized view [7] finds the workload permutation that produces the overall highest net benefit. A genetic algorithm [7] based approach was used to search the N! solution space, and to avoid materializing seldom-used Materialized Query Tables (MQT), those are pruned. The methodology dynamically manages the workload to get benefit over existing methods.

In some of research work on materialized views it focus on certain application areas. Here we consider few XML applications as XML is widely used in web applications. Answering XPATH queries using multiple materialized views is relatively a new problem, traditional methods work with one materialized view in XML applications. An NFA based approach called VFILTER [8] to filter views that cannot be used to answer a given query. Furthermore based on the output of VFILTER a heuristic method was proposed to identify a minimal view set that can answer a given query. An interesting problem in XML domain is to handle keyword queries. Materialized views could be used to solve the problem. The concept of Smallest Lowest Common Ancestor (SLCA) [9] was adopted for query result definition. It [9] identifies the relevant materialized views for a given query and develops an algorithm to find a small set of relevant views that can answer a query. Materialized views are often needs to be defined over data cubes in OLAP applications. Exact and appropriate functional dependencies and conditional functional dependencies (CFD) are redefined over previous summarization techniques such as condensed and quotient cubes [10]. This results in storage reduction however ensuring query performance. This also takes care whenever data is inserted or deleted from fact table (corresponds to base cuboid) materialized views are accordingly maintained. In another approach, materialization of cuboids is experimented on QC-tree which is most commonly used structure for data cubes in MOLAP. Though QC-tree achieves high compression ratio, still it is a fully materialized data cube. An algorithm was proposed in [11] to select and materialize some of the cells where as traditional methods require all the cells.

Modern day database system majorly run on relational databases and the corresponding OLAP application is called ROLAP. In relational model data is represented in the form of table and every table consists of attributes. The attributes within the table are functionally co-related. The analysis on the attribute affinity gives an idea of relationship among them. An analysis on attribute relationship is depicted in [12] where a numeric scale is constructed to enumerate the strength of associations between independent data attributes. However [12] don't propose any methodology to construct materialized view. In another research work linear regression [13] is used to measure the inter-association among attributes and this knowledge is used to form materialized view. The drawback of [12] and [13] is that both compute attribute relationship as a pair (two attributes) and this knowledge is guiding materialized view construction process. In this research work this drawback is identified and thus, after computing the pair wise relationship among attributes, materialized views are formed as cluster after analyzing the association among all the attributes. The different clusters are treated as different views, but however these views are further tested for validity. Among the created clusters, the clusters which are found to be valid by statistical analysis represent the final set of materialized views.

2   Proposed Methodology

In previous section a survey work was carried out to describe different methodologies of constructing materialized views and identifying the drawback, a new technique of materialized view creation is proposed here based on attribute similarity and formation of clusters using weighted connected graphs.

The similarity function that is used to measure similarity between attributes is the Jaccard Index. Here the set of attributes along with the set of queries form a categorical data set in which each attribute can be treated as a categorical variable. There are few well established similarity functions to compare the similarity .between categorical variables. Here the Jaccard Index [14] is used to measure the similarity between the attributes.

Based on the similarity between attributes a novel weighted graph based clustering algorithm is proposed to construct the views. Similar attributes are grouped together to form every cluster. To form the cluster pair wise attribute similarity is considered but each of these clusters is not considered as materialized views immediately. The validity of is these clusters is checked by considering the similarity of every cluster member with all other members within a particular cluster. Only the valid clusters represent materialized views.

At first based on m queries and the participating n attributes in the m queries, Attribute Usage Matrix (m× n) is formed. From the Attribute Usage Matrix the attribute similarity is carried out here using Jaccard Index. After the similarity calculation between attributes the n× n Attribute Similarity Matrix is formed. In the Attribute Similarity Matrix all the values which are greater or equal to a cut-off average similarity value are considered for the construction of graphs to form the clusters. For each of these similarity values a set of weighted connected graphs are constructed. Every graph represents a cluster where the intra cluster members are tied together by a particular similarity function value. After the creation of the clusters they are tested for validation process. Here the similarity between each possible pairs of attributes within a cluster is calculated and accordingly the average similarity measure for each cluster centroid is calculated. After this step only the valid clusters are considered to be the materialized views.

2.1   Definition of Jaccard Index

The Jaccard Index measures similarity between two attributes expressed in vector form and is defined as the size of the intersection divided by the size of the union of the two vectors.

So, if A_i and A_j be two attributes then similarity between them is calculated as

$J(Ai, Aj) = (A_i \cap A_j) / (A_i \cup A_j)$ (Equation 1)

$A_i \cap A_j$ = Total number of occurrences where both $(A_i)_n$ and $(A_j)_n = 1$,

$A_i \cup A_j$ = Total number of occurrences where either any one or both

$(A_i)_n$ or $(A_j)_n = 1$; $[(i \neq j)$ are the attribute indexes and n is the query index]

2.2   Relevance of Using Jaccard Index for Attribute Similarity Calculation

Measuring similarity or distance between two data points is a core requirement for several data mining and knowledge discovery tasks that involve distance computation. Here too the similarity between the pair of attributes is needed to be measured. The more similar or lesser distanced attributes are said to have greater affinity between themselves. For continuous data sets, the Minkowski Distance is a general method used to compute distance between two multivariate points. In particular, the Minkowski Distance of order 1 (Manhattan) and order 2 (Euclidean) are the two most widely used distance measures for continuous data. However it is not possible to directly compare two different categorical values where the values are not inherently ordered. In this scenario one way to compare the variables is to express each of these categorical variables in the form of vectors with multiple dimensions. Jaccard similarity is particularly used in positive space, where the outcome is neatly bounded in [0,1]. Here in the Attribute Usage Matrix output is either 1 or 0. Moreover in the attribute usage matrix every attribute is treated as a vector. Here the different queries form the dimensions and the attribute usage values of different queries are the value of each dimension corresponding to any attribute. Say, Q= $\{Q_1,Q_2,Q_3\}$ be the set of queries. The attribute usage values corresponding to A_i is say, [1,0,1]. So in the attribute usage matrix A_i is represented as [1,0,1] which forms a vector suitable for comparison with other attributes using Jaccard Index.

2.3   Components of Proposed Methodology

Attribute Usage Matrix
An mxn binary valued matrix in which the value of each entry denoted by use (A_j, Q_i) is either 0 or 1. Let Q = $\{Q_1,Q_2,....Q_n\}$ be the set of user queries (applications) that

will run on relation $R(A_1, A_2, \ldots A_n)$. Then, for each query Q_i and attribute A_j, Attribute Usage Value, denoted by use(A_j, Q_i) is defined as use (A_j, Q_i)=1   if attribute A_j is referenced by query q_i, else use (A_j, Q_i)=0.

Attribute Similarity Matrix
Attribute Similarity matrix is an n×n matrix, each element of which is the similarity measure J (A_i, A_j) between any two attributes A_i and A_j according to equation 1. The diagonal elements in this matrix are similarity between the same attributes as i = j. So in the diagonal elements' #' is placed.

Cut-off Average Similarity
The similarity values between any pair of attributes range between [0, 1]. The average similarity value is 0.5. In this paper this value is chosen as the cut-off similarity value between any pair of attributes. This cut-off similarity is to be considered as an important parameter for the cluster formation and validation process. This cut-off value actually regulates the number of possible clusters and also number of attributes present as the members in a cluster. The value could be fixed to any value between 0 and 1, based on application.

Construction of Connected Graphs from Attribute Similarity Matrix
A set of disjoint connected weighted graphs are constructed from the Attribute Similarity Matrix. In each of these graphs G_i, the attributes represent the nodes and for any pair of attributes (A_i, A_j) which are expressed as node A_i and A_j in the graph, the Jaccard Index Value J (A_i, A_j) between them is the weight of the edge connecting them.

The method of construction of connected graphs is stated as below:
a) At first all the similarity values which are greater or equal to Cut-off Average Similarity are identified. If no such value is found then graph construction process fails and therefore no views can be constructed whereas if some values are found they are inserted in a list L in descending order. So each element in L is a similarity measure value.

b) The number of elements in L is stored into a variable count. Starting from the first element (The highest Similarity value between any pair of attributes) each element is popped out until the list L is empty and for each element step c is repeated.

c) All the attribute pairs that have the similarity value equal to the currently popped out value from L are identified in the Attribute Similarity Matrix. After that each pair of the identified attributes are included as nodes in graph G_i (1≤ i ≤ count). Graph G_i is a connected weighted graph where every edge has the same weight values and is equal to the currently popped out similarity value from L.

For example let the popped out similarity value form L which is x (0 ≤ x ≤ 1) which is the similarity measure between A_i and A_j. Then an edge of weight x is inserted between A_i and A_j in graph G_i. Similarly if the similarity between A_i and A_k is x, an edge is inserted between A_i and A_k. As A_i is a common node for similarity value x, so A_i, A_j & A_k form a connected weighted graph G_i.

d) If there are n number of similarity values in the Attribute Similarity Matrix which are greater or equal to the cut-off value then n number of connected disjoint graphs will be formed where each G_i (1≤ i ≤ n) represents a graph for a particular similarity value.

Formation of Clusters from Connected Graphs
Each connected graph G_i is treated as a cluster C_i, where the nodes (attributes) of graph G_i are the cluster members. If there are n numbers of graphs then n number of clusters will be formed.

Average Similarity Value for Each of the Cluster Centroid
a) The Average Similarity Value is a measure of similarity of every attribute with all other attributes present in a particular cluster. If there are n number of attributes present in a particular cluster, then for any cluster C_i the Average Similarity Value for its centroid

$$(C_i)_{avg} = \frac{\sum_{i=1}^{\binom{n}{2}} J(A_i, A_j)}{\binom{n}{2}} \text{ where } i \neq j \qquad \text{(Equation 2)}$$

The numerator of equation 2 gives the total similarity value for all possible pair of attributes inside cluster C_i and the denominator gives the number of possible combinations that can be made by taking 2 attributes together (Attribute- pair) from n number of attributes. So, equation 2 actually gives a measure of average similarity between all pairs of attributes inside a cluster, which is the average similarity value for that cluster centroid.

Importance of Average Similarity Value for Cluster Centroid
The Jaccard Index $J(A_i, A_j)$ gives the measure between any two attributes. Say from the Attribute Similarity Matrix it is found that $J(A_i, A_j) = J(A_j, A_k) \geq$ cut-off. So according to the graph construction method A_i, A_j & A_k belong to a cluster C_i. The graph construction method considers similarities between the pair A_i, A_j and A_j, A_k but does not consider similarity between A_i and A_k. A_i and A_k might be very dissimilar yet they are present in a single cluster. Hence the similarity between A_i and A_k should also be considered. If the cluster centroid average similarity is calculated then it gives the measure of association of any attribute with all other attributes present in that cluster. So if A_i and A_k are very dissimilar their similarity measure $J(A_i, A_k)$ will be very small. This value will make a very small contribution to the overall value of $(C_i)_{avg}$. Obviously the value of $(C_i)_{avg}$ will be less for this. If the cluster centroid average similarity is less then it means the intra cluster members don't have higher association between themselves. Therefore C_i will not be a valid cluster.

3   Proposed Algorithm

Input: $R(A_1, A_2, \ldots A_m)$: The relation; $Q = \{Q_1, Q_2, \ldots Q_n\}$: The set of user queries that will run on R; cut-off: Cut-off Average Similarity .

Output: C: The set of materialized views.

Step 1: Construct the mxn Attribute Usage Matrix where m is the number of attributes and n is the number of queries.

Step 2: Construct the nxn Attribute Similarity Matrix from the Attribute Usage Matrix.
/* In step 3 the Graphs & the corresponding clusters are constructed*/

Step 3: ∀ (A_i, A_j) ∈ Attribute Similarity Matrix, identify the attribute pair similarity values so that J (A_i, A_j) ≥ cut-off.
Store these values in a list L in descending order.
Store the number of elements in L into a variable count.

a) If count=0 then go to step 5. /* The algorithm fails to draw any graph. Therefore no materialized view can be constructed */

b) If count > 0 then Repeat until list L is empty

i) Pop the ith (1≤ i ≤ count) element from L. Store the value of the element into a variable x (0 ≤ x ≤ 1).

ii) ∀ Attribute pairs (A_i, A_j) ∈ Attribute Similarity Matrix
If J (A_i, A_j) = x, then G_i ←G_i ∪ A_i ∪ A_j /* Pair of attributes is inserted in G_i, where G_i represents the ith graph for i^{th} highest similarity value.*/

iii) C_i ← G_i /*C_i represents the ith cluster for i^{th} highest similarity value.*/

iv) C ← C ∪ C_i /* Each cluster C_i is added to the set of clusters C */

/* In step 4 the clusters are validated and materialized views are formed*/

Step 4: ∀ C_i ∈ C, calculate (C_i) $_{avg}$ by equation 2.
If (C_i) $_{avg}$ < cut-off then C ← C - C_i
/* C represents the set of materialized views where each cluster C_i represents a valid materialized view */

Step 5: End.

4   Illustration by Example

Let's consider a small example set of queries. This is only for the sake of a lucid explanation of the steps to be followed in the proposed algorithm

Say, there are ten queries (Q_1, Q_2, ... ,Q_{10}) in the set which use 12 different attributes namely (A_1, A_2,.......,A_{12}).

The queries are not given here due to space constraint, the example is shown starting from Attribute Usage Matrix.

Step 1: The use of these 12 attributes, by these 10 queries is shown in the Attribute Usage Matrix (Table 1) .If Attribute A_1 is considered we can say A_1 is used by query Q_2,Q_4 and Q_7 .So in vector from A_1 can be expressed as A_1=[0,1,0,1,0,0,1,0,0,0].

Step 2: The similarities J (A_i, A_j) between each pair of attributes (A_i, A_j) (1≤ i ≤12 , 1≤ j≤12 and A_i ≠ A_j) are stored in Attribute Similarity Matrix. Here the Attribute Similarity Matrix is a 12 × 12 matrix where the diagonal elements are indicated by '#'. Due to space constraint we can't represent the Attribute Similarity Matrix as a 12 × 12 matrix; rather we have given the similarity values between each possible combination of attribute pairs below:

(A_1, A_2)=0.166667, (A_1,A_3) = 0.333333, (A_1,A_4) = 0.333333, (A_1,A_5) = 0, (A_1,A_6) = 0.142857, (A_1,A_7) = 0.285714, (A_1,A_8) = 0.125, (A_1,A_9) = 0.285714, (A_1,A_{10}) = 0, (A_1,A_{11}) = 0.285714, (A_1,A_{12}) = 0.142857, (A_2,A_3) = 0.285714, (A_2,A_4) = 0.285714, (A_2,A_5) = 0.5, (A_2,A_6) = 0.5, (A_2,A_7) = 0.125, (A_2,A_8) = 0.428571429,   (A_2,A_9) = 0.25, (A_2,A_{10}) = 0.5, (A_2,A_{11}) = 0.111111, (A_2,A_{12}) = 0.285714, (A_3,A_4) = 0.428571429, (A_3,A_5) = 0.375, (A_3,A_6) = 0.428571429, (A_3,A_7) = 0.375, (A_3,A_8) = 0.222222, (A_3,A_9) = 0.375, (A_3,A_{10}) = 0.25, (A_3,A_{11}) = 0.375, (A_3,A_{12}) =

0.428571429, $(A_4,A_5) = 0.375$, $(A_4,A_6) = 0.428571429$, $(A_4,A_7) = 0.222222$, $(A_4,A_8) = 0.222222$, $(A_4,A_9) = 0.57428571$, $(A_4,A_{10}) = 0.428571429$, $(A_4,A_{11}) = 0.57428571$, $(A_4,A_{12}) = 0.25$, $(A_5,A_6) = 0.57428571$, $(A_5,A_7) = 0.333333$, $(A_5,A_8) = 0.5$, $(A_5,A_9) = 0.5$, $(A_5,A_{10}) = 0.833333$, $(A_5,A_{11}) = 0.333333$, $(A_5,A_{12}) = 0.428571429$, $(A_6,A_7) = 0.222222$, $(A_6,A_8) = 0.375$, $(A_6,A_9) = 0.57428571$, $(A_6,A_{10}) = 0.428571429$, $(A_6,A_{11}) = 0.375$, $(A_6,A_{12}) = 0.666667$, $(A_7,A_8) = 0.5$, $(A_7,A_9) = 0.5$, $(A_7,A_{10}) = 0.222222$, $(A_7,A_{11}) = 0.5$, $(A_7,A_{12}) = 0.375$, $(A_8,A_9) = 0.333333$, $(A_8,A_{10}) = 0.375$, $(A_8,A_{11}) = 0.333333$, $(A_8,A_{12}) = 0.375$, $(A_9,A_{10}) = 0.375$, $(A_9,A_{11}) = 0.714285714$, $(A_9,A_{12}) = 0.375$, $(A_{10},A_{11}) = 0.222222$, $(A_{10},A_{12}) = 0.428571429$, $(A_{11},A_{12}) = 0.222222$.

If the similarity between A_1 and A_2 is considered we find the value is 0.166667.

Table 1. Attribute Usage Matrix

	Q_1	Q_2	Q_3	Q_4	Q_5	Q_6	Q_7	Q_8	Q_9	Q_{10}
A_1	0	1	0	1	0	0	1	0	0	0
A_2	0	0	1	0	1	0	1	0	1	0
A_3	1	0	1	1	0	0	1	0	0	1
A_4	1	1	1	0	0	1	1	0	0	0
A_5	1	0	1	0	1	1	0	0	1	1
A_6	0	0	1	0	1	1	1	0	0	1
A_7	1	1	0	1	1	0	0	1	0	1
A_8	0	1	1	0	1	0	0	1	1	1
A_9	1	1	0	0	1	1	1	0	0	1
A_{10}	1	0	1	0	1	1	0	0	1	0
A_{11}	1	1	0	0	0	1	1	1	0	1
A_{12}	0	0	1	1	1	1	0	0	0	1

Explanation: From the Attribute usage Matrix we find that $A_1= =[0,1,0,1,0,0,1,0,0,0]$ and $A_2= [0,0,1,0,1,0,1,0,1,0]$.

$J(A_1, A_2) = (A_1 \cap A_2) / (A_1 \cup A_2)$ [From equation 1]

$(A_1 \cap A_2) = 1$; because only for query Q_7 both A_1 and A_2 are '1'.

$(A_1 \cup A_2) = 6$; because A1 is '1' for queries Q_2, Q_4 and Q_7. So for A_1 number of occurrences= 3.

A_2 is '1' for queries Q_3, Q_5, Q_7 and Q_9. So for A_2 number of occurrences=4.

So total number of occurrences = (3+4) - 1 =6. Here 1 is subtracted since both A_1 and A_2 are '1'for query Q_7. According to the definition of Jaccard Index this common occurrence should be considered only once not twice.

Therefore, $J(A_1, A_2) = 1/6 = 0.166667$.

Step 3: The cut-off similarity is taken as 0.5 in this paper.

The similarity values between attribute pairs which are greater or equal to cut-off are:

i) $(A_5, A_{10}) = 0.833333$ ii) $(A_9, A_{11}) = 0.714285714$ iii) $(A_6, A_{12}) = 0.666667$

iv) $(A_4, A_9) = (A_4, A_{11}) = (A_5, A_6) = (A_6, A_9) = 0.57428571$

v) $(A_2, A_5) = (A_2, A_6) = (A_2, A_{10}) = (A_5, A_8) = (A_5, A_9) = (A_7, A_8) = (A_7, A9) = (A_7, A_{11}) = 0.5$

a) As there are 5 similarity values greater or equal to cut-off so 5 graphs can be constructed from them.

b) The members of these 5 graphs are:
$G_1 = \{A_5, A_{10}\}$, $G_2 = \{A_9, A_{11}\}$, $G_3 = \{A_6, A_{12}\}$, $G_4 = \{A_4, A_5, A_6, A_9, A_{11}\}$ and
$G_5 = \{A_2, A_5, A_6, A_7, A_8, A_9, A_{10}, A_{11}\}$

Explanation of Construction of Graphs: Let's for example consider graph G_4 shown in Figure 1.

This connected weighted graph is constructed for similarity value 0.571428571, where the nodes are A_4, A_5, A_6, A_9 and A_{11}. The edge weights between (A_4, A_9), (A_4, A_{11}), (A_5, A_6) and (A_6, A_9) are all 0.571428571.

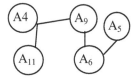

Fig. 1. Graph G_4 where the weight value of each edge is 0.571428571

According to the algorithm, each graph is treated as a cluster. As 5 graphs are constructed so, 5 clusters (C_1, C_2, C_3, C_4 and C_5) are formed from them.

Hence after step 3, the set of materialized view C contains:

$C = \{C_1 = (A_5, A_{10}), C_2 = (A_9, A_{11}), C_3 = (A_6, A_{12}), C_4 = (A_4, A_5, A_6, A_9, A_{11}), C_5 = (A_2, A_5, A_6, A_7, A_8, A_9, A_{10}, A_{11})\}$.

Step 4: The average similarity value $(C_i)_{avg}$ for each of the cluster centroid is calculated as: $(C_1)_{avg} = 0.833333$, $(C_2)_{avg} = 0.714285714$, $(C_3)_{avg} = 0.666667$, $(C_4)_{avg} = 0.5011905$ and $(C_5)_{avg} = 0.411918$ (Calculated according to equation 2)

Explanation of Cluster Centroid Average Similarity Calculation: Let's consider the calculation of cluster centroid average similarity for cluster C_4.

In fig. 1 only the edges which had weights 0.571428571 were drawn and a connected graph G_4 was formed between the nodes A_4, A_5, A_6, A_9 and A_{11}. The edges between (A_4, A_6), (A_4, A_5), (A_5, A_9), (A_5, A_{11}), (A_6, A_{11}) and (A_9, A_{11}) were not drawn and hence their weights were not considered in the graph construction method. Since each weight between the pair of nodes is the measure of association or similarity between the attributes. This fact is taken care of in this step.

If complete graph with all the possible edges and their weights is drawn it would look like fig. 2.

Cluster C_4 has 5 attributes (n=5), hence $\binom{n}{2} = \binom{5}{2} = 10$. The similarity values between all pair of attributes inside cluster C_4 are taken from section (4.Step 2) and rewritten below:

$(A_4, A_5) = 0.375, (A_4, A_6) = 0.428571429, (A_4, A_9) = 0.571428571, (A_4, A_{11}) = 0.571428571$
$, (A_5, A_6) = 0.571428571, (A_5, A_9) = 0.5, (A_5, A_{11}) = 0.333333, (A_6, A_9) = 0.571428571, (A_6, A_{11}) = 0.375, (A_9, A_{11}) = 0.714285714$.

The Total $(\sum_{i=1}^{(10)} J(A_i, A_j))$ of the above values = 5.011905.

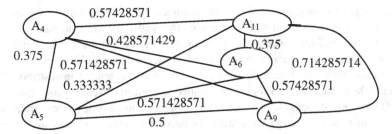

Fig. 2. Modified graph G_4 with all possible pair of nodes connected

The average (C_4) $_{avg}$ = (5.011905 /10) = 0.5011905 (From equation 2).
Similarly for cluster C_5 (n=8), (C_5) $_{avg}$ can be calculated as (C_5) $_{avg}$ = Total / $\binom{8}{2}$ = (11.53371 / 28) =0.411918. [Refer to section (4.Step 2) for relevant data]
We find that only for cluster C_5 the cluster centroid average similarity is less than cut-off .So, C_5 is rejected and the valid clusters are C_1, C_2, C_3 and C_4.
Since every valid cluster is treated as a materialized view, so finally we have 4 materialized views created for the given database: View-1 (A_5, A_{10}),
View-2 (A_9, A_{11}), View-3 (A_6, A_{12}) and View-4 (A_4, A_5, A_6, A_9, A_{11}).

5   Performance of the Proposed Clustering Algorithm

K-means algorithm is most widely used clustering algorithm in different applications. The major drawbacks of the k-means clustering algorithm are: a) Number of desired clusters are predefined. However in this problem domain the numbers of clusters or materialized views can't be fixed. b) There is a continuous shifting of cluster members to form the final valid clusters. This increases the time and computational complexity of the algorithm.
In the proposed clustering algorithm the numbers of desired clusters is unknown at the beginning. There is no need to predefine the desired number of clusters. Secondly, the validation process of each cluster considers the cluster centroid similarity measure only and does not require any shifting between inter cluster members. After validation either a cluster is considered to be valid or is rejected. The valid clusters form the materialized views. In this way the proposed weighted graph based clustering algorithm outperforms k-means algorithm.

6   Conclusion and Future Work

The paper contributes to the formation of materialized views using clustering technique. The existing techniques worked with pair wise attribute association only and at no stage considered the association or similarity of multiple attributes at a time. This research gap is identified in this paper and a method is introduced which measures the similarity function of every attribute with all other attributes present and this knowledge guides the construction of materialized views in the forms of cluster. Further a method is introduced which measures the quality of the materialized views in terms of intra attribute association. Only those views which have a predefined intra attribute association are therefore considered as the final materialized views.

This clustering based methodology may be further extended in distributed environment where the data servers are physically located in different geographical location. The proposed methodology need to be upgraded to consider access frequency of different queries at different sites, network bandwidth etc. to address the constraints of distributed systems. Apart from using the Jaccard Index the formation of distributed materialized views can also be done using other established similarity functions like Cosine Based Similarity and Tanimoto Coefficient. A comparative study of these methods and simulation in distributed environment would help to choose the appropriate methods for constructing materialized views.

References

1. Hu, Y., Zhai, W., Tian, Y., Gao, T.: Research and Application of Query Rewriting Based on Materialized Views. In: Qi, L. (ed.) ISIA 2010. CCIS, vol. 86, pp. 85–91. Springer, Heidelberg (2011)
2. Li, G., Wang, S., Liu, C., Ma, Q.: A modifying strategy of group query based on materialized view. In: IEEE 3rd International Conference on Advanced Computer Theory and Engineering (ICACTE), Chengdu, China, vol. 5, pp. 381–384 (2010)
3. Lee, M., Hammer, J.: Speeding up materialized view selection in data warehouses using a randomized algorithm. International Journal of Cooperative Information Systems 10(3), 327–353 (2001)
4. Vijay Kumar, T.V., Kumar, S.: Materialized View Selection Using Simulated Annealing. In: Srinivasa, S., Bhatnagar, V. (eds.) BDA 2012. LNCS, vol. 7678, pp. 168–179. Springer, Heidelberg (2012)
5. Derakhshan, R., Stantic, B., Korn, O., Dehne, F.: Parallel simulated annealing for materialized view selection in data warehousing environments. In: Bourgeois, A.G., Zheng, S.Q. (eds.) ICA3PP 2008. LNCS, vol. 5022, pp. 121–132. Springer, Heidelberg (2008)
6. Rashid, A.N.M.B., Islam, M.S., Hoque, A.S.M.L.: Dynamic materialized view selection approach for improving query performance. In: Das, V.V., Stephen, J., Chaba, Y. (eds.) CNC 2011. CCIS, vol. 142, pp. 202–211. Springer, Heidelberg (2011)
7. Phan, T., Wen, L.S.: Dynamic Materialization of Query Views for Data Warehouse Workloads. In: IEEE 24th International Conference on Data Engineering (ICDE), Cancun, Mexico, pp. 436–445 (2008)
8. Tang, N., Yu, X.J., Ozsu, T.M., Choi, B., Wong, K.-F.: Multiple Materialized View Selection for XPath Query Rewriting. In: IEEE 24th International Conference on Data Engineering (ICDE), Cancun, Mexico, pp. 873–882 (2008)
9. Liu, Z., Chen, Y.: Answering Keyword Queries on XML Using Materialized Views. In: IEEE 24th International Conference on Data Engineering (ICDE), Cancun, Mexico, pp. 1501–1503 (2008)

10. Garnaud, E., Maabout, S., Mosbah, M.: Functional dependencies are helpful for partial materialization of data cubes. In: Garnaud, E., Maabout, S., Mosbah, M. (eds.) Springer Journal on Annals of Mathematics and Artificial Intelligence (August 14, 2013)

11. Li, H.-S., Huang, H.-K., Liu, S.: PMC: Select Materialized Cells in Data Cubes. In: Tjoa, A.M., Trujillo, J. (eds.) DaWaK 2005. LNCS, vol. 3589, pp. 168–178. Springer, Heidelberg (2005)

12. Sen, S., Dutta, A., Cortesi, A., Chaki, N.: A new scale for attribute dependency in large database systems. In: Cortesi, A., Chaki, N., Saeed, K., Wierzchoń, S. (eds.) CISIM 2012. LNCS, vol. 7564, pp. 266–277. Springer, Heidelberg (2012)

13. Sen, P.G.S., Chaki, N.: Materialized View Construction Using Linear Regression on Attributes. In: IEEE Proc. of the 3rd International Conference on Emerging Applications of Information Technology (EAIT), Kolkata, India, pp. 214–219 (2012)

14. Schaeffer, S.E.: Survey on Graph Clustering. Elsevier Computer Science Review, 27–64 (2007), doi:10.1016/j.cosrev, 05.001

Big Data Spectra Analysis Using Analytical Programming and Random Decision Forests

Petr Šaloun[1], Peter Drábik[1], Ivan Zelinka[1], and Jaroslav Bucko[2]

[1] VŠB-Technical University of Ostrava FEE&I, 17. listopadu 15/2172
CZ-708 33 Ostrava-Poruba, Czech Republic
[2] Slovak Technical University Bratislava FIIT, Ilkovičova 2,
SK-84216 Bratislava 4 Slovakia
{petr.saloun,peter.drabik.st,ivan.zelinka}@vsb.cz,
bucko.jaroslav@gmail.com

Abstract. Spectra analysis on large datasets is in focus of this paper. First of all we discuss a method useful for spectra analysis – analytical programming and its implementation. Our goal is to create mathematical formulas of emission lines from spectra, which are characteristic for Be stars. One issue in performing this task is symbolic regression, which represents the process in our application, when measured data fits the best represented mathematical formula. In past this was only a human domain; nowadays, there are computer methods, which allow us to do it more or less effectively. A novel method in symbolic regression, compared to genetic programming and grammar evolution, is analytic programming. The aim of this work is to verify the efficiency of the parallel approach of this algorithm, using CUDA architecture. Next we will discuss parallel implementation of random decision forest (RDF) to classify huge amounts of various spectra. The mathematical formulas obtained via AP will be used to reduce attributes of explored spectra. Our goal is to propose scalable algorithm for classification of such data, which will preferably need only one pass over data, while maintaining acceptable accuracy. Later we will try to create module compatible with VO and DAta Mining and Exploration project.

Keywords: analytical programming, spectra analysis, CUDA, evolutionary algorithm, differential evolution, parallel implementation, symbolic regression, random decision forest, data mining, virtual observatory.

1 Introduction

Nowadays, astronomy is one of the scientific disciplines which produce enormous amounts of data per day, which needs to be processed automatically. With advancement of surveillance methods the data grows in amount and complexity. In our work we focused on the spectra analysis of Be star-candidates. Be stars are hot B-type stars (effective temperature $10\,000\,\mathrm{K}$ to $30\,000\,\mathrm{K}$) with luminosity class III to V (i.e. not supergiant stars) whose spectrum has shown at least

K. Saeed and V. Snášel (Eds.): CISIM 2014, LNCS 8838, pp. 266–277, 2014.

once an emission line – usually hydrogen in the Balmer line, see Figure 1. Sometimes, other emission lines are visible, for example neutral helium. Even when the spectrum goes back to *normal*, the star remains in the Be star class [9]. Some of them are among the brightest stars in the sky [2]. With the high complexity, the data attributes need to be reduced to less dimensions. The spectra attributes will be reduced from value for every observed wavelength in spectra to lines in certain wavelength ranges, which represent features of object the spectra belongs to.

Non-image data, such as spectra, are also mainly distributed in astronomy in Flexible Image Transport System (fits) format, standardized in 1981 [1]. This format can have the *.fts, *.fits, *.fit extensions and a major feature it has is that images metadata are store in a human readable ASCII header. In our work we processed fits format data files with fv FITS Editor, available from the standard Ubuntu repository.

Astronomical data are obtainable from various virtual observatories (VO). A set of standards to access and manipulate such data was created by International Virtual Observatory Alliance. They describe API to communicate with VO web services. The services provide not only FITS files, but VOTable formatted data too.

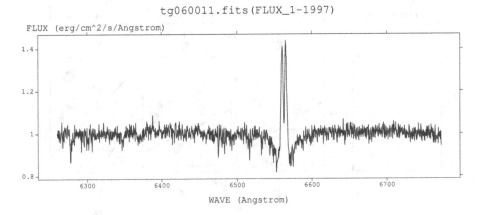

Fig. 1. An example of spectra with a characteristic Be star emission

2 Data Mining with Random Decision Forests, an Introduction

Random decision forests are a data mining structures proposed in 2001 by Leo Breiman [14] for supervised classification. Random decision forests are ensembles of classification and regression trees. They main difference from other decision trees and ensembles is a way of splitting nodes in trees to make decisions.

2.1 Training

During training the bagging is used. Each tree in ensemble is grown using subset consisting of cases, drawn random from training set. From this part of training data, a random subset of features is selected. Node split is selected randomly from best splits. The trees are not pruned, unlike in other classification trees. The trees grown during training can be tested for error using out-of-bag estimates.

2.2 Prediction

During prediction the sample is classified by every tree in the forest. After that, the final class of sample is class with the most "votes" from trees as shown in Figure 2, or can by selected from mean of probabilities of classes from each tree.

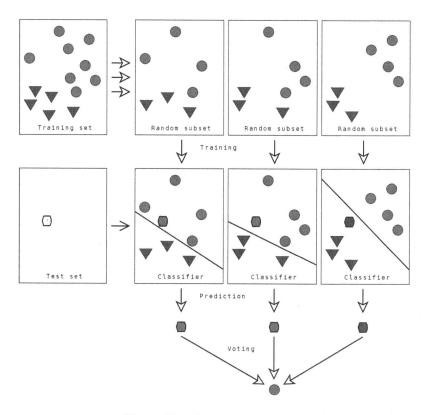

Fig. 2. Classification with bagging

2.3 Advantages of Random Forests

Random selection of features brings following advantages to RDF:

– robustness to noise and outliers,

– faster than bagging and boosting,
– simply and easily parallelized,
– no over-fitting.

RDF is considered one of the best learning algorithms, by its performance [16,17].

2.4 Scalable Implementation

Parallel implementation of RDF seems to be simple, by growing multiple trees at a time during training stage, and running prediction for multiple trees in forest at prediction stage. An optimal ratio between trees in ensemble and number of computing units should be found to minimize idle time waiting for new spectra samples to be loaded into memory. Since the working data is very large, a single pass over data is very time consuming. Everything should be done in that single pass, or at least in as few passes as possible. This makes decisions for best node split difficult. For this a histogram of values can be used like proposed by Ben-Haim for streaming parallel decision trees in 2010 [18] and used by Li [19]. In spectra analysis it is not necessary to worry about missing values, because missing value in astronomical spectra indicates, presence of certain chemical elements in object, what can be treated as another attribute. When not classifying spectra but other data, the missing values can be handled by substitution to median of values from histogram too. There are currently some scalable solutions for random forests:

Apache Mahout: is a data mining library based on Hadoop written in Java. With random forests allows the use of multiple classifiers.
Scalable random forest by Li B.: is a random forest implementation with MapReduce. It grows trees breadth-first. Uses histograms to calculate best split [19].
H2O: is a scalable machine learning platform, which uses L. Breimans implementation of random forests. It is capable to run on Apache Hadoop and Amazon EC2 (beta). Written in pure java.

2.5 Data Complexity Reduction

To improve speed and accuracy, data complexity reduction and relevant features of spectra selection is needed. The data reduction can be made with the help analytical programming by identifying interesting features and how they are represented in spectra and describing them by mathematical functions. It will not be necessary to break every observed spectra to set of features, instead, in every tree node, the spectra can be compared against one of the created mathematical functions and based on result, the decision of which child node descend to can be made.

3 Virtual Observatory

The Virtual Observatory is an international astronomical community-based initiative. It aims to allow global electronic access to the available astronomical data archives of space and ground-based observatories and other sky survey databases. To obtain data from VO we must follow IVOA standards for data access layer. DAL services are provided as HTTP REST web services. For spectra analysis are interesting following services:

Simple Spectral Access Protocol defines a uniform interface to remotely discover and access one-dimensional spectra and aggregations of 1D spectra. Discovered datasets are returned in VOTable format,

Simple Line Access Protocol defines interface to spectral lines search from Spectral Line Data Collections. Spectral lines are returned in VOTable format.

Simple Image Access Protocol allows retrieving on-the-fly created images of sky given the position and size of the desired output image. After client has described image, service returns list of possible images in VOTable format.Client then chooses image to retrieve. Retrieved image is stored in FITS format.

Simple Cone Access Protocol allows to retrieve records from a catalogue of astronomical sources. The query describes sky position and an angular distance, defining a cone on the sky. The response returns a list of astronomical sources from the catalog whose positions lie within the cone, formatted as a VOTable.

We will use these protocols to obtain spectra and metadata of spectra to process.

4 DAta Mining and Exploration

DAME[1] is an Italian project to provide Astrophysics community with easy to use data mining suit. This suit is called DAMEWARE. Its focus is on processing of massive data sets with machine learning methods. It is based on S.Co.PE.[2], a general-purpose supercomputing infrastructure of the University of Naples Federico II. DAMEWARE model library is extendable via plugins. The only requirement is to have executable of model and to supply parameters for model or configuration files without need to know underlying DAMEWARE architecture. We would like to create a model plugin from our implementation.

5 Overview of Analytical Programming

Analytical programming, proposed in 2005 [4], was inspired by Hilbert spaces and genetic programming. The principles and general philosophy behind analytical programming (AP) stem from these two methods. Into AP an idea about the evolutionary creation of symbolic solutions is taken from GP while from Hilbert spaces the idea of functional spaces and the building of the resulting function by means of the search process are adopted in AP. The core of AP is based on a

---

[1] http://dame.dsf.unina.it
[2] http://www.scope.unina.it

set of functions, operators and so-called terminals, which are usually constants or independent variables as well as in GP and GE. The main aim of AP is to synthesize a suitable program which would fit the measured data as well as possible (with the given precision). For this reason, a discrete set handling (DSH) idea [7,8] was adopted in AP [5]. Discrete set handling creates an interface between the Evolutionary Algorithm (EA) and the problem. Therefore, we can use in AP almost any evolutionary algorithm. The individual is represented as a nonnumeric value and a numerical value is added to the evolutionary process as an integer index. This index represents an individual from the General Function Set (GFS).

5.1   Versions of AP

There are three versions of AP. AP_{basic} is a basic version of AP and uses constants from the terminal set. AP_{meta} – in this version there are constants not defined in the terminal set; in the terminal set there is only one general constant K and every constant K is estimated by a different or the same evolutionary algorithm. We can mention one disadvantage of this version – because of running evolution under evolution; it could be very slow for a large number of steps. There are a big number of evaluations of the fitness function. The last version is AP_{nf} – constants are estimated by non-linear fitting algorithm.

5.2   General Function Set

The GFS is a set of all mathematical objects – functions, operators and terminals. GFS consists of functions with different numbers of arguments. GFS is user-defined, so the content may differ. We must split the content of GFS into classes based on the numbers of arguments: 0_{args} are terminals, 1_{args} $(sin, cos, tan, \ldots)$, 2_{args} $(+, -, *, /, \ldots)$, etc. Choosing the right set may have a large influence on the convergence of AP.

5.3   Evolutionary Algorithm

AP was designed to be a very robust method and we can use almost any evolutionary algorithm. Individual steps, such as mutation, crossover, etc. are fully handled by the chosen evolutionary algorithm. Operations which make EAs when the algorithm is run do not have any influence on performance. Thus the result performance depends mainly on the correct choice of GFS individuals. For every evolutionary algorithm, the main goal is generally to reduce the fitness value to below a user-defined threshold, or to achieve maximum number of migrations for a Self Organizing Migrating Algorithm (SOMA), or in the case of Differential Evolution (DE) – generations.

5.4   Mapping Operators

Mapping is the phase when an individual is transformed into a useful mathematical function. It consist of two parts, DSH and security functions, to exclude the

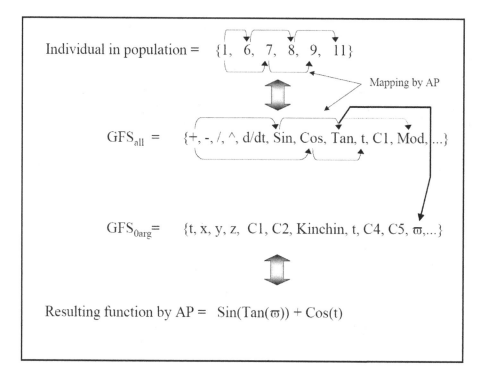

Fig. 3. Schema of mapping and security principles. Because of measuring distance to end of expression is *tan* replaced by ω [4]

creation of pathological individuals. In the evolutionary algorithm the individual is represented by a vector of indexes and is remapped to mathematical objects from GFS.

5.5 Reinforced Evolution

By running evolution, more or less suitable individuals are created, so one very good idea is to include the best individual as the terminal in GFS. The main idea of reinforcement is based on the addition of a just synthesized and partly successful program in an initial set of terminals [3]. The decision on whether the best value will be added to GFS is ensured by a user defined threshold value. If it is reached, from that moment it is added in GFS as a terminal, best solution and updated whenever a better solution with lower fitness is found.

5.6 Security Procedures

Evolution can result in an expression, which is not mathematically correct, thus we create a pathological individual (without argument). We can prevent this by distributing GFS into classes ordered by the number of arguments. By mapping from evolution space to GFS, we measure the distance to the end of the expression. When the number of arguments is greater than the distance to the end of the expression, we choose individuals from the lower class. We must also pay attention so as to exclude errors from the fitness function, such as division by zero, functions with an imaginary or real part (if not expected), frozen functions (an extremely long time to get a cost value), etc. [3].

6 Parallel Implementation Using CUDA – An Overview

CUDA (Compute Unified Device Architecture) is a platform for parallel computing, developing by NVIDIA. CUDA is SIMT (Single Instruction Multiple Threads). Its main feature is that one instruction is executed by thousands of threads. However, kernels can effectively perform only basic operations. In the CUDA device various types of memory reside, as you can see in Table 1. Note: registers are the fastest memory on the GPU.

Table 1. CUDA Memory Types and Characteristics [13], (u.c. $\equiv$ unless cached)

Memory	Location	Cached	Access	Scope
Register	On-chip	No	Read/Write	One thread
Local	On-chip	Yes	Read/Write	One thread
Shared	On-chip	N/A	Read/Write	All threads in a block
Global	Off-chip (u.c)	Yes	Read/Write	All threads + host
Constant	Off-chip (u.c.)	Yes	Read	All threads + host
Texture	Off-chip (u.c.)	Yes	Read/Write	All threads + host

The idea of implementing AP on parallel architecture is based on successful parallel implementation of evolutionary algorithms on CUDA, where a significant speeding up was achieved [10,11]. We were inspired to implement a parallel version of AP on CUDA, because of the good results achieved by the evolutionary algorithms when implemented on CUDA, although execution of this number of operations and structures may lead to worse performance results, as expected.

7 Testing Parallel Implementation – Methods, Datasets, Results

We cut the spectra from Figure 1 and obtained only the emission line in Figure 5 with 50 equidistant points, to satisfy our requirements. The data on the Be stars spectra come from the archive of the Astronomical Institute of the Academy of Sciences of the Czech Republic[3].

---

[3] Available from: http://astropara.projekty.ms.mff.cuni.cz/spectra/newest/

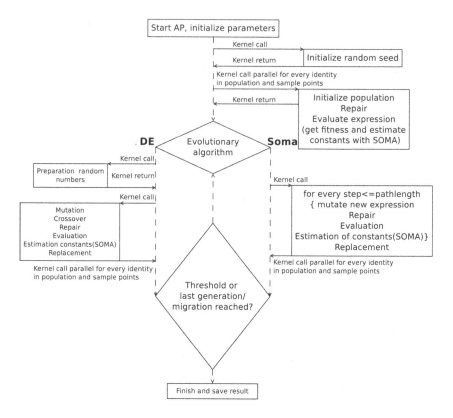

Fig. 4. The flowchart of AP implementation

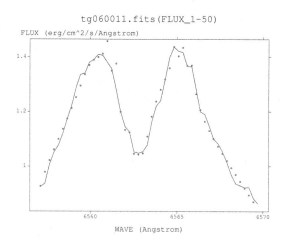

Fig. 5. Extracted emission line (blue) of Be star and our best result (red dots) of the SOMA algorithm with deterministic chaos

To be able to carry out a comparison in our tests we used a classical pseudo-random number generator and on the other site we tried to compare it to implemented deterministic chaos, with setting $A = 4$, which equation is as follows:

$$x_{n-1} = Ax_n(1 - x_n)$$

We carried out tests with SOMA and DE as the main evolutionary algorithm of AP. For estimating constants we chose the SOMA algorithm. The measured results are shown in Tables 2 and 3.

The settings for our implementation are shown in Table 2.

Table 2. Algorithm settings

DE		SOMA		SOMA constants	
NP	500	PopSize	500	PopSize	10
Dimensions	40	Dimensions	20	Dimensions	20
Generations	100	Migrations	10	Migrations	5
F	0.9	PRT	0.1	PRT	0.1
CR	0.5	PathLength	4	PathLength	3
		Step	0.21	Step	0.25

Table 3. Minimum, average and maximum fitness achieved from our tests. Each method was tested 10 times.

	DE PRNG	DE Chaos	SOMA PRNG	SOMA Chaos
MIN	4.02327	4.00432	0.85327	0.83326
AVG	4.30381	4.27877	1.41000	1.39508
MAX	4.57460	4.51520	1.84721	1.91367

Table 4. Execution of AP: with SOMA 95238096 evaluations of the cost function in the main EA, with DE 100000000

[s]	DE PRNG	DE Chaos	SOMA PRNG	SOMA Chaos
MIN	2688.59	1962.53	3161.47	2761.57
AVG	2805.84	2296.42	3305.62	2942.40
MAX	2873.77	3037.32	3372.46	3098.13

Thanks to the use of deterministic chaos against a pseudo-random number generator (PRNG) we speed up the running time by using simple mathematical operations, which is good for the CUDA kernel. Convergence of the fitness value is also a bit better.

8 Conclusion

We successfully implemented AP on CUDA and obtained relevant results. Both PRNG and deterministic chaos are suitable for running with parallel implementation of AP. The use of deterministic chaos seems to be a bit better. This is given by the fewer and simpler math operations needed to get a value. CUDA is not designed to run as long kernels, as we implemented, but there is a lot of room for future optimization of these kernels. We use lots of registers in the kernel, so performance falls from the ideal. In feature CUDA architecture, kernel under kernel will be probably run, which should bring a large improvement in performance. We want to compare our results with another parallel approach in the near future. On graphics hardware it will be Opencl, and OpenPM as a CPU variant respectively.

Acknowledgement. The following grants are acknowledged for the financial support provided for this research: Grant Agency of the Czech Republic – GACR P103/13/08195S, is partially supported by Grant of SGS No. SP2014/159, VŠB–Technical University of Ostrava, Czech Republic, by the Development of human resources in research and development of latest soft computing methods and their application in practice project, reg. no. CZ.1.07/2.3.00/20.0072 funded by Operational Programme Education for Competitiveness, co-financed by ESF and state budget of the Czech Republic.

References

1. Wells, D.C., Greisen, E.W., Harten, R.H.: FITS: A Flexible Image Transport System. Astronomy and Astrophysics Supplement Series 44, 363–370 (1981)
2. Rivinius, T., Carciofi, A.C., Martayan, C.: Classical Be stars. The Astronomy and Astrophysics Review, 1–86 (2013), doi:10.1007/s00159-013-0069-0
3. Zelinka, I., Davendra, D., Senkerik, R., Jasek, R., Oplatkova, Z.: Analytical Programming – a Novel Approach for Evolutionary Synthesis of Symbolic Structures. In: Kita, E. (ed.) Evolutionary Algorithms. InTech (2011), doi:10.5772/16166, ISBN: 978-953-307-171-8
4. Zelinka, I., Oplatkova, Z., Nolle, L.: Analytic Programming – Symbolic Regression by Means of Arbitrary Evolutionary Algorithms. Special Issue on Inteligent Systems, International Journal of Simulation, Systems, Science and Technology 6(9), 44–56 (2005) ISSN 1473-8031
5. Zelinka, I.: Symbolic regression – an overview, http://www.mafy.lut.fi/EcmiNL/older/ecmi35/node70.html
6. Zelinka, I., Oplatkova, Z.: Analytic programming – Comparative Study. In: CIRAS 2003: The second International Conference on Computional Intelligence, Robotics and Autonomous Systems (2003) ISSN 0219-6131
7. Lampinen, J., Zelinka, I.: New Ideas in Optimization – Mechanical Engineering Design Optimization by Differential Evolution, vol. 1, 20 p. McGraw-Hill, London (1999) ISBN 007-709506-5
8. Zelinka I.: Artificial Intelligence in The Problems of Global Optimization (in Czech). BEN, 190p. (2002) ISBN 80-7300-069-5

9. Thizzy: Be stars (2008), http://www.shelyak.com/contenu.php?id_contenu=30 &id_dossier=24

10. de Veronese, L.P., Krohling, R.A.: Differential evolution algorithm on the GPU with C-CUDA. In: IEEE Congress on Evolutionary Computation, CEC (2010)

11. Kralj, P.: Differential Evolution with parallelised objective functions using CUDA (2013), http://www.codehunter.eu/media/Kralj_Differential_Evolution_with_ parallelised_objective_functions_using_CUDA.pdf

12. Kromer, P., Platos, J., Snasel, V., Abraham, A.: Many-threaded implementation of differential evolution for the CUDA platform. In: Krasnogor, N. (ed.) Proceedings of the 13th Annual Conference on Genetic and Evolutionary Computation (GECCO 2011), pp. 1595–1602. ACM, New York (2011), http://doi.acm.org/10.1145/2001576.2001791, doi:10.1145/2001576.2001791

13. Farber, R.: CUDA Application Design and Development, 1st edn. Morgan Kaufmann Publishers Inc., San Francisco (2011)

14. Breiman, L.: Random Forests. Machine Learning 45, 5–32 (2001)

15. Breiman, L.: Bagging predictors. Machine Learning 24, 2:123–2:140 (1996), http://dx.doi.org/10.1023/A:1018054314350, doi:10.1023/A:1018054314350

16. Caruana, R., Niculescu-Mizil, A.: An Empirical Comparison of Supervised Learning Algorithms. In: Proceedings of the 23rd International Conference on Machine Learning, pp. 161–168. ACM, New York (2006), http://doi.acm.org/10.1145/1143844.1143865, doi:10.1145/1143844.1143865

17. Ho, T.K.: The Random Subspace Method for Constructing Decision Forests. IEEE Trans. Pattern Anal. 20(8), 832–844 (1998), http://dx.doi.org/10.1109/34.709601, doi:10.1109/34.709601

18. Ben-Haim, Y., Tom-Tov, E.: A Streaming Parallel Decision Tree Algorithm. J. Mach. Learn. Res. 11, 849–872 (2010)

19. Li, B., Chen, X., Li, M.J., Huang, J.Z., Feng, S.: Scalable random forests for massive data. In: Tan, P.-N., Chawla, S., Ho, C.K., Bailey, J. (eds.) PAKDD 2012, Part I. LNCS, vol. 7301, pp. 135–146. Springer, Heidelberg (2012), http://dx.doi.org/10.1007/978-3-642-30217-6_12

Man-Machine Interaction Improvement by Means of Automatic Human Personality Identification

Ryszard Tadeusiewicz and Adrian Horzyk

AGH University of Science and Technology,
Department of Automatics and Biomedical Engineering
{rtad,horzyk}@agh.edu.pl

Abstract. Creators of numerous information systems frequently concentrate on the semantic aspects of communication during planning and forming of man-machine interactions. Meanwhile emotions and adequate reactions to needs play equally essential role as rational reasoning when intelligence of a partner is judged. Intelligent behaviours and reactions usually deliberately affect the partner's needs. Therefore a computer could be accepted as an intelligent partner if it considers human needs affecting emotions. This paper presents a new method of automatic human needs recognition based on the extended personality typology that is described using characteristic verbal expressions. It enables to perform automatic passive classification of personality by means of psycholinguistic analysis during typical merit man-machine communication.

Keywords: man-machine interaction, natural language interfaces, emotional factor, psychological issues, human personality recognition.

1 Introduction to Recognition of Personality Needs

Communication with machines has become daily and common. It takes place through various man-machine interfaces that use menus, dialog boxes, or form elements. Sometimes there are used more advanced interfaces that use voice recognition, synthesis, or natural language analysis [3]. Computers are used to deliver, forward, process, and store various kinds of data that have information value for people and even for computers which change their behaviour and state after the read and processed data [5]. Nowadays we expect that computers will act and react in more human and intelligent way. 'Intelligent' means not only accurate, precise, efficient, and deliberately using knowledge that is based on the objectives but also taking into account the needs of interacting partners [3,7,9,14]. This paper focuses on recognition of human needs using extended personality typology which describes groups of needs associated with various personality types. These types can be recognized by means of psycholinguistic analysis of texts written by any analysed person, during chats or observation of actions on websites. The main challenge is to recognize individual human needs and adjust machine reactions to them to make the man-machine interaction

K. Saeed and V. Snášel (Eds.): CISIM 2014, LNCS 8838, pp. 278–289, 2014.
© IFIP International Federation for Information Processing 2014

pleasant, satisfactory, appropriate, and deliberate in view of his or her needs, so that modern intelligent machines could cooperate with people more efficiently.

Needs are not easy to identify when talking with another person, because people rarely talk about their needs directly. Much appropriate and fast solution can be delivered by automatic analysing of their personality, because it allows to easy identify many groups of needs, behaviours, likes, and dislikes. This paper introduces the extended personality typology in order to relate them to likes and dislikes that determinate predictable actions and reactions that can be influenced by changing the impact of machines on people.

Various needs of personality incline or avoid us to do something. They are also strictly associated with pleasure and satisfaction that can be achieved. People usually choose satisfaction or pleasure and avoid pain or problems, however, often the fulfilment of a given group of needs stands in contradiction with the others. Because some personality types are usually stronger than others, estimating their strength usually enables us to expect actions and predict reactions of individuals. It also can help machines to satisfy people when they are talking with machines capable to adjust interaction accordingly to the recognized needs of human partners. Similar personalities usually cooperate easier, because they mutually share pleasure. Different personalities can complement each other, although the cooperation cannot be easy.

As an alternative to the other known typologies [6,8], the introduced expanded character typology describes 10 extrovert and 10 introvert types (Fig. 1). Inborn character types induce us to act or react in a specific way. Some kinds of behaviours in accordance with character types and their strength can give us satisfaction and pleasure. On the other hand, behaviours that are at odds with character types cause us distress or dissatisfaction. The introduced types differ a lot in needs, likes, dislikes, actions, and reactions. Some group of needs are opposite for different character types and induce them to perform opposing behaviours. These differences can be favourable if people understand their diversity and learn to negotiate and cooperate. Understanding, respect, and wise interaction allow people to cooperate and obtain mutual benefits even if a part of their needs are opposing. Man-machine interfaces should also adapt according to the character types of a human user (customer) to make communication more efficient, personalized [1,10], and enjoyable by the user. Tables 1-2 show the most frequently used words, phrases, and forms for all introduced character types and enable a computer system to recognize them by text analysis. Some of the given words and phrases can be characteristic for more than one type of character or can be used in the other meaning or for the other reasons. They can be also extended and weighted according to their frequencies of use.

Dominant type (DOM, Opposite to SUB) likes to dominate, lead, guide, control (people and situations), direct, chair, conduct, rule, govern, recommend, suggest, counsel, influence, conquer, restrain, decide, determine, incline, select, choose, speak on behalf of himself and other people, operate, persuade, induce, teach, advise, instruct, program, regulate, designate, appoint, recommend, and convince somebody of his point of view. He is often a head, boss, manager, or

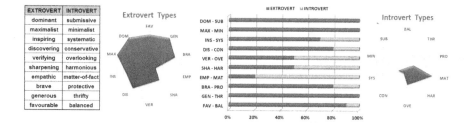

Fig. 1. The comparison of the strength of the character types of a person

president. He likes to own, have, possess, acquire, purchase, buy, obtain, and master something. He prefers new, original, intact, and untouched things. He likes to be asked for opinion, advice, suggestions, and recommendations, and be thanked for them, bowed, and curtsied. He likes accommodating, submissive, obedient, docile, and yielding people, acceptance of his ideas, decisions, and opinions but not always in partner relationships. He dislikes to be dominated, commanded, managed, determined, restrained, controlled, forced, ordered, steered, manipulated, persuaded, admonished, advised, instructed, depreciated, and humiliated. He likes freedom and independence, so leave him options, alternatives, and ability to choose or decide. He usually dislikes criticism of his opinion, choices, decisions, thoughts, ideas, and proposals. He hates to admit to his failures, mistakes, weaknesses, giving up, loss, inability, incapacity, powerlessness, helplessness etc. You can kindly ask him for various things, actions, and opinions, but do not forget to thank him. Neither ignore nor disregard his opinions, advises, or suggestions. You can lead him using evocative questions and proposals.

Submissive type (SUB, opposite to DOM) seems to be submissive, adjusting, accommodating, obedient, docile, yield, passive, indecisive, conformist, listening, and cooperative. He needs help, support, advice, suggestions, recommendations, assistance, and consultations to act, choice, decide, or operate. He likes to listen to opinions, analyses, experts, authorities, managers, bosses etc. He does not like to make decision or choices without advice, assistance, and support or take responsibility and control. He does not want to lead, guide, manage, and chair. He avoids or postpones choices and decisions. You can easily cooperate with him by taking control over him and inducing him to accomplish your targets or plans. Give him instructions and clarify your expectations.

Maximalist type (MAX, opposite to MIN) is ambitious, insatiable, unrestrained, excessive, optimistic, demanding, exacting, generalizing, striving to the sublime, unique, extravagant, extreme, and great things, properties, imaginations, actions, feelings etc. He likes to have, get, own, possess, obtain, and win more and more, first positions, something bigger, larger, longer, faster, better, or possibly all, everything, everywhere etc. He looks for something extreme, unique, rare, unusual, enormous, huge, super, great, significant, maximal, and the best. He dislikes restrictions, limitations, reductions, decreases, simplifications, half measures, compromises, mediocrity, minor, lesser, small, or insignificant things, goals, aims, targets, actions, features, parameters, experiences, or feelings. He avoids pessimists and people who cut off, discourage him or try to persuade him that his targets are beyond his scope. He likes challenges and to talk about significant plans, visions, concepts, targets, aims, and goals. Help him to overcome limitations and restrictions. You can easily offer him everything that will make him closer reaching his goals and visions. You can also raise the bar for him and give him challenging tasks to solve or manage. Do not give him too many options if you are not ready to give him all of them. Let him compete, rival, vie, emulate, and contend. It strengthens all other types of character and personality.

Minimalist type (MIN, opposite to MAX) seems to be minimizing, passive, with low expectations, and settling for what he already has. He can renounce, withdraw, or pull out when something requires too much effort, or he is pushed to do too many or too difficult things. He has no special or ambitious needs, requirements, or expectations. Almost everything he has is sufficient for him. He is satisfied with standards, and common things, actions, treatment, and features. He likes easy jobs and tasks, so he usually does not take up optional or challenging tasks. Competition or punishment will not motivate him to do something more or better, but you can assign simple tasks to him.

Inspiring type (INS, opposite to SYS) seems to be inspirational, creative, spontaneous, improvising, concocting, unconventional, enigmatic, surprising, inspiring, unpredictable, and sometimes impulsive, hasty, rash, irrational, disorganized, and chaotic. He likes new, different, various, interesting, inspiring, mysterious, fascinating, secretive, funny, artistic, unique, creative things, actions, and features. He looks for unusual arrangements, associations, things, features, actions, reactions, parameters, layouts, relations, feelings, experiences, knowledge, behaviours, ideas, concepts, targets etc. He likes surprises, astonishments, and unexpected things, and behaviours to act differently, intuitively, and creatively. He does not like well-worn phrases, trite words, outlines, rigid rules, plans, models, systematics, established procedures, stiff routines, regulations, categorizations, classifications, and stereotypes. He dislikes common, simple, normal, usual, and ordinary things, features, behaviours, and repetitions of the same operations. Do not cut his ideas or proposals. Let him inspire and positively surprise other people. Try not to limit or restrict him. Use his ideas and talk with him about them. Leave him create or find extraordinary solutions.

Systematic type (SYS, opposite to INS) seems to be systematic, organized, arranging, scheduling, steady, regular, predictable, and schematic. He likes plans, notes, regulations, models, rules, outlines, diagrams, formulas, schemes, recipes, systems, standards, norms, schedules, punctuality, lists, tables, grouping, arrangements, clusterization, classification, typologies, and systematics. He also likes to sort, order, arrange, organize, systematize, shape, categorize, classify, cluster, group, form a sequence or chronology, enumerate, list, and schedule everything. He operates in order and acts according to prepared schedules, plans, rules, and algorithms, and ticks and marks off the completed tasks. To him, everything should have its right place and time. He enumerates often and shows chronological dependencies between things, operations, and actions. He creates models, plans, and strategies for possibly all predictable situations. He dislikes mess, disorder, lack of arrangements or plans. He usually does not like surprises, twists that violate his plans or schedules. When dealing with him, try to be punctual, organized, and precise, and keep things in order and chronology. Map, reproduce, or copy his way of ordering things and enumeration. Try not to change his plans or schedules or give him time to plan again or reschedule.

Table 1. The characteristic words, phrases, and forms for the extrovert types

DOM	*I, my, we, us, our, self, want, need, decide, choose, select, elect, control, steer, drive, conduct, program, operate, order, book, recommend, autonomy, independent, sovereign, new, original, intact, untouched, have sth, own sth, owner, possess sth, option, alternative, power, selection, choices, powerful, strength, strong, big, huge, tall, high status/function; [on] my own, unaided; I/we [would] like, my/our opinion, my/our choice, from my/our point of view, to my mind, I/we think, I/we wish; you right, I/we have decided to/on, not to be dependent on sb/sth, believe me, do what I say, I/we recommend/suggest/advise, I/we agree with, I/we disagree with/on/about, I/we concur with; suggestions, recommendations, demands, commands and orders; speaking on behalf of a group of people; expressions of selections, choices and decisions; giving own opinions and points of view; possible various expressions of a refusal, contrary, revolt, rebel or mutiny*
MAX	*all, every, 100%, everything, collection, everywhere, never, always, everybody, nobody, entire, without restriction or limitation, great, large, huge, extreme, extra-, super-, mega-, ultra-, hyper-, enormous, maximal, optimal, fast, rapid, speedy, quick, nice, wonderful, exceptional, remarkable, revolutionary, modern, high-end, unique, rare, better, the best, more, the most, higher, the highest, big, bigger, the biggest, an extreme size, weight or height of physical or intellectual features or parameters, no problem, challenge, competitions, compete, rival, vie, emulate, contend; vision, concept, goal, target, aim; I/we manage to do sth, I/we cope with sth; I/we get by/along; asking for something more extreme (bigger, taller, faster etc.); describing extreme targets, goals, aims, visions or dreams; adjectives/adverbs in comparative or superlative forms*
INS	*idea, surprise, unexpected, unknown, new, revolution, inspiring, inspirational, inspired, remarkable, fantastic, mysterious, magic, enigmatic, special, unique, super, muse, mood, art, artistic, imaginatively, create, creative, fashion, improvisation, secrete, strange, dream, fascinating; I have thought about, I have invented/devised/concoct, I have been inspired/enthralled by something, I have been surprised; talking about invention, projects, conceptions, style, fashion, inspiration, surprise*
DIS	*why, ask, explain, test, compare, understand, discover, reveal, discern, check, check-up, compare, recognize, reconnoitre, examine, penetrate, integrate, understand, new, news, novelty, inventive, innovative, unknown, unusual, unordinary, curious, interesting, brilliant, inventive, riddle, mystery, relation, explore, penetrate, classify, examine, associate, think over/about, ponder over, make out, hypothesis, theory, observation, remark, proposal, invention, technology, progress; lot's of various questions, asks and request for explanations of something he would like to known or understand, asks for opinions and points of view, asks I would like to know/understand*
VER	*No, [verb] not, mis-, in-, im-, dis-, un-, -less, truth, exact, accuracy, sincere, disagree, incorrect, mistake, fault, error, break down, failure, gap, defect, bad, lie, mistakes, bugs, lacks, negligence, oversights, shortcomings, flaw, efficient, inconsistent, weakness, disparity, incompleteness, inaccurate, imprecise, inconsistent, misplaced, careless, omitted, dirty, spoiled, scratched, crooked, broken, careless, ambiguous, risk, show, look at, attention, note, control, quality, details, detailed, precise, inaccurate, neglected, controversy, inexact, verify, check, control, clean, improve, correct, repair, mend, fix, remedy, rectify, redress, neatness, remark, notice, watch, observe, point out, thorough, painstaking, meticulous, punctilious; manipulation, intrigue, hypocrisy, dishonesty, contradiction, ambiguous, conflict, misreading, miscalculation, misconception, carelessness, imprecise or inaccurate things and actions; underestimation, underrating; misrepresentation, stretching reality/truth; be meticulous in sth/in doing sth; put the emphasis on sth; critical and meticulous statements, point out various differences, impreciseness, faults, mistakes, inaccurateness, carelessness*
SHA	*no, not, sharp, hard, hot, tough, keen, precisely, adequate, right, keen, rough, steep, hard, clear, angular, controversial, defend, debate, discussion, disagree; intense, acute, sharpening, competing, conflicting, disagreeing, not permitting, not allowing, critical, rival, competitive, sharpen, fuel, bring matters to a head, edge, distinguish, indicate, label, mark, emphasise, split, break apart, strict, specify, make more specific, qualify, differentiate, difficult, point out; confront, compete, rival, struggle, stand up for something, wrestle, fight, taking up the gauntlet, throwing down the gauntlet to somebody; statements, orders, commands*
EMP	*nice, I am, children, family, friend, wife, husband, son, daughter, grandma, grandpa, uncle, aunt, nephew, hurt, wound, distress, unpleasantness, tribulation, understand, tell me about your problem/situation, how about you, for you, with you, intend, intention, reason, understand, disclose, show me, tell me, with a view to doing something, with the purpose of doing something, that is why, because, why, as, since, for, in order to, mean, what for, sympathy, sympathize with somebody, compassion, care, compassionate, condescend, pity somebody, regret, help, reciprocate, feel sorry for somebody, heart, disclose, confide; white lies to avoid unpleasant situation, diminutives, telling about intentions, reciprocate, weaken words, digressions, intentions, reasons and motivations behind behaviour and decisions*
BRA	*challenge, difficult, brave, courage, valiant, bold, brash, risk, stuntman, adrenaline, danger, hero, excessive, defend, fight, no fear; encouragements and hasten to act*
GEN	*give, bestow, convey, gift, lavish, opulent, showy, sumptuous, generous, expensive, striking, gesture, donation, support, assistance, help, charity, foundation, funds, donate*
FAV	*my, your, our, your, special, unique, individualistic, favourite, particular, selective, chosen, preference, award, recommendation, promotion, distinguish, differentiate, diversify, accent, highlight, opposed, in contrast to, depending on, respectively to, in relation to, by, unbalanced, different; distinguishing and differentiating*

Discovering type (DIS, opposite to CON) seems to be discovering, curious, inquiring, investigating, detective, open-minded, liberal, tolerant, and progressive. He likes to discover, examine, explore, test, check, try, experiment, decompose into prime factors, form various associations and understand unknown and undiscovered things, actions, reactions, behaviours, relations, features, or mysteries. He frequently queries himself and other people, so he likes open questions and discussions. He likes to watch, listen, touch, sniff, and taste various interesting thing in order to discover something new, unknown, unusual, curious, enigmatic, mysterious, obscure, and unusual happenings. He likes news, new hypotheses, technologies, statements, laws, rules, models, principles, theories, inventions, investigations, and their products. He dislikes stereotypes and simple, normal, unusual, common, and ordinary things, features, actions, reactions, rigid rules, plans, procedures, boredom, inactivity, lack of novelty, innovations, and changes, a repetition, a monotony, a humdrum, and a routine. He hates conservatism as well as immutable, primitive, and backward things and views. Try to use or reveal new hypothesis, theories, rules, or principles together with him.

Conservative type (CON, opposite to DIS) seems to be conservative, conventional, traditional, permanent, loyal, sentimental, faithful, stable, unchanging, hermetic, insular, and retaining the old. He likes permanent, immutable, unchanged things and behaviours. He likes conventions, rules, principles, fidelity, tradition, faith, and doctrines. He prefers old, checked, known, proven, well-tried, the same places, time, and people. He usually rejects new ideas, hypothesis, theories, principles, or rules and does not change his mind often. He hardly accepts any progress, changes, or innovations. He does not like revolution or evolution. He prefers solid, fixed, permanent things and behaviours and dislikes mixtures, hybrids, new combinations etc. Do not try to convince him too fast but gradually introduce and explain to him new ideas, hypotheses, and theories. He emphasizes faith, loyalty, and faithfulness.

Verifying type (VER, opposite to OVE) is always meticulous, pedantic, verifying, comparing, differentiating, discriminating, checking, inspecting, monitoring, controlling (quality, compliance), honest, truthful, evaluating, and commenting, looking for details, inconsistency, mistakes, incompatibility, and incoherency. He likes to watch, observe, listen, feel, and smell to compare, distinguish, and find out differences, faults, mistakes, errors, bugs, lacks, contradictions, breakdowns, misplacements, failures, defects, gaps, carelessness, omissions, shortcomings, oversights, negligence, inconsistencies, incoherency, incompatibility, inaccuracy, inexactness, inexactitude, weaknesses, disparity, misreading, miscalculations, misconceptions etc. He pays attention to dirty, spoiled, scratched, crooked, broken, careless, risky, and ambiguous things. He tries to check, point out, verify, control, clean, improve, correct, repair, mend, rectify, remedy, and fix them. He can easy disagree, deny, or oppose. He also likes to detect and uncover lies, manipulation, untruth, and falsehood. He does not like when somebody ignores or disregards his remarks and comments. You do not have to agree with him but take into consideration his remarks, suggestions, notices, critique, and comments. Neither quarrel nor argue with what he has said but thank him for them and ask for more details until he will not finish. Do not underestimate or underrate his notices. Treat them as a kind of help and allow him for notices, remarks, and observations. Weigh your words and choose them carefully.

Overlooking type (OVE, opposite to VER) seems to be overlooking, blurring, blending, unifying, joining, merging, generalizing, ascending, lifting, looking for similarities, aggregations, unification, grouping, classifying, clustering, and

Table 2. The characteristic words, phrases, and forms for the introvert types

SUB	he, she, you, they, his, her, your, their, experts, opinion, statistics, other, others; maybe, perhaps; I consult it; I (need/have to) ask sb an advise; I decide/choose later; I have to think about it; what would you advise me; what will you choose; tell me your opinion; give me an advise; ask for advise, suggestions, opinions or help to choose sth
MIN	O.K., enough, sufficient, fit, without, just, any, whatever, minimum, insignificant, unimportant, do not matter, little, less, the least, low, the lowest, settle for; normal, common, average, casual, ordinary, mediocre, typical, standard, usual, simple; usually short sentences, using of reducing words expressing sufficiency
SYS	first, second, third, fourth, fifth, previous, next, last, at last, now, earlier, later, at the beginning, start, start with, at the end, mess, tidiness, untidy, gradually, step, in steps, one by one, one after the other, chronologically, in turn, in its place, in order, order, sort, sequence, rank, systematize, step, level, stage, arrange, classify, cluster, chronology, enumerate, appointment, note, diary, timetable, layout, plans, models, rules, diagrams, outlines, formulas, schemes, schedules, recipes, systems, standards, norms, lists, tables, maps, notes, regulation, punctuality, compose, composition, group, structure, model, organization, organize, think, lay out, plan out, unfold, divide, spread out, time, on time, date, deadline, count, synchronize, schedule, reschedule; various expressions of time and date; enumeration or list something; temporal or spatial relations and order; construction of well-arranged statements, speeches, talks, articles and papers
CON	the same, proven, tradition, habit, affection, faithful, loyal, principle, rule, stable, old, common, typical, stylish, convention, doctrine, faith, permanent, immutable, unchanged; retaining rules and principles, faithful, fidelity, tolerance, restrain, religion, confidence, trust; lot's of statements, orders, appeals and refer to rules and principles
OVE	all, no, not any, everything, everybody, everyone, nobody, nothing, nowhere; blur, blend, unify, join, merge, classify, cluster, group, generalize, overlook, ascend, lift, similar, aggregate, consolidate, complete, broaden, widen, spread, increase, enhance, horizons, scope; unit, generally, usually, widely, overall, comprehensive, exhaustive, global, mostly, vaguely, majority, broad, wide, total, overall, miscellaneous, widespread, allow, permit, admit, enable, close, closer, near, similarity, cohesion, consolidation, globalization, grouping, over-, up-, every-, no-; generalizing, overlooking, flatten, oversimplifying
HAR	O.K., okay, yes, good, no problem, agree, confirm, bit, little, a bit, a little, gently, kindly, not so much, so, well, I agree, never mind, can happen to anyone, little, not many, small, slight, minor, almost, let off; peace, quiet, peace, harmony, melody, It is interesting, I ponder over this, I think about this; I ask my; do you mind if I; excuse me, forgive me, sorry, weepy; agreement, tuning, rhythm, match, soft, smooth, easy, round, harmonize, mitigation, conciliate, reconcile, appease, peace, symbiosis, adapt, accommodate, adjust, tune, fit, relieve, reduce, calm, appease, assuage, moderate; questions and asks, white lies, lies, telling to seek advice from somebody, diminutives and weaken words; handle somebody with kid glove; pull wool over somebody's eyes; beat about the bush; minces his words, excusing oneself, asking for permission
MAT	performance, efficient, fast, brief, quick, finish, complete, concisely, concrete facts, specifics, hurry, hurry up, hasten, quickly, talk sense, subject, task, issue, core, practical, sensible, business-like, precisely, accurately, exactly, concise, succinct, matter, substance, matter-of-fact, heart of the matter, hit the nail of the head, get on somebody with one's work, let's get down to facts / business / specifics, get down to brass tacks, talk sense, bring something to a conclusion; to get to the bottom of a matter; get down to brass tacks; rare or no intention and a little explanation, short matter-of-fact speech, talking without beating about the bush
PRO	but, problem, doubt, misgivings, careful, safe, strongbox, key, security, danger, cautious, reliable, sure, confident, certain, secure, warrant, sure, protect, provisions, stores, stock, alert, prevent, protect, precaution, protect, backup, firewall, alarm, be assured, guaranteed, warranted, insured, prudent, risk, threat, hazard, trouble, safeguard, precautionary measure against something, alarm, alert, warn, limit, precaution against risks, just in case, can be necessary, put away something for a rainy day; alerts, warnings, raise doubts, something but something; suspicious and mistrustful asks, questions and statements
THR	effective, efficient, saving, bank, account, spend, too much, too many, lose, loss, waste, cut, miss, safe, discount, cheap, promotion, share, utilize, eco, ecology, ecological, recycle, reuse, refactoring, turn off, switch off, cost-effective, energy-effective, LED, green energy, rate, percentage, commission, special offer, fuel-saving, energy-saving, -saving, minimize, maximize, optimize, profitable, cut one's loss
BAL	balance, balancing, in balance, counterbalance, compensation for sth, exact, accurate, precise, properly, evenly, evaluate, measure, measuring, assess, assessing, weight, weighting, weight out, level, calibrate, estimate, sizing, sort, grade, according to size, to bring things in balance, compare, compensate for, equal, be consistent, just, justice, fair, fairness, unfair, unfairly, judge, principle, rule, law, reciprocate, repay, be consistent, compensate, settle a debt, equalize, level, make something up to somebody, consistent, consequence, counterbalance; comparison, weighting, measuring, calibrating

consolidating. He likes to blur, blend, unify, join, merge, generalize, overlook, ascend, lift, broaden, widen, spread, and widespread. He allows permits, admits, and enables some unimportant or irrelevant mistakes, errors, faults, inconsistency, incompatibility, incoherency etc. He is tolerant and understanding. He usually passes over details, trifles, odds and sods. He does not like narrowing, reducing, or depleting. Assortments, types, sorts, differences, diversities, and discrimination are not as important for him as globalization, generalization, grouping, clusterization, and classification. Try to generalize and show tasks broadly, generally, and in a broad context or scope. Pass over the marginal, trifles and do not be too accurate and meticulous if not necessary.

Sharpening type (SHA, opposite to HAR) is sharp, hard, tough, hot, active, keen, intense, acute, sharpening, competing, conflicting, disagreeing, forbidding, disallowing, critical, rivalling, and competitive. He likes to sharpen, fuel, inflame, exacerbate, bring matters to a head, edge, distinguish, indicate, label, mark, emphasize, split, break apart, strict, specify, make more specific, qualify, differentiate, and point out. He also likes to confront, compete, rival, struggle, or stand up for something, wrestle, fight, take up the gauntlet, and throw down the gauntlet to somebody. He dislikes to resign, ease off, give up, withdraw, abandon, dispense, skip, smooth, moderate, and tone down. Try to explain, establish, fix, and arrange everything necessary.

Harmonious type (HAR, opposite to SHA) is harmonious, compliant, agreeable, tuning, avoiding conflicts, quarrels, critics, rows, brawls, fights, and disagreements, prone to compromises, reconciling, non-confrontational, gentle, symbiotic, forgiving, and softening. He likes rhythm, matching, softening, smoothing, rounding, harmony, mitigation, ease, conciliation, and reconciliation of people. He often arbitrates, mediates, alleviate stress and nervous situations, appeases disputes and conflicts, and makes peace with others or symbiosis between things. He can forgive, adapt, accommodate, adjust, tune, fit, and make things together. He relieves, reduces, calms, appeases, assuages, eases, and moderates all conflicting or difficult situations. He opens up very slowly. If you drive or force him to do something, he will lie or keep away from you in future.

Empathic type (EMP, opposite to MAT) seems to be empathic, personal, talkative, compassionate, caring, affectionate, sensitive, tender, emotional, gentle, open, warm, and soothing. He likes to listen to emotional confidences and secretes. He tries to be closer, friendlier, and reducing distance. He likes to personify and embody animals and even things. He reveals himself and expect the same from others. He does not like when somebody hides emotions or is cool, subjective, impersonal, and formal, does not explain his intentions or reasons of doing something, cuts personal reflections or moves immediately to the heart of the matter. Try to understand his intentions and do personal digressions.

Matter-of-fact type (MAT, opposite to EMP) seems to be subjective, businesslike, matter-of-fact, brief, concise, succinct, curt, productive, practical, efficient, focused, cool, impersonal, and often personally self-contained, introvert, and shy. He is focused on subjects and practical aspects. He dislikes uncompleted work and unfinished tasks or examinations. He also likes to finish previous tasks before he starts a new one. He comes straight to the point, gets to the heart of the matter, and hits the nail on the head. He does not like when somebody handles him with kid gloves, pulls wool over his eyes, beats about the bush, or minces his words. He dislikes irrelevant or personal reflections or digressions. He rarely reveals personal reasons, purposes, or intentions. He does not like vague and unsubstantial discussions and conversations. He usually hastens and pushes for concrete facts if somebody is beating about the bush. Talk to him briefly, concisely, in concrete terms, and go straight down to business. Use facts, specifics, and get down to brass tacks. Do not reveal yourself too much or too quickly. Avoid assigning to him next tasks before he finishes the previous ones.

Brave type (BRA, opposite to PRO) seems to be brave, courageous, surpassing, daring, valiant, heroic, bold, brash, and open to risk. He likes adrenaline, danger, hazard, and risk, so often behaves like a stuntman. He likes to take up difficult and dangerous challenges and puts out challenges to other people. He is usually skilful, fit, and active. He dislikes timid, fearful, and cowardly people. He avoids too much insurance, protection, and security, because it deprives him of pleasure. He does not like to talk about protection, security, risks, and threads. Allow him surpass and cross borders.

Protective type (PRO, opposite to BRA) seems to be protecting, insuring, ensuring, preventive, careful, restrained, and cautious, questioning, blocking, checking, and controlling safety. He likes guarantee, safeguards, and safe alternatives. He usually warns others against risks, threads, and danger, which he tries to limit by prevention, suitable planning, education, examination, or preparation. He purchases proven and reliable products. He always anticipates, expects risks, danger, troubles, and problems, so he demands guarantee, protection, and insurance. He wants to be prepared and know what to do when difficulties or troubles occur. He has some reserves, provisions, and stores for unexpected situations. He does not like underestimating, ignoring, or disregarding his warnings, rules, steps, plans, prevention, and means of caution, safety, and security. He always has a comprehensive policy, insurance, backups, and safe-locks.

Generous type (GEN, opposite to THR) is generous, lavish, and helpful. He can hardly refrain from giving, waiving, and remitting if he is asked for it. He likes opulent, showy, sumptuous, glamorous parties and receptions and to gratify, share, lend, distribute, donate, sponsor, or give gratuities. He gives back or helps using own and foreign resources. He dislikes storing money, economical solutions, and misers, so he rarely has reserves and savings. He often purchases splendid and opulent but disposable products. He likes spending money and takes loans. You can easily get his help, support, or a loan even without percentage.

Thrifty type (THR, opposite to GEN) seems to be thrifty, economical, optimizing, minimizing, maximizing, and saving. Saving is his way of earning money or supplementing it. He likes to recycle, refactor, and reuse, so he prefers to purchase multiply used things and products. He likes scalable and profitable products. He counts up and sums up possible or predictable profits, percentage, benefits, and advantages in a longer period of time. He avoids or cuts any predictable losses. He dislikes spoilage and throwaway things, wasting time, money, or unused resources, residues, and leftovers. He switches off the light, engines, and other appliance. He turns off the ovens, radios, computers, gas etc. He likes to use any kind of labour-saving, space-saving, fuel-saving, energy-saving, and cost-effective solutions. He likes promotional campaigns and special offers.

Favouring type (FAV, opposite to BAL) is favouring, preferring, biased, opposite, contrasting, advertising, promoting, recommending, selecting, opposing, distinctive, distinguishing, destabilizing, careerist, and tolerant. He does not like levelling, smoothing, equalling, balancing, compensating, ruling, adjusting everything, and comparing only similarities. He prefers special, unique, individualistic, particular, different, and contrasting things, features, and people. He likes to award, favour, promote, differentiate, distinguish, diversify, contrast, highlight, accentuate, select, and choose accordingly to one's abilities, knowledge, and talents. You can ask him to promote or support you. Try to stand out from other people and show your special features and abilities.

Balancing type (BAL, opposite to FAV) is balancing, equating, comparing, weighing, examining, tuning, measuring, assessing, sizing, levelling, calibrating, equally dividing, and usually striving for some kind of justice, compensation, or fulfilment. He likes to arbitrate, adjudicate, and work out rights. He expects balance, counterbalance, reciprocity, and mutual concessions. He expects compensation and usually justice. He dislikes injustice, imbalance, inequality, detuning, favouritism, biasing, corruption, unjust systems, unbalanced things or judgments, unfair, and inconsistent actions. Keep everything in balance, be fair, just, honest, reciprocating, self-critical, and compensating. Divide exactly, evenly, and equally. Do not promote or favour somebody or something too much without justification and arguments balancing such kind of behaviours.

Needs of intellect and spirit are related to the activities that lead to develop intelligence, knowledge, and express egocentric or non-egocentric attitude [5]. People who actively develop their intellect like to associate interesting facts in various contexts learn and seek for new information channels. They like to increase their possibilities of perception of incoming information. They clarify and expand their vocabulary of terms to increase possibilities to differentiate and discriminate. They try to make their knowledge reliable, coherent, consistent, verified, and well-associated with other facts. They like to receive, acquire, and purchase a variety of information sources. They also want to cooperate with other people who have interesting knowledge, experience, or abilities. They like to read books, magazines, papers, create efficient methods, techniques, algorithms, and solutions, so they often use the following words and phrases: *data, information, knowledge, learning, teaching, education, study, research, investigation, school, college, university, technology, magazine, book, newspaper, publication, article, science, scientific, cognitive, think, reason, cause, effect, motive, consider, reconsider, explore, apply, explain, understand, clever, smart, intelligent, intelligence, intellect, associate, associations, relation, relationship, correlation, development, progress, growth, evolution, revolution, transformation, adaptation, searching for, looking for, seek, find out, explain it to me, let me know, definition, accuracy, accurately, precisely, exactly* etc. Intelligence increase efficiency and boosts effectiveness. It optimizes behaviours and operations as well. When people cooperate, join, assist, work together, and are not selfish, the cooperation is more efficient. Egocentrism destroys relations, cooperation, and causes competition, rivalry, scrambling, fight for positions, and ineffective use of resources. The development of intelligence/intellect is associated with understanding wide context, relations, correlations, dependencies and needs.

2 Man-Machine Interaction Taking into Account Needs

Man-machine interaction can satisfy people if machines will be able to properly react on human needs and find out the answers for them. Machines should be able to automatically recognize and classify human needs even if people do not reveal or describe them. Linguistic communication is very natural for people, so it can be used to classify individual human personality in order to adjust machine reactions to it. Using the described personality systematics machines can sum weighted numbers of characteristic words, phrases, and inflection. The measurement of intensities of character types is based on counting characteristic linguistic objects that are weighted by their uniqueness in view of all types (Tab. 3). The presented systematics describes also the recommended treatment of the person of an established type of character. It makes possible to change the machine way of talking, presenting information, or automating correspondence [2,3,11,12]. Moreover, the answers for asked questions can take into account also the other recognized needs that were not expressed in given questions. It allows us to construct intelligent and personality sensitive man-machine interfaces that make the interaction between people and machines more human, pleasant, predictable, and friendly. We can even predict the most probable choices and decisions of a customer after gained knowledge about his character types. This knowledge can be used to adapt a way of further conversation and presentation to maximize the positive answer of a customer. Identification of human needs is also indispensable to a development of intelligent systems that are oriented to form the knowledge [5] and raise their intelligence [13,14].

Table 3. Psycho-linguistic analysis of character types

CHARACTER ANALYSIS		WEIGHTS FOR THE CHARACTER TYPES							
Word or phrase	No	INT	DOM	MAX	SYS	VER	HAR	MAT	EMP
all	1			4					
applications	1	1							
associate	1	3						1	
automatically	1	3			1				
be able	1			1	2				
choose, chosen	2		4						
computational	1	2				1			
could you	1	2					2		2
data	1	2			1		1		
description	1	1			1	2			
especially	1					2			
explore	1	3				3			
first	1				3				
functions	1		2				2		
group	1	1			2		1		
has to	1		3						
I'd like	1		3						
intelligence	1	3							
more	1			4					
need	1		2						
offers, offered	2		1						
pass to me	1		2						
possible	1		1	2					
precise	1			1		4			
quickly	1			2				3	
system	1	1			3				
will you be so kind	1	5							
WEIGHTED SUM:		27	24	15	12	11	8	8	5

Texts written by people are automatically parsed and analysed taking into account all important linguistic objects and their weights (Tab. 3), e.g.: "*I'd like to choose between two or more offers. Will you be so kind and could you pass them to me as quickly as possible? I need precise description of the offered applications, especially about the functions that provide new computational intelligence features. First of all, the chosen system has to be able to associate, explore, and group new data automatically.*" This text sample is very short but it enables us to gain fundamental knowledge about character types and intelligence of the person that has written it. Table 3 contains the list of the words and phrases that have occurred in the above text and the numbers of their occurrences. Namely, this person is intelligent (INT) and very dominant (DOM) - probably is a boss or a head. He is also maximalist (MAX), systematic (SYS), and verifying (VER). Probably he is also a bit harmonious (HAR) and matter-of-fact (MAT). About his emphatics (EMP) we cannot be sure, because any word uniquely defines this type and the total weighted sum is not significant.

3   Conclusion and Final Remarks

This paper has presented an extended model of psycholinguistic personality systematics that help to automatically classify human personality and recognize individual needs after the simple analysis of text written by an analysed human. The defined groups of needs allow the system to quickly adapt and foresee the other very probable needs, interests, businesses, behaviours, actions, and reactions of the human. The presented way of recognition and classification is automatic and passive, i.e. there is no need to ask a person to analyse or estimate his personality or reveal his or her needs. This kind of passive and automatic recognition of needs can supplement the information of a given person gathered in a traditional way by analysing his action, purchased products etc.

References

1. Jill, D.: CRM - relations with customers. Helion, Gliwice (2002)
2. Horzyk, A., Tadeusiewicz, R.: A psycholinguistic model of man-machine interactions based on needs of human personality. In: Cyran, K.A., Kozielski, S., Peters, J.F., Stańczyk, U., Wakulicz-Deja, A. (eds.) Man-Machine Interactions. AISC, vol. 59, pp. 55–67. Springer, Heidelberg (2009)
3. Horzyk, A., Magierski, S., Miklaszewski, G.: An Intelligent Internet Shop-Assistant Recognizing a Customer Personality for Improving Man-Machine Interactions. In: Recent Advances in Intelligent Information Systems, pp. 13–26. EXIT, Warsaw (2009)
4. Horzyk, A.: Negotiations: The Proven Strategies. Edgard, Warsaw, 1–192 (2012)
5. Horzyk, A.: Artificial Associative Systems and Associative Artificial Intelligence, pp. 1–280. Exit (2013)
6. Jung, C.G.: Psychological Types. In: Hull, R.F.C. (ed.) The Collected Works of C.G.Jung, vol. 6. Princeston University Press (1971)
7. Mirski, A.: Managing Creativity in the Enterprise Culture. Krakow, Wzorek (2013)
8. Myers, I.B., Myers, P.B.: Gifts differing: understanding personality type. Davies-Black Publishing, Mountain View, CA (1995)
9. Skowron, A., Wasilewski, P.: Interactive information systems: toward perception based computing. Theor. Comput. Sci. 454, 240–260 (2012)
10. Sae-Tang, S., Esichaikul, V.: Web personalization techniques for E-commerce. In: Liu, J., Yuen, P.C., Li, C.-H., Ng, J., Ishida, T. (eds.) AMT 2001. LNCS, vol. 2252, pp. 36–44. Springer, Heidelberg (2002)
11. Tadeusiewicz, R.: Speech in Human System Interaction. In: 3rd International Conference on Human System Interaction, Rzeszow (2010)
12. Tadeusiewicz, R.: New Trends in Neurocybernetics. Computer Methods in Materials Science 1, 1–7 (2010)
13. Tadeusiewicz, R.: Introduction to Intelligent Systems. In: The Industrial Electronics Handbook - Intelligent Systems, pp. 1–12. CRC Press, Boca Raton (2011)
14. Tadeusiewicz, R.: Place and Role of Intelligent Systems in Computer Science. Computer Methods in Materials Science 10(4), 193–206 (2010)

viaRODOS: Monitoring and Visualisation of Current Traffic Situation on Highways

Dušan Fedorčák, Tomáš Kocyan, Martin Hájek,
Daniela Szturcová, and Jan Martinovič

IT4Innovations, VŠB - Technical University of Ostrava,
17. listopadu 15/2172, 708 33 Ostrava, Czech Republic
{dusan.fedorcak,tomas.kocyan,martin.hajek,daniela.szturcova,
jan.martinovic}@vsb.cz

Abstract. This paper describes methods of traffic monitoring based on
on-line retrieval of big data both from cars equipped with GPS devices
and stationary sensor systems. Various visualization methods and styles
of presentation are discussed with focus on linear structure of gathered
traffic data along observed routes. Visualized data is available via interactive web interface which uses modern vector graphic standard and
enables presentation of as much information as possible with common,
well-known traffic symbolism.

Keywords: Traffic Monitoring, Traffic Visualisation, Current Traffic
Situation, Floating Car Data.

1 Introduction

Increasing number of new mobile devices, touch-screen and alson large video
screens has brought about the need to publish information in a different way.
These new trends emerge also in the field of traffic data processing and result
in publishing of current traffic status based on on-line information transmission
directly from the road network. There are several aspects that affect the way
in which the results of traffic data processing are made accessible. New type
of screens force the developers to adjust graphic concept of the output so that
users receive important information. This has to be selected in an appropriate
way and placed on a screen area.

An attempt to control traffic resulted in building of Intelligent Transportation
System (ITS). Several projects focused on traffic data processing were established, for example [6] and [9]. The projects address different aspects: detection
of current traffic, modelling of traffic flow, traffic data publication, traffic control,
etc. All of these activities rely on valid input data. Processed data is offered for
a variety of users. Different types of users need different styles of presentation of
results. In order to satisfy users' needs several styles of visualization have been
introduced: [1], [5], [2].

In our work, we focused on selection of a visual concept that considers such
effects and we make an attempt to outline possible ways of traffic data publishing

K. Saeed and V. Snášel (Eds.): CISIM 2014, LNCS 8838, pp. 290–300, 2014.

in specific tasks. First we describe data types and sources and then we indicate necessary traffic information characteristics. We also introduce visualization approach that was selected for our application with regards to above mentioned trends.

2   Car Data Sources in the Czech Republic

As number of cars has been growing and growing, traffic gets heavy and the probability of an accident or other problems increases. Every such unnecessary delay during the delivery of goods means a waste of resources, an increase in costs and a reduction in profits. For these reasons, drivers and shipper dispatchers need up to date information describing current traffic situation in order to efficiently plan routes and necessary stops. Generally, data sources describing actual traffic situation can be divided into two groups - stationary data sources and floating car data sources. The following paragraphs briefly describe both types of data sources and summarize their advantages and disadvantages. Finally, benefits of both data types are also outlined.

2.1   Stationary Data

In the Czech Republic, traffic situation is mostly monitored and evaluated using the stationary data. Stationary devices are integrated in traffic infrastructure and can have a form of: *camera systems* presenting current traffic situation; *inductive loop systems* detecting traffic intensity; *electronic toll system* collecting data from vehicles; *complex systems* combine more traffic detectors. This type of data is usually collected through a network of toll gates and inductive loops installed along the road.

Advantages: One of the biggest advantages of this approach is the fact that there is no need for equipping vehicles with special electronic devices. By this way, absolutely all vehicles (both personal and corporate, including foreign visitors) going through a measuring point are recorded. For example, camera systems or inductive loops work properly without any car alteration. Moreover, since the position of measuring devices is well known, it is easy to immediately calculate some important traffic indicators, such as average speed, traffic density, spacing between cars, etc.

Disadvantages: However, in the Czech Republic, this network of measuring points is relatively sparse and only about 17% of the road network is covered (about 1200 of the total of 7000 kilometres). This low density is caused, of course, by related necessary expenses – installation of such measuring points is quite expensive. For instance, installation of inductive loops requires disruption of asphalt surface, electronic toll requires building of special masts or gates etc.

Regardless of this density, there are other limitations. Electronic toll gates divide roads into fragments of various length, some of them may extend to many kilometres. Thus, data obtained from electronic tolls relate to the fragment as a whole. For example, it is possible to detect that there is a congestion on a fragment, but it is impossible to detect if its cause is located just a few metres behind electronic toll gate or many kilometres from it.

2.2 Floating Car Data

The opposite to stationary data is Floating Car Data (FCD), which describes exact movement of individual vehicles, including their trajectories, actual speed etc. Nowadays, an on-board unit including a GPS receiver becomes a standard equipment of corporate fleet cars. Moreover, increasing expansion of smart phones brought GNSS technology to our personal lives, where with combination of cheap connectivity, each vehicle can become a source of this type of data. There are many available applications which can send its data to a data centre. For example, Open Street Map gained most of its data in this way.

Advantages: The number of cars equipped with a GPS unit has doubled over the past five years. It can be expected that the trend will continue. It implies that the number of potential data sources will increase. Moreover, data from GPS receivers cover is not limited to predefined places. It is, unlike stationary data, available for all roads.

Disadvantages: On the other hand, GPS device as a part of GNSS technology, fails to provide precise outputs or the outputs can be intentionally distorted. The quality of outputs can also be influenced by the device quality, location, weather or other unpredictable and uncontrollable phenomena. All of this can have an impact on positioning, ranging from meters to tens of meters.

GNSS is based on satellite technology. GPS receiver has to be able to receive signals from several satellites. However, in some cases it is difficult. Typical example is an urban area with tall buildings which form obstacles between receiver and satellites. Then, GPS receiver is not able to report its position.

Both stationary and floating data has its strengths and weaknesses. The main goal of our work is to eliminate the above drawbacks and improve presentation of current traffic. The strength of one data type may overcome weakness of the other.

3   viaRodos Data Processing

The viaRodos system is not only a visualizer of collected stationary and floating car data. It also aggregates other essential data sources for assessment of the situation and decision support. The following paragraphs briefly introduce main viaRodos' inputs.

Traffic Data: There are two sources of stationary data:

- Toll Gates Electronic system of performance imposition of a charge [7] provides data related to vehicles above 3.5 tons. System retrieves data from 220 stations (gates) refreshed every minute. Every car record consists of information such as timestamp, gate identification, car category, car emission class.
- ASIM [11] triple-tech traffic detectors use a combination of Doppler radar, ultrasound and passive infrared technologies in a single unit. Data is retrieved from 52 profiles located on highways, processed and offered every 5 minutes in form of aggregated value—intensity, speed, occupancy for 7 categories of vehicles.

Floating Car Data: At the moment there is nearly 130 thousand vehicles providing the data. That is enough to calculate current traffic on the majority of significant roads. Data is dispatched from cars every minute and consists of information such as timestamp, location, speed and azimuth. Floating Car Data is associated with direction-oriented segments according to TMC tables.

Maps: Map basis associates traffic information with traffic infrastructure segments [4]. It is retrieved from RDS-TMC system.

Meteodata: Local meteodata is retrieved from web pages with meteoinformation and associated with traffic infrastructure segments.

JSDI: Uniform system of traffic information for the Czech Republic (JSDI) provides data representing occurrences and events related to traffic capacity and passability in the Czech Republic.

4   Visualization

As stated above, the FCD can provide useful information of different kinds than stationary sensors data. The key feature is the mobility of the sensors (the cars), and consequently, detailed segmentation can be used for roads with high FCD density (highways, main roads). There were situations observed where the FCD data signalized significant slowdown in the traffic flow 10–15 minutes before the national incident service system confirmed that there was a situation figure 1.

On the other hand, the stationary data (where present) can provide different types of information (e.g. vehicle counting) and also helps validate the FCD set thus it should not be omitted.

For these reasons, it was decided to build a visualization which merges the stationary sensor data and FCD data. The basic visualization should contain static data which defines the route of interest (road infrastructure, places of interests, road network information etc.). The next layer of visualization should contain dynamic data (i.e. FCD and stationary sensors data). Moreover, other types of dynamic data can be incorporated into visualization (weather information, known incidents etc.).

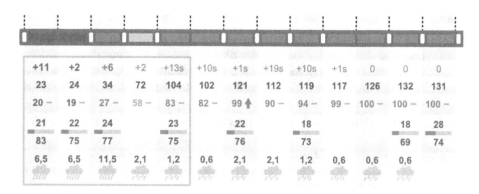

Fig. 1. FCD set an incident emergence: heavy rain caused a significant slowdown in the measured traffic flow (see the next section for detailed information about visualized data)

4.1 Selection of Features

There are many indicators present in the FCD set (see chapter above) and it is difficult to judge what kind of information is crucial and should be prioritized in the visualization. Also, we believe that the human recognition abilities along with the local experience of the real traffic managers is far better than any analytical/classification system we are able to implement right now and a rich visualization will enhance such abilities. For these reasons, the visualization should contain as many data types as possible without overwhelming the user. Finally, due to the experimental nature of the FCD set, there can be undiscovered flaws in the system and such visualization may help to identify them.

Unfortunately, these requirements appeared to be very difficult to implement with common types of traffic flow visualizations. The most serious problem is the amount of data we want to show for every road segment. The usual way how to visualize such data is put them in a geographically accurate map. But, if one wants to show more than one or two data elements for every road segment then it is almost impossible to build a well-arranged and clear visualization based on a map. Our solution to this problem was to sacrifice the spatial context in favour of the readability of the visualization.

4.2 Linear Visualization

We decided to use linear visualization [8] of a set of selected routes that were identified as interesting by traffic experts. Such simplification allows us to incorporate many "layers" of data with no degradation in readability. The linear visualization structure is shown in the figure 2.

As it is shown above we choose a tabular visualization structure as it is suitable for a large amount of data per segment. In the real application (*ViaRODOS*) the user interface allows to enable or disable every row and thus the user can customize the visualization according to his or her needs. Also, the natural shape

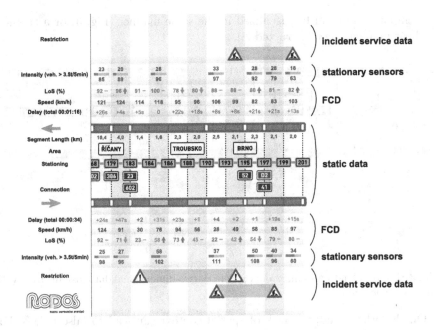

Fig. 2. Linear data visualization – detailed view: merged dynamic data is visualized above and below static route data

of visualization (long horizontal box) comply with front displays used in most control centers.

4.3 Spatial Relationships Versus Topology

Even though the spatial context is omitted and the user might not know the real geographical layout, there are some advantages this approach brings:

A natural view focused on route and from/to paradigm, which might be more suitable for many people. It is important to point out that the map layout is usually learned from other instances of maps than from reality. In real life, people think more topologically in terms of starting points and destinations.

The ability to represent detailed information where needed. From traffic management point of view, there are locations which have to be visualized in a higher level of detail, for example highway crossings, exits etc.. When the real scale is applied (i.e. on a map), there is significantly less space to provide necessary information in such areas. In our visualization, this is solved by higher segment granularity.

Extensibility based on linear approach. There is only one dimension used for the road itself and the other one can be used for some continuous value, e.g.

temporal data can be visualized in the same manner (Fig. 3) or a classical heat map can be constructed [3].

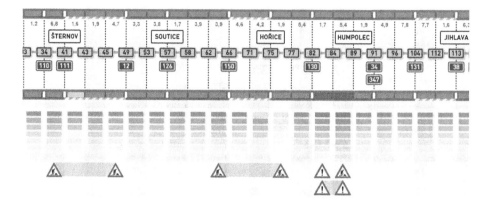

Fig. 3. Temporal data visualization: concept of two-dimensional data visualization with time as vertical axis

On the other hand, the lack of spatial context can lead to false beliefs. For example, segments appear to be of the same length (which is not true) and consequently, incident which is visualized halfway the road might not be spatially present and one neesd to be aware of this when analyzing such situations.

Also, we found that the "route" visualization is not enough when dealing with more complex road network and if relations between the routes need to be shown. For example, there is a large reconstruction of the national main highway in progress and it is important to visualize other possible routes and traffic status there. For such cases we build a two level linear visualization. The first level shows the topological view of the road network, where only basic attributes are shown. On the detailed level, accessible by hyperlink, the customizable linear route visualization is used (as described above). Figure 4 shows the first level of the two-phased visualization and its real geographical shape.

Finally, there are situations, for example city centres, where the topology is quite complicated and the planar visualization tends to be almost identical to the real geographical shape. In such scenarios, we are forced to switch back to the common map visualization and show only basic traffic status data. Figure 5 shows Prague city center visualization along with congestion info depicted as estimated minutes of delay.

4.4   Visualization Style – Traffic Signs

When such complex visualization is made, one must stick to as many known features as possible to maintain the visualization clear and understandable. Usually, attributes like visual style used to be marginalized but in areas where it is strictly specified (i.e. traffic rules and traffic signs) there is no reason to not follow the same visual style. Therefore, as a rule of a thumb, our visualization

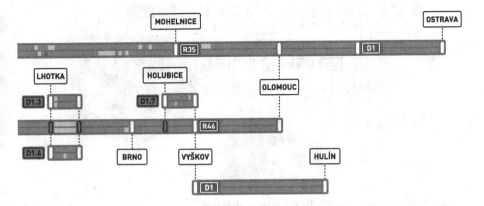

Fig. 4. Topology preserving linear visualization: Same nodes (towns) are visualized as vertical lines connecting roads at their crossings

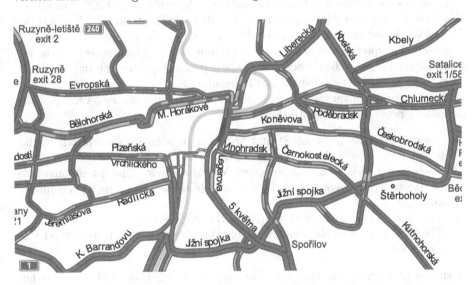

Fig. 5. Common map visualization of Prague city center: complexity of city topology disallows linear visualization

uses the same colours, shapes and symbols as traffic signs defined by the national traffic ordinance (Fig. 6). We believe that such approach makes the visualization familiar and more readable.

4.5 Implementation – ViaRODOS

The whole visualization of ViaRODOS system is based on web standards i.e., HTML5 & JavaScript languages. These technologies provide many advantages. For example, HTML5 standard is widely supported among various browsers thus the cross-platform support is assured. However, the main reason why the web

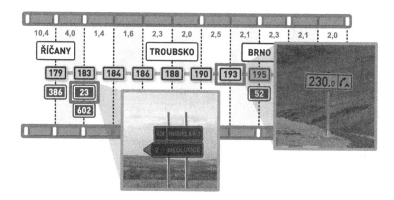

Fig. 6. Traffic signs: The ViaRODOS visualization uses the same signs, colours and symbols as defined by national traffic rules

technologies were chosen is the SVG support. The main advantage of the SVG (*Scalable Vector Graphics*) approach [10] is its scale independence. It is a standard XML based markup language which is send to the client (web browser), where it is interpreted and arranged as a graphic object. This means that the visualization will always be rendered at the best possible quality as it only depends on the size of the client's display and its resolution.

For the project purposes, a component model was built where several cascading phases provide the visualization:

1. Logical elements are created and arranged to a tree structure where the topmost element is the SVG page itself.
2. There is an SVG template for every logical element. These templates are parametrized through logical elements attributes and resulting SVG snippets are created.
3. The final SVG document is built from the snippet tree.
4. The SVG is send to the client. Possibly, JavaScript is used if interactivity is requested.

It should be pointed out that we are aware of the existing SVG wrappers for various programming languages but we decided to not use any of them. The main reason for this decision was that we are not interested in the low-level SVG elements but rather in topic related logical elements (e.g. traffic signs, symbols etc.). It would be inefficient to build such a complex SVG page through assembling basic SVG elements manually where annotated SVG snippets can supply the same functionality with only a little flexibility sacrifice.

4.6   Dynamic Visualization

As explained above, the first step in the visualization building process is the construction of a logical-element tree. Such a tree must be defined somehow, and we are using proprietary XML format for this purpose, and therefore, the visualization process is dynamic but the input XML must be manually constructed.

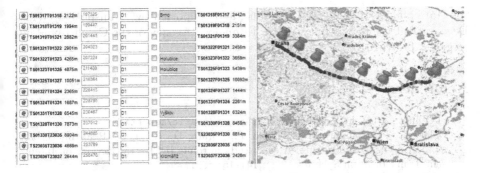

Fig. 7. Road Designer: an application for a user-friendly construction of route definition data

We are currently implementing a back-end user interface for route definitions as the construction of the XML input files are not very intuitive and user friendly. Figure 7 shows the first snapshot of the *Road Designer* application currently developed by our team.

5 Conclusion

Overall concept of the applicable visualization approach has been created in co-operation with the dispatchers from the National Traffic Information Centre. The developed visualization design was tested in NDIC in the daily operation. This allowed subsequent addition of the dispatchers' feedback. Their knowledge of traffic monitoring and management in real situations has been taken advantage of.

Roads classified as highways and expressways have been selected for current version of the viaRODOS system based on analysis of the road network in the Czech Republic. The selected roads present significant transport network segments within the framework of transport serviceability. They have been included to our outputs and visualized in a way appropriate for a dispatching centre.

Our future research will focus on new methods of visualization of the traffic flow prediction based on the historical traffic data analysis for selected lines. For this purpose, methods from the field of time series analysis, pattern mining, string alignment and neural network will be used. As a next promising area of interest, a utilization of wireless mobile services for mutual communication between vehicles will be studied [12]. The information about weather forecast will be used for the more accurate traffic prediction.

Acknowledgments. This work was supported by the European Regional Development Fund in the IT4Innovations Centre of Excellence project (CZ.1.05/1.1.00/02.0070) and the national budget of the Czech Republic via the Research and Development for Innovations Operational Programme, and supported by the project New creative teams in priorities of scientific research (reg. no. CZ.1.07/2.3.00/30.0055), supported by Operational Programme Education for Competitiveness and co-financed by the European Social Fund and the state budget of the Czech Republic, and supported by 'Transport Systems Development Centre' co-financed by Technology Agency of the Czech Republic (reg. no. TE01020155).

References

1. ITO map (2014), `http://www.itoworld.com/static/map.html`
2. Calabrese, F., Colonna, M., Lovisolo, P., Parata, D., Ratti, C.: Real-time urban monitoring using cell phones: A case study in rome. IEEE Transactions on Intelligent Transportation Systems 12(1), 141–151 (2011)
3. CATTLab: Vehicle probe project suite (2011), `http://www.cattlab.umd.edu/?portfolio=vehicle-probe-project-suite`
4. Central European Data Agency: Localization tables (2014), `http://www.ceda.cz/page.php?sid=838&Lang=en`
5. SENSEable City Laboratory MIT: REAL TIME ROME (2006), `http://senseable.mit.edu/realtimerome/`
6. Eisele, B., Schrank, D., Lomax, T.: Tti's 2011 congested corridors report. Tech. rep (2011), `http://mobility.tamu.edu`
7. Hassett, J.: Electronic vehicle toll collection system and method. US Patent 5,805,082 (September 8, 1998)
8. Le, Y.: Visualization of dynamics in linear referenced transportation data. In: Proceedings of the International Conference of ASPRS/CaGIS 2010, pp. 15–18 (2010), `http://www.isprs.org/proceedings/xxxviii/part4/files/Le.pdf`
9. Otaegui, O., Desenfans, O., Plault, L., Lago, A.: TAXISAT: A driverless gnss based taxi application capable of operating cost effectively. In: 9th ITS European Congress (2013)
10. W3C: Scalable vector graphics (svg) 1.1 (2011), `http://www.w3.org/TR/SVG11/`
11. Xtralis: ASIM by xtralis intelligent traffic detectors (2014), `http://xtralis.com/p.cfm?s=22&p=381`
12. Zelinka, T., Lokaj, Z., Svitek, M.: Service quality management for the its mobile wireless multipath telecommunications subsystems. In: Zapater, J.J.S., Martínez-Durá, J.J., López, V.R.T (eds.) EATIS. pp. 317–324. ACM (2012), `http://dblp.uni-trier.de/db/conf/eatis/eatis2012.html/ZelinkaLS12`

Computation of Swing-up Signal
for Inverted Pendulum
Using Dynamic Optimization

Stepan Ozana, Martin Pies, and Radovan Hajovsky

VSB-Technical University of Ostrava,
Faculty of Electrical Engineering and Computer Science,
Department of Cybernetics and Biomedical Engineering,
17. listopadu 15/2172, 70833 Ostrava, Czech Republic
{stepan.ozana,martin.pies,radovan.hajovsky}@vsb.cz
http://www.fei.vsb.cz/en

Abstract. The paper deals with computation and implementation of swing-up pulse for inverted pendulum educational model. It presents derivation of the full nonlinear mathematical model, formulation of dynamic optimization task and its solution by use of DYNOPT toolbox that finds control signal which causes rising of the pendulum into upright position. The control scheme containing this control signal is implemented in PAC (programmable automation controller) WinPAC-8000 with the use of REX Control System. The computed swing-up pulse is used for simulation in Simulink environment. The real measurement of state variables is also presented.

Keywords: Control design, Educational products, MATLAB, Regulators.

1 Introduction

The paper deals with design of swing-up control signal for physical model of inverted pendulum. The regulation of the pendulum itself in the upright position is quite complex model to control, therefore it is highly recommended to use algorithms based on so called modern control theory. So far, linear quadratic control has been successfully tested under real conditions. This work is inspired by other articles, for example the one referred in [1]. The previous work of this papers authors has been extended by adding swing-up problem so that the regulation of the model starts with special input signal that lifts up the pendulum. As soon as the angular position is within predefined interval, the regulation is switched to the automatic mode and the model becomes controlled by the state LQR controller designed according algorithms [3]. This is the most common way how to tackle the swing-up problem, yet there are more ways and algorithms how to compute the appropriate control signal responsible for lifting up [2]. For the work described in this paper a numerical approach based on DYNOPT tool which is a special MATLAB third-party product designed to compute basic problems of dynamic optimization.

K. Saeed and V. Snášel (Eds.): CISIM 2014, LNCS 8838, pp. 301–314, 2014.

2   Mathematical Model

To be able to design and implement controller for inverted pendulum model, it is necessary to derive accurate mathematical model. This paper describes method of Lagrange equations of the second kind. Lagrange equations make up general form of Newton equations, because they make it possible to form movement equation even in the fields where Newton equations have no sense. The used method allows creating movement equations for a set of mass points (bodies) by introducing so called generalized coordinates. Other frequent methods use Newton movement rules themselves.

2.1   Lagrange Equations

Derivation of Lagrange equations of the second kind is based on principle of virtual work, by which the plant is in a balance if virtual work $\delta\omega$ caused by all forces in the system is zero.

$$\delta\omega = \sum_{i=1}^{n} Q_i \delta q_i = 0$$

Q_i generalized force acting in the direction
of i-th coordinate
q_i i-th generalized coordinate

Forces acting in the systems can be divided into conservative and nonconservative. Conservative forces keep energy balance of the system, total sum of kinetic and potential energy is not affected by conservative forces. On the other hand, due to nonconservative forces the energy balance of the system change. These forces are for example dampening forces that depends on velocity.
The basic form of Lagrange equations is (1):

$$\frac{d}{dt}\frac{\partial L}{\partial \dot{q}_i} - \frac{\partial L}{\partial q_i} = Q_i^* \text{ for } i = 1, 2, \ldots, n \tag{1}$$

Lagrange function L, also referred to as kinetic potential, is defined as (2):

$$L = K - P \,[\text{J}] \tag{2}$$

K kinetic energy of the whole system
P potential energy of the whole system

Movement equations for introduced generalized coordinates thus can be set up by use of scalar quantities only (kinetic and potential energy).
General procedure for application of Lagrange equations of the second kind is as follows:

1. Definition of independent generalized coordinates $q_1, q_2, \ldots, q_n$.
2. Determination of kinetic energy K as a function of derivatives (velocities) of generalized coordinates $\dot{q}_1, \dot{q}_2, \ldots, \dot{q}_n$, and generalized coordinates $q_1, q_2, \ldots, q_n$.
3. Determination of potential energy P as a function of generalized coordinates $q_1, q_2, \ldots, q_n$. This function characterizes influence of all conservative forces.
4. Determination of Lagrange function.
5. Determination of generalized nonconservative forces $Q_1^*(t), Q_2^*(t), \ldots, Q_n^*(t)$.
6. Performing derivation of movement equations.

2.2 Physical Analysis of the Model

The scheme of physical model of inverted pendulum and its basic variables and parameters is given in Fig. 1. Its physical realization can be seen from Fig. 2.

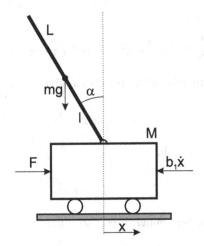

Fig. 1. Analysis of inverted pendulum model

m mass of the pendulum
g gravity
M mass of the cart
L length of the pendulum
l length between mass center and joint, $l = L/2$
F force (manipulated value)
x cart position
α pendulum angle
b_1 friction of the cart
b_2 friction of the pendulum
J inertia of the pendulum

Having introduced parameters of the system it is possible to move on towards determination of movement equations. Overall kinetic energy of the system is given by (3):

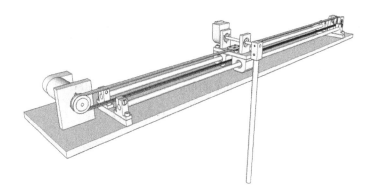

Fig. 2. Physical model of inverted pendulum

$$K = \frac{1}{2}M\dot{x}^2 + \frac{1}{2}m\dot{x}^2 + \frac{1}{2}J\dot{\alpha}^2 + ml\dot{x}\dot{\alpha}\cos\alpha\,[\text{J}] \tag{3}$$

Where J represents inertia of the pendulum given by (4)

$$J = \frac{1}{3}mL^2 \tag{4}$$

or, by use of Steiner formula (5),

$$J = \frac{1}{12}mL^2 + ml^2 \tag{5}$$

The equations for the first generalized coordinate (x) are given by (6)–(10):

$$\frac{\partial K}{\partial \dot{x}} = M\dot{x} + m\dot{x} + ml\dot{\alpha}\cos\alpha \tag{6}$$

$$\frac{\partial K}{\partial x} = 0 \tag{7}$$

$$Q_x = F - b_1\dot{x} \tag{8}$$

$$\frac{d}{dt}\left(\frac{\partial K}{\partial \dot{x}}\right) = (M+m)\,\ddot{x} + ml\ddot{\alpha}\cos\alpha - ml\dot{\alpha}^2\sin\alpha \tag{9}$$

$$\frac{d}{dt}\left(\frac{\partial K}{\partial \dot{x}}\right) - \frac{\partial K}{\partial x} = Q_x \tag{10}$$

The first output movement equation is then (11):

$$(M+m)\,\ddot{x} + ml\ddot{\alpha}\cos\alpha - ml\dot{\alpha}^2\sin\alpha = F - b_1\dot{x} \tag{11}$$

The equations for the second generalized coordinate (α) are given by (12)–(16):

$$\frac{\partial K}{\partial \dot{\alpha}} = J\dot{\alpha} + ml\dot{x}\cos\alpha \tag{12}$$

$$\frac{\partial K}{\partial \alpha} = -ml\dot{x}\dot{\alpha}\sin\alpha \tag{13}$$

$$Q_\alpha = mgl\sin\alpha - b_2\dot{\alpha} \tag{14}$$

$$\frac{d}{dt}\left(\frac{\partial K}{\partial \dot{\alpha}}\right) = J\ddot{\alpha} + ml\ddot{x}\cos\alpha - ml\dot{x}\dot{\alpha}\sin\alpha \tag{15}$$

$$\frac{d}{dt}\left(\frac{\partial K}{\partial \dot{\alpha}}\right) - \frac{\partial K}{\partial \alpha} = Q_\alpha \tag{16}$$

The second output movement equation is then (17):

$$J\ddot{\alpha} + ml\ddot{x}\cos\alpha = mgl\sin\alpha - b_2\dot{\alpha} \tag{17}$$

Equations (11) and (17) make up the full nonlinear model of the system.

2.3   State Nonlinear Model

Firstly, we obtain the formulas (18) and (19) that represent evaluation of second derivatives $\ddot{x}$ and $\ddot{\alpha}$. This is easily carried out by use of equations (11) and (17):

$$\ddot{x} = \frac{F - b_1\dot{x} + ml\dot{\alpha}^2\sin\alpha - ml\ddot{\alpha}\cos\alpha}{M + m} \tag{18}$$

$$\ddot{\alpha} = \frac{mgl\sin\alpha - b_2\dot{\alpha} - ml\ddot{x}\cos\alpha}{J} \tag{19}$$

Introducing the state variables, input variables and output variables, we get

$$\begin{aligned}
x_1 &= x \\
x_2 &= \dot{x}_1 = \dot{x} \\
x_3 &= \alpha \\
x_4 &= \dot{x}_3 = \dot{\alpha} \\
u &= F \\
y_1 &= x_1 \\
y_2 &= x_3
\end{aligned} \tag{20}$$

With the following physical meanings

x_1 position of the cart   [m]
x_2 velocity of the cart $[\mathrm{m \cdot s^{-1}}]$
x_3 angular position of the pendulum   [rad]
x_4 angular velocity of the pendulum $[\mathrm{rad \cdot s^{-1}}]$
u force (manipulated value)   [N]
y_1 position of the cart   [m]
y_2 velocity of the cart $[\mathrm{m \cdot s^{-1}}]$

by substitution into (18) and (19) we get (21) and (22)

$$\dot{x}_2 = \frac{u - b_1 x_2 + mlx_4^2 \sin x_3 - ml\dot{x}_4 \cos x_3}{M + m} \tag{21}$$

$$\dot{x}_4 = \frac{mgl \sin x_3 - b_2 x_4 - ml\dot{x}_2 \cos x_3}{J} \tag{22}$$

Having substituted $\dot{x}_4$ described in (21) by (22) we get (23)

$$\dot{x}_2 = \frac{u - b_1 x_2 + mlx_4^2 \sin x_3}{M + m}$$
$$- \frac{ml \cos x_3 \left(mgl \sin x_3 - b_2 x_4 - ml\dot{x}_2 \cos x_3 \right)}{J \left(M + m \right)} \tag{23}$$

Similarly, having substituted $\dot{x}_2$ described in (22) by (21) we get (24)

$$\dot{x}_4 = \frac{mgl \sin x_3 - b_2 x_4}{J} - \frac{ml \cos x_3 \left(u - b_1 x_2 \right)}{J \left(M + m \right)}$$
$$- \frac{ml \cos x_3 \left(mlx_4^2 \sin x_3 - ml\dot{x}_4 \cos x_3 \right)}{J \left(M + m \right)} \tag{24}$$

Making $\dot{x}_2$ and $\dot{x}_4$ single from (23), (24), and adding $\dot{x}_1$, $\dot{x}_3$ (that stayed the same during adjustments), we get the full final state description of the model, described by (25)–(28).

$$\dot{x}_1 = x_2 \tag{25}$$

$$\dot{x}_2 = \frac{gl^2 m^2 \cos x_3 \sin x_3 - Jlmx_4^2 \sin x_3 + Jb_1 x_2 - Ju - b_2 lmx_4 \cos x_3}{l^2 m^2 \cos^2 x_3 - J \left(M + m \right)} \tag{26}$$

$$\dot{x}_3 = x_4 \tag{27}$$

$$\dot{x}_4 = \frac{\left(M + m \right) \left(b_2 x_4 - glm \sin x_3 \right) + lm \cos x_3 \left(lmx_4^2 \sin x_3 + u - b_1 x_2 \right)}{l^2 m^2 \cos^2 x_3 - J \left(M + m \right)} \tag{28}$$

3   Dynamic Optimization

3.1   Introduction

The mathematical theory of dynamic programming used for solution of dynamic optimization problems dates to the early contributions of Bellman [4] and Bertsekas [5]. Dynamic programming was systematized by Richard E. Bellman. He began the systematic study of dynamic programming in 1955. The word "programming," both here and in linear programming, refers to the use of a tabular solution method and not to writing computer code.

As the analytical solutions are generally very difficult, chosen software tools are used widely. These software packages are often third-party products bound for standard simulation software tools on the market. As typical examples of such tools, TOMLAB and DYNOPT could be effectively applied for solution of problems of dynamic programming. We can classify the dynamic programming tasks concerning the type of final time (free/fixed) and final point (free/fixed), thus we can distinguish 4 combinations: problem with free time and free end point, problem with free time and fixed end point, problem with fixed time and free end point, problem with fixed time and fixed end point.

3.2   DYNOPT

DYNOPT is a set of MATLAB functions for determination of optimal control trajectory by given description of the process, the cost to be minimized, subject to equality and inequality constraints, using orthogonal collocation on finite elements method.

The actual optimal control problem is solved by complete parameterization both the control and the state profile vector. That is, the original continuous control and state profiles are approximated by a sequence of linear combinations of some basis functions. It is assumed that the basis functions are known and optimized are the coefficients of their linear combinations. In addition, each segment of the control sequence is defined on a time interval whose length itself may also be subject to optimization. Finally, a set of time independent parameters may influence the process model and can also be optimized.

4   Solution of the Task in DYNOPT

4.1   Adjusting of the Model for DYNOPT

It is the problem with free time and fixed end point, because we dont know the time when the pendulum reaches the vertical position. The objective function is defined as (29):

$$J = \int_{0}^{t} dt \tag{29}$$

and it has to be minimized, finding the unknown final time t_f. For that reason, the current model of the system will be added by one more state variable $x_5 = t$. Overall system is then described by basic equations (25)–(28), plus (30).

$$\dot{x}_5 = 1 \tag{30}$$

Then the objective function becomes as described by (31).

$$J = x_5\left(t_f\right) = \int_0^{t_f} \dot{x}_5 dt \tag{31}$$

This is required by Dynopt toolbox as the assignment has to be set up in so called Mayer form.

4.2   Solution on DYNOPT

The solution of the problem in DYNOPT lies in setup of needed scripts confun.m, graph.m, objfun.m, process.m according DYNOPT guide [6]. The core of the computation is defining the system itself as $F = f\left(x, u, p, t\right)$ represented by equations (25)–(28) plus (30), then the derivatives $\frac{\partial F}{\partial x}$ and $\frac{\partial F}{\partial u}$. The numerical computation consists of iterations which leads to the final control signal as shown in Fig. 3.

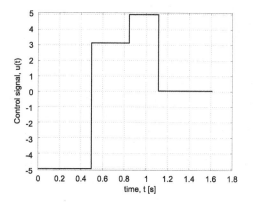

Fig. 3. Result of DYNOPT numerical computation finding the swing-up control signal

Following pictures Fig. 4 to Fig. 7 show the variables x_1, x_2, x_3, x_4 computed by DYNOPT compared to simulation in Simulink.

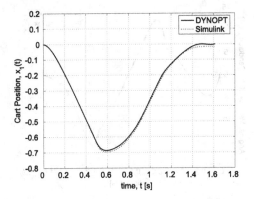

Fig. 4. Comparison of Cart Position in Simulink and DYNOPT

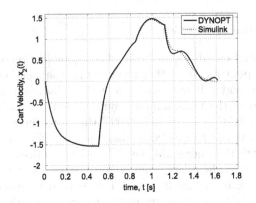

Fig. 5. Comparison of Cart Velocity in Simulink and DYNOPT

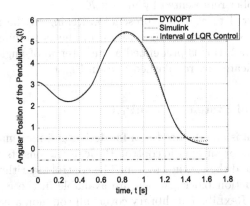

Fig. 6. Comparison of Angular Position in Simulink and DYNOPT

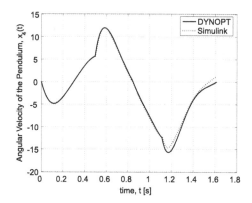

Fig. 7. Comparison of Angular Velocity in Simulink and DYNOPT

5   Implementation

5.1   Block Scheme of Solution

The scheme of control circuit given in Fig. 8 is a combination of control scheme and electronic components, altogether representing the idea how to control the inverted pendulum model. It uses analogue and digital input and output modules (AI, AO, DO) of the programmable automation controller. It also shows electronic elements SG3524N and LM18200T that represents hardware current (torque) controller, according functional diagram, see reference [7], page 2. Connection diagram with the bridge LM18200T can be seen from reference [8], page 11. The middle part of the scheme represents system observer designed based on LQG technique, using Kalmann filter. This is used to generate approximations of two state variables which are not measured (velocities of the cart and pendulum $\dot{x}$, $\dot{\alpha}$). These approximated state variables together with two other measured variables (cart and pendulum position x, α) are then used as input to state (LQR) controller represented by matrix K.

The switch referred to as "T" represents switching to the automatic mode which is triggered once the angular position of the pendulum is close to the vertical position 0 rad, this is predefined as an interval of angles between -0.5 to $+0.5$ rad, as indicated by red dashed lines in Fig. 6.

5.2   REX Control System + WinPAC

REX control system is an advanced tool for design and implementation of complex control systems for automatic control. Basically it consists of two parts: the development tools and the runtime system. The control algorithms are composed from individual function blocks, which are available in the extensive function block library called RexLib. This library covers all common areas of automation and robotics. Moreover, several unique advanced function blocks are contained [11].

The algorithms are composed of individual function blocks, which are available in extensive function block libraries. These libraries cover not only all common fields of automation and regulation but offer also a variety of elements for high-level control algorithms. Runtime version of the REX control system is available for industrial PLC/PAC WinPAC and ViewPAC or their predecessor WinCon of the ICPDAS company.

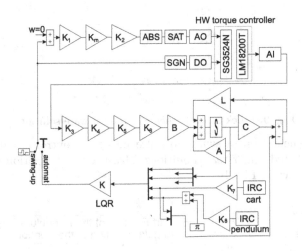

Fig. 8. Block control scheme of the software solution

The block scheme in Fig. 8 has been implemented on programmable automation controller PAC WinPAC-8000, see [9]. The creation of control algorithm for this PAC is performed at two steps.

Firstly, it is creation of executive task that defines target platform and the main tick (time period) of the process. The executive can handle up to 5 tasks, particularly one fast QuickTask, and 4 slower tasks referred to as Level0 – Level3. Each of slower tasks has predefined its own tick based on the main tick and factor (priority). Currently the inverted pendulum model is connected to a QTask with 4 ms sampling period. Processor scheduling is controlled by REX core executive running on a target platform (WinCE), [10].

The second step of implementation of control algorithm is creation of control scheme containing blocks for reading/writing from/to IO modules of the automation controller. The control scheme is similar and compatible with Simulink environment. This scheme together with executive scheme is stored as *.mdl* file so as it can be open and even edited in Simulink provided REXLib library is installed on the computer, [11]. The advantage of compatibility between REX and Simulink is the possibility of tunning and verification of the algorithms without loading the program to the real hardware.

Besides described hardware setup (WinCE, WinPAC-8000, REX) the proposed approach using REX Control System allows implementation on many other modern and common platforms, such as Embedded PC/Single-Board PC + Linux/Xenomai + B&R I/O modules or usage of Raspberry PI or Arduino boards.

Swing-up pulse was implemented in REX Control System according Fig. 3 with use of DELM and CNR blocks, see Fig. 9

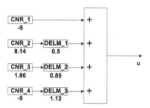

Fig. 9. Block control scheme of the software solution

After implementation of swing-up pulse into real control circuit, the functionality was tested under real conditions. Measured cart position and angular position are shown in Fig. 10.

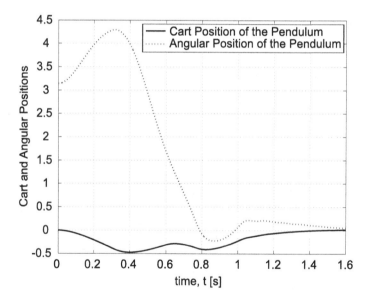

Fig. 10. Cart and Angular Positions Measured on Real Inverted Pendulum

6   Conclusions

The paper demonstrates use of DYNOPT Toolbox to design and implement swing-up control signal for physical model of inverted pendulum. The swing-up impulse for inverted pendulum designed and calculated by DYNOPT toolbox was implemented by a sequence of four pulses according Fig. 3 and Fig. 9, with overall length (final time) $T_f = 1.685$ s.

As it can be seen from Fig. 4 to Fig. 7, all of the state variables in T_f must be close to zero value because all positions and velocities are zero in upright position. After the system is agitated by swing-up pulse, the rod is getting close to upright position and automatic LQR control is applied immediately. Based on long-term experience, the swing-up problem is sensitive to constructional features of the system. Not all the swing-up attempts are successful when the cart moves through the railways, as even slight friction changes may cause a failure. Further work will require adding a signal of cart absolute position that can represent a flag indicating successful or unsuccessful swing-up. Based on this absolute position, the swing-up impulse may be adjusted in case of need. For example, it can handle some situations and conditions under which the swing-up is impossible at all. Typically, the cart needs approximately 2/3 of the length to be able to erect so if the cart is in the middle at the beginning than the swing-up is impossible due to insufficient space for swaying the rod.

Fig. 11. Laboratory model of inverted pendulum at the Department of cybernetics and biomedical engineering

The model is currently used for educational purposes at the Department of cybernetics and biomedical engineering for analysis and synthesis of the systems, representing a nonlinear very complex control system but attractive at the same time. Both swing-up and consequent LQR control have been successfully implemented and tested. The results implemented on a real system are documented in the form of YouTube video accessible through reference [12].

Acknowledgements. This work was supported by project SP2014/156, "Microprocessor based systems for control and measurement applications" of Student Grant System, VSB-TU Ostrava.

References

1. Przemyslaw, H.: Stabilization of the cart-pendulum system using normalized quasi-velocities. In: Proceedings of the 17th Mediterranean Conference on Control & Automation, pp. 827–830 (2009)
2. Kocian, J., Koziorek, J., Ozana, S.: An approach to identification procedures for PID control with PLC implementation. In: 2012 IEEE 17th International Conference on Emerging Technologies and Factory Automation, ETFA 2012 (2012)
3. Tewari, A.: Modern Control Design With MATLAB and SIMULINK. Wiley, Chichester (2002)
4. Bellman, R.: Dynamic Programming. Princeton University Press, Princeton (1998)
5. Bertsekas, D.: Dynamic Programming and Stochastic Control. Academic Press, New York (1976)
6. Cizniar, M., Fikar, M., Latifi, M.A.: Matlab DYNamic OPTimisation code – DYNOPT, Institute of Information Engineering, Automation, and Mathematics, Department of Information Engineering and Process Control, Bratislava, Slovak Republic, Tech. Rep (2013), http://www.kirp.chtf.stuba.sk/moodle/mod/resource/view.php?id=5464 (accessed on May 25, 2014)
7. Texas instruments, Regulating pulse width modulators SG3524 datasheet (2009), http://www.ti.com/lit/ds/symlink/sg2524.pdf (accessed on May 25, 2014)
8. National Semiconductor, 3A 55V H-bridge LMD18200 datasheet (2012), http://www.ti.com/lit/ds/symlink/lmd18200.pdf (accessed on May 20, 2014)
9. ICP DAS Co. Ltd., Winpac-8441/8841 WinCE Based Programmable Automation Controller (2013), http://www.icpdas-usa.com/documentation/Quickstarts/wp-8441_wp-8841.pdf (accessed on May 20, 2014)
10. Balda, P., Schlegel, M., Stetina, M.: Advanced Control Algorithms + Simulink Compatibility + Real-time OS = REX. In: 16th Triennial World Congress of International Federation of Automatic Control, Prague, vol. 16, pp. 121–126 (2005)
11. REX Controls, ZCU Plzen, Czech Republic (2009), http://www.rexcontrols.com (accessed on May 22, 2014)
12. Ozana, S.: Inverted pendulum with swing-up (2013), http://www.youtube.com/watch?v=rOt1FiJNVjA (accessed on May 20, 2014)

System and Application Scenarios
for Disaster Management Processes,
the Rainfall-Runoff Model Case Study

Antoni Portero, Štěpán Kuchař, Radim Vavřík, Martin Golasowski,
and Vít Vondrák

VŠB – Technical University of Ostrava, IT4Innovations, Ostrava, Czech Republic
{antonio.portero,stepan.kuchar,radim.vavrik,martin.golasowski,
vit.vondrak}@vsb.cz

Abstract. In the future, the silicon technology will continue to reduce following the Moore's law. Device variability is going to increase due to a loss in controllability during silicon chip fabrication. Then, the mean time between failures is also going to decrease. The current methodologies based on error detection and thread re-execution (roll back) can not be enough, when the number of errors increases and arrives to a specific threshold. This dynamic scenario can be very negative if we are executing programs in HPC systems where a correct, accurate and time constrained solution is expected. The objective of this paper is to describe and analyse the needs and constraints of different applications studied in disaster management processes. These applications fall mainly in the domains of the High Performance Computing (HPC). Even if this domain can have differences in terms of computation needs, system form factor and power consumption, it nevertheless shares some commonalities.

Keywords: HPC Systems, disaster management, reliability models.

1 Introduction

Application requirements, power, and technological constraints are driving the architectural convergence of future processors towards heterogeneous many-cores. This development is confronted with variability challenges, mainly the suscepti- bility to time-dependent variations in silicon devices. Increasing guard-bands to battle variations is not scalable, due to the too large worst-case cost impact for technology nodes around 10 nm. The goal of next generation firmware is to enable next-generation embedded and high-performance heterogeneous many-cores to cost-effectively confront variations by providing Dependable-Performance: cor- rect functionality and timing guarantees throughout the expected lifetime of a platform under thermal, power, and energy constraints. An optimal solution should employ a cross-layer approach. A middle-ware implements a control en- gine that steers software/hardware knobs based on information from strategically dispersed monitors. This engine relies on technology models to identify/exploit

K. Saeed and V. Snášel (Eds.): CISIM 2014, LNCS 8838, pp. 315–326, 2014.

various types of platform slack - performance, power/energy, thermal, lifetime, and structural (hardware) - to restore timing guarantees and ensure the expected lifetime and time-dependent variations.

Dependable-Performance is critical for embedded applications to provide timing correctness; for high-performance applications, it is paramount to ensure load balancing in parallel phases and fast execution of sequential phases. The lifetime requirement has ramifications on the manufacturing process cost and the number of field-returns. The future firmware novelty must rely in seeking synergies in techniques that have been considered virtually exclusively in the embedded or high-performance domains (worst-case guaranteed partly proactive techniques in embedded, and dynamic best-effort reactive techniques in high-performance). This possible future solutions will demonstrate the benefits of merging concepts from these two domains by evaluating key applications from both segments running on embedded and high-performance platforms. The intent of this paper is to describe the characteristics and the constraints of disaster management (DM) applications for industrial environments. When defining the requirements and their evaluation procedure, a first analysis of the DM applications modules (HW platform, OS and RT engines, monitors and knobs, reliability models) is provided.

From this perspective, this paper focuses on the description of system and application scenario for disaster management processes. The paper is divided in five main sections. Section 2 explains related work and the mitigation tools, basically, two environments for error attenuation. Section 4 provides information about System Scenarios for Disaster Management Processes, section 5 presents application scenarios in HPC environment. Final section 6 shows some results and conclusions, results.

2   Related Work

System scenarios classify system behaviours that are similar from a multi dimensional cost perspective, such as resource requirements, delay, and energy consumption, in such a way that the system can be configured to exploit this cost. At design-time, these scenarios are individually optimized. Mechanisms for predicting the current scenario at run-time and for switching between scenarios are also derived. These are derived from the combination of the behaviour of the application and the application mapping on the system platform.

These scenarios are used to reduce the system cost by exploiting information about what can happen at run-time to make better design decisions at design-time, and to exploit the time-varying behaviour at run-time. While use-case scenarios classify the application's behaviour based on the different ways the system can be used in its over-all context, system scenarios classify the behaviour based on the multi-dimensional cost trade-off during the implementation trajectory [1]. The following sections present system scenarios based on the mapping of an HPC application. The application is stressed with injection of faults and a trade-off between number of mitigated errors and overhead of the used mechanics (Operating System [2] and run-time [3]) is presented.

3   Mitigation Tools

Transient errors are a major concern for the reliable operation of modern digital systems. A new environment is needed for performance evaluation of a software mitigation technique on an industrial grade in many-core computation platform. Error mitigation is performed by re-computing erroneous data in a demand-driven manner with minimal hardware support. Monitoring the runtime performance [3] application is performed illustrating the mitigation overhead without violating the application real time constraints.

3.1   Runtime Environment – RTE

The runtime specifies a firmware that detects transient errors in the executed application. A possible way to detect transient errors is using parity detectors or the use of costly Error-correcting code (ECC) in memories. When a transient error is detected in the execution of a thread, a re-execution of such thread can happen. There are small cache memories where data and instructions are loaded without transient errors. The idea behind this runtime is the fast fine-grain faulty threads re-execution. The runtime daemon has to detect the execution threads with errors in micro seconds. The current state of the art detects the errors at program level and the re-execution time is in the order of milliseconds. In case the number of errors is high, the fine grained mitigation has to provide better performance in terms of executed time and power consumption. In the case when the runtime detects permanent errors in the infrastructure, the re-execution of the threads is performed in other healthy parts of the system. We define the runtime environment as HARPA RTE [4].

3.2   Operating System with RTRM

The HARPA framework [2],[4] is the core of a highly modular and extensible run-time resource manager which provides support for an easy integration and management of multiple applications competing on the usage of one (or more) shared MIMD many-core computation devices. The framework design, which exposes different plug in interfaces, provides support for pluggable policies for both resource scheduling and the management of applications coordination and reconfiguration.

Applications integrated with this framework get a suitable instrumentation to support Design-Space-Exploration (DSE) techniques, which could be used to profile application behaviours to either optimize them at design time or support the identification of optimal QoS requirements goals as well as their run-time monitoring. Suitable platform abstraction layers, built on top of Linux kernel interfaces, allow an easy porting of the framework to different platforms and its integration with specific execution environments. We define this operating System as HARPA OS [4]. The Operating System [2] with an efficient Run-Time Resource Manager (RTRM) exploits a Design-Time Exploration (DSE), which performs an optimal quantization of the configuration space of run-time tunable applications, identifying a set of configurations. The configuration of a run-time tunable application is defined by a set of parameters. Some of them could impact the application behaviour (for example the calibration of Rainfall-Runoff (RR) models can produce different accuracy for different situations) while other have direct impact on the amount of required resources. For example, the amount of Monte Carlo iterations in uncertainty modelling and the time between batches of simulations lead to different requirements for allocating system resources.

3.3   Error Mitigation Environment

Different combinations of tools produce different trade-offs between the amount of errors mitigated and the computation overhead. The overhead can be measured in terms of extra execution time and power consumption compared with the same system without HARPA. The HPC application without any error mitigation tool can then be used as the baseline scenario to which all other scenarios will be compared. When hardware errors are injected into the platform [5], the results of the simulations are going to be incorrect with a high percentage of confidence. Figure 1 shows an example of the expected results. Where a methodology schema, trade-off between quantity of errors mitigated versus computational overhead and energy versus execution time is shown. The confidence thresholds are provided by the number of injected errors that the system is able to support; below the threshold the framework is able to run the application without providing wrong results with a high percentage of confidence. This confidence threshold can be different for each system scenario and also their computation overhead. When the number of injected errors is higher than this threshold, the framework is not able to provide exact results and/or violates the time constraints. The threshold without error attenuation tools is relatively low compared to the situation when the runtime daemon, the Operating System or both are running on the platform at the same time. We expect an attenuation of the errors which are injected by the model of faults. There is the trade-off between the amount of errors that the platform can support and the overhead in terms of computation. The computation overhead means more lines of executed code, more re-execution of threads, and more re-mapping of threads in healthy parts of the system. This overhead leads to the increase in execution time and power consumption, but the additional code can be used to support better balancing of the workload and a better management of the temperature. Following sections describe different scenarios from the baseline scenario, baseline with error injection, roll-back case with error injection when HARPA runtime is used, the HARPA Operating System case for error mitigation and finally using both HARPA tools (Operating System and runtime) at the same time.

4   System Scenarios for Disaster Management Processes: Rainfall-Runoff Model Case

We can simulate different system scenarios to obtain different trade-offs. The first scenario is baseline or normal execution. This execution provides the correct values after a period of time and without any hardware injected error. But what happens if we start to inject errors to the normal execution. Then, without any attenuation tool the system will crash. We have to run the HARPA tools to attenuate these errors and still obtain correct results. The following system scenarios will be used for evaluating individual requirements of applications in the HARPA our environment.

4.1 Methodology

The starting point is a parallel code of the DM application running in multiple processes and threads [6,7]. A hybrid OpenMP and MPI [8] is used to deploy the computation to an HPC cluster. The cluster contains a set of x86-64 multi core computers, connected in a fat tree organization, infiniband technology network. The DM application runs under a specific real time operating system and a runtime engine (suggested structure shown in Fig. 1). Both tools manage the workload of the application and help in the attenuation of hardware errors.

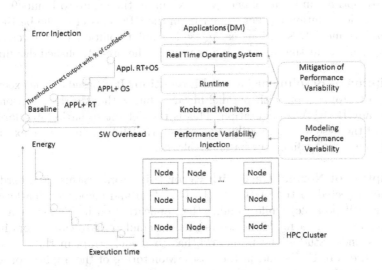

Fig. 1. Methodology Schema, Trade-off: Quantity of errors mitigated vs computational overhead and Energy vs Execution time

The *Real Time Operating System* is in charge of managing the resources. It can benefit from the performance counters in order to take advantage of both workload execution time and energy consumption. The response time of the operating system has to be lower than one second.

The *Runtime Engine engine* actuates the knobs to bias the execution flow as desired, based on the state of the system and the performance (timing / through-put) requirements of the application. It is the runtime engine that implements the various control strategies, aiming to provide dependable-performance in the presence of (highly) unreliable time-dependent variations. The goal is to exploit different manifestations of what we call as platform slack (i.e., slack in performance, power, energy, temperature, lifetime, and structures/components), in order to ascertain timing guarantees throughout the lifetime of the device (in spite of time-dependent variability) and maintain the expected lifetime of the system. The *runtime engine* must respond to the different knobs, monitors and operating system request in order of one microsecond.

The *knobs and monitors* in the platform allow to modify and control parts of the system like temperature sensors, program counters and provide useful information to the upper layers (RT OS and RTE) about where to map the workload more efficiently. Finally, *Performance variability injection* is a *daemon* that simulates the system as it would be built in a technology of 10nms. This submicron technology has a higher variability and then much more hardware errors appears during the application required execution time. The trade-off between the RTOS and RT engine is that produces an overhead (Fig. 1 up left) in the software, but this new environment will on the other hand enable a higher level of error mitigation. At the design time, we are able to detect which points are optimal in terms of energy vs execution time (Pareto Points[9]). The multi-threaded solution has not to be run on the HPC cluster at the best-effort. A set of intermediate solutions can provide similar solution with lower power consumption and at the same time finish before the pre-established deadline.

Description of Baseline or Normal Execution. It is based on the execution of the HPC application with parallel libraries but without error injection and without any HARPA configuration. This is the default scenario (standard operation of the system before utilization of any HARPA engine). This execution with all the values defines our baseline solution.

Description of Normal Case with Error Injection. In this case, hardware errors are injected to the platforms (HPC system and embedded platform for comparison if possible) while running the application on it. The system operation description is a model of errors used to emulate hardware errors in the platforms under study. The framework has to model errors in the memories, errors in the core CPUs and in the buses. Monitoring of the application when errors are injected: When the number of injected hardware errors increases then the percentage of incorrect solution also increases. Thus, a supervision of the platforms has to be considered under this scenario to find out the threshold of injected errors that still leads to a correct solution provided by the system.

Description of HARPA Runtime: Rollback Case with Errors Injection. In this scenario, errors are injected to the application, but the runtime HARPA daemon is able to detect hardware errors. This runtime daemon also rollbacks the execution of each faulty thread and re-executes it rollback and re-execution of the faulty threads increase the global execution time of the application. There is a threshold level of errors that are acceptable in the system before the required execution time of the program exceeds the threshold. The description of system operation is related with the HARPA runtime daemon that is in charge of rollback and re-execution of faulty threads. It is also possible to change the clock frequency to the maximum in the part of the system (cores) and during re-execution. System becomes more tolerant in comparison to the system scenarios without rollback. When more errors are injected, more mitigation has to be performed by the daemon. There is a threshold where the output solution provided by the system is still correct (Fig. 1).

Description of HARPA Operating System Case. In this case, application is running in the HARPA OS with the RTRM environment that manages the workload and resource allocation for error mitigation in the system. When errors are injected into the application, the HARPA environment identifies and manages them, decreasing the number of re-executions in the platform. An improvement of this scenario is using procrastination scheduling technique, where task execution is delayed to maximize the duration of idle intervals. This technique [10] has been proposed to minimize leakage energy drain. We will address dynamic slack retrieval techniques under procrastination scheduling to minimize the static and dynamic energy consumption. The description of system operation in this scenario is similar to the baseline scenario with error injection but Run-time Resource Management of the HARPA OS is used as a middleware when the application is running. This middleware allocates the workload of the system at runtime and it works in two steps:

1. design time, a suitable Design Space Exploration (DSE) activity identifies a set of resource requirements that are worth to be considered at runtime, namely Application Working Modes (AWM), and a set of application specific parameters defining different QoS levels, namely Operating Points (OP).
2. run-time, resource management is enforced in a hierarchical and distributed way: For each running application, the RTRM assigns the most promising AWM, as a result of a system-wide multi-objective optimization. The application can optionally perform a QoS fine tuning by switching among its OPs. Platform specific mechanisms (e.g. DVFS) are exploited to avoid risky conditions. Delaying task execution and maximizing idle periods (i.e. decreasing global power consumption) [10].

Description of HARPA OS + HARPA Runtime with Dynamic Slack Case. This new scenario is the combination of the rollback with error injection scenario with the features from HARPA OS. HARPA OS serves as a base for running the application in this extended environment with the rollback daemon that re-executes faulty threads with maximum clock frequency and with dynamic slack. In previous sections, we showed the need to work in different working points to align computation with resources. Fig. 2 shows a node of x86-86 cores with memory and accelerators. With OpenMP *pragmas*, we can decide the resources used to compute the HPC application. There are diverse Pareto points [9] from a sequential execution to an execution with all resources available (16 cores and the accelerators). In some cases, resources do not have to be available due to temporal or permanent hardware errors (greyed out in Fig. 3). The attenuation tools are able to detect this situation and remap the application in a new Pareto point from a new Pareto curve.

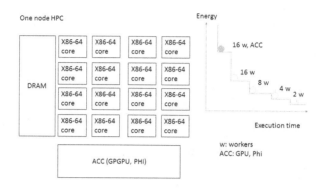

Fig. 2. HPC Node Schema without errors injection and Pareto curves (Energy vs Execution time)

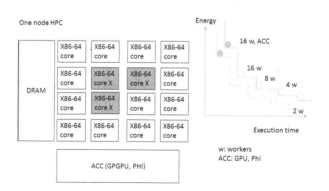

Fig. 3. HPC Node Schema with errors injection and Pareto curves (Energy vs Execution time)

5   Application Scenarios

Application scenarios describe different triggers and states of the application that influence the system responsiveness and operation (e.g. critical flooding level, critical state of patient's health, voice & data, etc.). Based on these scenarios, the system can be in different states with different service level requirements.

5.1 Critical Modules and Their Operation in HPC Environment. Case: Rainfall-Runoff Modelling

One of the applications that are used to develop, test and validate the HARPA architecture is the Floreon+ system [11,12]. It is an automatized flood prediction system for the Moravian-Silesian region in Czech Republic developed at IT4Innovations National Supercomputing Centre. One type of flood prediction models that we are working with are rainfall-runoff (RR) models. Hydrometeorological data for these models are collected from a network of gages and by methods of remote sensing (e.g. radar estimation of precipitation rates) together with the precipitation forecast. Meteorological inputs include the amount of precipitation in particular, air temperature and data about snow pack (thickness and water equivalent) during winter seasons. Hydrological inputs cover data on discharge volumes and water levels from the hydrologic gages. RR models compute how the precipitation over a specified area influences the stream flow over a specified period of time. These results is described by a function of discharge change over time (also called as hydrograph, example in Fig. 4). The complexity of RR models comes with a wide range of problems, one of them being a static setting of model parameters. This setting is done by hydrologists during the creation of model schematization for each modelled geographical area. This process cannot correctly support automatic runs in the system that have to behave accordingly to dynamic changes in weather and current state of the river and its catchment areas. The correct setting of model parameters can be done by inverse modelling and calibration methods, but these methods require repeated executions of the model with different parameters that converge to optimal configuration of these parameters in the model for current situation [12]. Taking these specifics into account, we identified two main application scenarios that support the different workload of the system based on the flood emergency situation.

Standard Operation. In this scenario, weather is favourable and the flood warning level is below the critical threshold. Here, the computation can be relaxed; some kind errors and deviations can be allowed. The system should only use as much power as needed for standard operation; one automatic batch of simulations only has to be finished before the next batch starts. The results do not have to be available as soon as possible, so no excess use of resources is needed. Fig. 4 shows a possible working point (energy vs execution time) where only 8 cores in one node of the HPC cluster are used for the standard operation. It is not necessary to use the accelerators of the system (GPU, and/ or Intel Phi). But resource allocation can be much larger in an emergency operation.

Emergency Operation. Several days of continuous rain raise the water in rivers or a very heavy rainfall on a small area creates new free-flowing streams. These conditions are signalled by the discharge volume exceeding the flood emergency thresholds or precipitation amount exceeding the flash flood emergency thresholds. Much more accurate and frequent computations are needed in this

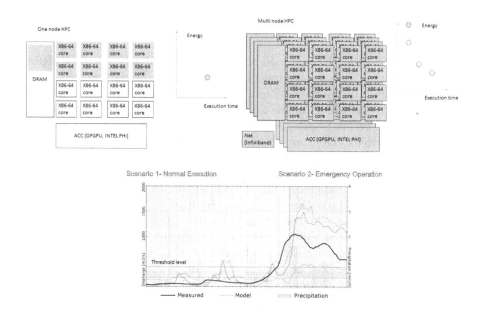

Fig. 4. Scenarios: Normal execution and Emergency Operation

scenario and results should be provided as soon as possible even if excess resources have to be allocated. The Fig. 4 shows real results from a real case [11], where the black curve presents the measured discharge and the orange curve shows the simulated discharge. The threshold level for switching to the emergency scenario depends on the location of the measurement station and is defined by flood activity degrees at the station that are specified by local catchment authorities. The figure also shows that several simulated values at the middle of the simulation exceed the threshold level for a short period while the measured values do not reach the threshold at all.

6 Preliminary Experiments and Conclusions

We have executed several experiments of the baseline scenario (see section 4) to see how the standard runs of RR models perform. Experiments were done on a RR schematization of Ostravice river basin (Czech Republic) with our in-house developed RR model [11] that was parallelized by OpenMP [6] and its calibration parallelized by MPI [7]. The measured input data used for this model were provided by the measurement gages operated by the Czech Odra basin management office [13] and the Medard model [14] was used for precipitation forecast. This configuration serves as the basis for further experimentation with other introduced system scenarios. All experiments were performed on the Anselm supercomputer operated by IT4Innovations. This cluster contains 209 computational nodes where each node is a x86-64 computer, equipped with 16 cores, at least 64GB RAM, and local hard drive. These nodes are interlinked by high speed InfiniBand (3600MB/s) and Ethernet networks. All nodes share a Lustre parallel file system with a throughput of 6 GB/s. The durations of experimental runs of the baseline scenario models are shown in Table 1.

Table 1. Durations of Experimental Runs of the Baseline Scenario Models

OMP threads per process	Simulation without calibration	Simulation with calibration				
		1 MPI process	2 MPI processes	4 MPI processes	8 MPI processes	16 MPI processes
1	0.5316s	691.5s	404.5s	196.7s	96.5s	59.3s
2	0.3854s	492.4s	288.6s	140.6s	70.0s	46.1s
4	0.2747s	339.5s	200.2s	98.3s	50.2s	33.6s
8	0.2609s	321.1s	185.2s	93.2s	48.6s	47.1s
16	0.3746s	488.2s	307.2s	234.1s	132.3s	143.1s

There are several conclusions in the results concerning the parallelization. The first one is the fact that durations for 16 OMP threads per process are significantly higher than for 8 threads. This shows that the overhead of creating and managing more threads along with the NUMA architecture for each node of the cluster (each node contains 2 independent processors, each with 8 cores) hinders the performance and scalability of the algorithm. Another interesting result is that the gain from 4 to 8 threads is very small and it is not enough to cover the overhead for configurations with more MPI processes. These results show that parallelization of the calibration process is very important for our operational execution of RR models, because there are 4 main basins in the Moravian-Silesian region and we plan to run 3 different RR models for each of these basins automatically every hour. This could not be done without parallelization as it would take more than 2 hours (4 x 3 x 11.5 = 138 minutes if all models would take the same time) to run one batch of simulations, without even considering error mitigation practices introduced in this paper.

Acknowledgements. This article was supported by Operational Programme Education for Competitiveness and co-financed by the European Social Fund within the framework of the project New creative teams in priorities of scientific research, reg. no. CZ.1.07/2.3.00/30.0055, by the European Regional Development Fund in the IT4Innovations Centre of Excellence project (CZ.1.05/1.1.00/02.0070), by the project Large infrastructures for research, development and innovation of Ministry of Education, Youth and Sports of Czech Republic with reg. no. LM2011033, and by 7 [th] EU framework programme project no. FP7-612069 HARPA - Harnessing Performance Variability.

References

1. Gheorgita, S.V., Palkovic, M., Hamers, J., Vandecappelle, A., Mamagkakis, S., Basten, T., Eeckhout, L., Corporaal, H., Catthoor, F., Vandeputte, F., De Bosschere, K.: System scenario based design of dynamic embedded systems. Transactions on Design Automation of Electronic Systems (ToDAES) 14(1), Article No. 3 (January 2009)
2. Bellasi, P., Massari, G., Fornaciari, W.: A rtrm proposal for multi/many-core platforms and reconfigurable applications. In: ReCoSoC (2012)
3. Rodopoulos, D., Papanikolaou, A., Catthoor, F., Soudris, D.: Software mitigation of transient errors on the single-chip cloud computer. In: Workshop on Silicon Errors in Logic - System Effects, SELSE (2012)
4. Harpa harnessing performance variability fp7 project (2013), http://www.harpa-project.eu
5. Broekaert, F., Sassi, F., Kuchar, S., Portero, A.: D.5.1.- requirements analysis and specification of the project application domain. In: FP7-612069, FP7-ICT-2013-10 (2014)
6. Openmp: Application program interface, version 4.0 (July 2013)
7. Mpi: A message-passing interface standard version 3.0 (2012)
8. Portero, A., Scionti, A., Yu, Z., Faraboschi, P., Concatto, C., Carro, L., Garbade, A., Weis, S., Ungerer, T., Giorgi, R.: Simulating the future kilo-x86-64 core processors and their infrastructure. In: SpringSim(ANSS) (2012)
9. Portero, A., Talavera, G., Moreno, M., Catthoor, F., Carrabina, J.: Methodology for energy-flexibility space exploration and mapping of multimedia applications to single-processor platform styles. IEEE Transactions on Circuits and Systems for Video Technology 8(21), 1027–1039 (2011)
10. Jejurikar, R., Gupta, R.: Dynamic slack reclamation with procrastination scheduling in real-time embedded systems. In: ACM (ed.) Proceedings of the 42nd Annual Design Automation Conference DAC 2005, Anaheim, California, USA, pp. 111–116. ACM, New York (2005)
11. Martinovic, J., Kuchar, S., Vondrak, I., Vondrak, V., Nir, B., Unucka, J.: Multiple scenarios computing in the flood prediction system floreon. In: ECMS 2010, pp. 182–188 (2010)
12. Vavrik, R., Theuer, M., Golasowski, M., Kuchar, S., Podhoranyi, M., Vondrak, V.: Automatic calibration of rainfall-runoff models and its parallelization strategie. In: Proceedings of International Conference of Numerical Analysis and Applied Mathematics ICNAAM, Rhodes, Greece (in print, 2014)
13. Czech odra basin management office (August 2014), http://www.pod.cz
14. Medard model (August 2014), http://www.medard-online.cz/index.php

An Approach to Continuous Pervasive Care of Remote Patients Based on Priority Based Assignment of Nurse

Paramita Sarkar[1] and Ditipriya Sinha[2]

[1] AKCSIT, Calcutta University, Kolkata, India
mailtoparo@gmail.com
[2] Megnadh Saha Institute of Technology, Kolkata, India
ditipriyasinha87@gmail.com

Abstract. Remote care of patient is now becoming a subject of major concern in healthcare services. Proposed work describes a pervasive system to assist continuously the patients who are at remote place from the connected hospital using a priority based classification and assignment of nurses to the high risk patients. The challenge lies in storage and management of the vast amount of real-time data originating from heterogeneous sources under dynamic situations. This paper attempts to design a new system consisting of several modules for managing real-time heterogeneous data. The overwhelming data could cause difficulty to decide over numerous patients to whom the care should be given first and then onwards. To solve this, the proposed system attempts to derive fuzzy rules to make decision based on priority among selected groups in a dynamic environment. This proposed model formulates an indexed hash key for high risk patients and proper nurse relatively.

Keywords: pervasive, context data, fuzzy rules, dynamicity, wearable sensor, hash key.

1   Introduction

Pervasive Computing is nowadays a growing research topic to improve the quality of remote healthcare service. It integrates seamlessly different heterogeneous technologies without user's awareness and intervention for the sake of user's benefit. Emerging ubiquitous or pervasive computing technologies offer 'anytime, anywhere, anyone' computing by decoupling users from devices. Context information used in pervasive environment provides adequate information regarding the changes occurred in any characteristics of users, place, and any event. This paper involves remote patient monitoring integrating body sensor network devices [1,2] that can upload a patient's real time contextual physiological information through a wrist worn wearable sensor device and a personal Smartphone for triggering risk alarm and dissemination to professional caregivers. Dynamic context are handled here by measuring automatic changes during a prolonged time and by mapping them into a predefined group. Some context data changes every second, and some every hour due to their dynamic nature. Recent advancement of pervasive computing has led increased accessibility to

K. Saeed and V. Snášel (Eds.): CISIM 2014, LNCS 8838, pp. 327–338, 2014.
© IFIP International Federation for Information Processing 2014

healthcare providers, centralized database storage, telemedicine services. Due to the growth in the number of chronically ill and weak people, it is becoming more difficult to take care of the patients in a central place. Therefore continuous monitoring of a remote patient in a pervasive way avoids the presence of a number of medical staff all-time at the patient's place. When the numbers of victims overwhelm the number of medical staff in a hospital in any emergency event, there are many challenges issues need to ration the medical staffs with proper assignment to patients [3]. Here this works attempts to search an appropriate nurse based on the computed hash key [section 4.3]. Continuous monitoring of patients from a remote hospital is highly desirable to take care of patients and providing suitable guidelines with proper medicine [4]. This paper includes heart rate variability as a new vital sign [5, 6] with other existing parameters. The design of proposed model inherits different existing real time systems for continuous monitoring [17], [19]. On the other hand, it develops a prioritised decision making using fuzzy inference and assignment of appropriate nurse to remote patient.

2   Related Work

In recent years lots of research, work and study in the related field have been carried out. A study of the review in this field revealed that several context aware pervasive system have been used regarding the services in emergency responses in rescue system, public healthcare system, other patient monitoring and alarm system, etc. This section is categorised into following subsection on the basis of real time implementation of pervasive computing.

2.1   Priority Assignment

Prioritized emergency operation plays an important role in remote healthcare services and evacuation system a lot. "Priority Assignment in Emergency Response" [3] is one of the application of priority assignment in pervasive environment. It formulated the priority assignment problem for each patient in triage system where each patient is evacuated from the mass casualty site to the hospital according to the priority set to them. This paper analysed the state dependent partial optimized policy and proposed a number of heuristic policies. Another "User-driven design of a context-aware application: an ambient-intelligent nurse call system" [8] focuses on the reasoning context data by the caregivers from various ambient sensors in the patient's room to answer a call from the patient. This paper describes the priority based of the proper nurse to the patient on the basis of the relation with patient.

2.2   Knowledge Representation in Cloud Database

It becomes crucial to store such huge and heterogeneous sensor real time data in a large database with proper representation and semantics of huge knowledge. Cloud computing is an obvious solution to access this large database from anyplace anytime in pervasive domain. "An approach for pervasive homecare environments focused on care of patients with dementia" [9] uses the ontology OWL [10] for homecare environment in pervasive system to represent the various relationships among domains and knowledge in the database implementing Semantic Web Rule Language (SWRL) and Semantic Query-Web Enhanced Language [11]. "Ontology for Context-Aware Pervasive Computing Environments" [12] discussed the solution to the limitation of that problem using the architecture of the centralized pervasive context aware distributed system named as Context Broker architecture (CoBrA) which is a collection of different ontology (COBRA-ONT).

2.3   Continuous Monitoring in Pervasive Environment

For continuous monitoring of disable/older people and other patients in pervasive environment it is desirable to detect whether they have any risk factor or not. Several researches and designing approaches were performed to detect fall in recent few years [13, 14]. "Evaluation of a threshold-based tri-axial accelerometer fall detection algorithm" [15] derives the threshold level for the fall detection. Different Body Sensors were developed for collecting and transmitting patient's physiological data for vital sign and activity recognition. "Human Activity Surveillance based on Wearable Body Sensor Network" [16] has proposed the advantages of a Body Sensor Network based architecture for wearable wireless monitoring system using an algorithm optimized for real time computing. To measure the impact of temperature as sleep deprivation in a human body "Accurate Temperature Measurements for Medical Research using Body Sensor Networks" [17] proposes a prototype of a body sensor network. Another vital sign of human body is heart rate/pulse rate. "Designing Heart Rate, Blood Pressure and Body Temperature Sensors for Mobile On-Call System" [18] paper describes the comparative study between different techniques and design issues for measuring heart rate, blood pressure and temperature. This paper focuses the different parameter used in measuring the vital signs of human body using ECG sensors and the Photoplethysmography (PPG). An unobtrusive method in "AMON: A Wearable Multiparameter Medical Monitoring and Alert System" [19] proposes the architecture and design of a miniature system for measuring heart rate using ECG, blood pressure, activity recognition and SpO2 for continuous monitoring high risk of cardiac and respiration patients. This system is optimized to collect vital signs of human body and evaluate these parameters continuously for communication through a gateway to the external database.

3   Scope of the Work

To implement pervasive environment in the system, heterogeneous data are needed to be stored in remote server. The state of the art study leads to the observation that not much attention has been paid to any mechanism to maintain heterogeneous real time dynamic data in the database. This proposed protocol describes a pervasive system to assist continuously the patients who are at remote place from the connected hospital using a priority based classification and assignment of nurses to the high risk patients.

4   Proposed Work

The proposed work is to design a system on the pervasive care environment for remote patient. This system emphasizes on the allotment of a caregiver to the remote patients according to the condition of the patients.

4.1   Assumption

- The wearable device analyses and processes every sensor signal in such a way that after every 5 minutes it can send data to the patient's Smartphone.
- Threshold value has been determined for Heart Rate, Blood Pressure, Temperature, Accelerometer (for Activity Recognition, Fall Detection) and Heart Rate Variability [5, 6] and [15, 16, 17, 18, 19].
- The continuous monitoring is attempted as long as the patient's wearable 4-array sensor wrist band is connected with server through the Bluetooth.
- Only the dynamic context data are considered for classification in every 30 minutes.
- The priority of a patient is classified into five groups **Urgent, High, Medium, and Low,** and **Very Low** depending on the severity of the context data coming from the Smartphone.
- Work Constraints: The following work constraints should not be violated during the allotment of the nurse to patients. They are as follows:

1. No nurses will have workload more than 8 hours in a whole day.
2. More experienced resources in a particular department should be   allocated to high priority job.
3. Expertise of a resource in a particular department should be given preferred most.
4. Minimum number of working days in a week is 5.
5. Minimum gap between two shifts is 12 hours.
6. Maximum number of consecutive days of duties in a week will be 3.

- At the server site, the schedule of nurses for each department and for each day of a week stored in its database. The existing schedule of nurses is updated every 30 minutes inside the server to calculate the remaining duty hours and key value of a nurse.
- Weights are provided to represent for the level of importance for each constraint.
- The allotment of the nurses is prioritized according to the lower value of the key c.
- Two different priority queues are needed for prioritizing the patients and the nurses.

4.2   Data Dictionary

- E_{di} = number of experience in years of ith nurse of a particular department say d
- H_i = total duty hours of ith nurse in a day.
- D_i = highest qualification of ith nurse in a particular domain related to the particular department

- nw_i = Minimum number of working day (w) of ith in a week
- ng_i = minimum gap (g) between two successive shift of duty of ith nurse.
- xcd_i = Maximum number of consecutive duties (c) of ith nurse in days of a week.
- w_i = weight factors for i^{th} indices where i=1,2,3,4,5,6.
- p_id_i = i^{th} patient's id given by the hospital
- $threshold_{ni}$ = corresponding threshold value of nth feature and i^{th} patient
- $feature\_value_{ni}$ = value of the nth context data of ith patient
- $num\_gr\_f_{ni}$ = associating group numbers to which n^{th} feature of ith patient belongs to.
- $cnt\_gr\_f_{ni}$ = total number of groups to which n^{th} feature of ith patient belongs to.
- $feature\_priority_{ni}$ = priority of nth feature of ith patient
- gr_id_i = group id of ith feature
- gr_mem_i = feature_name of nth patient in the ith gr_id
- p_hr_i = Heart Rate of ith patient, p_bp_i = Blood Pressure of ith patient, p_acc_i = of accelerometer data i^{th} patient, p_temp = temperature of ith patient, p_hrv_i = Heart Rate Variability of ith patient.
- $p\_arr\_time_i$ = arrival time of a sensor data of ith patient

Table 1. Database Record Table

Record	Field Name
Patient's record	{p_id_i, p_name_i, p_age_i, p_gen_i, p_dept_i, p_date_i, p_temp_i, p_bp_i, p_hr_i, p_acc_i, p_hrv_i, $p\_curr\_medicine_i$, p_pri_i, $p\_arr\_time_i$, $p\_allot\_status_i$, n_p_i, p_rel1_i, p_rel2_i, p_med_i, $p\_app\_dr_i$}
Nurse's Record	{$n\_department_i$, n_id_i, n_name_i, n_age_i, n_exp_i, $n\_prof\_degree_i$, $n\_date\_duty_i$, n_dhalf_i, $n\_totalhr_i$, $n\_allot\_status_i$, n_pri_i, n_time_i, p_n_i}
Feature's record	{$feature\_name_i$, $feature\_status_i$, $num\_gr\_f_{ni}$, $cnt\_gr\_f_{ni}$, $feature\_value_{ni}$, $threshold_{ni}$, $difference\_f_{ni}$, x_{ni}, $feature\_priority_{ni}$}
Doctor's record	{$dr\_department_i$, dr_name_i, dr_degree_i, dr_time_i, dr_date_i }
Group record	{gr_id_i, gr_mem_i }
Key record	key_i, $hfnc_i$

4.3   Definition

Definition 1. Indexed Key defines-the minimum key is defined to search the appropriate nurse from the database without avoiding all work constraints is defined as the total cost function:

$$C = E_{di} \times w_1 + H_i \times w_2 + D_i \times w_3 + nw_i \times w_4 + ng_i \times w_5 + xcd_i \times w_6 \qquad (1)$$

w_i [Section 4.2] is in the range from 1 to 6 according to the value of six indices, such that if a nurse has highest experience in a particular department (E_{di}), the weight factor w_i for that constraint will be 1. This minimum cost function will be treated as the key for index in the hash function.

Definition 2. The hash function is required to search proper nurse_id from the hash table. A hash function of key is

$$\text{hash(key)} = \text{key \% hash table size} \tag{2}$$

where key is defined as total cost function C. Searching will be performed based on the indexed key such that the hash function of that key would probably returns the location of the key value of the corresponding nurse.

Definition 3. The difference_f_{ni} is defined as the difference between the threshold of a particular feature n of ith patient.

$$\text{difference\_}f_{ni} = |(\text{threshold}_{ni} - \text{feature\_value}_{ni})| \tag{3}$$

This value will be computed in the computation module inside the server at the time of arrival of every context data.

4.4 Proposed Pervasive Remote Patient Care with Proper Nurse Assignment Model

In order to assist this work, a proposed model of the system's architecture is implemented at the server of the particular hospital. The server communicates with the Smartphone of the patient and the nurse through GSM. The proposed model can finally generate an assignment of appropriate nurses to high risk remote patients on the basis of the proposed priority inside the classification model. Figure 1 shows architecture of the proposed model inside the server. The proposed system has four connected parts labelled here as COMPUTATION MODULE, DATA MODULE, CLASSIFICATION MODULE,SCHEDULING MODULE, and UPDATATION MODULE.

Table 2. List of Abbreviation used in the Figure 1

No.	Abbreviation	Meaning
1	R_p,n,k	Record of patients, nurses and index key
2	R_p,n,	Record of patients and nurses
3	R_p	Record of patients
4	R_p,n,k,f,g	Record of patients, nurses, features and group
5	s_data	Sensor data coming from wearable device
6	MSG, con	Message and computed context data
7	N_MSG	Notification message

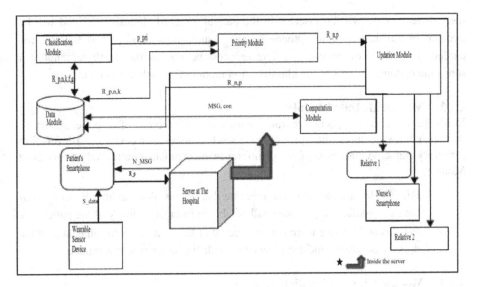

Fig. 1. Architecture of the Proposed Pervasive care Environment of remote patients

4.4.1 Module I: Computation Module

Data are coming continuously from the patient's wearable device to the Smartphone via Bluetooth.

1. Patient's records [Section 4.2] are sent from patient's Smartphone to the hospital server. Smartphone can send this updated record of the corresponding patient every 5 minutes until any notification received from the hospital.

2. Option is created for new patient to be registered to the connected hospital whenever he/she wears the device first time as follows.

3. **Registration:** On the particular page of the website of the hospital, responsive staff will check for registration of the patient wearing the sensor/

a) if $p_id_i== $ NULL

then, Set status: = "Not registered" and server sends REQ_MSG to the patient's Smartphone with Accept or Ignore option.

b) If the patient accepts this message then, server asks for confirmation of sending patient id to the new patient

c) After confirming that message, new patient will receive the new p_id_i and p_dept_i. Patient's records are received from the Smartphone by the server.

d) At this time two phone numbers of patient's most close relatives/friends are required for further notification.

4. Existing i^{th} patient's record [Section 4.2] is sent from the Smartphone at regular time interval to the server.

5. At the hospital terminal, those data are automatically compared to the threshold$_{ni}$ [Section 4.2] for different context data.

if difference$\_f_{ni} \neq 0$ [Equation (3)]

then, difference_f_{ni} will be inserted in the patient's record [Section 4.2]and will be updated in the data module. Otherwise, the context data of ith patient will be discarded. Thus the Computation module reduces the size of the database. Finally it sends the updated records to the classification module for further processing.

4.4.2   Module II: Data Module

Inside the server there will be separate database to store records of all patients, nurses, doctors, context features, their group, nurse's schedule and for key with hash function for every nurse. A database of fuzzy inference mechanism is attached in this Data Module.

- Fuzzy rules are stored in the separate database of this module. From this database classification module will be able to infer the priority of the patient.
- For this architecture there is also a record of five contextual health data [Section 4.2]. These are the most vital sign to decide the health risk of a patient.

4.4.3   Module III: Classification Module

Phase 1: Checking Dynamicity of Real–Time Contextual Data. In every 5 minutes patients' record at the hospital will be updated by the coming data.

1. Initialize time duration t_0:= 0 sec
2. Repeat the step 4 while t_i< 1800sec
3. [check changes frequently in 30 minutes duration]
    if |difference_f_{ni}| at t_{i+1} $\neq$ |difference_f_{ni} | at t_i [Equation (3)]
    then Set feature_status$_i$ = "dynamic"
    send feature_value$_i$ in data module
4. Else save the old feature_value$_i$

Fuzzy Sets for "priority". In the proposed system, "priority" is defined as a linguistic variable to x. Linguistic variable are termed as x, F(x), U and M. F(x) is termed as the set of x, the set of names or linguistic values assigned to x, with each value is a fuzzy variable defined in U. M is membership where semantic rules are associate with each variable [20]. T(priority) = {low, very low, high, medium, urgent}.U = {-α, + α}. M defines the membership function of each fuzzy variable for example, M(very low)= fuzzy set priority below 20% with membership of $\mu_{very\ low}$. The M (low) and M (high) are expressed as μ_{low} and μ_{high} respectively.

$$\mu_{low}(x) = 1/[1 + (x/20)]^4 \tag{4}$$

$$\mu_{high}(x) = 1/\left[1 + \left((x - (+\alpha))/20\right)^6\right] \tag{5}$$

Concentration and Dilation of fuzzy membership function. M (Urgent) = $\mu_{urgent}(x)$. Not low not high means M (medium) = $\mu_{medium}(x)$. Low but not too low means M (medium) = $\mu_{medium}(x)$.

$$\mu_{urgent}(x) = \left\{1/\left[1 + \left((x - (+\alpha))/20\right)^6\right]\right\}^{0.5} \tag{6}$$

$$\mu_{medium}(x) = min\left\{\left(\frac{1}{1-1/[1+(x/20)^4]}\right); \left(1 - \frac{1}{[1+((x-(+\alpha))/20)^6]}\right)\right\} \tag{7}$$

$$\mu_{medium}(x) = min\left\{\frac{1}{[1+(^x/_{20})^4]}; \left(\left(\frac{1}{[1+((x-(+\alpha))/20)^6]}\right)^{0.5}\right)\right\} \tag{8}$$

$$\mu_{very\ low}(x) = min\left\{1/[1 + (x/20)]^4; \left(\left(1/[1 + ((x - (+\alpha))/20)^6]\right)^{0.5}\right)\right\} \tag{9}$$

Phase 2: Priority Based Classification Algorithm. Group Assignment of specific feature in one or more than one group of clinically related context data has been done. At this phase a priority based classification algorithm is derived using Fuzzy memebership is computed according to the different range and that are assigned to each patient.

1. Compute the difference between the received feature_value$_{ni}$ and the threshold$_{ni}$ [Section 4.2] in percentage and that will be stored.
2. Set x$_{ni}$: = |(difference_f$_{ni}$ / 100)| [Equation (3)]
3. Set gr_no$_1$:= [p_h$_{ri}$, p_b$_{pi}$, p_ac$_{ci}$] in 1st group. gr_no$_2$:= [p_h$_{ri}$, p_b$_{pi}$, p_temp$_{pi}$] in 2nd group. gr_no$_3$:= [p_ac$_{ci}$, p_temp$_{pi}$] in 3rd group. gr_no$_4$:=[p_hr$_{vi}$] in 4th group [Section 4.1]
4. if (feature_name$_i$!= NULL) then
   a)   search its group members using num_gr_f$_i$ and cnt_gr_f$_{ni}$ [Section 4.2]
   b)   [Initialize counter count for checking in all groups] Set c:= 1
   c)   Repeat the following step while c <= cnt_gr_f$_{ni}$ for nth feature in ith group.
   a)   Make decision for priority assignment according to the following Decision Tree based on the value of x$_{ni}$.
   b)   if |20|<=x$_{ni}$<=|80| of feature_value$_{ni}$ then, Set feature_priority automatically according to the following decision.
5. Repeat the following steps until the final priority assignment is completed and the communication link is active. Let x$_i$ is any sensor data of ith patient
6. if M[x$_{ni}$]= $\mu_{urgent}(x)$ [Equation (6)] then, Set feature_priority$_i$: = "urgent" and p_pri$_i$:= 5 Else
7. if M[x$_{ni}$]= $\mu_{high}(x)$ [Equation (5)] then Set feature_priority$_i$: = "High" and p_pri$_i$:= 4 and if (num_gr_f$_n$!=NULL) then
   a)   if all feature_values$_{ni}$ of gr_mem$_i$ have x$_{ni}$ is in the range {|50%-80%|} then, Set feature_priority$_i$: = urgent I high I medium| low according to the relative group
   b)   Else Set feature_priority$_i$: =high I medium I low according to the relative group
8. Else   Set feature_priority$_i$: = "High" and p_pri$_i$:= 4
9. Repeat the above steps for all group and for all ranges according to the following decision structure.

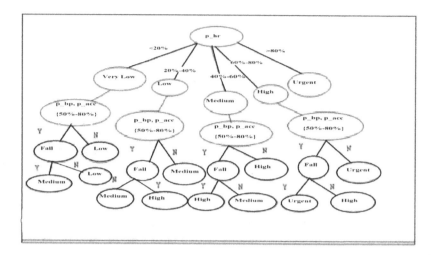

Fig. 2. Decision Tree architecture for priority assignment for group2 with Heart rate, Blood pressure, and temperature

4.4.4   Module IV: Priority Module

This module receives the list of all critical patients that have rapid variation in their physiological context information compared to the threshold value.

1. if ($p\_pri_i == 5$) then p_name_i are brought to the hospital immediately. The details information of that patient is available with all in his/her record [Section 4.2] in the data module.

2. Else Higher p_id_i takes place at the front of the priority queue and deleted from it [Section 4.1] according the higher priority.

3. if ($p\_pri_i == p\_pri_{i+1}$) then if ($p\_arr\_time_i < p\_arr\_time_{i+1}$) then Set $p\_pri_i > p\_pri_{i+1}$.

4. if ($n\_dep_i == p\_dep_i$),then key_i and hash function ($hfnc_i$) [Section 4.2 and 4.3] of all nurses [Equation (1) and (2)] are stored.

5. n_id_i of lowest key_i and fnc_i are fetched. Set $n\_p_i := n\_name_i$, $p\_n_i := p\_name_i$ records are also updated.

6. Until the first allotment is complete, the next patient should have to wait in the priority queue.

7. This new record is sent to the next module of the architecture.

4.4.5   Module V: Updation Module

The updation module performs like the informer from the server to the users.

1. After the allotment of the available nurses, Set $p\_alott\_status_i$: = 'yes' and $n\_alott\_status_i$: = 'yes'

2. The patient will receive a NOTI_MSG_p from the remote server about the allotment, and updated n_id_i, n_time_i. At the same time, the corresponding nurse will also receive the same alert message N_MSG with updated p_id_i and p_add_i and updated schedule record.

3. If no available nurse is found then Set $p\_alott\_status_i$: = "wait". It sends a list of prescribed $p\_curr\_medicine_i$ and app_dr_i [Section 4.2] to patient's Smartphone.

4. N_MSG [Section 4.4.1] are also sent to relatives' smartphone with the same updating for providing better support of this mechanism.

5   Conclusion

This paper designs the pervasive system to alert the healthcare providers for allotting a suitable nurse to the high risk patients. Some vital signs have been used as contextual sensor data which are continuously gathered and updated at the remote server at a regular interval. The focus of this work is to meet the challenges of existing work in the related field. A priority based classification using fuzzy logic is devised for alerting the health risk of the registered patients of a particular hospital. This work needs to be compared with other prioritized nurse assignment protocol in future so that this work can be validated. A scheduling plan will be generated in dynamic real time environment as well as a proper knowledge representation mechanism will be implemented using Semantic Web Rule Language (SWRL) [10] and Semantic Query-Web Enhanced Language [11] for generating updated knowledge and rules in huge database. Intelligent and a faster method for group assignment of the context data in the server will also a challenging task for future work.

References

1. Ullah, S., Higgin, H., Siddiqui, M.A., Kwak, K.S.: A Study of Implanted and Wearable Body Sensor Networks. In: Nguyen, N.T., Jo, G.-S., Howlett, R.J., Jain, L.C. (eds.) KES-AMSTA 2008. LNCS (LNAI), vol. 4953, pp. 464–473. Springer, Heidelberg (2008)

2. Lo, L.P.B., Thiemjarus, S., King, R., Yang, G.Z.: Body sensor network – A wireless sensor platform for pervasive healthcare monitoring. In: Adjunct Proceedings of the 3rd International Conference on Pervasive Computing (PERVASIVE 2005), pp.77-80 (May 2005)

3. Jacobson, U.E., Argon, T.N., Ziya, S.: Priority Assignment in Emergency Response. Journal Operations Research. ACM Digital Library 60(4), 07-08, 813–832 (2012)

4. Mirkovic, J., Norway, B.H., Rulland, C.M.: Framework for the development of ubiquitous patient support systems. In: 6th International Conference on Pervasive Computing Technology for Health Care, May 21-24. IEEEXPLORE (2012)

5. Malik, M.: Heart Rate Variability, Standards of Measurement, Physiological Interpretation, and Clinical Use. AHA Journals, Circulation 93, 1043–1065 (1996), doi:10.1161/01.CIR.93.5.1043

6. Norton, C.L., Fair, M.J., Taylor-Piliae, E.R., Mahbouba, H.M., Iribarren, C., Fortmann, P.S.: Cardiovascular Risk Factors and Heart Rate Variability in an Older Cohort. Abstract 2096 114:II_425 (2006)

7. Kung, H.-Y., Lin, M.-H., Hsu, C.-Y., Liu, C.-N.: Context-Aware Emergency Remedy System Based on Pervasive Computing. In: Yang, L.T., Amamiya, M., Liu, Z., Guo, M., Rammig, F.J. (eds.) EUC 2005. LNCS, vol. 3824, pp. 775–784. Springer, Heidelberg (2005)

8. Ongenae, F., Duysburght, P., Verstraete, M., Sulman, N., Bleumerst, L., Jacabst, A., Ackaert, A., Zutter, D.S., Verstichel, F., Turck, D.: User-driven design of a context-aware application: an ambient-intelligent nurse call system. In: 6th IEEE - International Conference on Pervasive Computing Technologies for Healthcare, pp. 205–210 (2012)

9. Bastiania, E., Librelottoa, R.G., Freitasa, O.L., Pereirab, R., Brasilc, B.M.: An approach for pervasive homecare environments focused on care of patients with dementia. In: Bastiani, E., et al. (eds.) Procedia Technology, vol. 9, pp. 921–929. Elsevier (2013), doi:10.1016/j.protcy.2013.12.103

10. Bechhofer, S., van Harmele, F., Hendler, J., Horrocks, I., McGuinness, L.D., Patel-Schneid, F., Stein, A.: Owl web ontology language reference. W3C Recommendation (2004), http://www.w3.org/TR/owl-ref/

11. Horrocks, I., Patel-Schneider, F.P., Boley, H., Tabet, S., Grosof, B., Dean, M.: SWRL: a semantic web rule language combining OWL and ruleML (2004), W3C Member Submission, http://www.w3.org/Submission/SWRL/

12. Chen, H., Finin, T., Joshi, A.: An Ontology for Context-Aware Pervasive Computing Environments. supported by DARPA contract F30602-97-1-0215, NSF award 9875433, NSF award 0209001, and Hewlett Packard (2003)

13. Diaz, A., Prado, M., Roa, L., Reina-Tosina, J., Sa´nchez, G.: Preliminary evaluation of a full-time falling monitor for the elderly. In: Proceedings of the 26th Annual International Conference of the IEEE-EMBS, pp. 2180–2183 (2004)

14. Hwang, J.Y., Kang, J.M., Jang, Y.W., Kim, H.C.: Development of Novel algorithm and real-time monitoring ambulatory system using Bluetooth module for fall detection in the elderly. In: Proceedings of the 26th annual international conference of the IEEE-EMBS (2004)

15. Bourke, K.A., O'Brien, V.J., Lyons, M.G.: Evaluation of a threshold-based tri-axial accelerometer fall detection algorithm. Elsevier, ScienceDirect, Gait & Posture 26, 194–199 (2007)

16. Kantoch, E., Augustyniak, P.: Human Activity Surveillance based on Wearable Body Sensor Network. In: AGH University of Science and Technology, Kraków, Poland, Computing in Cardiology, vol. 39, pp. 325–328 (2012)

17. Boano, C.A., Lasagni, M., Römer, K., Lange, T.: Accurate Temperature Measurements for Medical Research using Body Sensor Networks. In: 14th IEEE International Symposium on Object/Component/Service-Oriented Real-Time Distributed Computing Workshops, Newport Beach, CA, pp. 189–198 (2011)

18. Designing Heart Rate, Blood Pressure and Body Temperature Sensors for Mobile On-Call System (2010), http://digitalcommons.mcmaster.ca/ee4bi6/39/

19. Anliker, U., Ward, J.A., Lukowicz, P., Tröster, G., Dolveck, F., Baer, M., Keita, F., Schenker, E., Catarsi, F., Coluccini, L., Belardinelli, A., Shklarski, D., Alon, M., Hirt, E., Schmid, R., Vuskovic, M.: AMON: A Wearable Multiparameter Medical Monitoring and Alert System. IEEE Transaction on Information Technology in Biomedicine 8(4), 415–427 (2005)

20. Artificial Intelligence Application in Construction, http://osp.mans.edu.eg/elbeltagi

Abbreviation Method for Some Jointed Relations in Displaying Genealogy

Seiji Sugiyama[1], Daisuke Yokozawa[2], Atsushi Ikuta[2], Satoshi Hiratsuka[1],
Susumu Saito[3], Miyuki Shibata[2], and Tohru Matsuura[4]

[1] Ritsumeikan University, Kusatsu, Shiga, Japan
seijisan@hr.ci.ritsumei.ac.jp, hiratsuka@spice.ci.ritsumei.ac.jp
[2] Otani University, Kyoto, Japan
dyokozawa@gmail.com, a.ikuta@sch.otani.ac.jp, neko@res.otani.ac.jp
[3] Institute of Land Use Reorganization, Kyoto, Japan
ssm3110@gmail.com
[4] Hokkaido University Hospital, Sapporo, Hokkaido, Japan
macchan@med.hokudai.ac.jp

Abstract. In this research, a new method, named "Joint ABBReviation for Organizing WHIteBasE (JaBBRoW)", for abbreviating some jointed relations in displaying genealogy using our previous WHIteBasE method, is proposed. The WHIteBasE method has perfectly been able to integrate each relation that includes a married couple and their children, and has been able to display various complex relations with segment intersections easily. This method has a problem that all of inputted layouts are always displayed. The solution is to use the JaBBRoW. It is a hidden boundary that can organize information of some positions using a square area that is set by user's requirements to abbreviate. Not only the area is movable but also its scale can be compacted and recovered seamlessly by only mouse operations. As a result, arbitrary relations with horizontal and vertical connections in genealogy can be abbreviated easily. Our software that can display genealogy with abbreviation is presented.

Keywords: Family Trees, Pedigrees, GEDCOM, WHIteBasE.

1 Introduction

In genealogy on paper media, it is natural to write one individual only once using segment intersections even if there are complex relations that include multiple remarriages with children. This simple rule makes easy to understand all of complex relations at a glance. In contrast, almost all of existing genealogy display software often display one individual in multiple places when complex relations are inputted [1]-[21]. The displaying results cause confusion to understand the correct relations. They consider only simple family trees and have no idea to display complex relations because GEDCOM [22], a de facto standard for recording genealogy data exchange format, considers no layout information.

To cope with this difficulty, new genealogy display software has already been constructed on our previous research by using the WHIteBasE (Widespread

K. Saeed and V. Snášel (Eds.): CISIM 2014, LNCS 8838, pp. 339–350, 2014.
© IFIP International Federation for Information Processing 2014

Fig. 1. A regular family layout in genealogy **Fig. 2.** Connection model of WHIteBasE

Hands to InTErconnect BASic Elements) method [23]-[25]. The WHIteBasE is a hidden node for integrating relations that include not only a married couple and their children but also information of those positions. As a result, one individual have been displayed only once using segment intersections easily. In addition, not only various layouts such as paper media have been displayed but also intuitive inputs and inspections such as map display systems have been realized.

On the other hand, there is a requirement to abbreviate some jointed relations in genealogy on restrictions of displaying area, or the convenience of explanation. In this case, it is needed that not only the inputted information of relations is maintained but also the users can always find which relations are abbreviated. No software realizes this requirement.

New algorithm for abbreviating a part of relations in genealogy is necessary because all of inputted layouts are always displayed on the WHIteBasE method. In this research, a new method, "Joint ABBReviation for Organizing WHIteBasE (JaBBRoW)", is proposed so that it can solve this problem. The JaBBRoW is a hidden boundary that can organize information of some positions using a square area that is set by user's requirements to abbreviate. Not only the area is movable but also its scale can be compacted and recovered seamlessly by only mouse operations. As a result, arbitrary relations with horizontal and vertical connections in genealogy can be abbreviated easily. Our software that can display genealogy with abbreviation is presented.

2   WHIteBasE

In this section, the WHIteBasE method that is our previous proposal [23]-[25] is briefly introduced. A regular family relation between a married couple and their child is managed as an event by a Hidden Node, WHIteBasE as shown in Fig. 1. The connection model of WHIteBasE is shown in Fig. 2. WHIteBasE has three keyholes, S_L, S_R (Substance) and D (Descendant). Individuals have two keys, A (Ascendant) and M (Marriage). A can connect with D, and M can connect with S_L or S_R, where denote one family.

For brothers and sisters, D is extended to multiple keyholes D_j as shown in Fig. 3. For multiple remarriages, M is extended to multiple keys M_k and plural WHIteBasEs are used as shown in Fig. 4. For adoptions, A is extended to multiple keys A_l as shown in Fig. 5 where A_p, one of A_l, denotes ID for handling the biological parents, and the others denote IDs for handling social parents.

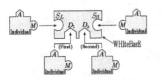
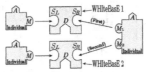
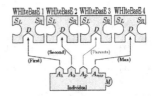

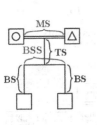
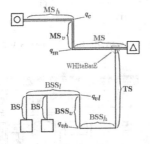
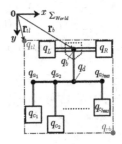

Fig. 3. Brothers and sisters   **Fig. 4.** Multiple Remarriages   **Fig. 5.** Adoptions

Fig. 6. Regular layout   **Fig. 7.** Various Layouts   **Fig. 8.** Coordinate System

Fig. 6 shows the regular Japanese layout style. It includes a double horizontal segment MS (Marriage Segment), a vertical segment TS (Trunk Segment), a horizontal segment BSS (Brothers and Sisters Segment), and a vertical segment BS (Branch Segment). The '△' denotes a male, and the '○' denotes a female that are a couple connected by using MS. For various layouts, MS is extended to MS, MS_v, and MS_h named DB (Double Bend), and BSS is extended to BSS_h, BSS_v, and BSS_l named HS (Hooked Segment), as shown in Fig. 7.

A set of W_i that defines WHIteBasEs and a set of I_j that defines Individual Nodes are represented by

$$W_i = \{S_L, S_R, D_j, \mathbf{Q}\} \qquad \begin{cases} i = 0, 1, \cdots, i_{max} \\ j = 0, 1, \cdots, j_{max} \\ k = 0, 1, \cdots, k_{max} \\ l = 0, 1, \cdots, p, \cdots, l_{max} \end{cases} \qquad (1)$$

where i, j, k, l and $i_{max}, j_{max}, k_{max}, l_{max}$ denote the IDs and their maximum values on the data table respectively, p denotes the ID for handling a biological parents, S_L and S_R denote the IDs for handling a couple, D_j denote the IDs for handling descendants, M_k denote the IDs for handling marriages, and A_l denote the IDs for handling ascendants. Individuals are managed by using data table including names and annotation data. WHIteBasEs are managed by using data table separated from Individuals.

A set of $\mathbf{Q}$ that defines coordinate values for each position managed by a WHIteBasE measured from the origin in the displaying area is represented by

$$\mathbf{Q} = \{q_b, q_L, q_R, q_d, q_{c_j}, q_{a_j}, q_{vl}, q_{vh}, q_m, q_e, q_{tl}, q_{rb}\} \qquad (2)$$

where q_b denotes the WHIteBasE's position, q_L, q_R denote the parents' positions, q_d denotes a junction's position between MS and TS, q_{c_j} denotes children's

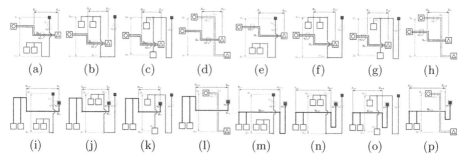

Fig. 9. Search pattern of segment intersections for various layouts

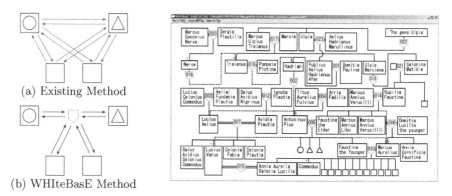

(a) Existing Method

(b) WHIteBasE Method

Fig. 10. Number of references   **Fig. 11.** Displaying Result by using WHIteBasE [26]

positions, q_{a_j} denotes junctions' positions between BSS and BS, q_{vl}, q_{vh} denote the corners on DB, q_m, q_e denote the corners on HS, q_{tl}, q_{rb} denote positions of top-left and bottom-right of all area managed by a WHIteBasE, as shown in Fig. 7 and Fig. 8.

There are only four kinds of horizontal segments and four kinds of vertical segments in the WHIteBasE method. The positions of segment intersections can be calculated by using only 16 patterns of line crossing as shown in Figs. 9(a)-(p). The half arcs are displayed on the positions of segment intersections. The detailed information has already been written in our previous research [25].

This algorithm is very fast because it skips when two WHIteBasEs' areas do not overlap. In addition, when adoptions are set, the segment style changes to the dashed segments named AS (Adopted Segment) and the arcs are not used.

One of advantages using WHIteBasE is the decreased reference volume. If the existing software is used, all of individuals connect with other individuals as shown in Fig. 10(a). In contrast, if the WHIteBasE is used, two reference links per a child decrease as shown in Fig. 10(b). Moreover, the users can understand the complex relations intuitively and can input and inspect them easily.

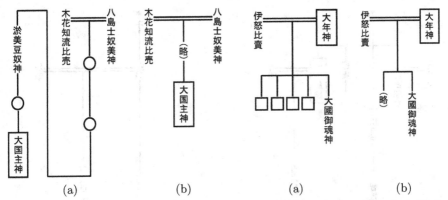

(a)   (b)   (a)   (b)

Fig. 12. Abbreviation of Generations   **Fig. 13.** Abbreviation of Brothers/Sisters

Fig. 11 shows the sample demonstrations by using our previous genealogy display software that can display complex relations with segment intersections automatically and seamlessly by only mouse operation [26].

3   Genealogy with Abbreviation

First of all, it is considered what is abbreviation in genealogy. Genealogy with abbreviation has three types as the following:

(A) There is no individual's data to input.

(B) Some names and/or generation numbers have to abbreviate.

(C) Some relations are abbreviated temporarily after inputting data.

In the case (A), no abbreviation layout is necessary because of no individual's data. In the case (B), intermediate relations are skipped but abbreviation layouts are used because of ambiguous information. In the case (C), abbreviation layouts are used temporarily by user's requirement, and this case is the abbreviation in our research. Note that the cases (A) and (B) are lack of data.

3.1   Abbreviation of Only Individuals' Names

Figs. 12(a) and 13(a) show the samples of genealogy with abbreviation of only individuals' names. In these cases, three '○'s in 12(a) and four '□'s in 13(a) are used instead of individuals' names. These abbreviation layouts are the cases that unknown names are displayed by using only '○' or '□', and all of existing individuals are displayed. As a result, numbers of the individuals can be found.

To display these abbreviation layouts are very simple. If a switching function between names and symbols such as '○' or '□' on the individual's text-box is available, these abbreviation layouts can be displayed easily.

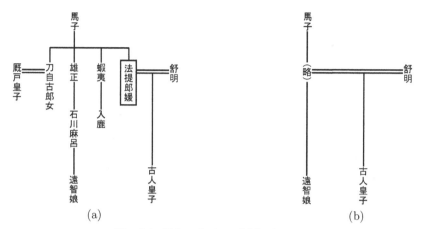

(a)   (b)

Fig. 14. Abbreviation of Marriages

3.2   Abbreviation Both of Generations and Brothers and Sisters

In the cases of Figs. 12(a) and 13(a), large displaying area is required according to increasing individuals, because all of the existing individuals are displayed. To cope with this difficulty, there is a case that abbreviation layouts of plural individuals are set to one. Figs. 12(b) and 13(b) show the samples of genealogy with abbreviation both of generations and brothers and sisters.

Comparing Fig. 12(a) with Fig. 12(b), it can be found that three '◯'s and one individual's name are changed to a symbol '略' by using the Japanese Kanji characters that means '(Abbreviation)' or '(Skip)'. Similarly, comparing Fig. 13(a) with Fig. 13(b), it can also be found that four '□'s are changed to the same abbreviation symbol '略'. In these cases, the abbreviation symbols do not display the abbreviated numbers of individuals. As a result, the numbers both of generations, and brothers and sisters cannot be found. In contrast, the space of Figs. 12(b) and 13(b) is wider than Figs. 12(a) and 13(a).

To display these abbreviation layouts are not simple. If the switching function in 3.1 is used, displaying the abbreviation symbol can only be realized. However, two or more than three inputted individuals text-box can not be combined to abbreviate because this function can be used in only one individual.

3.3   Abbreviation of Marriages

Fig. 14(b) shows the abbreviation result in the case that the individual with a rectangle as shown in Fig. 14(a) is only abbreviated using the same symbol '略'. However, seven individuals that are her brothers and sisters and their children and a partner are also abbreviated to one symbol simultaneously. Because this layout around the abbreviated individual has a lot of horizontal relations and vertical relations. As a result, the space becomes wider, however, the number of abbreviated individuals cannot be found.

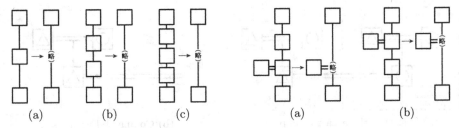

(a)   (b)   (c)   (a)   (b)

Fig. 15. Abbreviation of Generations   **Fig. 16.** Abbreviation of Marriages

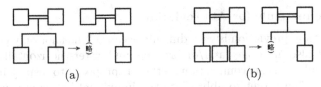

(a)   (b)

Fig. 17. Abbreviation of Brothers and Sisters

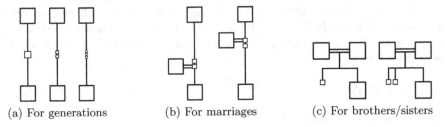

(a) For generations   (b) For marriages   (c) For brothers/sisters

Fig. 18. Abbreviation Display using scale compaction

3.4 Problem of the Abbreviated Symbol

Figs. 15(a)–(c) show the abbreviated patterns for generations. (a), (b), and (c) denote abbreviation of one generation, two generations and three generations respectively. In these cases, all of layouts become the same style using the same abbreviation symbol. It is difficult to find the number of abbreviated generations.

Figs. 16(a),(b) show the abbreviated patterns for marriages. (a) and (b) denote abbreviation of marriages in different generation. In these cases, two layouts also become the same style using the same abbreviation symbol. It is also difficult to find the connecting generation for marriages.

Figs. 17(a),(b) show the abbreviated patterns for brothers and sisters. (a) and (b) denote abbreviation of brothers and sisters in different numbers. In these cases, two layouts also become the same style using the same abbreviated symbol. It is also difficult to find the numbers of brothers and sisters.

If paper media is used, these problems do not occur. On the other hand, if genealogy display software is used, it has to avoid to input the same individual twice. It is necessary that abbreviated individuals can be found continually.

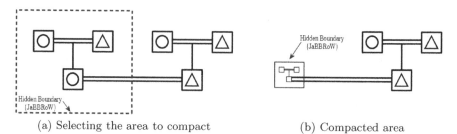

(a) Selecting the area to compact   (b) Compacted area

Fig. 19. Compacted and Recovered Operation by using the Hidden Node, JaBBRoW

3.5 Displaying Rule for Abbreviation

Genealogy with abbreviation is very difficult because it has not only generations vertically but also marriages and/or brothers and sisters horizontally. To cope with the difficulty, a scale compaction method is proposed to display individuals and segments. The target to abbreviate the individuals' sizes and positions is only compacted. Figs. 18(a)-(c) show the displaying rule for abbreviation.

As a result, not only these layout styles look like almost abbreviation display but also information of relations can always be found. In addition, all texts of abbreviated individuals should be non-display because it is not necessary to display texts while abbreviating. The size of compaction should be set freely by user's requirements.

4 JaBBRoW

4.1 Hidden Boundary

This is a new data management method for adding the abbreviation method to the WHIteBasE model. A selected area of genealogy with abbreviation is managed as an event by a Hidden Boundary as shown in Fig. 19(a). The Hidden Boundary can be displayed on the genealogy display area, and it can also be non-displayed as user's requirements. An arbitrary shape for the Hidden boundary is allowed, but a dotted rectangle is used in this research for convenience of mouse operations, and when the area is compacted, the rectangle becomes solid line as shown in Fig. 19(b).

This Hidden Boundary is not the normal selecting area in mouse operation. Once the Hidden Boundary is set, it can be kept until deleting it. As a result, the compacted and recovered operation can always be performed. In addition, all of relations in genealogy can be maintained while compacting, and all of relations in the Hidden Boundary can be scale down to the very small area. The model using the hidden boundary is named "Joint ABBReviation for Organizing WHIteBasE (JaBBRoW)".

4.2 Coordinate System in JaBBRoW

Positions of each node managed by one WHIteBasE is measured from the origin in the displaying area using the absolute coordinate system $\sum_{world}$ as shown in

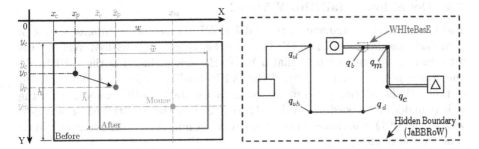

Fig. 20. Coordinate system in JaBBRoW   **Fig. 21.** Managed nodes by JaBBRoW

Fig. 8. On the other hand, the JaBBRoW is represented by using the moving coordinate system $\sum_J$ different from $\sum_{world}$. They have different scales. The scale of $\sum_J$ can be changed to increase/decrease according to the mouse wheel count by mouse operation on the inside of JaBBRoW rectangle. This means that if the mouse position is on the outside of JaBBRoW rectangle, the scale of all genealogy area is changed. $\sum_{\tilde{J}}$ is defined as the moving coordinate system after scale changing by one count of mouse wheel. This scale changing is set that the increasing rate is $\frac{1}{0.9}$, and the decreasing rate is 0.9 in this research. The compaction using JaBBRoW is defined as the coordinate transformation from $\sum_J$ to $\sum_{\tilde{J}}$ of each node in the JaBBRoW.

Fig. 20 shows the coordinate system in JaBBRoW where XY-coordinate system from the left-top origin denotes $\sum_{world}$, the rectangle 'Before' denotes $\sum_J$, the rectangle 'After' denotes $\sum_{\tilde{J}}$. The left-top position on 'Before' is (x_c, y_c), its width and height are w, h respectively, the mouse point is (x_m, y_m). If the left-top position on 'After' $(\tilde{x}_c, \tilde{y}_c)$ is represented by

$$\tilde{x}_c = x_m - (x_m - x_c)\frac{\tilde{w}}{w}, \quad \tilde{y}_c = y_m - (y_m - y_c)\frac{\tilde{h}}{h}, \tag{3}$$

the JaBBRoW rectangle can be scaled as center on the mouse position, where $\tilde{w}, \tilde{h}$ denote the width and height of 'After' rectangle. In addition, an arbitrary point inside the rectangle 'Before' is (x_p, y_p). If the position of the rectangle 'After' $(\tilde{x}_p, \tilde{y}_p)$ is represented by

$$\tilde{x}_p = \tilde{x}_c + (x_p - x_c)\frac{\tilde{w}}{w}, \quad \tilde{y}_p = \tilde{y}_c + (y_p - y_c)\frac{\tilde{h}}{h}, \tag{4}$$

the JaBBRoW rectangle can be scaled in maintaining all of the position relations of each node inside the rectangle. As a result, each node on the JaBBRoW is compacted to the mouse point when compacting, and each node keeps away when recovering. Finally, the position's values of each node can be updated to the next position data in $\sum_{world}$ and the previous WHIteBasE calculation method can be used without changing.

4.3   Definition of JaBBRoW Model

The information to manage in the JaBBRoW is a set of coordinate values of each node inside the JaBBRoW. Because the range of JaBBRoW rectangle is set arbitrarily, there is a case that a WHIteBasE is included in the JaBBRoW, and, there is no case. Basically, if the WHIteBasE position q_b is not included in the JaBBRoW, the q_b is not managed by the JaBBRoW. In contrast, if the q_b is included, the coordinate values $\mathbf{Q}$ managed by the WHIteBasE is searched whether all of $\mathbf{Q}$ is included in the JaBBRoW or not. As a result, computational time can be reduced.

JaBBRoW is defined using a set of hyper-graph G represented by

$$G = (\ V,\ \epsilon\ ) \tag{5}$$

where ϵ denotes a hyper-edge given by

$$\epsilon = \{\ J_0,\ J_1,\ J_2,\ \cdots\ \in V \mid J_i \cap J_j = 0,\ i \neq j\ \} \tag{6}$$

where J_k $(k = 0, 1, 2, \cdots)$ denote a Hidden Boundary JaBBRoW, each JaBBRoW is a disjoint set, and one node is not managed by plural JaBBRoW. On the other hand, V denotes a set of each node inside the JaBBRoW represented by

$$V = \{\ V_0,\ V_1\ \} \tag{7}$$

where V_0 and V_1 denote a set of Individuals and a set of WHIteBasE respectively represented by

$$V_0 = \{\ I_0,\ I_1,\ I_2,\ \cdots,\ \mid I_j \notin J_k \text{ then } I_j \notin V_0,\ k = 0, 1, 2, \cdots\ \} \tag{8}$$

$$V_1 = \{\ W_0,\ W_1,\ W_2,\ \cdots,\ \mid W_i \notin J_k \text{ then } W_i \notin V_1,\ k = 0, 1, 2, \cdots\ \} \tag{9}$$

where I_j are coordinate values on the $\sum_{world}$, and W_i are coordinate values of only corner points in the WHIteBasE as shown in Fig. 21 represented by

$$W_i = \{q_b, q_d, q_{vl}, q_{vh}, q_m, q_e | q_b \notin J_k \text{ then } q_d, q_{vl}, q_{vh}, q_m, q_e \notin W_i, k = 0, 1, 2, \cdots\}. \tag{10}$$

As a result, a set of each node inside the JaBBRoW is scaled in each J_k. Note that q_{vl}, q_{vh}, q_m, q_e are not calculated when various layouts are not used.

4.4   Registration Procedure to the JaBBRoW

Each node to manage by the JaBBRoW can be given by the following:

1. Add a new JaBBRoW rectangle from the menu of the WHIteBasE software.
2. Select the area to abbreviate by changing the size and position of JaBBRoW.
3. Spin the mouse wheel once to compact on the JaBBRoW rectangle.
4. Register all nodes inside the JaBBRoW rectangle.
5. Change the scale to all registered nodes for compaction.
6. Register the JaBBRoW ID to the all registered nodes.
7. All registered nodes are maintained until the JaBBRoW is recovered. As a result, to register a node twice can be avoided.

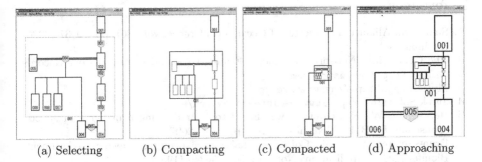

(a) Selecting   (b) Compacting   (c) Compacted   (d) Approaching

Fig. 22. Sample of Genealogy with Abbreviation using JaBBRoW

5   Demonstration of Our New Software

The JaBBRoW function is constructed on our previous WHIteBasE software. Fig. 22(a) shows the initial condition of JaBBRoW. Select the individuals and segments to abbreviate. Fig. 22(b) shows the intermediate condition by compacting of JaBBRoW. All registered nodes can be scale down and text is non-displayed. Fig. 22(c) shows the complete condition to compact. Even if the JaBBRoW is compacted, all individuals and segments can be seen, can be moved, and can be added/deleted such as previous WHIteBasE software. Fig. 22(d) shows some individuals are approached and genealogy scale is changed to large. In addition, even if JaBBRoW is used, the result of our previous research such as segment intersections and various layouts can be used as user's requirements.

6   Conclusion

In this research, a new method, "Joint ABBReviation for Organizing WHIteBasE (JaBBRoW)" have been proposed. Genealogy with Abbreviation could be constructed by using the JaBBRoW on our previous WHIteBasE method.

Using the JaBBRoW, an arbitrary area in genealogy can be compacted and recovered seamlessly by only mouse operations maintaining horizontal and vertical connections. It is possible to display a lot of genealogy information in a narrow displaying area because some relations can be abbreviated temporarily after inputting data. Understanding a whole genealogy with both a bird's-eye view in its totality and a detailed view can be easy. This method can give us the legibility of genealogy. Moreover, this idea is applicable also to another displaying matter that relations information has horizontal and vertical connections.

Future research will be conducted to construct automated layouts, generation search, grid layouts, improving GUI, etc.

Acknowledgement. This research has received the assistance of the *"Shin Buddhist Comprehensive Research Institute, Otani University, JAPAN"*.

References

1. Sugito, S.: Alliance. news letter of Oceania conference, vol. (86), pp. 10–37 (2006) (in Japanese)
2. The Generations Network: Genealogy, Family Trees and Family History Records on line, http://ancestry.com
3. MyHeritage, http://myheritage.jp
4. Jurek Software, http://www.pedigree-draw.com/
5. He, M., Li, W.: PediDraw: A web-based tool for drawing a pedigree in genetic counseling. In: BMC Medical Genetics, pp. 1–4 (2007)
6. Brun-samarcq, L., et al.: CoPE: a collaborative pedigree drawing environment. Bioinformatics 'Applications Note' 15(4), 345–346 (1999)
7. Dudbridge, F., et al.: Pelican: pedigree editor for linkage computer analysis. Bioinformatics 'Applications Note' 20(14), 2327–2328 (2004)
8. Trager, E.H., et al.: Madeline 2.0 PDE: a new program for local and web-based pedigree drawing. Bioinformatics 'Applications Note' 23(14), 1854–1856 (2007)
9. Makinen, V.P., et al.: High-throughput pedigree drawing. European Journal of Human Genetics 13, 987–989 (2005)
10. Mancosu, G., Ledda, G., Melis, P.M.: PedNavigator: a pedigree drawing servlet for large and inbred populations. Bioinformatics 'Applications Note' 19(5), 669–670 (2003)
11. Tores, F., Barillot, E.: The art of pedigree drawing: algorithmic aspects. Bioinformatics 17(2), 174–179 (2001)
12. Loh, A.M., et al.: Celestial3D: a novel method for 3D visualization of familial data. Bioinformatics 'Applications Note' 24(9), 1210–1211 (2008)
13. Aida, M.: Construction of a Japanese classic genealogy database. In: IPSJ SIG Computers and the Humanities, 2001-CH-051-6, pp. 39–46 (2001) (in Japanese)
14. Bennett, R.L., et al.: Recommendations for Standardized Human Pedigree Nomenclature. Journal of Genetic Counseling 4(4), 267–279 (1995)
15. PED Pedigree Software, http://www.medgen.de/ped/
16. PAF, http://www.familysearch.org/
17. ScionPC, http://homepages.paradise.net.nz/scionpc/
18. XY Family Tree, http://www.xy-family-tree.com/
19. WeRelate, http://www.werelate.org/wiki/Main_Page/
20. GenoPro, http://www.genopro.com/
21. Naito, M.: Topic Map for Displaying Genealogy. SIG-SWO-A603-04, pp. 1–7 (2007) (In Japanese)
22. GEDCOM LETTER, http://en.wikipedia.org/wiki/GEDCOM
23. Sugiyama, S., Ikuta, A., Shibata, M., Matsuura, T.: A Study of An Event Oriented Data Management Method for Displaying Genealogy: Widespread Hands to InTErconnect BASic Elements (WHIteBasE). International Journal of Computer Information Systems and Industrial Management Applications (IJCISIM), 2150–7988 (2011) ISSN: 2150-7988/2
24. Sugiyama, S., Ikuta, A., Yokozawa, D., Shibata, M., Matsuura, T.: Displaying Genealogy with Various Layouts by using the "WHIteBasE" Method. International Journal of Computer Information Systems and Industrial Management Applications (IJCISIM), 102–115 (2014) ISSN: 2150-7988/6
25. Sugiyama, S., Ikuta, A., Yokozawa, D., Shibata, M., Matsuura, T.: Displaying Genealogy with Adoptions and Multiple Remarriages Using the WHIteBasE. In: Saeed, K., Chaki, R., Cortesi, A., Wierzchoń, S. (eds.) CISIM 2013. LNCS, vol. 8104, pp. 325–336. Springer, Heidelberg (2013)
26. Nerva–Antonine dynasty, http://en.wikipedia.org/wiki/Nerva

Proposing a Novel Architecture of Script Component to Incorporate the Scripting Language Support in SCADA Systems

Muhammad Waseem Anwar and Farooque Azam

Department of Computer Engineering,
College of Electrical and Mechanical Engineering,
National University of Sciences and Technology, H-12, Islamabad, Pakistan
waseem12@ce.ceme.edu.pk, farooq@ceme.nust.edu.pk

Abstract. Scripting language support in SCADA systems significantly enhances their flexibility in performing diverse industry automation functions. Although SCADA vendors do provide rich scripting support in their automation solutions, development and integration aspects of SCADA Script Component are rarely presented in the contemporary research literature. This paper proposes a novel architecture of Script Component in SCADA systems to perform miscellaneous industry automation functions through any scripting language of choice. This architecture is validated by implementing and integrating Script component in a large scale SCADA automation solution. Moreover, series of experiments are performed to validate the working of Script Component after its integration. Empirical results prove that Script Component is capable to perform various SCADA functions through JavaScript by providing enhanced flexibility and simplicity.

Keywords: SCADA, JavaScript, SCADA scripting, industry automation.

1 Introduction

In modern factory and industry automation paradigm, SCADA (Supervisory Control and Data Acquisition) systems are commonly employed. These systems allow efficient monitoring and controlling of industrial processes. Various SCADA vendors provide rich-featured components for automation of miscellaneous industries and factories through single automation solution. However, due to the diversity of industry automation requirements, it becomes difficult to customize the SCADA functions according to particular industry requirements.

Therefore, scripting languages support in SCADA systems are commonly introduced to customize the SCADA functions according to industry automation requirements. Scripting languages support enables the simple and flexible customization of SCADA functions. Hence, it is supported by all renowned SCADA products. For example, GeniDAQ [5] provide scripting support as *Script Designer* and GENESIS32 [4] provide scripting facility as *ScriptWorX32* with rich VB script support.

K. Saeed and V. Snášel (Eds.): CISIM 2014, LNCS 8838, pp. 351–362, 2014.

Although SCADA vendors do provide rich scripting support, this increases the overall complexity of SCADA products especially for system integrators. The primary reason is syntax and programmatic semantics of scripting languages. Furthermore, complex GUI for script development and lack of proper help documentation makes it more complicated. Moreover, development and integration aspects of scripting languages support in SCADA systems are rarely presented in the contemporary research literature. These factors lead to limited utilization of scripting languages within SCADA systems regardless of their very powerful features.

Therefore, in this paper, a novel architecture of Script Component is proposed to incorporate any scripting language of choice in SCADA systems. Thereafter, proposed architecture is validated by developing and integrating Script Component in SCADA automation solution OpenControl [11]. Empirical results prove that Script Component is capable of executing various SCADA functions with enhanced flexibility and simplicity. Various integration aspects of Script Component are also investigated for security and flexibility of SCADA systems.

This paper is further organized as: Section 2 provides state of the art review. Section 3 provides details of major SCADA components. Architecture of Script Component is proposed in Section 4. Key benefits of proposed architecture are highlighted in Section 5. Implementation and integration details of Script Component are described in Section 6 and Section 7 respectively. Validation of Script Component is performed in Section 8. Future work and Conclusion are presented in Section 9 and Section 10 respectively.

2   State of the Art Review

As the primary idea of this study is to customize various SCADA operations through any scripting language of choice, therefore, it is necessary to first identify the major SCADA software components. Hence, we investigate the renowned SCADA products in order to identify major SCADA components. This comprises Invensys Wonderware [1], Siemens WinCC V7.2 [2], National Instruments LabVIEW [3], ICONICS GENESIS32 Automation Suite [4], Advantech GeniDAQ [5]. We also consider various scientific research works for the identification of major SCADA components. For example, Phan and Truong [17] identified different objects and components of SCADA software. The details of major SCADA components are present in Section 3.

We further analyze the scripting language support in various SCADA products before proposing our Script Component architecture. For example, GeniDAQ [5] provide scripting support as *Script Designer* with user-friendly interface. GENESIS32 [4] provide scripting facility as *ScriptWorX32* with rich VB script support. Wonderware [1] offer powerful event driven scripting module as *QuickScripts*. We also consider scientific research work relevant to current research context. For example, Marciniak et.al [15] elaborates the concept and advantages of practical usage of scripting languages in SCADA systems by performing experiments on *iFix* Software using VB Script.

3   SCADA Components

The major SCADA components are identified by investigating well-known SCADA products. This comprises Invensys Wonderware [1], Siemens WinCC V7.2 [2], National Instruments LabVIEW [3], ICONICS GENESIS32 Automation Suite [4], Advantech GeniDAQ [5]. The major SCADA components are depicted in Fig. 1. Here broad overview of components is presented.

- **Runtime** is the core SCADA component which is responsible to fetch the live values of sensors from PLCs (Programmable Logical Controllers) and other hardware devices. Various implementations of OPC (OLE for Process Control) technology [6] are widely used in Runtime along with different SCADA protocols.
- *HMI Screen Designer* component is used for development of HMI screens for monitoring and controlling operations according to real time values of sensors.
- *Alarm* component is used to configure and execute desired alarming conditions on live values of sensors. OPC A&E (Alarms &Events) specifications [7] are commonly used in this component however latest OPC UA (Unified Architecture) [8] combine OPC DA (Data Access) [9], OPC A&E and OPC HDA (Historical Data Access) [10] specifications.
- *Data Logging* component is used to store live values of sensors into database to manage enormous data logging requirements of critical industrial processes.
- *Script* component is used to perform various SCADA functions through scripting languages. VB and Java scripting languages are most commonly used in this component.
- *Historical Display* component is used to display historical data in various formats to support management decision making process.

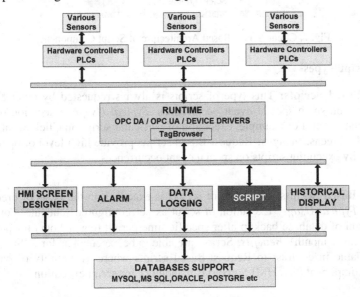

Fig. 1. Major SCADA Components

4   Architecture of SCRIPT Component

SCADA systems are usually developed on OPC technology which is based on Client-Server architecture. Moreover, SCADA systems are commonly used to automate industries where processes are physically distributed over great distances. Hence, Client-Server based architecture of Script Component is proposed as shown in Fig. 2.

SCADA applications are normally developed and deployed in two modes i.e. *Designer* mode and *Runtime* mode. In Designer mode, different designing and configuration operations are performed like designing of HMI screens, configuration of alarms, configuration of scripts etc. Once designing and configuration settings are completed, the SCADA application is deployed in Runtime mode where real time operations are performed according to the designing and configuration settings of designer mode. Therefore, Script editor and Script scheduler are only used in Designer mode. The detail of each sub-component is discussed in subsequent sections.

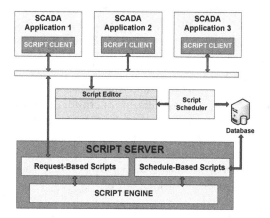

Fig. 2. Client-Server Based Architecture of Script Component

4.1   Script Types

Request-Based Scripts: This type of scripts is always requested by other SCADA components on some special event occurrences. *Typical Usage:* Execution of script on particular event. For example, execution of particular script on Click event of button in HMI screens. *Benefits:* Request-Based scripts provide high level of operational flexibility by executing scripts on special event occurrences.

Schedule-Based Scripts: This type of scripts is executed on the basis of predefined schedule. *Typical Usage:* Execution of script as per configured schedule. For example, creation of database backup after specific time period (e.g. 1 hour) for particular duration (e.g. 1 month). *Benefits:* Scripts are able to be executed as far as Script server is available in contrast to Request-Based scripts where availability of particular SCADA component (e.g. HMI Screen) is mandatory for script execution.

4.2   Script Client

Overview: Script client is responsible to initiate the request of configured scripts to Script sever and return the results back to corresponding SCADA application. *Typical Usage:* Script client provides connectivity with Script server for the execution of Request-Based scripts. *Benefits:* Concurrent processing of multiple scripts requests.

4.3   Script Editor

Overview: Script editor is used for development of scripts according to particular requirements. *Typical Usage:* Script editor provides script development and debugging features in Designer mode. *Benefits:* Script editor accelerates script development process due to its debugging feature, simple interface and inclusion of sample scripts.

4.4   Script Scheduler

Overview: Script scheduler is used to configure the various settings of Schedule-Based scripts. *Typical Usage:* Configuration of Schedule-Based scripts. *Benefits:* Script scheduler provides self-explanatory interface for configuration of scripts.

4.5   Script Server

Script server is the core of Script Component and primarily responsible for execution of scripts. It is further divided into various sub components as shown in Fig. 3.

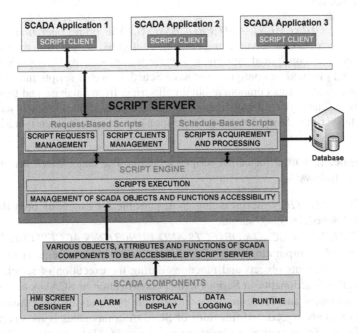

Fig. 3. Functional View of Script Server

Request-Based Scripts Component: This component is responsible to manage Script clients and corresponding script requests for Request-Based scripts as shown in Fig. 3. Major functions performed by this component are as follows: -

- *SCRIPT CLIENTS MANAGEMENT:* Request-Based scripts component incorporates the complete mechanism for management of script clients. It provides rich concurrent connectivity features to multiple Script clients. It also maintains list of active and inactive script clients in order to perform different optimization operations.

- *SCRIPT REQUESTS MANAGEMENT:* Request-Based scripts component further maintains the complete list of script requests. The major attributes of this list are Clientid, Requestid and Status. On receiving Script client request, respective Clientid and Requestid are stored in the list and Status is stored as "Processing". Thereafter, requested script is passed to Script Engine for execution which returns the result of script after execution. The result of script is returned to corresponding client by Request-Based scripts component and Status attribute is updated as "Completed" in request list. If there is some error (i.e. connection failure) while sending the result of script, Request-Based scripts component temporarily store the script result and update status attribute as "Pending". It will send the script result on availability of corresponding Script client.

Schedule-Based Scripts Component: This component is responsible to manage different operations for Schedule-Based scripts. The main function of this component is described below: -

- *SCRIPTS ACQUIREMENT AND PROCESSING:* The prime operation of Schedule-Based Scripts component is to obtain all configured scripts from database and investigate the configured attributes for further processing. Script Scheduler (Section 4.1) is used to configure and save Schedule-Based scripts into database. Schedule-Based Scripts component obtain all scripts from database and store them in structure. Thereafter, it investigates the configured attributes of each script and process the script to Script Engine for execution according to the configuration.

Script Engine: It is used for actual script execution. The major functions of Script Engine are as follows: -

- *SCRIPTS EXECUTION:* Script engine is responsible for executing both Request-Based and Schedule-Based scripts.
- *MANAGEMENT OF SCADA OBJECTS AND FUNCTIONS ACCESSIBILITY:* The key aspect of incorporating Script Component in SCADA systems is to modify SCADA components objects and functions during the execution of script. To accomplish this functionality in Script Engine, classification of SCADA components objects, attributes and functions is developed. On the basis of this classification, access to various objects and functions of SCADA components is incorporated in Script Engine. Script syntax and invoking matters of SCADA objects and functions are managed by Script Engine for smooth execution of scripts.

5 Key Benefits of the Proposed Architecture

1. **Cross Platform Development:** Proposed architecture is not targeted for specific development technology i.e. .NET, JAVA etc. Therefore, Script Component can be developed in any development technology.
2. **Rich Support for Integration in SCADA Systems:** Proposed architecture is highly supportive for integration of Script Component into any SCADA system of choice because it is based on major SCADA components and client-server architecture.
3. **Flexibility:** Proposed architecture provides high level of flexibility for both development and practical utilization of Script Component. Cross platform development and component-based design provide flexibility for the development of Script Component. On the other hand, inclusion of Request-Based and Schedule-Based scripts provide flexibility to system integrators for development and execution of scripts according to requirements.
4. **Simplicity:** Development and integration complexity is considerably reduced because of component-based design of Script Component. Furthermore, classification of scripts and sophisticated Script editor with enriched scripting features (e.g. debugging, sample scripts etc) further simplifies the utilization for system integrators.
5. **Customizability:** As proposed architecture is based on components, it has high customizability to be tailored as per development and integration requirements.
6. **Reduced Development Time:** Proposed architecture notably reduces development time of Script Component. The primary reason is component-based design and loose coupling between the components. For example, it is possible to develop different components concurrently i.e. develop Request-Based scripts and Schedule-Based scripts simultaneously because both are loosely coupled.

6 Implementation

Script Component is implemented according to proposed architecture (Section 4). Furthermore, developed Script Component is integrated in SCADA automation solution (OpenControl) which is based on Java technology. Therefore, Script Component is also developed in Java technology with JavaScript support in order to ease integration process. The implementation details of each Script Component are as follows: -

- *Script Client:* JAVA RMI technology [12] is used for client-server implementation.
- *Script Editor:* JAVA *Swing* technology is used to develop sophisticated Script editor. Rich script development and customization features are included in Script editor. Further details and relevant screenshots of Script editor can be viewed at [16].
- *Script Scheduler:* JAVA *Swing* technology is used to develop Script scheduler. *JDBC* drivers are used to establish connection with MYSQL database. Various attributes can be configured according to requirements as shown in Fig. 4. Only

Enable scripts are considered by Schedule-Based Script Component for further attributes evaluation and *Disable* scripts will never be processed for execution. *Frequency* describes the execution sequence of script and *start /end date* describes the overall duration for which script is applicable for execution. There is provision to select appropriate days for script execution between start and end date. For example, consider a script that is used to calculate the quantity of daily manufactured products in a factory for six month. For this script, frequency should be set to once a day (i.e. 12 hours etc) and start / end date should be set for six months. However, factory is closed on Saturday and Sunday. Therefore, by excluding Saturday / Sunday, script will not be executed on these days for the whole six month duration.

- *Script Server*: Java *RMI* technology is used to implement script client-server. Furthermore, *Java Scripting API* [13] and *Rino JavaScript Engine* [14] are used to incorporate JavaScript support in Script server. Java threads are used to provide maximum resource utilization and concurrent execution of scripts.

Fig. 4. Script Scheduler

7   Integration

7.1   Request-Based Script Integration

It is important to provide GUI in different SCADA components so that Script editor is invoked for script development on desired event occurrences. Therefore, event-based GUI is provided for the configuration of Request-Based scripts as shown in the Fig. 5.

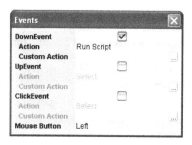

Fig. 5. Event-Based GUI for the Integration of Request-Based Scripts

Three types of events (Down, Up and Click) are provided for any button type in HMI Screen Designer component. Script execution is allowed through *action* attribute (by selecting run script from drop down list) and Script editor is invoked through *custom action* button.

7.2   Schedule-Based Script Integration

It is simple to integrate Schedule-Based scripts because of their independent execution methodology. Therefore, connection settings of database (MYSQL) are obtained from configuration file and SCRIPT table is created in the database for Schedule-Based scripts storage and retrieval.

7.3   Objects and Functions Accessibility

Security and flexibility aspects are analyzed while providing SCADA objects and functions accessibility in Script Component. *Security:* Integrating Script Component produces critical effects on overall security of SCADA system. Different script functions can be used to produce high security threats in SCADA system. *Flexibility:* On the other hand, limited access of SCADA objects and functions in Script Component significantly reduces its flexibility and strength.

By analyzing the security and flexibility issues, we try to provide reasonable SCADA objects and functions accessibility in order to keep flexibility and strength of Script Component while restricting SCADA security threads as low as possible.

8   Validation

Experimental Setup: Fatek FBS 24MC PLC is used where temperature sensor is attached at analog input and On/Off switch is attached at digital output. Acer Aspire 4720z laptop running Windows XP is used. For simplicity, Script client, Script server and MYSQL database server reside on the same machine. The necessary components (HMI Screen designer and Runtime) of OpenControl are also installed on same machine. As OpenControl is OPC based solution, Buraq Ethernet OPC Server is used for connectivity with PLC. Further details and relevant screenshots can be viewed at [16].

8.1   Request-Based Script Validation

Scenario1: Turn the Switch ON (By Modifying the Real Time Switch Value) by Investigating the Temperature Sensor Real Time Value. This scenario provides the model of very common example of real industry automation. For example, in industries, there is common situation where manufacturing plant is start only if temperature of hall is appropriate (e.g. less than 10.52 Celsius). The temperature and switch real time values are fetched via OPC Server and available in Script Component using OpenControl Runtime component. HMI screen is developed where script is executed on click event of button as shown in Fig. 6. The executed JavaScript is given below

```
/* including address space of tags */
var tag1="OpenControl.ModbusEthernetDA\\C1.Temperature";
var tag2="OpenControl.ModbusEthernetDA\\C1.ON/OFFSwitch";
/* Request preparation */
OpenGraphTagListener.addTag(tag1);
OpenGraphTagListener.addTag(tag2);
/* Fetching temperature value and Float conversion */
var temperature = parseF-
loat(OpenGraphTagListener.getValue(tag1));
/* Conditional Check */
if ( temperature <= "10.52" )
OpenGraphTagListener.writeValue(tag2,"true");
```

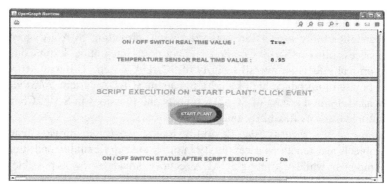

Fig. 6. HMI Screen for Request-Based Script Validation

We perform series of experiments to investigate the Request-Based scripts. Details of experiments, relevant screenshots and videos can be viewed at [16].

8.2   Schedule-Based Scripts Validation

Scenario2: Adding the Real Time Values of Two Unique Tags /Items and Write the Sum in Another Tag. In this scenario, three Read /Write tags are configured in OPC Server through Fatek PLC holding register. Tag1, tag2 and tag3 are used where sum of tag1 and tag2 is stored in tag3 according to configured schedule through Schedule-Based scripts. The value of tag3 can be used by any SCADA component without any interaction with Script Component. This scenario demonstrates the power of Script Component where low level programming functions (i.e. ladder logic) are achieved through scripting.

Further experiments are also performed in order to validate Schedule-Based scripts. More details, relevant screenshots and videos of experiments (including scenario 2) can be viewed at [16].

9   Future Work

In this paper, we discuss different features of Script Component to provide scripting language support in SCADA systems. However, certain open issues pertaining to integration and validation of Script Component still need to be researched, as briefly indicated below: -

Enhancement of Integration Capability: We will expand Script Component integration up to all SCADA components because only HMI screen component is integrated in current paper. Furthermore, enrich script calling events will be provided to meet diverse requirements as only few script calling events are included in this paper.

Investigation of Script Component in Distributed Environment: We also intend to investigate the potential response time of Script Component by deploying Script client and server on different machines in distributed SCADA environment.

10   Conclusion

Scripting language support in SCADA systems significantly enhances their flexibility in performing diverse industry automation functions. In this paper, client-server based architecture of Script Component is proposed in order to provide scripting language support in SCADA systems. We introduce Request-Based and Schedule-Based scripts types to perform various SCADA functions by making use of any scripting language of choice. Furthermore, sophisticated Script editor is introduced for the development and customization of scripts. Subsequently, proposed architecture is validated by developing and integrating Script Component in OpenControl. Java technology is used to implement Script Component. Empirical results prove that Script Component is capable of performing powerful SCADA functions through JavaScript.

The key benefits of proposed Script Component architecture are: cross platform development, rich support for integration in SCADA systems, flexibility, simplicity, customizability and reduced development time. This research also provides a strong foundation for *strengthening SCADA systems through scripting languages support.* The researchers in the field of industry automation and SCADA system can significantly benefit from this work as it elaborates various aspects of scripting languages support in SCADA systems.

Acknowledgement. We are thankful to the higher management of Buraq Integrated Solutions to provide source code access of OpenControl for integration and validation of Script Component.   Furthermore, rich technical support is always provided by development team during the implementation and integration process of Script Component.

References

1. Inves system, InTouch Wonderware (2014),
   `http://software.invensys.com/wonderware/`
2. Siemens winccv7.2 getting started manual (2013),
   `https://support.automation.siemens.com/WW/llisapi.dll/`
   `csfetch/73505596/GettingStarted_en-US.pdf`
3. Getting Started with LabView (2013),
   `http://www.ni.com/pdf/manuals/373427c.pdf`
4. ICONICS Genesis32 Version 9.3 (2014),
   `http://www.iconics.com/Home/Products/`
   `HMI-SCADA-Software-Solutions/GENESIS32.aspx`
5. GeniDAQ Automation Software,
   `http://www.advantech.gr/products/`
   `automation_software/GeniDAQ.htm`
   (accessed 2014)
6. OPC Foundation, `http://www.opcfoundation.org/` (accessed 2014)
7. OPC Alarms and Events Specifications,
   `http://www.opcfoundation.org/Downloads.aspx?CM=1&CN=KEY&CI=2`
   `69&CU=27` (retrieved 2014)
8. OPC Unified Architecture, `https://opcfoundation.org/about/`
   `opc-technologies/opc-ua/`
   (accessed 2014)
9. OPC DA specifications Version 3.0, `http://www.opcfoundation.org/`
   `DownloadFile.aspx?CM=3&RI=67&CN=KEY&CI=274&CU=34`
   (retrieved 2013)
10. OPC Historical Data Access Specifications, `http://www.opcfoundation.org/`
    `Downloads.aspx?CM=1&CN=KEY&CI=276&CU=33` (retrieved 2013)
11. OpenControl Open source SCADA automation solution (2010),
    `http://www.buraq.com/products/opencontrol.shtml`
12. Java RMI Technology,
    `http://docs.oracle.com/javase/7/docs/technotes/guides/rmi/`
13. Java Scripting API, `http://docs.oracle.com/javase/6/docs/technotes/`
    `guides/scripting/programmer_guide/` (accessed 2013)
14. Rhino JavaScript Engine, `https://developer.mozilla.org/en-US/docs/`
    `Mozilla/Projects/Rhino` (accessed 2013)
15. Marciniak, P., Kulesza, Z., Napieralski, A., Kotas, R.: Scripting languages for simulations
    in modern SCADA systems. In: MIXDES, pp. 613–618 (2010)
16. SCADA Research Group, College of E&ME, NUST (2013),
    `http://ceme.nust.edu.pk/scadaresearch/scadascript.html`
17. Anh, P.D., Chau, T.D.: Component-based Design for SCADA Architecture. International
    Journal of Control, Automation, and Systems, 1141–1147 (2010),
    doi: 10.1007/s12555-010-0523-y

Agent-Based Context Management
for Service-Oriented Environments

Adrija Bhattacharya, Avirup Das, Sankhayan Choudhury, and Nabendu Chaki

University of Calcutta, India
{adrija.bhattacharya,avirup0310,sankhayan}@gmail.com,
nabendu@ieee.org

Abstract. Context is an important aspect towards service discovery and selection. It is represented by a set of quality parameters. Any change in value of any one of the context parameter's (CP) changes the entire context. Relevance of the discovered services is often measured by similarity between service context and user's context. If these two does not match for a particular user's query; then corresponding services cannot be invoked or even if invoked, would perform poor. This paper proposes a novel context management framework. This holds the context information within a domain in a structured way such that the service discovery mechanism works faster as well as yields better result in terms of relevance of services specific to the queries from user. Autonomy, reactivity, and veracity properties of an agent help in achieving improved dynamics for the proposed framework. Implementation of the concepts and a comparative study is also reported. The proposed framework performs well with respect to search time, population size as well as varieties of queries.

Keywords: context, service discovery, agent programming, search time.

1 Introduction

Context plays a very important role in service engineering. The relevance of discovered services is highly dependent on the context from which the service is being searched. Context is described as collection of some parameters {Context Parameter (CP)}, either qualitative or behavioral parameters, and their specific values. The context of a service actually answers some 'wh' questions (Who, Where, Which, etc) and also hold some additional information. In this paper, each context is described as a tuple that represents a specific instance of those parameters. Any change in any of the parameter values indicates the change of context. There are two types of contexts; service context and user's context. Service context is declared at the time of service creation. It is included within the description of services and generally static in nature. In other words, the services have fixed answers with respect to the 'wh' questions. A single service can have multiple service contexts; i.e., that service can be invoked in multiple specified contexts. Similarly, user's context is about the circumstance under which the user queried or the services would be consumed. User context may be dynamic in nature. However, at a single point of time same service can satisfy multiple user queries with different context requirements.

K. Saeed and V. Snášel (Eds.): CISIM 2014, LNCS 8838, pp. 363–374, 2014.
© IFIP International Federation for Information Processing 2014

A service can only be invoked if its service context matches the user's context of the query. Alternatively a service's performance varies over the different user contexts. Thus, to serve users more efficiently (by returning more relevant set of services), there is a need of new context management system. The importance of the system is both in terms of speed of searching and relevance of search results.

There has been some works [8, 9 and 10] that aim to grab the user's context and match with service context. In [8] EASY has been proposed which considers only QoS (Quality of Service) parameters as key factor to judge at the time of service discovery and selection. This is held incomplete in the sense of searching more appropriate service according to user's context. The context has more parameters compared to only quality parameters. A graph matching based context aware system is also developed in [9] that use non functional information to match service and user's context by developing concept graph and their matching. These two methods neither consider all service contexts that can be queried for, nor these methods can identify relations among contexts that could be used further to make searching better. In [10], services are structured by hyperspace analogue to context (HAC) information for identifying the changes in user context and adapt accordingly. This method also failed to consider all valid service context and according user context. This approach [10] is also very application-specific, where changes in contexts are more emphasized.

Agent is an entity which has the property of autonomy, social adeptness, reactivity, pro-activity, mobility and learning capability [1]. An agent perceives from the environment and act on the environment autonomously as well as independently. Sensing (i.e. perceiving some information from the environment), Reasoning (after perceiving, the reasoning ability of agent takes decisions) and Action (is about actions on the environment to interact autonomously) are basic features of agent[2]. An agent senses its environments by its sensor. Sensors basically collect information in any form from the environment. An agent determines the current state of the environment based on sensor provided information and takes decision about suitable actions by the reasoning ability. The environment from the perspective of an agent changes continuously. Even the environment may change within the running time of an agent. However, an intelligent agent must have the flexibility to interact with the environment at run time also [3, 4]. Agents can form a community and interoperability among the members of the community leads to achieve a collective goal.

In this paper, a novel framework is proposed for efficient context management and service provisioning. This framework contains a model in the form of a hierarchical structure with some special properties for holding context information. Autonomous feature and the reasoning ability of an agent is exploited and used in the framework for service discovery. Agents generally communicate among them by message passing. This feature helps in finding appropriate matches according to user query by method of backtracking. Sharing of each combination's information within the hierarchical structure at run time is actually needed. Thus, the adaptability feature of agent is also needed in the proposed hierarchical model implementation.

Theory behind the hierarchical structure is discussed in brief in section 2 of this work for the sake of completeness. Section 3 presents a comparative study on agent based architectures. An emphasis is given to justify the selection of BDI (Belief-Desire-Intention architecture) for agent based implementation of the framework discussed in section 2. Section 4 describes the detailed implementation. Section 5 illustrates the performance and finally section 6 concludes.

2   Proposed Framework for Context Management

In this section we will discuss the proposed mechanism for context management in brief. The motivation behind the research work is discussed in previous section. The framework consists of a model that is nothing but a hierarchical structure. The framework consists of multiple levels. It holds the contexts information in a structured way. Each level contains multiple 'context-node'. Each node may have one or more parents adjacent to the next level. It helps in searching the all options across the levels. Here comes some sense of hierarchy with respect to contexts. Services within a closed domain can be arranged according to their described context within the unique structure.

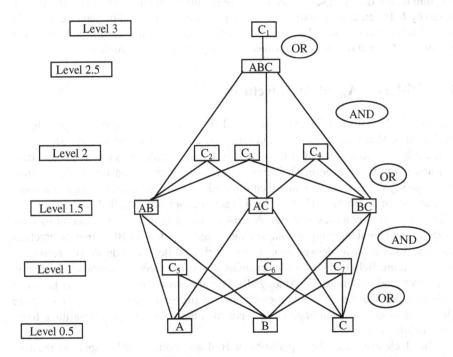

Fig. 1. Hierarchical Context Structure

At the time of matching user's context with that of the service; this structure is explored. This is to note that the structure is constructed previously at design time. However, it is explored at runtime, i.e., according to user's query. Figure 1 describes the structure for three goal levels (1, 2, and 3) and three intermediate levels (0.5, 1.5, and 2.5). It can be populated further.

At level-0.5, the contexts are specified by only one context parameter. These nodes are ORed at level-1. There are 3 context-nodes in level-1 and each node has some service and their context information integrated at a point. After that level-1.5 contains three nodes that are basically produced by ANDing level 0.5 nodes. Again level-2 has three context nodes and that are related with the level-1.5 nodes by OR. In each node the contexts are derived by generating combinations of the level 1.5 nodes. Level 2.5 again contains one intermediate node that is produced by ANDing level-2 nodes. Similarly, level-3 has by default only one node i.e. produced by ORing with only one previous level node; this node contains all the common contexts of all previous nodes. This way each level of the hierarchical structure is developed.

The offline formed hierarchical structure is searched based on the context information present in the users query online. Thus the structure of the services formed ac-cording to service context information, must be able to match service and user contexts in lesser time. The goal contexts are only at levels (1, 2 and 3). In figure 1context goals are defined by C1 to C7.The efficiency of the service hierarchical structure is that the valid service contexts are readily available in the structure and the hierarchy between consecutive level nodes provisions for switching among levels in case of context mismatch. The structure actually helps to decrease search time and fine tune the search results with various over varying subsets of contexts.

3   Different Agent Architectures

Reactive, Deliberative, BDI are three broad types of classifications of agent based architectures. Reactive agents only can sense the environment and respond accordingly. It can be easily modeled by if-then-else [5]. It can be called as a lower level abstraction and gives fast response. Deliberative agent architecture consists of deliberative agent sensing the environment and then to decide the next action using logical reasoning and pattern matching [11]. Actually this act of adaptively is called deliberation and it helps to design complex systems. A very powerful high level abstraction tool for designing and implementing a complex multi-agent system is BDI. It uses practical reasoning to achieve its desired goal. There are three different modules with respect to agents; that are Beliefs, Desires and Intentions. This architecture supports deliberation with means-end reasoning [7]. Among all of three plans a comparative study has been made to judge the most suitable architecture for implementing hierarchical structure with agent based programming. Table 1 contains the comparisons among three basic agent architectures.

Table 1 clearly states the superiority of BDI architecture with respect to reactive and deliberative agent architecture. The most important factor of BDI is that it enables the multi agent architecture and thus to build a complex structured system like hierarchical structure it held indispensable. At each level of the hierarchical structure there exists an agent. It will not be possible to design with Reactive or Deliberative agent architecture. The plan selection and execution process of an agent is completely separated and independent which makes it time efficient. The need of hierarchical structure also lies in optimizing the search time that can be possible through BDI. BDI is an event-driven architecture and maintains an even queue. Thus, the user query and each combination search are treated as a new event. All valid contexts are generated.

Table 1. Comparative study among popular agent architectures

Features \ Agent Architectures	Reactive	Deliberative	BDI
Building Complex System	N	Y	Y
Plan library exists	N	N	Y
Separation between plan selection and execution	N	N	Y
Event-driven	N	N	Y
Simple Communication	N	N	Y
Supports Multi-agent system	N	N	Y
Supports Deliberation	N	Y	Y
Supports Means-end reasoning	N	N	Y
Supports Deliberation & Means-end reasoning	N	N	Y
Dynamically changes intentions	N	N	Y
Multiple desires active simultaneously	N	N	Y
Strong Negation	N	N	Y
Rules	N	N	Y
Failure Handling	N	N	Y
Internal Actions	N	N	Y

Message passing is another essential feature of agents. Through messages an agent can shares its beliefs, goals and can ask about the situation of another agents which helps to implement hierarchical structure; as in the hierarchical structure if match at one level agent fails then it communicate to its previous level agent. BDI architecture has flexibility to dynamically update its intentions. That helps in implementing the backtracking in match algorithm in hierarchical structure. Due to the important rule that enables BDI agents to derive knowledge from existing knowledge, the Search mechanism is claimed to be efficient enough. There exists a set of BDI languages that supports different internal actions. All of the external features for construction of hierarchical structure as well as exploiting the hierarchical structure based on user query more or less can be mapped by the internal actions of the BDI language actions.

4   Implementation and Mapping to BDI Agents

In general, in BDI architecture an agent consist with four data structures i.e. Be-liefs, Goals, Plans and Intentions. Beliefs are represented the informative part of an agent that defines what an agent knows about the environment and itself. Goals or desires are represented the motivational part of an agent. It defines what an agent wants to achieve. Plans are represented as set of procedural knowledge and decide how an agent can achieve a desired goal. Each agent has a plan library that stores all the plans related to different situations. The plan library is consulted for a specific goal and a set of plan related to the goal is selected. Then the context part of a plan is checked using some expression evaluation and depending on beliefs. A specific plan among the selected set is chosen through the necessary matching of the context part of the plans and it becomes an Intention. If goal is a new arrived goal then the selected intention creates a new intention stack. But for a sub-goal, the selected intention is pushed at the top of the existing intention stack. Only then the Intention stack is selected and executed. It is an event-driven architecture since it maintains an event queue. This queue stores events which are perceived from the environment and sub-goals which are generated by executing another Goal as an event. A plan is represented as an event with two parts, a context part and the action part. In this particular agent paradigm the beliefs are basically the constraints of context parameters. Collectively some beliefs determine a typical context instance. The rest part of an event is singleton; that is an action or subgoal.   It looks like,

Event: belief$_1$ & belief$_2$ & …. & belief$_n$ ← actions / sub-goals

Using means-end reasoning an agent decides how to achieve a desired goal and the output of this reasoning are intentions. Here in the implementation of hierarchical structure by BDI agent based architecture, each goal level of the hierarchical structure is considered as agents. The information on context of services is stored in service database. It is mapped into an agent's beliefs and the user query into a goal of an agent. There exists a plan library consisting of different service records with context specifications, based on which the hierarchical structure is constructed offline (i.e., at design time). Now by means-end reasoning (incorporated within BDI) a most suitable step to response the user query is selected. The hierarchical relations among the different values of the same context parameter (CP) are expressed by derived knowledge of the BDI agents. Such as location parameter can take both the values 'Kolkata' and 'Westbengal'. But there exists a relationship among these two: Kolkata is a city in west Bengal. Thus, if a service has location context parameter as 'Westbengal'; it can be invoked from Kolkata also, but the reverse is not true. Again, it helps in backtracking at the time of searching services matching the user context in a query. BDI languages (such as AgentSpeak) give some internal actions like .print, .send, .broadcast which helps us to manipulate the output and messaging. In this implementation .print internal function is used to show the output and .send internal function to send a message from one agent to another agent and .broadcast internal function sends one message to all of the agents at a time.

Construction of the hierarchical structure is done mainly based on the two basic operations AND and OR. Agents at each level have information about the context combinations and their details service containment. Each agent is working as a level of abstraction for whole service data registry. In the implementation of the structure, all services in the service repository are represented as a belief of the agents. A service is represented in the belief base with N+2 fields (i.e. Id of the service, Context parameter1, Context parameter2, Context parameter3,…, Context parameter N, Functionality of the service) where N is the no. of context parameters as follows:

ID	CP$_1$	CP$_2$	CP$_3$	…	CP$_n$	Functionality

The following sub section illustrates the design details for service hierarchical structure and search procedures with the help of agent based programming using BDI.

Each goal node of the structure contains the services which have the same context parameters as the node have. Services in each node are arranged context wise; this helps in fast context matching and relevant service retrieval.

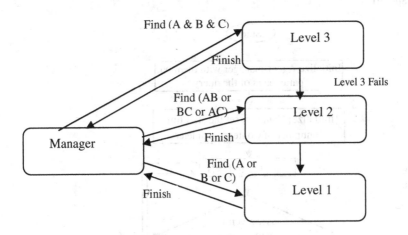

Fig. 2. Agent architecture and components

4.1 Basic Layout of Agent Based Architecture

The proposed framework is implemented with Multi-agent programming. Here define N+ 1 agent, when the number of context parameters is N. For example, if there are 3 CPs, then 4 agents are defined to handle the whole structure. For the hierarchical structure consisting of 3 CPs (A,B and C) the agents with their functions are depicted in figure 2. Different context parameter combinations generated are A, B, C, AB, AC, BC, ABC. At level-3 all context parameters are present (ABC) altogether. i.e. in this level context is defined by three CPs. In level-2, the responsible agent has information about the nodes in that levee specifies on CP combination. Here context is declared by two parameters at time. In this level there are three nodes (AB, AC and BC). Similarly at level 1 only (A, B and C) three nodes are there representing corresponding context (specified by one parameter at a time). The following subsection detailed out the agent's working algorithms.

4.2 Discussion on Algorithm for Different Agents

The algorithm for manager agent and other level agents are described in this subsection. In figure 3 the flow chart for a manager agent is described. When a user query arrives then, at first, the Agent-manager is initialized with the input parameters of the query. Then number of context parameters was declared as variable N. In case of searching at level N, the corresponding agent algorithm differs and becomes complex. An agent at Level N executes for user requested services at that level only. As shown in figure 2, if it fails then the search procedure is routed towards the next lower leve and so on. Similarly in figure 3 the flow of information and how it is all managed by manager agent is described.

In the manager algorithm, at first each of the CPs supplied by user's query is checked. The algorithm goes forward for only the valid CPs. After that the manager agent routes the search to appropriate level agent depending on the number of parameters specified in the query.

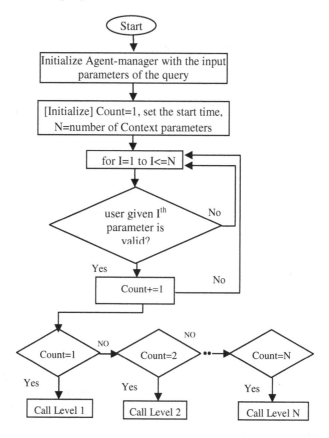

Fig. 3. Algorithm for Manager Agent

When the manager agent routes to a particular level agent; the search procedure starts. At first, the dedicated level agent searches according to the values of CP specified in the query. If it fails to find out any services matching user's requirement; it routs the search information to the next lower level agent. Then that agent also searches in the same way and so on. Algorithm for a any level agent is described in figure 4. It works in a generalized way for all level agents. In this algorithm the query CPs are collected and calculated that how many CPs are involved within the query. Then it collects all the services from the required node and checks individual CP specification of services. If the specification is same as in the user's query then the service is chosen as a relevant one. After successful completion of all level agents; the set of retrieved relevant services goes to the manager agent. Manager agent then decides and sends the relevant set of service to the user. A few methods and objects are declared in the figure for the sake of easy understanding of the complex algorithm.

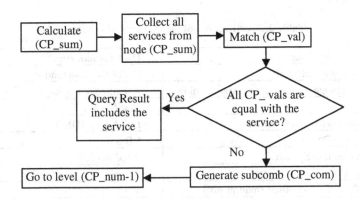

Fig. 4. Flow diagram for searching by any level agent

The definitions of those methods and variables are defined as follows:

CP_num: This is an integer value that denotes total number of CPs

CP_ sum: This is an integer value. It generates unique sum for each set of CP combination

CP_val: This may be any string. It denotes value of each CP. i.e. CP_1="c_1" CP_2="c_2" CP_3="c_3",…, CP_k="c_k" here all c_i's are considered as CP_val

CP_com: This is a particular cp combination, i.e., $CP_1 CP_2 CP_{k-1}$

Node(X): Node whose CP_sum is X

Level (X): It denotes the Level -X

Match(X): Here X is a set of CP_val. This method matches each CP_val of query with that of services stored previously.

Subcomb(X): X is a CP_com. Subcomb generates all possible sub components having CP_num-1 elements at a time from X. As for example, if X is ABCD then Subcomb will generate ABC, ABD, ACD, and BCD.

5   Performance Analysis

The construction of the hierarchical structure is done offline. Thus the overhead of construction is little. The structure is used for context matching and corresponding set of relevant services for dynamic user query. Complexity of the search mechanism is reduced by generating unique sum of CPs, i.e., in case of searching a particular CP the search procedure instantly finds out the CP combination that is matching with the combination provided in user query. This involves O(n) time complexity where n is the number of NFPs specified in user query.

A multi agent implementation of hierarchical structure is done with the notion of Belief-Desire-Intension architecture. The corresponding language used is AgentSpeak and complied in JASON 1.3.8 [6]. Each level of the hierarchical structure is managed by individual agents. An additional agent is responsible for coordinating among different level agents.

Table 2. Specifications of the agent based system

Specifications	Used components
Agent architecture	Belief-Desire-intention
Language used for agent programming	AgentSpeak language
Complier	JASON ver 1.3.8
Supported codes written	JAVA with JDK 7
Form Design	VB 6.0
Operating System	Windows XP
RAM size (minimum)	512 MB
Disk space required (minimum)	40 GB

A multi agent implementation of hierarchical structure is done with the notion of Belief-Desire-Intension architecture. The corresponding language used is AgentSpeak and complied in JASON 1.3.8. Each level of the hierarchical structure is managed by individual agents. An additional agent is responsible for coordinating among different level agents. Table 2 describes the system specifications. This experiment has been worked on almost 3000 Health care services. A portion of the list typically looks like figure 5, which is a snapshot of the partial belief base used in the agent based system.

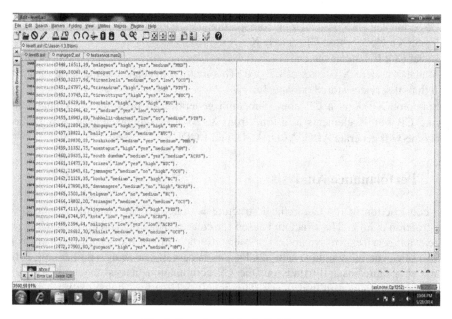

Fig. 5. Snapshot of the Belief-Base

A set of 70 queries were prepared (typically looks like Table 3). Here each column contains context parameter and corresponding value (from second to eighth column). Each tuple in the table is a query. The functional need of each query is specified by the value at column 1 and the rest is specified as the context. Randomly selected queries were run and a comparative study has been made between usual process and proposed hierarchical match model performances.

Table 3. Sample query set

Functionality	Relia-bility	Insurance rights	Where care needed	Accuracy	Cost	Waiting time	Location
Accidental care	"yes"	"yes"	"body"	"high"	20000	25mins	Burdwan
Diagnostic	"yes"	"no"	"body"	"medium"	12000	55mins	Kolkata
Nursing Care	"yes"	"no"	"arm"	"high"	1200	25mins	
Emergency	"yes"	"yes"	"arm"	"high"	1200	1hrs	Chennai
Diagnostic		"yes"	"body"		1500	2 hrs	Kolkata
Mental care	"yes"	"no"			1500	2hrs	Mumbai
Neonatal care	"yes"	"no"	"leg"	"high"	1700	1hrs	W. Bengal
General Medicine	"yes"	"yes"	"leg"	"high"	1700	25mins	Kolkata
Oldcare	"yes"			"high"	12000		Chennai
General Medicine	"yes"			"high"	9000	1 hrs	W. Bengal

A comparison between the two has been done in two manners. In first case, the queries are selected randomly from a wide varying query set. In any case our proposed mechanism works better with respect relevance of result. Another side of the comparison is time based. With the increasing size of service population; our proposed mechanism takes less amount of time. Thus the proposed mechanism works in an optimized way with respect to size of service population, wide varying context scenarios and off course for search time. The comparison graph is shown in figure 6.

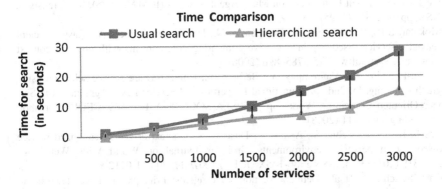

Fig. 6. Comparative Performance Analysis

6 Conclusions

Contexts defined in terms of service parameters for the users as well as services are to be matched before service provisioning. In this work, an effective Framework to represent all possible service contexts within its hierarchical structure is proposed. The offered hierarchical structure is built offline and is utilized for finding the most relevant services in terms of user context. The performance of the proposed framework is verified by an exhaustive simulation through agent based approach. As for experiment, the hierarchical structure is populated with service size 3500 and returns results within a feasible amount of time with respect to the existing alternative solutions. The most important contribution of this paper is that it delivers results considering all possible sub sets of CPs supplied in query and that will be beneficiary for the user as it offers the nearest match (may not be the exact match) based on his(her) choice. Thus the proposed framework should be considered to work in more flexible way, compared to their counterparts.

References

1. Nicholas, R., Jennings, Wooldridge, M.: Applications of intelligent agents, pp. 3–28. Springer-Verlag New York, Inc., Secaucus (1998)
2. Getchell, A.: Agent-based modeling. Physics 22(6), 757–767 (2008)
3. van der Hoek, W., van Linder, B., Meyer, J.-J.C.: An integrated modal approach to rational agents. In: Proceedings of 2nd AISB Workshop on Practical Reasoning and Rationality, pp. 123–159 (1997)
4. van der Hoek, W., Wooldrige, M.L.: Towards a logic of rational agency. Logic Journal of IGPL 11(2), 135–159 (2003)
5. Wooldridge, M., Jennings, N.R.: Intelligent agents: Theory and practice. Knowledge Engineering Review 10(2), 115–152 (1995)
6. Rafael, H., Bordini, J.F.H., Wooldridge, M.: Programming Multi-Agent System in AgentSpeak using Jason (Wiley Series in Agent Technology). John Wiley & Sons (2007)
7. Rao, A.S., Michae, P., Georgeff: BDI agents: From theory to practice. In: Proceedings of the 1st International Conference on Multi-Agent Systems (ICMAS 1995), San Fransisco, USA, pp. 312–319 (1995)
8. Mokhtar, S.B., Preuveneers, D., Georgantas, N., Issarny, V., Berbers, Y.: Easy: efficient semantic service discovery in pervasive computing environments with qos and context support. J. Syst.Softw. 81(5), 785–808 (2008)
9. Kirsch-Pinheiro, M., Vanrompay, Y., Berbers, Y.: Context-aware service selection using graph matching. In: 2nd Non Functional Properties and Service Level Agreements in Service Oriented Computing Workshop (NFPSLA-SOC 2008), ECOWS. CEUR Workshop Proceedings, vol. 411 (2008)
10. Rasch, K., Li, F., Sehic, S., Ayani, R., Dustdar, S.: Context-driven personalized service discovery in pervasive environments. Springer Journal on World Wide Web 14(4), 295–319 (2011) Print ISSN 1386-145X DOI 10.1007/s11280-011-0112-x
11. Castelfranchi, C., et al.: Deliberative normative agents: Principles and architecture. In: Jennings, N.R. (ed.) ATAL 1999. LNCS, vol. 1757, pp. 364–378. Springer, Heidelberg (2000)

Event Based Approaches for Solving Multi-mode Resource Constraints Project Scheduling Problem

Ripon Kumar Chakrabortty[*], Ruhul Amin Sarker, and Daryl L. Essam

School of Engineering and Information Technology
University of New South Wales, Canberra, Australia
ripon.chakrabortty@student.adfa.edu.au,
ripon_ipebuet@yahoo.com

Abstract. Over the last few decades, a number of mathematical models have been introduced for solving Multi-mode Resource Constrained Project Scheduling Problems (MRCPSPs). However the computational effort required in solving those models depends on the number of variables. In this paper, we attempt to reduce the number of variables required in representing MRCPSPs by formulating two new event-based models. A comparative study was conducted by solving standard benchmark instances using a common objective function for the developed as well as the existing mathematical models. The study provided interesting insights about the problem characteristics, model sizes, solution quality, and computational effort of these approaches.

Keywords: Multi-mode Resource Constrained Project Scheduling Problem, Mixed Integer Linear Programming formulations, Event based formulations.

1 Introduction

The Resource Constrained Project Scheduling Problem (RCPSP) has been a challenging research topic over the last few decades [1]. For it, each activity in RCPSP requires some resources for its processing, such as: machines and tools, human and their skills, raw materials, natural resources (energy, water, land, etc.), information and money. A variant of RCPSP is known as the Multi-mode Resource Constrained Project Scheduling Problem (MRCPSP) and for it each activity can be performed using one out of a set of different resources (known as modes), with specific activity durations and resource requirements. MRCPSP provides the most comprehensive framework for realistically representing the flexibilities that decision makers have [2]. MRCPSPs have many applications within computer integrated manufacturing, planning in make-to-order production, as well as other production planning problems, such as flow shop and job shop scheduling problem. These applications have stimulated many mathematical formulations for the MRCPSPs. From the last decades or so, CPM and PERT were the fundamental techniques to solve project scheduling problems that minimize the project completion time, while satisfying the precedence

---

[*] Corresponding author.

K. Saeed and V. Snášel (Eds.): CISIM 2014, LNCS 8838, pp. 375–386, 2014.

relationships among the activities, with an assumption that the resources are unlimited. In reality, as the resources are limited, the formulation of MRCPSPs becomes complex and the formulation varies with the assumptions made.

To solve RCPSPs, integers linear programming (ILP) based approaches are widely used [3]. In the formulation by Pritsker et al. [4], the binary decision variable x_{it} is defined to be one if activity i finishes at time instant t, and to be 0 otherwise. This formulation requires the use of at most nT binary decision variables and $O(n^2 + mT)$ constraints, where n is the number of jobs and m is the number of arcs. Later, Klein and Scholl [5] developed two different models where binary variable x_{it} is defined to be one if activity i is in progress in period t, and to be 0 otherwise. These formulations require nT binary decision variables and $O(n^2T)$ constraints, which is more than the previous one. Therefore, real life projects with many activities are impossible to solve by using exact algorithms, as they involve a large number of variables and constraints. Again, according to Lawler [6], the MRCPSP belongs to $\left(prec; r_j \middle| C_{max}\right)$ and the solution time is a function of $O(n^2)$, which is further increased exponentially with the modes, number of variables and constraints [7]. Many researchers have tested their approaches by solving benchmark instances from PSPLIB (Project Scheduling Problem Library), with different number of activities, such as 30, 60, 90 and 120 for single mode and 10-30 activities for multi-modes. According to Horroelen and Leus [8] and Alcaraz et al. [9], many of the 60-activity and most of the 90- and 120-activity instances from PSPLIB are beyond the capability of exact methods. Koné et al. [10] has recently indicated that MILP model can deal with up to 25–35 activities within the convenient computational time of 500 seconds. For this reason, any mathematical model that can reduce the number of variables and constraints in representing MRCPSPs would be very practically useful.

Pinto and Grossmann [11] provided an example from a plastic compound plant where the activity duration varied from 0.783 to 11.25 days. The conventional discrete-time formulations are not suitable to tackle this class of problem unless the processing time is rounded or the time horizon is decomposed into smaller time intervals, which only yields approximate solutions. Although Koné et al. [10] presented two event based approaches for single mode RCPSP that can deal with non-integer duration, there is no such model available for MRCPSP. In this regard, the continuous time formulation, along with the event based formulation, can be interesting approaches to study MRCPSPs. From the literature review, it is clear that the trend in MRCPSP research and practice is to formulate the problem as a mathematical model, such as Mixed Integer Linear Programming (MILP), and then solve the model using a conventional optimization technique. However, considering the state of current computational capability, the conventional methods are incapable of solving MILP models with a large number of variables and constraints. In some models, the number of variables increases exponentially with the number of time periods, which encourages the development of alternative mathematical models which by redefining the variables, attempt to minimize the number of variables and constraints.

In this paper, we have formulated two event based models for representing MRCPSPs. For reducing the number of binary decision variables, in those models, we have considered continuous time or time-independent approaches that are known as

'Start/End Event based formulation (SEE) and 'On/Off Event based formulation (OOE)'. The proposed formulations are variants of that of Zapata et al. [2], but with fewer variables. Thus, instead of the $3mn^2$ binary variables for Zapata et al. [2], it took $2mn^2$ variables for SEE and mn^2 binary variables for OEE, where m represents number of modes and n represents the number of activities. It was conjectured from the earlier researchers that the solution time of integer programming can be bounded as an exponential function of the number of variables [12]. So, the main intention of this paper is to reduce the number of variables and also the solution times for solving MRCPSP. Our developed mixed integer programming models were solved by using a commercial optimization solver. The proposed model is capable of dealing with MRCPSPs of up to 30-35 activities within reasonable computing time (500 sec). To demonstrate the applicability of the developed models, a number of 10-30 activity multi-mode benchmark instances from the Project Scheduling Library (PSLIB) were solved. The solutions were analyzed for problems with different levels of complexity and are compared with the traditional discrete time approach. The computational studies were also conducted to analyze the effects of different factors that relate to performance.

The structure of the paper is as follows: in section 2, we define the basic MRCPSPs. The terminologies, the proposed event based MILP formulations are described in section 3. In section 4, solution approaches are discussed. The experimental studies, along with the computational results and analysis are provided in section 5. Finally, we provide conclusions in the last section.

2   Problem Description

MRCPSP belongs to the set of combinatorial optimization problems [10]. The MRCPSP under study in this paper is based on the following assumptions: (i) the activities composing a project have certain and known durations that pertain to certain modes; all predecessors must be finished before an activity can start; (iii) resources can be either renewable or both renewable and non-renewable. Renewable resources are available in limited amounts, whereas non-renewable resources are fixed for the whole project; (iv) activities are non-preemptive (i.e., cannot be interrupted when in progress); (v) the main objective is to minimize the project completion time. Let I be the number of activities to be scheduled, R be the number of available renewable resources to be allocated and M_i be the number of modes available for activity i. The activities constituting the project are represented by a set $\{0,..., I+1\}$, where 0 and $I+1$ are the dummy nodes representing the start and end respectively. Accordingly, the set of renewable resources are defined by $\{0,1,...,r\}$, whereas the non-renewable resources are defined by $\{0,1,...,w\}$. The other important notations are depicted in the next section as Nomenclature. The traditional formulations for scheduling are discrete in manner, i.e., it depends on discretization of the time horizon, T, which is represented as $\{0, ..., t\}$. Each resource type has a certain capacity limit which cannot be exceeded throughout the project life.

3   The Mathematical Models

In this section, firstly, we have presented a discrete time approach and then two new formulations are developed.

3.1   Nomenclature

V_w *Capacity of non-renewable resource w*
U_{irm} *Resource usage of activity i for resource r at mode m*
L_{iwm} *Non-renewable resource 'w' usage for activity i on mode m*
d_{im} *Duration of activity i at mode m*
ES_i, LS_i *Earliest & latest starting time for activity i*
EF_i , LF_i *Earliest & Latest Finish time for activity i*
TF_i *Total Float time of activity i.*
T *Total planning horizon/upper bound of the project duration.*
P_{prec} *Represents the precedence set*
Y_k *Capacity of resource K*

3.2   Discrete Time Approach (DT)

The standard MRCPSP requires sequencing the project activities, so that the precedence constraints are met, the execution mode for each activity is determined, the resource constraints are met and the project duration is minimized. In spite of having several mathematical models for MRCPSP [2] and [13], the model from Talbot [14] is still being used as a basis for discrete time approach and hence is employed throughout this paper as the discrete time (DT) approach for comparing with our proposed models. In the MRCPSP model, a binary decision variable x_{imt} is defined to be 1 if activity i starts at mode m at time instant t, and 0 otherwise. The model can be presented as follows:

$$\text{Minimize Z} = \sum_{m \in M_i} \sum_{t \in T} t x_{Nmt}$$

Constraints:

$$\sum_{m}^{M_i} \sum_{t=0}^{T} x_{imt} = 1 \qquad \forall i \in I \qquad (1)$$

$$\sum_{m}^{M_i} \sum_{t=0}^{T} t x_{jmt} \geq \sum_{m}^{M_i} \sum_{t=0}^{T} (t + d_{im}) x_{imt} \qquad (i, j) \in P_{prec} \qquad (2)$$

$$\sum_{i=1}^{I} \sum_{m \in M_i} \sum_{q=t-d_{im}+1}^{T} U_{irm} x_{imq} \leq K_{rt} \qquad \forall r \in R \ \text{and} \ \forall t \in T \qquad (3)$$

$$\sum_{i=1}^{I} \sum_{m \in M_i} \sum_{t=0}^{T} L_{iwm} x_{imt} \leq V_w \qquad \forall w \in W \ \text{and} \ \forall t \in T \qquad (4)$$

$$f_i = \sum_{m \in M_i} \sum_{t \in T} (t + d_{im}) x_{imt} \quad \forall i \in I \qquad (5)$$

$$x_{imt} \in \{0,1\} \qquad \forall m \in M, \ \forall i \in I, \ t = 1, \dots, T \qquad (6)$$

Here, constraint equation (1) represents that every job or activity must be handled exactly one time for all modes. Constraint set (2) ensures that precedence relationships are maintained. Meanwhile constraint sets (3) and (4) respectively represent that the capacity of the renewable and non renewable resources are satisfied. Finally, constraint set (5) defines the finish time of activity i.

3.3 Start/End Event Based Continuous Time Formulations (SEE)

In discrete time formulations, the variables are indexed by time. In contrast to that formulation, in this section, a new event based formulation is proposed for MRCPSP. It is based on the concept of the single mode RCPSP model proposed by Koné et al. [10]. For classical MRCPSP, the numbers of activities are often considered as n+2 (where n is the activity number with 0 & n+1 being the dummy source and sink nodes). On the contrary, this event based formulation considers only $(n$+1) activities as events. Event-based formulations also have the advantage that they can deal with non-integer activity processing times. More importantly, for instances with long scheduling horizons, event-based models involve fewer variables in comparison to the models indexed by time. Here, we used only two types of binary variables one for start event (x_{ime}) at mode m and the other one is for the end event (y_{ime}) at mode m. A continuous variable t_e represents the date of event e and a continuous ble, r_{emk}, is used for the quantity of resource k that is required immediately after event e at mode m. That is why this proposed approach is termed as a start/end event based formulation (SEE).

$$\text{Min } t_n$$

$$t_0 = 0 \tag{7}$$

$$t_f \geq t_e + p_{im}x_{ime} - p_{im}(1 - y_{imf}) \quad \forall (e,f) \in \varepsilon^2, f > e, \forall i \in A, \forall m \in M_i \tag{8}$$

$$t_{e+1} \geq t_e \quad \forall e \in \varepsilon, e < n \tag{9}$$

$$\sum_m^{M_i} \sum_{e \in \varepsilon} x_{ime} = 1 \quad \forall i \in A \tag{10}$$

$$\sum_m^{M_i} \sum_{e \in \varepsilon} y_{ime} = 1 \quad \forall i \in A \tag{11}$$

$$\sum_m^{M_i} \sum_{\tau=e}^{n} y_{im\tau} + \sum_m^{M_i} \sum_{\tau=0}^{e-1} x_{jm\tau} \leq 1 \quad \forall (i,j) \in E, \forall e \in \varepsilon \tag{12}$$

$$r_{omk} = \sum_m^{M_i} \sum_{i \in A} b_{imk}x_{im0} \quad \forall k \in R \tag{13}$$

$$r_{emk} = r_{e-1,mk} + \sum_m^{M_i} \sum_{i \in A} b_{imk}x_{ime} - \sum_m^{M_i} \sum_{i \in A} b_{imk}y_{ime} \quad \forall e \in \varepsilon, e \geq 1, k \in R \tag{14}$$

$$r_{emk} \leq B_k \quad \forall e \in \varepsilon, \ k \in R, \ \forall m \in M_i \tag{15}$$

$$ES_i x_{ime} \leq t_e \leq LS_i x_{ime} + LS_{n+1}(1 - x_{ime}) \quad \forall i \in A, \ \forall e \in \varepsilon, \forall m \in M_i \tag{16}$$

$$ES_{n+1} \leq t_n \leq LS_{n+1} \tag{17}$$

$$(ES_i + p_{im})y_{ime} \leq t_e \leq (LS_i + p_{im})y_{ime} + LS_{n+1}(1 - y_{ime}) \quad \forall i \in A, \forall e \in \varepsilon, \forall m \in M_i \quad (18)$$

$$t_e \geq 0 \quad \forall e \in \varepsilon \quad (19)$$

$$\sum_{i=1}^{I} \sum_{m \in M_i} \sum_{t_e} L_{iwm} x_{imt} \leq V_w \quad \forall w \in W \ \text{and} \ \forall t \in T \quad (20)$$

$$r_{emk} \geq 0 \quad \forall e \in \varepsilon, \ k \in R, \ \forall m \in M_i \quad (21)$$

$$x_{ime} \in \{0,1\}, \ y_{ime} \in \{0,1\} \quad \forall i \in A \cup \{0, n+1\}, \ \forall e \in \varepsilon, \ \forall m \in M_i \quad (22)$$

Constraint (7) stipulates that event 0 starts at time 0. Inequalities (8) ensure that if activity i starts at event e and ends at event f, then $t_f \geq t_e + p_{im}$. Any other combination of values for x_{ime} and y_{ime} yield either $t_f \geq t_e$ or $t_f \geq t_e - p_{im}$, which are redundant with constraint (9). Constraints (10) and (11) ensure that the start and end events must have a single occurrence for all of its available modes respectively. Constraint (12) describes the precedence relationship between activities. Constraint (13) represents that the total resource demands for each resource starts at event 0. Constraint (14) defines that for each resource r, its demand immediately after event e is equal to its demand immediately after the previous event e-1, plus the demand required by the activities (on any mode m) that start at event e, minus the demand required by the activities that end at event e. Constraint (15) limits the demanded resources at each event to the availability of resources. Constraints (16)-(18) are valid inequalities based on activity time windows. Inequality (20) is for non-renewable resource w, while the usages of that resource throughout the whole event date t_e must to be within its maximum available limit.

3.4   On/Off Event Based Continuous Time Formulation (OOE)

In this section, we propose another model that uses only one type of binary variable per event. Similar to the last section, this is also an extension of an earlier model proposed by Koné et al. [10]. The SEE model needs more variables for representing events than doe the OEE model [3]. For it, the number of events is exactly equal to the number of activities. The representation of the resource constraints is also simpler and easier. Again, rather than using tree decision variables for start/end formulation, here in this model only two decision variables are used. A decision variable x_{ime} is set to be 1 if activity i starts at event e at mode m or if it is still being processed immediately after event e. Here, in the same way as in the previous model, a continuous decision variable (t_e) represents the date of event e. The OOE formulation is presented below.

$$\text{Min } C_{max}$$

$$\sum_{m}^{M_i} \sum_{e \in \varepsilon} x_{ime} \geq 1 \quad \forall i \in A \quad (23)$$

$$C_{max} \geq t_e + (x_{ime} - x_{im,e-1})p_{im} \quad \forall e \in \varepsilon, \forall i \in A, \ \forall m \in M_i \quad (24)$$

$$t_0 = 0 \quad (25)$$

$$t_{e+1} \geq t_e \quad \forall e \neq n - 1 \in \varepsilon \tag{26}$$

$$t_f \geq t_e + \left(\left(x_{ime} - x_{im,e-1} \right) - \left(x_{imf} - x_{im,f-1} \right) - 1 \right) p_{im} \quad \forall (e,f,i) \in \varepsilon^2 \times A, f > e, \forall m \in M_i \tag{27}$$

$$\sum_m^{M_i} \sum_{e'=0}^{e-1} x_{ime'} \leq e \left(1 - \left(x_{ime} - x_{im,e-1} \right) \right) \quad \forall e \in \varepsilon \backslash \{0\} \tag{28}$$

$$\sum_m^{M_i} \sum_{e'=e}^{n-1} x_{ime'} \leq (n - e) \left(1 + \left(x_{ime} - x_{im,e-1} \right) \right) \quad \forall e \in \varepsilon \backslash \{0\} \tag{29}$$

$$x_{ime} + \sum_m^{M_i} \sum_{e'=0}^{e} x_{jme'} \leq 1 + (1 - x_{ime})e \quad \forall e \in \varepsilon, \forall (i,j) \in E \tag{30}$$

$$\sum_m^{M_i} \sum_{i=0}^{n-1} b_{imk} x_{ime} \leq B_k \quad \forall e \in \varepsilon, \forall k \in R \tag{31}$$

$$ES_i x_{ime} \leq t_e \leq LS_i \left(x_{ime} - x_{im,e-1} \right) + LS_n \left(1 - \left(x_{ime} - x_{im,e-1} \right) \right) \quad \forall e \in \varepsilon, \forall i \in A, \forall m \in M_i \tag{32}$$

$$ES_{n+1} \leq C_{max} \leq LS_{n+1} \quad \forall e \in \varepsilon, \forall i \in A \tag{33}$$

$$t_e \geq 0 \quad \forall e \in \varepsilon \tag{34}$$

$$x_{ime} \in \{0,1\} \quad \forall i \in A, \forall e \in \varepsilon, \forall m \in M_i \tag{35}$$

The objective is once again to minimize the makespan. Constraints (23) ensure that each activity is processed at least once during the project. Constraints (24) build up the relationship between the makespan and the event dates: $C_{max} \geq t_e + p_i$ if i is in process at event e but not at event e-1, i.e., if i starts at event e. Constraints (25) and (26) ensure the basic definition of event sequencing. Constraints (27) link the binary optimization variable x_{ie} to the continuous variable t_e, and ensure that if activity i starts immediately after event e and ends at event f, then the date of event f is at least equal to the date of event e plus the processing time of activity i. Constraints (28) and (29) are called contiguity constraints, and they ensure non pre-emption (i.e. that the events after which a given activity is being processed are adjacent). Constraints (30) maintain the precedence relationship. Constraints (31) are the resource constraints limiting the total demand of activities in process at each event. Constraints (32) and (33) ensure that the start time of any activity is between its earliest and latest start time.

4   Experimental Study

The mathematical models developed in the previous section for MRCPSPs are integer programming models which can be solved using standard optimization algorithms. The developed models were coded with the LINGO optimization software, and were executed on an Intel core i7 processor with 16.00 GB RAM and a 3.40 GHz CPU. For solving the models, the Branch and Bound algorithm (B&B) algorithm within LINGO was applied. To compare the models, we have selected a number of MRCPSP benchmark instances from the popular test library known as PSPLIB-Project Scheduling Problem Library [15]. The characteristics of the MRCPSP instances vary a lot in terms of the average number of resources required (resource factor, RF), the resource feature incorporates time parameters (resource strength, RS) and finally the integration of resource and precedence features. For justifying the proposed formulations, we considered the RS and RF for both renewable and non renewable resource to be 0.5, which means that if the project has 4 renewable or non renewable resources then for any particular time each activity can demand two resources.

As suggested by the earlier models, the conventional DT approach needs mnT binary variables, where m is the number of modes, n is the number of activities including the dummy ones and T is the total project completion time. But for the SEE and OOE approaches, they need only $2mn^2$ and mn^2 binary variables to represent any MRCPSP. This indicates the binary variables required for SEE are twice that of OOE. To compare the above mentioned three models, we have considered a number of 10-activity test instances, with low activity duration time, that have an average makespan of 18. As shown in Table 1, the conventional DT approach needs on average 648 binary variables, while OOE and SEE require 432 and 864 respectively. After multiplying each activity duration time by 10 (now considered as a higher activity duration), the number of binary variables for DT becomes 6156 and the makespan increases from 18 to 81. However, the number of variables for SEE and OOE remain the same. As the number of variables is the dominating factor for the computational time required in solving a model, the time recorded in Table 1 consistently shows that the models with higher numbers of variables takes longer computational time than the same ones with lower numbers of variables.

Table 1. Binary variable and constraint based comparison among all mentioned approaches

10-activity Instances	Parameters	DT	SEE	OOE
With low activity-duration time	No. of Variables	648	864	432
	Solution time (sec)	2.0	3.0	1.5
With high activity-duration time	No. of Variables	6156	864	432
	Solution time (sec)	5.0	3.0	1.5

We have further analyzed and compared the above mentioned three models using a number of test instances from PSLIB with 10, 12, 14, 16, 18, 20 and 30 activities for both high and low duration times. Here, high duration means five times longer than low duration. For the low activity duration, the number of variables and the computational time required, with respect to the number of activities, are presented in Figures 1 and 2 respectively. For the high activity duration, these plots are shown in Figures 3 and 4. In these figures, for either low or high activity duration of all three models, the number of variables increases with the number of activities and the computational time consistently increases with the increase of the number of variables. There is no impact on the number of variables in SEE and OOE when the activity duration is changed (say changing from low to high). However, as can be seen in Table 1 and

Figures 1 and 3, the number of variables significantly increases in DT as activity duration increases. From these four figures, it is clear that OOE is the best model irrespective of the length of activity duration. However, SEE is better than DT only for high activity duration.

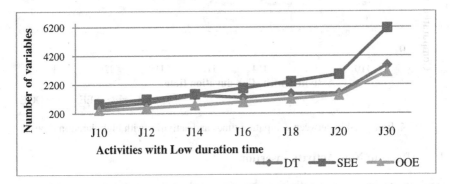

Fig. 1. Relationship between number of variables and activities with low duration time

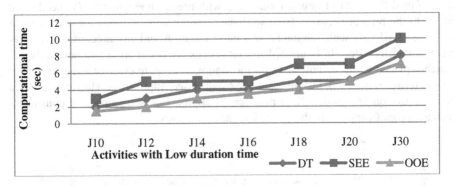

Fig. 2. Relationship between computing times and activities with low duration time

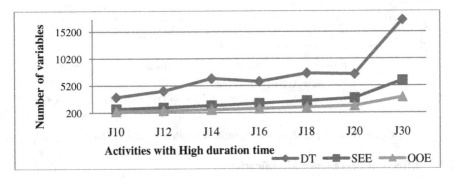

Fig. 3. Relationship between number of variables and activities with high duration time

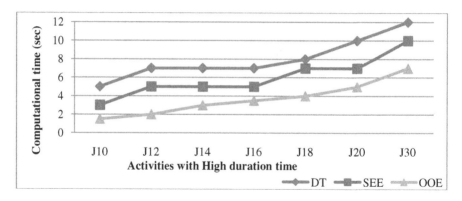

Fig. 4. Relationship between computing times and activities with high duration time

4.1   Effects of New Activity Insertion

In real life projects, some activities may be added or removed during project execution. In this section, we will analyze the impact of new activity insertion. To do this, we assumed that a set of new activities A_N with precedence relations P_N need to be added to the project network. Here we have considered three cases for a 10-activity instance (J1010_4) with randomly generated duration and resource usage requirements on each mode. In figure 5, Ins-2 represents the insertion of two new activities which replaced 2 old activities. From the figure, it is quite clear that the impact of new activity insertion is insignificant for event based approaches. However it has a clear impact on DT model. Note that, for all approaches, the number of constraints increases significantly with the increase of new activities.

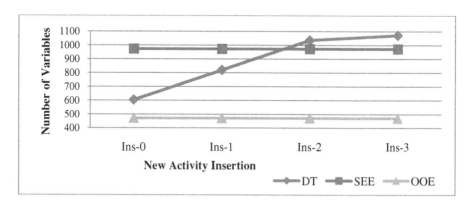

Fig. 5. Distribution of number of variables with new activity insertion

4.2   Effects of Precedence Modifications

In a project, the activity priority may be revised and this may change the precedence relationship. In this section, we have also analyzed the impacts of any particular precedence modifications. An example of precedence modification is when the project network for A needs to satisfy the additional precedence relationship P_A, and that it also no longer needs to satisfy the relations in P_R. We have considered four randomly generated precedence modifications for analyzing the impact on the three models. As shown in figure 6, similar conclusion can be drawn for precedence modifications as was earlier found for new activity insertions. From the figure, it can be observed that with increasing numbers of precedence modifications (PM), the number of variables remain same for both event based approaches, while for the DT approach, the number of variables is increased. So, it can be claimed, that the proposed event based approaches are independent of precedence modifications. But for all approaches, the number of constraints is slightly increased with the increase of precedence modifications.

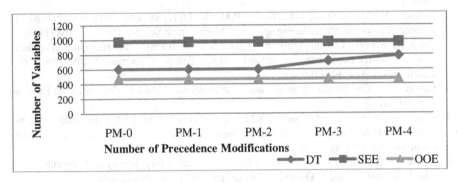

Fig. 6. Distribution of number of variables with precedence modifications

5   Conclusions

In this paper, we have developed two new event based mathematical models (mixed integer linear program) for MRCPSP that reduced the number of variables and hence the required solution times. For solving the models, the branch and bound techniques were implemented within LINGO. A number of benchmark problems with different numbers of activities and resources were solved and compared. From the comparisons, it can be concluded that (i) there is no impact on the number of variables in SEE and OOE with activity duration, (ii) the number of variables significantly increases in DT with increases of activity duration, (iii) OOE is the best model irrespective of the length of activity duration, (iv) SEE is better than DT only for high activity durations, (v) the effect of new activity insertion or precedence modification on the number of variables are insignificant for SEE and OOE, and (vi) there is a clear negative effect for new activity insertion or precedence modification on the DT model. So practitioners will benefit by choosing the proposed event based model (OOE) for MRCPSP, as it requires the lower number of variables and lower computational time in comparison to other existing models. The future research should be on proposing some real time event based RCPSP approaches for handling uncertainties or research disruptions. Implementing this model for more complex problems with large number of activities could be another important extension of these proposed models.

References

1. Hartmann, S., Briskorn, D.: A survey of variants and extensions of the resource-constrained project scheduling problem. European Journal of Operational Research 207(1), 1–14 (2010)
2. Zapata, J.C., Hodge, B.M., Reklaitis, G.V.: The multimode resource constrained multiproject scheduling problem: Alternative formulations. AIChE Journal 54(8), 2101–2119 (2008)
3. Koné, O., Artigues, C., Lopez, P., Mongeau, M.: Comparison of mixed integer linear programming models for the resource-constrained project scheduling problem with consumption and production of resources. Flexible Services and Manufacturing Journal 25(1-2), 25–47 (2013)
4. Pritsker, A.A.B., Waiters, L.J., Wolfe, P.M.: Multiproject scheduling with limited resources: A zero-one programming approach. Management Science 16(1), 93–108 (1969)
5. Klein, R., Scholl, A.: Computing lower bounds by destructive improvement: An application to resource-constrained project scheduling. European Journal of Operational Research 112(2), 322–346 (1999)
6. Lawler, E.L.: Combinatorial optimization: networks and matroids. Courier Dover Publications (1976)
7. Sabzehparvar, M., Seyed-Hosseini, S.M.: A mathematical model for the multi-mode resource-constrained project scheduling problem with mode dependent time lags. The Journal of Supercomputing 44(3), 257–273 (2007)
8. Herroelen, W., Leus, R.: Project scheduling under uncertainty: Survey and research potentials. European Journal of Operational Research 165(2), 289–306 (2005)
9. Alcaraz, J., Maroto, C., Ruiz, R.: Solving the Multi-Mode Resource-Constrained Project Scheduling Problem with genetic algorithms. Journal of the Operational Research Society 54(6), 614–626 (2003)
10. Koné, O., Artigues, C., Lopez, P., Mongeau, M.: Event-based MILP models for resource-constrained project scheduling problems. Computers & Operations Research 38(1), 3–13 (2011)
11. Pinto, J., Grossmann, I.: A continuous time MILP model for short term scheduling of batch plants with pre-ordering constraints. Computers & Chemical Engineering, 20, S1197–S1202 (1996)
12. Lenstra Jr, H.W.: Integer programming with a fixed number of variables. Mathematics of Operations Research 8(4), 538–548 (1983)
13. Beşikçi, U., Bilge, Ü., Ulusoy, G.: Different resource management policies in multi-mode resource constrained multi-project scheduling. In: 2011 World Congress on Engineering and Technology, Shanghai, China (2011)
14. Talbot, F.B.: Resource-constrained project scheduling with time-resource tradeoffs: The nonpreemptive case. Management Science 28(10), 1197–1210 (1982)
15. Kolisch, R., Sprecher, A., Drexl, A.: Characterization and generation of a general class of resource-constrained project scheduling problems. Management Science 41(10), 1693–1703 (1995)

Non-cooperative Games Involving Type-2 Fuzzy Uncertainty: An Approach

Juan Carlos Figueroa-García[1], Emanuel Jonathan Medina-Pinzón[2], and Jannan David Rubio-Espinosa[2]

[1] Universidad Distrital Francisco José de Caldas, Bogotá, Colombia
[2] Industrial Engineering Department,
Universidad Distrital Francisco José de Caldas, Bogotá, Colombia
jcfigueroag@udistrital.edu.co,
ejmedinap@gmail.com, darubios@hotmail.com

Abstract. Classical games theory is based on a set of deterministic payoffs that represent different strategies taken by its players. Deterministic (crisp) payoffs are used by homogeneous players while in many social and business scenarios, different uncertainties such as numerical, linguistic, stochastic, etc are involved. This way, we proposed a model for a two-player game problem involving non-probabilistic uncertainty coming from uncertain fuzzy payoffs, through Interval Type-2 fuzzy numbers. A method for solving this kind of uncertain games is proposed, and an introductory example is shown.

1 Introduction and Motivation

Game theory became an important discipline, widely applied in fields such as economics, financial, engineering, etc (see Nash [1], and Neumann and Morgenstern [2]). In some cases, uncertainty affects the payoffs of a game, so in real scenarios both the behavior of the payoffs and the strategies taken by players become an important topic in game theory. In classical (crisp) two-person games the payoffs are deterministic numbers, but in some cases the payoffs contain imprecision that can be handled through fuzzy numbers; in this case the game is called a *Fuzzy Game*.

Fuzzy games in literature are based on the use of classical fuzzy sets (a.k.a Type-1 fuzzy sets) alongside Linear Programming *(LP)* methods. The most important works have been proposed by Bector and Chandras [3], Campos [4], Delgado, Verdegay and Vila [5], Li [6], Butnariu [7, 8], Vijay et al [9], Monroy et al [10], Cunlin and Qiang [11], and Larbani [12]. All those works handle imprecision around the payoffs in the game using Type-1 fuzzy sets/numbers.

It is commonly assumed that the payoffs of a game are perfectly defined without uncertainty. In some cases the payoffs cannot be surely defined due to multiple uncertainties, and they are defined by multiple people who express their perceptions about the payoffs of a game. As usual, those perceptions are not deterministic values and they involve multiple aspects that every person believes possible, so different people's thoughts lead to have multiple fuzzy sets. This way, a fuzzy game composed by multiple people defining its payoffs needs special tools to handle this kind of fuzzy uncertainty.

Our proposal is based on the use of Type-2 fuzzy numbers to involve all perceptions and opinions of who define the payoffs of a game, dealing with non-consensus

K. Saeed and V. Snášel (Eds.): CISIM 2014, LNCS 8838, pp. 387–396, 2014.

and linguistic uncertainty around their perceptions. Using LP methods, the extension principle, and the decomposition theorem, we provide a mathematical framework for solving a matrix game conformed by two-players under uncertainty coming from disagreement and non-consensuses on the definition of the payoffs of the game.

We also use interval Type-2 fuzzy numbers to represent the set of possible solutions that the players may use, given a particular perception about the payoffs. A method based on α-cuts to solve such games is proposed and explained through an example.

The paper has seven sections. Section 1 shows the Introduction and Motivation. In Section 2, the classical two-players game and its LP formulation are presented. In Section 3, basics on Type-2 fuzzy numbers are recalled. In Section 4, a Type-2 fuzzy game model is presented. Section 5 presents the proposal for solving the problem; Section 6 shows an application example, and Section presents 7 some concluding remarks.

2   The Classical Two-Players Game

In a two-players game, they are trying to make a move to earn the best possible benefits, given possible moves of the other player and known payoffs of every move. In zero-sum games, a move gives a gain to a player while its opponent losses the same. Then a game G is conformed by a set S^m of strategies of the Player I and a set S^n of strategies of the Player II. If Player II selects the pure strategy s_j and the Player I selects the pure strategy s_i, then Player II has to pay a_{ij} units to Player I.

All payoffs of the game are comprised into a *payoff matrix* namely A, where each element a_{ij} is the payoff of the Player I, and a negative value means that Player I has to pay a_{ij} to Player II, as shown next:

$$A = \begin{pmatrix} a_{11} & a_{12} & \cdots & a_{1j} & \cdots & a_{1n} \\ a_{21} & a_{22} & \cdots & a_{2j} & \cdots & a_{2n} \\ \vdots & \vdots & \ddots & \vdots & \dots & \vdots \\ a_{i1} & a_{i2} & \cdots & a_{ij} & \cdots & a_{in} \\ \vdots & \vdots & \ddots & \vdots & \dots & \vdots \\ a_{m1} & a_{m2} & \cdots & a_{mj} & \cdots & a_{mn} \end{pmatrix}$$

where $a_{ij} \in \mathbb{R}$, $i \in \{1, 2, \cdots, m\}$ and $j \in \{1, 2, \cdots, n\}$.

This matrix A was originally defined with deterministic (crisp) payoffs, which leads to have only one strategy that maximizes the game. Decision making for Player I uses a $\max - \min$ principle which seeks to maximize its income through the worse possible movings done by its opponent, so the final decision consists in doing a move i that earns the maximum of the minimum payoffs given all possible moves j of its opponent ($\max - \min$ principle is applied to Player II).

2.1   LP Formulation

Basically, an LP formulation of a two-players game is intended to find the optimal frequency of moves x_i^* which maximizes the value of the game. To do so, Player I has to select a move $x_i^*(S^m)$ to obtain the best expected payoff (a_{ij}).

$$\underset{x \in S^m}{\text{Max}} \left\{ \text{Min} \left(\sum_{i=1}^{m} a_{i1}x_i, \; \sum_{i=1}^{m} a_{i2}x_i, \cdots, \; \sum_{i=1}^{m} a_{in}x_i \right) \right\}$$

$$s.t.$$

$$\sum_{i=1}^{m} x_i = 1 \tag{1}$$

$$x_i \geqslant 0$$

Dantzig [13] proposed the first LP model for games based on the works of Nash [1], and Neumann & Morgenstern [2]. His proposal uses an auxiliary variable v that represents the min operator. The LP formulation for Player I is shown next.

$$\text{Max } z = v$$

$$s.t.$$

$$v - \sum_{i=1}^{m} a_{ij}x_i \leqslant 0 \quad \forall \, j \in S^n \tag{2}$$

$$\sum_{i=1}^{m} x_i = 1$$

$$x_i \geqslant 0, \; v \in \mathbb{R}$$

v is an auxiliary variable which operates as $v = \text{Min} \left(\sum_{i=1}^{m} a_{i1}x_i, \cdots, \sum_{i=1}^{m} a_{in}x_i \right)$.

The LP model for Player II is the dual model of Player I, so the optimal value of the game is the same for both players. Further details can be found in Dantzig [13].

3 Type-2 Fuzzy Sets

A Type-2 fuzzy set $\tilde{A}$ (see Mendel [14]) is an ordered pair $\tilde{A} = \{(x, \mu_{\tilde{A}}(x)) : x \in X\}$, where A is its linguistic label and u represents uncertainty around the word A:

$$\tilde{A} = \{((x, u), \mu_{\tilde{A}}(x, u) \mid \forall x \in X, \forall u \in J_x \subseteq [0, 1]\}$$

where $J_x \subseteq [0, 1]$ is the set of primary memberships of $\tilde{A}$, $\mu_{\tilde{A}}(x, u) \in [0, 1]$, and u is its domain of uncertainty.

An *Interval Type-2 fuzzy set (IT2FS)* (see Figure 1) is a special kind of T2FS in which $\mu_{\tilde{A}}(x, u) = 1$. Hence, an IT2FS $\tilde{A}$ is composed by an infinite amount of Type-1 fuzzy sets embedded into J_x. In other words (see Mendel, John & Liu [15])

$$\tilde{A} = \{(x, \mu_{\tilde{A}}(x)) \mid x \in X\}$$

where $\mu_{\tilde{A}}(x)$ is completely characterized by $J_x \subseteq [0, 1]$.

Here, $\tilde{A}$ is an Interval Type-2 fuzzy set defined over a domain (usually $\mathbb{R}_+$), its support $supp(\tilde{A})$ is enclosed into the interval $a \in [A^{L(+)}, A^{R(+)}]$. $\mu_{\tilde{a}}$ has a linear Type-2 fuzzy

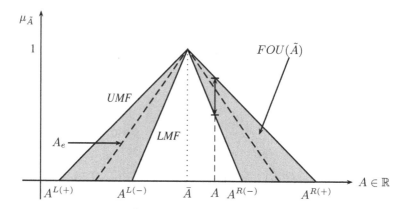

Fig. 1. Interval Type-2 Fuzzy set $\tilde{A}$

set with parameters $A^{L(+)}, A^{L(-)}, A^{R(-)}, A^{R(+)}$ and $\bar{A}$. FOU is the *Footprint of Uncertainty* of the Type-2 fuzzy set and A_e is an embedded Type-1 fuzzy set into its FOU. Uncertainty A is defined by its FOU as the union of all primary memberships, i.e.

$$\text{FOU}(\tilde{A}) = \bigcup_{x \in X} J_x \tag{3}$$

The FOU of $\tilde{A}$ involves all J_x weighted by a secondary membership function $f_x(u)/(x,u)$, in this case $1/(x,u)$. Any FOU is bounded by two membership functions: an *Upper* membership function *(UMF)*$= \overline{\mu}_{\tilde{A}}$ and a *Lower* membership function *(LMF)*$= \underline{\mu}_{\tilde{A}}$ which have e embedded sets (A_e).

3.1 The Zadeh's Extension Principle

The selected approach to to model fuzzy functions is the *Zadeh's Extension principle* (see Klir and Yuan [16] which is presented as follows

Theorem 3.1. *Let f be a function such as $f : X_1, X_2, \cdots, X_n \to z$, and A_i is a fuzzy set in X_i, $i = 1, 2, \cdots, n$ with $x_i \in X_i$, then we have*

$$f(A_1, A_2, \cdots, A_n)(z) = \sup_{z=f(x_1,x_2,\cdots,x_n)} \min_i \{\mu_{A_1}(x_1), \mu_{A_2}(x_2), \cdots, \mu_{A_n}(x_n)\} \tag{4}$$

Then, we can project any function $z = f(x_1, x_2, \cdots, x_n)$ into a fuzzy set using their membership functions $\mu_{A_1(x_1)}, \mu_{A_2(x_2)}, \cdots, \mu_{A_n(x_n)}$. For simplicity, we compute the set μ_z using a mapping of $A_i(x_i)$ instead of x_i. This is by using α-cuts and the representation theorem of fuzzy set (See Klir and Yuan [17]), presented next.

3.2 The Extended Representation Theorem

The α-cut of A is defined as $^{\alpha}A = \{x \mid \mu_A(x) \geqslant \alpha\}$. The function $z = f(x^*)$ comes from $f(\tilde{A}_i)(z)$, so $f(\tilde{A}_i)(z)$ can be easily computed through α-cuts instead of mapping

x_i. Then, we compute a function of $f^{-1}(\mu_{\tilde{A}}) \rightarrow x$ to finally compute functions of fuzzy sets. The extension of the α-cut of A to the α-cut of $\tilde{A}$ has been proposed by Figueroa [18] as the union of all possible α-cuts over A_e, $^{\alpha}A_e = \{x \mid \mu_{A_e}(x) \geqslant \alpha\}$:

$$^{\alpha}\tilde{A} = \{(x,u) \mid J_x \geqslant \alpha\}\, u \in J_x \subseteq [0,1],\ \alpha \in [0,1]$$

Now, the boundaries of each α-cut are defined as follows (see Figure 2):

$$^{\alpha}\tilde{A}_{ij}^{L} = \left[{}^{\alpha}\tilde{A}_{ij}^{L(+)},\ {}^{\alpha}\tilde{A}_{ij}^{L(-)} \right] \tag{5}$$

$$^{\alpha}\tilde{A}_{ij}^{R} = \left[{}^{\alpha}\tilde{A}_{ij}^{R(-)},\ {}^{\alpha}\tilde{A}_{ij}^{R(+)} \right] \tag{6}$$

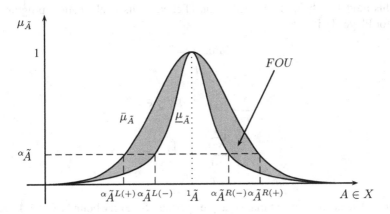

Fig. 2. Fuzzy set $\tilde{A}$

Using (4), we can extend z to a Type-2 fuzzy environment, as follows:

$$f(\tilde{A})(z) = f^{\alpha}(\tilde{A}_1, \tilde{A}_2, \cdots, \tilde{A}_n)(z) = f(^{\alpha}\tilde{A}_1(x_1),\ {}^{\alpha}\tilde{A}_2(x_2), \cdots,\ {}^{\alpha}\tilde{A}_n(x_n))(z) \tag{7}$$

3.3 Type-2 Fuzzy Numbers (IT2FN)

A Type-2 fuzzy number *(T2FN)* can be seen as the extension of a Type-1 fuzzy number. Then $\tilde{A}$ is a T2FS whose UMF and LMF are normalized fuzzy numbers, $^{\alpha}A$ is a closed interval for all $\alpha \in [0,1]$, and bounded support *supp*(A). Now, if both the UMF and LMF of $\tilde{A}$ are fuzzy numbers, then $\tilde{A}$ is an IT2FN. Figure 1 depicts a Type-2 fuzzy number since both its UMF and LMF are fuzzy numbers as well.

In some applications, a crisp measure (seen either as the expected or most possible value) of an IT2FS, is required. The computation of the expected value of an IT2FN is possible using a centroid-based method, whose details can be found in Figueroa [18], Karnik & Mendel [19], and Melgarejo [20].

4   The IT2FS Games Model

We have based our proposal on the Li's α-cuts method for fuzzy games (see Li [6]). In our paper, the payoffs matrix has been defined using Interval Type-2 fuzzy uncertainty, so the problem (in terms of Player I) is as follows:

$$\underset{x \in S^m}{\text{Max}} \left\{ \text{Min} \left(\sum_{i=1}^{m} \tilde{a}_{i1} x_i, \sum_{i=1}^{m} \tilde{a}_{i2} x_i, \cdots, \sum_{i=1}^{m} \tilde{a}_{in} x_i \right) \right\} \tag{8}$$

$$s.t.$$

$$\sum_{i=1}^{m} x_i = 1 \tag{9}$$

$$x_i \geqslant 0 \tag{10}$$

In this model each $\tilde{a}_{ij}$ is defined as an IT2FN, so its mathematical programming form (for Player I), is:

$$\text{Max } z = \tilde{v}$$

$$s.t.$$

$$\tilde{v} - \sum_{i=1}^{m} \tilde{a}_{ij} x_i \precsim 0 \ \forall \ j \in S^n \tag{11}$$

$$\sum_{i=1}^{m} x_i = 1$$

$$x_i \geqslant 0$$

Every $^{\alpha}\tilde{A}$ leads to four optimal strategies per cut. So every boundary of $^{\alpha}\tilde{A}$ reaches an optimal value namely $^{\alpha}\tilde{Z}^{L(+)}$, $^{\alpha}\tilde{Z}^{L(-)}$, $^{\alpha}\tilde{Z}^{R(-)}$ and $^{\alpha}\tilde{Z}^{R(+)}$:

$$^{\alpha}\tilde{A}^{L(+)} \to {}^{\alpha}\tilde{Z}^{L(+)} \tag{12}$$

$$^{\alpha}\tilde{A}^{L(-)} \to {}^{\alpha}\tilde{Z}^{L(-)} \tag{13}$$

$$^{\alpha}\tilde{A}^{R(-)} \to {}^{\alpha}\tilde{Z}^{R(-)} \tag{14}$$

$$^{\alpha}\tilde{A}^{R(+)} \to {}^{\alpha}\tilde{Z}^{R(+)} \tag{15}$$

After computing all values of the game regarding α then the fuzzy set of optimal solutions namely $\tilde{Z}$ is composed by using $f^{-1}(^{\alpha}\tilde{A})(z)$.

5   Solving IT2FGs

The problem of solving IT2FLPs has been investigated by Figueroa [18, 21–23], so the optimization of IT2FGs become a natural extension of his results. Note that we face a problem of having infinite Type-1 fuzzy sets into the FOU of $\tilde{A}$, so we have to deal with the FOU of $\tilde{a}_{ij}$ instead to solve infinite fuzzy LPs.

Now, the proposed method to compute a solution of IT2FG modeled as an LP when having a Type-2 fuzzy payoff matrix is described as follows:

Proposed α-cut Based Method

1. Select $k \in \mathbb{N}$ amount of α-cuts
2. Compute all the α-cuts of $\tilde{A}$
3. Solve the $4k$ LP related problems regarding (12), (13), (14) and (15)
4. Compose $f(\tilde{A})(z)$ using equation (7)
5. Compose $\tilde{Z}$ using $f^{-1}(^\alpha\tilde{A})(z)$
6. Compute $C(\tilde{Z})$, z_l and z_u using Figueroa [18]
7. Return $[z_l, z_u]$ as the interval of expected values of the game
8. Defuzzify $\tilde{Z}$ using $c_z = (z_l + z_u)/2$

5.1 Decision Making

Fuzzy Decision making is not based on having a single (global) optimum of the problem, they are based on the idea of having a set of optimal solutions coming from fuzzy information, so our problem needs to compute a set of possible solutions of the game called $\tilde{Z}$, as a function of the initial fuzzy payoffs $\tilde{a}_{ij}$.

Every particular value of $^\alpha\tilde{a}_{ij}$ leads to a particular value of the game z^* which is satisfactory in different degrees $J_z \in [\underline{\mu}_{\tilde{Z}}, \bar{\mu}_{\tilde{Z}}]$, so the idea is to cover as much as possible scenarios. The centroid of $\tilde{Z}$ provides an idea of what an expectation of the game is, so the analyst can use it to have an idea of the expected value of the game.

Finally, what it is proposed is a map of all possible values of a_{ij} in order to provide the analyst a better idea of the behavior of the fuzzy game.

6   Application Example

The example is based on a classical example introduced by Lieberman [24]. The original example is a crisp 4×5 two-players zero-sum game, where the solution is easily computed using an LP model. Now suppose there is no consensus about the payoffs of the game, so different uncertainties affect its definition (i.e ambiguity, multiple people's opinions, imprecision, etc).

The analyst only has crisp payoffs, but they are not reliable. This way, some experts of the game are asked for their opinions about its payoffs, so we have to comprise all the information given by the experts using Type-2 fuzzy numbers which collects linguistic uncertainty (coming from experts opinions and perceptions) around a_{ij} to finally provide a solution. The initial crisp payoffs are shown next:

Table 1. Crisp payoffs of the example

(i,j)	$j = 1$	$j = 2$	$j = 3$	$j = 4$	$j = 5$
$i = 1$	1	-3	2	-2	1
$i = 2$	2	3	0	3	-2
$i = 3$	0	4	-1	-3	-2
$i = 4$	4	0	-2	2	-1

For simplicity, experts were asked to express their opinion around the crisp payoffs shown in Table 1 using the statement *"What is your opinion about optimistic and pessimistic payoffs of the strategy (i, j)?"*. The words *Optimistic* and *Pessimistic* are used to compose triangular fuzzy numbers (namely $T(a, b, c)$) for every UMF and LMF. Note that a means pessimistic, b means crisp (see Table 1), and c means optimistic payoff. The collected IT2FNs are presented in Table 2.

Table 2. Parameters of the example

Lower membership functions (UMF) of the example					
(i,j)	$j = 1$	$j = 2$	$j = 3$	$j = 4$	$j = 5$
$i = 1$	T(0.7,1,1.5)	T(-4,-3,2)	T(1,2,5)	T(-2.5,-2,0)	T(0.8,1,5)
$i = 2$	T(1.5,2,3)	T(1.5,3,5)	T(-1,0,2)	T(-1,3,4)	T(-3,-2,1.5)
$i = 3$	T(-1,0,5)	T(3,4,6)	T(-3,-1,1.5)	T(-4,-3,1)	T(-3.5,-2,3.5
$i = 4$	T(-5.5,-4-0)	T(-0.5,0,1)	T(-4,-2,1.5)	T(0,2,3)	T(-2.5,-1,0.5)
Upper membership functions (UMF) of the example					
(i,j)	$j = 1$	$j = 2$	$j = 3$	$j = 4$	$j = 5$
$i = 1$	T(0,1,2)	T(-5,-3,3)	T(0,2,6)	T(-3,-2,2)	T(0.5,1,6)
$i = 2$	T(0.5,2,4)	T(1,3,7)	T(-2,0,3)	T(-3,3,5)	T(-5,-2,2)
$i = 3$	T(-2,0,6)	T(,1,4,7)	T(-5,-1,2)	T(-5,-3,3)	T(-4,-2,5)
$i = 4$	T(-6,-4,2)	T(-1,0,3)	T(-6,-2,2)	T(-2,2,5)	T(-4,-1,1.5)

Our example uses the values shown in Table 2 to compose the matrix $\tilde{A}$ whose elements are $\mu_{\tilde{a}_{ij}}$. Now, the game is solved using the α-cuts decomposition and the representation theorem.

6.1 Computational Results

We have selected $k = 21$ equally distributed α-cuts and computed $^{\alpha}\tilde{A}$ using (5) and (6). After solving the $4k$ LP problems related to (1) and (2) (this is, an LP for (12), (13), (14), and (15)), we compose $f(\tilde{A})(z)$ using step 3) and equation (7). The set of optimal solutions $\tilde{Z}$ is shown in Figure 3.

A clearer clear idea of the behavior of the game is given by the centroid of $\tilde{Z}$, so we compute z_l and z_u using Figueroa [18], whosse results are shown next:

$$C(\tilde{Z}) \in [z_l, z_u] = [-0.17637, 0.47788] \quad \rightarrow \quad c_z = 0.15075$$

Now, $C(\tilde{Z})$ is expected interval of values that both groups of players can expect. Different strategies can be taken in the game, for which we provide a set of possible solutions x_i^* and y_j^* (Player I and II respectively) that fits into $C(\tilde{Z})$. This is, a set of solutions whose values z^* fit into $C(\tilde{Z})$ having different membership degrees. Note that as more α-cuts are computed, we have more strategies into $C(\tilde{Z})$.

6.2 Discussion of the Results

We have obtained different solutions coming from different payoffs. For instance, the value $z^* = 0.427$ is within $C(\tilde{Z})$ and comes from $^{0.8}\tilde{A}^{L(-)}$. The optimal strategy

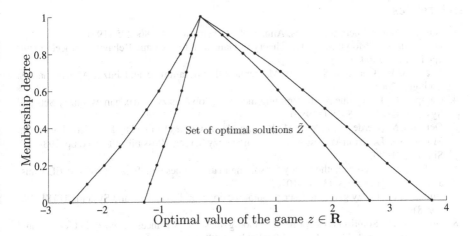

Fig. 3. Set of optimal values of the game $\tilde{Z}$

(probabilities) for Player I is $x^* = [0.554, 0.425, 0.021, 0]$, and the optimal strategy for Player II is $y^* = [0, 0.274, 0, 0.097, 0.629]$. Other example comes from $^1\tilde{A}^{R(+)}$ which is equivalent to the crisp solution of the game (outside $C(\tilde{Z})$); its optimal value is $z^* = -0.306$, the optimal strategy for Player I is $x^* = [0.565, 0.354, 0.081, 0]$, and the optimal strategy for Player II is $y^* = [0, 0.291, 0, 0.048, 0.661]$.

Other choice is to select a particular payoff. Suppose that players select a payoff, for instance $^{0.8}\tilde{A}^{L(-)}$. This selection leads to $z^* = 0.427$ whose set of memberships is $\bar{\mu}_{\tilde{Z}} = 0.8$ and $\underline{\mu}_{\tilde{Z}} \approx 0.9057$. Note that the value of $\bar{\mu}_{\tilde{Z}}$ is the solution of the game for $^{0.8}\tilde{A}^{R(-)}$, and the value $\underline{\mu}_{\tilde{Z}}$ is computed using the Type-reduction algorithm proposed by Figueroa [18], so the solution satisfies both groups of players in the interval $\alpha \in [0.8, 0.9057]$.

7 Concluding Remarks

We have presented a method to solve games involving Type-2 fuzzy uncertainty, using the results presented by Li [6] combined with IT2FNs. It is possible to deal with this kind of uncertainty using well known algorithms, so its applicability to real scenarios is promissory.

The α-cuts approach is a map of the optimal solutions of the IT2FG, so as more complete the map of $\tilde{A}$ is, the more complete $\tilde{Z}$ is, giving more information to the analyst. Although there is no a single solution of the IT2FG, we provide a map of the possible strategies that players can take in different scenarios, which is important in decision making under uncertainty.

The use of natural language in optimization and decision making has opened a door to use hybrid methodologies such as the presented in this paper. Different approaches can be proposed to solve this kind of games, so our proposal is just a method for modeling and solving the game.

References

1. Nash, J.: Non cooperative games. Annals of Mathematics 54, 286–295 (1951)
2. Neumann, J.V., Morgenstern, O.: Theory of Games and Economic Behavior. Princeton University Press (1944)
3. Bector, C.R., Chandra, S.: Fuzzy Mathematical Programming and Fuzzy Matrix Games. Springer (2005)
4. Campos, L.: Fuzzy linear programming models to solve fuzzy matrix games. Fuzzy Sets and Systems 326(1), 275–289 (1989)
5. Delgado, M., Verdegay, J., Vila, M.: Playing Matrix Games Defined by Linguistic Labels. In: Multiperson Decision Making Models Using Fuzzy Sets and Possibility Theory, pp. 298–310. Springer (1990)
6. Li, D.F.: An effective methodology for solving matrix games with fuzzy payoffs. IEEE Transactions on Cybernetics 43(2), 610–621 (2013)
7. Butnariu, D.: Fuzzy games a description of the concept. Fuzzy Sets and Systems 1, 181–192 (1978)
8. Butnariu, D.: Solution concept for n-Person games. In: Advances in Fuzzy Set Theory and Application, vol. 1. North-Holland Publishing (1979)
9. Vijay, V., Chandra, S., Bector, C.: Bimatrix games with fuzzy payoffs and fuzzy goals. Fuzzy Optimization and Decision Making 3, 327–344 (2004)
10. Monroy, L., Hinojosa, M., Mármol, A., Fernandez, F.: Set-valued cooperative games with fuzzy payoffs. the fuzzy assignment game. European Journal of Operational Research 225(1), 85–90 (2013)
11. Cunlin, L., Qiang, Z.: Nash equilibrium strategy for fuzzy non-cooperative games. Fuzzy Sets and Systems 176(1), 46–55 (2011)
12. Larbani, M.: Non cooperative fuzzy games in normal form: A survey. Fuzzy Sets and Systems 160, 3184–3210 (2009)
13. Dantzig, G.: Linear Programming and Extensions. Princeton University Press (1963)
14. Mendel, J.M.: Uncertain Rule-Based Fuzzy Logic Systems: Introduction and New Directions. Prentice Hall (2001)
15. Mendel, J.M., John, R.I., Liu, F.: Interval type-2 fuzzy logic systems made simple. IEEE Transactions on Fuzzy Systems 14(6), 808–821 (2006)
16. Klir, G.J., Folger, T.A.: Fuzzy Sets, Uncertainty and Information. Prentice Hall (1992)
17. Klir, G.J., Yuan, B.: Fuzzy Sets and Fuzzy Logic: Theory and Applications. Prentice Hall (1995)
18. Figueroa-García, J.C.: An approximation method for type reduction of an interval Type-2 fuzzy set based on α-cuts. In: IEEE (ed.) Proceedings of FEDCSIS 2012, pp. 1–6. IEEE (2012)
19. Karnik, N.N., Mendel, J.M.: Centroid of a type-2 fuzzy set. Information Sciences 132(1), 195–220 (2001)
20. Duran, K., Bernal, H., Melgarejo, M.: Improved iterative algorithm for computing the generalized centroid of an interval type-2 fuzzy set. In: 2008 Annual Meeting of the IEEE North American Fuzzy Information Processing Society (NAFIPS) (2008)
21. Figueroa, J.C.: A general model for linear programming with interval type-2 fuzzy technological coefficients. In: 2012 Annual Meeting of the North American Fuzzy Information Processing Society (NAFIPS), pp. 1–6. IEEE (2012)
22. Figueroa-García, J.C., Hernandez, G.: Computing optimal solutions of a linear programming problem with interval type-2 fuzzy constraints. In: Corchado, E., Snášel, V., Abraham, A., Woźniak, M., Graña, M., Cho, S.-B. (eds.) HAIS 2012, Part III. LNCS, vol. 7208, pp. 567–576. Springer, Heidelberg (2012)
23. Figueroa-García, J.C., Hernández, G.: A transportation model with interval type-2 fuzzy demands and supplies. In: Huang, D.-S., Jiang, C., Bevilacqua, V., Figueroa, J.C. (eds.) ICIC 2012. LNCS, vol. 7389, pp. 610–617. Springer, Heidelberg (2012)
24. Hillier, F.S., Lieberman, G.J.: Introduction to Operations Research. McGraw-Hill Science (2012)

Joining Concept's Based Fuzzy Cognitive Map Model with Moving Window Technique for Time Series Modeling

Wladyslaw Homenda[1], Agnieszka Jastrzebska[1], and Witold Pedrycz[2,3]

[1] Faculty of Mathematics and Information Science, Warsaw University of Technology
ul. Koszykowa 75, 00-662 Warsaw, Poland
[2] Systems Research Institute, Polish Academy of Sciences,
ul. Newelska 6, 01-447 Warsaw, Poland
[3] Department of Electrical & Computer Engineering, University of Alberta,
Edmonton T6R 2G7 AB Canada
{homenda,A.Jastrzebska}@mini.pw.edu.pl, wpedrycz@ualberta.ca

Abstract. In the article we present a technique for time series modeling that joins concepts based Fuzzy Cognitive Map design with moving window approach. Proposed method first extracts concepts that generalize the underlying time series. Next, we form a map that consists of several layers representing consecutive time points. In each layer we place concepts obtained in the previous step. Fuzzified time series is passed to the map according to the moving window scheme. We investigate two most important aspects of this procedure: division into concepts and window size and their influence on model's accuracy. Firstly, we show that extraction of concepts plays a big role. Fitted models have low errors. Unfortunately, it is not always possible to extract appropriate number of concepts. The choice of the number of concepts is a compromise between model size and accuracy. Secondly, we show that increasing window size improves modeling accuracy.

1 Introduction

Time series modeling has been a vital area of research for many years now. Time series are basic stochastic processes, extremely important and common. Beside classical approaches, there are plenty alternative time series modeling methods, among which we find Fuzzy Cognitive Maps.

Fuzzy Cognitive Maps allow to process knowledge on an abstract, conceptual level, which is far more understandable and interpretable for human beings. Fuzzy Cognitive Maps are directed graphs-based models, where nodes are concepts that represent phenomena, for example high unemployment, high crime rate, low incomes, and weighted arcs represent relationships between concepts.

The major advantage of FCM-based models is their human-centered knowledge representation interface. Therefore, time series modeling with Fuzzy Congitive

K. Saeed and V. Snášel (Eds.): CISIM 2014, LNCS 8838, pp. 397–408, 2014.

Maps may not beat well-researched classical approaches in terms of accuracy, but FCMs offer superior practical features.

In this article authors continue presentation of their research on Fuzzy Cognitive Maps-based time series modeling. The basics of our methodology have been presented in [3]. Cited paper provides information about a simple moving window FCM-based model, but processed information is crisp, scaled to $[0, 1]$, no concepts are designed and discussed. The objective of this paper is to continue with a presentation of our model. We stress and discuss the conceptual representation of time series for the model. Concept's based time series representation is joined with moving window approach. Introduced methods and ideas are illustrated with a series of experiments on synthetic time series.

The remainder of this paper is organized as follows. Section 2 covers literature review. In Section 3 we discuss proposed approach to time series modeling and prediction. In Section 4 we present a series of experiments. Section 5 concludes the article.

2   Literature Review

Fuzzy Cognitive Maps (FCMs) are abstract, graph-based knowledge representation models introduced in 1986 by B. Kosko in [4]. Time series modeling is one of many successful applications' areas of FCMs.

There are two major streams in research on time series modeling with FCMs. First, has been initiated in 2008 by W. Stach, L. Kurgan and W. Pedrycz in [7]. Named authors decided to design FCM's nodes as concepts describing the character of the value of input signal $a(t)$ and its difference $\delta a(t)$.

Second approach is rooted in classification. Examples of research in these stream are: [2], [5], and [6]. On the input to classification-oriented time series modeling methods are multivariate time series. Each node corresponds to a different variable.

In this article are we propose an alternative, original approach to time series modeling.

3   Methods

Fuzzy Cognitive Maps offer a noteworthy time series processing framework. FCMs operate on abstract level of concepts that represent aggregates of knowledge, or in other words knowledge granules. Proposed modeling method translates a numerical problem (the input sequence of scalars - the time series) into concepts and generates all necessary elements to train a Fuzzy Cognitive Map. Information passed to FCM's input is processed and FCM responses with concept-based time series models or predictions.

In brief, the proposed method for time series modeling with Fuzzy Cognitive Maps can be divided into following phases:

1. FCM design.
2. FCM training.
3. FCM exploration (time series modeling and prediction).

In the following subsections we introduce step-by-step the proposed approach.

3.1 Fuzzy Cognitive Map Design – Extraction of Concepts

Time series modeling with Fuzzy Cognitive Maps requires an algorithmically aided translation method from numerical problem to abstract concepts.

The only exception from this rule is when a time series is reported in a form of concepts, not in a form of crisp values. This is very rare, because typically time series are collected with the use of crisp measurement systems and represented with, for example money units, distance units, velocity units, etc. Let us denote such crisp input scalar time series as a sequence of numbers: $a_0, a_1, \ldots, a_M$.

The first task then is to elevate a scalar time series to concepts, which will become nodes in the designed FCM.

At the beginning, model designer has to decide on the number of concepts that will generalize the underlying time series. Concepts may be represented with any granular knowledge representation scheme. In this article we use fuzzy sets. For even more human-centered design, each concept has a linguistic variable, which describes the information that it aggregates. Proposed concepts should represent values of the underlying experimental data (the time series). Therefore, examples of concepts are: Small values, Moderate values, etc. Concepts in this study are realized with fuzzy sets. Thus, time series data points will be represented with degrees of membership to the fuzzy sets of proposed concepts.

The number of concepts, let us denote it as u, defines the level of model's specificity. The more concepts we decide on, the more specific model we get. The fewer concepts we have, the more general model we get. The balance between specificity and generality affects accuracy. Model's accuracy is typically measured with discrepancies between actual, observed phenomena and modeled values. As an indicator for model's accuracy in this study we use Mean Squared Error, which is a very common statistics. More specific models have lower errors, than general models. The other aspect of specificity/generality conflict is the ease of interpretation. Models based on fewer concepts are less complex and therefore easier to interpret and to apply. In this light, in all experiments presented in this paper we use 3 concepts with following linguistic terms: Small, Moderate, High, abbreviated as S, M ad H respectively. We have chosen the value of 3, which is enough to clearly illustrate method's properties.

Ideally, the number of concepts should match the experimental data and be as small as possible at the same time. This topic is out of the scope of this paper, we are currently working on an algorithmic approach to a selection of appropriate number of concepts.

To facilitate an efficient extraction of concepts we apply well-known fuzzy c-means algorithm, [1]. On the input to fuzzy c-means we pass the scalar time series and the desired number of concepts-clusters. On the output of fuzzy c-means we receive proposed cluster's centers and degrees of membership of all time series points to the proposed clusters. By assumption, the levels of belongingness are evaluated as a number from the $[0, 1]$ interval, while cluster's centers are best found representatives of the underlying data set.

3.2   Fuzzy Cognitive Map Design – Moving Window Technique

In the subsequent step of Fuzzy Cognitive Map design it is necessary to collect all elements required for Fuzzy Cognitive Map training. The initial design, described in the previous subsection, resulted in a scratch of the FCM. Let us remind, that after the first steps of the method we have extracted u concepts that generalize the underlying time series. Concepts are realized with fuzzy sets, obtained with the use of fuzzy c-means. To calculate the level of membership for an a_i-th observation to j-th concept the standard Fuzzy C-Means objective function is used:

$$z_{ij} = \frac{1}{\sum_{k=1}^{u} \left(\frac{||a_i - v_j||}{||a_i - v_k||} \right)^{2/(m-1)}} \tag{1}$$

where u is the number of concepts, m is the fuzzification coefficient ($m > 1$) and $|| \cdot ||$ is the Euclidean distance function, a_i is i-th time series data point, v_j is j-th concept.

As a result, each i-th time series data point is now fuzzified into u concepts. We can denote elevated granular time series as: $\mathbf{a}_0, \mathbf{a}_1, \ldots, \mathbf{a}_M$, where $\mathbf{a}_i = [z_{i1}, z_{i2}, \ldots, z_{iu}]$, and u is the number of concepts.

At this point we join the discussed concept's extraction procedure with moving window-based time series representation.

The moving-window technique analyzes data points by creating a series of different subsets of the full data set. The idea of moving window is perhaps most commonly applied and acknowledged in moving averages method. Moving window method for time series representation creates different sequences of consecutive data points from the time series. There are two parameters for the moving window method for time series representation: window size and window step size. Window size is the number of data points in each window. Window step size is the tempo at which the window moves. Window step size is typically equal 1, and in this case if current sequence starts with i-th observation from the time series, then the next window starts with i+1-th, then i+2-th, and so on. If the window step size is equal p, then if current sequence starts with i-th observation from the time series, then the next window starts with i+p-th, then i+2·p-th, and so on. In the experiments in this paper we always assume window step size equals 1.

The most important parameter in this technique is window size. In the experiment's section of this article we investigate the relation between window size and FCM-based model's accuracy.

3.3   Fuzzy Cognitive Map Learning

Moving window representation joined with extracted concepts provide necessary data to train the FCM.

At this point, let us briefly introduce necessary formalisms for Fuzzy Cognitive Maps.

The crux of each Fuzzy Cognitive Map is its weights matrix $\mathbf{W}$, which size is $n \times n$. n is the number of nodes in the FCM. The weights matrix contains values of all connections between nodes in the map. A single weight is denoted as w_{ij}, and $w_{ij} \in [-1, 1]$ with exception for elements above r-diagonal, which are set to 0. Weights that are fixed to 0 represent relationships from future to past. This is conceptually impossible, hence we set them to 0. We will elaborate on this topic later in this subsection.

FCM learning is based on activations $\mathbf{X}$ and goals $\mathbf{G}$. Goals are actual, reported states of phenomena. FCM responses are denoted as $\mathbf{Y}$. Map responses model phenomena, hence they should be as close to goals as possible. Activations', responses' and goals' matrices size is $n \times N$, where N is the number of training observations. Single activation is denoted as x_{ji}, single map response is denoted as y_{ij}, and single goal is denoted as g_{ij}, they all are real numbers from the $[0, 1]$ interval.

FCM exploration is performed according to the formula:

$$\mathbf{Y} = f(\mathbf{W} \cdot \mathbf{X}) \tag{2}$$

where f is a sigmoid transformation function:

$$f(t) = \frac{1}{1 + exp(-\tau t)} \tag{3}$$

The value of parameter τ was set to 5 based on literature review.

The shape of weights matrix $\mathbf{W}$ is obtained by a learning procedure. The goal is to adjust weights' matrix so that differences between FCM responses $\mathbf{Y}$ and goals $\mathbf{G}$ are the smallest. Typically in the literature, and also in our experiments, we minimize the Mean Squared Error:

$$MSE = \frac{1}{n \cdot N} \cdot \sum_{j=1}^{N} \sum_{i=1}^{n} (y_{ij} - g_{ij})^2 \tag{4}$$

In our experiments we select first 70% of data points for FCM training. We call this dataset 'train'. Consecutive 30% data points are for one-step-ahead predictions only. We call this dataset 'test'. Test dataset is not involved in FCM training and thus it is used to confirm quality of models proposed by our FCMs.

Moving window representation of fuzzified time series becomes activations and goals. Observations falling to an i-th window become i-th activations vector: $\mathbf{x}_i = [\mathbf{a}_{i+1}, \mathbf{a}_{i+2}, \ldots, \mathbf{a}_{i+r}]$, where r is window size. Goals are activations shifted one observation forward: $\mathbf{g}_i = [\mathbf{a}_{i+2}, \mathbf{a}_{i+3}, \ldots, \mathbf{a}_{i+r+1}]$. The actual number of elements in such vectors is $u \cdot r$. In our experiments it is then $3 \cdot r$.

Nodes in FCM correspond to consecutive concepts that fall to window of size $u \cdot r$. The number of nodes $n = u \cdot r$; $u = 3$, so:

- first triple of nodes corresponds to i-th crisp observation,
- second triple of nodes corresponds to i+1-th crisp observation,
- ...
- last triple of nodes corresponds to i+r-th crisp observation.

Note, that the triples of nodes are ordered and they represent consecutive time points. One may visualize it as layers.

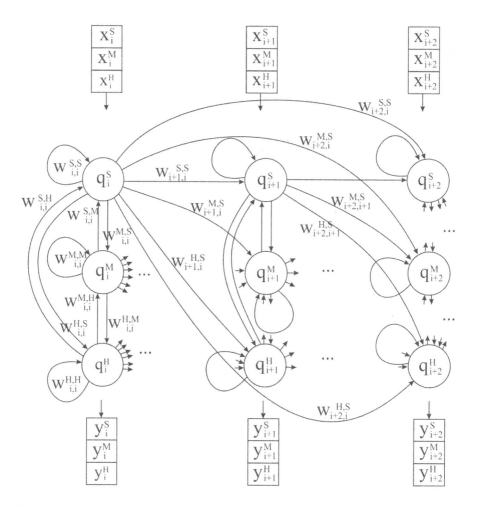

Fig. 1. Generic schema of FCM with window size $r = 3$, division for $u = 3$ concepts for time series modeling

Figure 1 illustrates the discussed scheme for window of size $r = 3$ and $u = 3$. FCM is a collection of nodes, denoted as $q_i^S, q_i^M, q_i^H, \ldots, q_{i+2}^S, q_{i+2}^M, q_{i+2}^H$. Notice, nodes form layers, each with 3 concepts. S, M, H abbreviate concepts' names.

First triple of nodes in Figure 1 corresponds to i-th time point, second triple to i+1-th time point, etc.

To improve readability we have not drawn all weights. Missing connections are represented with short arrows. Arrows are directed towards respective modes. Activations (x) and map responses (y) are symbolically in boxes.

There are no connections from future to past. Hence, weights matrix is a block lower triangular matrix. Block lower triangular matrix is a combination of lower triangular matrix with r-diagonal matrix. For example if window size $r = 3$, then lower block triangular matrix is a combination of lower triangular matrix and a tridiagonal matrix. Such special block matrix visually forms steps. Steps' height is 1, steps' width is u.

FCM training can be conveniently preformed with a search metaheuristics, such as PSO. In experiments presented in this article we use PSO implementation from R package 'pso' with all default parameters listed under: [8]. After we have learned the FCM's weights matrix we can use it to model time series.

3.4   Illustration on an Example of a Synthetic Time Series

Let us illustrate the described procedure on an example of a synthetic time series. The time series was constructed by replicating a sequence 2, 5, 8, 8, 5, 2 500 times, what gave total 3000 observations. We have distorted the sequence with a random value drawn from normal distribution with mean equals 0 and standard deviation 0.7. The time series has a period equals 6 and no trends. Left plot in Figure 2 illustrates first 200 observations from this synthetic time series.

With the use of fuzzy c-means we extract 3 concepts to represent the underlying data set. Concepts' centers are in: 1.91, 5.01, and 8.04. Right plot of Figure 2 illustrates extracted concepts with first 200 data points of the synthetic time series in the background.

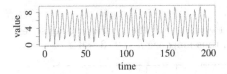 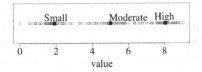

Fig. 2. Synthetic time series based on sequence 2, 5, 8, 8,5, 2. Left: first 200 data points in 2-dimens. space of time and values. Right: first 200 data points in 1-dimens. plot with extracted 3 concepts representing Small, Moderate and High values.

For the illustration let us assume window size $r = 2$. $u = 3$, so the number of nodes in the map is $n = 2 \cdot 3$. Figure 3 illustrates learned FCM. We have removed all weights weaker than 0.3 to improve visibility. Removing weak weights from the map may allow to simplify generated model, reduce dimensionality and improve

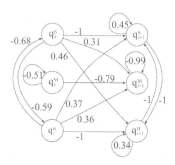

Fig. 3. Trained FCM with $n = 6$ nodes for the $(2, 5, 8, 8, 5, 2)$ synthetic time series

readability. By analogy to the removal of weights we can remove nodes that weakly influence other nodes. An example of the weakest node in FCM from Figure 3 is node denoted as q_{i+1}^S, which sum of absolute values of outgoing weights is 0.45.

Table 1 gathers activations and goals for this FCM. It is easy to notice that goals are activations shifted forward by 1. Also, each activation and goal is a collection of r triples of membership values to concepts described as Small, Moderate, and High.

The outcomes of modeling and predictions for this time series, among others, are discussed in the next section.

4 Experiments

In this Section we present a series of experiments on several synthetic time series.

The considered time series were built on three sets of numbers of cardinality 3 and 5: $\{2, 5, 8\}$, $\{2, 6, 8\}$, and $\{1, 3, 5, 7, 9\}$. Cardinalities correspond to the number of real concepts, that have a support in the underlying data. The length

Table 1. The matrices of activations $\mathbf{x}_i$ and goals $\mathbf{g}_i$ for the synthetic time series, window size $r = 2$, number of concepts $u = 3$, thus map size $n = 2 \cdot 3 = 6$

$\mathbf{x}_1$	$\mathbf{x}_2$	$\mathbf{x}_3$	...	$\mathbf{x}_{N-1}$	$\mathbf{x}_N$	$\mathbf{g}_1$	$\mathbf{g}_2$	$\mathbf{g}_3$	...	$\mathbf{g}_{N-1}$	$\mathbf{g}_N$
0.78	0.04	0.00	...	0.00	0.00	0.04	0.00	0.00	...	0.00	0.01
0.03	0.10	0.98	...	0.98	0.98	0.10	0.98	0.98	...	0.98	0.01
0.19	0.87	0.02	...	0.01	0.02	0.87	0.02	0.02	...	0.02	0.99
0.04	0.00	0.00	...	0.00	0.01	0.00	0.00	0.00	...	0.01	0.88
0.10	0.98	0.97	...	0.98	0.01	0.98	0.97	0.97	...	0.01	0.03
0.87	0.02	0.02	...	0.02	0.99	0.02	0.02	0.02	...	0.99	0.09

Table 2. Summary of synthetic time series constructions

time series	period	number of concepts
268	3	3
258852	6	3
258582	6	3
225825558822885	15	3
268682826286286	15	3
15739	5	5
1573993751	10	5
1573971593	10	5
153791377195395	15	5
157393975117359	15	5

of each generated dataset was 3000. Datasets were distorted by adding to the original sequence random values drawn from the normal probability distribution with mean equals 0 and standard deviation equals 0.7. Synthetic time series have different periods. Summary of properties of generated time series is in Table 2.

Objective of the experiment's section is to investigate properties of the proposed time series modeling technique. We take closer look at the following issues:

- relation between window size (r) and accuracy,
- influence of appropriate selection of the number of concepts (u) on accuracy.

For each artificial time series we have built 9 FCMs for various values of window size: $r = 1, 2, \ldots 9$. In each case the number of concepts was $u = 3$. Thus, the sizes of tested maps were $n = 3, 6, \ldots, 27$ respectively.

With such selection of different time series we were able to investigate quality of built models. For each FCM we have repeated the procedure 3 times to verify if the model was stable. To compare the results we use Mean Squared Error both on train and test data sets.

Figure 4 presents an overview of the results. Plots illustrate MSE on train and test data sets for synthetic time series from Table 2. Left column is for time series based on three elements: $\{2, 5, 8\}$ and $\{2, 6, 8\}$. Right column of Figure 4 is for synthetic time series based on 5 digits: $\{1, 3, 5, 7, 9\}$.

Figure 4 confirms that the proposed scheme's performance largely depends on characteristics of time series and on the window size. Note, that MSE for test does not differ much from MSE on train data set.

If the division into concepts directly fits time series, results are most accurate. For example, time series constructed on (2,6,8) sequence is exactly matching the division into $u = 3$ concepts. In this case both period is equal 3, and the number

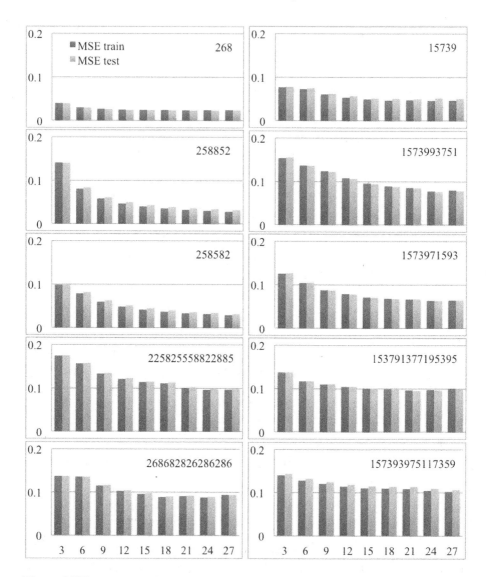

Fig. 4. MSE on train and test data for map sizes $n = 3, 6, \ldots, 27$ (OX axis). FCMs were constructed for $u = 3$ concepts and window sizes $r = 1, 2, \ldots, 9$. In the top right corner of each plot there is a base sequence of the corresponding synthetic time series.

of real concepts is equal 3. This is the time series that fits the most to our experiment scheme and we expect that in this case the results are the best. Indeed, in this case MSE on train and test are the smallest - in top left corner of Figure 4 bars are the lowest.

Other time series are less fitted to the division into $u = 3$ concepts. Therefore, errors are higher. Time series synthesized based on (2,5,8,8,5,2) and (2,5,8,5,8,2) sequences are in partial accordance with division into $u = 3$ concepts. These are second and third plots in left column of Figure 4. In these cases period is 6 and the number of real concepts is 3. Observe, that errors are higher than for the perfect fit of a time series based on (2,6,8), but smaller than in other cases. In contrast, fourth and fifth plots in left column of Figure 4 are for time series based on 3 real concepts and period equals 15. Here the error is higher, than for the cases above.

Similarly, in the right column of Figure 4 one can observe, that the number of clusters that we split data into is important. For a fixed number of concepts, the more complex time series we discuss, the higher the MSE. Experiments prove, that results are the worst for time series that are the furthest from perfect fit.

Second objective of the conducted experiments was to investigate the influence of window size. It turned out that the larger the window size, the smaller the MSE. The decrease of MSE is not linear though. Observe, in all plots that there is an inflection point, which we can indicate by calculating the tempo of model's improvement. This is why we do not need to aim at the highest possible window size, but we shall accommodate at a value that provides us with a reasonable map size and accuracy. The larger the window size, the bigger the map. Big models are inconvenient to train, to visualize and to interpret. Hence, depending on application one may decide, for example, to set window size to $r = 4$, what in almost all cases in Figure 4 is a convenient balance between size of the map and accuracy.

The second conclusion is that the improvement in modeling accuracy gained by increasing the window size depends on the character of the time series. For models with concepts fitted to the time series, like in the case of the (2,6,8)-based time series, increasing the window size moderately influences accuracy. MSE drops when we increase the window size, but the change is smaller than for time series that do not fit the model this well. In the case of (2,6,8)-based time series the best model (accurate and simple) is for window size $r = 2$. Unfortunately, it is very unlikely that in real-world time series we would be able to propose concepts that match the time series this well. Real-world data is not as regular as synthetic ones. Therefore, increasing window size is a valid approach to improve accuracy of proposed model.

5   Conclusion

Proposed time series modeling approach is based on Fuzzy Cognitive Maps that represent concepts arranged in r consecutive time points. One may perceive such structure as layers of concepts. In each layer we have u concepts that generalize values of the underlying data set. Proposed modeling scheme provides a clear, structured concept-based model for time series.

We have investigated two major parameters of the proposed method: the number of concepts and the number of layers. We have shown that both elements largely influence the MSE between model and actual values. We have shown that in general, when we increase window size, we improve accuracy. Second, we have shown, that if proposed division into concepts match the real time series characteristics, we get better results. The biggest indifference to the increase of the window size is for models that fit the data to the greatest extent. Unfortunately, typically real-world data is not as regular as synthetic data sets. This is why we have conducted meticulous study on the influence of window sizes on MSE for several synthetic data sets with the number of concepts that not exactly match time series. Experiments show that there is an inflection point, after which increasing window size does not influence the MSE this much.

In future research we will focus on finding an algorithmic approach to determine the best set of concepts to generalize the underlying dataset.

Acknowledgment. The research is partially supported by the Foundation for Polish Science under International PhD Projects in Intelligent Computing. Project financed from The European Union within the Innovative Economy Operational Programme (2007- 2013) and European Regional Development Fund.

The research is partially supported by the National Science Center, grant No 2011/01/B/ST6/06478.

References

1. Bezdek, J.C.: Pattern Recognition with Fuzzy Objective Function Algorithms. Plenum Press, New York (1981)
2. Froelich, W., Papageorgiou, E.I.: Extended Evolutionary Learning of Fuzzy Cognitive Maps for the Prediction of Multivariate Time-Series. In: Fuzzy Cognitive Maps for Applied Sciences and Engineering, pp. 121–131 (2014)
3. Homenda, W., Jastrzebska, A., Pedrycz, W.: Modeling Time Series with Fuzzy Cognitive Maps. In: Proc. of WCCI 2014 (in press, 2014)
4. Kosko, B.: Fuzzy cognitive maps. International Journal of Man-Machine Studies 7, 65–75 (1986)
5. Lu, W., Yang, J., Liu, X.: The Linguistic Forecasting of Time Series based on Fuzzy Cognitive Maps. In: Proc. of IFSA/NAFIPS, pp. 649–654 (2013)
6. Song, H.J., Miao, C.Y., Wuyts, R., Shen, Z.Q., D'Hondt, M.: An Extension to Fuzzy Cognitive Maps for Classification and Prediction. IEEE Transactions on Fuzzy Systems 19(1), 116–135 (2011)
7. Stach, W., Kurgan, L., Pedrycz, W.: Numerical and Linguistic Prediction of Time Series. IEEE Transactions on Fuzzy Systems 16(1), 61–72 (2008)
8. http://cran.r-project.org/web/packages/pso/pso.pdf

Time Series Modeling with Fuzzy Cognitive Maps: Simplification Strategies
The Case of a Posteriori Removal of Nodes and Weights

Wladyslaw Homenda[1], Agnieszka Jastrzebska[1], and Witold Pedrycz[2,3]

[1] Faculty of Mathematics and Information Science, Warsaw University of Technology
ul. Koszykowa 75, 00-662 Warsaw, Poland
[2] Systems Research Institute, Polish Academy of Sciences,
ul. Newelska 6, 01-447 Warsaw, Poland
[3] Department of Electrical & Computer Engineering, University of Alberta,
Edmonton T6R 2G7 AB Canada
{homenda,A.Jastrzebska}@mini.pw.edu.pl,
wpedrycz@ualberta.ca

Abstract. The article is focused on the issue of complexity of Fuzzy Cognitive Maps designed to model time series. Large Fuzzy Cognitive Maps are impractical to use. Since Fuzzy Cognitive Maps are graph-based models, when we increase the number of nodes, the number of connections grows quadratically. Therefore, we posed a question how to simplify trained FCM without substantial loss in map's quality. We proposed evaluation of nodes' and weights' relevance based on their influence in the map. The article presents the method first on synthetic time series of different complexity, next on several real-world time series. We illustrate how simplification procedure influences MSE. It turned out that with just a small increase of MSE we can remove up to $\frac{1}{3}$ of nodes and up to $\frac{1}{6}$ of weights for real-world time series. For regular data sets, like the synthetic time series, FCM-based models can be simplified even more.

1 Introduction

Fuzzy Cognitive Maps offer compelling modeling environment of phenomena and relations between phenomena.

Since their definition in 1986, Fuzzy Cognitive Maps have been applied to systems' modeling, to classification and prediction tasks, and also to time series modeling. Our recent research efforts are in the latter direction. During studies and experiments in this area we have faced a vital obstacle: complexity and dimensionality of modeled problems. The size of a model based on Fuzzy Cognitive Map is rapidly growing as we add new nodes. This is because each new node in the map requires taking into account all new connections from it to other nodes and from all other nodes to new node. Complexity is an undesirable feature of Fuzzy Cognitive Maps. Large maps are very difficult to interpret and to use. Moreover, learning large maps consumes a lot of computational resources.

K. Saeed and V. Snášel (Eds.): CISIM 2014, LNCS 8838, pp. 409–420, 2014.
© IFIP International Federation for Information Processing 2014

Named inconveniences inclined us towards research on simplification strategies for Fuzzy Cognitive Maps trained to model time series. This topic is our
contribution to the area of Fuzzy Cognitive Maps applications and to our best
knowledge, it has not been addressed in any previous works in this field.
The objectives of this paper are:

- to discuss Fuzzy Cognitive Maps design process for time series modeling and
  prediction,
- to introduce Fuzzy Cognitive Maps a posteriori simplification strategies,
- to present experimental evaluation of the proposed methods.

The remainder of this article is organized as follows. Section 2 presents brief
literature study in the area of time series modeling with Fuzzy Cognitive Maps.
Section 3 discusses time series modeling framework. Section 4 introduces Fuzzy
Cognitive Map a posteriori simplification strategies. Section 6 concludes the
paper and indicates future research directions.

2   Literature Review

B. Kosko introduced Fuzzy Cognitive Maps (FCMs) in 1986 in [3]. Since then
FCMs have been intensively researched. Among successful FCM's applications'
area is not only but also time series modeling.

In 2008 in [8] W. Stach, L. Kurgan and W. Pedrycz proposed first widely
accepted technique for FCMs-based time series modeling. In brief, their methodology can be decomposed into the following steps: 1. Input fuzzification, 2. FCM
training, 3. Modeling/prediction, 4. Defuzzifcation. In this method FCM's nodes
represent aggregates that describe a pair of input value $a(t)$ and increment $\delta a(t)$.

There were several attempts to time series modeling similar to the methodology described by Stach et al., but all of them focused only on technical aspects
of the original procedure. For example, [5,6] considered the application of neural
networks to facilitate Fuzzy Cognitive Map training procedure.

Alternative approaches to FCM-based time series modeling are related to
classification. Published works in this stream of research include for example:
[1,2,4,7]. In this method FCM's nodes represent attributes of a multivariate
time series. Next, the discussed approach is transferable into a typical FCM-
based classification problem.

In this article we present FCM a posteriori simplification procedures for FCMs
trained to model and predict time series. The origins of FCM design approach
are in the methods fathered by Stach et al. There are several shared elements in
ours and the cited FCM design procedure, but there also are several important
dissimilarities that differentiate the two. Shared is the general idea, both approaches are based on fzzified data, both train FCMs and require deffuzification
at the end. The difference is that we represent the time series in an unprocessed
manner, while Stach et al. use time series amplitude and increments. Moreover,
the original method stops after the FCM is designed. In contrast, we continue
modeling process with a posteriori FCM simplification methods.

3   Time Series Modeling with Fuzzy Cognitive Maps

The proposed modeling framework is based on Fuzzy Cognitive Maps trained to model and forecast future values of scalar time series. Therefore, in this section we present a brief discussion on Fuzzy Cognitive Maps training and we shortly introduce the FCM design approach.

FCMs represent the knowledge with weighted directed graphs. Nodes correspond to phenomena. Labeled arcs join the nodes and inform about relationships between the phenomena. Arc from phenomenon A to phenomenon B with a negative weight informs that a decrease in A results in a decrease in B. Arc from phenomenon A to phenomenon B with a positive weight says that an increase in A results in an increase in B. Arc weighting 0 represents lack of relation.

Numerically Fuzzy Cognitive Map is represented with its weights' matrix $\mathbf{W}$, collecting individual weights, denoted as $w_{ij} \in [-1,1], i,j = 1,\ldots,n$. n is the number of nodes in the FCM. There are two strategies of obtaining weights' matrix. First, expert(s) can determine weights' matrix. Secondly, weights' matrix can be learned from available training data. In our time series modeling method the second strategy is employed: the shape of weights' matrix is determined with customized learning procedure.

FCM exploration is based on its weights' matrix and it occurs as follows:

- FCM receives i-th input activation: $\mathbf{x}_i = [x_{1i}, x_{2i}, \ldots, x_{ni}]$; $\mathbf{x}_{1i}$ is passed to node 1, $\mathbf{x}_{2i}$ is passed to node 2, $\ldots$, $\mathbf{x}_{ni}$ is passed to n-th node,
- FCM processes input activation according to the following formula:

$$\mathbf{y} = f(\mathbf{W} \cdot \mathbf{x}) \tag{1}$$

where $\mathbf{y}_i = [y_{1i}, y_{2i}, \ldots, y_{ni}]$ denotes map responses, $\cdot$ is matrix product, f is a sigmoid transformation function with parameter τ:

$$f(t) = \frac{1}{1 + exp(-\tau t)} \tag{2}$$

In our experiments the value of τ was set to 5 based on literature review.

Map responses $\mathbf{y}_i$ are the states that we expect to observe in phenomena $1, 2, \ldots, n$ modeled by the map after the influence of an i-th activation. In Fuzzy Cognitive Maps activations and map responses are realized with fuzzy sets, so $x_{ik} \in [0,1]$ and $y_{ik} \in [0,1]$, $i = 1, \ldots, n$, $k = 1, \ldots, N$. In general, we are equipped with N activations and we expect to obtain N map responses. Then, the notation looks as follows:

- activations: $\mathbf{x} = [\mathbf{x}_1, \mathbf{x}_2, \ldots, \mathbf{x}_N]$,
- map responses: $\mathbf{y} = [\mathbf{y}_1, \mathbf{y}_2, \ldots, \mathbf{y}_N]$.

In the case of time series modeling and forecasting the k-th FCM response $(\mathbf{y}_k)$ codes the levels of phenomena predicted for the k-th time point. In order to learn weights' matrix $\mathbf{W}$ we conduct a training procedure. In general, it is realized in a following manner:

- initialize weights' matrix **W**, random initialization was applied,
- iteratively adjust weights' matrix so that the error between FCM responses **y** and goals **g** is the smallest.

Goals, denoted as **g**, are real, observed states of modeled phenomena. The learning procedure minimizes the expression:

$$error(\mathbf{y}, \mathbf{g}) \tag{3}$$

where error is a measure of difference between map responses **y** and observed states **g**. In our programs we use Mean Squared Error (MSE):

$$MSE = \frac{1}{n \cdot N} \cdot \sum_{j=1}^{N} \sum_{i=1}^{n} (y_{ij} - g_{ij})^2 \tag{4}$$

Training procedure stops when error is smaller than an ϵ threshold or after a fixed number of optimization algorithm's iterations has been exceeded. Weights' matrix adjustment can be performed, for example, with the use of search heuristics, such as Particle Swarm Optimization or Evolutionary Algorithms. In this study Particle Swarm optimization was arbitrarily chosen as a tool for solving an optimization problem. Our tests showed that other search methods give qualitatively similar results, what is sufficient for this study. Therefore, we do not discuss this topics in details.

We continue to use MSE for model quality evaluation throughout the article as well though we are aware that it is sensitive to occasional large error. Due to space limitations we do not elaborate on other error measures. Note, that this paper focuses on our method and we do not compare obtained results with other methods. In order to fully compare two different models in our future works we plan to extend the statistics to Mean Absolute Error (MAE) and Mean Absolute Percentage Error (MAPE).

In the proposed time series modeling method we distinguish following steps:

- data division into train/test. Input time series comprises of $a_0, a_1, \ldots, a_N$, $a_{N+1}, \ldots, a_M$ observations. It is divided into training dataset: $a_0, a_1, \ldots, a_N$ and testing dataset: $a_{N+1}, \ldots, a_M$. In our experiments we split data in proportions 70% for training and 30% for testing,
- model building phase. With training data we learn the weights' matrix **W**. In order to proceed to this phase we have to transform scalar time series so that the FCM, which is a model on a higher level of abstraction can process it,
- model tuning phase,
- FCM exploration. FCM responses corresponding to first $0, \ldots, N$ activations model time series. FCM responses for $N+1, \ldots, M$ activations are one-step-ahead forecasts for the time series.

Experiments presented in this article follow this convention. As for technical details, we aimed at comparability, so each experiment has been conducted in the same environment. FCM learning procedure has been written in R and it uses Particle Swarm Optimization "psoptim" function from "pso" package to minimize the Mean Squared Error between map responses and goals. All parameters are default, listed under: [9]. The number of algorithm repetitions was 1000 (also default).

Let us discuss how based on any scalar time series one can design a Fuzzy Cognitive Map on an example of two synthetic time series. The synthetic time series are used for illustrative purposes. First synthetic time series was constructed based on sequence (2,5,8,5,8,2) replicated 500 times, what gave 3000 data points. The second was constructed based on sequence (1,5,7,3,9,3,9,7,5,1,1,7,3,5,9) repeated 200 times, also total of 3000 data points. The original data points were subsequently distorted by adding random number from normal distribution with mean 0 and standard deviation 0.7. First synthetic time series is based on 3 numbers: $\{2, 5, 8\}$, second on 5 numbers: $\{1, 3, 5, 7, 9\}$. The shorter one has a period of 6 values, the longer of 15 values. Hence, the first time series can be considered as easier to learn, the second as harder.

Over the scalar time series we form concepts that aggregate the underlying data set. Formation of concepts is data-driven and aided with Fuzzy C-Means algorithm. We extract arbitrary number of $2, 3, \ldots, u$ cluster centers (k-th cluster center is denoted as v_k). Each cluster becomes a new concept. In this article we set $u = 3$ in each experiment. A posteriori simplification strategy behaves similarly for other architectures (for different u's) so we chose $u = 3$ as it is a good fit for clear illustration. It is worth to notice that other number of concepts still exhibit similar behavior with regard to properties outlined in this study. Of course, studying other properties requires more detailed discussion on valuing this parameter.

Extracted 1-dimensional concepts are described with linguistic variables. Examples of linguistic terms: Small, Moderate, Moderately High, High, etc. As an output of clustering procedure we obtain also membership values for time series data points: $a_0, a_1, \ldots, a_N$ to fuzzy concepts v_1, v_2, v_3.

In the example of the two synthesized time series Fuzzy C-Means extracted the following cluster centers:

- first time series: 1.95, 5.00, 8.06
- second time series: 1.56, 5.04, 8.52

To the concepts above we attach following linguistic interpretation: Small for 1.95 and 1.56, Moderate for 5.00 and 5.04, High for 8.06 and 8.52, abbreviated as S, M and H respectively. Because of properties of the two synthetic time series clustering into 3 concepts fits better to the first example, which is based on 3 numbers - the same as u. Clustering into 3 concepts is qualitatively in disagreement with character of the second synthetic time series based on 5 numbers. Figure 1 illustrates first 150 data points of the first (left plot) and of the second (right plot) time series and extracted 3 concepts with linguistic terms attached. Plots are drawn in 1-dimensional space of time series values. Determined concepts with their linguistic variables are marked with squares.

Fig. 1. First 150 data points of two synthetic time series with extracted concepts. Left: (2,5,8,5,8,2)-based time series. Right: (1,5,7,3,9,3,9,7,5,1,1,7,3,5,9)-based time series.

Subsequently, we move from 1-dimensional space of time series values $(a_0, a_1, a_2, \ldots, a_N)$ into 3-dimensional space of: current value, past value, and before past value. In such system each observation is characterized with 3 values representing its history. We can represent any time series in this manner as follows: $((a_2, a_1, a_0), (a_3, a_2, a_1), \ldots, (a_{N-2}, a_{N-1}, a_N))$. Interpretation of such triple is the following (current value, past value, before past value).

Next, 1-dimensional concepts are elevated to 3-dimensional concepts. Coordinates of new concepts' centers are determined by applying Cartesian product to the extracted values. Each new concept is characterized with 3 linguistic terms describing current, past and before past values. Examples of 3-dimensional concepts for the first synthetic time series are: (1.95, 1.95, 8.06), (1.95, 1.95, 5.00), (1.95, 5.00, 8.06). By analogy, concept with coordinates (1.95, 5.00, 8.06) is described linguistically as (Small, Moderate, High). 3-dimensional concepts form a sort of lattice points in the system of time series current values, past values and before past values. As a result we get u^3 3-dimensional concepts.

Figure 2 illustrates synthetic time series transformed to the 3-dimensional space of current, past and before past values. 3-dimensional concepts centers are marked with squares.

The synthetic time series form easily separable clouds of points. The first synthetic time series was distributed into 6 clouds, second into 15. Clouds for the second time series overlap more than in the first case. Several concepts proposed for the first time series match its character. Observe, that there is one concept falling to each cloud. There are some potentially redundant concepts as well. In contrast, concepts proposed for the second time series do not fit this well. We have used two distinct examples on purpose, to clearly illustrate the developed method. Broadly speaking the simplification procedure will take advantage from the fact that not all concepts and not all connections fit time series.

In order to relate each time series triple (current, past, before past) with the new fuzzy concepts we have to calculate level of membership for each such triple to the concepts. Membership value is at the same time the level of activation for a given triple. We compute level of activation for $\mathbf{a}_i$-th observation to j-th concept with the standard Fuzzy C-Means objective function:

$$\mathbf{x}_{ij} = \frac{1}{\sum_{k=1}^{n} \left(\frac{||\mathbf{a}_i - \mathbf{v}_j||}{|| \mathbf{a}_i - \mathbf{v}_k ||} \right)^{2/(m-1)}} \tag{5}$$

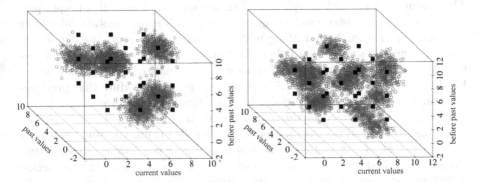

Fig. 2. Synthetic time series in 3-dimensional space of current, past and before past values with extracted 27 concepts (black squares). Left: (2,5,8,5,8,2)-based time series. Right: (1,5,7,3,9,3,9,7,5,1,1,7,3,5,9)-based time series.

m is the fuzzification coefficient ($m > 1$) and $|| \cdot ||$ is Euclidean norm. In the sequel, we arrange the all activations into $u^3 \times N$ matrix, where membership values are activations and goals are activations shifter forward by 1. The number of concepts is the number of nodes in the map.

To sum up, in this article we consider Fuzzy Cognitive Maps designed with a procedure discussed above. As a result we get a FCM with $n = 27$ nodes and 729 connections (weights).

4   Fuzzy Cognitive Maps a Posteriori Simplification Strategies

The key element of the research investigated in this paper are a posteriori FCM simplification methods. Scheme of the simplification procedure is the following:

- design and train a full FCM-based model.
- simplify the model.

Simplification occurs after we train the full map, this is why we call it a posteriori. In contrast, we can also simplify a FCM before we train it (a priori simplification). We have discussed this alternative method in our previous publications. The both strategies are not exclusive, they are complementary.

Why do we need to investigate FCM simplification strategies? Large models are difficult to understand and to use. Therefore, we agree that at the cost of accuracy we simplify models to make them more usable. In the case of a posteriori simplification we have to acknowledge that the more we simplify, the bigger the error, but for practical reasons we consider this as a reasonable trade-off. In order to simplify the map we can:

- remove weak nodes,
- prune weak weights.

The justification for such simplification strategies is that not all concepts proposed with the Cartesian product are supported with experimental evidence. It was shown in Figure 2, that along with potentially good concepts, the design procedure proposes also potentially redundant concepts. The proportions of useful/unfit concepts depends on the time series. Complexity of modeled data makes FCM design a challenging task. Therefore, the design procedure that produces an overflow of concepts can be tuned by simplification procedures.

Experiments presented in this paper are for time series models and predictions (one-step-ahead forecasts). Model data is called train, because it was used to train the FCM. Part of data for which we made predictions is called test. Proposed method was extensively tested on a series of synthetic time series, where we were able to investigate its properties. Next, we have applied it on several real-world time series. In this paper we present selection of results both on synthetic and real data.

4.1   FCM Simplification by Removing Weak Nodes

In order to determine the quality of nodes after FCM training procedure we evaluate how particular concepts/nodes interact with other concepts/nodes. In other words, we assesses how strongly nodes influence other nodes. Weak nodes are candidates for removal. The following index:

$$\sum_{j=1}^{N} |w_{ji}| \tag{6}$$

can be used to evaluate influence of i-th node on other nodes in the map. The stronger the node, the greater the sum of absolute values of it's outgoing weights.

We pose a question, how removing weak nodes affects model's accuracy. Figure 3 illustrates in detail how this simplification strategy influences MSE on the examples of two synthetic time series.

Figure 3 shows the MSE for model and for forecasts for the synthetic time series for increasing number # rej of rejected nodes. Removing weak nodes makes the MSE grow, but there is an inflection point, up to which the growth is very slow. For FCM architectures, which fit time series well we are able to detect and remove more redundant nodes. This is the case of time series based on 3 numbers divided into 3 concepts (top plot Figure 3), where we have reduced FCM size from 27 to 9 at relatively low cost. In this case for FCM with $n = 27$ MSE on train is 0.001. After simplification procedure by nodes removal for FCM with $n = 8$ we get MSE equal 0.009. At the same time reducing FCM dimensionality from 27 to 9 caused also elimination of weights from 729 down to 81. One can observe that such substantial simplification came at reasonable cost.

For time series models that do not fit this well the underlying data the improvement ranks are smaller, but still impressive. This is the case of the second synthetic time series, bottom plot Figure 3. In comparison, we were able to decrease FCM dimensionality from $n = 27$ with MSE equal 0.001 to $n = 11$ with MSE equal 0.009.

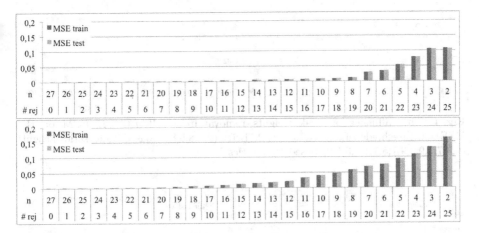

Fig. 3. MSE on time series model (train) and predictions (test) after a posteriori FCM simplification by removing #rej weak nodes. Top: (2,5,8,5,8,2)-based time series. Bottom: (1,5,7,3,9,3,9,7,5,1,1,7,3,5,9)-based time series.

4.2 FCM Simplification by Pruning Weights

Second approach to FCM simplification is based on evaluation of significance of weights in the trained FCM. The weaker is the absolute value of given weight, the less influence it has on the model. Hence, we can simplify the map by pruning such relations. A criterion here is the absolute strength of the weight. We set a threshold *thresh*, below which we consider the weight as insignificant and set its value to 0 indicating no relation.

Figure 4 shows how synthetic time series react to this simplification strategy. It illustrates change in MSE for increasing value of weights rejection threshold *thresh*. When we prune weights weaker than 0.5 the increase in MSE is not significant. Conclusion is as before. For well-fitted models we are able to reduce dimensionality more.

To conclude, the proposed technique of a posteriori FCM simplification allows reducing the complexity of the model at a reasonable cost in the form of the increase of the MSE. The better is FCM initial design, the more we can simplify it, but even not fortunate FCM designs have high capacity for simplification.

Figure 5 completes this topic it illustrates how many weights, measured as % share, we have removed for the thresholds *thresh* of 0, 0.1, ..., 0.9.

5 Experiments on Real-World Time Series

In this section we present a series of experiments on 6 real-world time series. Modeling and prediction quality is assessed with MSE on train (model) and test (prediction) data. Time series illustrated in this section were downloaded from [10,11]. The selection of time series was based on their character. We tested

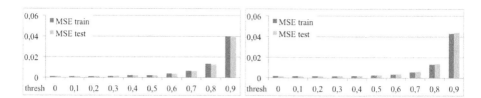

Fig. 4. The influence of weak weights removal from full $n = 27$ FCM on the MSE for thresholds of 0, 0.1, ..., 0.9. Left: (2,5,8,5,8,2)-based time series. Right: (1,5,7,3,9,3,9,7,5,1,1,7,3,5,9)-based time series.

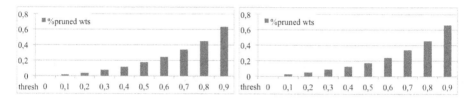

Fig. 5. Percentage of removed weights from full $n = 27$ FCM for thresholds of 0, 0.1, ..., 0.9. Left: (2,5,8,5,8,2)-based time series. Right: (1,5,7,3,9,3,9,7,5,1,1,7,3,5,9)-based time series.

different data sets, with various characteristics (seasonality, trends, length, etc.) Due to space limitations we do not elaborate more on selected time series.

Table 1 illustrates change in MSE for the 6 real-world time series models and predictions for a posteriori simplification procedure of weak nodes removal. Names of time series are the same as in the source repositories. Proposed procedure maintains the same properties for the synthetic and real data sets. We can remove over $\frac{1}{3}$ nodes with very little negative impact on the MSE.

The same observation concerns one-step-ahead predictions for the real-world time series, see lower part of Table 1. The more we simplify the map, the higher the error, but the increase has an inflection point. We can significantly improve time series model without a substantial decrease in its quality.

Table 2 illustrates the influence of a posteriori simplification by weights' pruning on MSE. In the experiment we have successively removed weights that were weaker than threshold $thresh = 0.2, 0.4, 0.6$. Table 2 illustrates the results for the 6 real-world time series. It was confirmed that weak weights can be removed without significant impact on map's quality. For real-world time series the simplification by removing weak weights does not allow to remove as many arcs as for very regular, synthetic data without a big increase in MSE. Nevertheless, maps can be simplified to some extent in this manner as well. We can drop around $\frac{1}{6}$ of weights without a substantial loss in FCM quality.

Table 1. 100·MSE on train (model) and test (one-step-ahead predictions) after removing a posteriori #rej weakest nodes

#rej	0	2	4	6	8	10	14	18	22
series	train								
Bicup2006	0.07	0.08	0.09	0.10	0.12	0.15	0.36	0.84	2.91
DailyIBM	0.01	0.02	0.02	0.02	0.05	0.08	0.43	0.85	2.86
Kobe	0.11	0.12	0.14	0.17	0.28	0.43	0.83	2.50	5.75
Nv515	0.26	0.29	0.35	0.44	0.71	0.92	1.75	4.87	9.28
Sunspots	0.09	0.10	0.11	0.13	0.15	0.20	0.78	2.35	9.27
Wave2	0.03	0.04	0.06	0.09	0.12	0.16	0.46	1.26	4.31
series	test								
Bicup2006	0.10	0.11	0.12	0.14	0.17	0.20	0.37	0.99	3.28
DailyIBM	0.01	0.02	0.02	0.03	0.07	0.12	0.58	1.22	4.04
Kobe	0.12	0.14	0.16	0.20	0.33	0.47	0.95	2.80	7.28
Nv515	0.25	0.28	0.34	0.45	0.73	0.96	1.72	4.75	9.22
Sunspots	0.11	0.12	0.13	0.15	0.18	0.23	0.98	2.56	9.97
Wave2	0.03	0.04	0.06	0.08	0.12	0.16	0.43	1.17	4.02

Table 2. 100·MSE for model (train) and predictions (test) and the number of pruned edges (#pr) for different weight's thresholds

threshold	0.2			0.4			0.6		
series	train	test	#pr	train	test	#pr	train	test	#pr
Bicup2006	0.08	0.11	36	0.08	0.11	78	0.31	0.35	149
DailyIBM	0.01	0.01	37	0.02	0.03	87	0.35	0.22	164
Kobe	0.11	0.12	28	0.15	0.14	72	0.19	0.20	167
Nv5150	0.26	0.25	52	0.29	0.27	111	0.52	0.48	217
Sunspots 0	0.09	0.11	38	0.10	0.12	81	0.26	0.26	156
Wave2	0.03	0.03	40	0.03	0.04	81	0.19	0.22	138

6   Conclusion

In this article we have investigated the issue of complexity and proposed simplification strategies in the context of the design method for time series modeling and prediction with Fuzzy Cognitive Maps.

Fuzzy Cognitive Map design procedure for time series modeling and prediction by assumption extracts an overflow of concepts. Having this in mind, we have proposed appropriate a posteriori FCM simplification strategies. Discussed methods evaluate nodes and weights by their influence in the map. Weak nodes and weights are candidates for removal. We have extensively tested this approach.

First, on very uniform and regular synthetic time series. Next, on several real-world time series. Experiments show that we can significantly simplify models with only a slight increase of Mean Squared Error.

In future research we will continue the research on time series modeling and prediction with Fuzzy Cognitive Maps. We plan to focus on interpretation of trained Fuzzy Cognitive Maps.

Acknowledgment. The research is partially supported by the Foundation for Polish Science under International PhD Projects in Intelligent Computing. Project financed from The European Union within the Innovative Economy Operational Programme (2007- 2013) and European Regional Development Fund.

The research is partially supported by the National Science Center, grant No 2011/01/B/ST6/06478.

References

1. Froelich, W., Papageorgiou, E.I.: Extended Evolutionary Learning of Fuzzy Cognitive Maps for the Prediction of Multivariate Time-Series. In: Fuzzy Cognitive Maps for Applied Sciences and Engineering, pp. 121–131 (2014)
2. Froelich, W., Papageorgiou, W.E.I., Samarinasc, M., Skriapasc, K.: Application of evolutionary fuzzy cognitive maps to the long-term prediction of prostate cancer. Applied Soft Computing 12, 3810–3817 (2012)
3. Kosko, B.: Fuzzy cognitive maps. International Journal of Man-Machine Studies 7, 65–75 (1986)
4. Lu, W., Yang, J., Liu, X.: The Linguistic Forecasting of Time Series based on Fuzzy Cognitive Maps. In: Proc. of IFSA/NAFIPS, pp. 649–654 (2013)
5. Song, H., Miao, C.Y., Shen, Z.Q., Roel, W., Maja, D.H., Francky, C.: Design of fuzzy cognitive maps using neural networks for predicting chaotic time series. Neural Networks 23(10), 1264–1275 (2010)
6. Song, H., Miao, C., Roel, W., Shen, Z.: Implementation of Fuzzy Cognitive Maps Based on Fuzzy Neural Network and Application in Prediction of Time Series. IEEE Transactions on Fuzzy Systems 18(2), 233–250 (2010)
7. Song, H.J., Miao, C.Y., Wuyts, R., Shen, Z.Q., D'Hondt, M.: An Extension to Fuzzy Cognitive Maps for Classification and Prediction. IEEE Transactions on Fuzzy Systems 19(1), 116–135 (2011)
8. Stach, W., Kurgan, L., Pedrycz, W.: Numerical and Linguistic Prediction of Time Series. IEEE Transactions on Fuzzy Systems 16(1), 61–72 (2008)
9. http://cran.r-project.org/web/packages/pso/pso.pdf
10. http://lib.stat.cmu.edu
11. http://robjhyndman.com/tsdldata

An Effective Initialization
for ASM-Based Methods

Hong-Quan Hua[1], T. Hoang Ngan Le[2], and Bac Le[1]

[1] Faculty of Information Technology, VNUHCM,
University of Science, Ho Chi Minh, Vietnam
[2] Department of Electrical and Computer Engineering (ECE),
Carnegie Mellon University, Pittsburgh, USA

Abstract. Locating facial feature points is an important step for many facial image analysis tasks. Over the past few years, Active Shape Model (ASM) has become one of the most popular approaches to solve this problem. However, ASM-based methods are sensitive to initialization errors caused by poor face detection results. In this paper, an effective initialization for the ASM-based methods is proposed by our improved initial 8-landmarks ASM model together with Viola-Jones eye detection. In particular, we apply the 8-landmarks ASM model with the position of eyes from eye detector as reference points. After that, we choose several 76-landmark candidates from the training set that have the key feature points related to the result of the previous 8-landmark model. The best candidate has the lowest fitting errors with the test image and is used as initialization. To evaluate the performance of our work, we conduct the experiments on the MUCT and LFPW database. Compared to the latest ASM implementation, MASM, our proposed can improved the MASM by an average accuracy of 44% when dealing with poor initialization.

Keywords: Active Shape Models, Facial feature points, Initialization errors.

1 Introduction

Facial feature points play an important role for face analysis in many computer vision systems such as human-machine interface, face recognition and expression analysis. For this reason, the problem of facial feature points localization has attracted large amount of attention. As shown in the recent research by Chen, et al.'s [2], leading performance in face verification can be acquired with simple features if facial feature points are detected accurately; therefore the problem of feature localization has become significant and attracted in the past years. Many approaches to extract facial feature points has been studied extensively including the active contour [10], deformable template [19], Active Shape Model [5], Active Appearance Models [4]. Most of above methods combine the local texture around each point and the shape of the whole face. ASM is known as one of the most popular methods that finds the landmarking points by Principle Component Analysis (PCA).

K. Saeed and V. Snášel (Eds.): CISIM 2014, LNCS 8838, pp. 421–432, 2014.

Active Shape Models (ASM) [5] proposed by Cootes, et al. has achieved great success in extracting facial feature points. In ASM, the feature points are modeled by the gray-scale texture whereas the geometrical information is defined by PCA. In order to implement a ASM system, a face detection is first used to find face regions and initialize a starting shape, then ASM is used to refine feature positions to the best locations based on the learned texture model. ASM is like deformable methods like snakes [10], but ASM's feature points are constrained to be a valid shape by the learned statistical shape model. Though many methods have been proposed to improve the fitting accuracy of ASMs [7],[13], [9], facial feature points localization remains a very challenging problem. The challenge comes from the variations of facial appearance in illumination, pose, expression, aging and so on. Especially, ASM methods are very sensitive to the initialization perturbations (translation, rotation and scaling in size) caused by the poor face detection [16]. To overcome these defects, Cootes et al. [3] propoesd a multi-resolution method, Wang et al. [18] added edge information into the model. Milborrow and Nicolls [12] achieved fairly accurate fitting results by combining 1D and 2D search model in the multi-resolution approach. Seshadri and Savvides [15] proposed a new robust method, called Modified Active Shape Model (MASM). MASM contains many theoretical changes to the traditional ASM and gains better results than above methods. However, MASM is still sensitive to initialization errors, especially while dealing with in-plane rotations and scaling effects. This is because the faces used to train the methods were upright and the initialization is too far from the optimal positions.

In our work, we focus on a new method to overcome the poor initialization. We select the initialization based on trained shapes instead of using mean shape as starting shape. Our selection process takes advantage of eye detector, support vector machine. Our selected feature points are almost in the optimal positions, which can prevent problems due to local minima. We also inherit the optimization metric of MASM [15] to determine the best location for each feature point. However, we weaken the important of edge information while fitting the facial boundary.

The remainder of this paper is organized as follows. In Section 2, the basic of Active Shape Model and improvements in Modified Active Shape Model are introduced. Our proposed method is described in Section 3. Experimental results are given in Section 4. A conclusion and future work are drawn in Section 5.

2   Related Works

This section gives an overview of Active Shape Models and the latest ASM-based methods called MASM. First, we explain the basic of training and testing stage in ASM method. Then, we show improvements of MASM to the basic ASM model since we use it as our main ASM-based method.

2.1   Active Shape Model

The following gives a brief review of the original ASM containing two main procedures: Training Stage and Testing Stage.

Training Stage. Shape Model and Local Appearance Model are built from a training set of manually annotated images. The Local Appearance Model is used to optimize the location for each landmark. On the other hand, the Shape Model constrains the landmark points to be in a valid shape.

The Shape Model: A *landmark* represents a distinguishable feature point in facial images. Locating landmarks is the same as locating feature points. Each face shape can be described by the coordinates of N landmarks points. The landmark points are (manually) annotated by a set of K training images. In our experiment, we use MUCT face database [11] which contains a total of 3755 faces with 76 manual landmarks at the resolution of 640 x 480 pixels. Figure 1 shows some example images of MUCT database.

Fig. 1. Example images from MUCT database. The green dots indicate the manually labeled landmark points.

The coordinates of each landmarks for each image are stacked as a shape vector **x**.

$$\mathbf{x} = [x_1 \ x_2...x_N \ \ y_1 \ y_2...y_N]^T \tag{1}$$

where x_i and y_i are the x and y coordinates of the ith landmark and N is the number of landmarks used.

The training images shape are all aligned by using Generalized Procrustes Analysis (GPA) [8] for minimizing the sum of squared distances between corresponding landmark points. PCA is then applied to reduce the dimensionality of the shape vectors, such that any shape **x** can be approximated as follows.

$$\mathbf{x} \approx \bar{\mathbf{x}} + \mathbf{Pb} \tag{2}$$

Here $\bar{\mathbf{x}}$ is a mean shape vector, **P** is a matrix of eigenvectors and $\mathbf{b} = (b_1 \ b_2...b_t)^T$ is a vector of shape parameters. When fitting the shape model to a face, the value of b_i is constrained to lie with the range ± 3 standard deviations to ensure that generated face shapes are valid.

The Local Appearance Model: The statistical models of appearance models (grayscale pixel intensities) of local regions around each landmark is used to optimize the location for each landmark in the search process. The 1D profiles are constructed by sampling the pixel intensities along a line, which is perpendicular to the landmark contour and centered at that landmark. The length of this line is $2k + 1$ with k pixels sampled on either side of the landmark. The normalized derivative of this vector is computed to form the profile vector, $\mathbf{g}$. The mean of such profiles (over the training images) at each landmark is called the mean profile vector, $\bar{\mathbf{g}}$ and the covariance matrix of such vectors is $\mathbf{S_g}$. To improve the accuracy and robustness, the process is repeated in a multi-resolution framework. The pyramid image contains L_{max} levels, where image at level i is formed by smoothing the image at level $i - 1$ and scaling by 50 percent. The fitting process is carried out at the coarse level first, then the results is refined in the finer level.

To compare the difference between a new sampled profile and the mean profile, we use the Mahalanobis distance measure as follows:

$$f(\mathbf{g_i}) = (\mathbf{g_i} - \bar{\mathbf{g}})^T \mathbf{S_g}^{-1} (\mathbf{g_i} - \bar{\mathbf{g}}) \tag{3}$$

By minimizing $f(\mathbf{g_i})$, we can get the optimal position for the landmark.

At each landmark position, a 2D profile is constructed by sampling a local patch around the landmark. The center of this local patch is the current landmark. The 2D local patch is then vectorized and normalized into vector $\mathbf{g}'$ using a constant parameter c at each element of the profile, g_i as shown in (4).

$$g_i' = \frac{g_i}{g_i + c} \tag{4}$$

where g_i' is the ith element of the vector $\mathbf{g}'$

Testing Stage. The search process of ASM can be implemented two iterative steps: (1) update the best location for each landmark point, (2) update the shape parameter b to ensure a valid shape. In the first step, we need to sample m pixels on both side of each landmark $(m > k)$. We then compute the Mahalanobis distance as above for each sub-profile with the length of k. The sub-profile with the minimum distance is chosen and the the center of that sub-profile is the update position for the current landmark. Once all landmarks have been moved to the best position, we obtain the new shape vector $\mathbf{x_{ini}}$ by using the shape model. The parameter vector $\mathbf{b}$ is calculated by minimizing the cost function in (5)

$$|\mathbf{x_{ini}} - T(\bar{\mathbf{x}} + \mathbf{Pb})|^2 \tag{5}$$

In (5), b is the vector of shape parameter, T is the similarity transform that minimizes the Euclidean distance between $\mathbf{x_{ini}}$ and $\bar{\mathbf{x}} + \mathbf{Pb}$. The detail of the process to find b and T can be found in [6].

The adjusting process is repeated until no significant change in the landmark points in observed. Once convergence is reached at the lowest resolution level, the landmark coordinates is scaled and the entire process is repeated in lower level until convergence at the finest level. Figure 2 gives overview of ASM steps at testing stage.

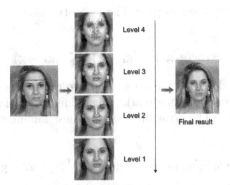

Fig. 2. Overview of ASM steps at testing stage. The blue box is the result of face detector. Red dots indicate the starting shape for each step and Green dots indicate the landmark result.

2.2 Modified Active Shape Model

In this section, we describe the Modified Active Shape Model (MASM) proposed by Keshav Seshadri and Marios Savvides [15]. This approach gives significant improvements to the traditional ASM. MASM can handles faces with slight pose variations, in-plane rotations and varied expressions.

Firstly, MASM uses an optimal number of landmark points to represent face shapes. The landmarking scheme used in MASM contains 79 points which can perform accurately and model varied facial expressions. Secondly, edge detection is used to better fit points around the facial boundary. The main contribution of MASM is the development of new metric to determine the best location of the landmarks compared to the minimum Mahalanobis distance in traditional method.

MASM metric can be described as follows. MASM extracts 2D profiles and builds a subspace to model the pixel variation in the local patch around each landmark. They obtains the mean profile vector for each landmark and computes the eigenvectors of the covariance matrix $\mathbf{S_g}$ corresponding to the dominant eigenvalues that models 97% of variation. Eigenvectors are stored along the columns of matrix $\mathbf{P_g}$. In the testing stage, a profile $\mathbf{g}$ around a candidate landmark is projected onto the subspace using equation (6) to obtain the shape parameter vector $\mathbf{b_g}$ and is then reconstructed using this parameter vector to obtain $\mathbf{g_r}$ using equation (7).

$$\mathbf{b_g} = \mathbf{P_g}^T(\mathbf{g} - \bar{\mathbf{g}}) \tag{6}$$

$$\mathbf{g_r} = \bar{\mathbf{g}} + \mathbf{P_g}\mathbf{b_g} \tag{7}$$

The metric for determining the best candidate point is the Mahalanobis distance between the original profile $\mathbf{g}$ and the reconstructed profile $\mathbf{g_r}$. The candidate with lowest reconstruction error is the best fit because it is the one that can be best modeled by the subspace. The reconstruction error can be computed as in equation (8).

$$error(\mathbf{g}, \mathbf{g_r}) = (\mathbf{g_r} - \mathbf{g})^{\mathbf{T}} \mathbf{S_g}^{-1} (\mathbf{g_r} - \mathbf{g}) \tag{8}$$

MASM also use edge information to improve the fitting accuracy for facial boundary. They assume that landmark points along the facial boundary usually lie along strong edges. The error function for these landmark is now defined in equation (9).

$$error(\mathbf{g}, \mathbf{g_r}) = (c - I)(\mathbf{g_r} - \mathbf{g})^{\mathbf{T}} \mathbf{S_g}^{-1} (\mathbf{g_r} - \mathbf{g}) \tag{9}$$

where c is a constant, chosen to be 2 in MASM implementation and I is the Sobel edge intensity at the candidate point which can only take on the values 1 or 0.

These modifications allow MASM to gain a significant improvement over the traditional ASM model.

3   Our Proposed Method

In this section, we introduce our proposed method for choosing initialization. In our method, each landmark is lie in an optimal location even when slightly expression and initialization errors are present. Moreover, we also introduce a modification to the cost function of MASM to improve the fitness of facial boundary. Figure 3 shows the comparison of initialization between our proposed method and MASM.

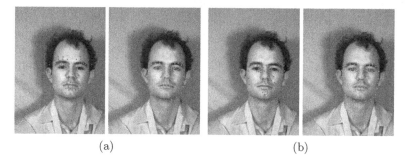

(a)   (b)

Fig. 3. Initialization of MASM and our proposed method without initialization errors a) and with initialization errors b). The Red dots indicate the initialization of MASM. The Green dots indicate the initialization of our proposed method.

3.1   New Method for Choosing Initialization

Most of previous ASM methods can not recover from poor initialization. The initialization is usually provided by the bounding box around the face which is the result of face detector. However, face detection algorithms such as Viola-Jones face detector [17] have no guarantees that the localization is perfect. There are many errors in translation and size. Especially, the bounding box from face detector is usually upright so the localization is poor when dealing with in-plane rotation of a face.

To overcome this problem, we propose a new method to reduce the sensitivity of ASM model to poor initialization. In our method, we use the location of eyes, nose and mouth to find 20 shape candidates from the training test that have the geometrical structure similar with the testing image. After that, we will use the local appearance information around each landmark to decide the best shape candidate. This shape candidate will be used as initialization instead of mean shape in previous ASM methods. Since we use the eyes, nose and mouth locations as well as the local appearance information, the resulting initial landmarks are almost in their optimal locations. The performance of this approach is shown in Section 4.

There are two different ASM model in our method, *full-shape model* and *minimal-shape model*. Full-shape model contains all the landmark points as in training set. On the other hand, *minimal-shape model* only contains 8 landmark points including 4 for eyes corners, 2 for nose and 2 for mouth corners. Figure 4 shows examples of both models. A flowchart of the overall process is depicted in Figure 5. First, we use Viola-Jones face detector to extract the face regions from the test image. Then, we detect the eyes using Viola-Jones algorithm. Since the detected regions contain many false positives, we apply a simple linear Support Vector Machine (SVM) to select true positive eye regions. After that, we apply the *minimal-shape model* with eyes positions as reference points. The result is the optimal positions for 8 landmark points and the corresponding shape parameter vector b_{min}. The key idea is that we will use this b_{min} to select 10 nearest shape parameter vector of known minimal shape in training set. This means that we now have 10 candidates of full shape for initialization purpose.

Fig. 4. Examples of *full-shape model* on the left and *mini-shape model* on the right

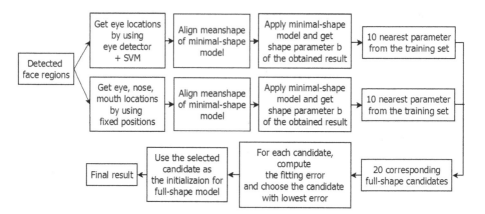

Fig. 5. Sequence of operations to select the suitable initialization for MASM model

Because the eye detector doesn't guarantee perfect results, we repeat the above process to have 10 more candidates of full shape. However, we use fixed positions in the bounding box as reference points for *minimal-shape model* instead of eyes positions. The ratio for fixed positions is described in Figure 6.

Fig. 6. The position of fixed *minimal-shape* points in the face region

After obtaining 20 candidates for initialization, we will select the candidate that has lowest error value. The error value of each candidate is the summation of fitting error of the profile around each landmark point. The selected candidate will be use as initialization points for *full-shape model*.

3.2   Use of Edge Information

In MASM, Keshav Seshadri and Marios Savvides assume that facial landmark usually lie along strong edges. However, we suggest that we should weaken that assumption because Sobel edge detector don't guarantee that strong edges will lie on facial boundary. In that case, the candidate points may be chosen inaccurately and then the performance of fitting process is reduced.

For the landmarks in the facial boundary, we will use the cost function as in equation (10) to measure Mahalanobis distance between the original profile $\mathbf{g}$ and the reconstructed profile $\mathbf{g_r}$.

$$error(\mathbf{g}, \mathbf{g_r}) = (1 - c * I)(\mathbf{g_r} - \mathbf{g})^{\mathrm{T}} \mathbf{S_g}^{-1}(\mathbf{g_r} - \mathbf{g}) \qquad (10)$$

where c is a constant, chosen to be 0.2 in our implementation, I is the Sobel edge intensity at the candidate point and $\mathbf{S_g}$ is the covariance matrix of the current landmark's subspace.

4 Experiments and Results

In this section, we will evaluate the performance of our proposed method and show the experimental results. The comparison experiments between our method and the Modified Active Shape Model (MASM) are conducted on MUCT [11] and LFPW [1] database. All model are trained with 300 face images from MUCT database. The landmark scheme used in MUCT database contains 76 landmark points as in Figure 4. Some original sample images of MUCT database are shown in Figure 1. We conducted two experiments in testing stage. In the first test, we evaluate with two test set from MUCT and LFPW with the assumption that initialization errors were not present. The first set consisted of 450 images from the MUCT database. The second set consisted of 300 images from LFPW database. In the second experiment, we added various of initialization errors to the face detector results.

To evaluate the performance of the method, we use the distance between the predicted landmark positions and the manually annotated points.

$$E = \frac{1}{n} \sum_{i=1}^{n} \{ \frac{1}{N} \sum_{j=1}^{N} dist(\mathbf{s_{ij}}, \mathbf{m_{ij}}) \} \qquad (11)$$

where n is the number of test images, N is the number of landmark, $\mathbf{s_{ij}}$ and $\mathbf{m_{ij}}$ are the coordinate vectors of the automatic landmark and the manually labeled landmark respectively. The Euclidean distance $dist(\mathbf{s_{ij}}, \mathbf{m_{ij}})$ between $\mathbf{s_{ij}}$ and $\mathbf{m_{ij}}$ is normalized so that the distance between the nearest corners of both eyes is 30 pixels. For these experiment, we used Viola-Jones face detector to get the face bounding box. Then, we refined manually the incorrectly detected results in translation and scaling to prevent initialization errors.

The results of first test are illustrated in Table 1. We can find that our method can enhance the accuracy of the MASM by 23.66 % in MUCT test and 14.59% in LFPW test. Figure 7 shows plots the errors for each landmark. The landmark scheme of MUCT database is 76 points. However, the ground truth landmark points in LFPW is 68 points, as labeled by IBUG [14]. Therefore, we choose the corresponding landmark points in both scheme to compute fitting errors. The resulting scheme contains 61 points. As can be seen, our proposed method has better result than the MASM method, especially while fitting the landmarks

Table 1. Results for first test without initialization errors

	Fitting Errors		Improvement
	Our method	MASM	
MUCT	1.5777	2.0666	23.66%
LFPW	7.6756	8.9873	14.59%

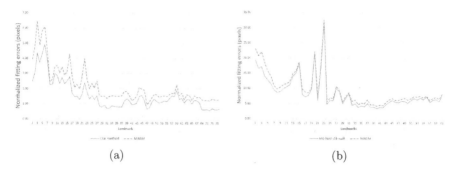

(a)   (b)

Fig. 7. Plots of fitting errors vs landmark number for (a) MUCT test (b) LFPW test

along the facial boundary (1-15). This is the effect of the modification in using edge information. On the remaining landmark points, our method just gives slightly improvements because we focus on the problem of initialization errors while these experiments assume that there is no initialization errors. Besides, other processing steps are almost the same as MASM. Hence, we don't have much improvement on others part. In the LFPW test, the errors are higher than the first test because LFPW images are captured in real-world scenario which contain many pose changes and expressions. However, our method can gain better results than MASM.

For our second experiments, we estimate the performance of our method when dealing with initialization errors. In this experiments, we test the effect of translation and scaling to the accuracy of our proposed method and MASM. Figure 8 shows the results of our test. In the translation test, we move the face bounding box with a same value along x and y coordinates. The translation value is: -50, -25, 0, 25, 50. In the scaling test, we scale the face bounding box with ratios of [1.5, 1.2, 1, 0.8, 0.6]. In Scaling test, we achieve the fitting errors of 2.32048 compared to 3.9663 of the MASM. In translation test, the error of our method is 1.8742 while MASM's error is 3.4945. In both cases, our proposed method can gains better performance, 46.37% and 41.49% in translation and scaling test respectively , which means that our method are more robust to the initialization errors.

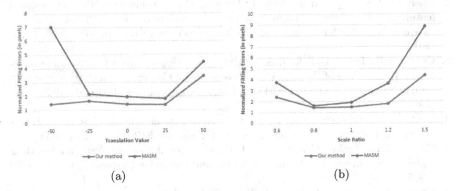

(a)   (b)

Fig. 8. Plots of fitting errors with the effects of scaling a) and translation b)

5   Conclusion and Future Work

In this paper, we presented a novel Active Shape Model for facial feature points detection in frontal-view face images. Our method focus on dealing with initialization errors due to the failure of face detector. In order to recover from poor initialization, we use an eye detector with Support Vector Machine to effectively extraction the location of the eye. Then, we apply a minimal ASM model with 8 key landmark points to obtain an optimal initialization. This optimal initialization is used as the starting point for the full ASM model with 76 landmark points instead of using mean shape. Moreover, we consider the usage of edge information carefully to prevent misalignment on facial boundary. Experimental results show that our proposed method can achieve better fitting accuracy even with poor initialization. In the future work, there are still many rooms to improve the performance of our proposed method. First, our method uses the eye location to obtain the initialization. Hence, our method can't deal with occlusion effectively, especially when the target face has sun glasses. Such problems can be solve by combing the location of nose and mouth in addition to eye location. Secondly, the feature descriptor is very simple. We can improve it with HOG or Gabor features which are robust to illumination.

Acknowledgments. This research is supported by research funding from Advanced Program in Computer Science, University of Science, Vietnam National University - Ho Chi Minh City.

References

1. Belhumeur, P.N., Jacobs, D.W., Kriegman, D., Kumar, N.: Localizing parts of faces using a consensus of exemplars. In: 2011 IEEE Conference on Computer Vision and Pattern Recognition (CVPR), pp. 545–552 (2011)

2. Chen, D., Cao, X., Wen, F., Sun, J.: Blessing of dimensionality: High-dimensional feature and its efficient compression for face verification. In: 2013 IEEE Conference on Computer Vision and Pattern Recognition (CVPR), pp. 3025–3032. IEEE (2013)

3. Cootes, T.F., Taylor, C.J., Lanitis, A.: Multi-resolution search with active shape models. In: Proceedings of the 12th IAPR International Conference on Pattern Recognition, onference A: Computer Vision & Image Processing, vol. 1, pp. 610–612. IEEE (1994)

4. Cootes, T.F., Edwards, G.J., Taylor, C.J.: Active appearance models. IEEE Transactions on Pattern Analysis and Machine Intelligence 23(6), 681–685 (2001)

5. Cootes, T.F., Taylor, C.J., Cooper, D.H., Graham, J.: Active shape models-their training and application. Computer Vision and Image Understanding 61(1), 38–59 (1995)

6. Cootes, T.F., Taylor, C.J.: et al.: Statistical models of appearance for computer vision (2004)

7. Cristinacce, D., Cootes, T.F.: Boosted regression active shape models. In: BMVC, pp. 1–10 (2007)

8. Gower, J.C.: Generalized procrustes analysis. Psychometrika 40(1), 33–51 (1975)

9. Gu, L., Kanade, T.: A generative shape regularization model for robust face alignment. In: Forsyth, D., Torr, P., Zisserman, A. (eds.) ECCV 2008, Part I. LNCS, vol. 5302, pp. 413–426. Springer, Heidelberg (2008)

10. Kass, M., Witkin, A., Terzopoulos, D.: Snakes: Active contour models. International Journal of Computer Vision 1(4), 321–331 (1988)

11. Milborrow, S., Morkel, J., Nicolls, F.: The muct landmarked face database. Pattern Recognition Association of South Africa 201(0) (2010)

12. Milborrow, S., Nicolls, F.: Locating facial features with an extended active shape model. In: Forsyth, D., Torr, P., Zisserman, A. (eds.) ECCV 2008, Part IV. LNCS, vol. 5305, pp. 504–513. Springer, Heidelberg (2008)

13. Romdhani, S., Gong, S., Psarrou, A., et al.: A multi-view nonlinear active shape model using kernel pca. In: BMVC. vol. 10, pp. 483–492 (1999)

14. Sagonas, C., Tzimiropoulos, G., Zafeiriou, S., Pantic, M.: A semi-automatic methodology for facial landmark annotation. In: 2013 IEEE Conference on Computer Vision and Pattern Recognition Workshops (CVPRW), pp. 896–903. IEEE (2013)

15. Seshadri, K., Savvides, M.: Robust modified active shape model for automatic facial landmark annotation of frontal faces. In: IEEE 3rd International Conference on Biometrics: Theory, Applications, and Systems, BTAS 2009, pp. 1–8. IEEE (2009)

16. Seshadri, K., Savvides, M.: An analysis of the sensitivity of active shape models to initialization when applied to automatic facial landmarking. IEEE Transactions on Information Forensics and Security 7(4), 1255–1269 (2012)

17. Viola, P., Jones, M.J.: Robust real-time face detection. International Journal of Computer Vision 57(2), 137–154 (2004)

18. Wang, W., Shan, S., Gao, W., Cao, B., Yin, B.: An improved active shape model for face alignment. In: Proceedings of the 4th IEEE International Conference on Multimodal Interfaces, p. 523. IEEE Computer Society (2002)

19. Yuille, A.L.: Deformable templates for face recognition. Journal of Cognitive Neuroscience 3(1), 59–70 (1991)

A Multiple Refinement Approach in Abstraction Model Checking

Phan T.H. Nguyen and Thang H. Bui

Faculty of Computer Science & Engineering,
Ho Chi Minh City University of Technology, Vietnam
nguyenthihongphan@gmail.com, thang@cse.hcmut.edu.vn

Abstract. Abstraction in model checking is the most effective method to overcome the state explosion problem, the most serious problem in model checking when the size and the complexity of the system-under-check are increasing. Unfortunately, when the abstraction goes wrong, the answer must be validated with the concrete system, so it faces the state explosion problem again. Moreover, the techniques in checking the abstraction and in validating must not be obstructions in the checking process. Research recently has shown that, the way to abstract a model and the approach to use abstraction are the main concerns in abstraction model checking.

In this work, we report our study on both two questions: (1) a model analyzing method to find a way of abstraction effectively, and (2) an error refinement approach using multiple abstraction in symbolic model checking. The experimentation shows that the new approach has a great performance in checking both 'buggy' and 'correct' models.

1 Introduction

In model checking, a model is a specification of the under-the-check system for detecting violations of desired properties. When a violation is found, a counter-example is generated to help system engineers in allocating defects. Unfortunately, when the size and the complexity of system-under-check grows up, the state space will be exposed, the checking process is more intractable. To deal with the explosion, abstraction can be used to reduce the size of the model, and thus the effort. However, abstraction may introduce a 'fake' behavior that violates the specification, but that behavior is not present in the original system (false alarm).

When abstracting a system, domain abstraction [1], that reduces domains of the model, and predicate abstraction, that uses (pre-defined) predicates in reducing the model, are mostly employed. The research in [1] has discovered that in most system there are some *collar variables* that play an important role in representing the behavior of the system. Base on that idea, Qian et al. proposed that some 'weak' *system variables* that almost play no role in the system can be abstracted away [2,3]. A simple variable dependency analysis [2] can be used to classified variables based on their impact to the system. Note that, the research

K. Saeed and V. Snášel (Eds.): CISIM 2014, LNCS 8838, pp. 433–444, 2014.

focused only on *directed model checking* [4]. The research in [5] proposed a propagation variable dependency analysis method to discover the impact of variables to each other. The experimentation has shown that, it outperforms the simple analysis method.

However, good abstract methods still introduce spurious counter-examples. Clarke et al. [6] states that refinement on a false alarm counter-example can eliminate it. Whenever a counter-example is found on the abstraction, it should be refined in the concrete system to validate the error. Therefore, abstraction refinement approach must deal with the state explosion on the concrete model when the abstraction is too bad to generate many 'fake' counter-examples.

Qian et al. [2] instead uses multiple abstraction and indicates that if there is no error on some abstraction, the system is verified without examine the original one. Of course, if all abstractions contain errors, the concrete system should be checked. When a defect is found on an abstraction, the next abstraction will be used. However, the multiple abstraction does not reduce the state space of the next search as in abstraction refinement [6].

In this report, we propose a new analysis method as an improvement of the former method [5] to analyze system variables so that weak ones are eliminated to make the model simpler. It takes the *convergence* into account to analyze the variable dependency in domain abstraction. Moreover, we applied the methods to symbolic model checking when states (and the transition relation) of the model can be represented as an expression of system variables, and then can be simply abstracted by domain abstraction.

Besides, a method that takes the advantages of the abstraction refinement [6] and multiple abstraction [2,3] is also proposed. In other words, the new so-called multiple abstraction refinement (MAR) method is a combination of multiple abstraction and abstraction refinement. It currently *supports only for directed model checking*, a research direction that considers only invariant properties.

The rest of paper is constructed as follows: Section 2 is to provide some technical background, Section 3 is for the convergent propagation variable dependency analysis, Section 4 is for multiple abstraction refinement. The conclusion and future work is in the last section.

2   Technical Background and Related Work

2.1   Symbolic Model Checking

Model checking is a problem to answer is a given model M satisfies the checking property.The problem has two related sub-problem: model representation and model checking approach. There are two main model representation: symbolic model checking, that represents the state space as symbolic expressions, and explicit state model checking, that represent states explicitly. When the state spaces in symbolic model checking are in expressions, In symbolic model checking, the state spaces are in symbolic expressions. one can capture more states than that of the explicit state model checking [7].

Definition 1 (Transition Systems). *A finite state transition system is a tuple* $M = (S, S_0, T)$, *where* S *is a finite set of states*, $S_0 \subseteq S$ *is a set of initial states and* $T \subseteq S \times S$ *is a transition relation.*

In symbolic model checking, a state $s_i \in S$ is represented as an expression over a non-empty set of system (or state) *variables* $X = (x_0, x_1, \ldots, x_n)$, where each variable x_i ranges over a finite domain D_i, $s_i = f(x_0, x_1, \ldots, x_n)$.

2.2   Abstraction

Abstraction is the concept using in model checking to make the model smaller. In general, if the abstract system is correct, so does the concrete system [8]. But there is no guarantee that there is an error in the concrete system if there is an error in the abstraction. For example, an abstraction of the concrete system [9] is depicted in Fig. 1, in which the error concrete state 10 is unreachable in the concrete system even though its abstract state IV is reachable from the (abstract) initial state.

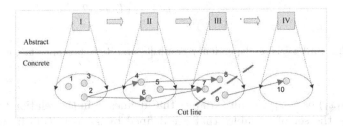

Fig. 1. An abstraction system [9]

Support that, there is a set of surjections $H = (h_1, h_2, \ldots, h_n)$, where each h_i maps a finite domain D_i to another domain $\hat{D}_i$ with $|\hat{D}_i| \leq |D_i|$. An domain abstraction of a transition system is defined as follows [2,3].

Definition 2 (Homomorphic Abstraction). *A homomorphic abstraction of a transition system* M *is* $\hat{M} = (\hat{S}, \hat{S}_0, \hat{T})$, *where* $\hat{S} = H(S) = \{\hat{s}_i \mid \hat{s}_i = h_i(s)\}$, $\hat{S}_0 = H(S_0)$, *and* $\hat{T} = \{(\hat{s}_i, \hat{s}_j) \mid (s_i, s_j) \in T, \hat{s}_i = h_i(s_i), \hat{s}_j = h_j(s_j)\}$.

For example, if we want to omit a system variable x_k of a model in making an abstraction, we can simply abstract its domain to an empty domain, and apply the above definition. It has been proved that, the (homomorphic) abstraction preserves the checking properties of the concrete system [2,3].

Based on that definition, the *restriction operation* can be defined as: let S_M is a set of states of a model M, $S_{\hat{M}}$ is a set of abstract states of an abstract model $\hat{M}$ of M, the restriction of S_M according to $S_{\hat{M}}$ is $\{s_i \in S_M \mid \hat{s}_i = h_i(s_i), \hat{s}_i \in S_{\hat{M}}\}$.

2.3 Variable Dependency Analysis

There are many way to abstract a model such as predicate abstraction [10], that uses predefined predicates to abstract the system, and lazy abstraction [11], that prunes branches of execution by abstracting and refines the pruning to allocate errors. Suppose that, the state space of a model in symbolic model checking can be defined over a set of system variables, Qian et al. [2] proposed that, pruning 'weak' system variables will set off the main features of the model. They have shown that, a simple variable dependency analysis can be used to find 'important' and 'weak' variables. The research in [5] suggested to use a propagation approach to the variable dependency analysis and achieved good results.

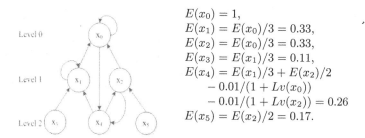

$$E(x_0) = 1,$$
$$E(x_1) = E(x_0)/3 = 0.33,$$
$$E(x_2) = E(x_0)/3 = 0.33,$$
$$E(x_3) = E(x_1)/3 = 0.11,$$
$$E(x_4) = E(x_1)/3 + E(x_2)/2$$
$$\qquad - 0.01/(1 + Lv(x_0))$$
$$\qquad - 0.01/(1 + Lv(x_2)) = 0.26$$
$$E(x_5) = E(x_2)/2 = 0.17.$$

Fig. 2. A variable dependency graph [5] and its importance factors

Let $Prv(x_i)$ be the set of all variables that defines x_i in the relation transition, $Nxt(x_i)$ be the set of variables that are defined by x_i, $varOf(f)$ be the set of variables in the expression f and φ be the checking property of the model. The variable dependency graph is defined as follows.

Definition 3 (Variable Dependency Graph). *A (variable) dependency graph is a directed graph* $VDG = (V, E)$, *where V is a set of variables as vertices, E is a set of edges* $E = \{x_i \to x_j \mid x_j \in Nxt(x_i)\}$.
We also defined a mapping Lv to map each variable to a 'layer'. It is defined as $Lv(x_j) = 0$ *iff* $x_j \in varOf(\varphi)$ *and* $Lv(x_j) = Lv(x_i) + 1$ *if* $x_i \in Prv(x_j)$.

In the case when x_i and x_j depend on each other, the propagation will be applied to calculate Lv. In the graph in Fig. 2, variable x_0 depends on itself and on x_4, x_2 and x_4 depends on each other.

Let $in(y)$ be the in-degree of the vertex y, the importance factor of a variable is defined as follows.

$$E(x) = \begin{cases} 1 & Lv(x) = 0 \\ \displaystyle\sum_{y \in Nxt(x) - \{x\}} \dfrac{E(y)}{in(y)} - \alpha(x) & Lv(x) > 0 \end{cases} \qquad (1)$$

where $\alpha(x)$ is the *counter-effect* on x and is defined as

$$\alpha(x) = \beta \sum_{y \in Prv, \ Lv(y) \, < \, Lv(x)(x)} \frac{1}{1 + Lv(y)} \qquad (2)$$

and $\beta \in [0\ldots1]$ is an adjustment, that controls how much the variables in a higher level affects a variable in a lower level. For example, let $\beta = 0.01$, the importance of variables in the graph in the left of Fig. 2 are given on the right of it.

2.4   Counter-Example Guided Abstraction Refinement – CEGAR

In order to find out the truth about a counter-example in an abstraction, Clarke et al. [6] proposed a method so-call Counter-Example Guided Abstraction Refinement (CEGAR). It is to determine if a counter-example on an abstract model can be confirmed on the concrete system. The main idea is that the search is performed on an abstraction and any found counter-example will be refined and confirmed on the concrete system to report an error. If there is no error on the abstraction, the concrete system has been proved its correctness. In this case, the performance of the model checking depends on the quality of the abstraction and the refinement algorithm. Moreover, the method faces the non-strong connectivity inside abstract state (See Fig.4 in [2]), when an abstract state represents a set of non-strong connected concrete states. The abstract state III in Fig. 1 is an example of the the issue.

2.5   Multiple Abstraction

Another abstraction approach had also been proposed by Qian et al. in [2,3]. It is a multiple abstraction strategy to reduce verification efforts. Based on an assumption that there are a series of abstractions $M_0 \preceq M1 \preceq \ldots$ such that some states $s_i^1, s_i^2, \ldots$ in M_{i+1} (more concrete) are abstracted into only one abstract state s_i in M_i (more abstract). The model checking searches through abstractions from $M_0, M_1, \ldots$ for any violation (in those abstraction). It can stop if there is no error found in any M_i. Otherwise, the search continuing detects the error on the remanding abstractions and even at last on the concrete system. The proposed method treats all abstractions as separated models and in the sequential order. However, it can take into account the counter-example found on the previous search as a heuristic to guide the search on the next abstraction (or concrete model). Of course, the problem of non-strong connected abstract state mentioned above still exists when it may lead the next search into the wrong direction. In the worst case, the search must be executed on the concrete model to find the actual counter-example. Although its performance is very good [2], it can be improved by concentrating on (only) dangerous areas in the next abstraction.

2.6   Other Direction on Reducing Model Checking Effort

There are some other directions on reducing model checking effort such as Partial Order Reduction [12], SAT-solving [13]. The latter is known as Bound Model Checking - BMC. In this work, we only focus on abstraction approach to reduce the size of the state space. We may try to apply the idea in this work to some other directions, including BMC in the future.

3   Convergent Variable Dependency Analysis

This section is to propose the convergent variable dependency analysis and some experimentation.

3.1   The Method – VRK

In this section, we try to add the convergent approach to the propagation approach mentioned in Section 2.3. In this approach, it captures the counter-effect from all related (or connected) variables. The idea of the convergent is actually came from the Page Rank algorithm [14], that had been used in the Google search engine to calculate the degree of related web pages for each web page.

Let d be the damping factor to the convergent (default value is 0.85), the formula to calculate the importance factors of a variable dependency graph $VDG = (V, E, Lv)$ is as follows.

$$PE(x) = \frac{1-d}{|V|} + d \left(\sum_{y \in Prv(x)} \frac{PE(y)}{|Nxt(y)|} \right) \tag{3}$$

$$E(x) = PE(x) + (Max(Lv) - Lv(x))/Max(Lv) \tag{4}$$

Let try to apply the new formula to the graph in Fig. 2.
(+) Apply equation (3):

$PE(x_0) = 0.16243,$ $PE(x_1) = 0.17687,$
$PE(x_2) = 0.1017,$ $PE(x_3) = 0.025,$
$PE(x_4) = 0.13348,$ $PE(x_5) = 0.025.$

(+) Apply equation (4):

$E(x_0) = 1.16243,$ $E(x_1) = 0.67687,$
$E(x_2) = 0.6017,$ $E(x_3) = 0.025,$
$E(x_4) = 0.13348,$ $E(x_5) = 0.025.$

Discussion: (1) It easy to see that the relationship among variables in this case is different to that of the proposed method in [5] (See Fig. 2). We captured more about the *inter-effect* between any two variables. (2) Especially, the variable's level on the graph still has its effects to the variable important degree similar to the method in [5]. Convergent variable dependency analysis simply has focused on both sides.

3.2 Experimentation

To compare our new proposed variable analysis in abstraction with previous work [2,3,5], we re-use models from those works. They are *peterson, leader-election, needham* protocols and *sender-receiver* communication system. They are actually 'buggy' models.

The variable analysis algorithm is made into NuSMV (http://nusmv.fbk.eu), a famous symbolic model checking tool. We also re-use the guided search (A*) algorithm proposed in [2,3] to compare the abstractions made from our new approach and the previous ones. When [5] has shown that the propagation analysis is generally better than the simple analysis proposed in [2,3], we will only compare the new algorithm named **VRK** with the one in [5] named **PG** in this experiment. The experiment is taken on a Core 2 Duo 2.93 GHz with 2 GB of RAM computer running Ubuntu 13.10. The results are the average of running time in seconds. The experimentation is in Fig. 3.

In this experiment, 40% of the least important variables ('weak' variables) are abstracted away to make the abstraction. It is easy to see that, the searching time of A* using abstraction generated from **VRK** is generally smaller than that of from **PG**. The chart on the figure also shows that, the strength of running time of A* using **VRK** is smoother than that of **PG**.

Note that, a other configuration may results differently with that experimentation. The experimentation of abstracting away 90% of 'weak' variables is in Fig. 4. In this case, they are almost identical. We believe that, the topology of the dependency graphs (of those models) may effect the calculation on convergent. For example, after analyzing, some first variables of the most important ones are the same in both approaches, thus the removing of them makes similar abstractions in both case and the checking will have the same effort. Therefore,

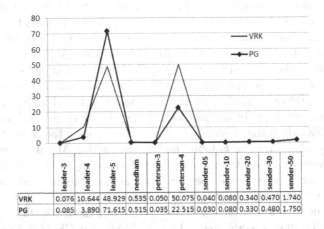

Fig. 3. Experimentation on A* using **VRK** and **PG** variable analysis methods

	leader-3	leader-4	leader-5
VRK	0.041	3.811	61.413
PG	0.047	3.808	61.407

Fig. 4. A* with 90% of weak variables abstracted away

the **PG** algorithm that has lest analysis computation effort, may take advantages. The similar issue has also been reported in [15].

Discussion: The VRK method in general has more computation effort than the PG method when it takes into account the relationship on all related variables in the system. This effort sometime effective, but in some other cases, it gives no advantages to the whole checking process. But when the development strength of the running time on the abstraction using VRK is smooth, it is likely better than other methods in general. We suggest to use VRK in general.

4   Multiple Abstraction Refinement – MAR

In this section, we present our new proposed approach named **MAR** that takes advantages from both CEGAR [6] and multiple abstraction methods [2,3].

4.1   MAR Algorithm

Suppose that there is a series of abstractions $M_0 \preceq M1 \preceq \ldots$ as in Section 2.5. The search is started in the M_0. If there is a violation (of the checking property), a series of counter-example refinements will be performed on the rest of abstraction M_i. If the counter-example is confirmed on all abstractions and then on the concrete system S, it is the actual counter-example. Otherwise, the search will continue on M_0 for another error. If there is no (or no more) counter-example, the concrete system S is proved to satisfy the checking property.

The flows of the algorithm are in Fig. 5. On the right, it is to show how to refine error on all abstraction M_i, and even on the concrete system S. The restriction operation is applied on the state space of the checking model based on the counter-example of the previous (more abstract) model. The difference to that of CEGAR is that instead of refining the error on the concrete system S immediately when an error is found on the abstraction M_0, it refines the error on the 'more concrete' abstraction M_1 (and then on M_2 and so on). In the worst case, the concrete system will be used to search. General speaking, it delays the refinement on the concrete system as long as possible. So, if there is a false alarm, this algorithm may have a chance to find out the truth without searching on the concrete 'huge' state space. In fact, MAR and CEGAR have the same idea when we only have only one abstraction M_0 such that they will refine the

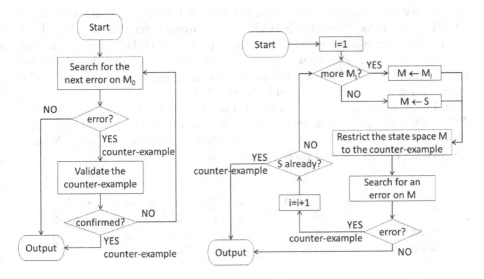

Fig. 5. The MAR algorithm

counter-example on the concrete state space immediately when it is found on the abstraction. Technically, they are not the same when CEGAR refines error on the concrete system using some complicated algorithms, and our MAR just search on the restricted area made from the (abstract) counter-example on the concrete state space. In this work, we assume that our MAR with one abstraction is CEGAR.

The MAR algorithm also differs to the multiple abstraction proposed in [2,3] when it uses the abstractions only for validating an error found on the previous abstraction. At every iteration, instead of searching the state space of M_i for a (new) error as in multiple abstraction method, it restricts the state space of M_i to the area that comes from the previous counter-example. The idea is that, when the counter-example found from the previous search is small, the restriction will help the algorithm to reduces the verification effort.

Remark 1. The MAR algorithm is sound and complete.

It is easy to prove the remark. When the algorithm returns no error, based on the algorithm, if there is no error on the abstraction M_0, or if there are some errors on M_0 but were rejected in the validation step, the concrete system has no error. When the algorithm returns a counter-example, it is confirmed on the concrete system, hence it is a counter-example.

4.2 Experimental Results on Multiple Abstraction Refinement

In this section, we compare our algorithm (MAR) to the that of [2,3] (named SAGA) using the variable dependency analysis VRK. To compare to CEGAR, we assume that our algorithm acts similar to CEGAR if there is only one abstraction M_0. We named that algorithm is MAR-1 in this experiment. The benchmark we use in this section is provided on the main page of NuSMV. They are named *brp, dme, gigamax, msi_ wtra, periodic*. All of them are correct models, so we can expect that only a few level of abstraction is enough to find the truth. The environment is the same as stated in Section 3.2.

In Fig. 6, we compare the algorithms. The abstractions are built by removing 80%, 60%, 40% and 20% of 'weak' variables, respectively. It is easy to see that, they almost have the same performance, when (in many cases) only the first abstraction is searched and no error ever returned.

	brp	dme1	dme2	gigamax	msi_wtrans	periodic
MAR	0.310	0.040	0.113	0.017	0.072	0.010
SAGA	0.333	0.041	0.112	0.026	0.073	0.010
MAR-1	0.265	0.040	0.113	0.017	0.072	0.010

Fig. 6. MAR vs. SAGA vs. MAR-1 on correct systems

We also re-use the benchmark in Section 3.2. When they are 'buggy' systems, the search in M_0 will return some error and the validation step will search on all the abstractions and the concrete system. The experimentation results in Fig. 7 confirms that the proposed method outperform both multiple-abstraction search (SAGA [2,3]) and single-abstraction refinement (MAR-1 as CEGAR). Only one exception that SAGA is extremely good on *sender* systems. [15] mentioned that this is a special case when the topology of the state space is skew to some buggy locations and thus the guided search algorithms like SAGA are the best to be used.

	leader-3	leader-4	leader-5	needham	peterson-3	peterson-4	peterson-5	sender-05	sender-10	sender-20	sender-30	sender-50
MAR	0.050	7.515	84.810	1.285	0.030	4.070	222.900	0.805	9.200	79.835	179.775	timeout
SAGA	0.085	79.570	timeout	0.160	0.065	6.765	timeout	0.050	0.115	0.530	0.940	7.110
MAR-1	0.040	7.690	81.920	1.310	0.040	4.090	251.870	0.790	9.420	80.070	178.840	timeout

Fig. 7. MAR vs. SAGA vs. MAR-1 on 'buggy' systems

To not be bias to the variable analysis methods, we repeated out experiments using random abstraction, in which the importances of system variables are assigned randomly. The experimentation results in Fig. 8 shown that the MAR is still the best.

	leader-3	leader-4	leader-5	needham	peterson-3	peterson-4	peterson-5	sender-05	sender-10	sender-20	sender-30
MAR	0.050	7.780	82.130	1.310	0.020	4.410	224.200	0.810	9.670	79.890	180.860
SAGA	0.090	8.710	82.300	2.250	0.030	4.960	timeout	5.430	189.220	timeout	timeout
MAR-1	0.050	7.790	82.050	1.310	0.030	4.080	224.400	0.810	9.900	79.680	181.880

Fig. 8. MAR vs. SAGA vs. MAR-1 on 'buggy' systems using random abstraction

Discussion: When we model check a system in practice, we actually do not known it is correct or not. The abstraction method MAR is a good choice when it works similarly to CEGAR or SAGA in correct systems and outperforms them in buggy systems. Moreover, it also works well on arbitrary abstraction such as random abstraction.

5   Future Work and Conclusions

In this paper, a new convergent variable analysis method has been proposed to enrich abstraction technique in model checking. It employees the idea of the convergent computation using in the Page Rank algorithm [14] to calculate the importance of system variables in domain abstraction. The less important variables can be omitted to make abstractions to reduce the state space. The experimentation shows that the new analysis generally gives a better solution in abstraction than some algorithm proposed in previous work. The study on when to use the new analysis and when to use the others is not carried out in this work and should be in the near future.

A new model checking based on counter-example refinement and multiple abstraction has also been proposed. It takes advantages from both methods such that it uses multiple abstraction to confirm a counter-example found on the finest abstraction and the idea of counter-example refinement to refine the counter-example. The modification is instead of refining the error on the concrete system, the new method validates it in the abstractions first. The modification allows the checking process works around the abstractions which are smaller than the concrete system and hence reduces the effort. The experimental results confirmed our assumption. Of course, our algorithm still faces the same problem with CEGAR and multiple abstraction algorithms that if there are errors, it still has to refer to the concrete system in generating a real counter-example.

Nevertheless, when we only support for directed model checking, we need to extend our approach to support other checking direction. It should be in our future work.

Acknowledgment. This research was supported by Vietnam National University - Ho Chi Minh City (Ho Chi Minh City, Vietnam) under the grant number C2013-20-07.

References

1. Menzies, T., Owen, D., Richardson, J.: The strangest thing about software. IEEE Computer 40(1), 54–60 (2007)
2. Qian, K., Nymeyer, A.: Abstraction-based model checking using heuristical refinement. In: Wang, F. (ed.) ATVA 2004. LNCS, vol. 3299, pp. 165–178. Springer, Heidelberg (2004)
3. Qian, K., Nymeyer, A., Susanto, S.: Experiments with multiple abstraction heuristics in symbolic verification. In: Zucker, J.-D., Saitta, L. (eds.) SARA 2005. LNCS (LNAI), vol. 3607, pp. 290–304. Springer, Heidelberg (2005)
4. Edelkamp, S., Lluch Lafuente, A., Leue, S.: Directed explicit model checking with HSF-SPIN. In: Dwyer, M.B. (ed.) SPIN 2001. LNCS, vol. 2057, pp. 57–79. Springer, Heidelberg (2001)
5. Bui, T.H., Dang, P.B.K.: Yet another variable dependency analysis for abstraction guided model checking. In: Proc. SEATUC 2012 (March 2012)
6. Clarke, E.M., Grumberg, O., Jha, S., Lu, Y., Veith, H.: Counterexample-guided abstraction refinement. In: Emerson, E.A., Sistla, A.P. (eds.) CAV 2000. LNCS, vol. 1855, pp. 154–169. Springer, Heidelberg (2000)
7. Burch, J.R., Clarke, E.M., McMillan, K.L., Dill, D.L., Hwang, L.J.: Symbolic model checking: 10^{20} states and beyond. In: Proc. the 5th Annual IEEE Symp. on Logic in Computer Science, pp. 1–33. IEEE Computer Society Press, Washington, D.C (1990)
8. Clarke, E.M., Grumberg, O., Long, D.E.: Model checking and abstraction. In: Proc. the 19th ACM SIGPLAN-SIGACT Sym. on Principles of Programming Languages, pp. 343–354 (1992)
9. He, F., Song, X., Hung, W.N., Gu, M., Sun, J.: Integrating evolutionary computation with abstraction refinement for model checking. IEEE Transactions on Computers 59(1), 116–126 (2010)
10. Ball, T., Majumdar, R., Millstein, T., Rajamani, S.K.: Automatic predicate abstraction of C programs. In: Proc. the ACM SIGPLAN 2001 Conf. on Programming Language Design and Implementation, pp. 203–213. ACM Press (2001)
11. Henzinger, T.A., Jhala, R., Majumdar, R., Sutre, G.: Lazy abstraction. In: Proc. the 29th SIGPLAN-SIGACT Symp. on Principles of Programming Languages, pp. 58–70. ACM (2002)
12. Peled, D.: Combining partial order reductions with on-the-fly model-checking. In: Dill, D.L. (ed.) CAV 1994. LNCS, vol. 818, pp. 377–390. Springer, Heidelberg (1994)
13. Eén, N., Sörensson, N.: Temporal induction by incremental SAT solving. In: Strichman, O., Biere, A. (eds.) Electronic Notes in Theoretical Computer Science, vol. 89, Elsevier (2004)
14. Brin, S., Page, L.: The anatomy of a large-scale hypertextual web search engine. In: Seventh International World-Wide Web Conference, WWW 1998 (1998)
15. Bui, T.H., Nymeyer, A.: Heuristic sensitivity in guided random-walk based model checking. In: Proc. the 7th IEEE Int. Conf. on Software Engineering and Formal Methods (SEFM 2009), pp. 125–134. IEEE Computer Society (November 2009)

Chaos Driven Particle Swarm Optimization with Basic Particle Performance Evaluation – An Initial Study

Michal Pluhacek, Roman Senkerik, and Ivan Zelinka

Tomas Bata University in Zlin, Faculty of Applied Informatics, T.G. Masaryka 5555,
760 01 Zlin, Czech Republic
{pluhacek,senkerik,zelinka}@fai.utb.cz

Abstract. In this paper, the novel concept of particle performance evaluation is introduced into the chaos driven particle swarm optimization algorithm (PSO). The discrete chaotic dissipative standard map is used here as a chaotic pseudo-random number generator (CPRNG). In the novel proposed particle performance evaluation method the contribution of each particle to the process of obtaining the global best solution is investigated periodically. As a reaction to the possible poor performance of a particular particle, its velocity calculation is thereafter altered. Through utilization of this approach the convergence speed and overall performance of PSO algorithm driven by CPRNG based on Dissipative map is improved. The proposed method is tested on the CEC13 benchmark set with two different dimension settings.

1 Introduction

Since its introduction in 1995 [1], the PSO algorithm [1], [2] has become one of the leading representatives of evolutionary computational techniques (ECTs) and also of the Swarm intelligence [2]. Various modifications have been proposed over the time [3–7] and the inner dynamic of the PSO has been subject of many detailed studies e.g. [8, 9]. One of the more recent trends with very satisfactory results is represented through the implementation of chaotic sequences into the PSO dynamic [10-17]. Within the previous research [13-17], the strong evidences have been collected to support the claim that utilization of CPRNGs based on different chaotic systems may lead to significantly different behavior of the swarm and overall performance of the algorithm. The dissipative standard map [18] in particular seems to be very promising chaotic sequence for the usage as the CPRNG inside the PSO algorithm. The performance of such algorithm has been investigated deeply in previous studies e.g. [13, 15, 17].

In this research a simple method called the "Particle Performance Evaluation" is designed to improve the performance of PSO algorithm driven by dissipative chaotic map and to address some of the main issues that were discovered during previous research.

The paper is structured as follows: In the next section the original PSO algorithm is described. Section three contains brief summary of the results and main points of previous research of PSO witch Dissipative map based CPRNG. The "Particle Performance Evaluation" is described in section four. Following sections contain the experiments design and results. The results discussion and conclusion follows afterwards.

K. Saeed and V. Snášel (Eds.): CISIM 2014, LNCS 8838, pp. 445–454, 2014.
© IFIP International Federation for Information Processing 2014

2   Particle Swarm Optimization Algorithm

The original (canonical) PSO algorithm was introduced in 1995 by Eberhart and Kennedy [1, 2]. Each particle in the swarm is defined by its "position" - the combination of cost function (CF) parameters, and "velocity". The new position of the particle in the following iteration is then obtained as a sum of actual position and newly calculated velocity. The velocity calculation follows two natural tendencies of the particle: To move to the best solution found so far by the particular particle (known in the literature as personal best: *pBest* or local best: *lBest*). And to move to the overall best solution found in the swarm or defined sub-swarm (known as global best: *gBest*).

According to the method of selection of the swarm or subswarm for *gBest* information spreading, the PSO algorithms are noted as global PSO (GPSO) [7] or local PSO (LPSO) [8]. Within this research the PSO algorithm with global topology (GPSO) [1,2, 7] was utilized.

In the original GPSO the new velocity is calculated according to (1):

$$v_{ij}^{t+1} = w \cdot v_{ij}^t + c_1 \cdot Rand \cdot (pBest_{ij} - x_{ij}^t) + c_2 \cdot Rand \cdot (gBest_j - x_{ij}^t) \qquad (1)$$

Where:

v_i^{t+1} - New velocity of the ith particle in iteration $t+1$.

w – Inertia weight value.

v_i^t - Current velocity of the ith particle in iteration t.

c_1, c_2 - Priority factors (set to the typical value = 2).

$pBest_i$ – Local (personal) best solution found by the ith particle.

$gBest$ - Best solution found in a population.

x_{ij}^t - Current position of the ith particle (component j of the dimension D) in iteration t.

$Rand$ – Pseudo random number, interval (0, 1). The CPRNG is used here.

The maximum velocity of particles in the GPSO is typically limited to 0.2 of the range of the optimization problem and this pattern was followed in this study. The new position of a particle is then given by (2), where x_i^{t+1} is the new position of the particle:

$$x_i^{t+1} = x_i^t + v_i^{t+1} \qquad (2)$$

Finally the linear decreasing inertia weight [5, 7] is used in the GPSO here. Its purpose is to slow the particles over time thus to improve the local search capability in the later phase of the optimization. The inertia weight has two control parameters w_{start} and w_{end}. A new w for each iteration is given by (3), where t stands for current iteration number and n stands for the total number of iterations. The values used for the GPSO in this study were $w_{start} = 0.9$ and $w_{end} = 0.4$.

$$w = w_{start} - \frac{((w_{start} - w_{end}) \cdot t)}{n} \qquad (3)$$

3   PSO with CPRNG Based on Dissipative Standard Map

Within the previous research [13-15, 17] strong evidences have been gathered hinting that through using of CPRNG based on Dissipative standard map inside the velocity calculation formula (1) of PSO algorithm the performance may be improved (in some cases). The detailed investigations [13 - 15] showed that the PSO driven by Dissipative map based CPRNG seems to achieve better results than canonical PSO in the cases of complex highly multimodal or high dimensional problems [13, 15, 17].

Recent research in chaos driven heuristics has been fueled with the predisposition that unlike stochastic approaches, a chaotic approach is able to bypass local optima stagnation. This one clause is of deep importance to evolutionary algorithms. A chaotic approach generally uses the chaotic map in the place of a pseudo random number generator. This causes the heuristic to map unique regions, since the chaotic map iterates to new regions. The task is then to select a very good chaotic map as the pseudo random number generator.

It seems that the performance of PSO is improved by altering the swarm behavior in such manner that the convergence speed is significantly slower, which may result in the lower chance of falling into local extremes. However the better achieved results are usually compensated by the significantly higher computational time demands given the higher number of iterations required for the algorithm to converge (for further details please see [13 - 15]).

The aforementioned behavior lead to conclusion: when strict time restrictions are applied, the PSO driven by chaotic Dissipative map based CPRNG is not able to achieve good results. As a reaction to these issues, the novel "Particle performance evaluation" approach is investigated and implemented into the GPSO driven by Dissipative standard map in this presented research. The goal is to enhance the overall performance of the algorithm through the improvement of the convergence speed together with maintaining the advantages of the original PSO driven by Dissipative map based CPRNG.

The Dissipative standard map is a two-dimensional chaotic map [18]. The parameters used in this work are $b = 0.6$ and $k = 8.8$ based on previous experiments [17, 15] and suggestions in literature [18].The map equations are given in (4).

$$X_{n+1} = X_n + Y_{n+1} \pmod{2\pi}$$
$$Y_{n+1} = bY_n + k \sin X_n \pmod{2\pi}$$

(4)

4   PSO with Particle Performance Evaluation (PSO with PPE)

The novel approach proposed in this study is based on the simple premise that all particles should take part in the process of finding and improving of the final solution. The only way of communication among the particles in the GPSO design [1] represents the shared knowledge of the position of the best globally found solution (*gBest*). In other words: To be beneficial for the swarm, the particle has to update the *gBest*. Therefore the first step in the particle performance evaluation (PPE) is the exact monitoring of the *gBest* updaters. A counter is allocated to each particle. On the start of each iteration the counter is incremented by 1 and is set to 0 when the particle triggers a *gBest* update. In this way, it is possible to measure the number of iterations since the last *gBest* was found by particular particle. The second step in the PPE approach is to alter the performance of the particular particle when it has not triggered the *gBest* update for a given maximum number of iterations. In this initial research the simple constant c_1 (1) is modified to vector (see (5)).

$$v_{ij}^{t+1} = w \cdot v_{ij}^t + c_{1i} \cdot Rand \cdot (pBest_{ij} - x_{ij}^t) + c_2 \cdot Rand \cdot (gBest_j - x_{ij}^t) \qquad (5)$$

Where:

c_{1i} – Priority factor 1 for the *i*th particle.

Subsequently when the particular particle does not trigger a *gBest* update for 1/10 of the total number of iterations, the c_1 value for that particle is set to 1. The value of c_1 is set back to 2 when the particle reaches the *gBest* update.

Through the following of this very simple pattern it is possible to reduce the number of particles with no *gBest* updates (triggers), further to reduce the number of iteration between *gBest* updates for the each particle and to improve the overall performance of the PSO algorithm driven by Dissipative map based CPRNG in some cases as it is presented in the following sections.

5   Experiment Setup

Within all performance testing three different GPSO versions were used. The first one was the original canonical GPSO with linear decreasing inertia weight (as described in the section 2), noted GPSO. The second version was the GPSO with Dissipative map based CPRNG in the velocity calculation (Noted GPSO Disi) and finally the third version represents the GPSO with Dissipative map based CPRNG and PPE as described in the section 4 (noted PSO Disi PPE).

For the performance tests the CEC 13 benchmark suite [19] was used. For each version, totally 20 separate runs were performed and statistically analyzed.

Control parameters were set up based on the previous numerous experiments and literature sources [1, 14, 15, 19] as follows:

Population size: 30

Dimension: 10, 50

Iterations: 2500, 12500 (according to [19])

Runs: 20

$v_{max} = 0.2 \cdot$ Range

$w_{start} = 0.9$

$w_{end} = 0.4$

6   Results

The mean results for all versions of PSO described in the previous section are given and compared in Tables 1 and 2. The bold numbers represents the best results. The mean results are presented alongside the total number of best results obtained.

Furthermore the performance of pairs of algorithms is compared, where 1 stands for "win" of the "algorithm 1" (the first from the pair - left); number 2 stand for "win" of algorithm 2 (the second from the pair - right) and 0 stands for draw. The final score is also given in Tables 1 and 2 as a sum of points for wins (1 point) and draws (0.5 point).

Table 1. Mean results comparison for dim = 10

$f(x)$	GPSO	GPSO Disi	GPSO Disi PPE	A1 vs. A2	A1 vs. A3	A2 vs. A3
$f(1)$	**-1400**	**-1400**	**-1400**	0	0	0
$f(2)$	**116137.6**	416672.8	238461.5	1	1	2
$f(3)$	2.73E+06	1.90E+06	**289907.1**	2	2	2
$f(4)$	-806.79	-471.1	**-957.38**	1	2	2
$f(5)$	**-1000**	**-1000**	**-1000**	0	0	0
$f(6)$	**-894.08**	-886	-890.78	1	1	2
$f(7)$	-795.82	**-796.74**	-793.61	2	1	1
$f(8)$	-679.67	**-679.69**	-679.67	2	0	1
$f(9)$	**-597.39**	-596.65	-596.82	1	1	2
$f(10)$	-499.51	-499.32	**-499.6**	1	2	2
$f(11)$	**-398.16**	-397.14	-397.61	1	1	2
$f(12)$	-287.02	-278.4	**-288.41**	1	2	2
$f(13)$	**-181.14**	-177.32	-180.41	1	1	2
$f(14)$	**73.36**	169.38	128.84	1	1	2
$f(15)$	835.16	949.55	**674.34**	1	2	2
$f(16)$	200.89	200.95	**200.79**	1	2	2
$f(17)$	314.23	329.04	**313.66**	1	2	2
$f(18)$	431.55	439.58	**422.38**	1	2	2
$f(19)$	500.68	501.48	**500.67**	1	2	2
$f(20)$	**602.48**	602.87	602.6	1	1	2
$f(21)$	1100.19	**1090.18**	1100.19	2	0	1
$f(22)$	**1031.51**	1045.12	1121.89	1	1	1
$f(23)$	**1623.05**	1726.28	1711.32	1	1	2
$f(24)$	1204.71	1209.16	**1204.64**	1	2	2
$f(25)$	1307.02	**1305.78**	1306.93	2	2	1
$f(26)$	1350.92	**1345.93**	1347.28	2	2	1
$f(27)$	**1640.26**	1656.97	1691.26	1	1	1
$f(28)$	1754.15	**1737.21**	1745.87	2	2	1
Best:	12	8	12	Score: 20 : 8	13 : 15	9.0 : 19.0

Table 2. Mean results comparison for dim = 50

f(x)	GPSO	GPSO Disi	GPSO Disi PPE	A1 vs. A2	A1 vs. A3	A2 vs. A3
f(1)	**-1400**	-1348.687	**-1400**	1	0	2
f(2)	**9.65E+06**	6.29E+07	2.18E+07	1	1	2
f(3)	3.01E+08	6.91E+09	**2.45E+08**	1	2	2
f(4)	1964.64	8114.369	**-742.66**	1	2	2
f(5)	**-1000**	-975.08	**-1000**	1	0	2
f(6)	-846.59	-832.96	**-853.21**	1	2	2
f(7)	**-749.31**	-732.56	-743.87	1	1	2
f(8)	-678.88	-678.879	**-678.9**	0	2	2
f(9)	**-558.06**	-550.86	-554.49	1	1	2
f(10)	-498.69	-377.11	**-499.88**	1	2	2
f(11)	-345.973	-202.754	**-346.22**	1	2	2
f(12)	-38.699	120.79	**-137.82**	1	2	2
f(13)	136.46	217.1	**88.27**	1	2	2
f(14)	**1582.63**	5858.16	1657.56	1	1	2
f(15)	12130.01	12897.36	**7891.71**	1	2	2
f(16)	203.04	**202.68**	202.89	2	2	1
f(17)	**432.469**	764.932	448.87	1	1	2
f(18)	868.08	947.15	**611.54**	1	2	2
f(19)	**507.03**	541.05	508.97	1	1	2
f(20)	621.37	621.67	**620.03**	1	2	2
f(21)	**1615.7**	1726.1	1661.8	1	1	2
f(22)	**2915.96**	7466.41	3205.45	1	1	2
f(23)	12395.47	14554.47	**10168.74**	1	2	2
f(24)	**1290.55**	1314.49	1306.99	1	1	2
f(25)	**1484.49**	1521.45	1510.91	1	1	2
f(26)	**1563.87**	1582.17	1586.17	1	1	1
f(27)	**2687.23**	2843.66	2863.93	1	1	1
f(28)	**1800**	1861.448	1960.31	1	1	1
Best:	13	1	12 Score:	26.5 : 1.5	14.0 : 14.0	4.0 : 24.0

Furthermore Fig. 1 depicts the illustrative comparison of the number of iterations since the last *gBest* update for each particle for GPSO Disi and GOPSO Disi PPE. It can be clearly observed the positive influence of PPE approach.

Finally two examples of mean *gBest* history plots are given in Fig. 2 and 3 to highlight the change in behavior of the chaos driven GPSO especially in terms of convergence speed. The results are further discussed in following section.

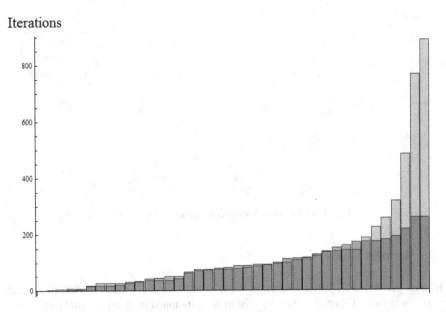

Fig. 1. Number of iterations since last *gBest* update for each particle (sorted). *f(1)*, *dim* = 10; comparison of GPSO Disi– blue, GPSO Disi PPE – red

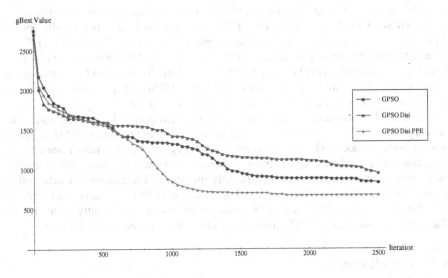

Fig. 2. Mean *gBest* history comparison *f(15)*, *dim* = 10

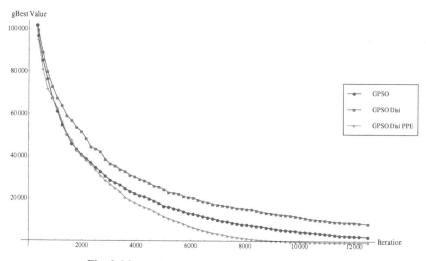

Fig. 3. Mean *gBest* history comparison *f(4)*, *dim* = 50

7   Results Discussion

The data presented in previous section seem to indicate that when the PPE is applied, the performance of GPSO driven by Dissipative standard map was in some cases significantly improved. In the first experiment (Table 1) the original chaotic GPSO (GPSO Disi) managed to obtain better results than the canonical version (GPSO) only for 8 functions. However when PPE was applied the number of better results (for the restricted number of iterations) has increased to 15. In direct comparisons the chaos driven GPSO with PPE (GPSO Disi PPE) managed to find better results for 19 different benchmark functions than the simple chaos driven GPSO (GPSO Disi). As an illustrative example, the effect of PPE (in case of *f(15)*) can be further observed from Fig. 2, where the *gBest* history is depicted and the improvement of convergence speed is clearly visible. It also seems that the GPSO Disi would improve its performance further if the number of iterations was increased.

The second experiment (with higher dimension setting) has brought up surprising results (Table 2) that were unprecedented in any previous research [13-15]. It seems that the performance of GPSO Disi is not satisfactory within the given dimension setting, function complexity and number of iterations. However when PPE is applied once again the performance was significantly improved. The example of mean *gBest* history for *dim*=50 and *f(4)* is given in Fig. 3. It seems that on this type of problem [19] the chaos driven PSO with PPE manages to obtain significantly better results than both the canonical (GPSO) and original chaos driven version (GPSO Disi).

8   Conclusion

In this initial research the behavior of GPSO algorithm driven by Dissipative standard map based CPRNG was altered by applying the "Particle performance evaluation".

The performance of newly designed algorithm was tested on the CEC 13 benchmark suite and compared to the performance of original GPSO with both canonical and chaotic PRNG.

It is necessary to mention, that the main aim of this paper was not to test the chaos embedding approach for evolutionary/swarm based algorithms, as the utilization of different CPRNGS and the very positive influence of inner chaotic dynamics to the performance of embedded algorithms was proved in many previous studies. Since the PPE approach was already successfully tested with canonical versions of PSO and with default PRNGs (no chaos embedded), the contribution of this paper is to show/prove the influence of PPE approach also in the different case of the chaos driven PSO algorithm, which takes advantages from the different swarm environment given by the chaotic dynamics.

The initial results presented in this paper seem to indicate that this approach may lead to significant performance improvements for certain types of optimization problems. Also it seems that the number of redundant cost function evaluations may be significantly reduced by using the PPE approach. There is however still a need for significant number of experiment with higher variety of problem types and control parameters settings to prove these claims. The future research will focus mainly on further improvements of this method by enhancing the PPE with variety of different behavior changes (rules) for the particles.

Acknowledgements. The following grants are acknowledged for the financial support provided for this research: Grant Agency of the Czech Republic - GACR P103/13/08195S, is partially supported by Grant of SGS No. SP2014/159, VŠB - Technical University of Ostrava, Czech Republic, by the Development of human resources in research and development of latest soft computing methods and their application in practice project, reg. no. CZ.1.07/2.3.00/20.0072 funded by Operational Programme Education for Competitiveness, co-financed by ESF and state budget of the Czech Republic, further was supported by European Regional Development Fund under the project CEBIA-Tech No. CZ.1.05/2.1.00/03.0089 and by Internal Grant Agency of Tomas Bata University under the project No. IGA/FAI/2014/010.

References

1. Kennedy, J., Eberhart, R.: Particle swarm optimization. In: IEEE International Conference on Neural Networks, pp. 1942–1948 (1995)
2. Kennedy, J., Eberhart, R.C., Shi, Y.: Swarm Intelligence. Morgan Kaufmann Publishers (2001)
3. Liang, J., Suganthan, P.N.: Dynamic multi-swarm particle swarm optimizer. In: Swarm Intelligence Symposium, SIS 2005, pp. 124–129 (2005)
4. Liang, J.J., Qin, A.K., Suganthan, P.N., Baskar, S.: Comprehensive learning particle swarm optimizer for global optimization of multimodal functions. IEEE Transactions on Evolutionary Computation 10(3), 281–295 (2006)
5. Nickabadi, A., Ebadzadeh, M.M., Safabakhsh, R.: A novel particle swarm optimization algorithm with adaptive inertia weight. Applied Soft Computing 11(4), 3658–3670 (2011)

6. Zhi-Hui, Z., Jun, Z., Yun, L., Yu-hui, S.: Orthogonal Learning Particle Swarm Optimization. IEEE Transactions on Evolutionary Computation 15(6), 832–847 (2011)
7. Yuhui, S., Eberhart, R.: A modified particle swarm optimizer. In: IEEE World Congress on Computational Intelligence, May 4-9, pp. 69–73 (1998)
8. Kennedy, J., Mendes, R.: Population structure and particle swarm performance. In: Proceedings of the 2002 Congress on Evolutionary Computation, CEC 2002, pp. 1671–1676 (2002)
9. van den Bergh, F., Engelbrecht, A.P.: A study of particle swarm optimization particle trajectories. Information Sciences 176(8), 937–971 (2006)
10. Caponetto, R., Fortuna, L., Fazzino, S., Xibilia, M.G.: Chaotic sequences to improve the performance of evolutionary algorithms. IEEE Transactions on Evolutionary Computation 7(3), 289–304 (2003)
11. Araujo, E., Coelho, L.: Particle swarm approaches using Lozi map chaotic sequences to fuzzy modelling of an experimental thermal-vacuum system. Applied Soft Computing 8(4), 1354–1364 (2008)
12. Alatas, B., Akin, E., Ozer, B.: Chaos embedded particle swarm optimization algorithms. Chaos, Solitons & Fractals 40(4), 1715–1734 (2009)
13. Pluhacek, M., Senkerik, R., Davendra, D., Kominkova Oplatkova, Z., Zelinka, I.: On the behavior and performance of chaos driven PSO algorithm with inertia weight. Computers & Mathematics with Applications 66, 122–134 (2013)
14. Pluhacek, M., Senkerik, R., Zelinka, I.: Particle Swarm Optimization Algorithm Driven by Multichaotic Number Generator. Soft Computing (accepted for publication, 2014), doi: 10.1007/s00500-014-1222-z
15. Pluhacek, M., Senkerik, R., Zelinka, I., Davendra, D.: On the Performance of Enhanced PSO Algorithm with Dissipative Chaotic Map in the Task of High Dimensional Optimization Problems. In: Zelinka, I., Chen, G., Rössler, O.E., Snasel, V., Abraham, A. (eds.) Nostradamus 2013: Prediction, Model. & Analysis. AISC, vol. 210, pp. 89–99. Springer, Heidelberg (2013)
16. Pluhacek, M., Budikova, V., Senkerik, R., Oplatkova, Z., Zelinka, I.: Extended Initial Study on the Performance of Enhanced PSO Algorithm with Lozi Chaotic Map. In: Zelinka, I., Snasel, V., Rössler, O.E., Abraham, A., Corchado, E.S. (eds.) Nostradamus: Mod. Meth. of Prediction, Modeling. AISC, vol. 192, pp. 167–177. Springer, Heidelberg (2013)
17. Pluhacek, M., Senkerik, R., Davendra, D., Zelinka, I.: Designing PID controller for DC motor by means of enhanced PSO algorithm with dissipative chaotic map. In: Snasel, V., Abraham, A., Corchado, E.S. (eds.) SOCO Models in Industrial & Environmental Appl. AISC, vol. 188, pp. 475–483. Springer, Heidelberg (2013)
18. Sprott, J.C.: Chaos and Time-Series Analysis. Oxford University Press (2003)
19. Liang, J.J., Qu, B.-Y., Suganthan, P.N., Hernández-Díaz Alfredo, G.: Problem Definitions and Evaluation Criteria for the CEC 2013 Special Session and Competition on Real-Parameter Optimization, Technical Report 201212, Computational Intelligence Laboratory, Zhengzhou University, Zhengzhou China and Technical Report, Nanyang Technological University, Singapore (January 2013)

Chaos Powered Grammatical Evolution

Ivan Zelinka[1], Petr Šaloun[1], and Roman Senkerik[2]

[1] VSB-Technical University of Ostrava, 17. listopadu 15,
708 33 Ostrava-Poruba, Czech Republic
{ivan.zelinka,petr.saloun}@vsb.cz
[2] Faculty of Applied Informatics, Tomas Bata University in Zlin
senkerik@fai.utb.cz

Abstract. In this paper we discuss alternative nonrandom generators for symbolic regression algorithms and compare its variants powered by classical pseudo-random number generator and chaotic systems. Experimental data from previous experiments reported for genetic programming and analytical programming is used. The selected algorithms are differential evolution and SOMA. Particle swarm, simulated annealing and evolutionary strategies are in process of investigation. All of them are mutually used in scheme Master-Slave meta-evolution for final complex structure fitting and its parameter estimation.

1 Introduction

The need of problem optimization is very old and covers various disciplines including engineering, economics, physics, biology and many others. In fact, many real-world problems can be defined as an optimization problem. The goal of a typical optimization is to maximize productivity or performance of some process or device or to minimize waste. Many more or less sophisticated optimization techniques have been developed over time. While the simplest problems involving functions of a single variable may be solved using basic math, many real-world problems require more complex tools. Evolutionary processes can be in general used for many practical tasks, like robot trajectory design, plasma or chemical reactor control, aircraft wings design, scheduling problems amongst the others.

For a long time in history optimization methods have been based on still more and more complicated methods usually involving exact mathematics. However, with increasing complexity of problems to be optimized need for more powerful and flexible optimization techniques arose. In mid-sixties, evolutionary algorithms were developed to address these demands. They are considered a powerful tool with many advantages over traditional optimization techniques.

One of the biggest advantages of evolutionary algorithms is that unlike many other traditional optimization techniques, they dont depend upon mathematical models of problems. Actually, the only precondition of using an evolutionary algorithm is the ability to evaluate candidate solution. In other words, the only thing that matter is whether or not it is possible to evaluate a solution once it is presented.

K. Saeed and V. Snášel (Eds.): CISIM 2014, LNCS 8838, pp. 455–464, 2014.

456   I. Zelinka, P. Šaloun, and R. Senkerik

An interesting extension of evolutionary algorithms is so called symbolic regression, that uses evolution to synthesize complex structures (formulas, el. circuits, computer programs) from simple building blocks (mathematical functions, el. elements, programming commands). The initial idea of symbolic regression by means of a computer program was proposed in genetic programming (GP) [1,2]. The other approach of grammatical evolution (GE) was developed in [3], [20] and analytical programming (AP) in [4]. Another interesting investigation using symbolic regression were carried out in [5] on AIS and Probabilistic Incremental Program Evolution (PIPE), which generates functional programs from an adaptive probability distribution over all possible programs. Yet another new technique is the so called *Transplant Evolution*, see [6], [7] and [8] which is closely associated with the conceptual paradigm of AP, and modified for GE. GE was also extended to include DE by [9]. Generally speaking, it is a process which combines, evaluates and creates more complex structures based on some elementary and noncomplex objects, in an evolutionary way. Such elementary objects are usually simple mathematical operators $(+, -, \times, ...)$, simple functions (sin, cos, And, Not, ...), user-defined functions (simple commands for robots – MoveLeft, TurnRight, ...), etc. An output of symbolic regression is a more complex "object" (formula, function, command,...), solving a given problem like data fitting of the so-called Sextic and Quintic problem [10,11], randomly synthesized function [11], Boolean problems of parity and symmetry solution (basically logical circuits synthesis) [12,4], or synthesis of quite complex robot control command by [2,19]. Examples mentioned in [13] are just few samples from numerous repeated experiments done by symbolic regression, which are used to demonstrate how complex structures can be produced by symbolic regression in general for different problems, see [13].

This paper focuses on grammar evolution which is an advanced evolutionary technique suitable for symbolic regression. Classical grammar evolution uses genetic algorithms as a computational core that manipulates genetic information. Further parts of this paper deal with an idea of *replacing the genetic-based core by DE or SOMA and pseudorandom generators by chaotic systems*. There has been made an experiment that measures performance of these alternative versions compared to the classical GE.

2   Used Methods and Motivation

For our experiments described here standard hardware and algorithms have been used. All important information about algorithms used in our experiments is mentioned and referred here. Standard as well as modern evolutionary algorithms were used for our experimentation. Comparing to the previous method, in this research GE with evolutionary algorithms like differential evolution (DE-Rand1Bin), [17] and SOMA (AllToOne), [18] are used. Application of alternative algorithms like Genetic Algorithms GA and Simulated Annealing (SA), ES and/or Swarm Intelligence is in process now.

The main difference comparing to similar experiments is the fact that we are using a) not only GE based on pseudorandom number generators (PRNG) but also on chaotic systems instead of PRNG use and b) instead of GE based operations are used algorithms DE and SOMA. All experiments were done in Mathematica 9, on MacBook Pro, 2.8 GHz Intel Core 2 Duo.

The master-slave approach was used in our experimentation, i.e. one kind of evolutionary algorithm was used like Master (to estimate general structure for data fitting with non-estimated parameters - constants) and second one s a Slave (to estimate just mentioned parameters - constants in formulas from Master process). Based on principles of DE and SOMA, individuals were of integer structure in the Master evolution.

The main motivation is based on use of chaotic dynamics instead of PRNG in previous research papers of various researchers (including our own, [26]-[28]). Till now chaos was observed in plenty of various systems (including an evolutionary one) and in the last few years it was also used to replace pseudo-number generators (PRGNs) in evolutionary algorithms (EAs). Let's mention for example research papers like one of the first use of chaos inside EAs [25], [26]-[28] discussing use of deterministic chaos inside particle swarm algorithm instead of PRGNs, [34] - [37] investigating relations between chaos and randomness or the latest one [38], [39], or another using chaos with EAs in applications, like [40] and [41], amongst the others.

Another research joining deterministic chaos and pseudorandom number generator has been done for example in [34]. Possibility of generation of random or pseudorandom numbers by use of the ultra weak multidimensional coupling of p 1-dimensional dynamical systems is discussed there. Another paper [29] deeply investigates logistic map as a possible pseudo-random number generator and is compared with contemporary pseudo-random number generators. A comparison of logistic map results is made with conventional methods of generating pseudo-random numbers. The approach used to determine the number, delay, and period of the orbits of the logistic map at varying degrees of precision (3 to 23 bits).

Logistic map that we are using here was also used in [30] like chaos-based true random number generator embedded in reconfigurable switched-capacitor hardware. Another paper [35] proposed an algorithm of generating pseudorandom number generator, which was called (couple map lattice based on discrete chaotic iteration) and combined the couple map lattice and chaotic iteration. Authors also tested this algorithm in NIST 800-22 statistical test suits and was used in image encryption.

In [36] authors exploit interesting properties of chaotic systems to design a random bit generator, called CCCBG, in which two chaotic systems are cross-coupled with each other. For evaluation of the bit streams generated by the CCCBG, the four basic tests are performed: monobit test, serial test, autocorrelation, Poker test. Also the most stringent tests of randomness: the NIST suite tests have been used. A new binary stream-cipher algorithm based on dual one-dimensional chaotic maps is proposed in [37] with statistic proprieties showing that the sequence is of high randomness. Similar studies are also done in [31], [25], [32] and [33].

Mutual comparison is discussed at the end.

2.1   Experiment Design

Our experiments have been set so that GE powered by classical pseudorandom number generator and deterministic chaos generators (see for example [14],
[15] and [16]), were used with above mentioned Master-Slave approach. Based
on the fact that deterministic chaos generators were successfully used in the
past [14], [15] and [16] for classical evolutionary algorithms, we have selected
logistic equation (1), and data series generated by this equation with setting
$A = 4$ as a random numbers to replace classical classical pseudorandom number
generator in symbolic regression. Algorithms selected for our experiments were
SOMA [18] and differential evolution (DERand1Bin) [17]. Another algorithms
like, simulated annealing (SA) [22] and [23], Evolutionary strategies (ES) [21]
and Particle Swarm (PSO) [24] are in process. Here we report results for GE
with SOMA (GSOMA) and GE with DE (GDE) test results.

$$x_{n+1} = Ax_n (1 - x_n) \qquad (1)$$

Both DE and SOMA are well regarded for their performance when applied on
various optimization problems. Genetic algorithms, on the other hand, are considered less performing. That said there is an assumption that also the grammar-
enabled variants of both (GDE and GSOMA) perform better than the classical
GE. This experiment aims to measure the GE, GDE and SOMA performance
and to compare it mutually.

Following paragraphs describe the problem of definition and control parameters that were used in the experiment. Each test was repeated 50 times for higher
accuracy.

All three mentioned evolutionary techniques were used to optimize a function
fitting problem. The goal was to find a function that describes given function
as closely as possible. The function was discretized into 50 points on a given
interval. Candidate solutions were evaluated as follows:

1. They were discretized the same way as the original function.
2. An absolute deviation was computed in each discretized point.
3. The cost value was determined as a sum of these absolute deviations.

An ideal solution would have a zero cost value while higher numbers mean that
the fitting was not perfect. That said no conversion was needed to transform
cost values into fitness values as lower values already represented better solution.
Furthermore, the ideal solution is represented by zero which is the optimal case.

There were two functions used in this experiment to achieve more accurate
results - formulas 3 and 4.

The cost function (2) has been defined according to Eq. 2 and the main aim
of the used evolution was to find formula, that gives the smallest value of Eq. 2.
To verify the functionality of AP more properly, set of comparative simulations
based on selected examples from Koza's GP has been done. Simulations were
focused on selected examples from [2] and [10], see its description in formulas
3 (sextic) and 4 (quintic).

$$f_{cost} = \sum_{1}^{n} |data_i - synthesized\_data_i| \tag{2}$$

$$x^6 - x^4 + x^2 \tag{3}$$

$$x^5 - 2x^3 + x \tag{4}$$

Different control parameters were used for each of the evolutionary techniques (GE, GDE and GSOMA). One reason is obvious each of these techniques uses a different set of control parameters. However, even if they would not, GE e.g. is known for requiring much bigger population sizes than DE to perform equally well so setting the same parameter values would not be fair even if it was technically possible. This is apparent with different GSOMA variants where highly different numbers of migration cycles are used, yet both variants evaluate the fitness function same times. To deal with this problem, we had to find three different sets of parameters that give the best results possible for each individual evolutionary technique. These parameter sets (described in tables 1, 2, 3, 4) were used for the experiment.

Table 1. GE Control Parameters

Parameter	Value
Cross Rate	0.85
Selection Strategy	Roulette-wheel selection
Population Size	300
Chromosome Length	50
Generation Count	500
Elitism Level	1

Table 2. GDE Control Parameters

Parameter	Value
Cross Rate	0.85
Mutation Constant	0.7
Population Size	50
Chromosome Length	50
Generation Count	20000

3 Results

This part contains graphs that visualize the experiment results in different ways. The first type of diagrams represent the evolution progress as it tries to approach the null fitness value. Many lines (specifically 50 but many of them overlap) can

Table 3. GSOMA All2One Control Parameters

Parameter	Value
Path Length	3.5
Step Size	0.11
Perturbation	0.3
Population Size	50
Dimension (Vector Length)	50
Migration Cycles	1000

Table 4. GSOMA All2All Adaptive

Parameter	Value
Path Length	3.5
Step Size	0.11
Perturbation	0.3
Population Size	7
Dimension (Vector Length)	50
Migration Cycles	20

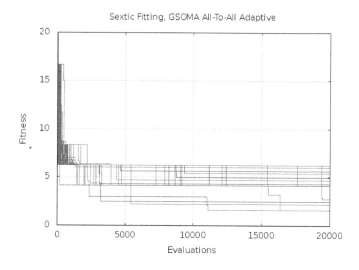

Fig. 1. An example of GSOMA

be seen in each of these diagrams, see Fig. 1. That is because each evolution has been run in 50 iterations as mentioned earlier and each chart visualizes these iterations all at once.

There were created diagrams for each evolutionary technique tested (GE, GDE and GSOMA) for each problem (Sextic, Quintic), see example at Fig. 2. That is obviously because two different problems were optimized. The diagrams are quite self-describing. There is a fitness value on the vertical axis and a number of fitness

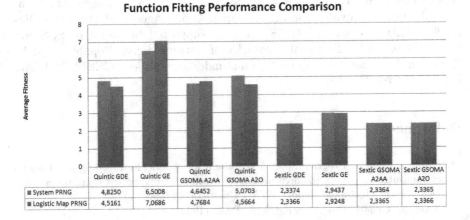

Fig. 2. Function fitting performance comparison

function evaluations on the horizontal axis. The individual lines consequently represent how many times the fitness function had to be evaluated to find a solution having the particular fitness value.

The second type of diagram shows the overall performance of each evolutionary technique depending of the PRNG used, see example at Fig. 2. There is a serie for each evolution technique measured (each of them with both PRNGs) on the horizontal axis. The vertical axis shows the average fitness values of the best solution of each iteration that has been created using 20,000 fitness function evaluation at maximum.

4 Conclusion

Based on the presented results, the chaotic PRNG based on logistic map proved itself suitable for use with GE, GDE and both GSOMA variants. As it turned out, neither of the techniques is sensitive to the non-uniform numbers distribution of the logistic map PRNG. The difference in performance using either of generators is within statistical error. It is surprising that such simple dynamic system can produce non random numbers which allows evolutionary techniques to run with almost unaffected performance. The uniformity of distribution is of course not the only attribute of quality and logistic map. PRNG may have some other qualities that the system PRNG is missing, although it offers much better (i.e. more uniform) number distribution. It also does not seem that logistic map PRNG would work better with some evolutionary techniques that with the others. Results for GE, GDE and GSOMA are all very similar for both PRNG types. There are open research questions like what is the best combination of algorithm parameters in Master-Slave approach, etc. The solution of those and other questions is mater on the next research.

Acknowledgement. The following two grants are acknowledged for the financial support provided for this research: Grant Agency of the Czech Republic - GACR P103/13/08195S, partially supported by Grant of SGS No. SP2014/159, VŠB - Technical University of Ostrava, Czech Republic, and by European Regional Development Fund under the project CEBIA-Tech No. CZ.1.05/2.1.00/03.0089.

References

1. Koza, J.: Genetic Programming: A paradigm for genetically breeding populations of computer programs to solve problems, Stanford University, Computer Science Department, Technical Report, STAN-CS-90-1314 (1990)
2. Koza, J.: Genetic Programming. MIT Press (1998)
3. Ryan, C., Collins, J.J., Neill, M.O.: Grammatical Evolution: Evolving Programs for an Arbitrary Language. In: Banzhaf, W., Poli, R., Schoenauer, M., Fogarty, T.C. (eds.) EuroGP 1998. LNCS, vol. 1391, pp. 83–96. Springer, Heidelberg (1998)
4. Zelinka, I., Oplatkova, Z., Nolle, L.: Analytic programming – Symbolic regression by means of arbitrary evolutionary algorithms. Int. J. of Simulation, Systems, Science and Technology 6(9), 44–56 (2005)
5. Johnson, C.: Artificial immune systems programming for symbolic regression. In: Ryan, C., Soule, T., Keijzer, M., Tsang, E., Poliand, R., Costa, E. (eds.) EuroGP 2003. LNCS, vol. 2610, pp. 345–353. Springer, Heidelberg (2003)
6. Weisser, R., Osmera, P.: Two-Level Transplant Evolution for Optimization of General Controllers, New Trends in Technologies, Sciyo (2010)
7. Weisser, R., Osmera, P.: Two-level Tranpslant Evolution, 17th Zittau Fuzzy Colloquium, Zittau, Germany (2010)
8. Weisser, R., Osmera, P., Matousek, R.: Transplant Evolution with Modified Schema of Differential Evolution: Optimization Structure of Controllers. In: International Conference on Soft Computing MENDEL, Brno, Czech Republic (2010)
9. O'Neill, M., Brabazon, A.: Grammatical Differential Evolution. In: Proceedings of International Conference on Artificial Intelligence, pp. 231–236. CSEA Press (2006)
10. Koza, J., Bennet, F., Andre, D., Keane, M.: Genetic Programming III. Morgan Kaufmann, New York (1999)
11. Zelinka, I., Oplatkova, Z.: Analytic programming – Comparative study. In: Proceedings of Second International Conference on Computational Intelligence, Robotics, and Autonomous Systems, Singapore (2003)
12. Koza, J., Keane, M., Streeter, M.: Evolving inventions. Scientific American, 40–47 (2003)
13. Zelinka, I., Davendra, D., Senkerik, R., Jasek, R., Oplatkova, Z.: Analytical Programming - a Novel Approach for Evolutionary Synthesis of Symbolic Structures. In: Kita, E. (ed.) Evolutionary Algorithms, InTech (2011),
http://www.intechopen.com/books/evolutionary-algorithms/analytical-programming-a-novel-approach-for-evolutionary-synthesis-of-symbolic-structures ISBN: 978-953-307-171-8, doi: 10.5772/16166
14. Zelinka, I., Senkerik, R., Pluhacek, M.: Do Evolutionary Algorithms Indeed Require Randomness? In: IEEE Congress on Evolutionary Computation, Cancun, Mexico, pp. 2283–2289 (2013)

15. Zelinka, I., Chadli, M., Davendra, D., Senkerik, R., Pluhacek, M., Lampinen, J.: Hidden Periodicity - Chaos Dependance on Numerical Precision. In: Zelinka, I., Chen, G., Rössler, O.E., Snasel, V., Abraham, A. (eds.) Nostradamus 2013: Prediction, Model. & Analysis. AISC, vol. 210, pp. 47–59. Springer, Heidelberg (2013)

16. Zelinka, I., Chadli, M., Davendra, D., Senkerik, R., Pluhacek, M., Lampinen, J.: Do evolutionary algorithms indeed require random numbers? Extended study. In: Zelinka, I., Chen, G., Rössler, O.E., Snasel, V., Abraham, A. (eds.) Nostradamus 2013: Prediction, Model. & Analysis. AISC, vol. 210, pp. 61–75. Springer, Heidelberg (2013)

17. Price, K.: An Introduction to Differential Evolution. In: Corne, D., Dorigo, M., Glover, F. (eds.) New Ideas in Optimization, pp. 79–108. McGraw-Hill, London (1999)

18. Zelinka, I.: SOMA – Self Organizing Migrating Algorithm. In: Babu, B.V., Onwubolu, G. (eds.) New Optimization Techniques in Engineering, pp. 167–218. Springer, New York (2004)

19. Oplatkova, Z., Zelinka, I.: Investigation on artificial ant using analytic programming. In: Proceedings of Genetic and Evolutionary Computation Conference, Seattle, WA, pp. 949–950 (2006)

20. O'Neill, M., Ryan, C.: Grammatical Evolution, Evolutionary Automatic Programming in an Arbitrary Language. Springer, New York (2003)

21. Beyer, H.-G.: Theory of Evolution Strategies. Springer, New York (2001)

22. Cern, V.: Thermodynamical approach to the traveling salesman problem: An efficient simulation algorithm. J. Opt. Theory Appl. 45(1), 41–51 (1985)

23. Kirkpatrick, S., Gelatt Jr., C.D., Vecchi, M.P.: Optimization by Simulated Annealing. Science 220(4598), 671–680 (1983)

24. Clerc, M.: Particle Swarm Optimization. ISTE Publishing Company (2006) ISBN 1905209045

25. Caponetto, R., Fortuna, L., Fazzino, S., Xibilia, M.: Chaotic sequences to improve the performance of evolutionary algorithms. IEEE Trans. Evol. Comput. 7(3), 289–304 (2003)

26. Pluhacek, M., Senkerik, R., Davendra, D., Kominkova Oplatkova, Z.: On the Behaviour and Performance of Chaos Driven PSO Algorithm with Inertia Weight. Computers and Mathematics with Applications (in print) ISSN 0898-1221

27. Pluhacek, M., Budikova, V., Senkerik, R., Oplatkova, Z., Zelinka, I.: Extended initial study on the performance of enhanced PSO algorithm with lozi chaotic map. In: Zelinka, I., Snasel, V., Rössler, O.E., Abraham, A., Corchado, E.S. (eds.) Nostradamus: Mod. Meth. of Prediction, Modeling. AISC, vol. 192, pp. 167–177. Springer, Heidelberg (2013)

28. Pluhacek, M., Senkerik, R., Zelinka, I.: Impact of Various Chaotic Maps on the Performance of Chaos Enhanced PSO Algorithm with Inertia Weight – an Initial Study. In: Zelinka, I., Snasel, V., Rössler, O.E., Abraham, A., Corchado, E.S. (eds.) Nostradamus: Mod. Meth. of Prediction, Modeling. AISC, vol. 192, pp. 153–166. Springer, Heidelberg (2013)

29. Persohn, K.J., Povinelli, R.J.: Analyzing logistic map pseudorandom number generators for periodicity induced by finite precision floating-point representation. Chaos, Solitons and Fractals 45, 238–245 (2012)

30. Drutarovsky, M., Galajda, P.: A robust chaos-based true random number generator embedded in reconfigurable switched-capacitor hardware. In: 17th International Conference Radioelektronika, April 24-25, vol. 1 and 2, pp. 29–34. Brno, Czech Republic (2007)

31. Bucolo, M., Caponetto, R., Fortuna, L., Frasca, M.,, R.: Does chaos work better than noise? IEEE Circuits and Systems Magazine 2(3), 4–19 (2002)
32. Hu, H., Liu, L., Ding, N.D.: Pseudorandom sequence generator based on the Chen chaotic system. Computer Physics Communications 184(3), 765–768 (2013), doi:10.1016/j.cpc.2012.11.017
33. Pluchino, A., Rapisarda, A., Tsallis, C.: Noise, synchrony, and correlations at the edge of chaos. Physical Review E 87(2) (2013), doi:10.1103/PhysRevE.87.022910
34. Lozi, R.: Emergence Of Randomness From Chaos. International Journal of Bifurcation and Chaos 22(2), 1250021 (2012), doi:10.1142/S0218127412500216
35. Wang, X.-Y., Qin, X.: A new pseudo-random number generator based on CML and chaotic iteration. Nonlinear Dynamics An International Journal of Nonlinear Dynamics and Chaos in Engineering Systems, Nonlinear Dyn. 70(2), 1589–1592 (2012), doi:10.1007/s11071-012-0558-0
36. Pareek, N.K., Patidar, V., Sud, K.K.: A Random Bit Generator Using Chaotic Maps. International Journal of Network Security 10(1), 32–38 (2010)
37. Wang, X.-Y., Yang, L.: Design Of Pseudo-Random Bit Generator Based On Chaotic Maps. International Journal of Modern Physics B 26(32), 1250208 (9 pages) (2012), doi:10.1142/S0217979212502086
38. Zhang, S.Y., Xingsheng, L.G.: A hybrid co-evolutionary cultural algorithm based on particle swarm optimization for solving global optimization problems. In: International Conference on Life System Modeling and Simulation / International Conference on Intelligent Computing for Sustainable Energy and Environment (LSMS-ICSEE), Wuxi, PR China, September 17-20 (2010)
39. Hong, W.-C., Dong, Y., Zhang, W.Y., Chen, L.-Y., Panigrahi, B.K.: Cyclic electric load forecasting by seasonal SVR with chaotic genetic algorithm. International Journal of Electrical Power and Energy Sysytems 44(1), 604–614, doi:10.1016/j.ijepes.2012.08.010
40. Chadli, M.: Unknown inputs observer design for fuzzy systems with application to chaotic system reconstruction. Computers and Mathematics with Applications 66(2), 147–154 (2013)
41. Zelinka, I., Chadli, M., Davendra, D., Senkerik, R., Jasek, R.: An investigation on evolutionary reconstruction of continuous chaotic systems. Mathematical and Computer Modelling 57(1-2), 2–15 (2013)

Network Anomaly Detection Using Parameterized Entropy

Przemysław Bereziński[1], Marcin Szpyrka[2], Bartosz Jasiul[1], and Michał Mazur[1]

[1] Military Communication Institute, C4I Systems' Department
ul. Warszawska 22a, 05-130 Zegrze, Poland
{p.berezinski,b.jasiul,m.mazur}@wil.waw.pl
[2] AGH University of Science and Technology, Department of Applied Computer Science
al. Mickiewicza 30, 30-059 Kraków, Poland
mszpyrka@agh.edu.pl

Abstract. Entropy-based anomaly detection has recently been extensively studied in order to overcome weaknesses of traditional volume and rule based approaches to network flows analysis. From many entropy measures only Shannon, Titchener and parameterized Renyi and Tsallis entropies have been applied to network anomaly detection. In the paper, our method based on parameterized entropy and supervised learning is presented. With this method we are able to detect a broad spectrum of anomalies with low false positive rate. In addition, we provide information revealing the anomaly type. The experimental results suggest that our method performs better than Shannon-based and volume-based approach.

Keywords: anomaly detection, entropy, netflow, network traffic measurement.

1 Introduction

The number of anomalies in IP networks caused by wormlike activities is growing [2]. Widely used security solutions based on signatures or rules like firewalls, antiviruses and intrusion detection systems do not provide sufficient protection because they do not cope with evasion techniques and not known yet (0-day) attacks [12], [13]. Therefore, network anomaly detection as one of possible solutions is becoming an essential area of research. Anomaly detection is an identification of observations which do not conform to an expected behavior. In a supervised anomaly detection a labeled data set that involves training a classifier is required.

There are many problems with anomaly detectors which have to be addressed. The main challenge is setting up a precise boundary between normal and anomalous behavior to avoid high false positive error rate or low detection rate. Another problems are long computation time, anomaly details extraction and root-cause identification [7]. In our previous work [4], some generalizations of entropy were described in details and preliminary results of using parameterized entropies were presented. In this paper, we make two major contributions. Firstly, we present our method and results in comparison with Shannon-based and volume-based approach. Secondly, we describe data set as well as the method we used to generate anomalies.

K. Saeed and V. Snášel (Eds.): CISIM 2014, LNCS 8838, pp. 465–478, 2014.
© IFIP International Federation for Information Processing 2014

2 Related Work

Entropy-based network anomaly detection has been a hot research topic recently. This approach relies on traffic feature distributions [16]. In the past, anomalies were treated as deviations in the traffic volume [11]. The problem is that not all anomalous network activities result in substantial traffic volume change. Moreover, Brauckhoff [6] proved that entropy-based approach with traffic feature distributions performs better then volume-based where sampling of flows is used. Several traffic feature distributions, i.e. header-based (addresses, ports, flags), volume-based (host or service specific percentage of flows, packets and bytes) and behavior-based (in/out connections for particular host) have been suggested in the past [17], [21]. However, it is unclear which feature distributions perform best. Nychis in [17], based on his results of pairwise correlation reported dependencies between addresses and ports and recommended the use of volume and behavior-based feature distributions. In opposite, Tellenbach in [21] reported no correlation among header-based features. Parameterized entropy-based approach for network anomaly detection is promising, what is confirmed by Tellenbach [21], who employed Tsallis entropy in his Traffic Entropy Telescope prototype capable to detect a broad spectrum of anomalies, Yang [23], who applied Renyi entropy to early detection of low-rate DDoS attacks detection, and Kopylova [15], who reported positive results of using Renyi conditional entropy in detection of selected fast spreading or aggressive worms. There are some limitations of entropy based detection especially when it comes to detecting small or slow attacks. This is especially true for Shannon entropy which has a limited descriptive capability [21]. Apart from entropy, some other feature distributions summarization techniques are successfully used in the context of network anomaly detection, namely sketches [10] and histograms [14]. As the main disadvantage of this methods is the proper tuning, we decided not to include them in this work.

3 Entropy

In this section, we present some not commonly known theory regarding entropies used in our experiments. Definition of entropy as a measure of disorder comes from thermodynamic and was proposed in the early 1850s by Clausius. In 1948 Shannon adopted entropy to information theory. In information theory, entropy is a measure of the uncertainty associated with a random variable. The more random the variable, the bigger the entropy and in contrast, the greater certainty of the variable, the smaller the entropy. For a probability distribution $p(X = x_i)$ of a discrete random variable X, the Shannon entropy is defined as:

$$H_s(X) = \sum_{i=1}^{n} p(x_i) \log_a \frac{1}{p(x_i)} \tag{1}$$

X is the feature that can take values $\{x_1, \ldots, x_n\}$ and $p(x_i)$ is the probability mass function of outcome x_i. Depending on the base of the logarithm, different units can be used: bits ($a = 2$), nats ($a = e$) or hurtleys ($a = 10$). For the purpose of anomaly detection, sampled probabilities estimated from a number of occurrences of x_i in a time window t are typically used. The value of entropy depends on randomness (it attains maximum when probability $p(x_i)$ for every x_i is equal) but also on the value of n. In order to measure randomness only, normalized forms have to be employed. For example, an entropy value can be divided by n or by maximum entropy defined as $\log_a(n)$. If not only the degree of uncertainty is important but also the extent of changes between assumed and observed distributions, denoted as q and p respectively, a relative entropy, also known as the Kullback-Leibler divergence can be used:

$$D_{KL}(p\|q) = \sum_{i=1}^{n} p(i) \log_a \frac{p(i)}{q(i)} \qquad (2)$$

To measure how much uncertainty is eliminated in X by observing Y the conditional entropy may be employed:

$$H_S(X|Y) = \sum_{i=1,j=1}^{m,n} p(x_i, y_j) \log_a p(x_i|y_j) \qquad (3)$$

The Shannon entropy assumes a tradeoff between contributions from the main mass of the distribution and the tail. To control this tradeoff, two parameterized Shannon entropy generalizations were proposed, by Renyi (1970s) and Tsallis (late 1980s) respectively [18], [22]. If the parameter denoted as α has a positive value, it exposes the main mass (the concentration of events that occur often), if the value is negative – it refers to the tail (the dispersion caused by seldom events). Both parameterized entropies (Renyi and Tsallis) derive from the Kolmogorov-Nagumo generalization of an average:

$$\langle X \rangle_\phi = \phi^{-1} \left(\sum_{i=1}^{n} p(x_i)\phi(x_i) \right), \qquad (4)$$

where ϕ is a function which satisfies the postulate of additivity (only affine or exponential functions satisfy this) and ϕ^{-1} is the inverse function. Renyi proposed the following function ϕ:

$$\phi(x_i) = 2^{(1-\alpha)x_i} \qquad (5)$$

After transformations, Renyi entropy may be given in the following form:

$$H_{R\alpha}(X) = \frac{1}{1-\alpha} \log_a(\sum_{i=1}^{n} p(x_i)^\alpha) \qquad (6)$$

Tsallis extended the Renyi entropy with the following function ϕ:

$$\phi(x_i) = \frac{2^{(1-\alpha)x_i} - 1}{1 - \alpha} \qquad (7)$$

After transformations, the Tsallis entropy will be given by:

$$H_{T\alpha}(X) = \frac{1}{1-\alpha} \left(\sum_{i=1}^{n} p(x_i)^\alpha - 1 \right) \qquad (8)$$

Both parameterized (Renyi and Tsallis) entropies:

- expose concentration for $\alpha > 1$ and dispersion for $\alpha < 1$,
- converge to the Shannon entropy for $\alpha \rightarrow 1$,
- correspond to cardinality of X for $\alpha = 0$.

4   Flow Monitoring

There are two approaches to network traffic monitoring, namely, packet-based and flow-based. In our work we focus on flow-based network monitoring since it is more scalable in the context of network speed. This approach is based on the ability of network devices to aggregate packets in flows. Each flow is cached by device and when it is finished or a timeout is exceed it is exported to an element called collector. Modern approach assumes the use of dedicated probes transparently connected as a passive appliance via span ports or network taps rather than the usage of routers to export flows. This approach (presented in Fig. 1) can overcome some performance limitations of routers.

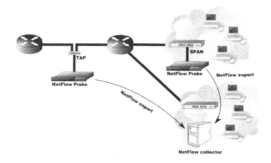

Fig. 1. Modern approach to flow exporting

The concept of network flows was introduced by Cisco and is currently standardized by the Internet Engineering Task Force (IETF). According to the IETF IPFIX working group [1], *"A flow is defined as a set of IP packets passing an observation point in the network during a certain time interval. All packets belonging to a particular flow have a set of common properties"*. In the simplest form, these properties are source and destination addresses and ports. A flow is typically defined as a unidirectional sequence of packets, which means that there are two flows for each connection between two endpoints – one from the server to client and one from the client to server. Recently, bidirectional flows (one record for each session between two endpoints) are also supported by vendors.

5   Data Set

For the purpose of this work, we created the data set containing labeled flows. Firstly, we captured two-day (Tuesday, Wednesday) legitimate traffic from a medium size

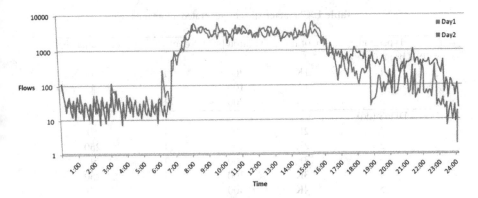

Fig. 2. Legitimate traffic profile by number of flows

corporation network connected to the Internet. This was accomplished using open source software – *softflowd* and *nfsen*. The profile of this traffic is depicted in Fig. 2.

We can see time t on x axis (5 minute fixed time window) and the number of flows on y (log scale) axis. Working day starts around 7 am. and finishes around 4 pm. The volume of traffic (expressed in number of flows) for both days is similar, but looking at the number of packets (Fig. 3), this similarity is a bit lower.

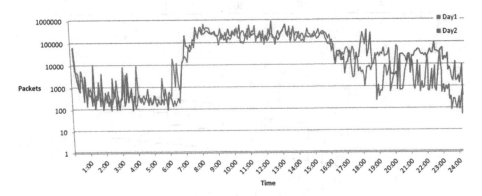

Fig. 3. Legitimate traffic profile by number of packets

In the next step, we generated *brute force*, *port scan*, *network scan* and *ddos* anomalies in different variants. More details concerning anomaly generation process is presented in the next section. Main characteristics of generated anomalies are presented in Table 1.

In the last step we mixed generated anomalies with the legitimate traffic from day2 (Wednesday) in the way presented in Fig. 4. We did not inject anomalies into the traffic from day1 (Tuesday) as it is used to build the profile of legitimate traffic in our approach.

As one can see, each anomaly is injected every 15 minutes mainly during working time. After injection only a few anomalies are visible in the volume expressed by number of flows or number of packets as depicted respectively in Fig. 5 and Fig. 6.

Table 1. Characteristics of generated anomalies

Type/kind	No. of flows	Duration [sec]	No. of victims	No. of attackers
SSH brute force (bf)				
1	1K	300	1	1
2	1K	100	1	1
3	2K	300	1	1
DDoS (dd)				
1	2K	200	1	50
2	2K	200	1	250
3	3K	300	1	50
4	3K	300	1	250
5	4K	400	1	50
6	4K	400	1	250
Network scan (ns)				
1	6K	60	6K	1
2	6K	300	6K	1
3	8K	80	8K	1
4	8K	400	8K	1
Port scan (ps)				
1	1K	50	1	1
2	1K	100	1	1
3	2K	100	1	1
4	2K	200	1	1

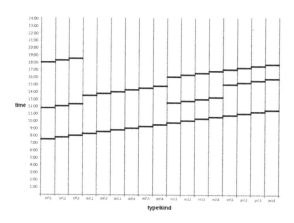

Fig. 4. Distribution of anomalies in time

6   Anomaly Generator

In order to produce flows that can mimic an anomalous behavior dedicated tool in Python language was developed. With this tool we can generate flows according to the predefined policy. The policy assigns a certain type of generation method to each field of flow record. In result we obtain a set of flows which meets given statistical profile.

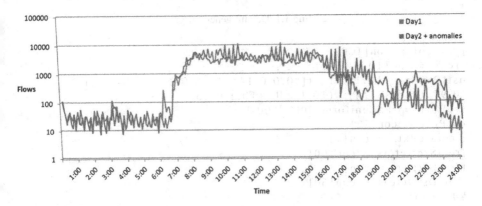

Fig. 5. Legitimate and anomalous traffic by number of flows

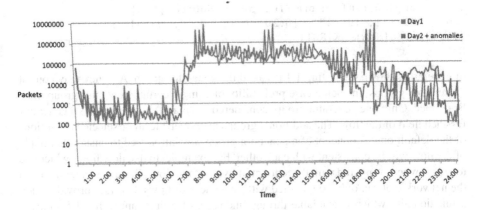

Fig. 6. Legitimate and anomalous traffic by number of packets

Internally, our tool operates on integer values which are manipulated by generation methods (introduced in [5]). They are as follows: *con* (constant), *ran* (random) and *per* (periodical). *Con* generator is straightforward and does not need further explanation, others are described below. *Ran* generators are used to obtain random values. There are two types of such generators: absolute (e.g. *srcPort* in Listing 1.1) or relative (e.g. *dstIP* in Listing 1.1). The value produced with the relative generator is summed with previously generated one. This feature can be used to sweep across certain range of values. Both generators can be initiated with either uniform or arbitrary distribution. Arbitrary distribution consists of two list: values and probabilities of these values. Relative generator additionally needs a start value and a range. *Per* generators are used to match a certain generating method with the sequence number of the currently generated flow. They are initiated with a list of key-value pairs out of which the first one represents the flow number and the second – the generator definition. On the last position, the default generator is placed. For example, *iar* definition in Listing 1.1 means that every 300th flow a uniform(10,50) generator will be applied and respectively every 800th flow generator returns 5000. In other cases, default generator will be applied. The set

Listing 1.1. Default generator group

```
[testgroup]
protocol = con[TCP]
srcIP = con[10.5.0.77]
dstIP = ran[10.1.0.1; (["0.0.0.1", "0.0.0.2", "-0.0.0.1"],
[0.97,0.15,0.15]); (10.1.0.1, 10.1.0.253)]
srcPort = ran[uniform(300, 500)]
dstPort = con[22]
fromSrcPkts = con[1]
fromSrcOctets = con[60]
fromDstPkts = con[1]
fromDstOctets = con[60]
#duration
dur = con[1]
#inter arrival time
iar = per[300:ran[uniform(10, 50)]; 800:con[500];
ran[ ([10, 11, 12, 13], [0.20, 0.30, 0.40, 0.10])]]
flags = con[SYN|ACK|RST]
```

of generators shown on Listing 1.1 is called the generator group. A policy may consist of multiple groups. In such a case probability of using a certain generator group must be defined. Only one generator group (considered as default) in a policy has a generator for each field of the flow. The additional groups may override all or selected definitions of the default one. A concept of a generator group was introduced to ensure that fields of the flow will be consistent with each other. For example, to disallow flows which are too short when compared with the amount of bytes of the flow. There are phenomena on the network that can only be modeled with sequences of flows. Our tool provides such a functionality which is available through indexing of group names. In such indexed groups, one can use mechanisms which allow sharing state between subsequent flows. For example, in Listing 1.2, we enforced value of *dstIP* not to be changed through the whole sequence.

Listing 1.2. Sequence modelling

```
[testgroup.1]
dstIP = args[usePrevValue]
dur = con[100]
[testgroup.2]
dstIP = args[usePrevValue]
dur = con[1000]
```

An example of a similar generator is Flame [5]. However, there are some significant differences. Flame comes with very basic support for generating flows, forcing users to implement all the generation logic by themselves, while our tool supports policy files. On the other hand it has fairly sophisticated functionality of inserting generated flows into the base traffic which our tool does not support at all. Another interesting concept was introduced in [19]. Authors proposed to describe network traffic (not only flows) by a set of so-called α- and β-profiles which can subsequently be used to generate a data set. α-profiles consist of actions which should be executed to generate a given event in the network (such as attack) while β-profiles are more similar to our policy files where behavior of certain entities (packet sizes, number of packets per flow) are represented by statistical model. On the whole this concept is similar to ours but far more complex.

7 Network Anomaly Detector

In this section we present entropy-based network anomaly detection module which is a component of the anomaly detection and security event data correlation system currently developed it the Secor project [8]. The goal of this module is to detect network anomalies with acceptable false positive error rate and high detection rate, classify anomalies and report some details (timestamps, related addresses and ports) to the correlation engine (output) which correlates events coming from different modules and external sensors in order to improve detection and limit false positive rate. The architecture of our network anomaly detection module is presented in Fig. 7.

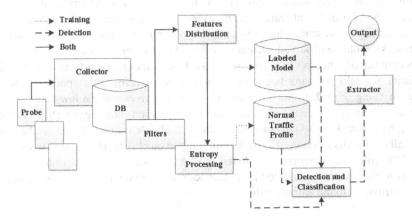

Fig. 7. Entropy-based network anomaly detection module

IP traffic is captured by NetFlow [1] probes. We decided to use bidirectional flows since, according to some works (e.g. [17]), unidirectional flows may entail biased results. In order to limit the area of search, filters per direction, protocol and subnet are used. Collected flows are analyzed within constant-length time intervals (every 5 min. by default). Next, depends on the version, Tsallis or Renyi entropy of positive and negative α values are calculated for traffic feature distributions presented in Table 2. Note: the Shannon version of our method use internally Renyi entropy with α set to 1.

Initially, during the training phase, a dynamic profile is built using min and max entropy values within a sliding time window for every $\langle feature, \alpha \rangle$ pair. Thus, we can reflect traffic changes during the day. In the detection phase, the observed entropy is

Table 2. Selected traffic feature distributions

Feature	Probability mass function
src(dst)address(port)	$\frac{number\ of\ x_i\ as\ src(dst)address(port)}{total\ number\ of\ src(dst)addresses(ports)}$
flows duration	$\frac{number\ of\ flows\ with\ x_i\ as\ duration}{total\ number\ of\ flows}$
packets, bytes	$\frac{number\ of\ pkts(bytes)\ with\ x_i\ as\ src(dst)\ addr(port)}{total\ number\ of\ pkts(bytes)}$
in(out)-degree	$\frac{number\ of\ hosts\ with\ x_i\ as\ in(out)-degree}{total\ number\ of\ hosts}$

compared with the min and max values stored in the profile according to the following rule:

$$r_\alpha(x_i) = \frac{H_\alpha(x_i) - k * \min_\alpha}{k * (\max_a - \min_\alpha)}, \qquad k \in \langle 1..2 \rangle \qquad (9)$$

With this rule, anomaly threshold is defined. Values $r_\alpha(x_i) < 0$ or $r_\alpha(x_i) > 1$ indicate abnormal concentration or dispersion respectively. This abnormal dispersion or concentration for different feature distributions is characteristic for anomalies. For example, during a port scan, a high dispersion in port numbers and high concentration in addresses should be observed. Detection is based on the relative value of entropy with respect to the distance between min and max. Coefficient k in the formula determines a margin for min and max boundaries and may be used for tuning purposes. A high value of k, e.g. $k = 2$, limits the number of false positives while a low value ($k = 1$) increases detection rate. We also take into consideration other approaches to thresholding based on standard deviation and quantiles. The detection is based on the results from all feature distributions. Classification is based on classifiers (decision trees, Bayes nets [20], rules and functions) employed in Weka software [3]. Extraction of anomaly details is also assumed – related ports and addresses are obtained by looking into the top contributors to the entropy value.

8   Results

Experiments were performed for Tsallis, Renyi and Shannon version of our method as well as traditional volume-based approach with flow, packet and byte counters. Final evaluation was performed with Weka tool. Some examplary results of entropies for a selected singular feature distributions are presented below. Abnormally high dispersion in destination addresses distribution for network scan anomalies exposed by negative value of α parameters is depicted in Fig. 8. One can see time t on x axis (5 minute time windows), result r on y axis and α values on z axis. Anomalies are marked with (A) on the time axis. Values of Shannon entropy are denoted as S.

Abnormal concentration of flows duration for network scans is depicted in Fig. 9. This concentration is typical for anomalies with fixed data stream.

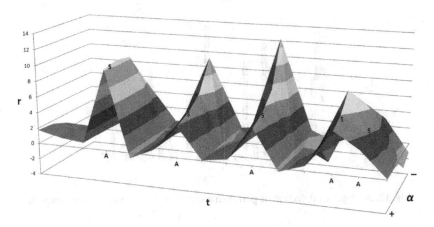

Fig. 8. Abnormally high dispersion in destination addresses for network scan anomalies (Renyi/Shannon)

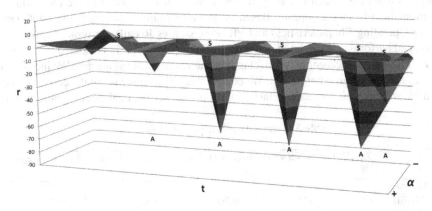

Fig. 9. Abnormally high concentration in flows duration for network scan anomalies (Tsallis/Shannon)

Fig. 10 shows ambiguous detection (no significant excess of $0 - 1$ threshold) of port scan anomaly with volume-based approach with flow, packet and byte counters. R on y axis corresponds to normalization applied in our method [equation (9)].

We noticed that measurements for all feature distributions as a group work better than single ones or subsets. The best results were obtained for addresses, ports and duration feature distributions, although we believe that the proper set of feature distributions is specific for particular anomalies.

Overall (whole data set, all feature distributions) multi-class classification was performed with Weka tool. We defined 4 classes for each anomaly type + 1 class for legitimate traffic. To properly asses predictive performance ten-fold cross-validation method was used. An ideal classifier should not produce false positive and false negative statistical errors. To evaluate non-ideal classifiers, one could measure proportion of correct

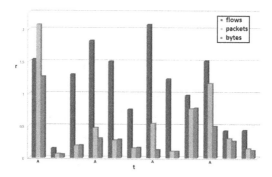

Fig. 10. Ambiguous detection of port scan anomaly with a volume-based approach

assessments to all assessments (Accuracy), the share of benign activities reported as anomalous (False Positive Rate) and the share of anomalies missed by the detector (False Negative Rate). Usage of Precision (proportion of correctly reported anomalies) and Recall (share of correctly reported anomalies compared to the total number of anomalies) is another option. Based on these measures some tools like ROC (Receiver Operating Characteristics) and PR (Precision vs Recall) are typically used [9]. Averaged performance of classification for different classifiers is presented in Table 3.

ZeroR is a trivial classifier which classifies the whole traffic as normal. We included it here as a reference to other results. We believe that an accuracy is not the correct choice to measure the performance of classification if data set is unbalanced – more normal

Table 3. Averaged performance of classification

	ZeroR|	Bayes Netw.|	Decision Tree J48|	Rand. Forest|	Simple Logistic Regress.
Accuracy					
Tsallis	0.66	0.89	0.90	0.92	0.93
Renyi	0.66	0.89	0.89	0.90	0.93
Shannon	0.66	0.84	0.86	0.90	0.92
Volume-based	0.66	0.71	0.77	0.78	0.80
ROC area					
Tsallis	0.44	0.97	0.94	0.99	0.98
Renyi	0.44	0.96	0.91	0.97	0.97
Shannon	0.44	0.95	0.88	0.97	0.98
Volume-based	0.44	0.80	0. 81	0.90	0.94
PR area					
Tsallis	0.45	0.96	0.90	0.97	0.96
Renyi	0.45	0.94	0.85	0.93	0.94
Shannon	0.45	0.93	0.83	0.94	0.96
Volume-based	0.45	0.75	0.72	0.79	0.85

than anomalous in our case. We suggest to look at ROC area and PR area instead. From the whole spectrum of tested methods the best performance was obtained by applying Logistic Regression, Bayesian Network, Decision Tree and Random Forest classifiers.

9   Conclusions and Future Work

Concluding the results of our studies, we can observe that, for our dataset: i) the Tsallis entropy performed best; ii) the Renyi entropy was slightly weaker; iii) the Shannon entropy was a bit worse than the Renyi (except from the Random Forest classifier); iv) the volume-based method performed poorly; v) among a large set of network traffic feature distributions, addresses, ports, and flows durations proved to be the best choices; vi) the most successful classifiers were Linear Regression, Bayes Network, Decision Tree and Random Forest. In general we believe that a broad spectrum of feature distributions provides a better flexibility to detect different types of anomalies.

While we admit that our experiments were limited to few number of cases, we also believe that these cases were representative. Our data set contains traces of network malicious activities which are typical for worm propagation, communication and attacks performed by group of machines infected by worms. Although, only one day legitimate traffic profile was built in our experiments, we have observed that this profile suits to each regular working day in the network we monitored. While more research work is necessary to validate the efficiency of the parameterized entropies, the poor performance of the Shannon entropy and volume-based methods allows to question whether they are the right approach to anomaly detection. In our method the precise traffic profile is the key, so future work will include optimization and experiments with more fluctuative legitimate traffic. We are also planning to model new anomalies and inject them into our data set to perform evaluation on a larger scale. We hope to retain good performance. Ś

Acknowledgements. This work has been partially supported by the National Centre for Research and Development project no. PBS1/A3/14/2012 "Sensor data correlation module for detection of unauthorized actions and support of decision process" and the European Regional Development Fund the Innovative Economy Operational Programme, under the INSIGMA project no. 01.01.02-00-062/09.

References

1. IETF IPFIX Working Group,
   http://datatracker.ietf.org/wg/ipfix/charter
2. Verizon. 2014 Data Breach Investigations Report,
   http://www.verizonenterprise.com/DBIR/2014/
3. Weka project homepage, http://www.cs.waikato.ac.nz/ml/weka
4. Bereziński, P., Pawelec, J., Małowidzki, M., Piotrowski, R.: Entropy-based internet traffic anomaly detection: A case study. In: Zamojski, W., Mazurkiewicz, J., Sugier, J., Walkowiak, T., Kacprzyk, J. (eds.) Proceedings of the Ninth International Conference on DepCoS-RELCOMEX. AISC, vol. 286, pp. 47–58. Springer, Heidelberg (2014)

5. Brauckhoff, D.: Network traffic anomaly detection and evaluation. ETH, Zurich (2010)
6. Brauckhoff, D., Tellenbach, B., Wagner, A., May, M., Lakhina, A.: Impact of packet sampling on anomaly detection metrics. In: Proceedings of the 6th ACM SIGCOMM Conference on Internet Measurement, IMC 2006, pp. 159–164. ACM (2006)
7. Chandola, V., Banerjee, A., Kumar, V.: Anomaly detection: A survey. ACM Computing Surveys 41(3) 15, 1–15 (2009)
8. Choraś, M., Kozik, R., Piotrowski, R., Brzostek, J., Hołubowicz, W.: Network events correlation for federated networks protection system. In: Abramowicz, W., Llorente, I.M., Surridge, M., Zisman, A., Vayssière, J. (eds.) ServiceWave 2011. LNCS, vol. 6994, pp. 100–111. Springer, Heidelberg (2011)
9. Davis, J., Goadrich, M.: The relationship between precision-recall and roc curves. In: Proc. of the 23rd Int. Conference on Machine Learning, ICML 2006, pp. 233–240. ACM (2006)
10. Dimitropoulos, X., Stoecklin, M., Hurley, P., Kind, A.: The eternal sunshine of the sketch data structure. Computer Networks 52(17), 3248–3257 (2008)
11. Fillatre, L., Nikiforov, I., Casas, P., Vaton, S.: Optimal volume anomaly detection in network traffic flows. In: Proceedings of the 16th European Signal Processing Conference, EURASIPCO 2008. EURASIP (2008)
12. Jasiul, B., Śliwa, J., Gleba, K., Szpyrka, M.: Identification of malware activities with rules. In: Proceedings of the Federated Conference on Computer Science and Information Systems, Warsaw, Poland (2014)
13. Jasiul, B., Szpyrka, M., Śliwa, J.: Malware behavior modeling with Colored Petri nets. In: Saeed, K., Snášel, V. (eds.) CISIM 2014. LNCS, vol. 8838, pp. 667–679. Springer, Heidelberg (2014)
14. Kind, A., Stoecklin, M.P., Dimitropoulos, X.: Histogram-based traffic anomaly detection. IEEE Trans. on Netw. and Serv. Manag. 6(2), 110–121 (2009)
15. Kopylova, Y., Buell, D.A., Huang, C.-T., Janies, J.: Mutual information applied to anomaly detection. Journal of Communications and Networks 10(1), 89–97 (2008)
16. Lakhina, A., Crovella, M., Diot, C.: Mining anomalies using traffic feature distributions. In: Proceedings of the 2005 Conference on Applications, Technologies, Architectures, and Protocols for Computer Communications, SIGCOMM 2005, pp. 217–228. ACM (2005)
17. Nychis, G., Sekar, V., Andersen, D.G., Kim, H., Zhang, H.: An empirical evaluation of entropy-based traffic anomaly detection. In: Proceedings of the 8th ACM SIGCOMM Conference on Internet Measurement, IMC 2008, pp. 151–156. ACM (2008)
18. Renyi, A.: Probability Theory. Dover Books on Mathematics Series. Dover Publ. Inc. (1973)
19. Shiravi, A., Shiravi, H., Tavallaee, M., Ghorbani, A.: Toward developing a systematic approach to generate benchmark datasets for intrusion detection. Computers and Security 31(3), 357–374 (2012)
20. Szpyrka, M., Jasiul, B., Wrona, K., Dziedzic, F.: Telecommunications networks risk assessment with bayesian networks. In: Saeed, K., Chaki, R., Cortesi, A., Wierzchoń, S. (eds.) CISIM 2013. LNCS, vol. 8104, pp. 277–288. Springer, Heidelberg (2013)
21. Tellenbach, B., Burkhart, M., Schatzmann, D., Gugelmann, D., Sornette, D.: Accurate network anomaly classification with generalized entropy metrics. Computer Networks 55(15), 3485–3502 (2011)
22. Tsallis, C., de Pesquisas Físicas, C.B.: Possible Generalization of Boltzmann-Gibbs Statistics. Notas de física. Centro Brasileiro de Pesquisas Físicas (1987)
23. Xiang, Y., Li, K., Zhou, W.: Low-rate ddos attacks detection and traceback by using new information metrics. Trans. Info. For. Sec. 6(2), 426–437 (2011)

Universal Central Control of Home Appliances as an Expanding Element of the Smart Home Concepts — Case Study on Low Cost Smart Solution

Jan Dvorak, Ondrej Berger, and Ondrej Krejcar[*]

University of Hradec Kralove, Faculty of Informatics and Management,
Center for Basic and Applied Research,
Rokitanskeho 62, Hradec Kralove, 500 03, Czech Republic
{Jan.Dvorak,Ondrej.Berger,Ondrej.Krejcar}@uhk.cz

Abstract. With the development of the electronic appliances, there is an increase in the usage of the so called Smart Homes concept. Nowadays, many standards and technologies exist which enable the control of the related home appliances. However, the common devices that support only the handeling via a controller on the basis of infrared transfer are not possible to be operated by these systems. In practical environment, the suggested solution is able to replace the function of such controllers and enable the user to operate the given devices using a website application that is available for example through a smartphone. The part of the solution is the interface for the connection of the application to current Smart Home systems and an intelligent recognition and an automatisation of user's actions with controllers. The result of the implementation is a functional prototype.

Keywords: Smart Home, Infrared, Remote Control, Automation, Mobile, Multimedia.

1 Introduction

The recent fast development in the field of electronic appliances also accompanies the development of the systems which contain elements of so called Smart Homes [1, 10-11, 13-15], the methods for the cooperation with electronic devices enabling the basic functions of a house. Originally, Smart House technologies were developed for the control of energetically advanced systems, such as heating or lighting. However, the current level of electronic equipment enables the connection of almost any components into the Smart Home system. Moreover, this is not only bound to switching on and off devices, it is also possible to create actions which would simplify the inhabitation of such environment and save time on the basis of pre-defined or intelligent algorithms. This is due to the instruments for monitoring of the presence and user's activity [2]. [3]

In relation to the intelligent buildings, recently the controlling and monitoring of their energy usage became a popular topic. The reason for the interest is for example the fact of up to 40% of spending on energy is in commercial buildings which can be reduced to

---

[*] Corresponding author.

K. Saeed and V. Snášel (Eds.): CISIM 2014, LNCS 8838, pp. 479–488, 2014.

70% [4] using automated systems for controlling of lighting. An example of an active operation in this field is the research of wireless control of lighting [5], technologies of smart transfer networks (Smart Grids [6]) or general usage of Smart Homes [7].

Current systems for intelligent homes usually contain a central controlling unit to which using star or bus line topology there are attached end nodes – sensors or action members. In relation to the supplier of the given solution, these nodes must support a specific standard of communication. The common representatives of such standards are for example C-Bus which communicated using the Ether network, international standard KNX [8] or a wireless system ZigBee [9].

The purpose of the project described in this paper was to suggest and implement a hardware and a software which would contribute to the centralised solution of the home appliances that are operated using the infrared controllers and do not support any of the standards for central controlling. The solution contains a website application which introduces a Human-Machine interface (HMI) and provides API for integration of current Smart Home systems.

Moreover, the system continuously monitors the usage of current controllers and on the basis of the user's activities suggests for example the unification of commonly consequential steps into mass actions (macros) or automatic implementation of regular actions. The result of this function should be the time saving and simplifying of everyday activities related to home appliances, which according to [3] corresponds to basic requirements of Smart Home technology users.

2   Problem Definition

The main reason for this project was the absence of the connection of most common multimedia appliances with current Smart Home solution. Some models support the standard HDMI CEC [20] that enables the operating of interconnected appliances using the HDMI cable. However, for the usage of such standard it would be necessary to connect to each device an individual module for its maintenance. This is technically, but also financially a very demanding solution. On the other hand, the traditional infrared remote controls are used by most multimedia home appliances. Moreover, the hardware for the transmitting and receiving is favourably priced. For example, the article [21] is concerned with the processing of the signals from IR controllers. This article suggests the system of automatic switch off of unused electric plugs and their repeated awakening using the IR signals.

Currently, there are a few products on the market which enable the functionality of the central controlling of the appliances using the IR signals. The product line Harmony from Logitech contains a wide spectrum of universal remote controls, from which Ultimate Hub, Smart control and Ultimate models have the Hub unit that provides similar functions as the suggested solution. For this solution, the company also offers applications for iOS and Android which are very well built and intuitive. Unfortunately, the Harmony product line is very closed and does not allow the connection with other systems. The prices range from 100 to 300 USD, depending on the specific model.

Moreover, the Open Source Universal Remote application is also worth mentioning when considering the open-source solutions. This application can be installed on any PC which contains IR controller and enables the transmitting of commands to appliances from any web browser in the network, for example even a smartphone.

The disadvantage of this application is that it does not offer the possibility to record signals of the current controller and consequently emulate them.

None of these above mentioned solutions has the ability to monitor the user's activities with the current controller and also does not suggest the optimisation of regular activities. The first two are introduced in the in the Fig 1.

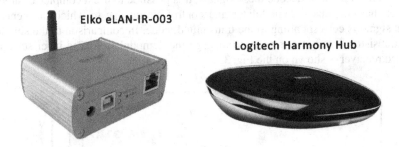

Fig. 1. Commercial device enabling the central control of IR appliances

3   New Solution

This chapter introduces the suggested solution for controlling of end devices. The schema (fig 2) shows the architecture of the whole system. It is important to notice the 3 basic communication directions:

- Through the web application, user can operate the end devices using the IR transmitter in the central point of the system.
- Central point captures commands which are sent from the original controller into the end devices.
- On the basis of the manual command, it is possible to duplicate the current controller and use it from the web application.

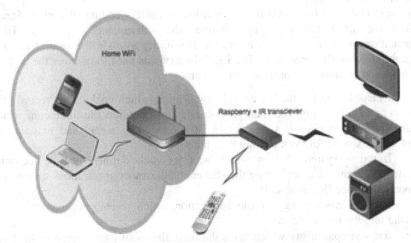

Fig. 2. Devices present in the system for the central control of the appliances

The requirements for the central point included the ability to receive and transmit IR signals which are compatible with remote controls and communicate with other devices using the HTTP protocol and LAN home network.

Most of the remote controls use the IR transfer with coding on the 38 or 36kHZ frequency. Manchester, Pulse distance or Pulse length coding is used for the modulation. In order to decode these signals, it is possible to use a completed three-pin receiver that contains a demodulator and control circuit due to which the generated digital signal is corresponding to the transmitted value. In comparison to the simple IR phototransistor, it is not necessary to manage the demodulation. The inner schema of the used receiver is shown on the Fig. 3.

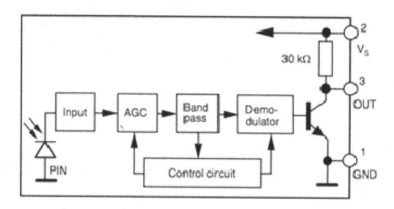

Fig. 3. The inner connection of the IR receiver TSoP 31238 [12]

The suggested transmitting circuit contains two IR diodes and a switching transistor (in order to not overwork the data pin by too much current). Two of the used diodes with the combination of wide-angle transmitting should provide the coverage of all appliances in an average room.

The next task was to ensure the recognition of correct coding of digital signals which come from the receiving module, the subsequent transfer to HEX representation of the pushed button and the possibility to code the value back and send it through the IR transmitter. The LIRC library was used to uncover the coding. It is composed of numerous basic sub-programmes:

• Irrecord – an interactive console application which enables to "record" the current remote controlling; the final product is a configuration file liircd.conf which contains for each operation a description of used coding signal and mapping of individual HEX codes of symbols into their aliases

• Liircd – system demon which acts on each defined end device with connected IR transmitter and using the socket enables other applications to send the previously recorded IR commands

• Irsend – associating console application which resends the entered saved command into the liircd socket

• Irw – simple utility which reads the lircd aliases of the received codes from the socket that is created by the demon and sends them to the standard output

Before the actual implementation, the structure proposal the user's interface of the application was conducted. The frequency of the expected usage of individual tasks which should be implemented was used for the distribution of the most important elements to the best reachable places. The most significant service of the application is the simulation of the push of the buttons for recorded controllers. Therefore, the accomplishing of the mass actions was placed at the original page.

The special page for recording of the controller functions on the basis of interactive navigator with simple commands. It can obtain text data from the users, such as the names of the recorded buttons, show the progress guide or the countdown of the remaining time. Physically, it is an interface which in real time [12,16-18], using the WebSockets communication technology [19]) conveys the commands of the irrecord application to the user and immediately returns to it the obtained data. The structure of the application and possible paths between individual functions are shown on the Fig. 4.

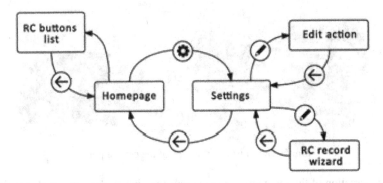

Fig. 4. Diagram of the transfers between individual pages of the application

The unique function of the suggested solution is the detection of the common actions. It is an implementation of an algorithm for searching of repeated sequences in the recorded time row. There are many papers which cover this problem, for example [24-27]. Most of them suggest the usage of algorithms based on the Markov chains or decision trees. However, in regards to their intended purpose for continuous data or even multi-dimensional data, they are too complicated for the needs of this paper.

The commonly used model of decision trees was used during the suggestion of a simpler algorithm which enabled the recognition of samples in recorded binary data that represent the buttons' push of the controllers. The recorded time line is processed by the algorithm for the detection of clusters and then each cluster and its metrics (for example the average delay between individual commands) are recorded in the form of a sequence into the graphic database. This obtains a system of sets of trees from which each represents a sequence of commands with identical first node. Therefore, each recorded sequence is connected to the current tree or there is a new tree created. When repeating the sequence, a counting mechanism is incremented only in the database.

From this continuously maintained database, it is possible to simply obtain the sequences which are most commonly used and may be for example suggested to the user for establishing of macros.

4   Implementation of the Solution

The compact computer Raspberry Pi [28] which functions on the platform ARM was used for the prototyping of the central point of the system (see Fig. 5). This platform is sufficiently powerful in order to carry out all the tasks and it has better dimensions and battery than common x86 PC platforms. It has the dimensions similar to the ones of a credit card and its price is around 25EUR. Moreover, it contains an integrated processor with 700MHz frequency and a 512MB RAM memory. In comparison with the simpler and cheaper device, such as Arduino, it has a significant advantage due to its support of fully-functioning operating systems on the basis of Linux which enable the usage of many software technologies.

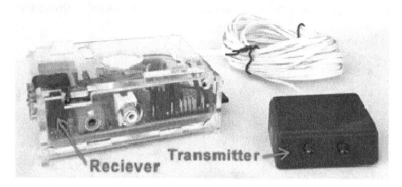

Fig. 5. The finished prototype of the central point

For the creation of the main application which contains all the functional logistics and offers the possibility of controlling through HTTP, the Node.js platform was chosen [30]. It is a server solution which functions with the JavaScript running environment V8 and is used in the Google Chrome browser. Its advantage is the orientation on the assynchronic utilisation of events and high power, even with a weaker hardware.

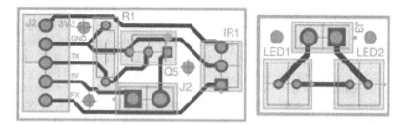

Fig. 6. The proposal PCB of IR module with separated transmitting part

The existing library was used for calling LIRC sub-programmes from Node.js on which even the competing solution Open Source Universal Remote is built. Unfortunately, it supports only the sending of the commands. Therefore, it was necessary to add the support for irrecord which enables the initiation of the record of the existing remote control from a smartphone or a PC. This was a significantly difficult task due to the fact that the given sub-programme has an interactive interface from which it is necessary to transfer all events from console through Node.js and into the browser, as well as back.

The whole structure of the application, described in the chapter III, was implemented in a way which enables a fully valuable and comfortable control from a web browser, as well as from a smartphone, independently of the resolution. An example of the application run from a smartphone which was adjusted to the resolution of the display is shown on the Fig. 7.

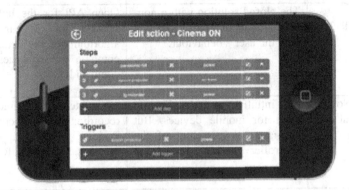

Fig. 7. Web application is responsive and adjusting its settings according to the type of device used

5   Comparison with Competing Devices

The result of this paper is the functional prototype of the device which ensured a centralised control of home multimedia appliances using the IR signals. In this chapter, the suggested solution is compared with competing products. The following table 1 shows the main advantages of the individual solutions which are comparable with the suggested one. The purpose is not to give a detail description of each product, but only to compare the important characteristics.

It is clear from the table that the main advantages of the suggested solution are the possibility of the linkage to other services using the public API and the ability to automatically recognise the most commonly used sequences. The commercial products offer more functions, but they are usually dependent on the hardware of the particular manufacturer.

Furthermore, the user testing on 10 sample subjects in the age 15-55 was run. It contained following tasks:

- Connect devices into the multimedia home system and run it,
- record the current controllers,
- try to use web application in a smartphone instead of controllers,
- let it create and name a mass action which is automatically suggested after a certain time period of usage.

After the evaluation of the results, it was found that users were able to fulfil given tasks with the success rate of 80% which shows a correctly designed users' interface and generally the principle of the solution. The created reminders were used for further improvement of the application.

Table 1. Comparison of Competing Solutions [33-35]

Name	Characteristics	Suggested solution
Logitech Harmony	Native application for Android and iOS. More expensive versions also have a hardware controller. It does not have API and does not learn according to the user's behaviour.	Instead of the native application, it is possible to use a web application which is optimised for mobile devices.
ELCO eLAN-IR-3	The closed solution with a non-intuitive application. Does not read the user's behaviour.	Open API for the linkage of services of 3 pages and algorithm for the detection of common sequences of commands.
Open Source Universal Remote (OSUR)	An intuitive web application even for mobile devices. But non-intuitive recording of the controller using command lines.	An interactive guide for recording of the controller. Princip web application originated from OSUR.
Traditional Smart Home solutions	Large selection of expensive specialised appliances which are able to be centrally controlled, but the inability to control common appliances	IR signals enable the controlling of most multimedia appliances with low expenses. For controlling of more advanced elements, it is necessary to link another system.

6   Conclusions

This paper suggests and open-source solution for centralised control of multimedia appliances which use IR controller. The suggested solution can be used as a supplement to the current Smart Home systems. Using the web application which is accessible from even a smartphone, it is possible to record commands of the current controllers, emulate their function using an individual approach and on the basis of long-term activity of the user, it suggests the unification of frequent sequences of commands into macros. This functionality can save time of the user and increase the comfort of working with multimedia appliances. The functional prototype was compared to the competing solutions and tested with users. One of the next directions of the development could be for example the improvement of the algorithm for detection of common usage patterns, independent of the order of carrying out the particular commands in the case when it does not matter.

Acknowledgment. This work and the contribution were supported by project "SP/2014 - Smart Solutions for Ubiquitous Computing Environments" Faculty of Informatics and Management, University of Hradec Kralove, Czech Republic.

References

1. Ricquebourg, V., et al.: The smart home concept: our immediate future. In: IEEE International Conference on -Learning in Industrial Electronics. IEEE (2006)
2. Naghiyev, E., Gillott, M., Wilson, R.: Three unobtrusive domestic occupancy measurement technologies under qualitative review. Energy and Buildings 69, 507–514 (2014)
3. Haines, V., et al.: Probing user values in the home environment within a technology driven Smart Home project. Personal and Ubiquitous Computing 11(5), 349–359 (2007)
4. Kim, C.G., Kim, K.J.: Implementation of a cost-effective home lighting control system on embedded Linux with OpenWrt. Personal and Ubiquitous Computing: 1–8
5. Daintree Networks Inc. The value of wireless lighting control (2010), http://www.daintree.net (accessed March 17, 2013)
6. Melike, E.K.: Wireless sensor networks for cost-efficient residential energy management in the smart grid. IEEE Trans. Smart Grid 2, 314–325 (2011)
7. Dhiren, T., Al-Kuwari, A.M.A.H., Potdar, V.: Energy conser- vation in a smart home. In: Digital ecosystems and technologies conference (DEST), pp. 241–246 (2011)
8. KNX Specification. v1.4AS (December 2007)
9. ZigBee Alliance, ZigBee Specifications, version 1.0 (April 2005)
10. Vanus, J., Novak, T., Koziorek, J., Konecny, J., Hrbac, R.: The proposal model of energy savings of lighting systems in the smart home care. In: IFAC Proceedings Volumes (IFAC-PapersOnline), vol. 12 (pt. 1), pp. 411–415 (2013) ISSN: 14746670. ISBN: 9783902823533
11. Vanus, J., Koziorek, J., Hercik, R.: Design of a smart building control with view to the senior citizens' needs, IFAC Proceedings Volumes (IFAC-PapersOnline), vol. 12 (pt.1), pp. 422–427 (2013) ISSN: 14746670. ISBN: 9783902823533
12. Machacek, Z., Slaby, R., Hercik, R., Koziorek, J.: Advanced system for consumption meters with recognition of video camera signal. Elektronika Ir Elektrotechnika 18(10), 57–60 (2012) ISSN: 1392-1215
13. Behan, M., Krejcar, O.: Modern Smart Device-Based Concept of Sensoric Networks. EURASIP Journal on Wireless Communications and Networking 2013(1), No. 155 (June 6, 2013), doi 10.1186/1687-1499-2013-155 ISSN 1687-1499 (received October 9, 2012) (accepted May 15, 2013)
14. Krejcar, O., Jirka, J., Janckulik, D.: Use of Mobile Phone as Intelligent Sensor for Sound Input Analysis and Sleep State Detection. Sensors 11(6), 6037–6055 (2011), doi 10.3390/s110606037, ISSN: 1424-8220 (received May 4, 2011) (in revised form May 31, 2011), (accepted June 1, 2011)
15. Krejcar, O., Frischer, R.: Smart Intelligent Control of Current Source for High Power LED Diodes. Microelectronics Journal 44(4), 307–314 (2013), doi 10.1016/j.mejo.2013.02.004, ISSN 0026-2692 (received July 30, 2012), (in Revised form February 01, 2013); (accepted February 05, 2013)
16. Benikovsky, J., Brida, P., Machaj, J.: Proposal of User Adaptive Modular Localization System for Ubiquitous. In: Pan, J.-S., Chen, S.-M., Nguyen, N.T. (eds.) ACIIDS 2012, Part II. LNCS, vol. 7197, pp. 391–400. Springer, Heidelberg (2012)

17. Cerny, M., Penhaker, M.: Wireless Body Sensor Network in Health Maintenance Systems. Journal Electronics and Electrical Engineering, vol 115(9), 113–116 (2011) ISSN 1392 – 1215 (print), ISSN 2029-5731 (online) Impact Factor (2010 Thomson JCR Science Edition): 0.659 (received December 15, 2010), (accepted March 29 2011)

18. Penhaker, M., Darebnikova, M., Cerny, M.: Sensor Network for Measurement and Analysis on Medical Devices Quality Control. In: Yonazi, J.J., Sedoyeka, E., Ariwa, E., El-Qawasmeh, E. (eds.) ICeND 2011. CCIS, vol. 171, pp. 182–196. Springer, Heidelberg (2011), doi:10.1007/978-3-642-22729-5_16

19. Krawiec, J., Penhaker, M., Krejcar, O., Novak, V., Bridzik, R.: Web System for Electrophysiological Data Management. In: Proceedings of 2010 Second International Conference on Computer Engineering and Application,s ICCEA 2010, Bali Island, Indonesia, March 19-21, vol. 1, pp. 404–407. IEEE Conference Publishing Services (2010), doi:10.1109/ICCEA.2010.85, ISBN 978-0-7695-3982-9

20. High Definition Multimedia Interface Specification. "Supplement 1. Consumer Electronics Control". version 1.3a (2009)

21. Han, J., Choi, C.-S., Lee, I.: More efficient home energy management system based on ZigBee communication and infrared remote controls. IEEE Transactions on Consumer Electronics 57(1), 85–89 (2011)

22. Vishay Semiconductors "Datasheet: IR Receiver Modules for Remote Control Systems". Dostupné, http://www.vishay.com/docs/82492/tsop312.pdf (visit on April 2, 2014]

23. Bartelmus, C., et al.: LIRC: Linux infrared remote controL (2002)

24. Ghassempour, S., Girosi, F., Maeder, A.: Clustering Multivariate Time Series Using Hidden Markov Models. International Journal of Environmental Research and Public Health 11(3), 2741–2763 (2014)

25. Wan, L., Liao, J., Zhu, X.: A frequent pattern based framework for event detection in sensor network stream data. In: Proceedings of the Third International Workshop on Knowledge Discovery from Sensor Data. ACM (2009)

26. Han, J., et al.: Frequent pattern mining: current status and future directions. Data Mining and Knowledge Discovery 15(1), 55–86 (2007)

27. Berndt, D.J., Clifford, J.: sing Dynamic Time Warping to Find Patterns in Time Series. In: KDD Workshop, vol. 10(16) (1994)

28. Pi, R.: Dostupné online: http://www.raspberrypi.org

29. Kurniawan, A.: Pocket Reference: Raspberry Pi. PE Press

30. Dahl, R.: Node. js: Evented I/O for V8 JavaScript (2012)

31. Turner, C.: Pebble Smart Watch Review (2014)

32. Labs, T.: Myo bracelet – Gesture Control Armband (2014)

33. Bain, Alex. Open Source Universal Remote, http://opensourceuniversalremote.com

34. Logitech. Harmony Remotes, http://www.logitech.com/en-us/harmony-remotes (visit on April 4, 2014)

35. ELKO EP s.r.o. eLAN-IR-003: "Převodník LAN na IR", http://eshop.elkoep.cz/elan-ir-003—detail-1LP1000101.aspx (visit on April 4, 2014)

An Off-the-Shelf Platform for Automatic and Interactive Text Messaging Using Short Message Service

Daniel Oliveira[1], Diana Oliveira[3], Nuno M. Garcia[1,2,4], and Graça Esgalhado[3]

[1] Computer Science Department, University of Beira Interior, Covilhã, Portugal
[2] Instituto de Telecomunicações, Covilhã, Portugal
[3] Psychology and Education Department
Universidade da Beira Interior, Covilhã, Portugal
[4] Universidade Lusófona de Humanidades e Tecnologias, Lisbon, Portugal
`danieloliveira@it.ubi.pt, dianapsoliveira@gmail.com,`
`ngarcia@di.ubi.pt, mgpe@ubi.pt`

Abstract. This paper describes the design and construction of a platform for the implementation of an automatic and interactive message handling system through the use of Short Message Service (SMS), also known as texting, devised to be used as support of a Psychology study. The platform was devised to use low cost off-the-shelf parts, yet allowing the design of an efficient and robust system. The research that prompted the platform's construction included researchers from the Psychology and Education Department and the Computer Science Department of the University of Beira Interior. The study's goal is to assess psychological changes of the research subjects after exposure to motivational SMS texts. The paper describes the strategies adopted to design the architecture of the platform and the setting in place of the system, including the description of the used software and hardware. The source code of this system is publicly available at the Assisted Living Computing and Telecommunications (ALLab) website.

Keywords: SMS, messaging, mobile, off-the-shelf, psychology, self-regulation, self-efficacy.

1 Introduction

It is considered that information and communication technologies play a major role in all aspects of current human interactions in the so-called developed countries and in particular for young humans.

Nowadays, mobile devices seem to be the first choice of graduate students to communicate, organize, actualize and eventually learn [1], in particular if smart phones are considered. When taken into account that only a very small percentage of students are not avid texters, we can assume that text messaging is one of the most privileged ways they use to communicate [2]. That might be why, even though the use

K. Saeed and V. Snášel (Eds.): CISIM 2014, LNCS 8838, pp. 489–500, 2014.
© IFIP International Federation for Information Processing 2014

of this technology is still taken with caution by colleges and lecturers, in the past decade there have been several studies concerning the use of Short Message Service (SMS) in an educational context. So far SMS technology has been used to send students administrative information [3], some educational content [4,5], or to send persuasive and motivational quotes [6], just to name some of its applications. Yet, there's not much research in this particular area, therefore we are just starting to analyze how SMS may be used as a tool to support teaching and learning in higher education.

With that in mind, in the context of research in the areas of Computer Science (CS) and Pedagogical Supervision (PS) at the University of Beira Interior (UBI) it was devised a joint research to study whether persuasive and motivational SMS texts could be used to increase the student's performance in mathematics classes, of students from four different undergraduate courses. This was done through a study that focused in establishing the effects of the SMS intervention in the student's self-regulated learning, general academic self-efficacy and learning strategies, and involved the definition of the architecture supporting that study.

This paper focuses mainly in the description of the computational issues of the study, although some other topics will be introduced to contextualize. As the results of the psychology study are not available at this time, it's not the goal of this paper to present conclusions regarding the impact of the use of the platform in the study subjects. The remainder of the paper is organized as follows: this paragraph concludes section 1; Section 2 presents a very brief overview of the state of the art; Section 3 describes the system's architecture; Implementation is discussed in Section 4; Section 5 concludes the paper, and references and acronyms are shown in the final part.

2   State of the Art

Globally, in the last decade, the telecommunications field has experienced a great increase not only in network coverage, but also in technological innovation [7]. Furthermore text messaging is now so popular, it is being used by people of all ages and technology expertise, and among university students texting is generalized [2,4].

Importing something as widespread as SMS and adapting it as a tool for teaching and learning purposes is only natural [2] considering we're not introducing something entirely new to colleges and classrooms.

Today's students use mobile phones and SMS, inside and outside school, therefore, the research was developed to assess whether SMS could have a motivational impact, as suggested by previous research [4,8].

In recent years, colleges and other higher education institutions have tried to come up with ways to introduce mobile phones in ways that may enhance lecturers supported in pedagogy. This means that from a pedagogical perspective, there may be opportunity to raise student engagement, considering the subjects studied at a higher education level [7] and use pervasive technologies such as the SMS.

The popularity of SMS is believed to have inspired some lecturers to explore their use in the educational context [9]. Besides studies that connect the usage of SMS with weight loss [10,11] and smoking cessation [12], in recent years investigators from the educational field have turned their sights into how this technology can be used in a producible way in their own work places: high education institutions. We can find such studies in many parts of the world, but as not to be exhausting some examples of such usage can be found in the following research: [3] published a study on how SMS could be used to send administrative content to students; [4,5] that focused on how to send educational contents through SMS; authors in [13] focused not only in the delivery of educational content, but also on how that might affect student engagement to class assignments; and [14] focused on how SMS exchange in class could increase its interactivity.

The development of the platform used in this study was made taking into consideration the requirements defined by the main stakeholders, the Pedagogical Supervision Master of Science (MSc) student and their supervisors. Although we found some commercial solutions that fulfilled some of the requirements, we didn't find an integrated solution that complied with them all and since we had a tight budget and tight time schedule to start the study, creating our own system architecture from the ground up was the obvious choice, especially when taking into consideration that there was previous expertise in this area and several in-house projects had been already developed at an experimental level.

3   System Architecture

The system was built taking into consideration the requirements and challenges posed by the psychology study it would be used for: (1) the system needs to work uninterrupted and unattended; (2) the system needs to address Mobile Network Operator (MNO) fair use policies, by not sending large amounts of SMS texts in a very short period of time; (3) the students have to receive a stream of messages at predefined times; (4) some messages require answers making this an interactive question-response system.

To comply with the requirements, a mechanism to control the message flow for each student was needed, *i.e.*, as each student responds on its own time, the message being processed for a particular student may be different from the message of the student that precedes him/her in the message queue.

The stream of SMS messages as well as the list of destinations were inserted as elements of a database (DB). The questions themselves, the admissible answers and the message flow was defined based on psychological validated literature as expressed in studies aiming to evaluate self-regulated learning and/or self-efficacy in the same population[17,18], which will be explored outside this paper.

To manage this flow of messages, a script was created which connected questions with their validated answers, and when admissible, gave predefined replies according to admissible options presented to the study subjects. After this process, discussed in more detail in the architecture section the script advances to the following question.

As to hardware it was decided to use three Global System for Mobile Communications (GSM) modems, one for each major Portuguese MNO: MEO (formerly known as TMN), Vodafone and NOS (formerly known as Optimus) (all trademarks and brands are property of their respective owners). This choice of operators was made because the researchers were confident that almost all students had subscribed to one of the free SMS plans that all MNO offer, which guaranteed that the research would be carried out with no costs to the end user, even when answers were required.

The modems were connected to a laptop via a powered universal serial bus (USB) hub, because the modems were too large to connect directly to the laptop and because that allowed extra power needed to support the modems, since the hub has an external power supply. To assure that the laptop was always ready to exchange SMS, an Uninterruptible Power Supply (UPS) was added to the hardware to increase power supply resiliency. The setting and operation of the solution cost 625€, as follows: Capital Expenditure (CAPEX) summed 505€ by adding 300€ for the small laptop used, 100€ for the UPS, 5€ for the USB hub, and 75€ for the three GSM modems (25€ each in average); Operational Expenditure (OPEX) summed 120€ (30€ per month), to allow the payment of 10€ per each MNO subscription (these values refer to early 2014 and include all legal taxes but not electricity expenses). Each Subscriber Identity Module (SIM) card was purchased with a free SMS plan, so sending messages had no cost. The architecture of the system is shown in Fig. 1.

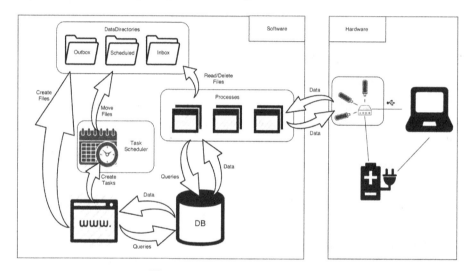

Fig. 1. System architecture diagram

Concerning software, a decision was made to assign the SMS exchange functionalities and the handling of the received SMS's to two separated processes, both sharing access to the three directories created for each MNO (Fig. 2). Because each process only has access to the directories of the assigned operator, each user only receives SMS sent from the operator. As depicted in Fig. 1, the computer runs six processes, each interacting with the DB, the computer's file system and one of the MNO GSM modems. One group of processes is in charge of processing the received messages and replies and implementing the interactive feature of the system. The other group of processes is in charge of sweeping its associated GSM modem, looking for incoming messages and retrieving and storing these messages in the respective Inbox folder. This group of processes is also in charge of sweeping the Outbox folder and sending the found outgoing messages to its associated GSM modem. More details on the tasks performed is given in Section 4.

The system also relies on (Fig.1):

— a web application to schedule the SMS's, add/remove users and disable the dispatch of messages to a given user, among others functionalities;
— a DB to store the messages (*text*) to be scheduled, the auto-reply messages, the users' information, the replies received from the users and all additional support tables;
— a task scheduler that creates the tasks requested from the web application.

No comparison between this solution and others available is given because most of them aren't neither free not open-source, which prevents comparability concerning, the underlying used architecture.

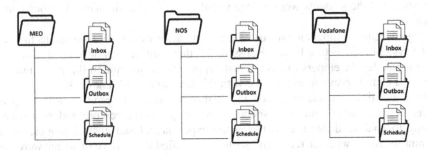

Fig. 2. Directories tree for each Mobile Network Operator

4   Implementation

The research started when MSc students from the DPE decided to develop their dissertations on the impacts of new technologies in the educational environment, but only the study entitled "The efficacy of the intervention through SMS in the learning's self-regulation and general academic self-efficacy in ungraduated students" will be mentioned.

The study focus on the use of SMS with persuasive and supportive messages to students from different courses: Computer Science Engineering, Electromechanical Engineering, Electrical and Computers Engineering and Optometry - Vision Sciences, which have in common poor academic performance and high dropout rate on their respective mathematics class. A three stages process was followed: a pre-study, the experiment, and a post-study. Both in the pre and post studies, the students were invited to fill a socio-demographic and data questionnaire prepared and managed by the DPE researchers and the experiment itself involves the use of the tool targeted by this paper. This study also included other relevant questions such as the students' mobile phone number and the desired MNO it would communicate with.

The pre-study started by initially contacting teachers who lectured math to the research subjects. The teachers were asked to collaborate and to make available 20 minutes of their first class of the semester for the researchers to invite students to participate in their study. Afterwards, the complete questionnaires were separated by course and class for the purpose of creating an experimental and a control group, where all classes and courses were represented: students were randomly rafted to one of the groups, by course and class.

Around 300 students were invited to participate, but only 184 filled the initial pre-study questionnaire; this roughly corresponds to the number of students met when visiting the classes at the start of the semester.

Considering that along the semester dropouts might occur, we didn't sort the students equally between our experimental and control group, instead we sorted 110 students (60%) to the experimental group and the other 74 (40%) to the control group.

During the experiment stage, while students normally attended classes, students rafted to the experimental group received a SMS twice a week, on Mondays and Thursdays and those of the control group didn't.

At the end of the semester the teachers lecturing the mathematics class were again contacted and the students were invited to fill the same questionnaire, by course and by class.

Regarding the computational side of the work, there were several decisions that led to the system architecture being discussed. All the software was developed using C# since it enables developers to easily create applications that run on the .NET Framework and there is previous experience with this language and framework.

At a later time, outside the scope and goal of this paper, researchers will compare scores between what students responded on the questionnaires pre and post-study, aiming to analyze differences between the experimental and control groups, in an attempt to assess whether receiving the texts modified the way students answered to the same set of questions.

4.1   Processes

The choice to create two different processes for each MNO resulted from the analysis made to the time spent between exchanging SMS messages, handling of received messages, including creating an answer if needed, saving the message, etc., since it wasn't desirable that the solution stopped exchanging SMS texts each time it had to handle received *texts*, whether they came from students, or operators (promotions, balance alerts, *etc.*). It was decided to call each of the processes "SMS Gateway" (send/receive) and "Auto-reply agent" (manage received messages). Along with time management, the other rationale for the separation of these two processes was to allow a layer of isolation between the management of the messages on the GSM modems (inbound and outbound), the management of messages received from a user, and the implementation of the necessary interactivity feature.

The "SMS Gateway" searches for new files in the "Outbox" directory of the assigned MNO. If it finds a new file it will process it by sending the SMS text to the recipients contained in the file, processing files in a last in first out manner using for this the time stamp for the creation of the file.

Since the modem cannot send and receive messages at the same time, it was decided to insert a delay between the dispatch of each message, not only to keep the buffers from overflowing and resulting in a faulty service, but also to allow incoming messages buffered at the MNO system to be delivered to the GSM modem and retrieved and stored in the respective folder ("Inbox" folder). To further take advantage of the delay, this time lapse is used to verify if any other message has been received at the modem, and if so download it from the SIM card to a file in the Inbox directory created for this purpose, (c.f. Fig. 2). The SMSLib [15] library was implemented in the gateways to easily exchange messages through the GSM modems, since it is an Application Programming Interface (API) available and tested in the Microsoft .Net framework.

The "Auto-reply agent" handles the received messages by always watching the "Inbox" directory for new files. If it finds one or more files it will decide how to handle them according to the system specifications: store it, delete it or answer it.

Internally, each of the outgoing message files has the following structure: FLOW_ID*MESSAGE*LIST_OF_RECIPIENT_NUMBERS. In the given example "230" represents the flow id of that message, the text to be sent spans from "SMS30UBI:" until "participaste." and +351000000000, +351111111111 and so on are the recipients' phone numbers, as shown in Fig. 3. The asterisk character "*" was used as field delimiter.

```
230*SMS30UBI: Esta é a última mensagem. Numa escala de 1 (nada útil)
a 6 (muito útil), indica o número que consideras reflectir a utilidade
do programa de SMS em que participaste. *+351000000000*+351111111111*+
351222222222*+351333333333*+351444444444*+351555555555*+351666666666*+
351777777777*+351888888888*+351999999999
```

Fig. 3. Outgoing message example (in Portuguese, phone numbers anonymized)

The list of *text* recipients is never larger than 10, in order to allow the GSM modems to receive incoming messages as the FAQ available in the SMSLib webpage suggests that if the library is being used with GSM modems the rate at which it can send SMS is about 6 messages per minute (a message each 10 seconds). However a compromise was reached to send each message with a random interval of 10 to 15 seconds in order to respect the fair use policy that each MNO demands from its' users. By limiting the amount of messages the system can send at once, it is guaranteed that no high priority message has a delay of more than 150 seconds before being sent. This is particularly relevant as the study aimed to implement a responsive interactive system to the user's point of view, thus allowing that, in the worst case scenario if a user's response is inversely buffered and all users respond at the same time to the received message, no user is left without response for more than 40 seconds.

As each individual message is part of a predefined flow, and each user may interact with the system at different points of each flow, the different messages have to be identified by a flow identifier (*flow id*). The *flow id* identifies the message that is being sent, giving also information as to if this message is waiting for an answer and what is the auto-reply to be delivered if the received answer is valid. The degree of interactivity of the system is limited to one question, several possible answers, and several corresponding replies, i.e., the dialog between the user and the system is limited to the depth of question-response-acknowledgment messages (Fig. 4). Nevertheless, more complex flows can be devised and stored at the DB without any influence to the complexity of the other parts of the system itself.

Inside a message, the numbers in the list of recipients are separated by the same control character used to separate the other fields (* in this example). The real control character is an extended ASCII character, chosen because it is highly improbable that it would be used in the text of a message, preventing a risk/abuse of the system. Message *text* is encoded in UCS2, a Unicode encoding that uses a 16-bit character format and allows accented characters along with other special ones (like c with cedilla 'ç'), in spite of losing the maximum length for each message (from 160 to 70 characters).

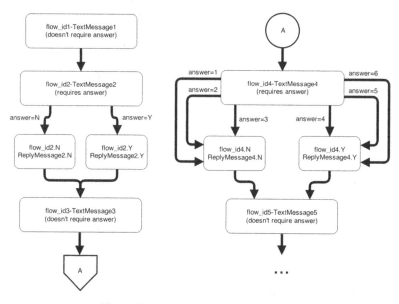

Fig. 4. Abstract example of message flow

A scheme for the processing of messages is presented in Fig.5 and consists of the system sending a message, leaving the system waiting for an answer. Assuming that the message is received by the recipient, two scenarios might occur: (1) the recipient sends one of the required response answers, this message is processed and a new message (the corresponding auto-response) is issued; (2) the recipient responds when no reply was expected: the response message is stored at the DB for further inspection and an alarm is raised in the control panel of the system, allowing the unexpected reply to be viewed by the system's administrator. If a response is expected but the user does not respond in a period of 1440 minutes (24 hours), the system administrator can decide what to do, for example, advance the flow of the user or send the message again (Fig.5).

4.2   Web Application

The application's main objective is to manage the scheduling of outgoing messages using a task scheduler, or preparing a message to be sent immediately, by creating files which contain the information needed to send a SMS. Since in this study the same message might be sent to several students at the same time, it was decided to create batches of files and each file has at most ten recipients. This way the process processes a file with many recipients and does not consider an interruption to allow, for example, the dispatch of a message might have a higher priority. Yet, as there are several processes running in parallel, there may be the case where all three modems are sending messages at the same time.

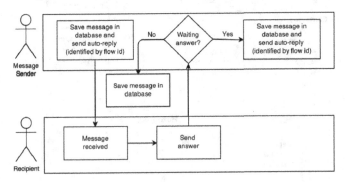

Fig. 5. Message flow scheme

The referred files are created in the respective MNO "Outbox" folder if it's a message to be sent immediately or in the "Scheduled" folder if it's a message destined to be sent later, usually, at a predefined time. When a scheduled message is created, the web application also creates the respective task in the Scheduler, including the details concerning the file's original location, when to move it, and to what directory it should be moved. In this study it was decided that the initial messages should always be sent between 18:30h and 20:30h, as not to disturb classes or sleep of the recipients.

4.3   Database

Microsoft SQL server was chosen since it has an easy integration with the web application (uses the same platform, the .NET framework), and it was used to save users information (message recipients), messages flow, log the messages exchanged with each user, courses' information, among other aspects, and its structure is shown in Fig. 6.

The following tables are responsible for the message flow control:

— Fluxo_EI – Has information about the flow identifier of each message, along with the respective message, response for a positive answer, for a negative answer and the type of message (if the message requires an answer or not);
— Fluxo_saida – Saves the sent message for each recipient, together with the respective timestamp, the flow at which corresponds and if the recipient has replied to the message;
— Fluxo_entrada – Used to store received messages for each recipient, along with the respective timestamp, the flow at which it corresponds and the text received.

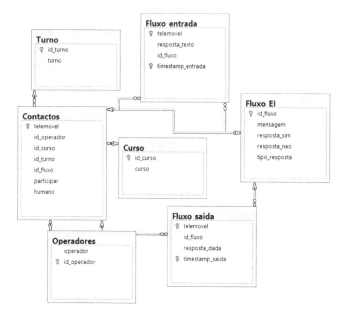

Fig. 6. Database table structure

4.4   Task Scheduler

This component creates tasks via the web application consisting of the following: for a given task, when the scheduled time arrives, the task scheduler will move the file defined in the task from the "Scheduled" directory to the respective "Outbox" directory, which will then be found by the process that handles the outgoing messages ("SMS Gateway"), sending them to the respective recipients.

It was decided to use the task scheduler available in the laptop operating system (Windows 7) on the grounds that this was more than adequate for the needed feature, therefore avoiding the creation of a proprietary task scheduler. This decision was also possible because the computer used for this task was dedicated to this study alone and no other scheduled tasks were added by other software components.

5   Conclusion and Future Work

Although the final results of the psychological study are neither the focus of this paper, nor available at this time, we may draw conclusions as to functionality of the support platform.

The auto-reply response time was generally perceived as very quick by the developers and the users, especially considering that it was an academic solution using low cost off-the-shelf hardware and simple software. Yet, one student complained that he couldn't read the *texts*. However when further questioned he told the researchers he was using a very old mobile phone that he no longer had with him, making it impossible to identify a possible solution to this problem. In future tests, the researchers will devise a pre-test to confirm that every subject is able to receive messages in a readable format.

Taking in consideration that we have sent and received a considerable number of messages (almost 7000), we conclude that the system ran as expected, having an up-time of 100% and zero system crashes. All this was achieved using a low-end laptop (Intel Atom N450, 1.66GHz clock, 2GB of RAM and a 64-bit operating system), having a workload of almost 100%. Moreover, the design of the messages and the request for replies was praised by several test subjects for being simple, user-friendly and not being too time consuming. The developed software source code is available at our research laboratory's MediaWiki [16]. The fact that the system was built using old off-the-shelf parts and components, and even so allowed for a free communication between the system and the users, makes it clear that the system was the exact response the requirements set. The system aimed not to abuse the MNO network with massive SMS messages and the fair use principle that applies to each of the subscribed plans was not violated.

It should be pointed out that the simplicity of this system allows for it to be easily adapted to other studies, subjects or businesses, not being limited to students or even academic environments (with the respective login account creation and credentials).

Acknowledgments. The authors would like to acknowledge the contribution of the COST Action IC1303 - AAPELE. This work was supported by FCT project PEst-OE/EEI/LA0008/2013.

References

1. Mellow, P.: The media generation: Maximize learning by getting mobile. ascilite 2005: Balance, Fidelity, Mobility: maintaining the momentum? p. 469–475 (2005), http://www.ascilite.org.au/conferences/brisbane05/blogs/proceedings/53_Mellow.pdf (retrieved March 12, 2014)
2. Lominé, L.L., Buckhingham, C.: M-learning: texting (SMS) as a teaching & learning tool in higher arts education. ELIA Teachers' Academy, Sofia. p. 1–6(2009), http://www.elia-artschools.org/images/activiteiten/18/files/Lomine%20-%20Texting%20as%20a%20tool%20for%20teaching.pdf (retrieved March 12, 2014)
3. Naismith, L.: Using text messaging to support administrative communication in higher education. Active Learning in Higher Education 8(2), 155–171 (2007), http://ganymedes.lib.unideb.hu:8080/udpeer/bitstream/2437.2/11817/1/PEER_stage2_10.1177%252F1469787407078000.pdf (retrieved March 12, 2014)
4. Lu, M.: Effectiveness of vocabulary learning via mobile phone. Journal of Computer Assisted Learning 24, 515–525 (2008)
5. Zhang, H., Song, W., Burston, J.: Reexamining the effectiveness of vocabulary learning via mobile phones. TOJET: The Turkish Online Journal of Educational Technology 10(3), 203–214 (2011), http://www.tojet.net/articles/v10i3/10323.pdf (retrieved March 12, 2014)

6. Goh, T., Seet, B., Rawhiti, L.: Persuasive and Affective SMS text messaging for Students' Learning (2011), `http://akoaotearoa.ac.nz/download/ng/file/group-6/persuasive-and-affective-sms-text-messaging-for-students-learning.pdf` (retrieved October 16, 2013)
7. Mockus, L., Dawson, H., Edel-Malizia, S., Shaffer, D., An, J.S., Swaggerty, A. (2011), The Impact of Mobile Access on Motivation: Distance Education Student Perceptions. Learning Design at Penn State's World Campus. World Campus Learning Design. p. 1–34, `http://learningdesign.psu.edu/research/MLRTWhitePaper.pdf` (retrieved March 12, 2014)
8. Thüs, H., Chatti, M.A., Yalcin, E., Pallasch, C., Kyryliuk, B., Mageramov, T., Schroeder, U.: Mobile Learning in Context. International Journal of Technology Enhanced Learning 4(5/6), 332–344 (2012), `http://learntech.rwth-aachen.de/dll154` (retrieved November 20, 2013)
9. Gasaymeh, A.M., Aldalalah, O.M.: The Impact of Using SMS as Learning Support Tool on Students' Learning. International Education Studies 6(10), 112–123 (2013)
10. Brug, J., Oenema, A., Kroeze, W., Raat, H.: The internet and nutrition education: challenges and opportunities. European Journal of Clinical Nutrition (59), 130–139 (2005)
11. Wang, Y., Tim, L.: Worldwide trends in childhood overweight and obesity. International Journal of Pediatric Obesity 1(1), 11–25 (2006)
12. Free, C., Knight, R., Robertson, S., Whittaker, R., Edwards, P., Zhou, W., Rodgers, A., Cairns, J., Kenward, M., Roberts, I.: Smoking cessation support delivered via mobile phone text messaging (txt2stop): a single-blind, randomised trial. The Lancet 378(9785), 49–55 (2011)
13. West, D.M.: Mobile Learning: Transforming Education, Engaging Students, and Improving Outcomes. Center for Technology Innovation at Brookings. Mobile Learning, 1–17 (2013)
14. Markett, C., Sánchez, I.A., Weber, S., Tangney, B.: PLS Turn UR Mobile On.: Short message service (SMS) supporting interactivity in the classroom pp. 1–5 (2004)
15. SMSLib – A universal API for sms messaging, `http://smslib.org` (last accessed June 05, 2014)
16. Oliveira, D., Garcia, N.M.: Interactive SMS Agent `http://allab.it.ubi.pt/mediawiki` (last accessed June 10, 2014)
17. Biggs, J.B.: The Study Process Questionnaire (SPQ): Manual. Hawthorn, Vic.: Australian Council for Educational Research (1987)
18. Torre Puente, J.C.: La autoeficacia, la autorregulación y los enfoques de aprendizaje en estudiantes universitarios. Tesis doctoral, Madrid, Spain: Universidad Pontificia Comillas (2006)

Application of PIL Approach for Automated Transportation Center

Stepan Ozana, Martin Pies, Radovan Hajovsky, Jiri Koziorek,
and Ondrej Horacek

VSB-Technical University of Ostrava,
Faculty of Electrical Engineering and Computer Science,
Department of Cybernetics and Biomedical Engineering,
17. Listopadu 15/2172, 70833 Ostrava, Czech Republic
{stepan.ozana,martin.pies,radovan.hajovsky,jiri.koziorek,
ondrej.horacek}@vsb.cz
http://www.fei.vsb.cz/en

Abstract. The paper describes the idea of design and implementation of Processor-in-the-loop (PIL) model of Automated Transportation Center (ATC) designed as a heavy laboratory operated by VSB-Technical University of Ostrava. It contains technical description of the real technology, the main concept of PIL model and its particular solution for ATC. As for means of design and implementation, the REX Control system was used as a real-time target running on ALIX system board that handles the software model of real technology while the real control system based on Simatic PLCs stays unchanged. The communication between PLCs and ALIX is provided by PROFINET protocol while all of the original I/O signals are re-mapped to match the PROFINET communication standard.

Keywords: Automation, PIL, PLC, SCADA/HMI, Transportation.

1 Introduction

This article gives an overview of control design and technical solution of PIL model for particular Automated Transportation Center but the principle of this solution can be easily applied in a wider scale to match various general technology complex units.

The main benefit of the paper and the project is to provide a tool for complex testing of real control systems without connecting to real technology.

During the construction of the new building of the Faculty of Electrical Engineering and Computer Science at VSB - Technical University of Ostrava (VSB-TUO) with financial support of European Union, a unique heavy laboratory – Automated Transportation Center (ATC) – was built. It is an absolutely rare real mechatronic system representing a fully automated pallet stacker machine that is able to reach four floors to store, for example, cars on pallets [1].

K. Saeed and V. Snášel (Eds.): CISIM 2014, LNCS 8838, pp. 501–513, 2014.

Within a single building, ATC deals with a connection between theory and practice – the research and development of security software and the real verification of the system of the automated, computer-controlled operation of the multi-story capacitive stacker machine with a direct transfer of R&D results to the application area.

The parcel designated for ATC – a square-shaped building with a space for a lab intended for teaching students on the ground floor, with technical facilities, four storage spaces and three other storage floors, and an automatic storage system with a total capacity of 37 cells – is situated on a free, unused area of the premises of VSB where, according to an area future development urban study, parking spaces are to be concentrated to eliminate the movement of motor vehicles within the university's large-scale campus. Fig. 1 shows a view of Automated Transportation Center located in VSB-TU Ostrava campus.

Fig. 1. A view of the Automated Transportation Center in Ostrava

Currently, when working on theses, students learn the lab's technology and their teachers participate in the further development and experimental verification of new features of the technology. The main usefulness of this infrastructure can be seen in the following points:

Faculty vehicles used for the purpose of educational and research activities can be safely stored here. Many of these vehicles were obtained as a gift from Hyundai Motor Manufacturing Czech in Nosovice and serve students as an educational tool. Other vehicles are a result of the faculty's own development activities, for example, Kaipan electric-drive cars. In ATC, these vehicles are protected against both weather conditions and vandalism.

It is a complex real mechatronic system equipped with a modern distributed control system, which demonstrates real issues associated with the operation of such a system. During lessons, when laboratory simulations are mostly performed, this can be seen as a great benefit and a unique experience for students.

The lab, which is located on the first floor, allows monitoring, analyzing, and storage of real-time data from the system's operation. Students can see this operation with their own eyes and become much more aware of potential risks related to errors in the control of such systems.

In the future, the concept of the automated parking system, which is the technological heart of the laboratory, could be used in densely populated urban agglomerations. Today, there are more and more places where such systems are being used. This laboratory allows teachers and students to participate in its further development.

In the future, the concept of the automated parking system, which is the technological heart of the laboratory, could be used in densely populated urban agglomerations. Today, there are more and more places where such systems are being used. This laboratory allows teachers and students to participate in its further development.

2   Educational and Research Activities within This Laboratory

Both the mechanical and control aspects of the laboratory's technological section have been analyzed so far. The technological section is a rather complex mechatronic system. When parking, it is necessary to avoid injury to persons or damage to vehicles. Therefore, the ATC technology is equipped with sophisticated sensors and control systems. The following steps must be performed in sequence: First, drive the car close to the front of the gate and open the outer gate by touching the smart card to the card reader attached to the gatepost. Then, drive the car on the pallet, put the handbrake on and leave the car in gear. After that, get out of the car and leave the check-in area. Finally, start the parking sequence by retouching the smart card to the card reader.

The parking sequence is divided into the following steps:

1. When the conditions checked and indicated on the information panel (vehicle size and weight) are met, the car is fixed to the pallet with linear actuators.
2. The fixed pallet, which is attached to the slewing unit, rotates 90 degrees in the direction of the first floor's ready skip.
3. After rotating the pallet and opening the inner gate, the pallet on the slewing unit is locked off and the skip's lift arm is released. The lift arm catches the pallet with the car and moves it to the skip.
4. The skip then moves to a designated parking spot on the first floor or change its position to reach the level of the lifting device (elevator).
5. Using the lift arm, which releases the pallet with the car to the opposite side, the car is moved to the elevator area.
6. The elevator brings the car to the designated floor where it is to be parked.
7. The ready skip on the particular floor, which is intended for moving the car on the pallet within the floor, releases its lift arm to catch the pallet in the elevator and move it to skip.
8. Once the car is positioned on the skip, the car is transported towards the designated parking spot.
9. The lift arm then moves the car to the parking spot.
10. Simultaneously with these steps, an empty pallet from another parking spot is moved to the slewing unit.

The heart of the system which controls the automatic operation of the parking sequence is a Siemens SIMATIC ET 200S PLC located in the switchboard of the technology's stationary section. Via a Wi-Fi network, this controller configures autonomous tasks which are performed on transport carts (skips) by a SIMATIC S7-1200 PLC.

Students are not allowed to interfere in the control algorithms in these PLCs so that the safe operation of the entire system is protected from being endangered. To visualize details of the entire parking sequence, which is subject to the conditions of dozens of sensors within the system, an application created in the Control Web development environment is used. This application assumes all information about the running process from an OPC server which runs on the same PC.

In addition to this basic automatic mode visualization, the system includes an operator's console in the form of a tablet which allows for turning off automatic mode and, in service mode, performing the parking sequence in a step-by-step manner.

In class, students can program their applications that visualize the entire process based on the values retrieved from the OPC server.

3   Scada/HMI Visualization

Thanks to the generosity of the Czech company GEOVAP, we managed, on very favorable terms, to equip the laboratory with their software product – the Reliance 4 SCADA/HMI system. Reliance is a professional SCADA/HMI system designed for the monitoring and control of various industrial processes and for building automation. Data is acquired from control or telemetry systems, logged to databases, and presented to end users in a graphical form (schemes, charts, tables, etc.).

Students will be assigned a number of tasks (projects) that will allow for visualizing and storing information from running parking sequences. Students will be able to carry out these tasks without endangering the safe operation of the entire process. Their applications will be based on reading data from a running OPC server. According to the results of the analysis of the system structure and parking sequences, they will visualize these sequences.

A complete application can be easily available to remote users. Reliance 4 Web Client is a Java-based program designed to run a visualization project over the Internet. Reliance 4 Smart Client is designed for use with smartphones and tablets running iOS, Android, Windows Phone, or BlackBerry OS. Students will thus be able to get acquainted with all these technologies while developing their applications.

Creating a visualization project is substantially accelerated by a well-arranged manager and wizard system. The basic features can be configured with no need for programming. Thanks to this, students can achieve significant time savings that can later be invested in creating further applications and their productivity should therefore increase rapidly with each newly created application.

To reliably detect errors and inconsistencies in an application, Project Diagnostics can be used. It is a tool built into the development environment that not only warns students of invalid links, non-existent tags, and syntax errors, but it also discovers unused tags. The results are displayed in a well-arranged list from which it is possible to access the respective property with just a mouse-click and fix the problem.

4 Concept of PIL Model

4.1 Motivation

PIL is a technique for a rapid prototyping when mathematic model is running in real-time, the control system is running on the target platform [2].

During the processor-in-the-loop (PIL) phase, the control is compiled and downloaded into an embedded target processor and communicates directly with the plant model via standard communications such as Ethernet. In this case, no I/O devices are used for the communication.

The scheme of PIL model is represented by Fig. 2 and it consists of 3 blocks:

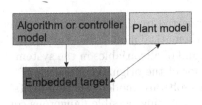

Fig. 2. Block scheme of PIL concept

The following conditions must be followed for PIL approach:

1. Mathematic model is running in real-time
2. Control system is running on the target hardware platform
3. No input/output devices are used, a data connection is used to exchange data between the control system and the model

It is mainly intended for testing the computing power of the target hardware platform and testing the control system by simulating machine malfunction.

4.2 Design of PIL Model for ATC

Control process of the technology is performed by a distributed control system which contains several PLC communicating over the deterministic protocol PROFINET. The main PLC is SIMATIC S7 300 and it communicates with the other PLCs (S7 1200) located in the center of each floor of the object. Furthermore, the technology contains two I/O modules and drive converters.

Due to the PIL concept, all of the signals from PLCs, I/O modules and drive converters are subject to PIL simulation and thus must be re-mapped to match the PROFINET protocol standard with the aim of establishing communication with the "slave" side of the system that is ALIX PC with PROFINET slave card CIFX90-RE\F.

The particular structure of PIL model of ATC is represented by Fig. 3. It contains the following parts:

1. Control system on target hardware
   It is embedded target with the current control system. Usually it is the original control system with no changes. For the purposes of this project we used the identical copy of the control system except I/O modules that have been emulated (re-mapped) to profinet communication while the control algorithms of course stay unchanged.

2. Mathematical model (CPU+HW)
   This the CPU declared by the definition of PIL model. Technically it is a computer board with a slave profinet card with the running real-time target, particularly the REX Control System. This part (software simulation) emulates the real technology and thus it has to act in the same way.

3. Host PC
   Any remote PC connected by the Ethernet. It can serve for design and implementation of mathematical model, SCADA/HMI visualization, diagnostic and remote control and of all variables in the system. Its main goal is to perform tests of behavior of the original control algorithms because unlike the real technology, the software model can represents any states of the system that can occur, including possible dangerous constellation representing highly non-standard, unlikely or impossible situations.

Mathematical models of the particular technology units can be created by means of function blocks of the REX Control System. It is composed of many blocks for various purposes: configuration of real-time executive, processing of analogue signals, logic control, dynamic systems simulation, continuous control, math blocks, data archiving, and input/output blocks for reading/writing data to the real I/O modules matching the chosen hardware platform. There are two main applications for design and compiling of the control scheme (RexDraw) and diagnostic graphic tool (RexView) to upload the program, access the variables and trends. However, the detailed description of the REX Control System and its all features and capabilities is beyond the scope of this paper and all the relevant information can be found in [3]-[5].

Fig. 4 shows the example of software model for a part of the system, particularly for motors and skips. It consists of two parts that is executive and main task. An example of implementation of control structure is mentioned in [6].

It presents the way how the I/O data is read and written by so called "flags" from/into the PROFINET slave (Simatic PLCs). The particular flags represents step-by-step the signals defined in the original control system based on PLCs, while the definition is read from HW configuration of the PLC.

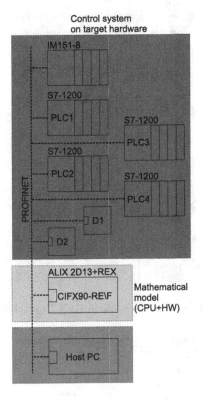

Fig. 3. PIL model of Automated Transportation Center in Ostrava

Hence, by use of standard or user-defined software blocks, it is possible to process the signals according users' needs and requirements, see the screenshot of RexView utility in Fig. 5. Typically, it helps to simulate the most common sequences in the system with the aim of either optimization or finding critical or weak links in the system during putting a car inside the ATC and out [7], [8].

5   Features and Novelty of the Solution

The main objective of using PIL model for Automated Transportation Center was to implement possibility to carry out various load tests of the designed control system performed by PLCs that control real technology. Unlike HIL model (hardware-in-the-loop), there is no need to use real i/o modules as all the signals are re-mapped for PROFINET protocol. Also, due to the large number of the signals, this approach helped to save up costs significantly.

The novelty of the solution lies in the use of a hard real-time target for the plant model of the complex technology that offers complex possibilities regarding processing input/output signals, mainly powerful libraries for mathematical operations, regulation, archiving and others. Of course there are more similar

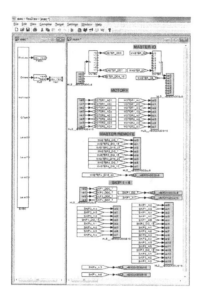

Fig. 4. Example of the source scheme in REX Control System (RexDraw)

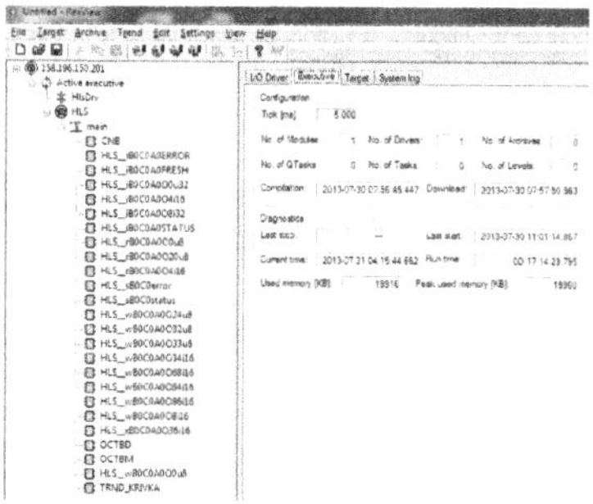

Fig. 5. A view of the diagnostic and visual utility (RexView)

solutions on the market, but not many of them follow the needs of hard real-time and low-cost budget or at least a good performance/costs ratio. The main reasons for use of the REX Control System are very good price and multiplatform support, see Fig. 6. Besides, it is compatible with the Matlab&Simulink platform, thus the control algorithms can be fully simulated before deployment to the target. It supports industrial OPC standard, visualization on the web through HTML5. It offers development of new function blocks (written in C language), use of a vast number of i/o drivers (for different hardware platforms, distributors and third- party products), and possibility to port to various operating system platforms (for example Windows CE, Windows Embedded, Linux/Xenomai, PharLap ETS, Windows7/Vista/XP.

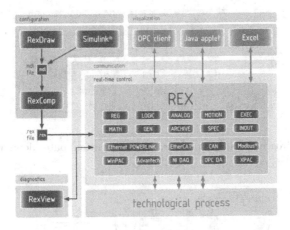

Fig. 6. Basic overview of REX control system configuration

6 Testing the Operation of PIL Model

This chapter briefly describes results of testing of two chosen case studies: outer doors and rotary unit.

6.1 Outer Doors

At the beginning of the experiment the outer doors are closed (down), see Fig. 7 (LY=true). This is in accordance with the overview of SCADA/HMI visualization. Once the Open button is clicked, the moving of outer doors is simulated by integrating the input signal to the integrator block, see visualization screenshot in Fig. 8 where both "Outer doors open" and "Outer doors closed" indicators are grey (false value), corresponding to false values of and LY and HY in Fig. 9 – doors are not either down nor up. After predefined time the doors reach the final upper position, as indicated in Fig. 10 in visualization (green indicator) screenshot and in Fig. 11 in REX control system screenshot.

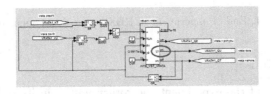

Fig. 7. Start of experiment in REX: outer doors closed (down)

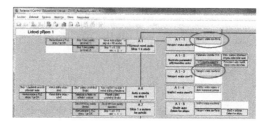

Fig. 8. Progress of the experiment in visualization: outer doors moving

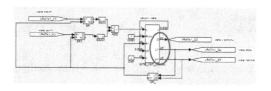

Fig. 9. Progress of the experiment in REX: outer doors moving

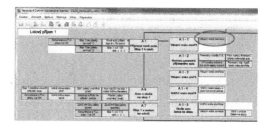

Fig. 10. End of experiment in visualization: outer doors open (up)

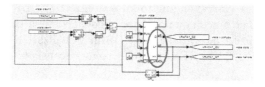

Fig. 11. End of experiment in REX: outer doors open (up)

6.2 Rotary Unit

At the beginning of the experiment the rotary unit is in its right position, as indicated in Fig. 12. Once the model received the command to rotate, the PIL model starts bidirectional communication with PLC distributed system to handle all control and states concerning the frequency drives. When all other conditions are followed to enable rotary unit to slide (for example release of blockade of the rotary unit and others), the moving of rotary unit is simulated by integrating the input signal to the integrator. After predefined time the output signal reaches the final value that means rotary unit finished its moving and came to its left position, see Fig. 13.

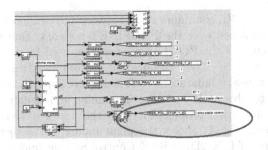

Fig. 12. Start of experiment in REX: rotary unit on the right position

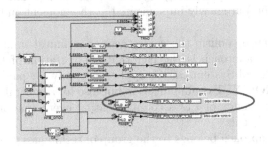

Fig. 13. End of experiment in REX: rotary unit on the left position

Fig. 14. PIL model of the technology of ATC

7 Conclusion

The main idea of the presented paper is to describe the concept of Automated Transportation Center and the use of the REX Control System for processor-in-the-loop model.

At present day, the PIL communication between physical control system and CPU has been established over the PROFINET network. Due to the security reasons, identical copy of the PLC CPUs have been used to work with the PIL model (1x IM 151-8, 4x S7-1200). Besides, the Automated Transportation Center is declared as a heavy laboratory so it will serve for educational purposes, too. Students will be able to deal with programming and visualization of typical real example of automation problematic with the use of modern software and hardware equipment. Fig. 14 shows the plant model of the technology implemented on computer ALIX 2D13+REX Control System under Linux OS with CIFX90-RE-\F PROFINET Slave card in mini-PCI Express.

The software blocks representing all of the particular technology units (lift, skips, and the others) are newly implemented at the moment and it is currently under tests.

Existing experience confirm the correctness of technical solution. The main contribution of the approach is the fact that configuration of the PIL model with the REX Control System can be applied not only for particular Siemens PLCs with the PROFINET communication but also for a general control system based on different brands of PLCs communicating over some of the standard communication protocols.

The objective approach belongs to the group of techniques generally referred to as "Model based design" and recently intensively developed by many software companies, for example by MathWorks as a part of Matlab&Simulink real-time tools.

Acknowledgments. Research supported by project SP2014/156, "Microprocessor based systems for control and measurement applications." of Student Grant System, VSB-TU Ostrava.

References

1. VysokeSkoly.cz, Automatizované dopravní centrum Ostrava na VŠB-TUO, http://www.vysokeskoly.cz/clanek/novy-clanek-5309
2. Francis, G., Burgos, R., Rodriguez, P., Wang, F., Boroyevich, D., Liu, R., Monti, A.: Virtual prototyping of universal control architecture systems by means of processor in the loop technology. In: The APEC 2007: Twenty-Second Annual IEEE Applied Power Electronics Conference and Exposition, Anaheim, vol. 1 and 2, pp. 21–27 (2007)
3. Balda, P., Schlegel, M., Stetina, M.: Advanced Control Algorithms + Simulink Compatibility + Real-time OS = REX. In: 16th Triennial World Congress of International Federation of Automatic Control, Prague, vol. 16, pp. 121–126 (2005)

4. Kocanek, M., Balda, P.: General sequential function charts editor. In: 12th International Carpathian Control Conference, Velke Karlovice, pp. 191–194 (2011)
5. REX Controls, ZCU Plzen, Czech Republic, http://www.rexcontrols.com
6. Ozana, S., Pies, M., Slanina, Z., Hajovsky, R.: Design and Implementation of LQR controller for Inverted Pendulum by use of REX Control System. In: 12th International Conference on Control, Automation and Systems, Jeju, pp. 343–347 (2012)
7. Kocian, J., Tutsch, M., Ozana, S., Koziorek, J.: Application of Modeling and Simulation Techniques for Technology Units in Industrial Control. In: 3rd International Conference on Computer, Communication, Control and Automation, 3CA 2011, Zhuhai. Lecture Notes in Electrical Engineering (2011)
8. Kocian, J., Tutsch, M., Ozana, S., Koziorek, J.: Modeling and Simulation of Controlled Systems and Technologies in Industrial Control. In: ICACTE 2011: Proceedings of the 4th International Conference on Advanced Computer Theory and Engineering, pp. 213–217. ASME Press, New York (2011)

A Model of a System for Stream Data Storage and Analysis Dedicated to Sensor Networks of Embankment Monitoring

Anna Pięta, Michał Lupa, Monika Chuchro, Adam Piórkowski,
and Andrzej Leśniak

Department of Geoinformatics and Applied Computer Science
AGH University of Science and Technology
al. Mickiewicza 30, 30-059 Cracow, Poland
{chuchro,apieta}@geol.agh.edu.pl,
{mlupa,pioro,lesniak}@agh.edu.pl
http://www.geoinf.agh.edu.pl

Abstract. Contemporary monitoring systems are a source of data streams. Processing of this data is an interesting issue from both a performance and data storage perspective. It is worth paying attention to the concept of stream database management systems, which are a hybrid that allows for efficient analysis of the data stream and provide a set of implemented statistical methods.

This article presents the issues raised by embankment monitoring systems, a sensor network which generates a large stream of measured signals that should be analyzed in real-time. Warning or crash scenarios are also generated which are compared to the incoming data. A model of this data is presented and a construction of stream data analysis is proposed.

Keywords: stream databases, sensor networks, time series.

1 Introduction

The protection of built-up areas against flooding poses modern technology with a very important task. Despite progress, every year floods occur both in Poland and around the world. Some phenomena are sudden and unexpected, while others are avoidable through the construction and control of embankments. Monitoring systems of environmental hazards have been the subject of research, both in terms of flooding [1,15,22,26] and landslides [7,8].

There are many types of monitoring systems. While there are existing solutions, in most cases a dedicated system which incorporates a complex software solution is required.

The monitoring system is usually a source of data streams that represent measurements taken from a line or a grid of points, or, sometimes, from a mobile sink [23]. The amount of data involved is usually large, therefore in the past decade many data stream processing proposals have been put forward, some

K. Saeed and V. Snášel (Eds.): CISIM 2014, LNCS 8838, pp. 514–525, 2014.

of them involving a data stream management system (DSMS). For example, DSMS's such as Aurora [4], Tribeca [25] or GigaScope [6] were created especially for the purposes of telecommunications and networks.

An interesting trend is the subgroup of solutions focused mainly on sensor networks [16,14], including for example, Fjord [17], Cougar [28] or TinyDB [18].

These solutions, although they are no longer under development, are very interesting because they can be used in the implementation of embankment monitoring systems. It is also worth drawing attention to some constantly developed commercial products, such as StreamBase [24]. There are also other, academic, non-commercial projects, such as [11].

1.1 Sensor Network for Embankment Monitoring System

An embankment monitoring system consists of a network of sensors in wells which measure selected physical and geotechnical (e.g. temperature, pressure, pore water, humidity, stress and strain, electrical conductivity, etc.) parameters at given time intervals. The network should cover the embankments on both sides of the riverbed, initially assuming a distance of approximately 5 meters between successive measurement points (Fig. 1). The entire system thus creates a grid of sensors, from which a constant feed of the parameters studied at each measurement point is flowing. This data must then be monitored by software that raises an alarm only if the changes are not caused by the normal diurnal cycle, or seasonal and annual fluctuations.

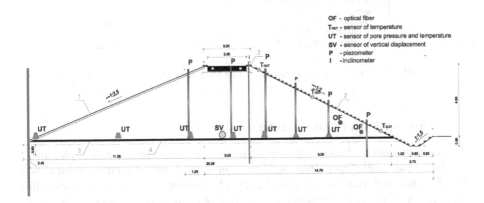

Fig. 1. The schema of experimental flood embankments

2 The Data Model and Query Language for the Dedicated Stream of Data from Sensor Networks

Analysis of the data measured and transmitted over a sensor network placed at given points in embankments is essential in order to assess the condition of the levees and provide early warning about changes in the value of the measured physical parameters. Two different types of data management systems are used in order to implement an embankment's flood control system; a stream database and a relational database. The streaming database is responsible for storing records received from point or linear sensors placed in flood embankments. The data transmitted by the sensors will carry information about parameters such as temperature, saturation and pore pressure that can be collected every minute (Fig. 2a). The relational database collects such parameters as temperature, saturation and pore pressure, obtained by numerical modeling (Fig. 2b). The modeling will be carried according to dynamically determined scenarios created for different initial and boundary conditions, and various mechanical properties of the embankment.

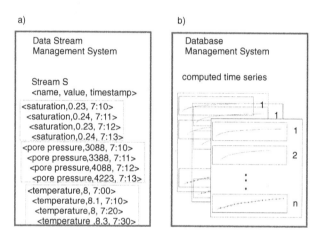

Fig. 2. The two data types used in embankment state monitoring

2.1   Description of Data Streams

The data stream is defined as a set of pairs $< s, t >$, where s is a tuple, and t is a time stamp [3]. Data streams differ from data stored in relational databases because stream data arrives in real time, so the database management system has influence neither on the content nor the order of the data. Another property of the stream data is that there is no restriction on the amount of data. In practice it is assumed that the stream contains an infinite amount of data. Another disadvantage of stream data is that analysis can only be easily carried out after the data has been downloaded from the stream. After data processing decisions concerning data archiving or destruction are taken and the system can proceed to analysis of the next packet from the data stream. A typical query implemented by the stream database can be in the form of an unlimited iteration which is characterized by a sequence of query-response, response, response. The main problem in the processing of stream data is the need to make decisions during the analysis of data packets that continuously arrive at the system database. Operations performed on data recorded by sensors should include a range of operations related not only to their analysis, but also to their initial segregation and processing. The most important operations that should be implemented are:

- selection,
- operations based on nested aggregation that compares the current value retrieved from the data stream with the moving average calculated for the specified range of data,
- operations similar to traditional query-based operations, using union operators and group by clauses, used to merge or decompose data stream
- analysis of the stream corresponding to data mining procedures such as pattern matching, similarity searching, and forecasting,
- operations which combine streams coming from different sensors and display them together with types of static data, queries executed in given time windows [9,10].

2.2 Description of Relational Data

The aim of the designed system is the comparison of data packets obtained from the flood embankments monitoring network with theoretical results obtained from numerical modeling. The calculations were performed using FLAC 2D software v. 7.0 and FLAC 3D v. 5.0 Itasca Consulting Group [12]. Calculations were performed for two-dimensional and three-dimensional models. Numerical calculations were done in order to determine the behavior of the embankments with different initial and boundary conditions. Dynamic module analysis was used to examine the impact of water filtration and temperature changes on the stability of flood embankments. A timed series of parameters such as pore pressure, temperature and saturation were recorded for given points of a computational grid. The governing equation describing the interaction of the water filtration and mechanical processes is described by generalized Biot's theory [2]. The numerical analysis of thermal processes, described by equation (1) incorporates both the conduction and advection processes. The equation describes the phenomenon of the spreading of temperature within the model and the impact of this process on the stresses and strains fields, as well as the advection phenomenon.

$$ - \nabla \cdot q^T + q_v^T = \rho C_v \frac{\partial T}{\partial t} \tag{1}$$

where:

- T - temperature,
- q^T - thermal flux,
- q_v^T - volumetric heat source intensity,
- ρ - reference density,
- C_v - specific heat of the fluid.

The numerical simulations of embankment behavior included scenarios that do not affect the stability of embankments, as well as scenarios that led to the violation of their stability. Embankment behavior scenarios were constructed for different sets of initial and boundary parameters and for different physical parameters that reflected the weakening of the embankments. The results of modeling that simulated sensor readings and powered a relational database were used as comparative material for the analysis of the data stream coming from the sensors placed in the real embankment. The modeling process is presented in the figure (Fig. 3).

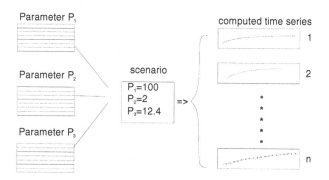

Fig. 3. Generation method of the relational database data used in the analysis step of streaming data. Modeling was conducted for given parameters values that describe the conditions that the embankment is subjected to.

3   Implementation of the System

Analysis of how existing flood embankments behave during floods leads to the conclusion that the state of the fortifications in different parts of the river change dynamically. This is caused by a number of factors, from the size of the flood and the time of its impact on the embankment to the geology and topography of the area. Therefore, one of the main principles of the system is the division of the embankment monitoring running along the river into segments. This procedure will maximize the effectiveness and accuracy of the expected embankment behavior that will be generated by the decision algorithms.

3.1   Stream Data Processing

The measurement network, depending on the section of embankments, will consist of 500-1000 sensors placed at different levels, which will collect data at a specified interval. Therefore, the minimum number of handled streams $S < s, t >$ must be consistent with the number of sensors (~1000), and the process should not have any delays which lead to a decline in data processing productivity.

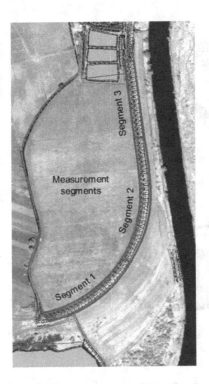

Fig. 4. Arrangement of the measurement segments on the embankment, Czernichow, Poland

A project map of the sensors' locations in the embankment (one segment contains one measurement network) is shown in Figure 4. Data reading will occur through an interface that handles the binary streams that will be generated by the sensor network. It will follow SOA (Service Oriented Architecture) principle where measured data will be processed by services deployed on the sensor nodes and on the server side of the system. Data between services will be transmitted using MoM (Message Oriented Middleware) [27] over IP and GPRS communication protocols [26]. Such a sensor network should adapt itself to the changing execution environment caused by the varying weather conditions that may result, among others, in network connection interruptions and delays [29]. One portion (tuple) s of data will include, in addition to the time stamp t, nine attributes, which will provide the current sensor readings; pore pressure, temperature, stress, etc. An exemplary system scheme is shown in the figure below (Figure 5).

3.2 Processing Data Operators

Each data stream is processed immediately by the implemented operators (logical operators, grouping clauses) that manipulate incoming data, sorting and

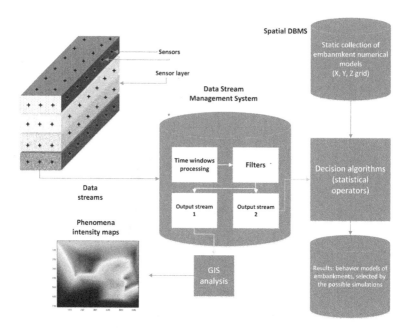

Fig. 5. System schema

grouping them according to the size of the measured parameters and the location of the sensor in the embankment. Since the measured values are often noisy due to the conditions prevailing inside the embankments, an important step in processing is a noise reduction process. For this purpose median filtering operators will be implemented, allowing the measurement to be authenticated. The flow of the data stream being processed using the implemented operators is presented in Figure 6. The processed streams are aggregated using time windows that generate an assumed time series, allowing the isolation of the most probable scenarios of embankment behavior by matching the size measurements to static stored (in a relational database) models. Implemented decision algorithms enable the selection of the n-best fit scenarios for the behavior of the embankment, on the basis of matching the measurement time series and modeled data [5].

3.3 DBMS

The decision algorithms proposed in the previous section are on one hand based on the data stream, on the other hand on the behavior of the embankment scenarios, which were prepared based on the numerical modeling. Due to the very high computational complexity, the numerical modeling of the embankment stability is not possible in real time. Therefore, the scenarios are prepared in advance based on many hours of simulations of embankment behavior, using the software package FLAC. Metodology of generation of a single scenario and exampled results are described in [21]. The result of each simulation is a

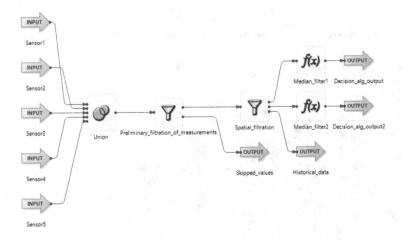

Fig. 6. Stream data processing

scenario and corresponding three-dimensional coordinates grid of the embankment model. Such prepared data sets will supply a relational database, which is the reference point for incoming measurements. The system should also be able to store historical data, ie, the knowledge base, supplied by the data collected during each previous flood. Due to this the decision algorithms will "learn", in order to increase their efficiency.

3.4   Used Technologies

Since one of the principles of the system is its reliability, a decision was made to use commercial solutions. The stream database system is StreamBase LiveView (Server, Desktop), which provides an API, enabling customers to implement tools (operators of median filters, time windows, TCP/IP interfaces). A relational database will be created based on MS SQL Server 2014. Numerical modeling is carried out based on the FLAC software.

4   Construction of the Stream Data Analysis System

The data interpretation procedure relies on the synthetic scenarios realized by numerical modeling in a Flac system. The scheme of the procedure is shown in Figure 7. The particular scenario S_{ij} consists of a set of time series. Each of them describes dynamic changes of the measured physical quantity in the particular node of the computational grid. The static, relational data basis stores time series generated for each node of the grid in the assumed time observation window (e.g. two weeks). The data covers a large number (over 500) scenarios constructed for different initial and edge conditions. Let's assume that the measurements are taken using N digital sensors mounted in the embankment.

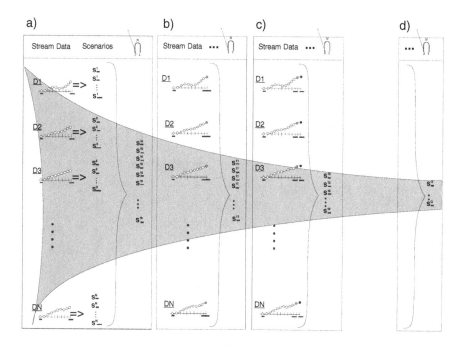

Fig. 7. Method of application of the relational database data for the analysis of streaming data

Sensors are located in same nodes of a grid used for the numerical modeling. We assumed that each sensor measures a single physical parameter probing a physical field with a constant sampling rate. The first stage of the proposed procedure is presented in part A of figure 7. The measurement system is activated in cases of flood risk, usually by the local authority responsible for crisis management. The sensors start measurements and the data is continuously transmitted to the database over the wireless transmission system. The data interpretation starts after a predetermined number of data samples have been received, for example 10. The samples are used in the scenario identification procedure. The recorded time series is compared with the synthetic time series modeled in the same place (in the same node) for different scenarios. As a result of the procedure the scenarios that give the best-fitted models are selected. The maximum misfit is selected empirically. Finally, for each sensor the set of characteristic scenarios that best reflect the dynamic processes are chosen. In the final step of the procedure the scenarios that were identified for most of sensors are recognized as scenarios common for all sensors. If we decide that only the scenarios that were identified for each sensor should be accepted we have to choose the common part of all identified scenarios (logical product). The second stage of the procedure is presented in Fig 7b. When the new sample appears on the sensor it is appended to the existing time series. Next, similarly to the previous step, the right scenarios for each sensor are identified and a common part of all the scenarios is chosen. As a result, we obtain common models, most probable for all parts of the embankment, valid for step two. The same operations are repeated in the following steps (see Fig. 7 c,d). In each step we obtain a set of permissible scenarios. Step by step the scenarios are identified with better precision, because the time series increases in length. Eventually, step by step, the number of permissible scenarios decreases. Preferably, only the scenarios that were present in the previous step should be accepted in the next one. Finally, in the last step of the procedure, the relatively small number of acceptable scenarios is identified. They optimally characterize the dynamic conditions in the examined structure. What is important is that the assessment of admissible scenarios can be evaluated for any starting time of the experiment. The number of accepted scenarios will be larger for that case because the time series is shorter. Consequently the assessment of the real embankment state will be less reliable.

5   Conclusions and the Further Work

The problem of processing stream data from a flood embankment monitoring system is presented in this article. The authors have introduced a real application for flood embankment monitoring into stream data systems, especially sensor networks. A model has been proposed for storing the data acquired from sensors (saturation, pore pressures, temperature), dedicated to data stream storing and processing. Another proposal considers a method for comparing input stream data with scenarios that assume stability of embankments as well as the scenarios that led to the violation of its stability. The key features of the proposed model (schema, scenario analysis) are included in this article. Future work involves consideration of such problems as efficient spatial indexing of data acquired from different measurement points on the grid of sensor networks. Another problem is the sizing of the sliding windows in order to perform proper scenario analysis [19,20]. This case and its related issues is a topic for further consideration. It may be also considered to use machine learning methods to assess the embankment stability. For example, support vector machines can be trained with large amount of data using the framework proposed in [13].

Acknowledgments. This work is financed by the National Centre for Research and Development (NCBiR), Poland, project PBS1/B9/18/2013 - (no 180535).

This work was partly support by the AGH - University of Science and Technology, Faculty of Geology, Geophysics and Environmental Protection, as a part of statutory project number No.11.11.140.032.

References

1. Balis, B., Kasztelnik, M., Bubak, M., Bartynski, T., Gubała, T., Nowakowski, P., Broekhuijsen, J.: The urbanflood common information space for early warning systems. Procedia Computer Science 4, 96–105 (2011)

2. Biot, M.A.: Theory of elasticity and consolidation for a porous anisotropic solid. Journal of Applied Physics 26(2), 182–185 (2004)
3. Botan, I., Derakhshan, R., Dindar, N., Haas, L., Miller, R.J., Tatbul, N.: Secret: a model for analysis of the execution semantics of stream processing systems. Proceedings of the VLDB Endowment 3(1-2), 232–243 (2010)
4. Carney, D., Çetintemel, U., Cherniack, M., Convey, C., Lee, S., Seidman, G., Stonebraker, M., Tatbul, N., Zdonik, S.: Monitoring streams: a new class of data management applications. In: Proceedings of the 28th International Conference on Very Large Data Bases, pp. 215–226. VLDB Endowment (2002)
5. Chuchro, M., Lupa, M., Pięta, A., Piórkowski, A., Leśniak, A.: A concept of time windows length selection in stream databases in the context of sensor networks monitoring. In: Bassiliades, N., Ivanovic, M., Kon-Popovska, M., Manolopoulos, Y., Palpanas, T., Trajcevski, G., Vakali, A. (eds.) New Trends in Database and Information Systems II. AISC, vol. 312, pp. 173–183. Springer, Heidelberg (2015)
6. Cranor, C., Johnson, T., Spataschek, O., Shkapenyuk, V.: Gigascope: a stream database for network applications. In: Proceedings of the 2003 ACM SIGMOD International Conference on Management of Data, pp. 647–651. ACM (2003)
7. Flak, J., Gaj, P., Tokarz, K., Wideł, S., Ziębiński, A.: Remote monitoring of geological activity of inclined regions – the concept. In: Kwiecień, A., Gaj, P., Stera, P. (eds.) CN 2009. CCIS, vol. 39, pp. 292–301. Springer, Heidelberg (2009)
8. Gaj, P., Kwiecień, B.z.: The general concept of a distributed computer system designed for monitoring rock movements. In: Kwiecień, A., Gaj, P., Stera, P. (eds.) CN 2009. CCIS, vol. 39, pp. 280–291. Springer, Heidelberg (2009)
9. Golab, L., Özsu, M.T.: Issues in data stream management. ACM Sigmod Record 32(2), 5–14 (2003)
10. Golab, L., Özsu, M.T.: Processing sliding window multi-joins in continuous queries over data streams. In: Proceedings of the 29th International Conference on Very Large Data Bases , vol. 29, pp. 500–511. VLDB Endowment (2003)
11. Gorawski, M., Gorawska, A., Pasterak, K.: Evaluation and development perspectives of stream data processing systems. In: Kwiecień, A., Gaj, P., Stera, P. (eds.) CN 2013. CCIS, vol. 370, pp. 300–311. Springer, Heidelberg (2013)
12. Itasca Consulting Group, Inc.: FLAC Fast Lagrangian Analysis of Continua and FLAC/Slope – User's Manual (2008)
13. Kawulok, M., Nalepa, J.: Support vector machines training data selection using a genetic algorithm. In: Gimel'farb, G., Hancock, E., Imiya, A., Kuijper, A., Kudo, M., Omachi, S., Windeatt, T., Yamada, K. (eds.) SSPR & SPR 2012. LNCS, vol. 7626, pp. 557–565. Springer, Heidelberg (2012)
14. Konieczny, M.: Enriching WSN environment with context information. Computer Science 13(4) (2012), http://journals.agh.edu.pl/csci/article/view/47
15. Krzhizhanovskaya, V.V., Shirshov, G., Melnikova, N., Belleman, R.G., Rusadi, F., Broekhuijsen, B., Gouldby, B., Lhomme, J., Balis, B., Bubak, M., et al.: Flood early warning system: design, implementation and computational modules. Procedia Computer Science 4, 106–115 (2011)
16. Madden, S.: Data management in sensor networks. In: Römer, K., Karl, H., Mattern, F. (eds.) EWSN 2006. LNCS, vol. 3868, p. 1. Springer, Heidelberg (2006)
17. Madden, S., Franklin, M.J.: Fjording the stream: An architecture for queries over streaming sensor data. In: Proceeding of 18th International Conference on Data Engineering, pp. 555–566. IEEE (2002)
18. Madden, S.R., Franklin, M.J., Hellerstein, J.M., Hong, W.: TinyDB: an acquisitional query processing system for sensor networks. ACM Transactions on database systems (TODS) 30(1), 122–173 (2005)

19. Patroumpas, K., Sellis, T.: Window update patterns in stream operators. In: Grundspenkis, J., Morzy, T., Vossen, G. (eds.) ADBIS 2009. LNCS, vol. 5739, . pp. 118–132. Springer, Heidelberg (2009)
20. Patroumpas, K., Sellis, T.: Subsuming multiple sliding windows for shared stream computation. In: Eder, J., Bielikova, M., Tjoa, A.M. (eds.) ADBIS 2011. LNCS, vol. 6909, pp. 56–69. Springer, Heidelberg (2011)
21. Pieta, A., Bala, J., Dwornik, M., Krawiec, K.: Stability of the levees in case of high level of the water. In: 14th SGEM Geoconference On Informatics, Geoinformatics And Remote Sensing – Conference Proceedings, vol. 1, pp. 809–815 (2014)
22. Piórkowski, A., Leśniak, A.: Using data stream management systems in the design of monitoring system for flood embankments. Studia Informatica 35(2), 297–310 (2014)
23. Płaczek, B., Bernaś, M.: Optimizing data collection for object tracking in wireless sensor networks. In: Kwiecień, A., Gaj, P., Stera, P. (eds.) CN 2013. CCIS, vol. 370, pp. 485–494. Springer, Heidelberg (2013)
24. Stonebraker, M., Çetintemel, U., Zdonik, S.: The 8 requirements of real-time stream processing. ACM SIGMOD Record 34(4), 42–47 (2005)
25. Sullivan, M.: Tribeca: A stream database manager for network traffic analysis. In: VLDB, vol. 96, p. 594 (1996)
26. Szydlo, T., Nawrocki, P., Brzoza-Woch, R., Zielinski, K.: Power aware MOM for telemetry-oriented applications using GPRS-enabled embedded devices – levee monitoring use case. In: Federated Conference on Computer Science and Information Systems (FedCSIS), September 7-10 (in print, 2014)
27. Szydlo, T., Zielinski, K.: Adaptive Enterprise Service Bus. New Generation Computing 30(2-3), 189–214 (2012)
28. Yao, Y., Gehrke, J.: The cougar approach to in-network query processing in sensor networks. ACM Sigmod Record 31(3), 9–18 (2002)
29. Zielinski, K., Szydlo, T., Szymacha, R., Kosinski, J., Kosinska, J., Jarzab, M.: Adaptive SOA Solution Stack. IEEE Transactions on Services Computing 5(2), 149–163 (2012)

Analysis of Social Influence and Information Dissemination in Social Media: The Case of Twitter

Chien-Wen Shen and Chin-Jin Kuo

Department of Business Administration, National Central University
No.300, Jhongda Rd., Jhongli City 32001, Taiwan
cwshen@ncu.edu.tw

Abstract. To understand how the influencers of event information dissemination on social media can be identified, we propose three perspectives for investigating this topic: the number of related messages posted by the influencers, the number of related messages in which the influencers are mentioned by other users, and the number of influencers' messages that are reposted. The findings regarding social influencers can help companies identify the key people or organizations with whom they must engage. In addition, we used a social network diagram to depict how event information is disseminated from the influencers. This diagram shows the top influencers at different stages of information dissemination. Effectively modeling relationships among top users and accordingly using them to filter or recommend information are fundamental for mining social networking services. To illustrate our approach, we used the tweets from the Windows 8.1 launch event as a case study.

Keywords: Social Influence, Information Dissemination, Social Networks, Twitter.

1 Introduction

In an era of social media, people do not merely rely on traditional media that delivers information through one-way communication channels. People directly engage and become "the media" by using various online platforms such as content communities, social networking sites, blogs and microblogs to share their opinions, insights, information, experiences, and perspectives with each other [1]. On social networking services such as Facebook and Twitter, users build their own friendship networks and widely share, discover, and spread information by using various formats such as words, pictures, audio, and video. Because of the extraordinary popularity of social media, more than 10 billion messages are currently on Facebook daily, and more than 300 billion messages have been sent on Twitter [2]. Hence, understanding the characteristics of information dissemination in social media has become a crucial topic both in academia and business. Related research from Cha et al. [3] investigated the 11 million photos shared by 2.5 million users on Flickr to determine how widely and quickly the information spread through the social network as well as regional influences on popularity. Kwak, Lee, Park, and

K. Saeed and V. Snášel (Eds.): CISIM 2014, LNCS 8838, pp. 526–534, 2014.
© IFIP International Federation for Information Processing 2014

Moon [4] collected 41.7 million user profiles and 106 million tweets to study the topological characteristics of Twitter and its power as a new medium of information sharing from the perspectives of connectivity, influencers, and retweets. Ediger et al. [5] used data sets comprising H1N1 tweets and Atlanta Flood tweets from 2009 to identify the top vertices of tree-structured message connections in Twitter. Their findings indicated that major media outlets and government organizations are usually the highest-degree vertices in news dissemination. Aral and Walker [6] designed and conducted a randomized field experiment that evaluate the effectiveness of active-personalized referrals and passive-broadcast notifications in creating peer influence and social contagion among the 1.4 million friends of 9,687 experimental users on Facebook. Yoganarasimhan [7] examined a dataset of 1939 YouTube videos uploaded in 2007 to understand how the size and structure of a user's local network affect its ability to disseminate information on YouTube. Lin, Lazer, and Cao [8] introduced a visualization tool that highlights the social and spatiotemporal processes of information diffusion through social media in real time. This tool was designed based on a metaphorical sunflower of which the seeds are often dispersed far away.

To provide further insight into information sharing using social media, one of the objectives of this study is to discuss how the influencers of event information dissemination on social media can be identified. We propose three perspectives for investigating this topic: the number of related messages posted by the influencers, the number of related messages in which the influencers are mentioned by other users, and the number of influencers' messages that are reposted. Because the perceptions of brands and companies are largely driven by the rapid expansion of social media channels through which influencers communicate with their social networks [9], findings regarding influencers can help companies identify the key people or organizations with whom they must engage. In addition, we used a social network diagram to depict how event information is disseminated from the influencers. This diagram shows the top influencers at different stages of information dissemination. Analyzing the process of information dissemination on social media is complex because a numerous people use social media and their complex topological relationships must be considered. Effectively modeling relationships among top users and accordingly using them to filter or recommend information are fundamental for mining social networking services. The methodology used for the aforementioned objectives is detailed in the next section. To illustrate our approach, we used the tweets from the Windows 8.1 launch event as a case study, which is discussed in Section 3. Finally, Section 4 concludes our study.

2   Methodology

To analyze the characteristics of an event information dissemination on social media, the related key words must first be identified, and the related posts are then retrieved by using the tools provided by social networking services. For example, on Twitter, the streaming application programming interface (API) can be used to stream tweets in real time, or the search API can be used to perform ad hoc user queries from a limited corpus of recent tweets. Based on the collected data set, the most intuitive method for identifying the influencers of event information dissemination on social media is to count the number of related messages posted by users. Because different social networking services have distinct data structures or metadata tags, the related data fields must be understood. For example, on Twitter, the user who posted a message can be identified by referring to the user_screen_name data field. Hence, the users who have the highest frequency numbers in user_screen_name among the tweets related to the target event in a given observation time can be considered the influencers of information dissemination. In this study, we selected only the top 10 influencers to avoid generating excessively complex discussions. Moreover, a user mention in social media is any message update that contains a person's username in the body of the message. Hence, the users who receive the highest frequencies of mentions in the target social media feeds can also be considered influencers of information dissemination. On Twitter, user mention data can be retrieved by a code like the follows.

```
if doc['entities'].get('user_mentions'):
        for user_mention in
doc['entities']['user_mentions']:
            yield ('@' + user_mention
['screen_name'].lower(), [doc['_id'], doc['id']])
```

Because the value of the attribute screen_name in user_mentions indicates the username mentioned in a message, the users with the highest counts of screen_name in the target tweets can be considered the influencers of the related information disseminated on Twitter. In addition, the users who frequently repost information related to an event were also considered influencers. On Twitter, reposting of another person's tweet is called a retweet. This feature allows a user's retweets to be disseminated to all of the user's followers. The number of times that a username appears after the metadata tags "RT" or "via" in the target tweets can be counted to determine how many related tweets user has retweeted. After identifying the influencers, we further investigated how information is disseminated from these influencers by depicting a social network diagram. A node representing an influencer is allocated in the center of a network diagram and is associated with the top five users who have reposted the most messages from this influencer. This procedure can be repeated to obtain a social network diagram that illustrates how event information is disseminated from influencers as well as the influencers of information dissemination at different stages. The influencers at the first and the second stages are essential for the initial distribution of event information, and the influencers at the remaining stages are responsible for the subsequent information circulation.

3   Case Study

In this study, we used Twitter as the form of social media example to illustrate our approach. Twitter is the most popular microblogging platform, and its prominence as a social media platform is growing [10]. According to a report conducted by the Pew Research Center [11], 72% of U.S. adults online use social networking sites and 18% of them are Twitter users. Because of its great popularity, Twitter has been exploited as a platform for the viral marketing of content, products, and political campaigns [12]. In this case study, we used the Windows 8.1 product launch event to demonstrate how the information from this event was disseminated on Twitter. Microsoft launched Windows 8.1 on October 17, 2013, and a 1-month collection of tweets that included the key word "Windows 8.1" was obtained by using the Twitter search API. A total of 450,250 messages published by 206,792 users were collected. Fig. 1 shows that nearly 60% of the related tweets were published during the first week after the Windows 8.1 launch date. The daily tweets drastically dropped from more than 100,000 to less than 20,000 within 4 days. However, the number of tweets increased to more than 20,000 on October 21 because Microsoft temporarily pulled the Windows RT 8.1 update from the Windows Store. Since that date, the tweets regarding Windows 8.1 continued decreasing. One month after the Windows 8.1 launch date, the number of related tweets was only approximately 2,000. Hence, one month of data collection is sufficiently to effectively investigate the issues of social influence and information dissemination regarding Windows 8.1 launch event on Twitter.

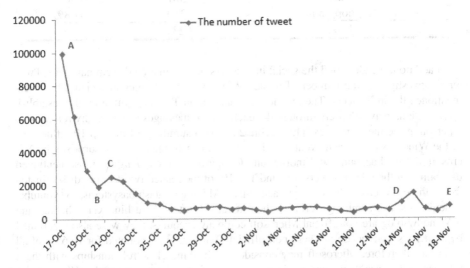

Fig. 1. Distribution of Windows 8.1 tweets during the first month after the launch date

To identify the social influencers of information dissemination regarding Windows 8.1 event on Twitter, we commenced with an investigation of the top users who posted the greatest number of related tweets. According to the results shown in Table 1, the top 10 users (@Windows, @hatiwin, @WindowsSupport, @atlazone, @arsenico, @NotebookDeal, @softpediadriver, @WinObs, @jorin5712, @scoop_india) posted an average of 723 related tweets during the first month following the launch of Windows 8.1. However, the average number of tweets related to Windows 8.1 posted by general users was only 2.18. Hence, these influencers shared 100 times more related tweets than the average users did. Among the top 10 users, only the users @Windows and @WindowsSupport are from the official Microsoft accounts. Besides, the total tweets of the top 10 users account for only 1.60% of the investigated Windows 8.1

tweets posted by 206,792 Twitter users. This number indicates that numerous people were engaged in sharing information regarding the Windows 8.1 launch event on Twitter, and that this information dissemination was not limited to a small group of users.

Table 1. Top 10 influencers by the number of tweets

Rank	Username	Number of Tweets	Percentage
1	@Windows	1,110	0.25%
2	@hatiwin	1,102	0.24%
3	@WindowsSupport	1,037	0.23%
4	@atlazone	775	0.17%
5	@arsenico	708	0.16%
6	@NotebookDeal	683	0.15%
7	@softpediadriver	669	0.15%
8	@WinObs	427	0.09%
9	@jorin5712	361	0.08%
10	@scoop_india	359	0.08%
	Total	7,231	1.60%

In addition, we identified the social influencers of information dissemination on Twitter by investigating the number of related Windows 8.1 messages in which other users mentioned the influencers. The mention mechanism on Twitter is often used to establish conversations between users through the exchange of messages or simply by referring to a person in the message's text [13]. Table 2 shows a summary of the top 10 influencers of the Windows 8.1 launch event based on the number of mentions. Unsurprisingly, Microsoft's official accounts @Windows and @Microsoft were among the most mentioned usernames in the related tweets. Around 13.21% of the related tweets were disseminated from these Microsoft's official accounts. Although @ishibasystems, @youtube, @detiknews5, @sambung_cerita, @henextweb, @artem_klyushin, @mashable, and @Windowsblog are not official Microsoft company accounts, they were also mentioned by numerous Twitter users. These non-official Twitter users accounted for 16.65% of all mentions; therefore, Microsoft may consider establishing close relationships with these influencers because they were crucial sources of information regarding the Windows 8.1 launch event for Twitter users.

Another key mechanism Twitter provides is the retweet feature, which enables people to quickly share tweets with their followers. This feature enables individual tweets to be propagated throughout social networks and serves as a method for people to endorse their perspectives regarding specific topics [13]. Therefore, the influencers of information dissemination on Twitter can be identified according to the number of retweets by other users. Among the 450,250 related tweets during the first month since the Windows 8.1 launch date, 19.92% were retweets. Table 3 lists the top 10 users who had the greatest number of messages reposted by other users. Because the retweets from these influencers accounted for 26.87% of total retweets, these influencers were vital to the Windows 8.1 event information disseminated on Twitter.

In addition to the Windows and Microsoft official accounts, most of the influencers were non-official users. Hence, Microsoft must quickly update these users with current information because many of their followers spread news regarding Windows 8.1 provided by these influencers.

Table 2. Top 10 influencers by the number of mentions

Rank	User ID	Count	Percentage
1	@Windows	14,362	10.06%
2	@ishibasystems	4,967	3.48%
3	@Microsoft	4,505	3.15%
4	@youtube	4,125	2.89%
5	@detiknews5	3,599	2.52%
6	@sambung_cerita	3,216	2.25%
7	@thenextweb	2,437	1.71%
8	@artem_klyushin	2,034	1.42%
9	@mashable	1,777	1.24%
10	@Windowsblog	1,615	1.13%
	Total	42,637	29.86%

Table 3. Top 10 influencers by the number of retweets

Rank	User ID	Count	Percentage
1	@ishibasystems	4,597	5.13%
2	@Windows	4,137	4.61%
3	@detiknews5	3,595	4.01%
4	@thenextweb	2,365	2.64%
5	@artem_klyushin	2,034	2.27%
6	@Microsoft	1,685	1.88%
7	@sambung_cerita	1,607	1.79%
8	@mashable	1,380	1.54%
9	@cnet	1,371	1.53%
10	@kakocom	1,327	1.48%
	Total	24,098	26.87%

A social network diagram illustrating how the Windows 8.1 tweets were disseminated from the official Windows and Microsoft Twitter accounts to the other users is depicted in Fig. 2. In this diagram, the Windows and Microsoft nodes are centrally located and are tied to the nodes that represent the top users (followers) who have reposted the most Windows 8.1-related messages from the official Windows and Microsoft accounts. Fig. 2 shows that the top followers of the Windows account were @microsoft_now, @windowsphone, @MicrosoftID, and @WinObs. The top followers of the Microsoft account were @MicrosoftASIA, @dovellonsky, @MicrosoftTH, @BenThePCGuy, and @lee_stott. In addition, the top followers that resent the tweets from the top followers of @Windows and @Microsoft were also illustrated in Fig. 2.

Hence, a total of 3 layers of top influencers related to the information dissemination of Windows 8.1 launch event were identified.

Fig. 2. A social network diagram that identifies the top influencers related to the information dissemination of Windows 8.1 launch event

In addition, we measured the strength of the ties between a social influencer and their top followers according to the number of the user's tweets that were reposted by followers. Table 4 shows the results regarding the strength of the tie between the nodes in Fig. 2. The results revealed that 4,137 retweets were from the official Windows account, and that 1,647 retweets were from the official Microsoft account. Users who exhibit strong retweet influence are highly capable of generating content with pass-along value. The influences at the two initial stages were essential for the initial distribution of Windows 8.1 event information. The social influencers at the later stages were critical for the dissemination of this information on Twitter.

Table 4. Strength of the ties between social influencers and their followers

Stage-1 Influencer	Stage-2 Influencers	Number of Retweets	Stage-3 Influencers	Number of Retweets
@Windows (4137)	@Microsoft	1647	@MicrosoftASIA	29
			@dovellonsky	21
			@MicrosoftTH	13
			@BenThePCGuy	13
			@lee_stott	12
	@microsoft_now	334	@windows8_ai	52
			@WinOPZ	33
			@syuu1228	23
			@TakuKKaseda	7
			@keno1977	4
	@windowsphone	305	@bing	45
			@MSHelpsThai	37
			@MS_SurfaceEvang	34
			@akipekka	34
			@MicrosoftTH	13
	@MicrosoftID	268	@MicrosoftSA	25
			@masajirjb	21
			@isfahanighiyath	7
			@irfansaflawi	4
			@Dollauchiha	4
	@WinObs	252	@edbott	207
			@WinBetaDotOrg	155
			@BogdanSPD	135
			@VTTechnology	132
			@Pureinfotech	122

4   Conclusion

Because of the viral nature of information dissemination on social media, identifying and analyzing the influential social media users is becoming increasingly important to business. This study not only provides different perspectives for investigating the influencers of event information dissemination, but also proposes a social network diagram approach to depict how event information is disseminated from the influencers. Our proposed approaches can help companies identify the key users during an event information dissemination as well as model the relationships among top influencers. A case study regarding the tweets from the Windows 8.1 launch event was also discussed to illustrate our approaches. Our results suggest that these social influencers did play important roles on the information dissemination of the Windows 8.1 launch event. We are also able to understand how event information was disseminated from the influencers based on the social network diagram. Future studies may explore other events to evaluate our proposed approaches on identifying the influencers. Besides, we can investigate how our approached can be applied on other social networking platforms such as Facebook and YouTube. We can also further examine how public sentiment towards an event can be assessed based on the related messages on social media.

Acknowledgements. This research was supported in part by the Ministry of Science and Technology, Taiwan (grant # MOST 103-2410-H-008 -029).

References

1. Thevenot, G.: Blogging as a Social Media. Tourism and Hospitality Research 7, 287–289 (2007)
2. Smith, C.: By the Numbers: 130 Amazong Facebook User & Demographic Statistics, http://expandedramblings.com/index.php/by-the-numbers-17-amazing-facebook-stats/
3. Cha, M., Mislove, A., Gummadi, K.P.: A Measurement-Driven Analysis of Information Propagation in the Flickr Social Network. In: Proceedings of the 18th International Conference on World Wide Web, pp. 721–730. ACM, Madrid (2009)
4. Kwak, H., Lee, C., Park, H., Moon, S.: What is Twitter, a Social Network or a News Media? In: Proceedings of the 19th International Conference on World Wide Web, pp. 591–600. ACM, Raleigh (2010)
5. Ediger, D., Jiang, K., Riedy, J., Bader, D.A., Corley, C., Farber, R., Reynolds, W.N.: Massive Social Network Analysis: Mining Twitter for Social Good. In: 2010 39th International Conference on Parallel Processing, pp. 583–593 (2010)
6. Aral, S., Walker, D.: Creating Social Contagion Through Viral Product Design: A Randomized Trial of Peer Influence in Networks. Management Science 57, 1623–1639 (2011)
7. Yoganarasimhan, H.: Impact of Social Network Structure on Content Propagation: A Study Using YouTube Data. Quantitative Marketing and Economics 10, 111–150 (2012)
8. Lin, Y.-R., Lazer, D., Cao, N.: Watching How Ideas Spread Over Social Media. Leonardo 46, 277–277 (2013)
9. Booth, N., Matic, J.A.: Mapping and Leveraging Influencers in Social Media to Shape Corporate Brand Perceptions. Corporate Communications 16, 184–191 (2011)
10. Efron, M.: Information Search and Retrieval in Microblogs. Journal of the American Society for Information Science and Technology 62, 996–1008 (2011)
11. Brenner, J., Smith, A.: 72% of Online Adults are Social Networking Site Users. Pew Research Center's Internet & American Life Project, Pew Research Center (2013)
12. Jin, F., Dougherty, E., Saraf, P., Cao, Y., Ramakrishnan, N.: Epidemiological Modeling of News and Rumors on Twitter. In: Proceedings of the 7th Workshop on Social Network Mining and Analysis, pp. 1–9 (2013)
13. Borondo, J., Morales, A., Losada, J., Benito, R.: Characterizing and Modeling an Electoral Campaign in the Context of Twitter: 2011 Spanish Presidential Election as a Case Study. Chaos: An Interdisciplinary Journal of Nonlinear Science 22, 23138 (2012)

Multi–criteria Route Planning in Bus Network

Vo Dang Khoa*, Tran Vu Pham, Huynh Tuong Nguyen, and Tran Van Hoai

Faculty of Computer Science & Engineering - Ho Chi Minh City University
of Technology
268 Ly Thuong Kiet Street, District 10, Ho Chi Minh City, Vietnam
{khoa.v.dang}@gmail.com
{t.v.pham,htnguyen,hoai}@cse.hcmut.edu.vn
http://www.cse.hcmut.edu.vn/

Abstract. In this paper, we consider the problem of finding itineraries
in bus networks under multiple independent optimization criteria, namely
arrival time at destination and number of transfers. It is also allowed to
walk from one stop to another if the two stops are located within a small
distance. A time–dependent model is proposed to solve this problem.
While focusing on the network where the size of the Pareto set in the
multi–criteria shortest path problem might grow exponentially, we
develop an efficient algorithm with its speed–up techniques. An evaluation on the qualities of found paths and the empirical results of different
implementations are given. The results show that the allowance of walking
shortcuts between nearby stops gives a better route planning.

Keywords: Time–dependent model, shortest path problem, public
transport system, bus system, labelling algorithm.

1 Introduction

Route planning becomes essential for bus users when the size of the timetable
gets larger. A manual planning is mainly based on individual experience and is
hardly optimal. Therefore, the planning should be done automatically and in an
algorithmic way. The user then makes a query that consists of a *source bus stop*
(or stop) A, a *destination stop* B and a *departure time* t_A at A. The system
answers with the optimal route planning to reach B under the optimization of
multi–criteria, namely arrival time at B and number of transfers. Tradeoffs of
the multi–criteria optimization is that the improvement of one criterion comes
at the expense of decreasing other criteria. For instance, the planning with an
earlier arrival time at destination might have a greater number of transfers,
whereas the one with a smallest number of transfers might have a later arrival
time at destination. A set of Pareto–optimal paths [11] then allows to focus on
important tradeoffs without considering the full range of all possible values of
criteria. The multi–criteria route planning problem in the bus network then can
be solved by transforming the problem to a multi–criteria shortest path problem
in a graph model.

---

* Corresponding author.

K. Saeed and V. Snášel (Eds.): CISIM 2014, LNCS 8838, pp. 535–546, 2014.

The multi–criteria shortest path problem is an extension of the classical short-est path problem. The problem aims to find a set of *non–dominated* (Pareto-optimal) paths (Pareto set) from a *source vertex* to a *destination vertex* under *multiple* criteria. A path p dominates a path q iff p's weight is less than or equal q's weight in all criteria and one of the inequalities is strict. A path is called Pareto–optimal if it is not dominated by any other paths. The standard way to find the Pareto set in a non–negative weighted graph is *labelling algorithm*. The algorithm keeps candidate paths which can be further expanded in a prior-ity queue of labels. Labelling algorithm is distinguished by the order paths are extracted from the queue and the policy for the expansion at each vertex. In particular, *label setting method* [10,11,14,15] chooses paths in a *lexicographical* order. Given two path p and q with p's weight vector (x_p, y_p) and q's weight vector (x_q, y_q) respectively, p is lexicographically less than q iff $x_p < x_q$ or $(x_p = x_q$ and $y_p \leq y_q)$. Lexicographical ordering assures that established paths are the Pareto–optimal paths [11]. On the other hand, *label correcting method* [9,11,12,13] extracts paths in the FIFO order or the minimum weighted sum aggregate order, the chosen paths might be dominated by other paths later. As a result, the established paths which contain the chosen path have to be cor-rected. Regarding the expansion policy, it is either *label–selection* [10,11,14] or *vertex–selection* [9,12]. In label–selection policy, labels belonging to a particular vertex is treated separately. That means there is only one path expanded at each time for each outgoing arc. In contrast, vertex–selection policy extracts all paths which have a same destination vertex from the queue at the same time and then expands all of them for each outgoing arc.

As for the graph model, there are two main approaches: *time-expanded* [2,3], and *time-dependent* [4,5,6]. Hannemann and Schulz [1] gave a great survey on these models. In time–expanded approach, a static weighted graph is used to model *time events* (departure/arrival pairs) in the timetable. Schulz et al. [2] used the model to solve the simplified version of railway system problem. Han-nemann et al. [3] then extended the simplified model with the involvement of ticket cost, and number of transfers as well as traffic days. In time–dependent ap-proach, weights of arcs in the arc set E are determined by function $f : E \times T \to T$, with time set T in the timetable. Time–dependent model was first proposed by Brodal and Jacob [4]. The aim of their study is to propose a more effective model in comparison with the time–expanded model in [2]. Brodal and Jacob argued that in the simplified case where transfer from a train to another is not specified, Dijkstra's algorithm [16] considers many redundant arcs in the time–expanded graph. Pyrga et al. [5] then proposed an extended model which allows transfers between trains, and then they improved their model with the involvement of traffic days in [8]. Disser et al. [6] extend the model in [8] by introducing the criterion of *"reliability of transfers"* which presents the probability of catching all trains of the planing.

In this paper, we formulate a multi–criteria route planning problem in a bus network as a multi–criteria shortest path problem. A time–dependent model and a labelling algorithm with its speed–up techniques are then proposed to solve the problem. Our proposed model allows the possible transfer between nearby stops that are within a walking distance. Empirical results are therefore evaluated and presented using Ho Chi Minh City (HCMC) bus network. From the obtained results, we also discuss about the quality of the route planning when users are able to walk between stops. The remaining of the paper is organised as follows. In Section 2, we present how the bus network is modelled. The algorithm and speed–up techniques then are proposed in Section 3. The experimental studies are given in Section 4. Finally, the conclusion is presented in Section 5.

2 Route Planning Problem

2.1 Bus System

Generally, a bus system is formulated by $\mathfrak{J} = (N, R, T, TT)$ in which

- $N = (S, C)$ is a directed graph that presents the bus stop network where the vertex set S is a set of stops, and the arc set $C \subseteq S^2$ is a set of stop connections.
- R is a set of routes. For each route $x \in R$, let S_x and $C_x \subseteq S_x^2$ be a set of stops and a set of connections of route x such that $S = \bigcup_{x \in R} S_x$ and $C = \bigcup_{x \in R} C_x$. A route $x \in R$ is defined by an acyclic path $x = \langle s_1, s_2, ..., s_k \rangle$ on graph N with $(s_i, s_{i+1}) \in C_x, \forall i \in \{1, ..., k-1\}$. Route x means there are a set of buses starting their route from the stop s_1, then visiting consecutively $s_2, ..., s_{k-1}$ and finishing at s_k.
- $T \subset \mathbb{Z}^+$ is a set of time points appearing in the timetable. T depends on the period the timetable is considered, daily or weekly.
- TT is the timetable. The timetable TT consists of *elements* c which has the form $c = (Z, S_d, S_a, t_d, t_a)$. An element c then means there is a bus running on route $Z(c)$ which departs from stop $S_d(c)$ at time $t_d(c)$, and then arrives at stop $S_a(c)$ at time $t_a(c)$ in the timetable TT. For each $c \in TT$, c has the following constraints: $Z(c) \in R$; $S_d(c), S_a(c) \in S_{Z(c)}$; $t_d(c), t_a(c) \in T$; $t_a(c) \geq t_d(c)$.

2.2 Time–Dependent Model

The problem based on time–expanded model is simpler to model [2], but needs a higher space consumption due to the graph model structure [4]. Empirical results also show that time–dependent model gives a better performance in running time [7,8]. In this paper, we propose a time–dependent model which is extended from the model in [5], but allows walking between nearby stops. The idea of the extension is that arcs which model the walking shortcuts are introduced. Let $G = (V, E)$ be the directed graph that models the bus system $\mathfrak{J}$, and let $\xi : V \to S$ define the injective function mapping a vertex $u \in V$ to a stop $A \in S$. The graph G is constructed by the following steps:

1. Let $G_R = (V_R, E_R)$ be the directed graph that models the routes in R, with $V_R = \bigcup_{x \in R} W_x$ and $E_R = \bigcup_{x \in R} F_x$. For each route $x \in R$, create a *route vertex* $r_A^x \in W_x$ for every stop $A \in S_x$, and let $\xi(r_A^x) = A$, then create a *route arc* $(r_A^x, r_B^x) \in F_x$ for every connection $(A, B) \in C_x$.

2. Let $G_S = (V_S, E_{walk})$ be the directed graph that models the stops in S. Create a *stop vertex* $s_A \in V_S$ for every stop $A \in S$, and let $\xi(s_A) = A$, then create a *walking arc* $(s_A, s_B) \in E_{walk}$ for every pair of stop $A, B \in S$ that is allowed to walk between.

3. The graph $G = (V, E)$ is given by $G = G_R \oplus G_S$ with $V = V_R \bigcup V_S$, and $E = E_R \bigcup E_{walk} \bigcup E_{in} \bigcup E_{off}$ where $E_{in} \subseteq V_S \times V_R$ is the set of *get–in* arcs, and $E_{off} \subseteq V_R \times V_S$ is the set of *get–off* arcs. Then, create an arc $(u, v) \in E_{in}$ and an arc $(v, u) \in E_{off}$ for every pair of vertices $u \in V_S$ and $v \in V_R$ if $\xi(u) = \xi(v)$.

Figure 1 illustrates the graph model of the connection from stop A to stop B in which two routes α, β visit A then B; route γ visits A but not B; route δ visits B but not A; and walking is allowed from A to B and from B to A.

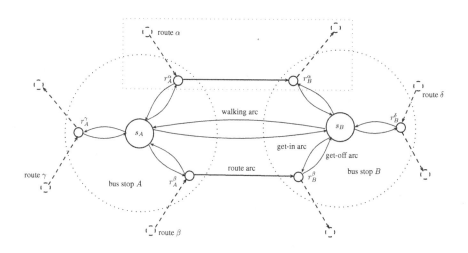

Fig. 1. The model for the connection from stop A to stop B

The graph model has the following properties: $\bigcap_{x \in R} W_x \bigcap V_S = \emptyset$, and $\bigcap_{x \in R} F_x \bigcap E_{walk} \bigcap E_{in} \bigcap E_{off} = \emptyset$. With these properties, the vertices and the arcs of the graph G capture all possible states and possible actions of a bus user respectively. The semantics of the vertices and the arcs are given as follows:

– A stop vertex $u \in V_S$ presents the state that one is waiting at stop $\xi(u)$.
– A route vertex $u \in W_x$ presents the state that one visits stop $\xi(u)$ on a bus of route x.

- A get–in arc $(u, v) \in E_{in}$, with $u \in V_S$ and $v \in W_x$, presents the action that one gets in a bus of route x at stop $\xi(u)$.
- A get–off arc $(u, v) \in E_{off}$, with $u \in W_x$ and $v \in V_S$, represents the action that one gets off a bus of route x at stop $\xi(v)$.
- A walking arc $(u, v) \in E_{walk}$ represents the action that one walks from stop $\xi(u)$ to stop $\xi(v)$.
- A route arc $(u, v) \in E_R$, with $u, v \in W_x$, represents the action that one travels from stop $\xi(u)$ to stop $\xi(v)$ on route x.

Given a path $p = \langle v_1, v_2, ..., v_k \rangle$, $k > 2$, on the graph model G, path p gives a route planning for a user query from stop A to stop B with the departure time t_A at A with the following constraints: $v_1, v_k \in V_S$; $\xi(v_1) = A$; $\xi(v_k) = B$; $(v_i, v_{i+1}) \in E, \forall i \in \{1, ..., k - 1\}$.

2.3   Multi–criteria Shortest Path Problem

Travel time – We consider three kinds of travel time, namely *routing time*, *transfer time* and *walking time*, as below.

Table 1. A part of the timetable TT which relates to the connection from stop A to stop B

bus	Z	S_d	S_a	t_d	t_a
...	...	...	...	...	...
bus 1	α	A	B	8:05	8:30
bus 2	β	A	B	8:18	8:39
bus 3	α	A	B	8:20	8:55
...	...	...	...	...	...

Table 2. The time table $TT^{\alpha}_{A,B}$ of route α from stop A to stop B

bus	t_d	t_a
...	...	...
bus 1	8:05	8:30
bus 3	8:20	8:55
...	...	...

- Let $\theta^{\alpha}_{A,B}(t_A)$ be the routing time from stop A to stop B on route α with the arrival time t_A at A, then

$$\theta^{\alpha}_{A,B}(t_A) = min\{t' \mid (t, t') \in TT^{\alpha}_{A,B}, t_A \leq t\} - t_A \tag{1}$$

$$TT^{\alpha}_{A,B} = \{(t_d(c), t_a(c)) \mid c \in TT, S_d(c) = A, S_a(c) = B, Z(c) = \alpha\} \tag{2}$$

where $TT^{\alpha}_{A,B}$ is the timetable of route α from A to B. If $TT^{\alpha}_{A,B} = \emptyset$, that means there is no connection from A to B via route α in the timetable. In other words, one cannot catch any bus of route α to travel from A to B. The min operation in Formula 1 yields the pair (t, t') in $TT^{\alpha}_{A,B}$ such that its departure time t is after t_A and its arrival time t' is minimum. Let the minimum arrival time (if exists) be t^*, the time to travel from A to B is $t^* - t$ and the waiting time at A before catching a bus of route α to B is $t - t_A$, then

$$\theta^{\alpha}_{A,B}(t_A) = t^* - t + t - t_A = t^* - t_A.$$

Table 1 gives a part of the timetable TT which relates to the connection from stop A to stop B. The timetable $TT_{A,B}^{\alpha}$ is presented in Table 2. For the route α, suppose we arrive at A at time $t_A = 8{:}15$, at the time t_A we cannot catch bus 1, since it has already left A at 8:05 and the next bus of route α is bus 3. The routing time from A to B on route α when we arrive at A at 8:15 then is 8:55 - 8:15 = 40 minutes.

- At every stop A, it is only possible to get in a bus of a route α if we arrive at A earlier than the departure time of that bus by a given non–negative transfer time, denoted by τ_A.
- Let $\omega_{A,B}$ be the time to walk from stop A to stop B, the walking time is computed by the walking distance from A to B divided by the average walking speed.

Let $f : E \times T \rightarrow T$ be the function that determines the travel time weight of an arc $(u,v) \in E$ at time $t_u \in T$ where t_u is the time arc (u,v) is traversed, then

$$
f(u,v,t_u) = \begin{cases} 0 & \text{if } (u,v) \in E_{off} \\ \tau_{\xi(u)} & \text{if } (u,v) \in E_{in} \\ \omega_{\xi(u),\xi(v)} & \text{if } (u,v) \in E_{walk} \\ \theta_{\xi(u),\xi(v)}^{x}(t_u) & \text{if } (u,v) \in F_x \subseteq E_R \end{cases} \tag{3}
$$

Number of Transfers – Let $g : E \rightarrow \{0,1\}$ be the function that determines the number of transfer weight of an arc $(u,v) \in E$, then:

$$
g(u,v) = \begin{cases} 1 & \text{if } (u,v) \in E_{in} \\ 0 & \text{otherwise} \end{cases} \tag{4}
$$

Combine Two Criteria – Let vector function $w : E \times T \rightarrow T \times \{0,1\}$ be weight function of an arc $(u,v) \in E$ at time $t_u \in T$ where w^1 is travel time weight and w^2 is the number of transfers weight, the function w is given by:

$$
w(u,v,t_u) = (f(u,v,t_u), g(u,v)) \tag{5}
$$

Multi–criteria Shortest Path Problem – Given a path $p = \langle v_1, v_2, ..., v_k \rangle$, $k > 2$, from vertex $v_1 = s$ to vertex $v_k = d$ with $w^{arrival}(p,t_s)$ being the arrival time at d if the departure time at s is t_s, and $w^{transfer}(p)$ being the number of transfers on p. The weight vector $w(p,t_s)$ of path p with the departure time t_s at s is formulated by

$$
\begin{aligned}
w(p,t_s) &= (w^{arrival}(p,t_s), w^{transfer}(p)) \\
&= (t_s,0) + \sum_{i=1}^{k-1} w(v_i, v_{i+1}, t_{v_i}) \\
&= (t_s,0) + \sum_{i=1}^{k-1} (f(v_i, v_{i+1}, t_{v_i}), g(v_i, v_{i+1}))
\end{aligned} \tag{6}
$$

where $f(v_i, v_{i+1}, t_{v_i})$, $g(v_i, v_{i+1})$ are given by Formula 3 and Formula 4 respectively, and

$$t_{v_{i+1}} = \begin{cases} t_s & \text{if } i = 0 \\ t_{v_i} + f(v_i, v_{i+1}, t_{v_i}) & \text{otherwise} \end{cases} \tag{7}$$

with t_{v_i} being the arrival time at vertex v_i, or the time the arc (v_i, v_{i+1}) is traversed. Then, the arrival time t_{v_i} is used as the input to compute the arrival time $t_{v_{i+1}}$ at vertex v_{i+1}, and so on.

Let $P_{s,d}$ be a set of all possible paths from vertex s to vertex d. The set of Pareto–optimal paths $\Pi_{s,d} \subseteq P_{s,d}$ is formulated by:

$$\Pi_{s,d} = \{p \in P_{s,d} \mid \nexists q \in P_{s,d} : q \prec p\} \tag{8}$$

where $\prec$ is a *strictly dominance* relation. Path q strictly dominates path p, denoted by $q \prec p$, or p is dominated by q iff:

$$w^{arrival}(q, t_s) \leq w^{arrival}(p, t_s)$$
$$w^{transfer}(q) \leq w^{transfer}(p)$$
$$w(q, t_s) \neq w(p, t_s)$$

In order to avoid arcs with negative travel time weights in the graph model, Assumption 1 on the elements in the timetable TT must be held [5]. It implies that buses of the same route need to follow the FIFO property in the traffic flow.

Assumption 1. *Given two elements $c_1, c_2 \in TT$ with $Z(c_1) = Z(c_2), S_d(c_1) = S_d(c_2)$ and $S_a(c_1) = S_a(c_2)$. If $t_d(c_1) \leq t_d(c_2) \Rightarrow t_a(c_1) \leq t_a(c_2)$ [5].*

Given a path $p \in \Pi_{s,d}$, p follows the optimality principle [11] if $w^1(u, v, t_u) \geq 0$ and $w^2(u, v) \geq 0$ for every arc $(u, v) \in p$. Indeed, with Assumption 1, the travel time function f is non–negative. Also, the function g is non–negative constant. The multi–criteria shortest path problem then can be solved by labelling algorithm.

3 Algorithm

3.1 Labelling Algorithm

For the labelling algorithm, we use the label setting method and the label selection policy. The used notations are defined as below.

- $\Pi_{s,i}$: a set of non–dominated paths from the source s to a vertex i.
- $\Diamond$: relation that concatenates a path p with an arc (i, j) or another path q.
- Q: the queue of candidate paths that can be further expanded.
- $\prec$: the dominance relation between two paths.

The pseudo code of the proposed algorithm is given in Algorithm 1. The key idea of the algorithm is one vertex associated with several labels, each corresponding with a non–dominated path from the source to that vertex. Since the number of non–dominated paths in $\Pi_{s,d}$ is nondeterministic, the algorithm only terminates when Q is empty (Line 4). For each iteration, path $p = \langle s, ..., i \rangle$ is extended along all its outgoing arcs (i, j) (Line 8). To relax an arc (i, j), we check if the new extended path $q = p\Diamond(i, j)$ is not dominated by any path $u \in \Pi_{s,j}$ (Line 12). $\Pi_{s,d} \neq \emptyset$ means some non–dominated paths have been found. For a given path q expanded via an arbitrary arc (j, k), if q is dominated by any path in $\Pi_{s,d}$, the path $q\Diamond(j, k)$ is also dominated since the weight of arc (j, k) is non–negative, and so on. Therefore, we can use paths in $\Pi_{s,d}$ as the upper bound to early prune all paths if they are dominated by any path in $\Pi_{s,d}$, since q will lead to dominated paths which have form of $q\Diamond\langle j, ..., d \rangle$ in $\Pi_{s,d}$. This early prune is illustrated in Line 10. If a path q satisfies two conditions in Line 10 and Line 12, that means q might lead to a non–dominated path at $\Pi_{s,d}$. Therefore q is put into Q for further expansion (Line 14). There is still the case that some paths in $\Pi_{s,j}$ are dominated by q, Line 13 is supposed to remove all these paths and update $\Pi_{s,j}$.

Algorithm 1. The labelling algorithm

Input : a graph G with a source s and a destination d and a departure time t_s.
Output: the Pareto set of optimal paths $\Pi_{s,d}$.

1   $\Pi_{s,s} \leftarrow \{\langle s \rangle\}$;
2   $\Pi_{s,i} \leftarrow \emptyset, \forall i \in V \setminus \{s\}$;
3   $Q \leftarrow \{\langle s \rangle\}$;
4   **while** $Q \neq \emptyset$ **do**
5      $p \leftarrow$ the lexicographically lowest path in Q;
6      $Q \leftarrow Q \setminus \{p\}$;
7      $i \leftarrow$ the destination vertex of p;
8   **for** $(i, j) \in E$ **do**
9          $q \leftarrow p\Diamond(i, j)$;
10   **if** $\nexists u \in \Pi_{s,d} : u \prec q$ **then**
11   continue;
12   **if** $\nexists u \in \Pi_{s,j} : u \prec q$ **then**
13          $\Pi_{s,j} \leftarrow (\Pi_{s,j} \cup \{q\}) \setminus \{ u \in \Pi_{s,j} \mid q \prec u \}$;
14          $Q \leftarrow Q \cup \{q\}$;

3.2 Speed–Up Techniques

1. **Backward Get–Off Arc Avoidance:** In the graph model, get–off arcs have zero weights. The labelling algorithm might explore back to stop vertices via these arcs. These labels are absolutely dominated later. The search therefore should avoid these arcs.

2. **Upper Bounds for Criteria:** The realistic assumptions can be used to set constraints on criteria. For example, it is undesirable for a path which has the number of bus transfers greater than 4 times or the travel time more than 3 hours. Given an upper bound for travel time α and an upper bound for number of transfers β, then any path p with $w^{arrival}(p, t) > \alpha + t$ or $w^{transfer}(p) > \beta$ should be early pruned.

3. **Search Area Reduction:** Depending on the locations of source and destination, only a part of the bus network is used for searching. In this paper, we propose the search area as a rectangle. The idea is as follows. Suppose we has a query for the route planning from stop A to stop B, then we can calculate the differences in x and y–coordinate of A and B, denoted as dx and dy respectively. Given $0 < \epsilon < 1$, the target search area is then obtained via the scaling up of the x and y–coordinate based on ϵ and the ratio dx/dy as illustrated in Figure 2.

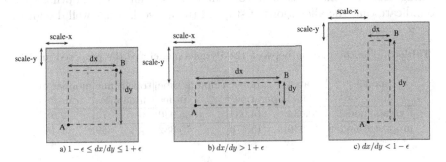

a) $1 - \epsilon \le dx/dy \le 1 + \epsilon$ b) $dx/dy > 1 + \epsilon$ c) $dx/dy < 1 - \epsilon$

Fig. 2. Three possible cases in which the target search area is scaled up based on the ratio dx/dy

4   Computational Study

4.1   The Graph Instance and the Testing Data Set

HCMC bus network consists of 4,090 stops, 220 routes and 8,833 stop connections. It is allowed for walking shortcuts between stops in the radius of 150 metres. Regrading the daily timetable, at some stops like the begin and the end of a route, the departure and the arrival times are fixed. These are used to estimate the departures and the arrival times of the remaining stops in the route. The graph model has 13,140 vertices and 29,161 arcs. Assume that the constructed graph and the timetable are stored in the primary memory and binary heap is used to implement the queue of candidate paths. We consider three criteria of measurements, namely the number of created labels (vertex visits), the number of queue operations and the running time. We also evaluate the quality of the solution, namely arrival time and number of transfers of found paths. The data set for testing is made up from 1,000 random user requests where the source, the destination and the query time are generated randomly. The empirical results then are the average value of the data set.

4.2   Empirical Results

The empirical study is conducted on 2.6 GHz dual–core Intel Core i5 4GB RAM on MAC OS X under Java Runtime Environment 1.6 (JRE 1.6). The tested database is MySQL 5.2.

First we compare the proposed model with Pyrga's model [5] in which it is not allowed to walk between nearby stops. In this case we use the implementation of label setting without any speed–up techniques. As seen from Table 3, the proposed model is inferior to Pyrga's model in term of the performance because it has additional walking arcs. But the proposed one produces more efficient route planning with lesser travel time and smaller number of transfers. Besides, there are 1,322 paths which contains walking arc amongst 1,376 non–dominated paths. That means the addition of walking options produce a more effective route planning. However, the appearances of walking arcs in majority of optimal paths also indicate that the allocations of stops in the network is not well designed.

Table 3. The comparison between the Pyrga's model and the proposed model

model	created label	queue operations	running time in ms	travel time in minutes	number of transfers
Pyrga's model	30,034	14,084	55.930	74	2.686
proposed model	42,936	15,470	75.882	49	1.450

Since there are only 1,376 non–dominated paths over 1,000 queries. In other words, only 1.357 non–dominated paths in the Pareto set per query on average. We compare the average quality of found paths in the Pareto set with the average quality of paths under single optimization. For the single optimization, we use Epsilon–constraint method in which arrival time is optimized and number of transfers is bounded. In this experiment, the used bound value is 4. As shown in Table 4, the average number of transfers of paths in the Pareto set is less than that of the paths which only optimize travel time. That means the Pareto set contains desirable paths with smaller number of transfers which are left out if we only consider the problem in single–criteria manner.

Table 4. The comparison between multi–criteria and single–criteria

algorithm	created label	queue operations	running time in ms	travel time in minutes	number of transfers
single–criteria	29,757	11,196	47.056	47	2.920
multi–criteria	42,936	15,470	75.882	49	1.450

Table 5. The comparison between different speed–up techniques

variant	backward avoidance	criteria upper bound	search area	created label	queue operations	running time in ms
plain version	no	no	no	42,936	15,470	75.882
backward avoidance	yes	no	no	36,249	15,470	75.417
upper bound	no	$\alpha = 5,\ \beta = 3\ hours$	no	42,783	15,397	75.632
search area reduction	no	no	yes	31,057	11,138	51.822
optimized version	yes	$\alpha = 5,\ \beta = 3\ hours$	yes	26,136	11,081	51.559

Table 5 gives the comparison between the different speed–up techniques with various parameters. The results show that the backward avoidance reduces significantly the number of created labels, but does not reduces the number of queue operations. This is consistent with what discussed in Section 3.2 because all backward get–in arcs will lead to dominated paths which are discarded before being put into the queue. Using the transfer bound and travel time bound decreases both the number of created labels and queue operations, that leads to improve the running time, but these improvements are not so significant. The search area reduction brings a huge speed–up. The drawback of the technique is losing optimal paths if the searching area is not estimated properly. Therefore, in the empirical result, we adjust the target search area in the way that no solution is lost. The technique reduces 25% number of created labels, 30% number of queue operations and 30% running time in comparison to the plain version.

5 Conclusion

We have developed in this paper the model for transforming a route planning problem in a bus network to a multi–criteria shortest path problem. An modified time–dependent model and an efficient labelling algorithm are proposed and evaluated. The results show that the size of Pareto set in HCMC bus network is quite small, and the addition of walking shortcuts gives a much better route planning. The quality of paths produced by the algorithm lies in the correctness of the timetable. However, in reality, arrival and departure times of buses might disobey the timetable when traffic condition is involved. Thus, in future work, we will develop the model combining the timetable and real–time data from the bus tracking system. Besides, the appearance of walking shortcuts in the majority of route planning also raises the question whether the allocation of stops is efficient.

Acknowledgments. The authors gratefully acknowledge the helpful comments offered by Professor Hai Le Vu in Intelligent Transport Systems Lab of Swinburne University of Technology, Melbourne, Australia. This research is supported by Ho Chi Minh City University of Technology, under grant number T-KHMT-2014-28 and T-KHMT-2014-32.

References

1. Müller-Hannemann, M., Schulz, F., Wagner, D., Zaroliagis, C.D.: Timetable Information: Models and Algorithms. In: Geraets, F., Kroon, L.G., Schoebel, A., Wagner, D., Zaroliagis, C.D. (eds.) Railway Optimization 2004. LNCS, vol. 4359, pp. 67–90. Springer, Heidelberg (2007)
2. Schulz, F., Wagner, D., Weihe, K.: Dijkstra's Algorithm On-Line: An Empirical Case Study from Public Railroad Transport. In: Vitter, J.S., Zaroliagis, C.D. (eds.) WAE 1999. LNCS, vol. 1668, pp. 110–123. Springer, Heidelberg (1999)

3. Müller-Hannemann, M., Schnee, M.: Finding All Attractive Train Connections by Multi-criteria Pareto Search. In: Geraets, F., Kroon, L.G., Schoebel, A., Wagner, D., Zaroliagis, C.D. (eds.) Railway Optimization 2004. LNCS, vol. 4359, pp. 246–263. Springer, Heidelberg (2007)
4. Brodal, G.S., Jacob, R.: Time–dependent networks as models to achieve fast exact time-table queries. Electronic Notes in Theoretical Computer Science 92, 3–15 (2004)
5. Pyrga, E., Schulz, F., Wagner, D., Zaroliagis, C.: Towards Realistic Modeling of Timetable Information through the Time–Dependent Approach. Electronic Notes in Theoretical Computer Science 92, 85–103 (2004)
6. Disser, Y., Müller–Hannemann, M., Schnee, M.: Multi-criteria Shortest Paths in Time-Dependent Train Networks. In: McGeoch, C.C. (ed.) WEA 2008. LNCS, vol. 5038, pp. 347–361. Springer, Heidelberg (2008)
7. Pyrga, E., Schulz, F., Wagner, D., Zaroliagis, C.: Experimental comparison of shortest path approaches for timetable information. In: 6th Workshop on Algorithm Engineering and Experiments (ALENEX04), pp. 88–99. SIAM (2004)
8. Pyrga, E., Schulz, F., Wagner, D., Zaroliagis, C.: Efficient Models for Timetable Information in Public Transportation Systems. Journal of Experimental Algorithmics (JEA) 12, Article No. 2.4 (2008)
9. Skriver, A.J.V., Andersen, K.A.: A label correcting approach for solving bicriterion shortest path problems. Computers & Operations Research 27, 507–524 (2000)
10. Gandibleux, X., Beugnies, F., Randriamasy, S.: Martins' algorithm revisited for multi–objective shortest path problems with a MaxMin cost function. In: 4OR, vol. 4, pp. 47–59 (2006)
11. Martins, E.Q.V., Santos, J.L.: The labeling algorithm for multicriteria shortest path problem. Departamento de Matematica, Universidade de Coimbra, Portugal (1999)
12. Brumbaugh, J., Smith: An empirical investigation of some bicriterion shortest path algorithms. European Journal of Operational Research 43, 216–224 (1989)
13. Mote, J., Murthy, I., Olson, D.L.: A parametric approach to solving bicriterion shortest path problems. European Journal of Operational Research 53, 81–92 (1991)
14. Paixao, J.M., Santos, J.L.: Labeling methods for the general case of the multiobjective shortest path problem–a computational study. Intelligent Systems, Control and Automation: Science and Engineering 61, 489–502 (2013)
15. Mali, G., Michail, P., Zaroliagis, C.: Faster multiobjective heuristic search in road maps. In: Proceedings ICT, vol. 3, pp. 67–72 (2012)
16. Dijkstra, E.W.: A note on two problems in connection with graphs. Numerische Mathematik 1, 269–271 (1959)

Enhanced LBP-Based Face Recognition System Using a Heuristic Approach for Searching Weight Set

Nhat-Quan Huynh Nguyen and Thai Hoang Le

Department of Computer Science, Ho Chi Minh City University of Science, Vietnam
1012337@student.hcmus.edu.vn, lhthai@fit.hcmus.edu.vn

Abstract. Local Binary Patterns is one of the most effective approaches for pattern recognition in general and face recognition in particular. There have been many studies on improving this method such as changing the input values or using another kind of histogram. Although weight set is also an important key leading to the success of this method, it does not seem to get much attention. A majority of LBP-based approaches are still using the weight set of Ahonen et al.'s study, one of the first researches applying LBP to face recognition. In this study, we introduce a powerful algorithm named Heuristic Weight Search, which finds a suitable weight set for not only LBP-based approaches but also other methods using weight set to improve performance. Experiments on the FERET database prove an ability of HWS thanks to their higher accuracy than original methods.

Keywords: Face recognition, Local binary patterns, Heuristic search, FERET, Weight set.

1 Introduction

Face recognition is a highly active area of researchers thanks to its real-world applications. Up to now, a large number of face recognition methods have been developed. Local Binary Patterns (LBP) is widely used for face recognition based on its potential for speed and accuracy. LBP can be applied for not only face recognition, but also many applications such as: texture classification, facial expression recognition and gender recognition. Since Ahonen et al. [2] introduced LBP as a powerful method for describing faces and reported impressive results in experiments on the FERET database in 2004, many LBP-based descriptors have been proposed. In 2012, a research from Ngoc-Son Vu et al. [9] introduced the Patterns of Oriented Edge Magnitudes (POEM) descriptor which uses LBP operator as a main part of this powerful descriptor.

According to Ahonen et al.'s research [1], a weight set is computed through a simple procedure. Although this weight set has been used for many researches to improve performance without any changes, it seems to be too general to fix the characteristic of each data set. That makes the problem how to create an

K. Saeed and V. Snášel (Eds.): CISIM 2014, LNCS 8838, pp. 547–558, 2014.
© IFIP International Federation for Information Processing 2014

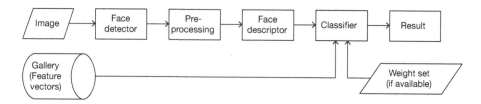

Fig. 1. Architecture of face recognition system in use

efficient weight set for a respective condition of images such as facial expression or illumination changes.

In this paper, we propose a Heuristic Weight Search (HWS) algorithm to solve the problem of generating weight set based on the properties of each image set. Applying this algorithm on any face recognition system using weight set helps to improve performance at all. A sample system integrating POEM descriptor into HWS algorithm is also introduced.

Our study is organized as follows: in section 2 and 3, LBP and POEM are introduced respectively; section 4 represents our algorithm to generate weight set of image sets; the sample system combining POEM descriptor and HWS algorithm is illustrated in section 5; the next section presents our experiments on FERET database; conclusion and references are in the rest of this paper.

2   Local Binary Patterns

Being introduced by Ojala et al. [5] in 1996, LBP operator is a powerful tool for texture description. This operator labels the pixels of an image and thresholds each neighbourhood of 3×3 pixels by using the central pixel value. The gray value of each pixel g_p in the neighborhood is compared to the gray value g_c of the central pixel. If g_p is greater than g_c, then it is assigned 1, and 0 if not. The LBP label for the central pixel of image is obtained as [1]:

$$LBP = \sum_{p=0}^{7} S(g_p - g_c)2^p, \quad \text{where } S(x) = \begin{cases} 1, & x \geq 0 \\ 0, & x < 0 \end{cases} \tag{1}$$

The basic operator was extended to use neighbourhood of different sizes to capture dominant features at different scales. Notation $LBP(P, R)$ denotes a neighborhood of P equally spaced sampling points on a circle of radius of R. For example, the original LBP operator can be denoted $LBP(8, 1)$.

According to [6], there is a small subset of 2^P patterns, called uniform patterns, accounted for the majority of the texture of images, over 90% of all patterns for $LBP(8, 1)$ and about 70% for $LBP(16, 2)$. These patterns contain at most two bitwise transitions from 0 to 1 or vice versa for a circular binary pattern. For instance, '00000000' (0 transition), '01111100' (2 transitions), and '10001111'

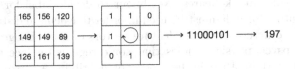

Fig. 2. $LBP(8,1)$ operator

(2 transitions) patterns are uniform while '11001110' pattern is not uniform due to its four bit transitions. The uniform patterns can be used to find the pixels that belong some texture primitives such as spot, flat area, edge, and corner. It can be denoted as $LBP_{(P,R)}^{u2}$, which was mentioned in [2].

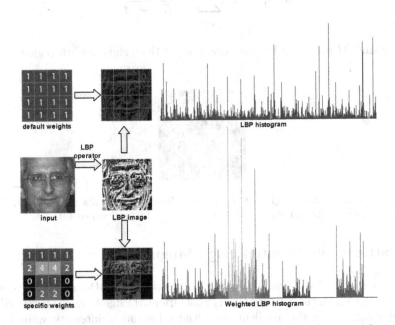

Fig. 3. LBP feature extracting procedure in two case of applying weight set

In the face recognition procedure of Ahonen et al. [2], a facial image is divided into m small same sized non-overlapping regions called patches from which LBP histograms are extracted and concatenated into a single vector, which enhanced the facial representative ability. A patch histogram is defined as [1]:

$$H_i = \sum_{x,y} I\{LBP(x,y) = i\}, \quad i = 0, 1, ..., n - 1 \quad (2)$$

in which n is the number of different labels produced by the LBP operator and

$$I(A) = \begin{cases} 1, & A \text{ is true} \\ 0, & A \text{ is false.} \end{cases} \quad (3)$$

In using classifier like k-Nearest Neighbour to decide label for input image, distance computing formula must be used in order to calculate distance between images which is difference between feature vectors of these images. It was also announced by psychophysics studies that some regions on face contain more useful information than others in the process of identifying a person. That means each region on face has its own contribution which can be represented as a number called weight. Difference between applying specific and default weight set is presented in Fig 3. In this research, we suggest using weighted Chi square statistics, which has been used to build a dissimilarity measure of face with the weight set W.

$$\chi^2_W (S, M) = \sum_{i,j} w_j \frac{(S_{i,j} - m_{i,j})^2}{S_{i,j} + M_{i,j}} \tag{4}$$

where S and M are two LBP histogram, w_j is the weight for jth region.

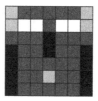

Fig. 4. Ahonen et al.'s weight set for the weighted χ^2 dissimilarity measure. Black square indicate weight 0.0, dark gray 1.0, light gray 2.0, and white 4.0.

3   Patterns of Oriented Edge Magnitudes

In their research, Ngoc-Son Vu et al. [9] introduce a LBP-based structure on oriented edge magnitudes called Patterns of Oriented Edge Magnitudes (POEM). This descriptor uses the gradient magnitudes instead of intensity value in the computing using LBP operator.

POEM feature is extracted through the process shown at Fig. 5. Firstly, the oriented edge magnitude image (oriented EMI) generated from an original input image is divided into m uni-oriented $EMIs$ $\left(uEMI^{\theta_i}\right)$ through gradient orientations of pixels, over $0 - \pi$ (*unsigned* representation) or $0 - 2\pi$ (*signed* representation). Then, each pixel on $uEMIs$ is then replaced by the sum of values of its $w \times w$ neighbour area called *cell*. The resulting images are called accumulated $EMIs$ ($AEMIs$). On the next stage, POEM images are created by applying LBP^{u2} operator on $AEMIs$. Finally, the output POEM feature called POEM-HS (POEM histogram sequence), which is the concatenation of LBP histograms of all POEM images, is generated:

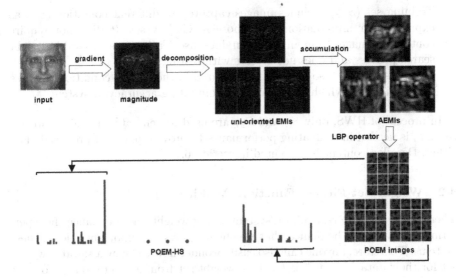

Fig. 5. POEM descriptor extracting procedure

$$POEM = \left[POEM^{\theta_1}, ..., POEM^{\theta_m}\right], \quad POEM^{\theta_i} = LBPH^{u2}\left(AEMI^{\theta_i}\right) \quad (5)$$

In their study, Ngoc-Son Vu et al. [9] made many experiments on the FERET database and got the optimal POEM parameters for face recognition as: an unsigned representation with three direction bins ($m = 3$) built on 7×7 pixels cell using $LBP_{(8,5)}^{u2}$. These experiments were made on face images of 110×100 pixels. The similar optimal parameters were obtained when testing with images of around 90×90 pixels.

4 Heuristic Weight Search (HWS)

Based on proposed approach presented on a submitted paper [8], we made some changes and show our work here. In this section, we introduce an algorithm called Heuristic Weight Search (HWS) which uses heuristic search to find an optimal weight set. Firstly, we show how to prepare data for HWS. Then, fitness function evaluating goodness of a weight set, a way to prioritize patches and a complete HWS algorithm is presented in order.

4.1 Organizing Data

A certain database is divided into three image sets for using through weight search and evaluating accuracy process:

– Gallery set (S_G) contains images of everyone in database, in which each person has only one image. Both training and testing stage need to use S_G to decide labels of images.

– Training set (S_{Tr}) includes images captured in different condition such as expression or illumination from those in Gallery set. It does not require containing images from all people in database. Training set is used in weight search process and does not involve with testing stage.
– Testing set (S_{Ts}) also has images captured in the similar condition to those in Training set, which is only used in computing accuracy of system.

In process of HWS, only S_G and S_{Tr} are used to generate an efficient weight set. S_{Ts} is needed in evaluating performance to prove a power of proposed algorithm. Detailed content is presented in section 6.

4.2 Weight Set Fitness Function (WsFitness)

There are many face recognition systems using weight set to enhance their performance. It cannot be denied that weight set plays an important role on these systems. Therefore, anyone can also easily wonder how to know a suitable weight set for their data, or which is the best weight set from a several ones. To solve this problem, we suppose each weight set has its own *fitness value* for a certain image set. A basic idea of fitness value of a weight set is a recognition rate of system in case of using that weight set. The higher value is, the better weight set is. We call a function calculating fitness value of a weight set $WsFitness$.

$$WsFitness(W) = \frac{\left| \left\{ \begin{matrix} I_{Tr} | I_{Tr} \in S_{Tr}, label(I_{Tr}) = label(I), \\ I = \underset{I_G \in S_G}{\operatorname{argmin}} \left(\chi_W^2(I_{Tr}, I_G) \right) \end{matrix} \right\} \right|}{|S_{Tr}|} \tag{6}$$

where $label(X)$ is identification of image X and $\underset{x \in S}{\operatorname{argmin}} (f(x))$ shows the object of x producing the smallest value in computing with function $f(x)$.

4.3 Different Contributions of Patches

Each region on a face has its own role in process of face recognition. Calculating contributions of all patches is needed before processing proposed algorithm. In this subsection, we define a single entry weights matrix denoted $sEM(i)$ whose values are zero except an element in position of i. If we apply this matrix to face recognition process, only nonzero patch will affect recognition rate. Therefore, we call a fitness value of $sEM(i)$ a contribution of ith patch. We also name the matrix containing these values a contribution matrix CM.

4.4 Heuristic Weight Search in Detail

After calculating a contributions of all patches, heuristic search is applied to find an optimal weight set whose elements are scaled on $[0, 1]$ range. First of all, we initialize a new weight set W_n with 0.0 for all weights except that the most

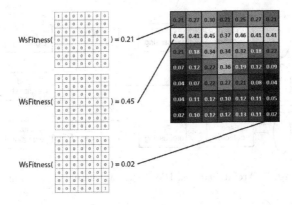

Fig. 6. Contribution matrix in an experiment

important patch, which gains the highest contribution, is assigned a value of 1.0. From now on, all changes in weight values are processed in W_n. Then, weight values of other patches are calculated in descending order of the contributions of patches, which use a similar procedure presented as follows: (1) weight of a certain patch decreases steady from 1.0 to 0.0 by small static changing step of 0.05 (read 6.2 for more details); (2) the value maximizing $WsFitness(W_n)$ is an optimal weight of that patch.

Heuristic Weight Search (HWS) algorithm

1. Compute a descending ordered contribution list CM.
2. Initialize new weight set $W_n = \{0, \}$; set weight for the most important patch $W_n[index(CM[0])] = 1$.
3. Loop for each remaining value in CM, find the best weight value for each patch, which is in range of $[0, 1]$ and maximizes $WsFitness(W_n)$.
4. The optimal weight set W_n is ready for application.

In above presentation of HWS, $index(X)$ returns a respective position of patch having fitness value of X.

5 Combination

In this part, we introduce a face recognition system applying POEM descriptor to HWS in order to show a boosting ability of the proposed algorithm.

Fig. 7 presents the system integrating POEM descriptor into HWS algorithm, which is called HWS-POEM system. As can be seen from that diagram, our proposed system follows the procedure of normal face recognition system, except a few changes. That means people can easily apply HWS-POEM combination to their certain system to improve performance.

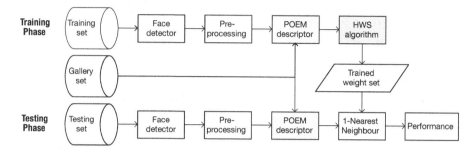

Fig. 7. Architecture of HWS-POEM evaluating system

5.1 Pre-processing

Condition of input images make a huge impact on recognition result. If we apply a powerful descriptor on bad quality images, we might get a worse result than applying a normal descriptor on good pre-processed images. In this work, we use pre-processing tool of CSU Face Identification Evaluation System [3] to ensure that condition of images are better. Fig. 8 shows five steps in converting a PGM FERET image to a normalized image.

1. Integer to float conversion - Converts 256 gray levels into floating point equivalents.

2. Geometric normalization - Lines up human chosen eye coordinates.

3. Masking - Crops the image using an elliptical mask and image borders such that only the face from forehead to chin and cheek to cheek is visible.

4. Histogram equalization - Equalizes the histogram of the unmasked part of the image.

Normalized image

5. Pixel normalization - Scale the pixel value to have a mean of zero and a standard deviation of none.

Fig. 8. Image normalization using pre-processing tool of CSU

Certainly, there are many better methods of image pre-processing, for instance, that of Ngoc-Son Vu et al. [9]. Although applying these methods improves performance, we only use CSU tools in all of our experiments in order to evaluate approaches on FERET database.

5.2 Discussion

This system inherits abilities from both POEM descriptor and HWS algorithm, so it has their characteristic.

POEM has many properties which are mentioned in [9]; two most important ones are: (1) POEM is an oriented feature so that it has the ability to capture image information with different levels of orientation accuracy, (2) using gradient magnitudes instead of intensity values makes POEM more robust to lighting variations than original methods of LBP.

HWS algorithm brings us a number of benefits. Firstly, HWS algorithm can be applied to any face recognition systems, provided weight set can be used in that system. In other words, if features of facial parts can be calculated separately using a face descriptor, we can use our algorithm there. Secondly, After finding weight for each patch, we could get the best weight in range of $[0, 1]$. With the first assigned value 1, a new calculated value could be better or equal to the weight of 1. Even in the worst case, we might still get the weight set whose elements are all 1, which means a new recognition rate of system applying weight set from HWS algorithm could not be less than that of original system. Finally, HWS algorithm just generate an efficient weight set without integrating into applications. Therefore, speeds of these applications are not be affected.

6   Experiments

6.1   Database

In our experiments, we use facial images from FERET database [7]. This database contains 14051 face images which are divided into many subsets based on their condition. According to FERET Tests September 1996, some frontal image subsets were classified as below, all changes of non-Gallery (we can name it Probe) images are in comparison with these ones in Gallery set.

Table 1. FERET frontal image subsets

Image set	Quantity	Description	Image list
Gallery	1196	Single images of all subjects	gallery.names
FAFB	1195	Images having changes in face expression	probe_fafb_*.names
FAFC	194	Images captured under different illumination	probe_fafc_*.names
DUP1	722	Images taken between 0 to 1031 days after	probe_dup_1_*.names
DUP2	234	Subset of DUP1, contains images captured at least 18 months after	probe_dup_2_*.names

For experiments, Gallery set of FERET database is used as Gallery set S_G of HWS algorithm. Training set S_{Tr} and testing set S_{Ts} is generated by cross-validation k-fold method with k = 2 for each FERET's Probe set. The final result of a certain Probe set is an average of experiments on that image set.

6.2   The Parameter of Step Value in Search

First of all, we made some experiments to compare effect on fitness (section 4.2) of weight change value in HWS process. Firstly, it can be easily to aware that a

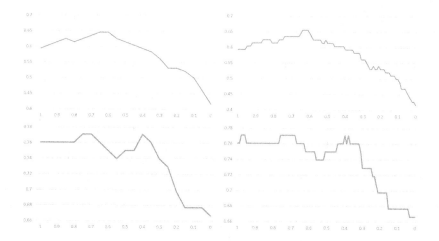

Fig. 9. Fitness changes in comparison between steps of 0.05 (left) and 0.01 (right) in weight search of the 2nd (top) and 4th (bottom) patches (based on an importance of patches). Vertical axis is fitness value; horizontal one is weight of a certain moment.

large step makes weight search faster. Secondly, as can be seen from Fig. 9, in the early stages of HWS process, both fitness graphs of 0.05 and 0.01 share the same pattern despite a difference of step value. It means effect of 0.05 step value on fitness is similar to 0.01 one. In addition, Fig. 10 shows the fitness values of a new weight set after searching weight for each patch. Although spending much time on calculating, the experiment using step of 0.01 reach the final fitness slower than that of another one. In another experiment in which a step value of 0.1 is used, it also reaches the final fitness slower than that of 0.05. This problem can be explained as 0.1 is such a large weight change that it pass through optimal weight values of patches while 0.01 is so small value that over fit training data. Finally, using a small step of weight change like 0.01 is too waste and brings no more benefits than a medium value like 0.05 while a weight change of 0.1 leads to some missing optimal values. Therefore, 0.05 is a suitable weight step for HWS algorithm.

6.3   Result

We made experiments using HWS algorithm to find an optimal weight set for some LBP-based methods. Experiments of the same descriptor use the same parameters. In the table of results below, we call Ahonen et al.'s weight set by Ahonen and weight set found by Heuristic Weight Search algorithm by HWS.

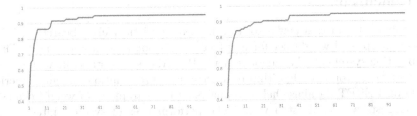

Fig. 10. Fitness of new weight set after completely searching weight for each patch in comparison between steps of 0.05 (left) and 0.01 (right). Vertical axis is fitness value; horizontal one is the completion of new weight set (maximum value is 100).

Table 2. Boosting performance ability of HWS algorithm in comparison with original approaches

Method	FAFB	FAFC	DUP1	DUP2
LBP [2]	93.0	51.0	61.0	50.0
LBP + Ahonen [2]	97.0	79.0	66.0	64.0
LBP + HWS	**98.33**	**84.07**	**67.88**	**71.90**
MLBP	92.38	28.28	61.09	49.59
MLBP + Ahonen	97.24	58.76	65.65	61.11
MLBP + HWS	**98.24**	**85.07**	**66.49**	**71.79**
POEM	96.82	77.85	72.73	71.08
POEM + Ahonen	98.22	86.88	71.83	70.21
POEM + HWS	**99.08**	**90.73**	**75.07**	**77.35**
LGBP	98.16	96.41	78.95	76.50
LGBP + Ahonen	98.91	**98.45**	80.47	80.77
LGBP + HWS	**99.16**	97.42	**82.41**	**83.33**

There are some differences (worse or better) between results of our experiments and those reported in original papers (POEM [9]; Multi-scale LBP - MLBP [4]; Gabor+LBP - LGBP [10]) because of different pre-processing methods (mentioned in 5.1) and matching algorithms (presented in section 2). However, in our experiments, each method gains a higher performance than its original when applying weight set found by HWS algorithm, which proves the effectiveness of proposed algorithm. As can be seen from the results of LGBP group, the performances of all experiments when applying our algorithm to find weight set are higher than those of LGBP approach and LGBP using weight set of Ahonen et al. [2], except an experiment on FAFC subset where the recognition rate of LGBP using this weight set is higher than found weight set from HWS algorithm. This can be explained that LGBP is so suitable for illumination changes on images in FAFC subset that it does not boost significantly a final performance when applying HWS algorithm for this experiment. In this case, a hand labeled weight set like that of Ahonen et al. [2] is good enough to use.

7 Conclusion

This paper introduces a new algorithm named Heuristic Weight Search (HWS) to find an optimal weight set for any face recognition system applying it. The combination system of HWS algorithm and POEM descriptor also shows an ease of integrating proposed algorithm to a certain face recognition system. Experiments on FERET database helps to analysing the parameter of weight change and suggests a suitable step value. The performances of systems integrating proposed algorithm proves its ability in comparison with other approaches.

Acknowledgement. This research is funded by Vietnam National University of Ho Chi Minh City (VNU-HCMC) under the project "Features descriptor under variation condition for real-time face recognition application", 2014. We are also supported by research funding from Advanced Program in Computer Science, University of Science, Vietnam National University - Ho Chi Minh City.

References

1. Ahonen, T., Hadid, A., Pietikäinen, M.: Face recognition with local binary patterns. In: Pajdla, T., Matas, J(G.) (eds.) ECCV 2004. LNCS, vol. 3021, pp. 469–481. Springer, Heidelberg (2004)
2. Ahonen, T., Hadid, A., Pietikainen, M.: Face description with local binary patterns: Application to face recognition. IEEE Transactions on Pattern Analysis and Machine Intelligence 28(12), 2037–2041 (2006)
3. Bolme, D.S., Beveridge, J.R., Teixeira, M., Draper, B.A.: The CSU face identification evaluation system: Its purpose, features, and structure. In: Crowley, J.L., Piater, J.H., Vincze, M., Paletta, L. (eds.) ICVS 2003. LNCS, vol. 2626, pp. 304–313. Springer, Heidelberg (2003)
4. Chan, C.-H., Kittler, J., Messer, K.: Multi-scale local binary pattern histograms for face recognition. In: Lee, S.-W., Li, S.Z. (eds.) ICB 2007. LNCS, vol. 4642, pp. 809–818. Springer, Heidelberg (2007)
5. Ojala, T., Pietikäinen, M., Harwood, D.: A comparative study of texture measures with classification based on featured distributions. Pattern Recognition 29(1), 51–59 (1996)
6. Ojala, T., Pietikainen, M., Maenpaa, T.: Multiresolution gray-scale and rotation invariant texture classification with local binary patterns. IEEE Transactions on Pattern Analysis and Machine Intelligence 24(7), 971–987 (2002)
7. Phillips, P.J., Moon, H., Rizvi, S.A., Rauss, P.J.: The feret evaluation methodology for face-recognition algorithms. IEEE Transactions on Pattern Analysis and Machine Intelligence, 22(10), 1090–1104 (2000)
8. Thai, L.H., Khoa, T.Q.D., Vu, N.D.: On approaching heuristic weight mask to improve face recognition. International Journal of Pattern Recognition and Artificial Intelligence (IJPRAI) (submitted)
9. Vu, N.S., Dee, H.M., Caplier, A.: Face recognition using the poem descriptor. Pattern Recognition 45(7), 2478–2488 (2012)
10. Zhang, W., Shan, S., Gao, W., Chen, X., Zhang, H.: Local gabor binary pattern histogram sequence (lgbphs): A novel non-statistical model for face representation and recognition. In: Tenth IEEE International Conference on Computer Vision, ICCV 2005 vol. 1, pp. 786–791. IEEE (2005)

A Local Gaussian Filter and Adaptive Morphology as Tools for Completing Partially Discontinuous Curves

Przemysław Spurek[1,*], Alena Chaikouskaya[1], Jacek Tabor[1], and Elzbieta Zając[2,**]

[1] Jagiellonian University, Faculty of Mathematics and Computer Science
Łojasiewicza 6, 30-348 Kraków, Poland
Przemyslaw.Spurek@ii.uj.edu.pl
[2] Jan Kochanowski University, Institute of Mathematics
Świętokrzyska 15, 25-406 Kielce, Poland

Abstract. This paper presents a method for extraction and analysis of curve–type structures, which consist of disconnected components. Such structures are found in electron–microscopy (EM) images of metal nano-grains, which are widely used in the field of nanosensor technology. The topography of metal nanograins in compound nanomaterials is crucial to nanosensor characteristics. The method of completing such templates consists of three steps. In the first step, a local Gaussian filter is used with different weights for each neighborhood. In the second step, an adaptive morphology operation is applied to detect the endpoints of curve segments and connect them. In the last step, pruning is employed to extract a curve which optimally fits the template.

Keywords: covariance matrix, Gaussian filter, mathematical morphology, electron microscopy.

1 Introduction

This paper presents a method for completing curve–type structures consisting of disjoint segments using Gaussian filter modification and adaptive morphology. Both of these methods modify images depending on the local properties.

It is known that in some nanostructural films one can observe the formation of percolation paths [1], which could be formed due to the influence of an electric or magnetic field on the film or, sometimes, due to film annealing. For example, such percolation paths have been observed for palladium-carbonaceous nanostructural films (nPd–C films) obtained by physical vapor deposition (PVD) in vacuum. The details of film preparation are described in paper [2]. The structure,

* The work of this author was supported by the Polish National Centre of Science Grant No. 2013/09/N/ST6/01178.
** The work of this author was supported by the European Regional Development Fund within the 2007–2013 Innovative Economy Operational Programme No. UDA-POIG.01.03.01-14-071/08-09.

K. Saeed and V. Snášel (Eds.): CISIM 2014, LNCS 8838, pp. 559–570, 2014.
© IFIP International Federation for Information Processing 2014

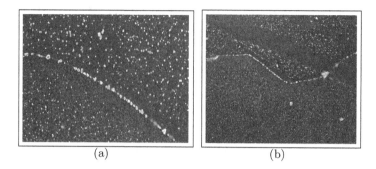

(a)   (b)

Fig. 1. Original EM images of a carbonaceous–nanopalladium film

morphology and topography of such films are described in papers [1, 3]. nPd–C films are composed of palladium nanograins (with a diameter of 1–4 nm), which are placed in a carbonaceous matrix. The effect of percolation paths generation has been observed for nPd–C films and is presented in paper [1]. These paths, composed of large agglomerated Pd grains, formed due to an electric field acting along the film surface. Such paths could be seen as wire-like structures, as it is shown in Fig. 1. The bright objects visible in this image are palladium nanograins while the dark background is the carbonaceous matrix. The objective is to detect these curve-type (wiretype) templates in EM images. The investigated features consist of nanoparticle clusters (nanograins) with various sizes and geometries. Some of the nanograins are hidden below the surface of a thin layer (a carbonaceous matrix in Fig. 1). Consequently, the wire–type nanostructures are represented in EM images as discontinuous curves with breaks of different width.

The proposed method consists of two steps: a local Gaussian filter and an adaptive morphological operation. The combination of these two methods allows one to fill in large gaps in curve templates. On the other hand, each of these methods gives good results in the case of a regular pattern with reasonably small breaks (see Figs. 6 and 10). The basic difference between these methods is that the former uses grayscale images, while the latter works with black and white images.

The first step is based on standard Gaussian filters [4, 5] and local scale selection [6], which are used to deal with noise in signal and image processing [7–9]. Our idea is based on blurring the elements of an image depending on the local properties, more precisely weighted covariance matrix.

The operation connects segments of a template and forms a blurred curve (see Fig. 2(a)). On the other hand, the background, which consists of quite regular patterns, is transformed into an uniform layer. Consequently, the curve template can be extracted by simple thresholding (see Fig. 2(b)). In our paper CEC (cross entropy clustering) [10–13] algorithm is used for binarization.

In some cases, gaps are too large (see the left upper corner in Fig. 2(b)) to be filled by a local Gaussian filter. To solve this problem, we used the other method – a modification of classical mathematical morphology [14, 15].

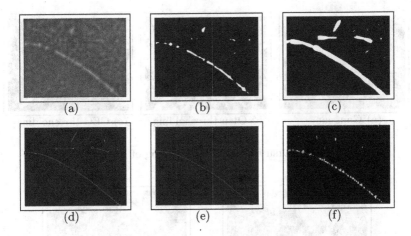

Fig. 2. Results of the proposed algorithm for the image presented in Fig. 1(a) with steps: a) Gaussian blur, b) Thresholding with a CEC algorithm, c) Adaptive morphology filter, d) Skeletonization, e) Pruning

This paper presents a new version of mathematical morphology which uses local covariance matrix. Similar approaches are presented in [16, 17, 4], where segments are connected by locally estimated lines or curves. In [18], the authors present a method based on a morphology operation which fills gaps by an elliptical structural element. Our approach also uses ellipses, but in contrast to the previous method, size and direction are extracted by using a covariance matrix instead of iteratively suited parameters. The results of our morphology are given in Fig. 2(c).

The presented approach can also be used for different types of images. For instance, one can use it to connect parts of rivers and roads divided by bridges in satellite images of Earth (see Fig. 6) [19].

The next section of the paper presents a local Gaussian filter which uses different Gaussian functions in each point of an image. Then, an adaptive morphology operation is presented, which is applied to connect curve fragments. The last section presents the final version of our algorithm.

2   Local Gaussian Filter

Gaussian filtering (also known as Gaussian smoothing) is the result of the blurring of an image by a Gaussian function. For processing images, one needs a twodimensional Gaussian density distribution. The normal random variable with the mean equal to zero and the covariance matrix Σ has a density

$$g_\Sigma(x) := \frac{1}{2\pi\sqrt{\det(\Sigma)}} \exp(-\frac{1}{2}\|x\|_\Sigma^2)$$

where by $\|x\|_\Sigma$ we denote the Mahalanobis norm [20] of $x \in \mathbb{R}^2$ by $\|x\|_\Sigma^2 := x^T \Sigma^{-1} x$.

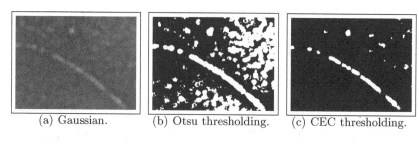

(a) Gaussian.   (b) Otsu thresholding.   (c) CEC thresholding.

Fig. 3. Otsu and CEC thresholding of Fig 3(a)

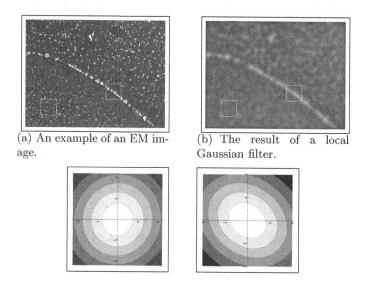

(a) An example of an EM image.   (b) The result of a local Gaussian filter.

Fig. 4. The result of a local Gaussian filter and levels for the Gaussian function estimated for the detail marked on the left and right side respectively

An image with dimensions $m \times n$ is interpreted as a function $J \colon [0, m - 1] \times [0, n - 1] \to [0, 1]$, where $J(k_1, k_2)$ describes the intensity of the pixel with coordinates (k_1, k_2). In this paper, the function is extended to $J \colon \mathbb{Z} \times \mathbb{Z} \to [0, 1]$ by assigning $J(k_1, k_2) = 0$ for $(k_1, k_2) \notin [0, m - 1] \times [0, n - 1]$.

All calculations are dedicated to the circular neighborhood of a fixed point $(k_1, k_2) \in \mathbb{Z} \times \mathbb{Z}$. A circle with its center at zero and a radius $r > 0$ is denoted by $\mathbb{B}_r := \{(i, j) \in \mathbb{Z}^2 \colon i^2 + j^2 \leq r^2\}$.

Classical Gaussian filtering is based on a convolution operation with a mask of the size $2 \cdot r + 1$ for $r \in \mathbb{N}$. Consequently, each pixel with coordinates $(k_1, k_2) \in \mathbb{Z} \times \mathbb{Z}$ is transformed into

$$(g_\Sigma \ast J)(k_1, k_2) := \sum_{\substack{i,j=-r \\ i^2 + j^2 \leq r^2}}^{r} g_\Sigma(i, j) J(k_1 + i, k_2 + j) \text{ where } \Sigma \text{ is fixed.}$$

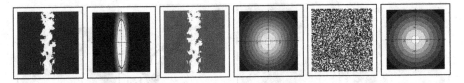

Fig. 5. Examples of simple images and Gaussian functions

In the classical approach, Σ is proportional to the identity matrix. The results of the standard Gaussian filter in the case of the image from Fig. 1(a) are presented in Fig. 3. As it can be seen, when one uses a covariance matrix proportional to the identity matrix, the curve template is uniformly blurred in all directions (see Fig. 3(b)). Moreover, one obtains more holes which are difficult to reduce (compare Fig. 2(b) and Fig. 3(c)).

As it was said, in this paper CEC thresholding [10, 11] is used instead of the classical Otsu [21] method. Fig. 3 presents the basic differences between these two approaches (compare Fig. 3(b)) and Fig. 3(c)).

Our method uses the coordinates of pixels and grayscale color. More precisely, the intensities of pixels in a neighborhood are used as weights. Note that a small change of background intensity radically deforms the shape of the estimated Gaussian function (see Fig. 5).

Since the color range of the image has major influence on the shape of the estimated Gaussian function, we reduce it by subtracting the mean color in a neighborhood and taking the maximum from point zero and the subtraction result. Consequently, in the neighborhood of point (k_1, k_2) the following function

is considered: $J^r_{k_1,k_2}(l, k) := \max\left\{ 0, J(l, k) - \frac{1}{\text{card}(\mathbb{B}_r)} \sum_{i,j \in \mathbb{B}_r} J(k_1 + i, k_2 + j) \right\}.$

In the case of EM images of a carbonaceous – nanopalladium film, one often deals with curves which separate two environments with different particle distributions (see Fig. 2(b)). This effect causes a distortion of the covariance matrix. Moreover, the weighted average of pixels (from the circular neighborhood) is far from the center of neighborhood. Consequently, it is impossible to detect the main direction of the curve. To deal with these problems, we take arithmetic average of pixels from the circular neighborhood so we fix the mean in zero.

Therefore, in the case of the circular neighborhood $\mathbb{B}_r$ at point $(k_1, k_2) \in \mathbb{Z} \times \mathbb{Z}$, a weighted covariance matrix is given by

$$\Sigma^r_J(k_1, k_2) = \frac{\sum\limits_{i,j \in \mathbb{B}_r} \left(J^r_{k_1,k_2}(k_1 + i, k_2 + j) \cdot [(i,j)^T \cdot (i,j)] \right)}{\sum\limits_{i,j \in \mathbb{B}_r} J^r_{k_1,k_2}(k_1 + i, k_2 + j)} \tag{1}$$

Gaussian filtering is obtained by replacing each pixel with coordinates (k_1, k_2) using the formula $(g_\Sigma * J)(k_1, k_2)$, where $\Sigma = \Sigma^r_J(k_1, k_2)$.

The effects of the proposed filter for EM images are presented in Fig. 4. This figure also shows differences between Gaussian density estimated from an element

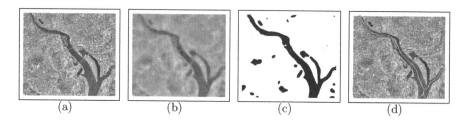

(a)   (b)   (c)   (d)

Fig. 6. Original image and the result of the proposed algorithm: a) Original image, b) Local Gaussian filter with the neighborhood $r = 21$, c) Thresholding with a CEC algorithm, d) The result of the proposed algorithm

of the image containing background (left hand side of Fig. 4) and part of the curve–type structure (right hand side of Fig. 4). Description of our algorithm is presented in Algorithm 1.

Algorithm 1. Local Gaussian blur:

input
$J: [0, m - 1] \times [0, n - 1] \to [0, 1]$ ▷ input image
$I: [0, m - 1] \times [0, n - 1] \to [0, 1]$ ▷ output image
$r > 0$ ▷ radius of the structural element
for $(k_1, k_2) \in [0, m - 1] \times [0, n - 1]$ **do**
    $\Sigma \leftarrow \Sigma_J^r(k_1, k_2)$ ▷ calculate local covariance
    $I(k_1, k_2) \leftarrow (g_\Sigma * J)(k_1, k_2)$
end for

At the end of this section, a possible application of local Gaussian filtering is presented. As was said in the introduction, the proposed algorithm can be used for locating curve structures such as rivers and roads, in satellite images (see Fig. 6). Our method identifies the main part of the river and can deal with barriers such as bridges and roads. In future, our method can be used to estimate the length of rivers.

In the case of templates containing equal elements with similar gaps our method gives good results. Unfortunately, EM images of carbonaceous – nanopalladium films present a more complicated situation. Curves contain segments of different size and geometry. Moreover, the gaps which need to be filled have different widths.

A local Gaussian filter and thresholding led to the elimination of most gaps, but some still persisted in the studied curve–type structure. An adaptive morphology operation will be used to deal with that problem.

3   Adaptive Morphology Operation

In the case of EM images, curves cannot be detected directly and some gaps remain after thresholding (see Fig. 2(b)). To solve this problem, a mathematical morphology operation is usually applied [14, 15], which uses a fixed structural

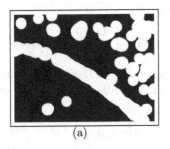 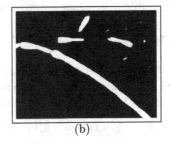

(a)   (b)

Fig. 7. Results of the classical version (Fig. 7(a)) and our modification of morphology operations (Fig. 7(b)) for the image from Fig. 2(b)

element in all pixels, although the size and shape of that element can be arbitrarily designed. Unfortunately, classical dilation increases data in all directions (see Fig. 7(a)).

This section presents an adaptive version of morphology and its application for filling gaps between segments (see Fig. 7(b)). Similarly as in the local Gaussian filter, local properties of images are used. More precisely, a covariance matrix is employed to fit the size and orientation of elliptical structural elements. Since the set should be extended only in the direction of the gaps, a morphology operation is used only if necessary.

Consequently, for each point one needs to answer the questions: *Should the morphology operation be applied in this place?* and *What size and orientation of the elliptical structural element should be used?*

In this section, similar to the previous one, a covariance matrix is used to address these questions. Before proceeding, let us recall some basic information about 2–dimensional ellipses.

Let Σ be a positive definite matrix of size 2×2. The 2–dimensional ellipse generated by matrix Σ with its center in zero is defined as follows $\mathbb{B}_\Sigma :=$ $\left\{ (k_1, k_2) \in \mathbb{Z}^2 \colon \|(k_1, k_2)\|_\Sigma^2 < 1 \right\}$. The eigenvectors of Σ define the principal directions of the ellipse and the eigenvalues of Σ are the squares of the semi–axes: a^2, b^2. On the other hand, the covariance matrix of uniform density of an ellipse $\left\{ (k_1, k_2) \in \mathbb{Z}^2 \colon \frac{k_1^2}{a^2} + \frac{k_2^2}{b^2} < 1 \right\}$ is given by $\Sigma_{a,b} := \begin{bmatrix} \frac{a^2}{4} & 0 \\ 0 & \frac{b^2}{4} \end{bmatrix}$. Therefore, elliptical structural elements with radiuses $2\sqrt{\lambda_1}$, $2\sqrt{\lambda_2}$ and the principal directions v_1, v_2 are used, where λ_1, λ_2 are eigenvalues and v_1, v_2 are eigenvectors of the covariance matrix. In other words, the square roots of eigenvalues are proportional to parameters a, b: $\frac{\sqrt{\lambda_2}}{\sqrt{\lambda_1}} = \frac{a}{b}$, assuming $a \leq b$.

The following observation presents a method for extracting an ellipse without eigendecomposition of Σ.

Proposition 1. *Let $a, b \in \mathbb{R}$ be given, then*

$$\left\{ (k_1, k_2) \colon \frac{k_1^2}{a^2} + \frac{k_2^2}{b^2} < 1 \right\} = \left\{ (k_1, k_2) \colon \|(k_1, k_2)\|_{\Sigma_{a,b}}^2 < 4 \right\}$$

Proof. By simple calculations, one obtains

$$\|(k_1, k_2)\|^2_{\Sigma_{a,b}} = (k_1, k_2)^T \Sigma_{a,b}^{-1}(k_1, k_2) = (k_1, k_2)^T \begin{bmatrix} \frac{4}{a^2} & 0 \\ 0 & \frac{4}{b^2} \end{bmatrix} (k_1, k_2) = \frac{4k_1^2}{a^2} + \frac{4k_2^2}{b^2}.$$

Thanks to these observations, one can easily draw an ellipse using only knowledge about Σ. More precisely, for point (k_1, k_2) and a fixed r, the structural element is given by the following formula:

$$\{(i, j) \in \mathbb{Z}^2 : \|(k_1 + i, k_2 + j)\|^2_{\Sigma_j^r(k_1, k_2)} < 4\}.$$

Now let us return to the proposed algorithm. Again, a neighborhood of size $2r + 1$ is used and the covariance matrix is determined by the formula (1).

Since the set should be increased only in the direction of the gap, one needs to verify whether the pixels in question are endpoints of a segment or intermediary points. This is explained in greater detail in the example:

Example 2. Let us consider the set presented in Fig. 9. Let $r = 2$ be arbitrarily fixed. The behavior of an adaptive morphology is described for two points, which are marked black.

We use coordinates of points from the neighborhood to determine a covariance matrix. In this example, elements of the curve are marked in light gray.

In the case of the first point (upper left corner in Fig. 9) the eigenvalues of the covariance matrix are: $\lambda_1 = 4.6$ and $\lambda_2 = 0.6$. Moreover, $\frac{\sqrt{\lambda_2}}{\sqrt{\lambda_1}} = 0.36$, so the structural element in this point is elliptical. Thus, the gap is filled without expanding our set in all directions.

In the second case, the covariance matrix is $\begin{bmatrix} 2.9 & 0.1 \\ 0.1 & 2.9 \end{bmatrix}$. The eigenvalues are: $\lambda_1 = 3$ and $\lambda_2 = 2.7$. Consequently, we obtain $\frac{\sqrt{\lambda_2}}{\sqrt{\lambda_1}} = 0.95$ which means that the structural element is circular. In general, circular structural elements expand the curve in all direction. Consequently, we do not want to apply morphology operation in this place.

Thus, a morphological operation is used only if eigenvalues are clearly different, or, more precisely, if $\frac{\sqrt{\lambda_2}}{\sqrt{\lambda_1}} \leq \alpha$ where α is fixed parameter.

The value of parameter α has a considerable influence on the final result of the morphology operation. Unfortunately, it is difficult to choose an optimal value. In fact, it depends on the size of the neighborhood and the geometry of the largest gaps that need to be filled.

Fig. 8 presents points in which a morphology operation is applied, for the image from Fig. 2(b).

Let us consider one more example. Fig. 10(a) shows different types of lines. The results of the proposed adaptive morphology operation are presented in Fig. 10(b) and Fig. 10(c), while the results of classical morphology operations are given in Fig. 10(d). The adaptive version allows one to increase the set in the direction of the gap, while the standard approach expands the set in all directions.

Algorithm 2 presents the pseudo code of the adaptive morphology method.

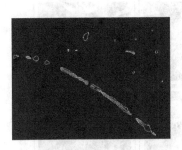

Fig. 8. Contours of elements from Fig. 2(b). Points in which a morphology operation was applied are marked in gray.

Fig. 9. Structural elements adjusted to different situations

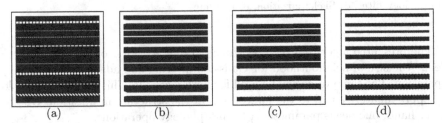

| (a) | (b) | (c) | (d) |

Fig. 10. Line detection: a) Original image, b) Local adaptive dilation for a neighborhood with $r = 25$ and $\alpha = 0.3$, c) Local adaptive dilation for a neighborhood with $r = 25$ and $\alpha = 1$, d) Classical dilation for a neighborhood with $r = 21$

4 The Final Method

The main objective of the presented algorithm is to detect curve-type structures in EM images of compound nanomaterials, such as carbonaceous–nanopalladium films. In the case of this kind of images one deals with small elements of different shapes and geometries which are separated by gaps of different sizes.

The presented method consists of two steps. In general, in simple situations (see Fig. 6) it is sufficient to use one of them. Local Gaussian filtering uses the grayscale color of images, since an adaptive morphology operation requires a binary version of images.

Since the procedure should lead to producing a curve, skeletonization is applied [22]. As after local morphology operations images exhibit some connected components with non-standard shapes, we use pruning [23] and thinning [24].

Our method can be described as follows:

1. apply a local Gaussian filter,
2. apply CEC thresholding,
3. apply an adaptive morphology filter,
4. apply skeletonization, thinning and pruning to extract a curve which describes the studied curve–type nanograin structures.

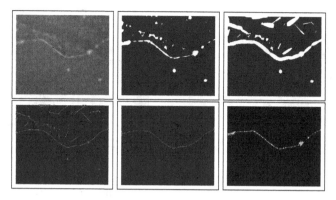

Fig. 11. Examples of detecting a curve–type template for the image presented in Fig. 1(b) with steps: a) Gaussian blur, b) Thresholding with a CEC algorithm, c) Adaptive morphology filter, d) Skeletonization, e) Pruning

The presented algorithm requires three parameters. First of all, one needs to define the size of neighborhood for Gaussian filtering and adaptive morphology operation. The same value can be used for both methods. This parameter should be approximately equal to the largest gap in the structure in question. On the other hand, one needs parameter α for morphology operations. The results of our method for EM images are presented in Fig. 11.

Algorithm 2. Adaptive morphology operation:

input
$J: [0, m-1] \times [0, n-1] \to [0,1]$ ▷ black and white image
$I: [0, m-1] \times [0, n-1] \to [0,1]$ ▷ output, copy of J
$r > 0$ ▷ radius of the structural element
$\alpha \in [0,1]$
for $(k_1, k_2) \in [0, m-1] \times [0, n-1]$ **do**
  if $J(k_1, k_2) = 1$ **then**   ▷ only in white pixels
    $\Sigma \leftarrow \Sigma_J^r(k_1, k_2)$ ▷ calculate local covariance
    $\lambda_1, \lambda_2 \leftarrow \mathrm{Eig}(\Sigma)$ ▷ eigenvalues ($\lambda_1 \geq \lambda_2$)
    if $\frac{\lambda_2}{\lambda_1} \leq \alpha$ **then**
      for $(i, j) \in [-r, r] \times [-r, r]$ **do**
        if $\|(i, j)\|_\Sigma^2 < 4$ **then**
          $I(k_1 + i, k_2 + j) \leftarrow 1$
        end if
      end for
    end if
  end if
end for

---

5 Conclusion

This paper presents a method for completing curve–type structures consisting of small elements of different shapes and geometries. In general, two approaches to this problem are presented. One is based on local Gaussian filtering. The use of weighted covariance makes it possible to find the direction of the position of the next element locally. The objective is to blur curve segments so that they could be connected.

The other method is based on an adaptive morphology operation with elliptical structural elements whose size and orientation are locally estimated by the use of a covariance matrix. Moreover, thanks to spectral analysis of the covariance matrix, one can verify which pixels are endpoints of a given curve element (dilation is applied) or intermediate points (a morphological operation is not applied).

By using a combination of these two methods, it is possible to detect curves, i.e., wire-type nanograin structures in EM images of compound nanomaterials. Furthermore, the presented method can be applied in various situations, such as road and river detection in satellite images.

The implementation of local Gaussian filter and Adaptive morphology operation as a plug–in for imageJ is available in ww2.ii.uj.edu.pl/ spurek/imageJ/ LocalGaussianFilter_AdaptiveMorphologyOperation/LocalGaussianFilter _AdaptiveMorphologyOperation.html.

References

1. Czerwosz, E., Dłużewski, P., Gierałtowski, W., Sobczak, J., Starnawska, E., Wronka, H.: Electron emission from c/c+ pd films containing pd nanocrystals. Journal of Vacuum Science & Technology B: Microelectronics and Nanometer Structures 1064 (2000)
2. Czerwosz, E., Dluzewski, P., Kozlowski, M., Sobczak, J., Starnawska, E., Wronka, H.: Electron emitting nanostructures of carbon+ pd system. In: Molecular Crystals and Liquid Crystals, pp. 237–242 (2000)
3. Czerwosz, E., Diduszko, R., Dłużewski, P., Keczkowska, J., Kozłowski, M., Rymarczyk, J., Suchańska, M.: Properties of pd nanocrystals prepared by pvd method. Vacuum 35, 372–376 (2007)
4. Russ, J.C.: The image processing handbook. CRC press (2011)
5. Waltz, F.M., Miller, J.W.: Efficient algorithm for gaussian blur using finite-state machines. In: International Society for Optics and Photonics, pp. 334–341 (1998)
6. Gomez, G., Marroquin, J., Sucar, L.: Probabilistic estimation of local scale. In: Proceedings of the 15th International Conference on Pattern Recognition, pp. 790–793. IEEE (2000)
7. Hu, H., de Haan, G.: Low cost robust blur estimator. In: Proceedings of the International Conference on Image Processing, pp. 617–620. IEEE (2006)
8. Berg, A.C., Malik, J.: Geometric blur for template matching. In: Proceedings of the 2001 IEEE Computer Society Conference on Computer Vision and Pattern Recognition, p. I-607. IEEE (2001)
9. Geusebroek, J.-M., Smeulders, A.W., Van De Weijer, J.: Fast anisotropic gauss filtering. IEEE Transactions on Image Processing, 938–943 (2003)

10. Tabor, J., Spurek, P.: Cross-entropy clustering. Pattern Recognition, 3046–3059 (2014)

11. Śmieja, M., Tabor, J.: Image segmentation with use of cross-entropy clustering. In: Proceedings of the Computer Recognition Systems CORES 2013, pp. 403–409 (2013)

12. Tabor, J., Misztal, K.: Detection of elliptical shapes via cross-entropy clustering. In: Sanches, J.M., Micó, L., Cardoso, J.S. (eds.) IbPRIA 2013. LNCS, vol. 7887, pp. 656–663. Springer, Heidelberg (2013)

13. Spurek, P., Tabor, J., Zając, E.: Detection of disk-like particles in electron microscopy images. In: Proceedings of the Computer Recognition Systems, CORES 2013, pp. 411–417 (2013)

14. Shih, F.Y.: Image processing and mathematical morphology: fundamentals and applications. CRC Press (2010)

15. Wilkinson, M.H., Roerdink, J.: Mathematical morphology and its application to signal and image processing. In: Proceedings of 9th International Symposium on Mathematical Morphology. Springer (2009)

16. Nevatia, R.: Locating object boundaries in textured environments. IEEE Transactions on Computers, 1170–1175 (1976)

17. Nalwa, V.S., Pauchon, E.: Edgel aggregation and edge description. In: Computer Vision, Graphics, and Image Processing, pp. 79–94 (1987)

18. Shih, F.Y., Cheng, S.: Adaptive mathematical morphology for edge linking. Information Sciences, 9–21 (2004)

19. Hinz, S., Baumgartner, A.: Automatic extraction of urban road networks from multi-view aerial imagery. ISPRS Journal of Photogrammetry and Remote Sensing, 83–98 (2003)

20. Mahalanobis, P.C.: On the generalized distance in statistics. In: Proceedings of the National Institute of Sciences (Calcutta), pp. 49–55 (1936)

21. Otsu, N.: A threshold selection method from gray-level histograms. Automatica, 23–27 (1975)

22. Blum, H.: A transformation for extracting new descriptors of shape. In: Models for the Perception of Speech and Visual Form, pp. 362–380 (1967)

23. Attali, D., di Baja, G.S., Thiel, E.: Pruning discrete and semicontinuous skeletons. In: Braccini, C., Vernazza, G., DeFloriani, L. (eds.) ICIAP 1995. LNCS, vol. 974, pp. 488–493. Springer, Heidelberg (1995)

24. Lam, L., Lee, S.-W., Suen, C.Y.: Thinning methodologies-a comprehensive survey. IEEE Transactions on pattern analysis and machine intelligence, 869–885 (1992)

Subspaces Clustering Approach to Lossy Image Compression

Przemysław Spurek[1,*], Marek Śmieja[1,**], and Krzysztof Misztal[2,***]

[1] Jagiellonian University
Faculty of Mathematics and Computer Science
Łojasiewicza 6, 30-348 Kraków, Poland
{przemyslaw.spurek,marek.smieja}@ii.uj.edu.pl
[2] AGH University of Science and Technology
Faculty of Physics and Applied Computer Science
al. A. Mickiewicza 30, 30-059 Kraków, Poland
Krzysztof.Misztal@fis.agh.edu.pl

Abstract. In this contribution lossy image compression based on subspaces clustering is considered. Given a PCA factorization of each cluster into subspaces and a maximal compression error, we show that the selection of those subspaces that provide the optimal lossy image compression is equivalent to the 0-1 Knapsack Problem. We present a theoretical and an experimental comparison between accurate and approximate algorithms for solving the 0-1 Knapsack problem in the case of lossy image compression.

Keywords: lossy compression, image compression, subspaces clustering.

1 Introduction

The vector quantization is the basic approach to lossy image compression [1–4]. The procedure relies on encoding a possibly large set of points from a multi-dimensional vector space into a finite set of values from a discrete subspace of lower dimension. Clustering algorithms are widely used in vector quantization [5–7]. In such cases the effect of the compression depends strictly on the selection of the clustering algorithm. In this paper we consider a special case of subspaces clustering [8–12] based on Principal Component Analysis (PCA) [13–15]. We focus on finding the division of data and clusters representation which have the highest possible level of compression and minimal error (loss of image quality).

* The work of this author was supported by the National Centre of Science (Poland) [grant no. 2013/09/N/ST6/01178].
** The work of this author was supported by the Polish Ministry of Science and Higher Education from the budget for science in the years 2013–2015 [grant no. IP2012 055972].
*** The work of this author was supported by the National Centre of Science (Poland) [grant no. 2012/07/N/ST6/02192].

K. Saeed and V. Snášel (Eds.): CISIM 2014, LNCS 8838, pp. 571–579, 2014.

We assume that a group of points $S \subset \mathbb{R}^N$ is compressed by its orthogonal projection onto a subspace generated by n principals components [16–18], i.e. the subspace spanned on n eigenvectors $\{v_1, \ldots, v_n\}$ associated with the n highest eigenvalues of the covariance matrix $\Sigma = \mathrm{cov}(S)$ shifted by the mean $\mathrm{m} = \mathrm{mean}(S)$. The compression error is given by the sum of squared distances between the points and their orthogonal projections [8, 19]:

$$
\mathrm{E}(S; n) = \sum_{x \in S} \left(\sum_{i=1}^{n} \mathrm{dist}(x; \mathrm{m} + \mathrm{span}(v_1, \ldots, v_i))^2 \right)^{1/2},
$$

where $\mathrm{dist}(x; \mathrm{m} + \mathrm{span}(v_1, \ldots, v_i))$ denotes the distance between the point x and the subspace $\mathrm{m} + \mathrm{span}(v_1, \ldots, v_i)$.

Consequently, given k-clusters $S_1, \ldots, S_k$ and the dimensions $n_1, \ldots, n_k$ of subspaces that are used for projection in appropriate clusters, the compression error equals

$$
\mathrm{E}(S; n_1, \ldots, n_k) = \sum_{j=1}^{k} \mathrm{E}(S_j; n_j).
$$

In the case of image compression, the objective is to cluster a dataset for which the total compression error does not exceed ε, i.e:

$$
\mathrm{E}(S; n_1, \ldots, n_k) \leq \varepsilon,
$$

and the number of parameters used to store the compressed data

$$
\sum_{j=1}^{k} n_j \cdot \#S_j
$$

is minimal, where $\#S_i$ denotes the cardinality of cluster S_i. In [8], where (k, ω)-means is presented, the authors proposed a possible solution for the selection of subspaces. The method is based on choosing the eigenvectors associated with the largest eigenvalues regardless of the cluster membership.

In this paper we show that the aforementioned optimization problem can be transformed into the 0-1 Knapsack Problem and that the solution proposed in [8] realizes its greedy approximation. Moreover, we consider an exact solution constructed with the use of dynamic programming algorithm which for the case of lossy image compression gives a slightly better results than the greedy method. An experimental study conducted on standard images of sizes 512×512 [20] showed that both approaches work in a comparable computation time. Therefore, it is more preferable to apply the dynamic algorithm. However, for high resolution images, the exact method can be numerically inefficient.

2   Image Compression

In this section we define a problem of lossy image compression based on PCA. We then show how to transform it into the 0-1 Knapsack Problem and present two approaches to solving it.

Suppose that a data-set S is divided into k clusters $S_1, \ldots, S_k$. Every cluster S_i is represented by a subspace $V^k = m^k + \text{span}(v_1^k, \ldots, v_N^k)$ where $m^k = \text{mean}(S_k)$ and $v_1^k, \ldots, v_N^k$ are eigenvectors of $\text{cov}(S_k)$ ordered increasingly respectively to corresponding eigenvalues $\lambda_1^k, \ldots, \lambda_N^k$. Such a representation can be obtained by applying PCA for every cluster S_i.

In order to compress the image, $n_i \leq N$ principal components are chosen for each cluster S_i, and vectors are projected onto constructed n_i dimensional spaces. The error associated with one cluster after projecting its elements onto n_i principal components can be calculated with the use of the following proposition.

Proposition 1. *Let S be a subset of $\mathbb{R}^N$ and let $n < N$. By $\{\lambda_1, \ldots, \lambda_N\}$ we denote the increasingly ordered eigenvalues corresponding to eigenvectors $\{v_1, \ldots, v_N\}$ of covariance matrix $\text{cov}(S)$. Then*

$$E(S; n) = \sum_{i=n+1}^{N} \#S \cdot \lambda_i.$$

Proof Compare with [21, Propetries A1-A5].

Given k clusters $S_1, \ldots, S_k$ the total compression error after projecting data onto appropriate $n_1, \ldots, n_k$ dimensional subspaces is given by

$$E(S; n_1, \ldots, n_k) = \sum_{j=1}^{k} \left(\#S_j \sum_{i=n_i+1}^{N} \lambda_i^j \right).$$

Let $\varepsilon > 0$ denote the maximal compression error allowed. We seek the minimal number of parameters to describe the image for which the overall compression error does not exceed ε:

Problem 1. *Let $\varepsilon > 0$ be given. Find the dimensions $n_1, \ldots, n_k$ of clusters $S_1, \ldots, S_k$, such that the total compression error does not exceed ε, i.e.*

$$\sum_{j=1}^{k} \sum_{i=n_i+1}^{N} \#S_j \cdot \lambda_i^j < \varepsilon$$

and which minimize the number of parameters, i.e.

$$\min_{n_1, \ldots, n_k} \left\{ \sum_{j=1}^{k} n_j \cdot \#S_j \right\} = \min_{n_1, \ldots, n_k} \left\{ \sum_{j=1}^{k} \sum_{i=1}^{n_j} \#S_j \right\}.$$

In [8] the authors proposed a method to select the subspaces dimensions. In general, their idea is based on choosing the eigenvectors related to the largest eigenvalues. This is not the optimal solution. Since the compression error is bounded by $E(S; 0, \ldots, 0)$ we transform the above minimization problem into an equivalent maximization one:

Problem 2. *Let $\varepsilon > 0$ be given. Find the dimensions $n_1, \ldots, n_k$ of clusters $S_1, \ldots, S_k$, such that*

$$\sum_{j=1}^{k} \sum_{i=n_j+1}^{N} \#S_j \cdot \lambda_i^j < \varepsilon$$

and which maximize

$$\sum_{j=1}^{k} \sum_{i=n_j+1}^{N} \#S_j.$$

This is the 0-1 Knapsack Problem. For a proper illustration of this matter, let us define the items parameters for the Knapsack Problem. The weights and values of $N = k \cdot n$ items are defined as follows:

$$w_{(i-1)n+j} = w_{i,j} = \#S_j \cdot \lambda_i^j,$$

$$v_{(i-1)n+j} = v_{i,j} = \#S_j.$$

The goal of the 0-1 Knapsack Problem is to select those items which maximize the overall profit and do not exceed the knapsack capacity, i.e. to define numbers $k_l \in \{0, 1\}$ which maximize:

$$\sum_{l=1}^{N} k_l v_l, \text{ subject to } \sum_{l=1}^{N} k_l w_l \leq \varepsilon.$$

Plenty of strategies have been proposed for the 0-1 Knapsack Problem which is NP-hard with respect to the number of items [22]. The greedy approach finds an approximated solution and relies on choosing elements ordered with respect to the highest density v_l/w_l. In the case of compression, it depends on sorting with respect to decreasing eigenvalues:

$$\frac{v_{i,j}}{w_{i,j}} = \frac{\#S_j}{\#S_j \cdot \lambda_i^j} = \frac{1}{\lambda_i^j}.$$

It is easily seen that this is exactly the method proposed in [8].

If m is the maximum value of items that fit into the knapsack (in the optimal solution), the greedy algorithm is guaranteed to achieve at least an overall value of items equal $m/2$ [23]. However, this is not a common situation in the image compression – more often the solution returned by both algorithms is similar. This can be seen in the following example.

Example 2. Let the cardinalities of all clusters be the same, i.e.

$$c := \#S_i = \#S_j, \text{ for all } i, j = 1 \ldots, k.$$

Then both algorithms return identical items. Indeed, we maximize

$$\sum_{j=1}^{k} \sum_{i=n_j+1}^{n} 1, \text{ subject to } \sum_{j=1}^{k} \sum_{i=n_j+1}^{n} \lambda_i^j < \frac{\varepsilon}{c}$$

Since all items are equally valuable, the optimal solution includes the lightest items. This strategy is also preferred by the greedy algorithm.

Also, many algorithms which construct an exact solution exist, e.g. the dynamic programming method. More precisely, let us denote by $F(l, v)$ the minimal overall weight of elements chosen from 1 to l such that their overall value is maximal and at least $v \geq 0$, i.e.

$$F(l, v) = \min_{k_1, \ldots, k_l} \left\{ \sum_{i=1}^{l} k_i w_i : \sum_{i=1}^{l} k_i v_i \geq v \right\}$$

for $l = 0, \ldots, N$, $v = 0, \ldots, V$, where $V = \sum_{l=1}^{N} v_l$ (we assume that $l = 0$ means that no items are included into knapsack – then $F(0,0) = 0$ and $F(0,v) = \infty$, for $v > 0$). The maximal value of items included in the knapsack is denoted by:

$$C^* := \max\{v : F(N, v) \leq \varepsilon\}.$$

This value can be calculated in a recursive procedure:

$$F(l, v) = \begin{cases} 0 & \text{, for } l = 0 \text{ and } v = 0 \\ \infty & \text{, for } l = 0 \text{ and } v > 0 \\ \min\{F(l-1, v), F(l-1, v - v_l) + w_l\}, \\ \qquad \text{for } l = 1, \ldots, N, \end{cases}$$

and is realized by a bottom up algorithm. The complexity equals $\Theta(N \cdot V) = \Theta(k \cdot n \cdot \#S)$, which for large datasets is quite high.

3   Experiments

In this section we present the results of numerical experiments illustrating the performance of the lossy image compression based on subspaces clustering with the use of the greedy and dynamic approaches.

We apply classical methods often used in such situations: PCA, k–means ($k = 5$) with PCA representation for each cluster and (k, ω)–means ($k = 5$ and ω with non zero elements on 11-15 coordinates). Table 1 contains the results of these compression methods with the use of greedy and dynamic algorithms. Dynamic approach delivers slightly better results for all methods except for the PCA method because only one cluster was considered. This is a consequence of Example 2.3. Both of these algorithms worked in a similar time. Moreover, (k, ω)–means algorithm gave the best results. Therefore, the further experiments will be performed with the use of this method.

Figure 1 presents sample compression results for the classical Lena image. Given the maximal compression error, the qualities of images are comparable for both Knapsack algorithms, while the number of parameters varies greatly. The advantage of using the dynamic programming algorithm is evident.

The comparison of the errors achieved by the greedy and the dynamic algorithms for the Lena image is showed in Figure 2. Since the dynamic algorithm constructs the optimal solution, the compression error is greater than in the

Table 1. Parameters needed to obtain the desired error level for compression of a few sample images using (k, ω)–means, PCA and k–means with PCA methods. We compared the greedy and dynamic strategies for choosing the optimal compression configuration. Among all, (k, ω)–means provides better compression level than other methods.

Error	(k, ω)–means		PCA		k-means	
	Dynamic	Greedy	Dynamic	Greedy	Dynamic	Greedy
1%	96 543	96 903	105 625	105 625	179 737	180 304
5%	18 995	20 140	21 125	21 125	48 313	48 948
10%	9 866	10 028	12 675	12 675	24 547	24 676
15%	6 333	6 495	8 450	8 450	15 723	16 582
25%	3 859	4 021	4 225	4 225	8 678	9 194
50%	2 801	2 963	4 225	4 225	3 541	3 850
1%	316 086	316 325	401 375	401 375	481 563	481 617
5%	103 642	103 721	143 650	143 650	240 836	241 061
10%	46 555	46 873	67 600	67 600	147 632	147 882
15%	24 099	24 178	33 800	33 800	104 404	104 441
25%	9 064	9 143	12 675	12 675	59 618	60 850
50%	2 064	2 536	8 450	8 450	16 312	17 123
1%	125 330	125 940	143 650	143 650	307681	308705
5%	21 283	21 283	25 350	25 350	83386	83788
10%	11 816	12 264	12 675	12 675	39869	40560
15%	8 158	8 938	8 450	8 450	24997	25444
25%	4 489	4 489	8 450	8 450	15048	15658
50%	977	977	4 225	4 225	5224	5224

case of the greedy approach (the results are closer to the black line). Moreover, the graph is smoother. In the case of the greedy algorithm, the ordering of eigenvalues is performed once for all error levels. Consequently, the graph is constant in the subsequent intervals. Clearly, the dynamic algorithm provides better compression level than the greedy solution (Figure 3).

The presented experiments confirmed that the dynamic approach delivers better results than the greedy one. The differences are especially evident for large dimension images that contain complicated patterns.

4   Conclusions

Subspaces clustering algorithms are very often used for image compression. In such a situation elements from each group are represented by the orthogonal projection onto low dimensional subspaces. The crucial problem lies in determining such subspaces that minimize the use of memory and do not exceed arbitrarily given loss of image quality. In this paper we showed that this optimization problem can be transformed into the 0-1 Knapsack Problem. Moreover, two possible solutions, the exact and the approximated one, were presented. Consequently,

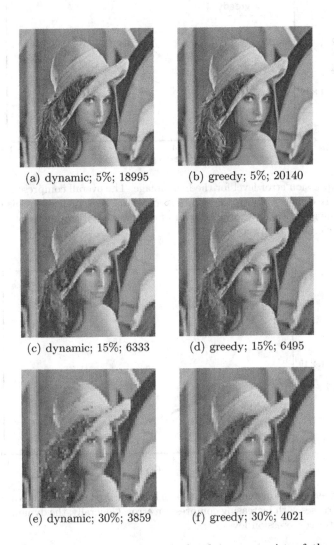

(a) dynamic; 5%; 18995   (b) greedy; 5%; 20140

(c) dynamic; 15%; 6333   (d) greedy; 15%; 6495

(e) dynamic; 30%; 3859   (f) greedy; 30%; 4021

Fig. 1. Compressed Lena image. Description of each image consists of: the name of the compression algorithm, the level of compression error and the number of parameters needed for compression. The algorithm using the dynamic approach for compression needs less parameters.

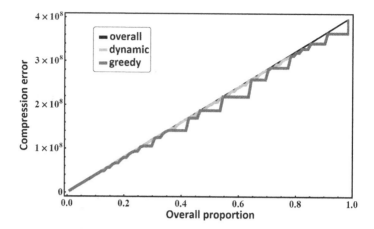

Fig. 2. Compression error level for the Lena image. The overall compression error level (black line) is compared with the compression error level realized by using the dynamic and the greedy algorithm. The error of compression with the use of the dynamic approach is closer to the overall one.

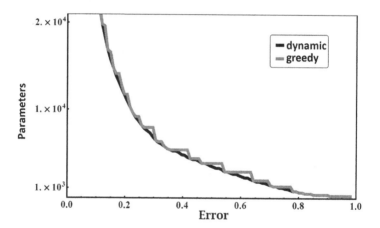

Fig. 3. Number of parameters needed to reach the desired error level. Number of parameters decreases with increasing compression error. Generally, the dynamic algorithm provides better compression level.

the method from [8] realizes a greedy approximation of the 0-1 Knapsack Problem. Experiments performed on standard images showed that both algorithms work in a similar computation time.

References

1. Gray, R.: Vector quantization. IEEE ASSP Magazine 1(2), 4–29 (1984)
2. Scheunders, P.: A genetic lloyd-max image quantization algorithm. Pattern Recognition Letters 17(5), 547–556 (1996)

3. Lin, Y.-C., Tai, S.-C.: A fast linde-buzo-gray algorithm in image vector quantization. IEEE Transactions on Circuits and Systems II: Analog and Digital Signal Processing 45(3), 432–435 (1998)
4. Gray, R.M., Neuhoff, D.L.: Quantization. IEEE Transactions on Information Theory 44(6), 2325–2383 (1998)
5. Equitz, W.H.: A new vector quantization clustering algorithm. IEEE Transactions on Acoustics, Speech and Signal Processing 10(37), 1568–1575 (1989)
6. Scheunders, P.: A genetic c-means clustering algorithm applied to color image quantization. Pattern Recognition 30(6), 859–866 (1997)
7. Chou, C.-H., Su, M.-C., Lai, E.: A new cluster validity measure and its application to image compression. Pattern Analysis and Applications 7(2), 205–220 (2004)
8. Spurek, P., Tabor, J., Misztal, K.: Weighted Approach to Projective Clustering. In: Saeed, K., Chaki, R., Cortesi, A., Wierzchoń, S. (eds.) CISIM 2013. LNCS, vol. 8104, pp. 367–378. Springer, Heidelberg (2013)
9. Agarwal, P.K., Mustafa, N.H.: k-means projective clustering. In: Proceedings of the twenty-third ACM SIGMOD-SIGACT-SIGART Symposium on Principles of Database Systems, pp. 155–165. ACM (2004)
10. Kriegel, H.P., Kröger, P., Zimek, A.: Clustering high-dimensional data: A survey on subspace clustering, pattern-based clustering, and correlation clustering. ACM Transactions on Knowledge Discovery from Data (TKDD) 3(1), 1–58 (2009)
11. Parsons, L., Haque, E., Liu, H.: Subspace clustering for high dimensional data: a review. ACM SIGKDD Explorations Newsletter 6(1), 90–105 (2004)
12. Vidal, R.: Subspace clustering. IEEE Signal Processing Magazine 28(2), 52–68 (2011)
13. Jolliffe, I.: Principal component analysis. Wiley Online Library (2005)
14. Abdi, H., Williams, L.J.: Principal component analysis. Wiley Interdisciplinary Reviews: Computational Statistics 2(4), 433–459 (2010)
15. Wold, S., Esbensen, K., Geladi, P.: Principal component analysis. Chemometrics and Intelligent Laboratory Systems 2(1), 37–52 (1987)
16. Bingham, E., Mannila, H.: Random projection in dimensionality reduction: applications to image and text data. In: Proceedings of the Seventh ACM SIGKDD International Conference on Knowledge Discovery and Data Mining, pp. 245–250. ACM (2001)
17. Ifarraguerri, A., Chang, C.-I.: Unsupervised hyperspectral image analysis with projection pursuit. IEEE Transactions on Geoscience and Remote Sensing 38(6), 2529–2538 (2000)
18. Kaarna, A., Zemcik, P., Kalviainen, H., Parkkinen, J.: Compression of multispectral remote sensing images using clustering and spectral reduction. IEEE Transactions on Geoscience and Remote Sensing 38(2), 1073–1082 (2000)
19. Grim, J.: Multimodal discrete karhunen-loève expansion. Kybernetika 22(4), 329–330 (1986)
20. USC-SIPI, USC-SIPI image database, http://sipi.usc.edu/database/
21. Jolliffe, I.: Principal component analysis. In: Encyclopedia of Statistics in Behavioral Science (2002)
22. Martello, S., Toth, P.: Knapsack problems: algorithms and computer implementations, John Wiley & Sons, Inc (1990)
23. Kellerer, H., Pferschy, U., Pisinger, D.: Knapsack problems. Springer (2004)

An Impact of the User and Time Parameters to Sequence Alignment Methods for Process Mining

Jakub Štolfa[1], Svatopluk Štolfa[1], Kateřina Slaninová[1,2], Jan Martinovič[1,2], and Václav Snášel[1,2]

[1] Department of Computer Science, FEECS, VŠB, Technical University of Ostrava, 17. Listopadu 15, 708 33, Ostrava-Poruba, Czech Republic
[2] IT4Innovations, VŠB, Technical University of Ostrava, 17. Listopadu 15, 708 33, Ostrava-Poruba, Czech Republic
{jakub.stolfa,svatopluk.stolfa,katerina.slaninova,jan.martinovic, vaclav.snasel}@vsb.cz

Abstract. Process mining is relatively new domain that opens many opportunities for process control and improvement. Anyway, the basis of the process mining is the examination of bunch of data from processes. There are many methods that already had been used in this domain and many other are still waiting for the discovery of their benefits. One of the main issues is to find out whether the new method is useful or not. The main purpose of this paper is to present the usability of sequence alignment method in process mining especially from the user and time perspective.

Keywords: Sequence Alignment Methods, Process Mining.

1 Introduction

Process mining is the examination of the data from processes. Data are taken especially from systems that support business processes. Processes are not sequential and the instances can follow different prescribed ways of process description, same activities are performed by different users, lasting of the activities varies etc. Therefore, there are many different types of information that can be logged by the supporting system. These logs are then used for the examination of process behavior, user behavior, entities behavior and many other ways. Another methods allows us to obtain result that can help to study the anomalies in process execution, social nets, timing aspects of activities and processes etc.

Our intention is to use and adopt sequence alignment methods as one of the tools that can be used to study the data from the processes. Since the sequence alignment methods work with the sequences, the issue is then to try preparing the proper sequence. The sequence must be prepared from the perspective of intended view of the process. Relatively easy task is to study the topology of the process. In that case, the sequence consists from the activities that are performed

K. Saeed and V. Snášel (Eds.): CISIM 2014, LNCS 8838, pp. 580–591, 2014.

by the process. In case that we would like to study other type of information, like to involve the time and user information, we have to prepare a sequence that obtains such type of data.

Ideas in this paper are based on our previous work that included process reconstruction and path analysis [15] and analysis of the process data that involved usage of the sequence alignment methods [7]. The approach was tested and used in other research areas, for example in e-learning area [9], in analysis of behavior of agents during the simulation [11] and in analysis of user behavior on the web [10].

The research follows our paper [6], where we discussed the usage of sequence alignment methods in the area of process mining. We have described four types of the sequences that allowed us to form four different points of view of the particular process. The aim of the current paper is to describe and explain the meaning of results of the similarities defined by the sequence alignment methods for the different types of sequences. We would like to prove that the proper creation of the sequences with this type of information - topology of the process, duration of the process, users involved in the process can be useful for the study of process instances and bring us new way how to study the process instances data.

The paper is organized as follows: Section 2 introduces the state of the art; Section 3 describes the analyzed process that was used for the experiments, Section 4 depicts the preparation and data structure, Section 5 presents the experiment that we have performed, shows the usage of our process mining method and explains obtained results; concluding Section 6 provides a summary and discusses the planned future research.

2   State of the Art

Business process definitions are sometimes quite complex and allow many variations. All of these variations are then implemented to supportive systems. If you want to follow some business process in a system, you have many decisions and process is sometimes lost in variations. Modeling and simulations can help you to adjust the process, find weaknesses and bottlenecks during the design phase of the process.

The idea of process mining was introduced by Aalst in 2004 [13,12]. This area of the research has been developing during the years, lot of methods were introduced to this topic. In 2005, ProM tool was introduced [14]. ProM aggregates methods and approaches in this area of study. There are a lot of papers that describe new ways or improvements of methods, techniques and algorithms used in the process mining, but only several papers are focused on the case studies [1].

In the area of process mining, the methods of the sequence alignment were introduced by Esign and Karagoz [2] in 2013. Focus of their work was quantitative approach for performing process diagnostics. The approach uses sequence alignment methods for delta analysis. It is comparison of actually performed process and prescriptive reference model [13]. Our paper provides another usage of the sequence alignment methods. We use these methods for comparison of extracted processes to find similarity in the process executions, i.e. some patterns of the process.

The basic approach to the comparison of two sequences, where the order of elements is important, is The longest common substring method (LCS). This is used in exact matching problems [4]. It is obvious from the name of the method that its main principle is to find the length of the common longest substring. The LCS method respects the order of elements within a sequence. However, the main disadvantage of this method is that it can only find the identical subsequences, which meet the characteristics of substrings.

Unlike substrings, the objects in a subsequence might be intermingled with other objects that are not in the sequence. The longest common subsequence method (LCSS) allows us to find the common subsequence [5]. Contrary to the LCS method, the LCSS method allows (or ignores) these extra elements in the sequence and, therefore, it is immune to slight distortions.

The important method is The time-warped longest common subsequence (TWLCS) [3]. This method combines the advantages of the LCSS method with dynamic time warping [8]. Dynamic time warping is used for finding the optimal visualization of elements in two sequences to match them as much as possible. This method is immune to minor distortions and to time non-linearity. It is able to compare sequences, which are for standard metrics, evidently not comparable.

The methods LCS and LCSS used for the comparison of sequences find the longest common subsequence z of compared sequences x and y, where ($z \subseteq x$) $\wedge$ ($z \subseteq y$). The relation weight $w_{seq}(x, y)$ between the sequences x and y was counted by Equation 1:

$$w_{seq}(x, y) = \frac{l(z)^2}{l(x)l(y)} \frac{Min(l(x), l(y))^2}{Max(l(x), l(y))^2}, \tag{1}$$

where $l(x)$ and $l(y)$ are lengths of the compared sequences x and y, and $l(z)$ is a length of a subsequence z. Equation 1 takes account of the possible difference between $l(x)$ and $l(y)$. Due to this reason, z is adapted so that $w_{seq}(x, y)$ is strengthened in the case of similar lengths of sequences x and y, and analogically weakened in the case of higher difference of $l(x)$ and $l(y)$. For the methods LCS and LCSS, w_{seq} meets all the similarity conditions: $w_{seq} \geq 0$, $w_{seq}(x, x) = 1$, $w_{seq}(x, x) > w_{seq}(x, y)$ and $w_{seq}(x, y) = w_{seq}(y, x)$.

The output z is only the sequence which characterizes the relation between the sequences x and y for T-WLCS method. Therefore, $w_{seq}(x, y)$ does not meet all the similarity conditions due to its characteristics. Respectively, it is possible that $w_{seq}(x, y) > w_{seq}(x, x)$. Although we know that $w_{seq}(x, y)$ is not a similarity for T-WLCS method, due to a simplification, the 'sequence similarity' will be used as a relation weight $w_{seq}(x, y)$ between the sequences x and y for all the methods of sequence comparison in the following text.

3   Process Context

We used data logs of the SAP system for running of testing examples. Current SAP system runs in the company that operates in five European countries. We chose business process of the invoice verification that is implemented in SAP system, user activities are controlled by SAP workflow system. Users participate in the invoice verification workflow in several different roles (creator, accountant completion, approver, and accountant   decision and posting). Generally, it is process in which the accountant should create the invoice, verify it, send to the approvers and finally, when he gets it back he does invoice posting.

We have loaded the log of the process between 1/1/2012 and 6/30/2012, totally we loaded 70,855 records for adjusting. Detailed description of the obtaining log and data preprocessing is described in our previous work [15]. We know that the log contains data from the three factories of the company. That means in the results we can also focus on that if the people, or users, cooperate or if the factories are separated.

We know the architecture of the process model because user activities in the SAP are controlled by SAP business workflow. It means that process execution should follow the process model. On the other hand, we can find out some deviations. This model is depictured in the Fig. 3. Process starts with event Creation. Next one is Verification. These two events Creation and Verification can be done repeatedly. Approval event can be done repeatedly too. If the invoice is not acknowledged, then process goes from the beginning. Last events are Posting.

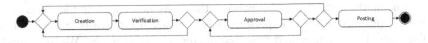

Fig. 1. Process Model

4   Data Preparation and Sequences Types

The main purpose of this paper is to prove that sequence alignment methods are useful for finding the similarity between the sequences with user and time parameters. We would like to prove that adding the parameters to the sequences has an appropriate impact to the results of these methods and can be used for the further analysis.

Like it was written in the introduction, our paper extends the finding in our previous paper in this area [6]. We have set up four sequence types. The sequence types represent four points of view that we are able to see according to the data in the log. These four types are:

- Type A - Events without Time and Users,
- Type B - Events with Time and without Users,
- Type C - Events without Time and with Users,
- Type D - Events with Time and Users.

We have solved the task about event duration. We have set up three categories of the duration of the events:

1. Category 1 - If the event lasts less than 32 hours it fits to the first category
2. Category 2 - If the event lasts more than 32 hours and less than 168 hours it fits to the second category
3. Category 3 - If the event lasts more than 168 hours it fits to the third category

We set up aliases for the type of the events in the sequence. It means that Verification event is in the sequence like V, Creation event is C, Approval is A, and Posting is P. Sequence type A focuses on the topological structure of the process only. Sequence type B focuses on the topological structure of the process and combines it with the information about the duration of the events. Tagging of the duration of the events is made by repeating the symbol of the event in the sequence. We use string comparison methods and thus we need to transform the duration to the strings. Repetition of the symbol depends on the duration category of the particular event. First category is represented by one single symbol, second category by two same symbols, and third category by three same symbols. Sequence type C combines the topological structure of the process and meta-information about the users. Sequence type D combines all possible views to the process - topological, time view and users view.

5   Experiments and Results

This section presents performed experiments and obtained results. Experiments were run on the data from the process that was described in the Section 3. The main purpose of these experiments is to analyze if there is any impact of adding user, time or user and time parameter to the sequence. We have made experiments for each sequence type - A, B, C and D.

Consideration of the useability of particular sequence alignment method for analyzed data collection was discussed in [6]. After several tests we have found that each sequence type requires different sequence alignment method. This finding follows the mentioned paper. We have more data in the experiments described in this paper. Therefore, we have decided that LCS, or LCSS method is more usable than T-WLCS method for this type of business process. The LCS method do not accept any differences in the middle of the sequence, that means that really similar sequences fits together only. This might be more usable for the business process described by sequence type A in our experiments. If we add other attributes like user and time (or both) then LCSS method is more suitable for the definition of sequence similarity.

5.1   Sequence Type A

We can see the most used case types in the examined process for sequence type A in the Table 1. Case type CVAAS has the most occurrences. It means that the most invoices in the reality went approved twice. The third one shows us

Table 1. Sequence Type A: Result Ordered by Occurrence

Case Type	Occurrence	Weighted Degree
C;V;A;A;S;	3788	9.79
C;V;A;A;A;S;	2952	27.03
C;V;A;S;	2007	6.51
C;V;A;A;A;A;S;	587	16.50
C;V;A;A;A;A;A;S;	209	18.57
C;V;C;V;A;A;A;S;	147	19.01
C;V;A;S;A;A;A;S;	142	18.93
C;V;C;V;A;A;S;	116	15.47
C;V;A;A;S;A;S;	114	15.78
C;V;A;S;A;A;S;	90	14.88

that 2007 cases went through only one approving, so the invoices might not be properly checked. The four eyes company rule is broken here. The four eyes rule means that the invoice is checked at least by two persons.

Other information is about weighted degree. This information is obtained using network analysis. The network (weighted undirected graph $G(V, E, w)$) was created by case types as nodes V, while the relation weight w represents the similarity between the case types. Weighted degree is the sum of the weights of the edges for the particular node. That tells us how much the current node is similar to the other nodes. If the weighted degree is higher then the node is more similar to at least some of its neighbor nodes.

The case type CVAAS had the most occurrences, CVAAAS had the second biggest number, and CVAS had the third biggest number of occurrences. We can see that other nodes that have deviation in meaning of number of the occurrences have a relatively high weighted degree. They have edges between each other with the high weight and create one cluster, which can be seen in Figure 2(a). We can see that these nodes are deviant from the biggest nodes (most used case types) in meaning of the number of the occurrences and also in meaning of the similarity and distance from the most used case types.

Weighted degree data range was from 0.62 to 62.42 for the LCS method. We can see that the case types with the most occurrences have relatively small weighted degree according the range of the weighted degree. It tells us that the most used case types are relatively out of the other nodes. It means that the other nodes, we can say deviation nodes in meaning of number of the occurrences, are quite a lot different from the nodes with the most occurrences (according to the chosen sequence alignment method and its settings). From the business process view, this information says that if some case type is deviation then the difference is quite big from the most used case types of the process. On the other hand, we have to look at it in a complex way in correlation with the particular graph or in correlation with the deep data examination. We can see whether the examined case type is really out of the other nodes, or if the examined case type has a lot of edges with small weight, or that it has only one or small number of edges with high weight. For example, if the node can have weighted degree 9 then we can think that this node is out of the other nodes. But but we have to examine if that node has 90 edges with weight 1, or only 5 edges with weight 18. The result can tell us completely other information. There are two issues that have two different meanings and have to be examined. In the first way, it is node out of the other nodes, and in the second way, it is a node that has some quite similar nodes.

Figure 2 shows the examples of undirected weighted sequence graph $G(V, E, w)$. The nodes V represent sequences (cases), the ties E represent relations between them. Weight w is determined by similarity between the sequences set by method for sequence alignment, LCS. As we can see, Figure 2(a) for the sequence type A shows that the most used case types are really out of the other case types which create one evident cluster. The graph was made by force atlas decomposition. The smallest node represents the lowest occurrence of the case type, the biggest one represents the higher occurrence. Node with minimal weighted degree has the blue color, then it continues through green, yellow and the maximal degree is colored by the red color.

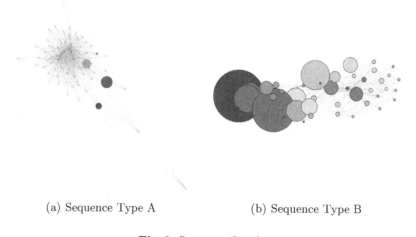

(a) Sequence Type A   (b) Sequence Type B

Fig. 2. Sequence Graphs

Next experiments with case types B, C, and D deal with the addition of time and user parameters to the sequence. We have performed the experiments for all case types from the previous experiment, but the results were not clearly visible for their visualization and study them from the overall overview. Therefore, we show the impact of the time and user parameters addition on the selected case type only. We have selected case type CVAAS from the previous example; this case type has the highest occurrence in the log.

5.2   Sequence Type B

Table 2 shows case types ordered according to their occurrence for sequence type B. These case types were created by addition of time parameter and were

Table 2. Sequence Type B: Result Ordered by Occurrence

Case Type	Occurrence	Weighted Degree
C;V;A;A;S;	573	2.99
C;V;A;A;A;S;	474	4.66
C;V;A;A;A;A;S;	312	9.25
C;V;A;A;S;S;	291	4.70
C;C;V;A;A;S;	222	5.14
C;V;A;A;A;S;S;	217	8.00
C;C;V;A;A;A;S;	203	10.52
C;C;V;A;A;A;S;S;	164	10.45
C;V;A;A;A;A;A;S;	150	10.08
C;C;V;A;A;A;A;S;	141	13.02
...	...	...

derived from the selected case type CVAAS in the sequence type A. Addition of this parameter caused a decomposition of the case type CVAAS to other 43 case types. Case type with the most occurrences is the CVAAS. The time parameter was added with following rules: if the event lasts less then 32 hours then it is repeated in the sequence once, 30-168 twice, more then 168 three times. Taking into account the rules for the time parameter we can see that the most used case type was the one with the shortest execution time. The second one was the sequence type CVAAAS that had 474 occurrences. This case type shows us that 474 cases were executed by the same way. This type of the sequence may be the case with the three approvals, and also it could be the case type with one approval that takes a lot of time. Anyway, according to the time parameter, these cases are signed as the same case type. This information can be easily obtained form the statistical analysis as well, but our methods can be seen as a different view of this data with possibility to easily set up adjusting parameters.

Figure 2(b) shows the distribution of the sequences from the time-sequence view. We can see several main nodes according to their occurrence. This graph shows mainly the distribution of the sequences according to their duration.

5.3   Sequence Type C

Table 3 depicts case types ordered by occurrence for the sequence type C. This case type reflects the topology of the process and user parameter. Case type CVAAS of the sequence type A by the addition of the user parameter has been augmented to 217 case types for the sequence type C. We can see that the most used case type is that one, where the user260 starts the process and ends the process as well. Mostly used user in the role approval is user074 followed by user202. In the perspective with the user parameter, we are able to see what user is the most frequented, as well as the process connection between the users. From this point of view, we can study for example whether the users do mostly only simple invoices where the process is easy, whether the user that creates the

Table 3. Sequence Type C: Result Ordered by Occurrence

Case Type	Occurrence	Weighted Degree
C_U260;V_U260;A_U074;A_U202;S_U260;	761	3.36
C_U068;V_U068;A_U074;A_U202;S_U068;	298	2.64
C_U068;V_U068;A_U249;A_U192;S_U068;	254	3.00
C_U162;V_U162;A_U074;A_U202;S_U162;	174	0.64
C_U068;V_U068;A_U227;A_U202;S_U068;	145	0.00
C_U040;V_U040;A_U102;A_U030;S_U040;	124	1.08
C_U087;V_U087;A_U126;A_U124;S_U087;	117	2.08
C_U110;V_U110;A_U114;A_U043;S_U200;	91	2.44
C_U260;V_U260;A_U249;A_U192;S_U260;	89	1.72
C_U178;V_U178;A_U249;A_U192;S_U178;	82	2.36
...	...	...

invoice occurs in more deviations (this can mean that there can be problem with the knowledge to whom the invoice should be send to approve it), etc.

Figure 3(a) shows the distribution of the sequences from the user-sequence view. We can see several main nodes. These nodes are made around the same user for C, V and S activities. These activities are mainly performed by the same user. For example the node (case type) in the graph down right has the main user U087, the node on the top has main user U068, and we can see there the case types with the second and the third highest occurrence. Case types around the user U260 are in the middle of the graph. We also can see that one cluster of nodes is separated (top right). We have analyzed the sequences in this cluster and had found out that this cluster contains the sequences from one factory only. Since we have used data from three factories of the current company, we can see that other two factories probably cooperate on the user level and the third one is separated.

5.4   Sequence Type D

The results for the sequence type D are shown in Table 4. Sequence type D combines a topology of the process, user and time parameter. We can see that the most used case type is a case type in which user U260 created the invoice in less then 32 hours, then verified the invoice in less then 32 hours, user U074 followed by user U260 approved the invoice in less then 32 hours, and finally, user U260 sent the invoice in less then 32 hours.

Figure 3(b) shows even more distribution of the same topological sequences based on the time and user view. There are more interesting findings. For example the cluster on the right side of the graph is made around the sequences performed by the user U260 (C, V, S activities), but even the sequences with different user for C, V and S activities are clustered here. The reason is that when the A activity took too long one user, his sequences where put together. The reason might be e.g. that one particular user worked on difficult invoices that took long time to approve.

Table 4. Sequence Type D: Result Ordered by Occurrence

Case Type	Occ.	W. Deg.
C_U260;V_U260;A_U074;A_U202;S_U260;	309	4.09
C_U260;V_U260;A_U074;A_U202;S_U260;S_U260;	97	6.48
C_U260;V_U260;A_U074;A_U074;A_U202;S_U260;	72	3.42
C_U260;C_U260;V_U260;A_U074;A_U202;S_U260;	57	6.03
C_U162;V_U162;A_U074;A_U202;S_U162;	51	2.32
C_U260;V_U260;A_U074;A_U202;S_U260;S_U260;S_U260;	46	7.84
C_U162;V_U162;A_U074;A_U074;A_U202;S_U162;	46	1.49
C_U068;C_U068;V_U068;A_U249;A_U192;A_U192;A_U192;S_U068;S_U068;	45	13.04
C_U068;C_U068;V_U068;A_U074;A_U074;A_U202;S_U068;S_U068;	38	8.59
C_U087;V_U087;A_U126;A_U126;A_U124;A_U124;S_U087;	37	2.73
...	...	...

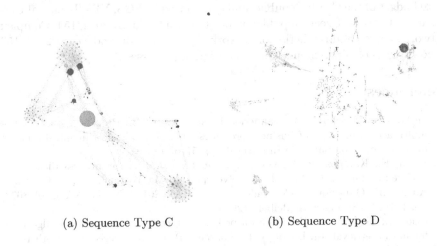

(a) Sequence Type C   (b) Sequence Type D

Fig. 3. Sequence Graphs

6   Conclusion

The paper was focused on various points of view to process mining, especially from the user and time perspective. The process instances were compared and similarity between them analyzed using methods for sequence alignment. We can relatively easily reach many different types of findings that have to be analyzed.

Our approach involves time and user metadata to the examination which enables us to find possible ways to see interesting results. For example, the particular person behavior can be showed and analyzed what are her/his process instances. The behavior patterns from the time perspective can be observed as well. The creation of different communities, user participation on deviations, etc. can be also examined using the proposed approach.

We would like to continue with the extension of this approach in the future. We intent to find out what exact types of results can be obtained by the usage of different methods, examine the methods and accustom them for the usage on different real examples. The detailed interpretation of different case studies will help us then to determine which method, adjustment and what views will be used then for data mining and real process examination in general. The idea is to have a very good control of the process by the usage of the data about already performed process instances.

Acknowledgments. This work was supported by the European Regional Development Fund in the IT4Innovations Centre of Excellence project (CZ.1.05/1.1.00/02.0070) and the national budget of the Czech Republic via the Research and Development for Innovations Operational Programme, and supported by the project New creative teams in priorities of scientific research, reg. no. CZ.1.07/2.3.00/30.0055, supported by Operational Programme Education for Competitiveness and co-financed by the European Social Fund and the state budget of the Czech Republic, and co-financed by SGS, VB - Technical University of Ostrava, Czech Republic, under the grants No. SP2014/154 'Complex network analysis and prediction of network object behavior' and No. SP2014/157 'Knowledge modeling, simulation and design of processes'.

References

1. de Weerdt, J., Schupp, A., Vanderloock, A., Baesens, B.: Process mining for the multi-faceted analysis of business processes - a case study in a financial services organization. Computers in Industry 64(1), 57–67 (2013)
2. Esgin, E., Karagoz, P.: Sequence alignment adaptation for process diagnostics and delta analysis. In: Pan, J.-S., Polycarpou, M.M., Woźniak, M., de Carvalho, A.C.P.L.F., Quintián, H., Corchado, E. (eds.) HAIS 2013. LNCS (LNAI), vol. 8073, pp. 191–201. Springer, Heidelberg (2013)
3. Guo, A., Siegelmann, H.: Time-warped longest common subsequence algorithm for music retrieval. In: Buyoli, C.L., Loureiro, R. (eds.) Proceedings of 5th International Conference on Music Information Retrieval, ISMIR 2004, pp. 258–261. Universitat Pompeu Fabra (2004)
4. Gusfield, D.: Algorithms on Strings, Trees and Sequences: Computer Science and Computational Biology. Cambridge University Press (2008)
5. Hirschberg, D.S.: Algorithms for the longest common subsequence problem. J. ACM 24, 664–675 (1977)
6. Štolfa, S.J., Štolfa, S., Slaninová, K., Martinovič, J.: Searching time series based on pattern extraction using dynamic time warping. In: Proceedings of the Dateso 2014 Annual International Workshop on DAtabases, TExts, Specifications and Objects. CEUR Workshop Proceedings, pp. 81–90 (2014)
7. Kocyan, T., Martinovič, J., Dráždilová, P., Slaninová, K.: Searching time series based on pattern extraction using dynamic time warping. In: Proceedings of the Dateso 2013 Annual International Workshop on DAtabases, TExts, Specifications and Objects. CEUR Workshop Proceedings, pp. 129–138 (2013)
8. Müller, M.: Information Retrieval for Music and Motion. Springer (2007)
9. Slaninová, K., Kocyan, T., Martinovič, J., Dráždilová, P., Snášel, V.: Dynamic time warping in analysis of student behavioral patterns. In: Proceedings of the Dateso 2012 Annual International Workshop on DAtabases, TExts, Specifications and Objects. CEUR Workshop Proceedings, pp. 49–59 (2012)

10. Slaninová, K., Martinovič, J., Novosád, T., Dráždilová, P., Vojáček, L., Snášel, V.: Web site community analysis based on suffix tree and clustering algorithm. In: Proceedings of the 2011 IEEE/WIC/ACM International Joint Conferences on Web Intelligence and Intelligent Agent Technology - Workshops, WI-IAT 2011, pp. 110–113 (2011)

11. Slaninová, K., Martinovič, J., Šperka, R., Dráždilová, P.: Extraction of agent groups with similar behaviour based on agent profiles. In: Saeed, K., Chaki, R., Cortesi, A., Wierzchoń, S. (eds.) CISIM 2013. LNCS, vol. 8104, pp. 348–357. Springer, Heidelberg (2013)

12. van der Aalst, W., Weijters, A.: Process mining: A research agenda. Computers in Industry 53(3), 231–244 (2004)

13. van der Aalst, W., Weijters, A., Maruster, L.: Workflow mining: Discovering process models from event logs. Transaction on Knowledge and Data Engineering 16(9), 1128–1142 (2004)

14. van Dongen, B.F., de Medeiros, A.K.A., Verbeek, H.M.W., Weijters, A.J.M.M., van der Aalst, W.M.P.: The prom framework: A new era in process mining tool support. In: Ciardo, G., Darondeau, P. (eds.) ICATPN 2005. LNCS, vol. 3536, pp. 444–454. Springer, Heidelberg (2005)

15. Štolfa, J., Kopka, M., Štolfa, S., Koběrský, O., Snášel, V.: An application of process mining to invoice verification process in sap. In: Abraham, A., Krömer, P., Snášel, V. (eds.) Innovations in Bio-inspired Computing and Applications. AISC, vol. 237, pp. 61–74. Springer, Heidelberg (2014)

An Implementation of a Paper Based Authentication Using HC2D Barcode and Digital Signature

Puchong Subpratatsavee[1] and Pramote Kuacharoen[2]

[1] Department of Computer Science, Faculty of Science at Siracha
Kasetsart University Siracha Campus
199 Sukumvit Rd. Siracha, Chonburi 20230 Thailand
[2] Department of Computer Science, Graduate School of Applied Statistics
National Institute of Development Administration
118 Serithai Rd. Bangkapi, Bangkok 10240 Thailand
puchong.sp@gmail.com, pramote@as.nida.ac.th

Abstract. Paper-based documents are important and still widely used in government agencies and private entities as some documents cannot be replaced by electronic documents. These include loan agreements, dispatch or contracts, household registrations and passports. They must be paper-based. Paper-based documents can be easily forged with a printer and a scanner, and imaging software can easily edit them. This paper presents a paper-based document authentication by applying a digital signature and HC2D barcode to verify the integrity of the text message and the sender of the document. This is useful both for a quick inspection of documents with large quantities and monitoring that may help prevent fraud and forgery which may have occurred.

Keywords: HC2D barcode, paper-based document, digital signature, authentication.

1 Introduction

The documents in a paper format are still important and still widely used in organizations or for personal proposes because some documents cannot be replaced by an electronic document. Examples are loan agreements, driver licenses, passports, etc. [1]. These documents are often forged and easily modified by criminals. The forged documents in the form of paper can be accomplished by using a printer and a scanner, and imaging software. The devices are relatively inexpensive and easily obtained and the image software can be used to edit the documents. Therefore, it is difficult to prevent the forgery from fraudster [2]. Although there are attempts to prevent forgery by putting chemicals or watermarks on the documents, it makes monitoring more difficult because some types of the protected documents require an expert for monitoring and inspecting. Consequently, this can take a significant amount of time.

This paper presents the process of authentication of text on a paper-based document by applying a digital signature and a 2D barcode, specifically, HC2D barcode. Using this method, text on a paper-based document can be authenticated. This can

K. Saeed and V. Snášel (Eds.): CISIM 2014, LNCS 8838, pp. 592–601, 2014.

verify the document author if the document has not been tampered with and can detect whether or not the document has been altered by an unauthorized person. The paper based document can be verified without the need of special equipment or expertise. Moreover, this method is very convenient and inexpensive.

2   Background and Related Work

This section provides background information and related work.

2.1   2D Barcodes

2D barcodes [3] are geometric patterns in two dimensions. The two-dimension barcodes have more data capacity than one-dimensional barcodes while using a smaller space because they can store data in both vertical pixel and horizontal pixel directions to support a large information distribution and detection without accessing the database or any storage tools. Generally, 2D barcodes contain black square pixels on a white color background. Currently, the 2D barcodes that are common are QR Code [4][5], PDF417 barcode [6], Maxi Code, Aztec Code [7], and Data Matrix [8] [9]. However, HC2D barcode [10] has a higher capacity. The characteristics and properties of the 2D barcodes are show in Table 1.

Table 1. The characteristics and properties of 2D barcodes

	PDF417	Data Matrix	Maxi Code	QR Code	Aztec Code	HC2D barcode
Code type	Multi-low	Matrix	Matrix	Matrix	Matrix	Matrix
Capacity (Characters)	1,850	2,355	93	4,296	3,067	7,250
Characteristic	High capacity	High capacity, small	High speed reader	High capacity, small, high speed reader	High capacity	High capacity, small,
Applications	Office	Plant, medical industry	Industrial products import and export	All industries	Aviation and transport industries	Paper-based Document

A HC2D barcode is a 2D barcode, which consists of a black square pattern on white background. The HC2D barcode contains information in the vertical direction as well as the horizontal direction. The data capacity can be at a maximum of 7,250 numeric characters and 10,100 ASCII characters. HC2D barcodes use the Reed-Solomon [11] error correction, which can detect and correct multiple errors and HC2D barcodes have an option to compress data which allows a large amount of data to be stored [12]. HC2D barcodes can be read using a standard scanner and supporting software. The HC2D barcode has a greater capacity than other common 2D barcodes. Moreover, the shape of the HC2D barcode is suitable for use with paper documents or print media.

2.2   Cryptographic Hash Function

Cryptographic hash function is the hash function used for the purpose of safety information such as confirmation of identity to login (authentication) or to check the validity of the content, such as SHA-1 and MD5. Input data to the hash function can be varied in size and the hash function does not require any key. This result is called a hash value or a message digest with a fixed length and cannot be calculated back to the original message which is a one-way property. Hash function is often used for creating digital fingerprints which is used for checking whether or not the data has changed [13].

2.3   Digital Signature

Digital signature [14] is signature electronic that can be used to prove the identity of the sender or the signed document. It can verify the content of the message or data in document that it is an original and has not been altered or modified in transit. A digital signature can be done easily, but it cannot be mimicked, forged or modified by an unauthorized person because the digital signature uses asymmetric cryptography. This makes counterfeiting impossible and sender cannot deny responsibility (non-repudiation) of the information or document with the corresponding signature. The process of creating a digital signature is shown in Fig. 1.

The message is inputted to a mathematical process called a hash function to get a fixed-size data called message digest, because the original data is often very long which makes the signing process take longer. After that, the message digest is encrypted with private key of the sender. The signature can be used to authenticate the sender of the message since only the sender has knowledge of the private key. The encrypted message digest is called a digital signature. The digital signature is then sent to the recipient along with the original data.

In order to verify the digital signature, a message digest is derived through a hash function from the received data. The digital signature is decrypted with the sender's public key to obtain a message digest. Then, the two message digests are compared. If both values are identical, the data has not been modified and the signed message was sent from the owner of the public key. Hence, the sender cannot deny transmitting the message. However, if the values are different, it indicates that the received data has been modified during transit. The process of verifying a digital signature is illustrated in Fig. 2.

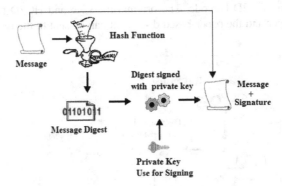

Fig. 1. The process of creating a digital signature

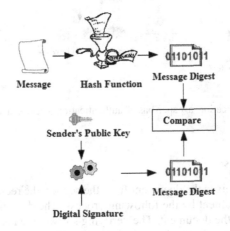

Fig. 2. The process of verifying a digital signature

3   Design and Implementation

In this section, the design and implementation of an implementation of a paper based authentication using HC2D barcode and digital signature is presented. By using our proposed method, the authentication of the paper-based document (plaintext) can be verified.

3.1   Sender Process

The sender prepares a message and starts the process of creating a digital signature. The message is passed through the hash function to obtain the corresponding message digest. The resulting value is then encrypted with the private key of the sender. The resulting value is a digital signature. Both original message and the digital signature are used in the process of creating HC2D barcode. The original message and HC2D barcode are then printed on the paper and the paper-based document can be sent to the recipient as shown in Fig. 3.

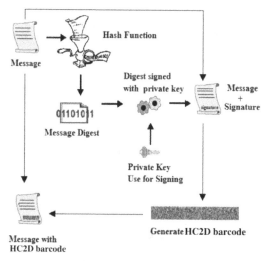

Fig. 3. The process of creating a paper-based authentication document using HC2D barcode and digital signature

3.2   Receiver Process

When the recipient receives the document from the sender, the recipient can verify the authenticity of the document by the following process. The document is first scanned to obtain the image of the document. The verifying software reads the HC2D barcode and then obtains the data in the barcode using the Reed-Solomon error correcting code to detect and correct errors that may occur during shipping. The HC2D barcode may have been distorted or damaged. After successfully decoding using the Reed-Solomon error correcting code, the obtained data is decompressed (if data is compressed) to obtain the actual data which is a message from a sender and a digital signature. The digital signature part is decrypted with a public key. The message part is inputted to the hash function to obtain the message digest. Both message digests are compared. If they are identical, the information in the barcode has not been altered.

The text on the document can be recognized using OCR function to obtain the original text of the document. The data is passed through the hash function to get message digest which is used to compare with the message digest obtained from the HC2D barcode. If both values are the same, the text on the document is accurate and has not been modified in transit. If they are different, it may be possible that the text on the document may have been modified during transit or may be possibly due to errors of the OCR. If this occurs, the recipient must visually compare the text on the document and the text in the HD2B barcode. The verifying software can overlay the documents or put them side by side and highlight the positions that are different. The verifying process is shown in Fig. 4.

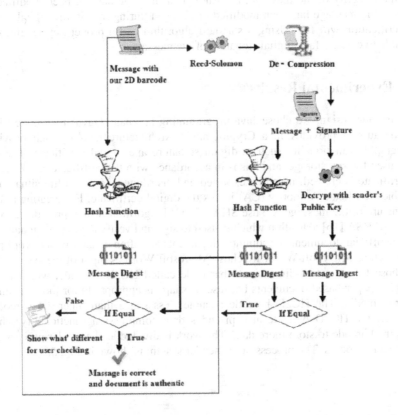

Fig. 4. The verifying process of the paper based authentication using HC2D barcode and digital signature

4   Security Analysis

This research uses a digital signature technique to provide security of the data on the document. This is because the digital signature can be used to verify whether or not the original content of the message or document has not changed or been modified in transit. The sender can efficiently create a digital signature. However, it is infeasible for an unauthorized person to modify the text or document and generate the digital signature as the sender. A digital signature is used for authentication because before the sender sends a message, the message digest of the message is encrypted with the sender's private key, which is only known by the sender, and only the sender's public key can be used to decrypt the digital signature. Successful digital signature verification implies that the message was actually sent by the sender and has not been modified in transit. As a result, the sender cannot deny responsibility for creating the message. This provides non-repudiation of the message since the sender has to encrypt the message digest with the corresponding private key. The capabilities of a digital signature, as mentioned above, would show that the digital signature also provides the integrity of the message; it ensures that message has not been modified in transit. If the message has been modified or changed during transit, the digital signature verification will fail. Using a standard algorithm and a proper key length, it is infeasible to create a fake digital signature of the message.

5   Experimental Results

To verify our design, we chose Java programming language (Java) for the development because it provides Java Cryptographic Architecture (JCA) which provides cryptographic functionality such as digital signature and digital certificate. The key tool is used for key storage, and this is in accordance with the certificate X.509. After the certificate is created, it can be exported and distributed. In a real life situation, a reputable Certificate Authority (CA) issues the digital certificate. For creating a digital signature of the message, we use SHA-256 [15] algorithm, which provides 256-bit output and RSA [16] algorithm which is used to sign and verify the digital signature.

Since official documents or common documents are often created with a word processor such as Microsoft Word, we chose Microsoft Word as input of the system. We also chose to use a two-dimensional bar code called HC2D barcode, which is designed for paper-based documents because its shape is appropriate for the attachment and print media. The HC2D barcode occupies less space than other 2D barcodes. Moreover, the HC2D barcode also provides data compression functionality which allows the barcode to store more data. The work is divided as the sender process and the recipient process. The process of the sender system is shown in Fig. 5.

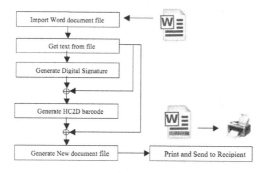

Fig. 5. The process of the sender system

The process begins as the sender enters Microsoft Word file into the system. The software obtains the text from the document, and then the system will create a digital signature from text with sender's private key, generate a HC2D barcode containing the message and the digital signature, and finally attaches it to the message. A new document which consists of the original text and the HC2D barcode is generated and can be printed on paper. The process of the receiver system is shown in Fig. 6.

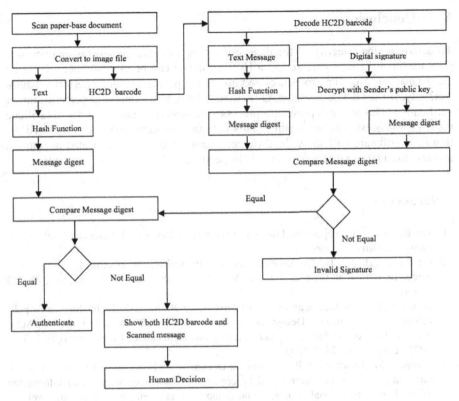

Fig. 6. The process of the receiver system

When the recipient receives the document from the sender, the paper document must be scanned as an image. The image of the HC2D barcode is processed. The system will decode HC2D barcode to get the message and the digital signature. Then the digital signature which is read from HC2D barcode is decrypted with the sender's public key to obtain the message digest. The text message from HC2D barcode is passed through a hash function to obtain another message digest. Subsequently, both message digests are compared. If they are equal, the HC2D barcode contains the original message which was sent by the sender and has not been modified in transit. The printed text message on the paper is also read using OCR. The obtained text is hashed to obtain a message digest which is used to compare with the message digest from HC2D barcode. If both message digests are identical, the document is valid and has not been modified in transit. It also confirms that the document was actually sent by the sender who is the owner of the public key. On the other hand, if they do not match, it may be possible that the text on the document may have been modified during transit or may be possibly due to errors of the OCR. The system will display the differences between the two texts. This allows the user to visually verify them.

6 Conclusion

To determine the integrity of the data in the form of paper documents or published print media, a digital signature and a HC2D barcode can be used without relying on the database or file. The procedures and inspection processes can be performed automatically, if the OCR is accurate. Otherwise, a human is required to perform further verification. This research presents a process with semi-automatic in order to facilitate the review process. The verification starts with the automatic process. If the verification fails, software will show the difference between the data on printed documents and text from HC2D barcode for human inspection.

References

1. van Renesse, R.L.: Paper-based document security–A Review. In: European Conf. on Security and Detection (1997)
2. Garain, U., Halder, B.: On automatic authenticity verification of printed security documents. In: 6th Indian Conf. on Comput. Vision, Graphics & Image Process., pp. 706–713 (2008)
3. Gao, J.Z., Prakash, L., Jagatesan, R.: Understanding 2D-BarCode Technology and Applications in M-Commerce – Design and Implementation of A 2D Barcode Processing Solution. In: 31st Annual Intl. Computer Software and Applications Conference (COMPSAC 2007), Beijing, July 24-27 (2007)
4. Warasart, M., Kuacharoen, P.: Paper-based Document Authentication using Digital Signature and QR Code. In: International Proceedings of Computer Science and Information Technology, International Conference on Computer Engineering and Technology, vol. 40, pp. 94–98 (2012) ISSN 2010-460X
5. QR Code, http://www.denso-wave.com/qrcode/
6. Rong, C., et al.: Coding Principle and Implementation of Two-Dimensional PDF417 Bar code. In: 6th IEEE Conference on Industrial Electronics and Applications, pp. 466–468 (2011)
7. Ke, H., Zhang, G.: An Algorithm Correcting Flex Distortion of Aztec Code. In: 2nd IEEE International Conference on Information Management and Engineering, pp. 457–460 (2010)
8. Biao, L.: A DataMatrix-based mutant code design and recognition method research. In: Proceedings of the 4th International Conference on Image and Graphics, pp. 570–574 (2007)
9. Data Matrix, http://en.wikipedia.org/wiki/Data_Matrix
10. Subpratatsavee, P., Kuacharoen, P.: An Implementation of a High Capacity 2D Bar-code. In: Papasratorn, B., Charoenkitkarn, N., Lavangnananda, K., Chutimaskul, W., Vanijja, V. (eds.) IAIT 2012. CCIS, vol. 344, pp. 159–169. Springer, Heidelberg (2012)
11. Mamidi, S., et al.: Instruction Set Extensions for Reed-Solomon Encoding and Decoding. In: 16th IEEE International Conference on Application-Specific Systems, Architecture Processors, pp. 364–369 (2005)
12. Islam, M.R., Ahsan Rajon, S.A.: An Enhanced for Lossless Compression of Short Text for Resource Constrained Devices. In: 14th International Conference on Computer and Information Technology, pp. 292–297 (2011)

13. Singh, M., Garg, D.: Choosing best hashing strategies and hash functions. In: Int. Advance Computing Conf., pp. 50–55 (2009)
14. Kuacharoen, P.: Design and Analysis of Methods for Signing Electronic Documents Using Mobile Phones. In: International Conference on Computer Applications and Network Security (ICCANS 2011), pp. 154–158 (May 2011)
15. SHA-2, http://en.wikipedia.org/wiki/SHA-2
16. RSA Cryptography Standard, PKCS #1 v2.1 (2002)

Grasping Action for Impaired Vision Action Using HC2D Barcode Technology

Puchong Subpratatsavee and Suchai Tanaiadehawoot

Faculty of Science at Siracha, Kasetsart University Siracha Campus
199 Sukumvit Rd. Siracha, Chonburi 20230 Thailand
puchong.sp@gmail.com, fscisut@ku.ac.th

Abstract. Nowadays, There are many people who have impaired vision. It is hard to do for weak-eyed man to sense a range because of their blurry vision. Therefore they often feel complication in grasping objects. It is useful to design and implement a system presenting the distance between a hand and an object for low vision people. In this paper, we propose a method to estimate the distance between a camera and an object surface on which a HC2D barcode is pasted. In this research, we assume the camera is worn on hand and the HC2D barcode with information embedded is pasted on the surface of object. The distance between the camera and the HC2D barcode, which is attached on the object, is estimated comparison the actual size of the HC2D barcode with the size of HC2D barcode that snap or capture from the camera.

Keywords: HC2D barcode, impaired vision, camera, grasping action.

1   Introduction

According to the recent day, the lot of number of people with visual impairment in the world is low vision people. And people with visual impairment are elderly people who are old. It seems that the number of low vision people in the world increases much more. From these facts, developing a system, which supports low vision people's daily life, is necessary. Compared to the healthy people's vision (Fig. 1), low vision people's visibilities vary according to every individual symptom, such as blurry, crooked, and restricted visions. The visibility, of which an example is as shown in Fig. 2, might bring on tipping things and missing in grasping. And also, these difficulties could give low visions much stress. Indeed a lot of studies have been devoted with respect to support systems in reading characters, but there are few attempts to support in grasping things. In this paper, we propose a grasp action support system for visually impaired persons using HC2D barcodes [1] and a camera. This system can present the distance between the camera and the HC2D barcode, which is attached on the object surface by comparing the real size of HC2D barcode with the apparent size of HC2D barcode in the camera. In addition, the system can guide hands to the object's direction. The proposed system can be easily applied to support system presenting the distance perception by wearing the camera on hand. The effectiveness of proposed system is verified through some experiments.

K. Saeed and V. Snášel (Eds.): CISIM 2014, LNCS 8838, pp. 602–614, 2014.
© IFIP International Federation for Information Processing 2014

Fig. 1. Vision of healthy people   **Fig. 2.** Simulated low vision people's visibilities

2   Overviews

In this section, the way to use the proposed system is explained. The purpose of system is to guide user's hand to the object on table safely by showing distance and direction information from the hand and an object. The user wears a small, lightweight camera on the hand. Cordless cameras are recommended so as to prevent the user from interfering in daily life. In using the system, captured images are transferred to processing equipment. And the distance and direction information are estimated when the system detects a HC2D barcode. It is useless for the visually impaired to show the distance and direction information in display because they cannot see anything. Therefore, this information are shown user by voice sound. If the captured HC2D barcode which is pasted on the object run off the center of camera coordinate at following the voice sound, voice sound guides the direction again to capture the HC2D barcode at the center. By repeating this operation, user's hand is guided to the object.

3   Background and Related Works

In this paper, we propose a new distance estimation method using a HC2D barcode and a camera. The reasons why we use HC2D barcode are shown as indicated below.

1. A special camera is unnecessary
2. It is easy to create HC2D barcode by using web sites.
3. The distance estimation can be quickly because HC2D barcodes can be read fast.
4. Extension of function is done easily by embedding some data in HC2D barcode such as the object's name.

In some research explain about distance estimation method using different-aperture images [2] using tilted lens optics. This method uses two different focus images. Comparing amount of the blur between these images performs distance estimation. However, this method needs to vary the aperture of camera at high speed in continuity. Therefore, it is hard to say this method is suitable for real-time processing. Some research show proposed method using a standing wave of audible sound. This method uses standing wave, which is generated by phase interference of transmitted and reflected waves. Using standing wave of audible sound [3], distance estimation is possible at the close distance. However, this method takes long time for calculating the distance. In addition, uses stereo images to estimate distance. Distance is estimated by the gap of corresponding areas. However, these methods do not use marker. It is not able to capture the target object. The purpose of this study is to guide a hand to object for visually impaired person. Therefore, it is hard to say this method is suitable for this study. As another approach, there is a method to use a compact compound-eye camera system: TOMBO [4]. However, TOMBO is special camera. In this study, a standard monocular camera is used from the viewpoint of availability and tractability.

4   Proposed Method

In this study, the distance between camera and the object is estimated by camera and HC2D barcode embedding the HC2D barcode's shape information. Let the camera focal length f [m], distance between HC2D barcode and camera z[m], size of HC2D barcode in the captured image a[pix], and real size of HC2D barcode b[m]. The relation of these symbols is shown in Fig. 3. As we can see, the distance between the camera and the HC2D barcode is calculated based two homologous triangles including camera focal length, the size of HC2D barcode in the captured image, and the real size of HC2D barcode. Processing flow of this study is shown as indicated below.

1. Get a captured image
2. Detect the region of HC2D barcode
3. Extract information of HC2D barcode
4. Estimate distance using the information of HC2D barcode
5. Show the distance the way to detect the region of HC2D barcode, way to estimate distance by using the information of HC2D barcode, and way to show the direction of object are explained in next section.

4.1   Detection of HC2D Barcode

In this section, the mathematical descriptions with respect to the distance estimation are explained. Suppose a camera coordinate is represented as (x; y; z) (Fig. 6), the coordinate is transformed into the image plane coordinate by perspective transformation as follows.

4.2   Distance Estimation

Three of four HC2D barcode's vertex has a distinctive mark called "finder pattern" (Fig. 4). HC2D barcode is distinguished by detecting these marks. To detect finder pattern, the following process are applied to the captured image.

1. Binarize the captured image.
2. Extract the contour information.
3. Detect and save a square using the contour information.
4. Check up the square whether it has Small Square in itself.

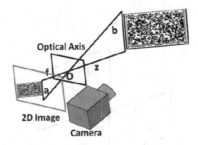

Fig. 3. Relationship of the camera and HC2D barcode

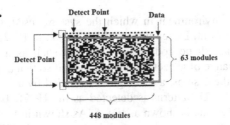

Fig. 4. HC2D barcode

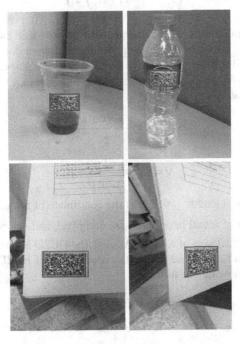

Fig. 5. Detection result of HC2D barcode

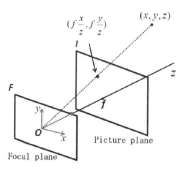

Fig. 6. Coordinate system

Assuming a realistic environment in which the systems used, the HC2D barcode is not always facing the front. Depending on the direction of HC2D barcode against for the camera, the square-shape code looks distorted such as a rectangle-shape one. Therefore, a certain range of aspect ratio is configured so that a little deviation is tolerated. At the end of these steps, a rectangle surrounded by a straight line connecting among the detected finder patterns is detected as the HC2D barcode. The result of detection of HC2D barcode is shown as Fig. 5. As shown in Fig. 5, if the HC2D barcode is taken on a skew in captured image, it is detected as HC2D barcode.

$$(x, y, z) \rightarrow (f\frac{x}{z}, f\frac{y}{z}). \tag{1}$$

Indeed the above notation "(1)," is true in case of an ideal model, but the angle formed by x-axis and y-axis in the camera coordinate system does not definitely correspond to the angle θ formed by u-axis and v-axis in image plane. By considering the actual angle θ, a coordinate $(x; y; z)$ is transformed to a point $(u; v)$ in the image plane by the following equations:

$$u = fk_u \bullet \frac{x + y\cot\theta}{z} + u_0 \tag{2}$$

$$v = fk_v \bullet \frac{y}{z\sin\theta} + v_0 \tag{3}$$

Where f [m] is the focal length, $(u0; v0)$ is the coordinate of image center, k_u [pix/m] is the inverse number of actual horizontal size of a pixel, and k_v [pix/m] is the inverse number of actual vertical size of a pixel. Assume the HC2D barcode is a-pixel square in the image plane and $u1$ and $u2$ are vertex coordinates of HC2D barcode, a[pix] is represented as the following equations:

$$a = u_1 - u_2 \tag{4}$$

Substituting the "(2)," to the "(4)," the following notation can be obtained:

$$a = fk_u \frac{x_1 - x_2}{z} \tag{5}$$

Assume the real size of HC2D barcode is b[m], it is represented by the following equation:

$$b = x_1 - x_2 \tag{6}$$

Substituting the "(6)," to the "(5)," the following equation is obtained:

$$z = fk_u \bullet \frac{b}{a} \tag{7}$$

According to the "(7)," camera's focal length f [m], distance between HC2D barcode and camera z[m], size of HC2D barcode in the captured image a[pix] and real size of HC2D barcode b[m] has proportional relation. From this point forward, the distance estimation is performed on the basis of the "(7)".

4.3   Guide Process

Two separated parts construct the guide method. One is a direction guide process to guide the user's hand to the object, and the other is distance guide process to announce the distance between the hand and the object.

4.3.1   Direction Guide

Captured image is separated 9 parts (Fig. 7). Direction guide is decided by detected position of HC2D barcode. There are 8 kinds of direction to guide the hand, such as "upper", "upper left", "upper right", "left", "right", "lower", "lower left", and "lower right". HC2D barcode's gravity center is calculated by detected HC2D barcode and direction of HC2D barcode is announced like "upper", "under left", by considering where the gravity point is found in separated parts. When the gravity point fit in the center of captured image, the hand is guided to the object after the distance between the hand and the object is announced.

4.3.2   Distance Guide

Distance between the camera and the object is calculated by "(7)," and user is informed the information of distance and direction by voice sound. When the HC2D barcode's gravity point fits in the center of captured image, the distance is read aloud for user. If the center of captured image does not fit the gravity point of HC2D barcode, voice sound announces the direction of the HC2D barcode again to fit the center point in gravity point. The system guides hand to the object by repeating this process. When the distance between hand and the object is short in under 5cm, voice sound saying that "please close your hand".

5   Experimental Results

5.1   Measuring the Accuracy of Distance Estimation

Distance estimation is conducted by HC2D barcode and camera using "(7)". In addition, the value of f in "(7)" is calculated by camera calibration. Value of is calculated by (Fig. 7). In "(7)" substituting a at z=0.05[m]. In this experiment, the values of f and are used 838 and 0.686, respectively. As described at section of "HC2D barcode detection", the camera does not always capture HC2D barcode from an anterior view in realistic environment. Within a captured image, there is a possibility of being reflected in the form where HC2D barcode was reflected aslant or was distorted. Therefore, distance estimations are attempted in some situations to evaluate the accuracy of estimated distance. The situation where distance estimation is performed is as follows.

1. When camera confront with HC2D barcode set as 0 degrees and measure distance which gradually changing the angle.
2. Estimate distance is performed at 3 patterns, which the HC2D barcode is attached on cylinder, prism and cone (Fig. 8).

The start of the estimate distance between HC2D barcode and camera is 0.03[m], and estimate distance interval is 0.005[m]. If distance between camera and HC2D barcode will be less than 0.03[m], HC2D barcode cannot fit within the captured image.

upper left	upper	upper right
left		right
lower left	lower	lower right

Fig. 7. Separate the captured image system

5.2   Distance Estimation When HC2D Barcode and a Camera Turn to the Front

At first, distance estimation is conducted by camera and HC2D barcode, which is attached on flat plate surface. The estimated distance and true distance is summarized in graph. Axis of abscissas is true distance D_t and axis of ordinate is error E. The error is calculated by estimated distance D_e and true distance. If estimated distance is longer than true distance, the error is plotted with a positive value. By contraries, if estimated distance is shorter than true distance, the error is plotted with a negative value. The equation to calculate the error is shown as "(8)"

$$E = \frac{D_e - D_t}{D_t} * 100 \tag{8}$$

Fig. 9 shows result of distance estimation when HC2D barcode and a camera turn to the front. The error was less than 5% and error was further reduced at close range.

According to this result, our proposed method can estimate correct distance in this situation.

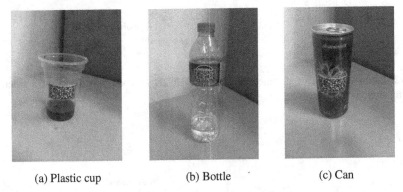

(a) Plastic cup   (b) Bottle   (c) Can

Fig. 8. Attached place of HC2D barcode

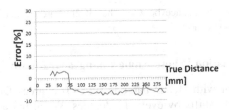

Fig. 9. Estimated error of distance between HC2D barcode and a camera turn to the front

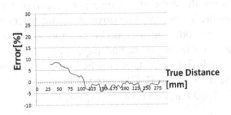

Fig. 10. Estimated error of distance between the HC2D barcode and the camera when the shooting angle is 15 degrees

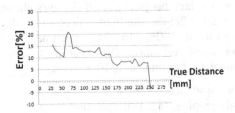

Fig. 11. Estimated error of distance between the HC2D barcode and the camera when the shooting angle is 30 degrees

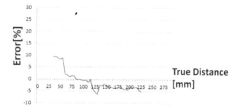

Fig. 12. Estimated error of distance between the HC2D barcode and the camera when the shooting angle is 45 degrees

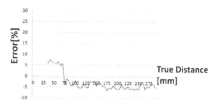

Fig. 13. Estimated error of distance between the HC2D barcode and the camera when the HC2D barcode is pasted on cone

5.3   Distance Estimation Whose Angle Changes Gradually

When camera confront with HC2D barcode set as 0 degrees Distance estimation is performed whose angle shifts by every 15 degrees. When the angle exceeds 60 degrees, HC2D barcode did not recognize as HC2D barcode even if it is in the capture image. According to Figs. 10-12, in each angle, the accuracy of close range is lower than Fig.9. However, when the error of distance is replaced to real distance, it is only a several millimeters error. Therefore, this error does not affect action of grasp. The next experiment, HC2D barcode was attached on cylinder, prism and cone. We used tin can as cylinder, PET bottle as prism, and paper cup as cone. According to Figs. 13-15, the error of which HC2D barcode is attached on cylinder and cone, is similar at Fig. 9. However, the error of which HC2D barcode is attached on prism is huge. Furthermore, detection of HC2D barcode is difficult in this case.

5.4   Assessment of Support System of Grasp Action

Next, proposed system is evaluated by examinee by grasping the object using the system. First, examinees (sighted peoples) cut off the eyesight by taking a blindfold and put the camera on hand. After the blindfold, object, which the HC2D barcode has attached on, is set up on the desk (Fig. 16). The experiment whether the examinees can grasp the object or not is performed. The experiment environment is shown as indicated below. The number of examinees is 10 persons.

1. Examinees take a blindfold and do not wear the camera. They grasp the object at cluttered desk by only groping (Fig. 17): Valuation 1.
2. Examinees take a blindfold and wear the camera. They grasp the object using the system at desk put on the object only: Valuation 2.

3. Examinees take a blindfold and wear the camera. They grasp the object using the system at cluttered desk: Valuation 3.

5.4.1   A. Valuation Method

Examinees are had a questionnaire at 5 grade evaluation. The item of the question-naire is shown as indicated below.

- Usability of the direction guide
- Usability of the distance guide
- Usability of this system

5.4.2   Result of Valuations

The result of valuation 1 is shown as Table 1. 7 of 10 blindfolded examinees could grasp the object at the cluttered desk by only groping. In this experiment, one exami-nee could grasp object, but he tipped other object on the desk. An average time the examinees grasp the object is 23 second. This experiment used only feeling of exami-nee's hand. Therefore, there are some cases that they tipped an object because of the difference between the examinee's imaged distance and the real distance. If it replaces to actual environment, it is dangerous for visually impaired persons to look for some-thing only groping. If the tipped thing is hot drink, they get burned. We feed off the feedback from the examinees.

- It takes a long time to recognize that a touched object is target object or not be-cause it is necessary that a touched object is confirmed carefully.
- It is dangerous that if there are some easily tipped things on the desk.

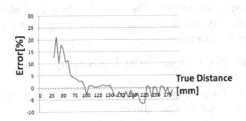

Fig. 14. Estimated error of distance between the HC2D barcode and the camera when the HC2D barcode is pasted on cylinder

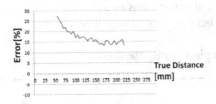

Fig. 15. Estimated error of distance between the HC2D barcode and the camera when the HC2D barcode is pasted on prism

Fig. 16. Object, which the HC2D barcode has attached on

Fig. 17. The experiment considering-actual environment

Next, the result of valuation 2 is shown as Table 2. The value of "Usability of the direction guide", "Usability of the distance guide", and "Usability of this system" are shown at average point. In this experiment, there was only the object on the desk. Therefore, all examinees could grasp the object without the tipping. All items of usability value is over 3.5. There is little variability among the examinees, but it seems to be good result. We feed off the feedback from the examinees. Sometimes, examinees feel difficulties that how long the camera moves. If the HC2D barcode's gravity point fits the center of captured image, it can grasp easily the object. It is necessary to get used to this system At last, the result of valuation 3 is shown as Table 3 and Table 4. The value of "Usability of the direction guide", "Usability of the distance guide", and "Usability of this system" are also shown at mean opinion score (MOS) [5]. As compared to the result of valuations 1, all examinees could grasp the object without the tipping. An average time is 4 second faster than the result of valuations 1. Therefore, the information from the camera could guide examinee to the object. In addition, the evaluation of usability is better than the result of valuation 2. It is because that the examinees get used to this system. These results show they alleviate their a burden on grasping action in daily life if users acquire proficiency in this system. We feed off the feedback from the examinees.

- When comparing the experiment 1, it is easily to grasp the object by using this system's information.
- If the HC2D barcode out of the captured image, the system cannot inform the information of distance and direction.

Table 1. Result of practical experiments on using only groping

	A number of examinee
The target was grasped, and nothing was tipped.	6
The target was grasped, but other object was tipped.	1
The target was tipped.	3
An average time the examinees grasp the object	23 Second

Table 2. Mean option score at valuation 2. higher score is better. A number of examinee is 10. (1: BAD, 2: POOR, 3: FAIR, 4: GOOD, 5: EXCELLENT.)

Average Operate time	Usability of the direction guide	Usability of the distance guide	Usability of system
15.5 Second	3.6/5	3.5/5	3.5/5

Table 3. Result of practical experiments on using the system

	A number of examinee
The target was grasped, and nothing was tipped	10
The target was grasped, but other object was tipped	0
The target was tipped	0
An average time the examinees grasp the object	19.3 Second

Table 4. Mean option score at valuation 3. higher score is better. A number of examinee is 10. (1: BAD, 2: POOR, 3: FAIR, 4: GOOD, 5: EXCELLENT.)

Usability of the direction guide	Usability of the distance guide	Usability of system
3.7/5	3.3/5	3.7/5

6   Conclusion

In this paper, we propose distance estimation and guide system using HC2D barcode and a camera. This system can present distance between camera and HC2D barcode, which is attached on the object surface by comparing the real size of HC2D barcode with the size of HC2D barcode in the camera. In addition, the system can guide hands to the object's direction by capturing the HC2D barcode's position. By using this system, the visually impaired person's daily life ameliorates much more. In the experiment, we performed two prominent types of performs considering the actually environment. One is the measure of accuracy about distance estimation. We performed some experiments considering the actually environment and got a good result for this. Another is the validation of usability of guide system. The target object is set up on the desk with other object, and examinee grasped the target object using this system or does not. As a result, the value of valuation is over 3.5 point. All examinees could grasp the object by using this system, but 40% of examinees could not grasp the object by only using groping. Therefore, these results show this system's effectiveness. However, some examinees felt difficulties that how long they move their hand and where they move the hand if the camera drop off the HC2D barcode. To resolve this problem, the separation of captured image must become finer, and the direction will be announced more properly.

References

1. Subpratatsavee, P., Kuacharoen, P.: An Implementation of a High Capacity 2D Barcode. In: Papasratorn, B., Charoenkitkarn, N., Lavangnananda, K., Chutimaskul, W., Vanijja, V. (eds.) IAIT 2012. CCIS, vol. 344, pp. 159–169. Springer, Heidelberg (2012)
2. Pentland, A., et al.: A simple, real-time range camera. In: IEEE Computer Society Conference on Computer Vision and Pattern Recognition, pp. 256–261 (1989)
3. Ohmata, N., Uebo, T., Nakasako, N., Shinohara, T.: A trial on implementation of distance estimation method based on standing wave of audible sound. IEEJ. Transactions on Electronics, Information and Systems 129, 314–319 (2009)
4. Tanida, J., Kumagai, T., Yamada, K., Miyatake, S., Ishida, K., Morimoto, T., Ichioka, Y.: Thin observation module by bound optics (TOMBO): concept and experimental verification. Applied Optics 40(11), 1806–1813 (2001)
5. Viswanathan, M., Viswanathan, M.: Measuring speech quality for text-to-speech systems: development and assessment of a modified mean opinion score (MOS) scale. Computer Speech & Language 19(1), 55–83 (2005)

Hardware Approach for Generating b-detectors by Immune-Based Algorithms

Maciej Brzozowski and Andrzej Chmielewski

Faculty of Computer Science, Białystok University of Technology,
ul. Wiejska 45a, 15-331 Białystok, Poland
{m.brzozowski,a.chmielewski}@pb.edu.pl

Abstract. The most interesting feature of negative selection algorithms is ability for detecting novel, never met anomalies. This is especially important in security systems like intrusion detection, spam, virus detection, etc. However, the main problem is scalability which occurs for both: binary and real-valued representation. This paper describes a hardware implementations of the process of generating b-detectors which allows for a fast generation the receptors as well as a very fast recognition of anomalies in high-dimensional datasets.

Keywords: artificial immune system, anomaly detection, hardware implementation.

1 Introduction

Natural immune system (NIS) prevents living organism against intruders called *pathogens*. It consists of a number of cells, tissues, and organs that work together to protect the body. The main agents responsible for the adaptive and learning capabilities of the NIS are white blood cells called *lymphocytes*. These differentiate into two primary types: B- and T-lymphocytes called also B- and T-cells for brevity. T-lymphocytes are like the body's military intelligence system, seeking out their targets and sending defenses to lock onto them. Next, B-lymphocytes, destroys detected invaders to protected the body. It is only a very short description of NIS; an unacquainted reader is referred e.g. to [3] for further details.

The mechanisms and procedures developed within NIS were an inspiration for *Artificial Immune Systems* (AIS). One of them is *negative selection* oriented towards fast and efficient discrimination between own cells (called *self*) and pathogens (called *nonself*). Additionally, it helps the body against self-reactive lymphocytes. A nice feature is that it does not need examples of *nonself* samples (counterpart of pathogens) to detect them. The information about own cells is sufficient. Hence, every organism has a unique "protection system", capable of detecting even new type of attacks. This is an inspiration to build a computer security systems (e.g. firewall).

A key problem when applying *negative selection algorithm* (*NSA*) in real-life application is scalability. To detect spam or intruders at computer networks *NSA*

K. Saeed and V. Snášel (Eds.): CISIM 2014, LNCS 8838, pp. 615–623, 2014.

should be able operate on high-dimensional data. Moreover, in such domains, the classification is performed online, without significant delays, what makes this task much more difficult to solve. This descriptions correspond to NIS, where only fast and effective response on intruders activity can protect organisms against damaging or even die. To overcome this problem, many solution were proposed, including hybrid b-v model [4], emloying binary (called b-detectors) and real-valued detectors (called v-detectors) to increase the efficiency, especially in case of classification process.

In this paper, we present hardware implementations of NSA for b-detectors, where most of computationally complex operations can be paralellized and done within a few ticks of clock. This is the first step towards hardware firewall embedded in a reprogrammable FPGA (see Section 3). Such solution makes that rules in security systems are not hardcoded and updating the set of detectors is possible. Finally, there are compared two possible approaches: combinational and pipeline.

2 Negative Selection Algorithm

The NSA, proposed by Forrest *et al.*, [6], is inspired by the process of thymocytes (i.e. young T-lymphocytes) maturation: only those lymphocytes survive which do not recognize any *self* molecules.

Formally, let $\mathcal{U}$ be a universe, i.e. the set of all possible molecules. The subset $\mathcal{S}$ of $\mathcal{U}$ represents collection of all *self* molecules and its complement $\mathcal{N}$ in $\mathcal{U}$ represents all *nonself* molecules. Let $\mathfrak{D} \subset \mathcal{U}$ stands for a set of detectors and let $match(d, u)$ be a function (or a procedure) specifying if a detector $d \in \mathfrak{D}$ recognizes the molecule $u \in \mathcal{U}$. Usually, $match(d, u)$ is modeled by a distance metric or a similarity measure, i.e. we say that $match(d, u) = \texttt{true}$ only if $dist(d, u) \leq \delta$, where $dist$ is a distance and δ is a pre-specified threshold. Various matching function are discussed in [7], [10].

The problem relies upon construction the set $\mathfrak{D}$ in such a way that

$$match(d, u) = \begin{cases} \texttt{false if } u \in \mathcal{S} \\ \texttt{true} \ \ \text{if } u \in \mathcal{N} \end{cases} \tag{1}$$

for any detector $d \in \mathfrak{D}$.

A naive solution to this problem, implied by biological mechanism of negative selection, consists of five steps:

(a) Initialize $\mathfrak{D}$ as empty set, $\mathfrak{D} = \emptyset$.
(b) Generate randomly a detector d.
(c) If $math(d, s) = \texttt{false}$ for all $s \in \mathcal{S}$, add d to the set $\mathfrak{D}$.
(d) Repeat steps (b) and (c) until sufficient number of detectors will be generated.

So far, there were considered two types of detectors: b- and v-detectors [9]. Usually, each of them were used separately, except b-v model [4]. In this paper, we focus only on binary representation.

In case of binary encoding, the universe $\mathcal{U}$ becomes l-dimensional Hamming space, $\mathbb{H}^l = \{0,1\}^l$, consisting of all binary strings of fixed length l:

$$\mathbb{H}^l = \{\underbrace{000...000}_{l}, \underbrace{000...001}_{l}, \ldots, \underbrace{111...111}_{l}\}$$

Hence the size of this space is 2^l. The most popular matching rules used in this case are:

(a) r-contiguous bit rule [5], or
(b) r-chunks [1].

Both the rules say that a detector bonds a sample (i.e. data) only when both the strings contain the same substring of length r. To detect a sample in case (a), a window of length r ($1 \leq r \leq l$) is shifted through censored samples of length l. In case (b) the detector $t_{i,\mathbf{s}}$ is specified by a substring $\mathbf{s}$ of length r and its position i in the string. Below an example of matching a sample by r-detector (left) and r-chunk for affinity threshold $r = 3$ is given

$$\overbrace{1\,0\,0\,0\,1\,1\,1\,0}^{l} \qquad \leftarrow \text{sample} \rightarrow \qquad \overbrace{1\,0\,0\,0\,1\,1\,1\,0}^{l}$$

$$0\,1\,\underbrace{0\,0\,1}_{r}\,0\,0\,1 \leftarrow r\text{-detector; } r\text{-chunk} \rightarrow *\,*\,\underbrace{0\,0\,1}_{r}\,*\,*\,*$$

Here it was assumed that irrelevant positions in a string of length l representing the r-chunk $t_{3,001}$ are filled in with the star ($*$) symbol. This way r-chunk can be identified with schemata used in genetic algorithms: its order equals r and its defining length is $r-1$. Although a single r-detector recognizes much more strings than a single r-chunk, this last type of detector allows more accurate coverage of the $\mathcal{N}$ space [1].

Further, the notion of the ball of recognition allows to define "optimal" repertoire $\mathfrak{D}$. Namely it consists of the detectors located in $\mathbb{H}^l$ in such a way that they cover the space $\mathcal{N}$ and their balls of recognition overlap minimally. A solution to such stated problem was given in [14]. To construct the r-detectors we split all the *self* strings into the templates represented identically as the r-chunks and we construct the detectors by gluing these r-chunks that do not belong to the set S. More formally, if $t_{i,\mathbf{s}}$ and $t_{j,\mathbf{w}}$ are two candidate r-chunks, we can glue them if both the substrings are identical on $r-1$ positions starting from position $i+1$.

Using such an optimality criterion we come to the conclusion that shortest detectors are more desirable as they are able to detect more samples. However, Stibor [12] showed the coherence between r and l values for various cardinalities of S in terms of the probability of generating detectors, P_g. He distinguished three phases:

- Phase 1 (for lower r) – the probability P_g is near to 0,
- Phase 2 (for middle r) – the probability P_g rapidly grows from 0 to 1 (so called *Phase Transition Region*),
- Phase 3 (for higher r) – the probability is very near to 1.

Hence, we should be interested in generating detectors with medium length r (belonging to the second region) and eventually with larger values of r if the coverage of $\mathcal{N}$ is not sufficient.

In case of software approach, the detectors can not be too long, due to exponential increase in the duration of learning process, which should be finished in reasonable time. That was a main reason why b-detectors were not used to solve problems in high-dimensional datasets. In litetaure, we find that longest binary samples ($l = 49$) were used to model the system for monitoring TCP SYN packets to detect network traffic anomalies (called LISYS) [8]. In Section 3, we show, that detectors even with $l = 95$ can be generated in just a few ticks of clocks in case of hardware implementation of NSA algorithm.

3 Hardware Implementation

Traditional software firewalls when analyzing and filtering packets flowing through the network use the processing power on which they are installed. This can lead to a significant reduction in responsiveness of the computer during a network attack. An alternative to software solutions are hardware firewalls, however, they are relatively expensive to use.

Another solution are firewalls embedded in a reprogrammable FPGA (Field Programmable Gate Array) architectures characterized by a high degree of flexibility during the design process. Usage of HDL (Hardware Description Language) languages reduces the cost of design and allows to transfer design between different architectures from manufacturers such as Xilinx or Altera. The use of reprogrammable architecture for the construction of a firewall reduces the cost of the final solution and increases the number of classified packets compared to pure software solution.

Construction of FPGA allows for parallelization of calculations and algorithms, so that they have wide range of applications during the HPC process (High Performance Computing). Another advantage of FPGAs is their low power consumption compared to the GPU (Graphics Processing Unit) solutions used in HPC, so that they represent better value performance-per-watt power consumption [13].

The use of FPGAs significantly shortens time to market (the length of time since the inception of the product concept to placing it on the market) compared to system based on ASIC (Application Specific Integrated Circuit).

The biggest advantage of FPGAs is that they can be reprogramed even after they have been installed in the target system. This allows to correct the errors or complement the design with new functionality. In the case of ASIC the process of design and manufacturing should be repeated and then replace a malfunctioning chip in the target system, which is associated with high costs.

The research are focused on building firewall with high throughput and latency as low as possible through the use of reprogrammable architectures. Designed in this way, the firewall will work independently without supervision of other (external) devices.

FPGAs contain programmable logic (configurable logic blocks) contains a set number of LUTs (LookUp-Table - small memory generate boolean function), flip-flops and multiplexers connected via programmable interconnects.

As the implementation language of hardware firewall has been chosen VHDL (Very High Speed Integrated Circuits Hardware Description Language) because is the most supported hardware description language by synthesis software and source code simulators.

3.1   Combinational Component Approach

In initial stage of work on the hardware firewall design was considered as a purely combinational circuit. The advantage of this approach is the clarity of its timing behavior (input/output response) analysis in oder to verify its correctness. Another advantage of this approach is the eases of making changes in the design description.

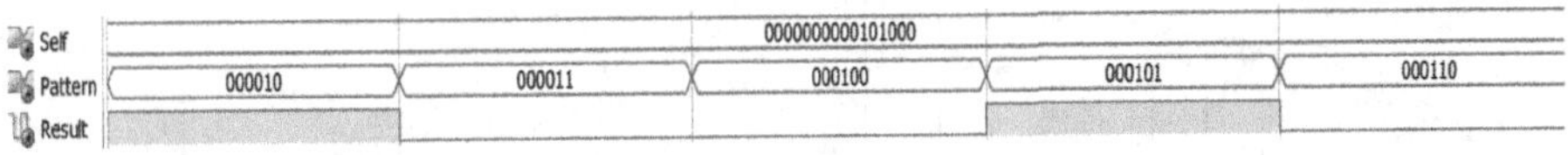

Self			0000000000101000			
Pattern	000010	000011	000100	000101	000110
Result					

Fig. 1. Combinational component approach: simulation waveform (timing diagram) of anomaly detection

Figure 1 shows a simulation of generating detectors for combinational component approach. In order to increase the readability of input/output values, results of operations component the were limited to a $l = 16$ for each sample and $r = 6$ for r-chunks. On simulation sample was market as Self - on the input might be inserted signal values of Self/NonSelf; detectors as *Pattern* - r-chunks; and the *Result* as the output of designed unit. *Value* of $'1'$ on output denotes that the detector bonds a sample. For example, if $Self = \{0000000000101000\}$ and $Pattern = \{000010\}$ then $Result = 1$ ($Self$ and $Pattern$ are matched). The same behavior is observed for larger values $l = 64$ and $r = 32$ or $l = 128$ and $r = 64$ etc. The only restriction is length of $1 \leq r \leq l$.

Diagram on Figure 2 is schematic representation of the combinational unit design in terms of logic elements optimized to the target Xilinx Virtex 4 device xc4vfx12-12sf363. Technology schematic was generated for $l = 6$ and $r = 3$ (design occupies 10 LUT tables) because generating schema for lengths greater than the specified would lead to difficulties in the analysis. Detailed schematic generated for $l = 16$ and $r = 8$ occupies more than four pages and 53 LUT tables.

The proposed solution indicates very regular structure. Therefore, a different approach - pipelined - should be considered.

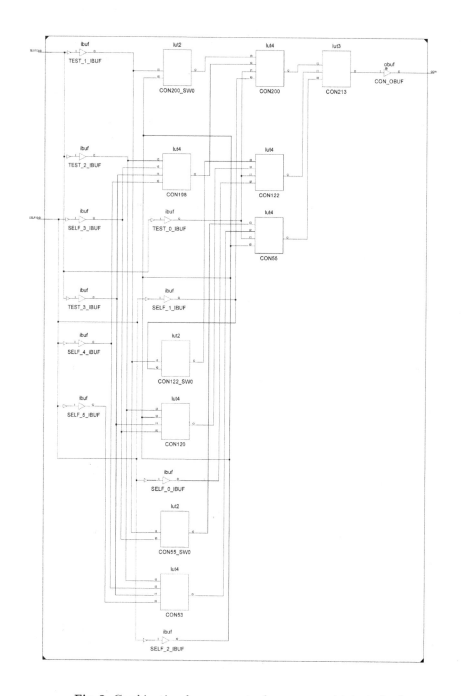

Fig. 2. Combinational component schema mapped into technology

3.2 Pipelined Approach

Throughput and delay are two critic performance criteria for designed component. Delay is the time that one task required to be completed, and throughput is the number of tasks that can be completed in one unit time. The major step of adding pipeline to immunologic anomaly detection design into stages. As was mentioned before combinational version indicates very regular structure. Comparison of r-chunk vector witch parts of self/nonself vector is realized on LUT tables which have the same or very close critical propagation delay time. An analogous situation occurs with the logical summation of the results of the comparison which is realized by a cascade connected LUT tables. Therefore when converting the combinational version of immunologic design to pipeline component version the system delay would not change but the system throughput will increase.

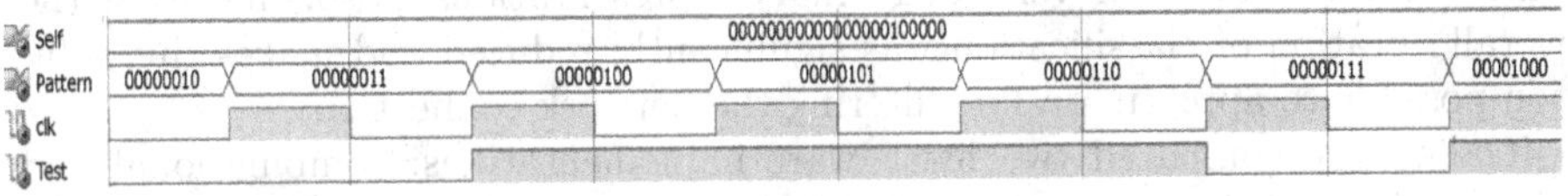

Fig. 3. Pipeline approach: simulation waveform (timing diagram) of anomaly detection

Figure 3 shows a simulation censoring samples for pipeline component approach. In order to increase the readability of input/output values results of operations component the were limited to a $l = 23$ for each sample and $r = 8$ for r-chunks. Clk is a signal used for computing stages synchronization. Test signal value is delayed for 4 ticks of the clock. It means that the system needs 4 ticks of the clock to calculate value of Test signal and its directly depend on length of l and r.

3.3 Comparison of Hardware Implementations

Table 1 shows comparison of two approaches, combinational and pipeline, of matching patterns and samples. All measurements were made for a Xilinx

Table 1. Comparison of combinational and pipeline versions

l	r	tc [ns]	tp [ns]	n
11	8	9.101	7.234	3
23	8	11.133	6.869	4
71	8	20.201	7.486	5
35	32	11.801	7.454	4
47	32	18.335	7.215	5
95	32	14.615	7.906	6

xc3s250e-5pq208 device from Spartan3E family. Parameter tc describe maximum combinational path delay for combinational version of matching system, tp - maximum combinational path delay for pipeline version and n how many ticks of the clock is needed to compute output value. It means that for the length $l = 47$ and $r = 32$ combinational system version may match 54M of sample/pattern pairs and pipeline - 138M - but the system response take 5 clock ticks (36,075ns).

4   Conclusions

Hardware implementations of negative selection algorithm are the way to overcome the scalability problem. The main advantage of this solution is a very short duration of both processes: generating detetors and censoring, as the most complex operations can be parallelized and aditionally computed without CPU utilization. Hence, in comparing to software approach, b-detectors can be generated very fast even for very long binary representations. Also, the result the overall duration of classification was significantly reduced and makes this solution possible to apply in on-line filtering the network connections.

There were compared two hwardware implementations: combinational and pipeline. Pipeline is commonly used technique to increase the performance of the design. Through a combination of pipelining and parallel processing, which is an advantage of FPGA devices, increases number of classified packets in network traffic using immunological methods.

This article is a first step for building dedicated (unique system security) hardware firewall with abbility to detect new types of attacks. In next step, implementation of V-Detector algorithm on FPGA will be performed to build hardware version of b-v model.

Acknowledgment. This work was supported by Bialystok University of Technology grants S/WI/3/13 and MB/WI/1/2014.

References

1. Balthrop, J., Esponda, F., Forrest, S., Glickman, M.: Coverage and generalization in an artificial immune system. In: Proc. of the Genetic and Evolutionary Computation Conference (GECCO 2002), New York, July 9-13, pp. 3–10 (2002)
2. Chu, P.P.: RTL Hardware Design Using Vhdl: Coding For Efficiency, Portability, and Scalability. Wiley-Interscience (2006)
3. de Castro, L., Timmis, J.: Artificial Immune Systems: A New Computational Intelligence Approach. Springer (2002)
4. Chmielewski, A., Wierzchoń, S.T.: Hybrid negative selection approach for anomaly detection. In: Cortesi, A., Chaki, N., Saeed, K., Wierzchoń, S. (eds.) CISIM 2012. LNCS, vol. 7564, pp. 242–253. Springer, Heidelberg (2012)
5. Forrest, S., Hofmeyr, S.A., Somayaji, A., Longstaff, T.A.: A sense of Self for Unix Processes. In: Proc. of the 1996 IEEE Symposium on Research in Security and Privacy, pp. 120–128. IEEE Computer Society Press (1996)

6. Forrest, S., Perelson, A., Allen, L., Cherukuri, R.: Self-nonself discrimination in a computer. In: Proc. of the IEEE Symposium on Research in Security and Privacy, Los Alamitos, pp. 202–212 (1994)
7. Harmer, P.K., Wiliams, P.D., Gunsch, G.H., Lamont, G.B.: Artificial immune system architecture for computer security applications. IEEE Trans. on Evolutionary Computation 6, 252–280 (2002)
8. Hofmeyr, S., Forrest, S.: Architecture for an Artificial Immune System. Evolutionary Computation J. 8(4), 443–473 (2000)
9. Ji, Z., Dasgupta, D.: Real-valued negative selection algorithm with variable-sized detectors. In: Deb, K. (ed.) GECCO 2004. LNCS, vol. 3102, pp. 287–298. Springer, Heidelberg (2004)
10. Ji, Z., Dasgupta, D.: Revisiting negative selection algorithms. Evolutionary Computation 15(2), 223–251 (2007)
11. Sayood, K.: Introduction to Data Compression. Elsevier (2005)
12. Stibor, T.: Phase transition and the computational complexity of generating r-contiguous detectors. In: de Castro, L.N., Von Zuben, F.J., Knidel, H. (eds.) ICARIS 2007. LNCS, vol. 4628, pp. 142–155. Springer, Heidelberg (2007)
13. Vanderbauwhede, W., Benkrid, K.: High-Performance Computing Using FPGAs (2013)
14. Wierzchoń, S.T.: Generating optimal repertoire of antibody strings in an artificial immune system. In: Kłopotek, M.A., Michalewicz, M., Wierzchoń, S.T. (eds.) Intelligent Information Systems. Proc. of the IIS 2000 Symposium, Bystra, Poland, June 12-16, pp. 119–133. Springer (2000)

Evaluating Industrial Control Devices Security: Standards, Technologies and Challenges

Feng Xie, Yong Peng, Wei Zhao, Yang Gao, and Xuefeng Han

China Information Technology Security Evaluation Center, Beijing, China
xief@itsec.gov.cn

Abstract. Cyber security for industrial automation and control systems has been a much discussed topic in recent years. Security evaluation of industrial control devices has been gaining rising attention. In this paper, the security evaluation standards for industrial control devices are analyzed, and the corresponding several certifications are compared. Meanwhile, this paper proposes several key testing technologies that can be used in evaluation of devices, and analyzes primary difference compared with traditional IT devices. Finally, this paper discussed the challenges facing us in evaluation of industrial control devices.

Keywords: Cyber security, industrial control device, standards, certifications, testing technologies.

1   Introduction

Industrial control systems have been widely used in petrochemical factories, power generation systems, manufacturing facilities, and many other critical infrastructures. Traditional industrial control systems typically consist of instrumentation, fuses, system simulation screen and control cables. With more information technology, modern industrial control systems are composed of the industrial control devices, historical data servers, engineer stations as well as HMIs. Industrial control devices (ICDs) usually locate in industrial fields and implement the core control functions. They are often directly connected to sensors and actuators, reading data from sensors, executing a predefined control algorithm, and sending an output to a final element (e.g. control valves or damper drives). Typical industrial control devices include distributed control system controllers (DCS controllers), programmable logic controllers (PLCs), intelligent electronic devices (IEDs) and remote terminal units (RTUs).

In the early development of industrial automation, industrial control system is a closed and proprietary environment, almost free from the threat of cyber attacks. Thus the design of industrial control device is focused on reliable and real-time requirements, which is solved by fault detection, redundancy, fault-tolerant control and other mechanisms. However, with more and more information technologies, such as TCP/IP network and embedded operating system, being applied to industrial automation controls, and with more requirements for interconnection between industrial network and business network, a lot of security incidents have occurred in recent years.

K. Saeed and V. Snášel (Eds.): CISIM 2014, LNCS 8838, pp. 624–635, 2014.
© IFIP International Federation for Information Processing 2014

Table 1 shows a part of industrial incidents, including the brief incident description, the potential impact and the most likely reason (root cause).

Table 1. A part of industrial security incidents occurred in recent years

Year	Incident Description	Root Cause	Impact
2000	An engineer attacked a sewage treatment system in Australia by radio, resulting in large amounts of sewage directly into the river and causing serious environmental disaster. [1,2]	Unauthorized access	An environmental disaster occurred.
2003	A computer virus named Sobig attacked train signaling, dispatching and other systems at CSX Corporation in Florida, U.S.[3]	Malware	Trains were delayed.
2008	A nuclear power plant in Georgia was shut down for 48 hours unexpectedly due to software updates.[4]	Software update	The nuclear power plant was closed unexpectedly.
2010	Stuxnet virus infected Iran's nuclear power plant, tampered programmable logical controller (PLC), and eventually led to centrifuges damaged. [5,6]	Malware	A lot of centrifuges were destroyed.
2011	Hackers claimed to have taken control of U.S. water treatment plant in South Houston by remotely cracking passwords of SCADA system.[7]	Password cracked	Hackers seized control of the public water facility.
2011	Conficker worm infected a steel system, resulting in unstable communication between the PLC and the monitoring station, and resulting in most of the surveillance system failure.	Malware	Plant surveillance was blocked, affecting industrial production.

From these accidents it can be seen that common cyber attacks, e.g. malware, password cracking, unauthorized access and denial of service attacks, have an ability of affecting industrial control systems. In particular, considering that control systems are often used in plant automation control, the impact would lead to industrial operation damage, or even failure, which inevitably would lead to affecting health, safety, and environment.

Nowadays the industrial control devices become more intelligent and networked, which means that they are more vulnerable to cyber attacks. For example, Stuxnet virus, as shown in Table 1, tampered the control program in PLC at the Iran nuclear facility, resulting in PLC sending the wrong instructions to controlled equipments and furthermore destroying about one-tenth of the centrifuges [5, 6]. Therefore, it becomes very important to improve the security of industrial control devices itself.

In this paper, the security evaluation of industrial control devices is reviewed, including the state-of-the-art cyber security standards for evaluating industrial control devices, the existed products certification, as well as some key testing technologies that could be used in evaluation. Further, the issues and challenges of security evaluation are discussed.

The rest of paper is organized as follows: Section II discusses the state-of-the-art security standards for industrial control devices. Section III compares several security certifications used in industrial control devices. Section IV proposes some technologies that can be applied to assess and test industrial control devices. Section V summarizes the current issues and challenges. Finally section VI concludes the paper.

2   Security Evaluation Standards

In recent years, many security standards for industrial control systems have been proposed. For example, NERC (North American Electric Reliability Corporation) CIP (Critical Infrastructure Protection) standards provide a cyber security framework for identification and protection of critical cyber assets to support reliable operation of the bulk electric system [8]. Meanwhile, the IEC 62351 standard defines end-to-end security methods for SCADA protocols and security in diverse protocol layers in layered communications architecture [9]. However, as far as security evaluation of industrial control devices, the condition is far from satisfactory. Whether comprehensiveness or feasibility, industrial control devices security evaluation is not only far behind IT devices security evaluation, but also far behind functional safety evaluation. These standards include ISA99 [10], ISO/IEC 62443 [11], WIB 2.0 [12] and so on.

2.1   ISO/IEC 62443

ISO/IEC 62443 is not a single standard, but a standard series. It derives from ISA 99, and has undergone several major changes in recent years. Now it becomes a very comprehensive standard suitable for industrial control products, vendors, system integrators and end users. There are 12 sub-standards in ISO/IEC 62443 and can be divided into four categories, as shown in table 2. However, only the fourth part is aiming to industrial control components or products including ICDs. It involves two security requirements of industrial control components: development requirements and technical security requirements. The former describes the security development process for products, covering 12 stages from security architecture design, threatening modeling, software detailed design, to security integration testing. The latter provides the information security function of industrial automation and control components. Figure 1 shows the framework of ISO/IEC 62443, in which each black point denotes that corresponding standards are applicable. For example, the part 2-4 is applicable for automation supplier and system integrator, and the part 4-1 as well as 4-2 are only applicable for device.

　　Due to the security development of industrial control devices are essentially like software security development, part 4-1 appears relatively mature. In contrast, industrial control devices are distinct with traditional IT products in hardware, software and architecture, therefore existed IT product security requirements cannot be directly applied to industrial products, which leads to part 4-2 is still incomplete.

2.2   WIB 2.0

WIB 2.0 is published by international instrument user's associations (WIB) [12]. Noticed that it is not fit for a product or a device, but rather for a product vendor or system integrator. It defines security requirements on the organizational policies, procedures as well as responsibilities, which should be fulfilled by vendors or integrators in process control domain. Now it is still in draft and is adopted as a part of ISO/IEC 62443 (i.e., ISO/IEC 62443-2-4).

Table 2. Four categories in ISO/IEC 62443

Category	Description
General	Composed of industrial control system security terminology, concepts, models, etc. They are applicable to entire standard series.
Policies & Procedures	Composed of requirements to the security organization and processes of the plant owner and suppliers. They can be seen as security operation and management of an organization.
System	Composed of requirements to a secure industrial control system. They can be adapted as construction guide.
Component	Composed of requirements to secure industrial control components including security development and security functions of ICDs.

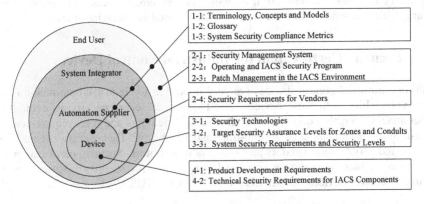

Fig. 1. The framework of ISO/IEC 62443 standard. It involves 12 sub-standards, covering the device, the automation supplier (vendor), the system integrator and end use. Each black point indicates that the sub-standard is applicable.

The purpose of this standard is to ensure industrial control devices security through a maturation process covering whole life cycle from design and development to maintenance of industrial control systems, which is clearly based on the capability maturity model (CMM). A total of 35 process areas (PAs) can be categorized as four classes: organizational, system capability, system acceptance testing and commissioning, as well as maintenance and support. Each PA is composed of many basic processes. These requirements basically seem to ensure that product capabilities defined in the product process area are properly used.

In order to identify security degree, different levels are divided based on the maturity of the process. Higher certification level indicates a more mature organization with advanced policies and procedures in place, which should be able to produce better security. Figure 2 shows the framework of WIB 2.0.

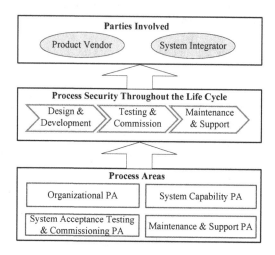

Fig. 2. The framework of WIB 2.0. It comprises of four process areas, covering the whole security life cycle, and is suitable for product vendors as well as system integrators.

3   Security Certification for Industrial Control Devices

Securing industrial control devices are very important for industrial automation. Are there vulnerabilities in these devices? Are the devices secure and robust enough for cyber attacks? Whether do they have some security features and meet requirements of industrial environments such as real-time and reliability? They all are urgent questions to industrial users, vendors and sector administrators. Security certification is a good way to identify a device security level. At present security certifications for industrial control devices include EDSA, APC, ACC, MUSIC, etc.

3.1   Embedded Device Secure Assurance (EDSA)

In order to promote industrial device evaluation and certification, ISA (International Society of Automation) developed a program, ISASecure, for industrial devices and systems [14], in which EDSA is the first step suitable for embedded devices. EDSA consists of three kinds of tests as follows:

— Communication robustness test (CRT). It tests a device's communication ability to resist large traffic and malformed packets. By CRT we can know the extent to which network protocol implementations on an embedded device defend themselves and other device functions against unusual or intentional malicious traffic received from network. Inappropriate message response or failure of device always implies there is something wrong in device due to the incorrect communication.

- Function security assessment (FSA). It tests whether or not security features of a device are correctly implemented. In EDSA all security functionality are divided into seven categories: access control, usage control, data integrity, data confidentiality, data flow restrictions, incident response, and network resource availability. It is noticed that these security features mainly come from ISO/IEC 62443 and NIST 800-53.
- Software development security assessment (SDSA). It derives from software security development process and is compliance with the ISO/IEC 62443 4-1. SDSA can detect and avoid the systematic design faults. The vendor's development and maintenance processes are audited, respectively.

To distinguish security capability, the devices are divided into three security levels in EDSA: low, middle, and high (Figure 3). The higher the level is, the more the content needed to assess, and the more secure the product. In figure 3, the number represents the number of test cases. For example, in level 1 SDSA involves 130 test cases, and in level 2 the number becomes 149. But CRT remains the same regardless of certification level.

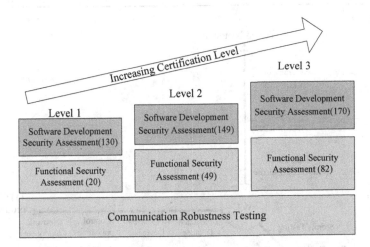

Fig. 3. The framework of EDSA. It consists of three kinds of tests: CRT, SDSA and FSA. Three security levels are determined in EDSA, and different security certification level involves different test cases.

3.2   Achilles Communications Certification (ACC)

ACC is a communication robustness certification for industrial devices [15]. It is provided by Wurldtect Corporation. In nature, ACC is focused on the assessment whether the communication process of a device is robust by testing network protocols covering the link layer, the network layer and the transport layer.

Because focused on protocol stack, ACC is not only fit for embedded control devices (e.g., PLC/DCS/RTU), but also for PC host devices (e.g., engineer station, history server and domain controllers), control applications (e.g., HMI software and control software), and network devices (e.g., routers and switches).

In order to identify security degree, two levels are provided in ACC: level 1 and level 2. Compared with level 1, level 2 has more testing cases.

Also three kinds of test cases are carried out in ACC (Table 3): traffic storms, protocol fuzz-testing (or negative testing), and known vulnerability testing.

Figure 4 shows the tested protocols, tested objects and key testing technologies in ACC.

Table 3. Three kinds of test cases categories in ACC

Category	Meaning
Traffic storms	Traffic storms simulate denial-of-service attack, in an attempt to exhaust resources, such as network, bandwidth, CPU time, or memory.
Protocol fuzz-testing	It iterates through the protocol to identify various implementation weaknesses/vulnerabilities, e.g. coding errors (buffer overflow, and format string bugs).
Known vulnerability	Identify existing weaknesses and security holes by appropriate tools and techniques.

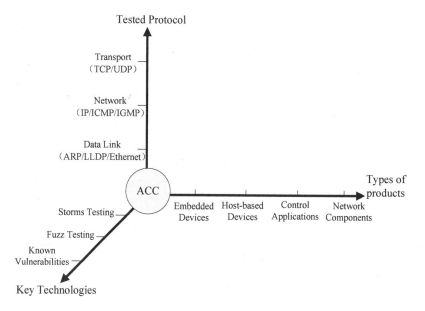

Fig. 4. Achilles communication certification (ACC). It mainly makes use of three key testing technologies: storm testing, fuzz testing and known vulnerabilities detection, and focuses on TCP/IP protocols. At present, four types of products can be certified by ACC.

3.3   Achilles Practices Certification（APC）

APC is also provided by Wurldtect Corporation [15]. Different from ACC, APC is more fit for practices of vendors. This certification is based on WIB 2.0. It is noticed that APC does not address a product itself, but rather a product vendor and/or system integrator. It defines requirements on the organizational policies and procedures as well as organizational responsibilities.

3.4   MUSIC Certification

MUSIC is an industrial device certification offered by Mu Dynamics, Inc. It requires the use of an evaluation platform for the testing for network protocols covering link layer, network layer, transport layer and application layer. Although it operates in a similar manner to that of the ACC program, the acceptance of MUSIC lags behind that of ACC.

3.5   Comparison among Several Certifications

Table 4 shows the comparison results among four certifications of industrial control devices, from which we can draw the following conclusions.

(a) Communication security is very important for a device and therefore is widely used in certification, even sometimes as the only requirement.
(b) EDSA is the only certification assessing security function of products.
(c) Process assurance is an effective way securing products, and is involved in many certifications. For example, EDSA involves security development process assessment, and APC is itself fit for process vendors.

Table 4. Comparision amoung several certifications

Certifi cation	Organization	TOE (Target of Evaluation	Description
EDSA	ISA	Device	Test the product's stack robustness, security functionality and security development practice being an acceptable level.
ACC	Wurldtect	Device	Test the product's stack robustness being an acceptable level.
APC	Wurldtect	Vendor	Test organizational preparedness being an acceptable level.
MUSIC	Mu Dynamics	Device	Test the product's stack robustness being an acceptable level.

4   Key Testing Technologies

The following technologies can be used in the security evaluation for industrial control devices.

4.1   Data Storm Testing

Usually industrial control systems require high real-time. Any short latency maybe has an immeasurable impact on industrial operations, therefore these devices should have a good performance. Data storms test is an important evaluation technique aiming at processing capability of a device by sending packets with different rates. Usually data storms consist of TCP SYN storm, TCP LAND attack, ICMP storm, UDP unicast/multicast/broadcast storm, ARP request storm, and so on.

4.2   Protocol Fuzz-Testing

Fuzz-testing is a popular security evaluation technique in which hostile inputs are crafted and passed to the target in order to reveal bugs. An industrial control device often communicates with HMI or field device based on different communication protocols. The vulnerability which can be exploited by hacker maybe exists for design and implement of protocols. Therefore identifying protocol vulnerabilities via fuzz-testing plays an important role in EDSA, ACC as well as MUSIC. The typical process is to inject a lot of erroneous or variation data to the target device and to monitor whether or not it runs normally. An abnormal behavior implies that a bug in protocol is triggered. Many researchers discovered vulnerabilities by this technique. To improve the efficiency, many fuzz-testing tools such as Spike [18], Sulley [19] and Peach [20] are developed. However when applied directly to industrial control devices, they encountered many problems as follows.

Problem 1. These tools are developed for conventional TCP/IP protocols which are open. However, most of industrial protocols are proprietary and not known by outsiders. As a result researchers have to crack the packet structure and session process before fuzz-testing for a proprietary protocol, which distinguishably increases the difficulty.

Problem 2. As far as exception monitoring is concerned, it becomes more difficult in industrial environment. Traditionally, network survival detection can be used to monitor exceptions when fuzz-testing is carrying out. In this approach, after each set of testing cases to send, a specific probing packet is sent to the target in order to detect whether or not the network is survival. Usually probing packet is ICMP or ARP packet. By the intermittent request-response, we can know whether or not the test cases trigger the exception and further crash the device. When fuzz-testing is used for industrial control devices, a new issue occurs. In fact an industrial control device can be seen as a device connecting the information space and physical space [13, 17]. It usually consists of two kinds of interface connected to other devices. One is network interface such as Ethernet and wireless network, by which ICDs can be connected with other host devices (e.g., HMI and engineering station) and network devices (e.g., switch and router), and can transmit all kinds of data such as monitoring status information and control instruction. The other is input/output signal interface such as analog I/O and digital I/O, by which ICDs can communicate with different field devices such as sensors and actors. Therefore, when testing an industrial control device, not only is the network exception detection needed, but also the output signal exception detection is needed. The former is used to monitor whether or not the network behavior is abnormal. Abnormal behaviors typically include the slowing network packet speed, the increasing latency, or even loss of response. These anomalies usually indicate that network protocol stack of control device are damaged by test cases. The latter is used to monitor whether the output signal is expected. Anomaly signal indicates that the test cases have an impact on control program running on the device. In order to do it, the expected output signal should be known before testing starts.

Problem 3. It is very difficult to debug the exceptions or errors on industrial control devices. Noticed that most industrial control devices are embedded devices with different platform from computers. As a result, many traditional debuggers (e.g. Ollydbg and Windbg) based on computers cannot be used on industrial control device, which makes it difficult to debug the exceptions to acquire root cause.

4.3   Penetration Testing

Penetration testing is directed toward finding vulnerabilities that enable a user to violate the security policy in the target (i.e. the device under test). It is based upon an analysis of the target that specifically seeks to identify vulnerabilities in the design and implementation, and can be simply considered as vulnerability assessment. Penetration testing becomes an important approach for security evaluation of devices as well as systems. For example, it is already widely used in common evaluation criteria for IT security (i.e. ISO/IEC 15408 [16]). Similarly, it also can be used to test industrial control devices.

Penetration testing involves a lot of attack techniques to identify, analyze and exploit vulnerabilities. The following techniques often can be used in penetration testing.

- Scanning. Scanning can be defined as "a method for discovering exploitable communication channels". Via scanning, we can know the open ports as well as existed services in a device. Unnecessary ports should be shut down to reduce attack surface.
- Known vulnerability exploit. It is well-known that many control devices nowadays often use COTS operating systems such as VxWorks and embedded Linux. The known vulnerabilities in the operating system are often acquired easily from Internet (such as CVE database [21]). It is a good approach to attack a control device by means of exploiting the known vulnerability in the operating system of the device.
- Firmware analysis. The firmware of a device is the set of all code running on the hardware's processor (machine code and virtual machine code). Undoubtedly, industrial control devices belong to firmware-driven devices. If the firmware of devices is not encrypted or protected well, it is can be reverse engineered by security researchers. Hereby, finding security issues become possible. In some cases, even hard-code usernames and passwords as well as undocumented access approaches such as back doors can be identified.

5   Current Challenges

At present, several key challenges in security evaluation for industrial control devices are as follows:

Firstly, although security has become an abstracting topic in recent years, it is not be widely accepted by industrial vendors and users. Security evaluation for industrial control equipments has drawn little attention. In contrast, the functional safety of devices has been emphasized in industrial automation sector for a long time. At present, security is not embedded in the whole life cycle of industrial products covering design, development, delivery and maintenance.

Secondly, most of industrial security standards are still in discussion and draft, which brings great challenges to industrial equipment assessment. Meanwhile, these standards are concentrated on basic concepts, frameworks and models, while detailed technical requirements still keep a blank. For example, although the fourth part of ISO/IEC 62443 can be regarded as technical requirements of industrial control products, most requirements in ISO/IEC 62443 4-2 are missing, which makes it difficult to evaluate the compliance with standards. Due to the reasons above, the current industrial equipment evaluation still mainly focused on communication robustness tests.

Thirdly, although many perfect testing techniques/tools are developed and used in IT security evaluation, they are often not suitable for industrial devices testing. For example, many protocol analyzers based on conventional TCP/IP protocols hardly know the industrial protocols, therefore they cannot identify the vulnerabilities inherent in industrial devices. Because industrial protocols are often proprietary and abundant, it is a horrible work to develop new analysis devices. Similarly, many existing tools cannot be directly used in the vulnerability analysis of control devices due to the huge difference between control devices and person computers in hardware and operating system, while vulnerability testing is very critical for security evaluation.

Fourthly, because the industrial control devices are often used for real-time control of physical process or industrial production, the security evaluation cannot be performed in plants to avoid the impact on the physical environment, which indicates the needs for simulated testing environment. This is a considerable investment!

Finally, automation security is related with many fields such as industrial automation, sectors (i.e. applications) and cyber security, therefore the knowledge and skills of testers become very important. They not only need to be familiar with different industrial applications and control devices with different architecture, but also need to master a number of security testing technologies to identify security vulnerabilities in control equipments. Unfortunately, the amount of staff with such knowledge is too little.

6   Conclusions

In this paper, the security evaluation standards, certifications, key testing technologies as well as challenges of industrial control devices are reviewed. Compared with functional safety assessment, the security evaluation for industrial control devices lags far behind. Most of security standards are still in draft, and the certification has not widely accepted by industrial vendors and users. Many traditional security testing techniques encounter unique problems when they are used to evaluate industrial control device. All these difficulties give us tremendous challenges.

References

1. Abrams, M., Weiss, J.: Malicious control system cyber security attack case study-maroochy water services, Australia
2. Miller, B., Rowe, D.: A survey of SCADA and critical infrastructure incidents. In: Proc. of the 1st Annual Conference on Research in Information Technology (2012)
3. Nicholson. SCADA security in the light of cyber-warfare. Computers & Security (2012)
4. http://www.waterfall-security.com/cyber-incident-blamed-for-nuclear-power-plant-shutdown-june-08/
5. Luders, S.: Stuxnet and the impact on accelerator control systems. In: Proc. of the 13th Conference on Accelerator and Large Experimental Physics Control Systems, pp. 1285–1288. JACoW, Geneva (2011)
6. Farwell, R.: Stuxnet and the futher of cyber war. Survival: global politics and strategy (2011)
7. http://www.dailymail.co.uk/sciencetech/article-2064283/Hackers-control-U-S-public-water-treatment-facilities.html
8. North American Electric Reliability Council (NERC), Critical Infrastructure Protection Committee, NERC Standard CIP-002 through -009, Cyber Security (2006)
9. IEC 62351 Power systems management and associated information exchange data and communication security (2007)
10. ANSI/ISA 99. Security for industrial automation and control systems. ISA, Research Triangle Park (2007)
11. ISO/IEC 62443. Security for industrial automation and control systems. International Electrotechnical Commission, Switzerland (2010)
12. M 2784 X10. Process control domain-security requirements for vendors
13. Rajkumar, R., Insup, L., Lui, S., et al.: Cyber-physical systems: the next computing revolution. In: Proc. of 47th Conference on Design Automation Conference, pp. 731–736. IEEE Press, Piscataway (2010)
14. ISA Security compliance institute. ISASecure Embedded Device Security Assurance Certification,
    http://www.isa.org/filestore/asci/isci/ISCI%20ISASecure%20ECSA%20Certification%20brochure.pdf
15. Wurldtech Security Inc. Achilles practices certification,
    http://www.wurldtech.com/product_services/certify_educate/achilles_practices_certification
16. ISO/IEC 15408. Evaluation criteria for IT security, Switzerland. ISO (2005)
17. Wang, Z., Xie, L.: Cyber-physical systems: a survey. Acta Automatica Sinica 37(10), 1157–1166 (2011)
18. Aitel, D.: An introduction to SPIKE, The fuzzer creation kit. In: BlackHat Conference
19. Sulley: fuzzing framework,
    http://www.fuzzing.org/wp-content/SulleyManual.pdf
20. http://peachfuzzer.com/
21. http://cve.mitre.org/

Protection Profile for Secure Sensitive Information System on Mobile Devices

Imed El Fray, Tomasz Hyla, and Włodzimierz Chocianowicz

West Pomeranian University of Technology, Szczecin
Faculty of Computer Science and Information Technology, Poland
{ielfray,thyla,wchocianowicz}@zut.edu.pl

Abstract. The mobility of the user and information is a factor that should be taken into account during the design and development of mechanisms protecting the sensitive stored, exchanged and processed information on mobile devices. This paper discusses the security profiles for the user and dispatcher subsystems protecting sensitive information on the mobile device called MobInfoSec. MobInfoSec is a system providing users with secure sensitive documents by using the specialized class SP cryptographic module, which protects directly the trusted system components through implementing ORCON access control rules. Protection Profile defines the security functional requirements for MobInfoSec system executing the encryption/decryption of documents based on addressed access policies. The article includes a general description of MobInfoSec system, including assets, assumptions, threats, policies and functional requirements necessary for the evaluation of security functions developed in accordance with requirements of the standard ISO/IEC 15408 (called the Common Criteria).

Keywords: Mobile device, Sensitive information, *Originator Controlled Access Control*, *Secure Protec*tion Module, Protection Profile.

1 Introduction

Today such terms as privacy, security, mobility of users and information or mobility of the information itself are important features of the information systems that must be considered during the design and development of protection mechanisms of sensitive information. The importance of the systems dedicated to the mobile platforms has grown significantly in recent years. Mobility of information requires that the level of information protection, regardless of its location, must be the same as in the case of local information. The achievement of this level of protection requires the design and implementation of systems in the manner preventing the access to information by unauthorized entity (especially if confidential or classified information is the case).

The growing number of mobile users (private or business ones) who store sensitive data on such devices requires strong access control mechanisms. These requirements can be met by using the Originator Controlled (ORCON) access control model [1].

K. Saeed and V. Snášel (Eds.): CISIM 2014, LNCS 8838, pp. 636–650, 2014.
© IFIP International Federation for Information Processing 2014

It is assumed in this model that each document has its owner. However, an access must be controlled by a dispatcher of the document (i.e. the entity that has the right to share the document on behalf of the owner). The owner can determine who shares a document, but the final decision is up to the document dispatcher. The user of the document (who was given the access right from the dispatcher) can't copy it or share it with other users without the consent of the dispatcher. The solution based on ORCON model will allow the achievement of two objectives:

- security of mobile information
- release of the user from the obligation to monitor any classified information contained in his/her mobile device.

A noticeable rapid increase in the number of identified vulnerabilities and attacks on mobile systems, and the lack of a system that clearly and transparently enforces the protection of sensitive information collected from various sources and stored on mobile devices, justify the need to design and develop new mechanisms to improve the security of information processed on mobile devices.

This paper presents protection profiles for the user system of information processed and stored on a mobile device, and the dispatcher system as well. It is assumed that the mobile device allowing an access to sensitive information will be a part of the proposed MobInfoSec system described in [2]. Typically, such systems must be centralized in a way enabling each entity to download the protected sensitive information properly. The access to the system can only be obtained by the entity or entities from the group who meet the conditions specified in the access policy integrally related to the downloaded sensitive information.

Due to such features, the sensitive information will be available not only within the information management system, but also on any mobile device (called an ORCON class), in contrast with existing systems.

This paper contains the description of the ORCON access control model (in Section 2) and the description of the MobInfoSec system (in Section 3). Section 4 contains the identified assets, assumptions, threats, the security policy and selected functional requirements of the above-mentioned system, all together realizing the security goals.

2   Originator Controlled Access Control

One of the biggest challenges for the protection of the sensitive information is to create such an access control system where, under the assumption that the creator of the document (or the institution acting on its behalf) has no control over the operating user system of the document, it would be possible to control the process of sharing documents distributed by the author to the others. By using the existing cryptographic mechanisms one can protect the documents in such a way, that only an authorized person has an access to them. In contrast, it is difficult to protect them against an internal attacks, when a dishonest user having access rights to the file intends to distribute these rights further without permission of the author.

The ORCON [1] access control rules, which require that the author of the document have full control over its dissemination, allow the creation of such a system to control an access to the classified information in order to protect the document against internal attacks. However, due to the fact that modern operating systems together with the software can be freely modified by an attacker, the effective implementation of the ORCON model is a difficult task. It results from the fact that the attacker can preview the contents of memory at any time, and thus can gain unauthorized access to a document which always must be decrypted before being displayed on the mobile device screen [2,3].

In order to achieve more functionality, the hybrid ORCON model has been created. This model combines the features of MAC and DAC models/strategies. In this model it is assumed that each resource (document) has its owner. The owner may be the author of the document, but this is not necessary. The document owner has the authority to manage his/her documents, for example he/she may have to read, write or update rights. The owner may transfer these rights to other users of the system. Users are endowed with such a right, but they cannot pass it on - this applies to the same document and all copies thereof. The access to the document can only be granted after its owner approval. This rule distinguishes ORCON model from the basic models (MAC, DAC, RBAC).

ORCON model rules proved to be particularly important in the case of the sensitive information of high importance (the security of the government institutions as an example), as suggested by the authors [4,5]. The example of using the ORCON model in this context is provided in [6].

As mentioned above, the hybrid ORCON model draws its principles from models of MAC and DAC. ORCON requirements can be fulfilled only by bringing together some of the features of MAC and DAC. The idea of this was presented in [1,6] and consists of describing the ORCON model as a function of the requirements which are fulfilled by MAC and DAC models:

- the owner of the resource cannot itself to change the access rules for MAC;
- when copying a resource, the access restrictions are copied along with the access to the resource and attributed to its copies (access to a copy is identical to the original);
- the resource originator can change the access rights of other entities too.

One can notice that the first two principles are under the control of MAC (not under the control of the owner), while the third rule is consistent with DAC and is subjected to the owner control.

The main problem related to ORCON model is of an architectural and implementation nature, i.e. how to meet ORCON objectives effectively. In this model it is important to define an arbitrary and dynamic access structure. There are many approaches for the implementation of access structures (ACL, cryptographic techniques using special SP hardware modules [1], etc.).

When building the flexible access structures, special attention should be paid to the secret sharing methods [7,8], which allow to create dynamic structures [9-11]. When designing advanced algorithms, secret sharing can tend to create structures with specific topologies or structure topology defined by the resource owner.

The detailed description of ORCON access control model (including examples) was presented in [1-3,6]. Below the protection profile of the MobInfoSec system is described. This system is evaluated for the compliance with the requirements of the Common Criteria (EAL4 level).

3   Description of MobInfoSec System

The subject of the protection profile is the system of cryptographic protection of the sensitive information on the mobile devices (MobInfoSec). The system consists of four basic subsystems:

- Dispatcher subsystem,
- User subsystem,
- Policies and assertions management subsystem,
- Cryptographic and PKI services subsystem and two auxiliary Subsystems: standard trusted subsystem and mobile device protection subsystem.

All the above mentioned subsystems are functionally combined into a single integrated system.

The following Figure 1 highlights the important software components included in MobInfoSec system.

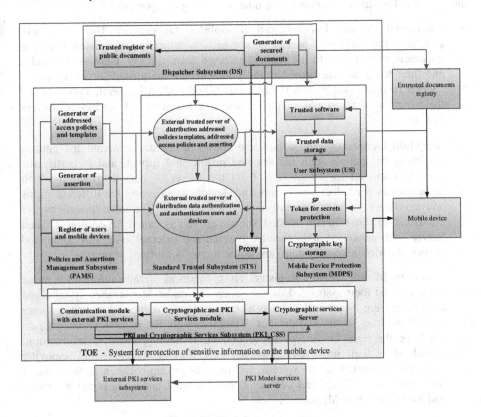

Fig. 1. MobInfoSec components

3.1   Dispatcher Subsystem (DS)

DS is used to generate the addressed access policies and to encrypt documents with sensitive information in accordance with those policies. DS can be embedded on a stationary device, and on a mobile device as well. The subsystem consists of two components:

–   **Trusted Register of Public Documents:** The component is responsible for collecting public documents developed by the authors, which can be encrypted by Generator of Secured Documents;.

–   **Generator of Secured Documents**: The component is responsible for issuing requests to generate addressed access policies and to encrypt the specified document under the terms of the policy.

3.2   Policies and Assertions Management Subsystem (PAMS)

PAMS is used to generate and provide an addressed access policy and its templates to a standard trusted subsystem, and to generate and make available information concerning assertion users and mobile devices based on the catalogue of trusted users and devices. The subsystem consists of three following components.

–   **Addressed Access Policies and Templates Generator:** The component generates the addressed access policy and its templates associated with the document in response to the request received from the DS. Generated Policies and their templates are provided and published by the trusted server, so called "Server of Addressed Access Policies and Templates". All generated policies and their templates are stored in the "Templates Magazine of Addressed Access Policies".

–   **Assertion Generator:** The component allows to register, generate and publish assertions compatible with the selected profile and format, and to certify the existing imported assertions (e.g. from the server of data distribution which authenticates trusted external users and devices, confirming the different rights and privileges of sensitive information users). The generated assertions are published in the standard trusted subsystem (STS) called "Assertion Trusted Server". All generated and cancelled internal and external assertions (generated outside the MobInfoSec system) are stored in the "Assertions Magazine".

–   **Users and Mobile Devices Register:** The component contains information about the users and their associated devices operating under MobInfoSec system, and their status (e.g. whether the unit is a combination of registered trusted software and SP module). Users and devices withdrawn from the registry (catalogue) do not have the right to decrypt any document containing sensitive information, regardless of their previously granted rights. Making available and removing users and devices from the system, and the relationship between them, is under the control of the "Users and Devices Trusted Server", and is registered in "Users and Mobile Devices Magazine".

3.3   PKI and Cryptographic Services Subsystem (PKI_CSS)

This subsystem is a service provider generating keys for the purpose of users and devices authentication, data encryption and decryption, and secure communication within the External PKI Services Subsystem and External PKI Services Module Subsystem. The subsystem consists of three following components.

- **Cryptographic Services Server:** The component generates and stores cryptographic keys used for authentication algorithms and data encryption/decryption (including threshold algorithms for keys sharing), assertions evidences, addressed policies templates and addressed policies.

- **Communication Module for External PKI Services:** The component implements the functionality of interface with PKI services provided by the external PKI service providers.

- **Cryptographic and PKI Services:** The component operates as a broker managing cryptographic service requests for the execution of service (e.g. service requests arising from the signing evidences from Dispatcher Subsystem, and Polices & Assertions Management Subsystem) and its results, or communicates with one of the two components described above.

3.4   User Subsystem (US)

US is used to authenticate and authorize users and mobile devices, and to distribute access policies to the mobile device. US is also used to enforce the access policy in the case of decryption. A trusted or untrusted (produced by external suppliers) application presenting the data subjected to access policy may be located in US. The subsystem consists of two main components (the Trusted Software and the Trusted Data Storage).

- **Trusted Software:** This component includes the software which integrity is protected by the main module of trusted software ("watchman") operating in MDPS (see: 3.5).

- **Trusted Data Storage:** This component is "the protected data storage" containing evidences concerning the user of the mobile device (certificates, optionally private keys and basic assertions), Root CAs certificates (trust points) and the decrypted document. The integrity of this storage is protected by the trusted software module ("watchman") operating in MDPS (see: 3.5).

3.5   Mobile Device Protection Subsystem (MDPS)

MDPS contains a dedicated cryptographic module called SP module. SP module protects directly the trusted US components implementing ORCON rules. This protection is possible by controlling the integrity of the code and configuration data. The subsystem consists of two following components.

- **Secret Protection Token:** This component provides the functionality of Trusted Platform Module (two keys, one for an authentication and one for an access to the storage), the encryption and decryption keys from Cryptographic Keys Storage, and it includes registers and codes needed to verify the integrity and enforcing certain behaviour in the case of incorrect integrity verification (blocking the action of a trusted code).

- **Cryptographic Key Storage:** This component is used to securely store keys used to authenticate users or devices, and to carry out the operations of encryption and decryption of data.

3.6   Standard Trusted Subsystem (STS)

STS is the subsystem intermediary between DS, US and PAMS. This subsystem is used to share and distribute the addressed access policies templates and assertions, data authentication of users and devices, and serves as the register of published addressed policies. STS also works with PKI_CSS under the control of e.g. PKI Proxy Gateway. The subsystem consists of two following components.

- **External Trusted Server of Addressed Policies Templates, Addressed Access Policies and Assertions Distribution:** This component retrieves addressed policies templates of PAMS. These templates are then made available for the preparation of PD addressed access policies. Prepared addressed access policies are taken by mobile devices. This component also provides assertions to mobile devices and PD in order to implement the process of authentication and encryption/decryption of data.

- **External Trusted Server of Authentication Data Distribution and Users/ Devices Authentication:** This component distributes information about the users and devices (such as information about their groups, roles) stored in the MobInfoSec system to other components of the system, and authenticates them on request.

The detailed description of all mentioned above components and architecture of individual subsystems, together with examples of business scenarios, are described in [2]. Below, in accordance with the guidelines of the Common Criteria [12-14], the following items are defined: assets, assumptions, threats and security policy, and then the policy goals counteracting security threats and supporting the security policy and security functional requirements. The security objectives rationale for threats, security policies, etc., were deliberately omitted, because they are an effect of the aggregation of data resulting from the specified chain of events describing the threat, politics, etc., contained in the following tables.

4   Protection Profile for MobInfoSec systems

4.1   The Assets off the System

This section describes the most important assets that should be protected by the system.

Table 1. The most important identified assets of the MobInfoSec system

A. Document	Electronic Document(s) for encryption/decryption. Data contained in this document must be protected against the loss of integrity and confidentiality.
A. Encrypted data	Includes encrypted document and document attributes. Data (ciphertext) must be protected against the loss of confidentiality and integrity.
A. Encrypted attributes	Data contained in addressed access policies and allowing to correct encrypt and decrypt the encrypted data. These attributes must be protected against the loss of integrity.
A. Addressed access policies	Defines the rules that should be used to encrypt and decrypt the data. Addressed access policy is managed by the system administrator and must be protected against the loss of integrity
A. Programming components of the system	Software includes executable code that implements sharing services and verification rules based on addressed access policies. This software must be protected against loss of integrity
A. Users and dispatcher data for authentication and authorization	Data allowing the user and the dispatcher to authenticate and authorize. The successful end of the authentication carries out the mobile device on standby to execute commands of an authenticated entity. These data must be protected against the loss of integrity and confidentiality
A. Validation Data	All data necessary to carry out the verification of the rights of the entity to decrypt the document. These data must be obtained from a Standard Trusted Subsystem and stored on the mobile device on which the verification is made. These data must be protected against the loss of integrity.
A. Cryptographic keys stored in the system	Cryptographic keys used by the system in order to enforce their security functions. Cryptographic keys can be present in SP module and Cryptographic Key Storage, and can be exchanged between them via a trusted channel only. These data must be protected against the loss of confidentiality
A. Audit Records	Records include the events that are audited. These events should be detected and recorded by the system. These data must be protected against the loss of availability

4.2   The Assumption of the System

This section describes the assumptions concerning MobInfoSec system security environment.

4.3   The Threats in the System

Threats must be identified in order to accurately determine the security requirements. Because the threat is a result of the attack on the assets, it is important to correctly identify these attacks, especially those which use the currently known vulnerabilities in mobile devices [15-16]. Table 2 shows the identified threats of MobInfoSec system.

Table 2. The main assumption of MobInfoSec system

AE. Configuration of MobInfoSec system	It is assumed that: –MobInfoSec is properly installed and configured (virus protection is ensured, dedicated access to the system functions, etc.); –all SF are properly configured in such a way as to ensure that the security policies will be enforced on all connections associated with the components of MobInfoSec.
AE. Access policies for sensitive information	It is assumed that an access to classified information is protected in MobInfoSec in accordance with the following principles of ORCON model: –the resource (document, classified information) has a creator who is authorized to process the document (he/she does not have permission to access rights management); –the dispatcher of resource (document, classified information) manages the access rights on behalf of the creator; –copies of the resource (document, classified information) have the same access restrictions as the original resource (nobody can create copies with other privileges); –the entity that granted the right to access the resource from the dispatcher may temporarily delegate the right to access to a third party, provided that confidence in the assertion and attribute certificates of that party will be at least at the same level as confidence in the assertion and attribute certificates of party delegating their rights of access.
AE. Authenticity of a policy origin	It is assumed that the addressed access policies used by TOE and their templates are authentic.
AE. Cryptographic module of a mobile device	It is assumed that the mobile device has a SP class security module. SP module directly or indirectly allows, among others: –secure storage of cryptographic objects (including keys) and data; –device authentication; –authentication and integrity check of local software enabling access to classified information; –authorize access to the document on the basis of policies, certificates and attribute assertions; –document decryption; –protection (or separation) of the portion of operational memory in which the decrypted document is stored (to protect against unauthorized reading).

Table 3. The most important identified threats of the MobInfoSec system.

T. Damage to the system	Accidental or intentional damage to the system. –Accidental damage to the functions and/or parameters of the system can occur, for example, when entity encrypting or decrypting data removes one or more components of hardware and/or software, which are part of the system. –Deliberate damage may occur as a result of attempts to modify the components of the system by an attacker, for example, by installing false programs or applications without the knowledge of users. This damage can lead to the creation of the invalid ciphertext, the creation of the ciphertext without the knowledge of the dispatcher of the document, the creation of the ciphertext using spoofed addressed access policies, the input data validation damage or the damage to the decrypted data, etc.
T. Unauthorized access to the system	Malicious user, process or an external entity may mask as an authorized entity to gain unauthorized access to data or system resources or misrepresent yourself as a system to obtain data authentication and authorization belonging to the entities having the rights to the encryption /decryption.
T. Modification of documents set	An attacker can modify the list of selected documents for encryption, e.g. by installing false software, applications, or as a result of damage to the system code.
T. Substituting data	One or several components responsible for the form of representation of the encrypted or decrypted data can be substituted (e.g. false application) during the process of creating the ciphertext or during the transfer of it to the mobile device in order to decrypt by the user. This threat could lead to the creation of the ciphertext based on data different from those that have been selected by the dispatcher. The same applies to the decryption process by the user.
T. Malicious or flawed applications	Applications run on a mobile device may contain malicious executable code. This code can be used unconsciously or deliberately by the author (e.g. programmer), may also be a part of the software library. Malicious applications may try to publish data to which they obtained unauthorized access. They can also perform the attacks on the system platform that will provide them with additional privileges. Malicious applications may be able to control mechanisms to capture the signals from the sensors embedded in devices (e.g. GPS, camera, microphone) and to collect in this way information and data transmitted or residing on the device.
T. Unauthorized application update	A malicious third party may attempt to deliver end-user application updates that may compromise the security functions of the system.
T. Access to communication channels	Attacker can gain access to data protected by cryptographic mechanisms during the transmission by using a trusted channel between the components of the system, modifying the data during their transfer in a manner undetectable by the user.
T. Disclosure of authenticated and authorized data	The authenticated and authorized data of an encrypting/decrypting entity may be disclosed. This includes interception by an attacker of data entered into the system, the use of any unattended mobile device without the use of adequate security during the operation decryption, performing incorrect operations misleading to the encryption/decryption entity, the attack using the full search method the value of authentication and authorizing or divining or as a result of unintentionally sent data to a destination other than that indicated by the original sender.
T. Modification of a set of addressed access policies	Malicious user can access in a manner allowing to add or remove one or more addressed access policies supported by the system. In the case of addition of policies the result can be correct validation of compliance with the policies invalid ciphertexts, and in the case of deletion it becomes impossible to verify the decrypted ciphertexts.

4.4   The Security Policy of the System

This section sets out the principles of an organizational nature, applicable to the system.

Table 4. Security Policy Supporting the MobInfoSec system

P. Data Presentation	The system must have the ability to present the entity encrypting/decrypting copy of encrypted or decrypted data and it should not be allowed to encrypt or decrypt the data if one can't present the entity or entities will not be informed. If the decrypted data are presented, the system should not be allowed to make a copy of data that is not following the rules set out in the addressed access policies.
P. Encryption/ decryption of documents	The system must allow for the encryption/decryption of single or multiple documents. The authorization granted by the encryption and/or decryption of the multiple documents must be based on the same encryption attributes that are necessary for a single document.
P. Compatibility attributes	To prevent the creation of improper ciphertexts or the loss of confidentiality of the ciphertexts, the system must check if all encryption attributes selected by ciphertexting person are compatible with the addressed access policies.
P. Interruption of encryption/decryption	The encrypting/decrypting entity must be able to interrupt the process before activation key encryption/decryption.
P. Explicit agreement from the Dispatcher and the user of a document	The system must oblige the Dispatcher/User for the implementation of a set of non-trivial operations to verify their willingness to encrypt/decrypt the document before running the proper process encryption /decryption of the document(s)
P. Compliance of Certificates:	To prevent the loss of confidential data contained in ciphertexts, the system must verify that the certificates (including certificates belonging to certification path), which are used during the authentication and authorization of shadows owners , are compatible with the addressed access policies.
P. Authenticity of certificate	The system should monitor the presence and validity of the certification path between the certified decryption entity and trusted point specified in the addressed access policies
P. Validity of certificate	To prevent improper ciphertexts or loss of confidentiality of the ciphertexts, the system must verify that the certificate selected by the dispatcher has been successfully applied in the period of its validity in accordance with the addressed access policies.
P. Integrity of validation data	The system should control the user data integrity validation on mobile devices.
P. Management	The system must allow the operator to manage addressed access policies, certificates and assertions (adding and removing them).

4.5   Security Objectives for the System

This section defines the security objectives that correspond to the identified assumptions and threats to the system, and support its security policy.

Table 5. The main assumptions and security objectives of MobInfoSec system

O. Management	The system must allow the dispatcher to define addressed access policies and their publication, and allow the operator to manage this addressed access policies, certificates and assertions (adding and removing them).
O. Secure communication	The system provides the opportunity to build a trusted communication channel between its components and to detect any violation.

Table 5. (*continued*)

O. Data protected in communication channel	System protects the encrypted data, authenticated encryption attributes, etc., against disclosure and modification when they are transmitted between its components.
O. Update and verification of mobile device software	System ensures that any updates to the user subsystem components and SP token must be automatically verified for their invariability and their origin.
O. Monitoring system and user application	System/user application provides the ability to generate event records for the audit and to send them on request to the administrator, operator and user.
O. Removal of resident information	System ensures that all data are permanently deleted and are not available.
O. Lock of the session	The system provides mechanisms that allow the temporary suspension of unattended user session, which can be captured and allow it to resume only after re-authentication.
O. End of the session	The system should impose a limit on the time that has elapsed between the taking by the dispatcher decision to start the encryption process and the time for calculating the value of the ciphertext. The same requirements apply to the process of decrypting the ciphertext by the user. In case of detecting the state of the system lock, the session ends.
O. Authentication and authorization of the administrator, operator, etc. of the system	The system should provide the administrator, operator and user to enter their authentication and authorization data before accessing its functions and before carrying out any specific measures provided therein.
O. Integrity of services	Before the system will allow users to access the provided services, it should check their integrity and the integrity of the parameters necessary for their proper operation.
O. User's warning	The system should alert the operator encryption/decryption and allow to interrupt the process of encryption/decryption in a situation where it is impossible to present the dispatcher and the user encrypted data or the encryption attributes indicated by the identifier addressed access policies, and/or where the data encrypted or decrypted are not conform to the syntax format describing it.
O. Integrity of encrypted data	It must ensure the integrity of encrypted data formats used from the time they were formatted for the creation of the ciphertext.
O. Consent of the dispatcher/user	The system should provide the dispatcher/user mechanism enabling (on a voluntary and explicit basis) the consent to initiate the process of selecting a document or documents in order to create/decrypt the ciphertext. In addition, the system should require the dispatcher/user a non-trivial initiation of the process excluding any randomness of this decision.
O. Process interruption	The system should provide the ciphering /deciphering with the mechanism that allows it to interrupt the process of encryption/decryption before activating the appropriate key.
O. Processes protection	The system must provide protection against arbitrary interference by untrusted processes, peripheral devices and communication channels, and intruders interfering with these processes, which are used during the encryption/decryption, and during the creation of encrypted data as indicated in the creation of ciphertext request.
O. Confidentiality of data authentication and authorization:	The system must ensure the confidentiality of authentication and authorization data which belongs to the encryption/decryption entity.

O. Integrity of addressed access policies:	Before each use, the system should inspect the integrity of the addressed access policies. The system should not allow to decrypt the ciphertext if the violations of the addressed access policies integrity is detected
O. Set of documents	After acceptance by the dispatcher a permission to encrypt documents, the system must ensure that the processed set of documents actually corresponds exactly to selected one, and encryption attributes used must be identical for each document.
O. Starting the application	The system must run the application upon the user request to allow it to present the attributes of data encryption and decryption after the encryption, without revealing their content to third parties. If the system can't run this application, it should warn the user
O. Compliance of attributes	The system should verify compliance of used encryption attributes with the addressed access policies.
O. Compliance of validation data	The system shall verify that the validation data supplied for the purpose of decrypting the data comply with the criteria of addressed access policies.
O. Time stamping	The system should provide the ability to bind to the ciphertext with the reliable timestamp, which will allow (according to the addressed access policies) to confirm the creation of the ciphertext before a certain date.
O. Validity of certificate	The system must control that the certificate selected by the encryption entity is used for its intended purpose and only during the period of its validity.
O. Certification path	The system should monitor whether there is a valid certification path between the certified entity decryption and certificate of one of the selected points of trust, as defined in the addressed access policies.
O. Compliance of certificates	The system shall verify that the certificates (including certificates belonging to certification path) used during the authentication and authorization owners of shadows addressed in accordance with a given access policy.
O. Compliance of decryption key reproducibility	The system should monitor whether the process of acquiring the shadows necessary to restore the decryption key is compatible with the target site access policies.
OE. TOE configuration	TOE must be properly installed and configured so that as soon as you start passing in a safe state. TSFs implemented on mobile devices must be configured by the administrator of TOE in order to properly support the adopted TSP.
OE. Authenticity of a policy origin	Before the addressed access policy to information and their templates are approved, the operator of TOE must ensure the authenticity of their origin.
OE. Access to PKI services	ICT environment of the TOE must ensure access to: ⊢certificates, assertions, and other necessary validation data; ⊢information about PKI services supporting group encryption/ decryption schemes and protocols for authentication and protection of exchanged messages; ⊢other PKI services necessary for the proper operation of the TOE (e.g. to support the secure establishment of distribution channels and revocation of certificates).

4.6 The Security Functional Requirements

To determine the security functional requirements for MobInfoSec system justifying the selection of security objectives and the relationship between these components, the requirements based on the CC [13,14] and the trust model described in [17,18] are used. The results of the selection of these security functional requirements are presented in Table 6.

Table 6. Functional requirements meeting the objectives of MobInfoSec system security

Security audit (FAU)	Audit data generation (FAU_GEN.1), User identity association (FAU_GEN.2, Audit review (FAU_SAR.1), Restricted audit review (FAU_SAR.2), Selective audit (FAU_SEL.1), Protected audit trail storage (FAU_STG.1), Action in case of possible audit data loss (FAU_STG.3), Prevention of audit data loss (FAU_STG.4),.
Cryptographic support (FCS)	Cryptographic key generation (FCS_CKM.1), Cryptographic key distribution (FCS_CKM.2), Cryptographic operation (FCS_COP.1),.
User data protection (FDP)	Export of user data with security attributes (FDP_ETC.2), Subset information flow control (FDP_IFC.1), Simple security attributes (FDP_IFF.1), Import of user data with security attributes (FDP_ITC.2), Full residual information protection (FDP_RIP.2), Advanced rollback (FDP_ROL.2), Stored data integrity monitoring and action (FDP_SDI.2),
Identification and authentication (FIA)	SSF Generation of secrets (FIA_SOS.2), Timing of authentication (FIA_UAU.1), User authentication before any action (FIA_UAU.2), Protected authentication feedback (FIA_UAU.7), Timing of identification (FIA_UID.1), User identification before any action (FIA_UID.2),
Security management (FMT)	Management of security functions behaviour (FMT_MOF.1), Management of security attributes (FMT_MSA.1), Static attribute initialisation (FMT_MSA.3), Management of SSF data (FMT_MTD.1), Specification of Management Functions (FMT_SMF.1), Security roles (FMT_SMR.1),
Protection of the SSF (FPT)	Basic internal SSF data transfer protection (FPT_ITT.1), Simple trusted acknowledgement (FPT_SSP.1), Time stamps (FPT_STM.1), Inter-SSF basic SSF data consistency (FPT_TDC.1), SSF testing (FPT_TST.1),
System access (FTA)	SSF-initiated session locking (FTA_SSL.1), SSF-initiated termination (FTA_SSL.3), Default system access banners (FTA_TAB.1), System session establishment (FTA_TSE.1)
Trusted path/channels (FTP)	Inter-SSF trusted channel (FTP_ITC.1), Trusted path (FTP_TRP.1),

5   Summary

This article provides an overview of a system for cryptographic protection of sensitive data on mobile devices, implementing the functionality resulting from the requirements of ORCON model and information mobility. It presents the most important security functional requirements imposed on this type of system working in a distributed environment. The law on protection of Sensitive Information [4], the most representative ISO/IEC standards [12,14,19], all analysed attacks, especially those that use currently known vulnerabilities in mobile devices [15,16], and security profiles for mobile devices [19-21] were taken into account in order to accurately identify the possible threats, define the security policy and security objectives to minimize the impact of threats and support the activities stated in the security policy.

Acknowledgment. This scientific research work is supported by National Centre for Research and Development (NCBiR) of Poland (grant No PBS1/B3/11/2012) in 2012-2015.

References

1. Chen, Y.-Y., Lee, R.B.: Hardware-Assisted Application-Level Access Control. In: Samarati, P., Yung, M., Martinelli, F., Ardagna, C.A. (eds.) ISC 2009. LNCS, vol. 5735, pp. 363–378. Springer, Heidelberg (2009)
2. Hyla, T., Pejaś, J., El Fray, I., Maćków, W., Chocianowicz, W.: Sensitive Information Protection on Mobile Devices Using General Access Structures. In: ICONS-IARIA, pp. 192–196 (2014)
3. Pejaś, J., Hyla, T., Kryński, J.: ORCON access control monitored by the initiator: theoretical and practical implementation method. In: National Conference on Cybercrime and Information Security, Warsaw, Poland, 21 pages (2012)
4. Protection of sensitive information, Polish Act of 5 August 2010, Dz.U. 2010 nr 182 position 1228
5. Hołyst, B., Pomykała, J.: Cybercrime, information security and cryptology. Prosecution and Law, 30 (2011)
6. Bishop, M.: Computer Security: Art and Science. Addison Wesley (2002)
7. Shamir, A.: How to share a secret. Communication of the ACM 22, 612–613 (1979)
8. Blakley, G.R.: Safeguarding cryptographic keys. In: AFIPS, pp. 313–317 (1979)
9. Benaloh, J., Leichter, J.: Generalized secret sharing and monotone functions. In: Goldwasser, S. (ed.) Advances in Cryptology - CRYPTO 1988. LNCS, vol. 403, pp. 27–35. Springer, Heidelberg (1990)
10. Tassa, T.: Hierarchical threshold secret sharing. Journal of Cryptology 20, 237–264 (2007)
11. Nakielski, B., Pomykała, J.: Simple dynamic threshold decryption based on CRT and RSA. Journal of Telecommunications and Information Technology 2, 70–73 (2009)
12. ISO/IEC 15408, Information technology — Security techniques — Evaluation criteria for IT security, Part 1: Introduction and general model (2012)
13. ISO/IEC 15408, Information technology — Security techniques — Evaluation criteria for IT security, Part 2: Security functional requirements (2012)
14. ISO/IEC 15408, Information technology — Security techniques — Evaluation criteria for IT security, Common Methodology for Information Technology Security Evaluation (2012)
15. Fortinet's FortiGuard Labs, Reveals Newest of mobile Malware Trends in Latest Threat Report, http://www.fortinet.com/resource_center/whitepapers/threat-landscape-report-2014.html
16. F-Secure, Mobile threat report, http://www.f-secure.com/static/doc/labs_global/Research/Mobile_Threat_Report_Q3_2013.pdf
17. El Fray, I.: Method of determining the trust in the information system based on the process of assessing and treating risk, monograph Informatics, West Pomeranian University of Technology of Szczecin (2013)
18. El Fray, I.: About some application of risk analysis and evaluation. Kluwer International Series in Engineering and Computer Science 752, 283–292 (2003)
19. Protection Profile for Mobile Device Fundamentals, NIAP (2013)
20. Protection Profile for Mobile Device Management, NIAP (2013)
21. Protection Profile for Network Devices, NIAP (2012)

Implicit and Explicit Certificates-Based
Encryption Scheme

Tomasz Hyla, Witold Maćków, and Jerzy Pejaś

West Pomeranian University of Technology, Szczecin
Faculty of Computer Science and Information Technology, Poland
{thyla,wmackow,jpejas}@zut.edu.pl

Abstract. Certificate-based encryption (CBE) combines traditional public-key encryption and certificateless encryption. However, it does suffer to the Denial of Decryption (DoD) attack called by Liu and Au. To capture this attack, they introduced a new paradigm called self-generated-certificate public key cryptography. In this paper we show that the problem of DoD attack can be solved with a new implicit and explicit certificates-based public key cryptography paradigm. More importantly, we propose a concrete implicit and explicit certificate-based encryption (IE-CBE) scheme that defends against DoD attack. This new scheme is enhanced version of CBE scheme and preserves all its advantages, i.e., every user is given by the trusted authority an implicit certificate as a part of a private key and generates his own secret key and corresponding public key. In addition, in the IE-CBE scheme trusted authority has to generate an explicit certificate for a user with some identity and a public key. We prove that our scheme is IND-CCA2- and DoD-Free secure in the random oracle model as hard is to solve p-BDHI and k-CCA problems.

Keywords: Pairing based cryptography, implicit certificate, explicit certificate, encryption scheme, random oracle model.

1   Introduction

In Asiacrypt 2003, S. Al-Riyami and K. Paterson [1] introduced a new cryptographic paradigm called Certificateless Encryption (CLE). The CLE scheme is an intermediate step between Identity-Based Encryption (IBE) schemes and Public Key Encryption (PKE) schemes based on traditional public key cryptography (see [1, 2, 3, 4, 5]). In the CLE schemes, a Trusted Authority (TA) is involved in issuing user partial private keys computed from TA's master secret. The user also independently generates an additional secret value and calculates both the private and corresponding public keys. Even if a TA knows the user's partial private key, impersonation is impossible.

In PKE approach, the message sender needs to retrieve the authenticated parameters from the Certificate Authority (CA), the user's public key, and the certificate signed by the CA. In CLE, the message sender also needs to retrieve the authenticated parameters from the TA and the user's public key, but not any certificate [5]. On the one side this last CLE feature allows to eliminate the third-party queries for the

K. Saeed and V. Snášel (Eds.): CISIM 2014, LNCS 8838, pp. 651–666, 2014.

certificate, but on other side the lack of a certificate does not allow to identify the proper public key. As a result, the sender may choose a wrong public key, or even use another one which is never owned by the intended recipient.

Liu J. K., *et al.* [6] were the first to notice that a CLE schemes did not prevent a sender from encrypting a message using an incorrect public key and termed this feature as a Denial of Decryption (DoD) attack, since this possibly denies the recipient's opportunity to get a correct decryption result. In DoD attack the adversary cannot gain any secret information, but any authorised user is also not able to decrypt this information and get the normal service. The adversary can succeed to launch this attack since there is no checking whether the public key is associated with the proper person or not.

Unfortunately, the certificate-based encryption (CBE) schemes introduced by Gentry in 2003 [7] also do not resist the DoD attacks. Each user in the CBE scheme achieves a certificate from a TA. However, this certificate is a part of a private key, so that certificate is implicit and should be kept in secrecy. The secrecy of the implicit certificate means that the encrypting subject implicitly assumes existence of a certificate related to the recipient of an encrypted message. However, is this assumption correct in any case? No, because CBE scheme did not prevent a sender from encrypting a message using a public key which does not correspond to the recipient's identity *ID* for which the message is intended.

In the literature a few solution of the DoD problem exists (e.g., [6], [8, 9]). One of the firsts belongs to Liu J. K., *et al.* [6], which propose the idea of self-generated-certificate public key encryption (SGC-PKE) to address this problem. Same as CLE and CBE schemes, the TA in SGC-PKE scheme is trusted to only issue a partial private key after user's authentication. The underlying idea for the construction of SGC-PKE scheme consists of asking the recipient to use one partial private key to certify (to sign) the public key and only then to share a correct copy of the public key, while the second one to decrypt the ciphertext received from the sender. As a result, there are two full private keys, one for CLE and the other for certificateless signature (CLS).

It is noteworthy that other SGC-PKE scheme given by Lai, J. and Kou, K. [8] essentially instantiates above generic construction of Liu J. K., *et al.* [6]. In Lai-Kou's scheme the receiver and the TA must undertake a protocol before the receiver can sign its identity and public keys using private key. This last operation means that the receiver creates a digital self-generated certificate which binds the receiver's encryption key to its identity.

Dent, A.W. [9] describes the certificate-chain certificateless encryption scheme that combines a SGC-PKE approach with a traditional public-key encryption scheme PKE. This scheme demonstrates that a PKI-based public-key encryption scheme with a certificate generated by the CA (Certificate Authority) can be used to instantiate a BSS certificateless encryption scheme [10] with receiver self-generated certificate.

The above-mentioned schemes have one fundamental advantage: they allow for the authentication of the receiver's identity and its public key. Therefore, if a sender wishes to encrypt a message, then the sender first checks whether the certificate correctly authenticates the encryption key for the receiver's identity. This procedure resembles a traditional public key encryption systems based on Public Key Infrastructure (PKI): the message senders still need to retrieve and verify the self-generated certificates. The only difference from the PKE approach is another certification process including the issuance and management of certificates. In SGC-PKE, the certificate is self-generated and managed by the receiver, while in the PKE, it is generated and managed by the CA. This last features cannot be rather treated as an advantage of SGC-PKE compared with PKE, because such SGC-PKE schemes do not allow building global encryption systems.

1.1   Our Contribution

In this paper, we introduce a new paradigm called Implicit and Explicit Certificates-Based Public Key Cryptography (IEC-PKC) to defend against the DoD attack and propose a concrete encryption scheme (IE-CBE). This scheme preserves all advantages of Certificate-Based Public Key Cryptography (CB-PKC), i.e., every user is given, by the TA, an implicit certificate as a part of a private key and generates his own secret key as well as corresponding public key. In addition, in the IE-CBE scheme the TA has to generate an explicit certificate for a user with some identity and a public key. The purpose of this explicit certificate is similar both to the self-generated certificate in SGC-PKE and the one in traditional PKC. However, the main difference is that in SGC-PKE schemes two secret keys are randomly generated, while in IE-SK-CBE only one. The implicit and explicit certificates should be related with each other in such a way that no one, even the entity of those certificates and their issuer (TA authority) should not be able to recreate an implicit certificate using the explicit certificate.

1.2   Paper Organisation

The remainder of this paper is organized as follows. In Section 2 we present a formal definition for the Implicit and Explicit Certificate-Based Encryption (IE-CBE) scheme and its security model. In Section 3, we present IE-CBE Scheme based on Sakai-Kasahara encryption scheme [3, 4] derived from CBE [12] schemes and provide a formal security proof of it in Section 4. The paper ends with conclusions.

2   An Implicit and Explicit Certificate-Based Encryption Scheme

2.1   Generic IE-CBE Encryption Scheme

In this section, we present a formal definition for the IE-CBE scheme. The three main entities involved in an IE-CBE scheme are a sender, a receiver and a trusted authority chosen by the sender. The scheme uses bilinear pairings [15] and using notions similar to those presented by S. Al-Riyami, et al. [1].

Definition 1. An implicit and explicit certificate-based encryption scheme (IE-CBE) is the 7-tuple of algorithms which are defined in Table 1.

Table 1. Generic IE-CBE encryption scheme definition

Algorithm	Input	Output	Run by
Setup	1^k	$params$, P_0, s_{TA}	TA; s_{TA} is secret
Create-User	$params$, P_0, ID_R	$s_{2_{ID_R}}$, Pk_{ID_R}, $\overline{CI}_{ID_R}$	User; $s_{2_{ID_R}}$ is secret
Extract-Partial-Private-Key	$params$, P_0, s_{TA}, $\overline{CI}_{ID_R}$	Sk'_{ID_R}, CI_{ID_R}	TA for each user
Certificate-Generate	$params$, P_0, s_{TA}, CI_{ID_R}	$Cert_{ID_R}$	TA for each user.
Set-Private-Key	$params$, $\overline{CI}_{ID_R}$, Sk'_{ID_R}, $s_{2_{ID_R}}$	Sk_{ID_R}	User; Sk_{ID_R} is secret
Encrypt	$params$, CI_{ID_R}, $Cert_{ID_R}$, m	$C^m_{ID_R}$ or $\perp$	User that encrypts m
Decrypt	$params$, CI_{ID_R}, Sk_{ID_R}, $C^m_{ID_R}$	m	User that decrypts m

Notations:

1^k — security parameter

$C^m_{ID_R}$ — a ciphertext

$Cert_{ID_R}$ — an user's certificate

$\overline{CI}_{ID_R}$ — user's partial certificate information (includes Pk_{ID_R}, P_0, ID_{TA}, ID_R,)

CI_{ID_R} — a full certificate information (includes Pk_{ID_R}, P_0, ID_{TA}, ID_R, τ) of user with ID_R

ID_R — receiver identity

ID_{TA} — trusted authority identity

m — a plaintext $m \in (0,1)^n$

n — number of bits

$params$ — system parameters

P_0 — master public keys

$s_{2_{ID_R}}$ — a secret key value

s_{TA} — master private key

$Sk_{ID_R} = \left(s_{2_{ID_R}}, \overline{Sk}_{ID_R} \right)$ the full user's private key

Sk'_{ID_S} — a blinded partial private key

$\overline{Sk}_{ID_R}$ — an unblinded value of Sk'_{ID_R}

τ — time period for which the information in CI_{ID_R} is valid

$\perp$ — not valid symbol

It is required that algorithms from Table 1 must satisfy the standard consistency constraint, i.e., for all $m \in \{0,1\}^n$, **Decrypt**($C^m_{ID_R}$, $params$, CI_{ID_R}, Sk_{ID_R}) = m, where **Encrypt**(m, $params$, CI_{ID_R}, $Cert_{ID_R}$) → $C^m_{ID_R}$, **Certificate-Generate** (s_{TA}, P_0, $params$, $\overline{CI}_{ID_R}$) → ($Cert_{ID_R}$, CI_{ID_R}) and (Pk_{ID_R}, Sk_{ID_R}, $Cert_{ID_R}$) is a valid public/private certified key pair.

2.2   Security Model

The security model should appropriately describe the real-world security needs to demonstrate that the scheme resists all practical attacks, but the model should not be so powerful that it would require to use overly complex and inefficient schemes in order to meet the security notions [9]. We require the IND-CCA2 [6], [8, 9], [12] notion of security for the encryption scheme. This captures the notion that no attacker can determine any information about a message from a ciphertext even, if they can obtain the decryptions of any other adaptively prepared ciphertext.

The security model of IE-CBE scheme is modified version of the models proposed by S. Al-Riyami and K. Paterson [1], A. Dent [9], Lai, J., Kou, K. [8] and J. K. Liu, et al. [6]. According to these models, there are two types of adversaries. **Type I** adversary is an uncertified user, who is allowed to impersonate an arbitrary victim by changing his public key with other public key of his own choice, that the sender uses to encrypt messages, but does not have access to the TA's master-key. It can also obtain partial and full secret keys of arbitrary identities, and the certificates of all users except the certificate for the forged certificate information of the victim. **Type II** adversary is a malicious TA that is equipped with master-key and can compute the master public key value maliciously (see [9], [11]), but is not allowed to replace public keys. The main goal of Type II adversary is to impersonate a victim with a given public key and without access to the corresponding secret private key chosen by the victim.

Typically, it is expected that the decryption oracle should be able to correctly respond to decryption queries made on identities whose public keys have been replaced by the Type I adversary and for which oracle does not know the corresponding private keys. However, such security model is to strong and does not reflect an attacker's real-life capabilities [9, 10]. In our IE-CIBE scheme we assumed that the challenger is not forced to attempt to decrypt ciphertext for which the public key has been replaced, if the corresponding secret key is not known. It is known as **Type I** adversary [6].

A security model is typically presented as a game played between an arbitrary (probabilistic polynomial-time, PPT) adversary A representing given an encryption scheme and a challenger (who represents a new algorithm B which uses A as a subroutine and supplies the answers to A's oracle queries). The challenger keeps a list of users in the system and all TA-issued certificates, their real public/private key pairs, and the public key value that the sender associates with each user. The adversary interacts with the challenger via a series of oracles which force the challenger to perform certain operations and model the different ways that the adversary can interact with the system.

Definition 2. (IND-CCA2⁻ security, compare [6], [8, 9], [12]). The IE-CBE encryption scheme is said to be IND-CCA2⁻ secure if no PPT adversary A of Type Ⅰ⁻ or Type II has a non-negligible advantage in the following game played against the challenger:

Setup. The challenger C takes a security parameter 1^k and runs the *Setup* (1^k) algorithm. It gives A the resulting system parameters *params* and a random TA public key P_0. If A is of Type Ⅰ⁻, the challenger keeps the master secret key s_{TA} to itself. Otherwise, it gives s_{TA} to A and additionally, a random public key Pk_* of some user.

Phase 1. In this phase, the adversary A can adaptively issue queries to the following oracles:

- *CreateUser-Query*(ID_R). On input an user's identity ID_R , the challenger first generates his public key $Pk_{ID_R} = \left(X_{ID_R}, Y_{ID_R}, Z_{ID_R}, R_{ID_R} \right)$. If a user with identity index $\left(ID_R, Pk_{ID_R} \right)$ is already created, then challenger responds with the public key Pk_{ID_R} associated with the identity ID_R . Otherwise, the challenger calculates the full private key Sk_{ID_R} and composes the certificate information CI_{ID_R} . Finally, the challenger calculates the explicit certificate $Cert_{ID_R}$ and outputs Pk_{ID_R} and CI_{ID_R} to A. The tuple ($\overline{ID}_R$, Sk_{ID_S} , Pk_{ID_R} , $Cert_{ID_S}$, CI_{ID_R}) is added to the $Users_{list}$ list and the user with identity $\overline{ID}_R = \left(ID_R, Pk_{ID_R} \right)$ is said to be created. We assume that other oracles defined below only respond to an identity which has been created.

- *Cert-Generate-Query*($\overline{ID}_R$, CI_{ID_R}). (*This oracle is applicable to Type I adversary.*) When adversary A queries a user with identity $\overline{ID}_R$ and the certificate information CI_{ID_R} , the challenger C returns the certificate $Cert_{ID_R}$ to A. If the identity $\overline{ID}_R \notin User_{list}$, the symbol $\perp$ is returned.

- *Extract-Partial-Private-Key-Query*($\overline{ID}_R$, CI_{ID_R}). (*This oracle is applicable to Type I adversary.*). On input of an identity index $\overline{ID}_R$ supplied by an adversary, challenger C returns a partial key $\overline{Sk}_{ID_R}$ whenever the user with identity index ID_{ID_R} has been created. Otherwise, a symbol $\perp$ is returned.

- *Private-Key-Extract-Query*($\overline{ID}_R$). (*This oracle is applicable to Type I adversary.*). On receiving a query for an identity index $\overline{ID}_R$, challenger C responds with the private key Sk_{ID_R} . If the identity $\overline{ID}_R$ has no associated private key or the user's public key has been replaced, the challenger C returns a symbol $\perp$.

- *Public-Key-Replace-Query*($\overline{ID}_R$, Pk'_{ID_R}). (*This oracle is applicable to Type I adversary.*) This oracle takes an identity $\overline{ID}_R$ and allows adversary A to replace a public key Pk_{ID_R} with a new value Pk'_{ID_R} chosen by him.

- *Certificate-Replace-Query*($\overline{ID}_R$, $Cert'_{ID_R}$). (*This oracle is applicable to Type I adversary.*) This oracle acts as *Public-Key-Replace-Query*, but this time the adversary A is able replace a previous certificate $Cert_{ID_R}$ with a new value $Cert'_{ID_R}$ chosen by him.

- *Decryption-Oracle*($\overline{ID}_R$, CI_{ID_R} , $C^m_{ID_R}$). This oracle takes as input an identity $\overline{ID}_R$, the user's certificate information CI_{ID_R} and the ciphertext $C^m_{ID_R}$ for some message m and returns the decrypted plaintext. If the user's public key has been replaced, it requires an additional input of the corresponding secret key for the decryption. If this secret key is unknown to oracle, then a symbol $\perp$ is returned (only in the case of Type Γ adversary).

Challenge. When the adversary A decides that Phase 1 is over, it outputs and submits two message (m_0, m_1), together with an identity $\overline{ID}_*$ of uncorrupted secret key and the corresponding certificate information CI_{ID_*}. If A is of Type II adversary, it is allowed additionally to generate the master public key P_0' of the TA different then its correctly generated static master public key P_0 and some state information [9], [11]. All information prepared by the adversary A are sent to the challenger C. The challenger picks a random bit $\beta \in \{0,1\}$ and computes $C_{ID_*}^{m_\beta}$, the encryption of the message m_β under the current public key Pk_{ID_*} for ID_*. If this ciphertext is correct, the challenger C sends $C_{ID_*}^{m_\beta}$ as the challenge to the adversary A. Otherwise the challenger C outputs $\perp$ and A loses the game.

Phase 2. In this phase, the adversary A may adaptively query the same oracles as in the Phase 1. In any moment it terminates game and outputs a guess $\beta' \in \{0,1\}$.

Guess. The adversary A wins this security game if $\beta \neq \beta'$ and the following restrictions are fulfilled:

- in Phase 2, the A cannot use *Decryption-Oracle* ($\overline{ID}_*$, CI_{ID_*}, $C_{ID_*}^{m_\beta}$) for the tuple ($\overline{ID}_*$, CI_{ID_*}) under which the message m_β was encrypted;

- in Phase 1, the adversary A of Type Γ cannot submit $\overline{ID}_*$ and/or CI_{ID_*} to *Cert-Generate-Query*, *Extract-Partial-Private-Key-Query* and *Private-Key-Extract-Query*;

- if A is Type II, the identity $\overline{ID}_*$ has not been submitted to *Private-Key-Extract-Query*.

The adversary's advantage is defined to be $Adv_{IE-CIBE}^{IND-CCA^-}(A) = |\Pr[\beta = \beta'] - 1/2|$ and the scheme IC-CIBE is said to be secure against the adversary A of Type Γ and II if this advantage is negligible.

For security, in addition to IND-CCA2$^-$, we require the IE-CIBE encryption scheme to be DoD-Free. The formal security model for DoD attacks is defined as a game played between the challenger and a PPT adversary (DoD adversary), which has the same power as the adversary A of a Type Γ.

Definition 3. (DoD-Free Security, see [6], [9]). We say that IE-CIBE encryption scheme is DoD-Free secure if no PPT adversary A has a non-negligible advantage in the following game played against the challenger:

Setup. The challenger C takes a security parameter 1^k and runs the *Setup (1^k)* algorithm. It gives A the resulting system parameters *params* and a random public key P_0 of the TA. The challenger keeps the master secret key s_{TA} to itself.

Queries. In this phase, the adversary A can adaptively issue queries to the same oracles which are given in Phase 1 to the adversary A of a Type Γ^- (see Definition 2).

Challenge. When the adversary A decides that Phase 1 is over, it outputs message m_* together with an identity $\overline{ID}_*$ and the corresponding certificate information CI_{ID_*}. All information are sent to the challenger C, which computes $C_{ID_*}^{m_*}$, the encryption of the message m_* under the current public key Pk_{ID_*} for ID_*. If the output of the encryption is $\perp$, then A immediately losses the game. Otherwise, it outputs $C_{ID_*}^{m_*}$.

Constrains. The adversary A wins the game if the following requirements are fulfilled:

- the ciphertext $C_{ID_*}^{m_*}$ computed in Challenge phase is not $\perp$;
- the output of the *Decrypt*($C_{ID_*}^{m_*}$, *params*, CI_{ID_*}, Sk_{ID_*}) is not equal m_* for the tuple ($\overline{ID}_*$, CI_{ID_*}) under which the message m_* was encrypted;
- the adversary has not been submitted $\overline{ID}_*$ and/or CI_{ID_*} to *Cert-Generate-Query*, *Extract-Partial-Private-Key-Query* and *Private-Key-Extract-Query*.

The DoD adversary's advantage is defined to be $Adv_{IE-CIBE}^{DoD-Free}(A) = \Pr[A\ wins]$.
The IND-CCA2$^-$ security model of IE-CIBE is a little different from the definition of the chosen ciphertext security model given in [8], [10], [12]. First, it contains two new queries on an explicit certificate extraction and its replacement, i.e., *Cert-Generate-Query* and *Certificate-Replace-Query* (the Type Γ^- adversary only), respectively. Second, the Type II adversary is challenged on a random partial public key of a user and the TA public key of its choice. Note that the Type II adversary is not required to show its knowledge of the matching private keys corresponding to these public keys. When using the IND-CCA2$^-$ and DoD-Free games we can define the security for the IE-CIBE scheme.

Definition 4. The IE-CBE encryption scheme is said to be secure if it is both IND-CCA2$^-$ secure and DoD-Free secure.

3   IE-CBE Scheme Based on Sakai-Kasahara encryption scheme

The IE-CBE scheme is constructed on the Sakai-Kasahara identity-based encryption scheme [3, 4] and is similar to the certificate-based encryption (CBE) scheme given by Y. Lu and J. Li [12].

3.1   Full Implicit and Explicit Certificate-Based encryption scheme (IE-CBE)

The proposed IE-SK-CBE scheme consists of eight algorithms: **Setup, Create-User, Extract-Partial-Private-Key, Certificate-Generate, Set-Public-Key, Set-Private-Key, Encrypt** and **Decrypt**:

Setup. For given security parameters 1^k and two cyclic groups $(G_1, +)$ and $(G_2, \times)$ of the same prime order $q>2^k$, a trusted authority (TA):

(a) generates P being a generator of G_1 and chooses the bilinear admissible pairing given as $\hat{e}: G_1 \times G_1 \to G_2$ (e.g., [1, 12, 15]);

(b) picks a random main key $s_{TA} \in_R Z_q^*$;

(c) calculates the public key $P_0 = (\overline{P_0}, \tilde{P})$, where $\overline{P_0} = s_{TA} P$ and $\tilde{P} = s_{TA} s_{TA} P$;

(d) selects five secure hash functions: $H_1 : \{0,1\}^* \to Z_q^*$, $H_2 : \{0, 1\}^* \times G_1^3 \to Z_q^*$, where notation G_1^3 is the Cartesian product of groups G_1 defined as $G_1^3 = G_1 \times G_1 \times G_1$, $H_3 : G_1 \times G_2 \times G_1 \to \{0, 1\}^n$, and $H_4 : \{0, 1\}^n \to \{0, 1\}^n$ for some integer $n>0$, where n is plaintext message $m \in \{0,1\}^n$ length in bits.

The message space is $M=\{0, 1\}^n$, while the ciphertext space is $C=G_1^* \times \{0, 1\}^n$.

Create-User. Decrypting entity R generates a key material that contains R private key and a partial public key.

(a) R chooses two secret random values $s_{1_{ID_R}}$, $s_{2_{ID_R}} \in_R Z_q^*$;

(b) R calculates a public key $Pk_{ID_R} = (X_{ID_R}, Y_{ID_R}, Z_{ID_R})$, where $X_{ID_R} = s_{2_{ID_R}} P$, $Y_{ID_R} = s_{2_{ID_R}} \overline{P_0}$ and $Z_{ID_R} = s_{2_{ID_R}} \tilde{P_0}$;

(c) R calculates parameters $userParams = \{UP_1, UP_2, X_{ID_R}, ID_R\}$, where $UP_1 = s_{1_{ID_R}} (s_{2_{ID_R}} + \overline{q}_{ID_R})^{-1} X_{ID_R}$ for $\overline{q}_{ID_R} = H_1(\overline{CI}_{ID_R})$ and $UP_2 = s_{1_{ID_R}} P$;

> Remark. The UP_1 value, as in the traditional PKC, proves by R to the TA the possession of secret key $s_{2_{ID_R}}$ corresponding to public key Pk_{ID_R} (see **Extract-Partial-Private-Key** algorithm).

(d) R composes the well-formed (i.e., using syntax rules specified by some data specification language like ASN.1 or XML) partial certificate information $\overline{CI}_{ID_R}$, filling it with desired values including the *userParams*, the public keys (P_0, Pk_{ID_R}) and identities for both the subject R and the TA;

(e) R sends $\overline{CT}_{ID_R}$ to TA.

Extract-Partial-Private-Key. *TA* authority calculates a blinded partial private key of an entity R:

(a) *TA* verifies and registers ID_R; if entity R is already registered, then TA omits registration and goes into key renewal mode;

(b) *TA* based on X_{ID_R} calculates Y_{ID_R} and Z_{ID_R}, then compares them with the content of $\overline{CT}_{ID_R}$, subsequently calculates a $\overline{q}_{ID_R} = H_1(\overline{CT}_{ID_R})$ and verifies if equation $\hat{e}(UP_1, X_{ID_R} + \overline{q}_{ID_R} P) = \hat{e}(X_{ID_R}, UP_2)$ is true; if it is false, the algorithm is ended; if it is true, TA has a proof, that identity ID_R is related to secret key $s_{2_{ID_R}}$ and to X_{ID_R}, Y_{ID_R}, Z_{ID_R};

(c) *TA* composes the full user certificate information CI_{ID_R}, including the public keys Pk_{ID_R} and P_0, identifiers of the user R and the *TA*, and the time period τ for which this information CI_{ID_R} is valid;

(d) TA calculates a blinded partial private key $Sk'_{ID_R} = (s_{TA} + q_{ID_R})^{-1} s_{TA} UP_1$, where $q_{ID_R} = H_1(CT_{ID_R})$ and together with CI_{ID_R} sends it to entity R.

Certificate-Generate. TA authority, using parameters received from R and values calculated during execution **Extract-Partial-Private-Key** algorithm, generates an explicit certificate $Cert_{ID_R}$ of an entity R.

(a) TA generates a certificate for an entity R, which binds identity with public key components:

$$Cert_{ID_R} = \frac{1}{s_{TA} + q_{ID_R}} P \tag{1}$$

(b) TA sends $Cert_{ID_R}$ to an entity R.

Set-Private-Key. An entity R calculates a full private key Sk_{ID_R}.

(a) R verifies correctness of Sk'_{ID_R}:

$$\hat{e}(Sk'_{ID_R}, Y_{ID_R} + q_{ID_R} X_{ID_R} + \overline{q}_{ID_R}(\overline{P}_0 + q_{ID_R} P)) = \hat{e}(P, s_{1_{ID_S}} s_{2_{ID_S}} \overline{P}_0) \tag{2}$$

(b) R calculates a second part of the private key:

$$\overline{Sk}_{ID_R} = s_{1_{ID_R}}^{-1}(s_{2_{ID_R}} + \overline{q}_{ID_R}) S'_k = \frac{1}{s_{TA} + q_{ID_R}} Y_{ID_R} \tag{3}$$

(c) R formulates a private key for entity R in the form: $Sk_{ID_R} = (s_{2_{ID_R}}, \overline{Sk}_{ID_R})$.

Encrypt. To encrypt the message $m \in \{0,1\}^n$, the sender S:

(a) calculates $q_{ID_R} = H_1(CT_{ID_R})$, and then verifies the authenticity of the certificate $Cert_{ID_R}$:

$$\hat{e}\left(Cert_{ID_R}, q_{ID_R}Y_{ID_R} + Z_{ID_R}\right) = \hat{e}\left(P, Y_{ID_R}\right) \tag{4}$$

$$\hat{e}\left(X_{ID_R}, \tilde{P}_0\right) = \hat{e}\left(Y_{ID_R}, \overline{P}_0\right) = \hat{e}\left(Z_{ID_R}, P\right) \tag{5}$$

Remark. When equations (4) and (5) are true, then components of public key Pk_{ID_R} are authentic, which implies that a public key Pk_{ID_R} belonging to the entity with an identity ID_R is authentic.

(b) if the verification result from previous step is positive, then S chooses a random number $v \in \{0,1\}^n$ and calculates:

$$r = H_2\left(v, m, ID_R, Pk_{ID_R}\right) \tag{6}$$

$$U = r\left(\overline{P}_0 + q_{ID_R}P\right) \tag{7}$$

$$k = H_3\left(U, \hat{e}\left(Cert_{ID_R}, r\left(Z_{ID_R} + q_{ID_R}Y_{ID_R}\right)\right), r\left(Y_{ID_R} + q_{ID_R}X_{ID_R}\right)\right) \tag{8}$$

$$V = v \oplus k, \ W = m \oplus H_4(v) \tag{9}$$

(c) S creates the ciphertext $C = (U, V, W)$ and sends it to a recipient R.

Decrypt. A decryption entity R reconstruct message m using ciphertext C.

(a) R calculates:

$$k' = H_3\left(U, \hat{e}\left(\overline{Sk}_{ID_R}, U\right), s_{2_{ID_R}}U\right) \tag{10}$$

$$v' = V \oplus k' \tag{11}$$

$$m' = W \oplus H_4(v') \tag{12}$$

$$r' = H_2\left(v', m', ID_R, Pk_{ID_R}\right) \tag{13}$$

(b) if $U \neq r'\left(H_1\left(CT_{ID_R}\right)P + \overline{P}_0\right)$, then decryption process is incorrect, otherwise m' is a correct plain text corresponding to the ciphertext $C = (U, V, W)$.

3.2   IE-CBE Scheme Correctness

Assume that the ciphertext $C = (U, V, W)$, the partial private key Sk_{ID_R} and the explicit certificate $Cert_{ID_S}$ were generated using the **Encrypt, Certificate-Generate** and **Extract-Partial-Private-Key** algorithms, respectively. Hence, combining equation (8) with equations (1), (3) and (10) shows the following:

$$k = H_3\left(U, \hat{e}\left(Cert_{ID_R}, r\left(Z_{ID_R} + q_{ID_R}Y_{ID_R}\right)\right), r\left(Y_{ID_R} + q_{ID_R}X_{ID_R}\right)\right) =$$

$$H_3\left(U, \hat{e}\left(\frac{1}{s_{TA} + q_{ID_R}}P, s_{2_{ID_R}}s_{TA}r\left(\overline{P}_0 + q_{ID_R}P\right)\right), s_{2_{ID_R}}r\left(\overline{P}_0 + q_{ID_R}P\right)\right) =$$

$$H_3\left(U, \hat{e}\left(\frac{1}{s_{TA} + q_{ID_R}}s_{2_{ID_R}}s_{TA}P, r\left(\overline{P}_0 + q_{ID_R}P\right)\right), s_{2_{ID_R}}U\right) = \tag{14}$$

$$H_3\left(U, \hat{e}\left(\overline{Sk}_{ID_R}, U\right), s_{2_{ID_R}}U\right) = k'$$

Furthermore, it is now easy to prove the correctness of equations (4):

$$\hat{e}\left(Cert_{ID_R}, q_{ID_R}Y_{ID_R} + Z_{ID_R}\right) =$$

$$\hat{e}\left(\frac{1}{s_{TA} + q_{ID_S}}P, \left(s_{TA} + q_{ID_R}\right)Y_{ID_R}\right) = \hat{e}\left(P, Y_{ID_R}\right) \tag{15}$$

3.3   IE-CBE Scheme Modification

Any certificate-based encryption (CBE) scheme contains an implicit certificate that is a part of a private key. Hence, it seems to be naturally to modify any particular encryption scheme based on both explicit and implicit certificate and produce a CBE scheme that can be proven secure.

Assume that this is possible in our case and we may remove the **Certificate-Generate** algorithm form IE-CBE scheme. The resulting scheme is a new scheme based on an implicit certificate (let's name it I-CBE, Implicit Certificate-Based Encryption scheme). Introduced change requires to remove certificate verification (Eq. 4) in the algorithm **Encrypt** and modify equation (8), which will be as follows (compare with Eq. 15):

$$k = H_3\left(U, \hat{e}\left(P, Y_{ID_R}\right), r\left(Y_{ID_R} + q_{ID_R}X_{ID_R}\right)\right) \tag{16}$$

<u>Remark.</u> It is easy to notice that a certificate $Cert_{ID_R}$ in relation with the scheme I-CBE plays in the IE-CBE scheme a similar role to self-generated certificate in relation with the underlying CL-PKE scheme in SGC-PKE scheme ([6], [8, 9]).

4   IE-CBE Scheme Security

In the IE-CBE construction, the implicit and explicit certificates are based on a short signature scheme given in [12, 16] that security depends on a k-CAA hard problem (see Definition 1). It means that if adversary is not able to counterfeit an explicit certificate, then it is not possible to execute a DoD attack and IE-CBE scheme is secure as hard is to solve k-CCA problem. Because IE-CBE scheme depends on the underlying I-CBE scheme complemented with an algorithm **Certificate-Generate**, hence it is natural to divide its security proof into two phases: in the first it must be shown that I-CBE scheme is IND-CCA2⁻ secure and in the second that IE-CBE scheme is DoD free.

A similar approach was used for a security model of SGC-PKE scheme [6], [8, 9], where they first examine the security of CL-PKE from which the SGC-PKE developed, and then consider the DoD-Free security. In our case, we construct the IE-CBE encryption scheme from an implicit certificate-based encryption (I-CBE) scheme and an explicit certificate built on a short signature defined in [16]. The security of resulting IE-CBE scheme needs to show that the requirements of Definition 4 are met and thus following Theorem should hold.

Theorem. The IE-CBE scheme is IND-CCA2⁻ and DoD-Free secure in the random oracle model.

To prove the above theorem, we first prove the *IND-CCA2* security of the IE-CBE scheme (Lemma 1 and 2) and then show that IE-CBE scheme is DoD-Free (Lemma 3).

Lemma 1. The IE-CBE scheme is IND-CCA2⁻ secure if IND-CCA2⁻ secure is the underlying I-CBE scheme.

Proof. The definition of IE-CBE given in Section 3.1 is the same as the definition of I-CBE from Section 3.3, except for **Certificate-Generate** algorithm which is used to generate the explicit certificates. This certificates have no influence on the semantic security of I-CBE scheme (see equation (16)), but provide the DoD-Free feature of IE-CBE scheme only (compare Lemma 2). Hence, it is clear that IND-CCA2⁻ security of I-CBE scheme implies IND-CCA2⁻ security of IE-CBE scheme.

Lemma 2. In the random oracle model, the I-CBE scheme is IND-CCA2⁻ secure under the p-BDHI assumption (p-BDHI problem, Boneh D., Boyen X. [14]).

The proof of Lemma 2 is similar to the proof of [13] and it is run on the basis of the IND-CCA2⁻ game (see Definition 2), in which the oracle **Cert-Generate-Query** is not accessible and no longer needed, as challenger C cannot now generate certificates and the adversary cannot use them in any operation. Due to its length the proof is not included here.

Besides the IND-CCA2⁻ security property, we require additionally IE-CBE scheme to be DoD-Free secure. The condition that IE-CBE scheme should meet are defined in Lemma given below.

Lemma 3. The IE-CBE scheme is DoD-Fee secure, assuming that the implicit and explicit certificates are existential unforgeable.

Proof. In IE-CBE scheme, the implicit and explicit certificates are short signatures computed using a signature scheme considered in [16]. According to Theorem 3 of [16] this signature scheme is existentially unforgeable under chosen message attack (EUF-CMA) in the random oracle model, assuming that k-CCA problem (k-CAA problem, Mitsunari S., et al. [13]) is believed to be computationally hard.

We now consider the DoD-Free game implemented with a Type Γ adversary A (see Definition 3), in which the adversary A models an uncertified entity. Suppose that algorithm F is a forger that breaks the short signatures. We wish to construct another algorithm B that uses A with algorithm F to solve the k-CAA problem. The algorithm B receives the k-CAA instance (a challenge) with $P, \overline{P}_0, \tilde{P} \in G_1$, $h_1, h_2, ..., h_k \in Z_q^*$ and $\dfrac{1}{h_1 + s_{TA}} P, ..., \dfrac{1}{h_k + s_{TA}} P$. Its goal is to compute a pair $\left(h^*, \dfrac{1}{h^* + s_{TA}} P \right)$ for some $h^* \notin \{h_1, ..., h_k\}$. As the algorithm B has access to the signing-oracle, hence B can answer all oracle queries given by A, including the queries for the implicit and explicit certificate signing.

When the queries phase of DoD-Free game is over, then the adversary A submits message m_* and an identity $\overline{ID}*$ to the B. An adversary A wins if following conditions hold (compare [6], [8]):

(a) the certificate $Cert_{ID_*}$ of CI_{ID_*} (with ID_* and Pk_{ID_*}) is valid (see Eq. 4);

(b) $Decrypt(C_{ID_*}^{m_*}, params, CI_{ID_*}, Sk_{ID_*}) \ne m_*$, where $Encrypt(m_*, params, CI_{ID_*}, Cert_{ID_*})$;

(c) the adversary never makes $Cert$-$Generate$-$Query$, $Extract$-$Partial$-$Private$-Key-$Query$ and $Private$-Key-$Extract$-$Query$ for $\overline{ID}*$ and/or CI_{ID_*}.

Due to the correctness of IE-CBE scheme (see Section 3.2), the equality $Decrypt(C_{ID_*}^{m_*}, params, CI_{ID_*}, Sk_{ID_*}) = m_*$ holds always if the condition (a) is satisfied. Because the hash function H_1 is collision-resistant and an adversary cannot find another distinct certificate information CI'_{ID_*} that is in collision with CI_{ID_*}, then the veracity of the condition (a) implies the public key Pk_{ID_*} associated with the certificate $Cert_{ID_*}$ (and the identity $\overline{ID}*$) has not been replaced. Hence, if the condition (b) holds, the public key Pk_{ID_*} had to be replaced. This means that $Encrypt(m_*, params, CI_{ID_*}, Cert_{ID_*}) \ne \bot$ and thus form the conditions (a) and (c) follows that the certificate $Cert_{ID_*}$ is a successful forgery. Consequently, challenger B can compute a group element $\left(s_{TA} + h^* \right)^{-1} P$, where $h^* = q_{ID_*} = H_1\left(CT_{ID_*} \right)$, which is the solution of the k-CAA problem.
This ends the proof.   □

5   Conclusions

This paper contains an encryption scheme IE-CBE that has been built on a new paradigm called Implicit and Explicit Certificates-Based Public Key Cryptography (IEC-PKC). The idea of this paradigm is similar to Self-Generated-Certificate Public Cryptosystem (SGC-PC) paradigm given in [6, 8] and provides a mechanism for strong authentication of the user's identity, its public key and relationship between these two elements. Moreover, any encryption scheme with this mechanism should be immune to the DoD attack. Our way of achieving this authentication mechanism is different from that used in SGC-PKE: we allow the TA to sign the user's identity and public key, instead of the user signing the self-certificate with TA-issued partial private key.

However, this explicit certificate is closely related to implicit certificate and its role is only technical (compare Eq. 14, 15 and 16). Following this approach we make formally analysis of the IE-CBE scheme security in the random oracle model and prove that the scheme is IND-CCA2- and DoD-Free secure, assuming p-BDHI and k-CCA problems to be computationally hard.

Our future works will focus on applying approach presented in this paper to our group encryption scheme CIBE-GAS [17, 18].

Acknowledgment. This scientific research work is supported by National Centre for Research and Development (NCBiR) of Poland (grant No PBS1/B3/11/2012) in 2012-2015.

References

1. Al-Riyami, S.S., Paterson, K.G.: Certificateless public key cryptography. In: Laih, C.-S. (ed.) ASIACRYPT 2003. LNCS, vol. 2894, pp. 452–473. Springer, Heidelberg (2003)
2. Boneh, D., Franklin, M.: Identity-Based Encryption from the Weil pairing. In: Kilian, J. (ed.) CRYPTO 2001. LNCS, vol. 2139, pp. 213–229. Springer, Heidelberg (2001)
3. Chen, L., Cheng, Z.: Security proof of Sakai-Kasahar's identity-based encryption scheme. In: Smart, N.P. (ed.) Cryptography and Coding 2005. LNCS, vol. 3796, pp. 442–459. Springer, Heidelberg (2005)
4. Sakai, R., Kasahara, M.: ID based cryptosystems with pairing on elliptic curve. Cryptology ePrint Archive, Report 2003/054 (2003)
5. Chow, S.S.M.: Certificateless Encryption. In M. Joye and G. Neven (Eds.) Identity-Based Cryptography, pp. 135-155. IOS Press, (2009)
6. Liu, J., Au, K., Susilo, M.H.: W.: Self-Generated-Certificate Public Key Cryptography and certificateless signature/encryption scheme in the standard model: Extended abstract. In: Bao, F., Miller, S. (eds.) ASIACCS 2007, pp. 273–283. ACM Press (2007)
7. Gentry, G.: Certificate-based encryption and the certificate revocation problem. In: Biham, E. (ed.) EUROCRYPT 2003. LNCS, vol. 2656, pp. 272–293. Springer, Heidelberg (2003)
8. Lai, J., Kou, W.: Self-generated-certificate public key encryption without pairing. In: Okamoto, T., Wang, X. (eds.) PKC 2007. LNCS, vol. 4450, pp. 476–489. Springer, Heidelberg (2007)
9. Dent, A.W.: A Brief Introduction to Certificateless Encryption Schemes and Their Infrastructures. In: Martinelli, F., Preneel, B. (eds.) EuroPKI 2009. LNCS, vol. 6391, pp. 1–16. Springer, Heidelberg (2010)
10. Baek, J., Safavi-Naini, R., Susilo, W.: Certificateless public key encryption without pairing. In: Zhou, J., López, J., Deng, R.H., Bao, F. (eds.) ISC 2005. LNCS, vol. 3650, pp. 134–148. Springer, Heidelberg (2005)
11. Au, M., Chen, H., Liu, J., Mu, J.K., Wong, Y., Yang, D.S., Malicious, G.: KGC Attacks in Certificateless Cryptography. In: ASIACCS, pp. 302–311 (2007)
12. Lu, Y., Li, J.: Constructing Efficient Certificate-based Encryption with Paring. Journal of Computers 4(1) (January 2009)

13. Mitsunari, S., Sakai, R., Kasahara, M.: A new traitor tracing. IEICE Transactions E85-A(2), 481–484 (2002)
14. Boneh, D., Boyen, X.: Efficient selective-ID secure identity-based encryption without random oracles. In: Cachin, C., Camenisch, J.L. (eds.) EUROCRYPT 2004. LNCS, vol. 3027, pp. 223–238. Springer, Heidelberg (2004)
15. Lynn, B.: On the implementation of pairing-based cryptosystems. PhD Thesis. Stanford University (2007)
16. Zhang, F., Safavi-Naini, R., Susilo, W.: An efficient signature scheme from bilinear pairings and its applications. In: Bao, F., Deng, R., Zhou, J. (eds.) PKC 2004. LNCS, vol. 2947, pp. 277–290. Springer, Heidelberg (2004)
17. Hyla, T., Pejaś, J.: A practical certificate and identity based encryption scheme and related security architecture. In: Saeed, K., Chaki, R., Cortesi, A., Wierzchoń, S. (eds.) CISIM 2013. LNCS, vol. 8104, pp. 190–205. Springer, Heidelberg (2013)
18. Hyla, T., Pejaś, J.: Certificate-Based Encryption Scheme with General Access Structure. In: Cortesi, A., Chaki, N., Saeed, K., Wierzchoń, S. (eds.) CISIM 2012. LNCS, vol. 7564, pp. 41–55. Springer, Heidelberg (2012)

Malware Behavior Modeling with Colored Petri Nets

Bartosz Jasiul[1], Marcin Szpyrka[2], and Joanna Śliwa[1]

[1] Military Communication Institute
C4I Systems' Department
ul. Warszawska 22a, 05-130 Zegrze, Poland
{b.jasiul,j.sliwa}@wil.waw.pl
[2] AGH University of Science and Technology
Department of Applied Computer Science
al. Mickiewicza 30, 30-059 Kraków, Poland
mszpyrka@agh.edu.pl

Abstract. We propose a solution which provides a system operator with a mechanism that enables tracking and tracing of malware behavior which – in consequence – leads to its detection and neutralization. The detection is performed in two steps. Firstly single malicious activities are identified and filtered out. As they come from the identification module, they are compared with malware models constructed in the form of Colored Petri nets. In this article we present our approach to malware modeling. Proposed method was implemented and practically verified in laboratory environment with emulated malicious activity at the hosts level.

Keywords: malware, cyber attack, Colored Petri net, malware detection, behavioral analysis.

1 Introduction

Computer systems are prone to cyber attacks even though they have number of security controls already deployed. Cyber criminals are focused on finding a way to bypass security controls and gain access into a protected network or a single host. For that reason organizations, companies, governments and institutions as well as ordinary citizens all over the world are interested in detection of all attempts of malicious actions targeted on their computer networks and single machines.

In general, the success rate of the applied method for malware detection depends on the reliability of the used malware model. Usually they are based on signatures which are bits of application code typical for malicious activity. Security controls (e.g. antivirus tools) might be maladjusted because signatures of new threats are not identified yet. Hackers often use existing parts of code in order to implement new types of malware. This allows, in return, to quickly develop signatures of new dangerous software. Therefore, the more signatures are deployed the more malicious applications are identified. On the other hand, one of the methods of misleading the signature-based detection systems is code obfuscation, the aim of which is generating – from already existing code – a new application that cannot be assessed yet as risky by security control [29],

K. Saeed and V. Snášel (Eds.): CISIM 2014, LNCS 8838, pp. 667–679, 2014.

[31]. This technique is simple to be used and potentially successful, so that also successful countermeasures are necessary. One of the examples is to follow behaviors of malicious software in order to identify them and eliminate from the protected system and computer machines. This article is focused on modeling of malware behavior with Colored Petri nets (CP-nets) [12], [30]. Our approach was implemented and verified in laboratory environment with success and various types of malware were detected.

2   Evading Virus Detection Technologies

The method of evading antivirus tools is generally called obfuscation. It is a technique aimed at generating new software that realizes the same functions as the original one but does not have its specific code signatures. It can be realized by modification of Java scripts, additional loops in the code that return to the point of execution (zero loops), encryption techniques run at program execution, etc.

The list of obfuscation techniques includes, but is not limited to:

- *Parasitic obfuscation* that is used to append, prepend, or insert code into data sections of files on disk [4].
- *Self-modification* that allows malware to modify its code during every infection. Thus, each infected file contains different variant of the virus [19].
- *Polymorphic coding* that is an obfuscation that consists in infecting files with an encrypted copy of the virus [1]. At each time an encryption key or even encryption method can be modified, therefore virus codes are different from one another in infections causing their signatures to be hard to detect [6]. If some part of code remains the same, an anti-virus tool can decrypt the code using an emulator. However, it is not always a successful technique. It allows to detect some malware and produce new signatures for them.
- *Metamorphic coding* that is a technique of rewriting the functions of software at each infection in a different way [5], [23]. Viruses that utilize this technique are very large and complex. Metamorphism makes viruses almost undetectable by signature-based tools.

Obfuscation techniques are very successful in hiding malicious code against byte-level content analysis [13], [15] and static analysis methods [8], [9] which make cyber attacks undetectable. Significant effort is made by cyber criminals in order to thwart detection by anti-malware tools. Moreover, methods of evading antivirus products will be developed as long as cyber crimes are profitable.

3   Malware Detection Techniques – An Overview

Great effort has been put lately in static analysis of malicious codes because this technique generally has brought good accuracy in malware detection [3], [14], [25]. Even though it is an appropriate technique [16] in case of traditionally compiled machine code, the most difficult problem it faces is difficulty to handle obfuscated binaries [28]. Additionally, obfuscation techniques are perceived as NP-hard for static analysis [20].

On the other hand, dynamic malware analysis is directed at reaching reliable tracks of executed malicious codes. Dynamic malware analysis may be based on setting up behavior clusters from sequences and measuring distances between single events [2], [18]. However, this approach suffers from the lack of external rules for data analysis. According to [7], [24] a successful method of dynamic malware analysis is comparison of specifications of malicious behavior with *hooked* processes at application level. Therefore one of the problems of dynamic malware analysis is necessity of building models of this malicious activity. The approach to malware modeling proposed in this article is based on utilization of Colored Petri nets used during the dynamic malware analysis.

It is worth to mention that Petri nets were already successfully adapted for identification of cyber threats. In work [17] authors observed that mathematical representation of Petri nets allows for modeling of computer misuse. Proposed mechanisms consisted in representation of known attack as a sequences of events. In this case the attack was presented as a Petri net graph. Comparing misuses with the Petri net graph allowed for detection of unwanted actions.

Colored Petri nets were also utilized for detection of DoS attacks in Wide Area Networks [10]. In this case Colored Petri nets were adapted to model router network connections in the area of The United States. It was proved that modifications in the network infrastructure made by DoS attacks can be detected by comparison of the current state to the modeled one. Moreover, this method was proposed as an early warning system against network attacks. Additionally, it can support development of network infrastructure security strategies.

Next major contribution in utilization of Colored Petri nets was identified in work [33] supported by US Air Force Office of Scientific Research. This outstanding research presents a new approach to formal specification of the malicious functionalities based on activity diagrams (Unified Modeling Language – UML diagrams) defined in an abstract domain. It introduces abstract functional objects that, along with system objects, could be used for creating generic specifications covering multiple functionality realizations. Methodology proposed in this work utilizes Colored Petri nets for recognition of functionalities at the system call level.

Our particular usage is also crucial in this article for CP-nets application in cyber defence, especially in malware modeling and detection, what has been shown in the following sections.

4 PRONTOnet – Malware Tracking

4.1 An Architecture of the Solution

In our work we proposed and developed behavior-oriented malware hunting tool, so-called PRONTO, that could be used in parallel to existing signature-based tools. The main assumption for the introduced method is that the malware was not recognized yet by the signature mechanisms. The aim therefore is to track its suspicious activities in order to find it while running in the system. PRONTO hunting tool performs its activity in two stages (Fig. 1):

- **Filtering of the system events** registered by the system monitors (sensors) to discover the main features of the hostile activity. These features are related to particular objects and actions triggered on that objects – e.g. registry (add entry, modify entry, delete registry entry, etc.), process (start, stop process, etc.), file (copy, delete, run, open, close file, etc.), domain (connect to, etc.), IP address (connect to, etc.);
- **Tracking suspicious activity** in order to discover malicious exploits running in the system. Filtered events are correlated in order to find similarities with the stored malware activities modeled in the form of Colored Petri nets. The result of malware tracking is the alarm that contains information vector about malicious activity, similarity to the known attacks and list of incidents that affected the system.

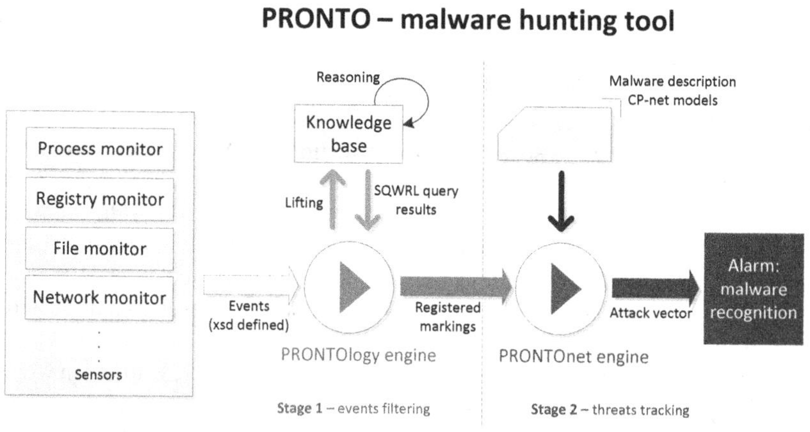

PRONTO – malware hunting tool

Fig. 1. PRONTO – malware hunting tool

The first stage which is related to capturing events from sensors and analyzing them with an expert system that uses – defined for the purpose of the method – comprehensive ontology, so called PRONTOlogy. Registered events in the form of XML objects are sent to the PRONTOlogy engine and lifted to add entries to the Knowledge Base. PRONTOlogy describes events registered by system monitors and is able, on the basis of rule engine and inference, with the use of specially defined rules [21], [22], to classify an event as potentially suspicious, malicious or regular. As a result, markings of the modeled malware in the form of CP-nets are delivered for further analysis.

This article presents only the second stage PRONTOnet which is related to malware modeling and detection with the use of Colored Petri nets. PRONTOnet provides formal model of malware behavior and allows to track suspicious activities potentially assigning them to the class of known malware types or identifying unknown ones. Known exploits can be invisible to signature-based malware detecting tools after their code has been obfuscated, although their activities can be easily observed. It also happens often that a new malware piece of software is composed of known components from other ones. This results in another behavior pattern that can be tracked as a new exploit, not identified yet. The result of threats tracking stage is an alert informing about identification of suspicious or malicious events with a certain similarity rate to the known malware types.

4.2 Colored Petri Nets

Colored Petri nets (CP-nets) [12] provide graphical notation typical for Petri nets, but net elements are described using high level programming language (e.g. CPN ML). They take the form of bipartite directed graph, with place nodes holding values (called *tokens*) of selected types (called *color sets*), transition nodes consuming and producing tokens, and arcs between these two kinds of nodes specifying dependencies between transitions and places, and the values on them (see Fig. 3, 4, 5, 6). A transition is *enabled* if sufficient tokens are available on its input places. Such an enabled transition can *fire* by consuming tokens along each input arc and producing tokens along each output arc. To cope with tokens of different types the inscription language uses variables and expressions typical for programming languages.

For an effective modeling CP-nets enable to distribute parts of the net across multiple subnets called modules. The result of such an approach is a hierarchical CP-net [12]. *Substitution transitions* and *fusion places* are used to combine modules. The former idea allows the user to refine a transition and its surrounding arcs to a more complex net, which usually gives a more precise and detailed description of the activity represented by the substitution transition. A fusion of places allows users to specify a set of places that should be considered as a single one. It means, that they all represent a single conceptual place, but are drawn as separate individual places (e.g. for clarity reasons).

4.3 An Approach to Malware Tracking

Let us assume we model malicious behavior of malware with the use of vocabulary applied in the theory of the Colored Petri nets. In this case, places are any nodes, files, protocols, processes or any other assets in the monitored system, transitions are any operations made on system assets, arcs are shifts that activate assets in the system, and color sets are sets of values or pointers indicating particular system assets.

Now let us assume the situation (as presented in Fig. 2) when in the monitored computer system a web browser is activated in order to visit some Internet resources (e.g. a web page). This web page contains malicious code which is downloaded to the system and then executed. After being activated it is responsible for logging user keystrokes when https sites are visited (e.g. banks) and sending registered streams to the command and control center (so called C&C). When analyzing this case it is assumed that the code of the malicious software program passed successfully rigorous verification by signature based mechanisms (an anti-virus application), was not recognized so far and is able to activate itself in the system. Firstly, a virus is setting up his presence in the system. This is called the establishing presence phase and includes downloading additional codes and commands from C&C, deactivating security metrics (switching off firewall, antivirus, other intrusion detection mechanisms and security controls). After this step, the exploit is able to execute malicious activities and disseminate itself to other systems.

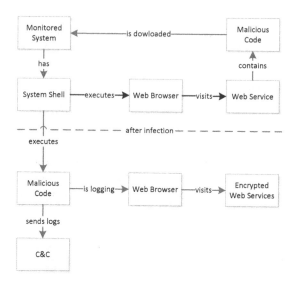

Fig. 2. Example of malicious activity

In order to follow our CP-net modeling approach and get familiar with the basis of CP-nets, one can investigate Fig. 2, which presents relationships among assets that take part in malicious activities that are run in the system. The assets such as System Shell, Web Browser, Malicious Code, Web Service, etc. are in fact places in the CP-net model. Transitions are actions realized on those system assets such as execution, logging, browsing, sending, etc. Arcs are arrows depicted in the picture. Color sets are e.g. names of registry entries, locations of files, their handlers after execution, sent data, IP addresses or domain names of C&Cs.

4.4   Utilization of CP-Net Models for Malware Tracking

Malware that is produced almost never is deployed without a obfuscation technology that hides malicious code against signature based anti-virus tools. Obfuscation is a fast and the most popular way for hackers to generate new malicious tools without much investment. These techniques cause signature based mechanisms insufficient for detecting new malicious activities. Regarding that, a new exploit which is composed of known malware executes the same functions and operations on the system. Therefore, even performed among many actually harmless actions, it is possible to detect some diverse actions like:

– operations on particular files,
– operations on registry entries,
– executed processes and applications,
– communication with specific IP addresses,
– communication with domains.

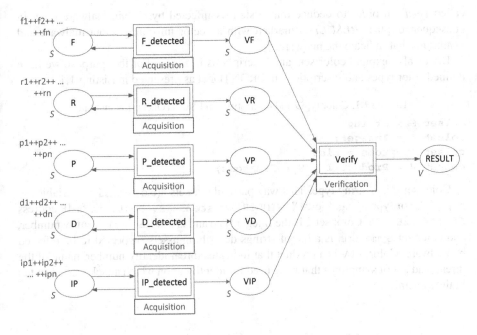

Fig. 3. CP-net model of PRONTOnet – prime module

The malware detection takes as an input a set of suspicious events received from process' hooking engine, so called PRONTOlogy, developed by authors of this article [11]. This engine is based on ontology reasoning [26], [27], [32] used for the purpose of filtering single malicious incidents among hundred thousands regular ones. These single events are passed to PRONTOnet engine for further investigation.

PRONTOnet uses CP-net models of malware and performs malware detection passing through particular places in the model, using CP-net vocabulary and characteristics. The CP-net model defined by the authors is hierarchical and has been described by four modules layers: *prime* (Fig. 3), *acquisition* (Fig. 4), *verification* (Fig. 5), and classifiers layer. A classifier module for the *Virut* malware is shown in Fig. 6.

The *prime module* of CP-net model representing PRONTOnet threat tracking tool is depicted in Fig. 3. On the left hand side of this figure there is a column of places storing tokens that represent particular assets that might be affected by malware:

- *F* – a place storing tokens indicating files;
- *R* – registry entries;
- *P* – processes;
- *D* – domains;
- *IP* – IP addresses that malware may communicate with.

The second column in Fig. 3 is composed of *substitute transitions* that are related to the *Acquisition* process depicted in Fig. 4. The next column is made up of places indicating particular assets affected by malware activated in the monitored system. Markings of these places (i.e. tokens stored in them) are processed by the substitute transition called *Verify* in order to deduce that system is infected by certain malware type. In consequence, place *RESULT* is marked with a vector informing about malware and symptoms that indicate the malware.

Let us also explain color sets and inscriptions in Fig. 3. For this purpose we have defined color types and inscriptions in PRONTOnet as presented in Listing 1.1.

Listing 1.1. Color types and inscriptions in PRONTOnet prime module

```
colset S = String;
colset I = Integer;
colset Symptoms = List S;
colset V = Product I * S * Symptoms;
```

Color set S is a string type. This way particular assets are described by variables f, r, p, d, ip of type S, e.g. file C:\[WINDIR]\System32\svchost.exe or IP address 66.232.126.195. Color set I is the Integer type and is used as threat identity number, and color set Symptoms is a list of strings describing assets suspected to be infected by malware. Color set V is a product that indicates threat identity number, name of the threat, and list of symptoms that were used for identification which attack was executed in the system.

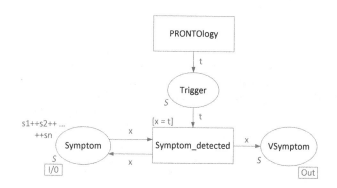

Fig. 4. CP-net – Acquisition module

Symptom acquisition process and co-operation with PRONTOlogy module is presented in Fig. 4. The module is assigned to each substituted transition from the higher level. Place *Symptom* is an input/output port that indicates appropriate places *F, R, P, D*, and *IP* from the higher level module (Fig. 3). In the *Acquisition module* tokens that represent filtered suspicious activities identified by PRONTOlogy are passed to the *VSymptom* place if the same token exists at *Symptom* place. Identified suspicious actions mark *VSymptom* place for further processing by the *Verify* transition. Marking of *Symptom* place contains all tracked elements of the monitored system, e.g. all IP addresses that the system may communicate with and download malicious software. Transition *Symptom_detected* is developed in order to test existence of appropriate token in *Symptom* place in case the *Trigger* place is marked. If compared tokens are different, the transition does not react. The conformity of tokens is required by the guard $[x = t]$. The module is also prepared to detect more than one exploit that uses the same *tricks* to switch off system security controls or even two or more malware using the same malicious code. Marking of *Symptom* place is not reduced while *Symptom_detected* transition is enabled. This module shows an important role of PRONTOlogy in detection of suspicious events and passing them to PRONTOnet module.

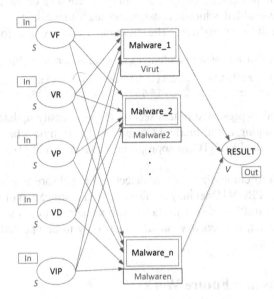

Fig. 5. CP-net – Verification module

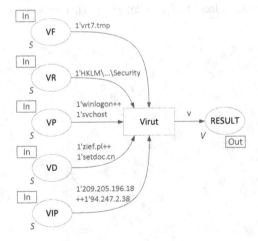

Fig. 6. CP-net – Virut module

Verification module is presented in Fig. 5. It must be noted that substitute transition *Verify* in *primary module* represents multiple transitions designed for identification of various malware types. This indicates that in particular marking of V places appropriate transition for particular malware (verification process) is enabled. An exemplary virus detection for chosen marking is shown in Fig. 6, which presents detection of malware called Virut. In the presented example, assuming appearance of the current marking, transition Virut is enabled, which in consequence leads to receiving vector v informing about detection of the Virut malware. The structure of vector v is as follows:

Listing 1.2. Structure of vector informing about detection of the Virut malware

```
1' 1 | Virut | vrt7.tmp, HKLM\...\Security, winlogon, svchost,
zief.pl, setdoc.cn, 209.205.196.18, 94.247.2.38.
```

The CP-net models presented in this section allow to easily update symptoms of a new attack by changing initial markings of places. Every time when a new malware model is entered to the PRONTOnet appropriate actualization of places markings must be realized.

It is also worth to emphasize that the detection of malware is not limited only to depicted resources. PRONTOnet may be also used to identification of exploits through analysis of network traffic and system statistics. If some resource is identified as useful for malware detection, the *primary module* needs only to be updated with additional places and transitions.

5   Conclusions and Future Work

On the basis of presented method an application for malware detection and modeling was developed. Symptoms of particular malware that form the CP-net model are edited with the use of the tool presented in Fig. 7. It offers *drag and drop* functionality which allows to add subsequent places to the model easily. This software is in the development

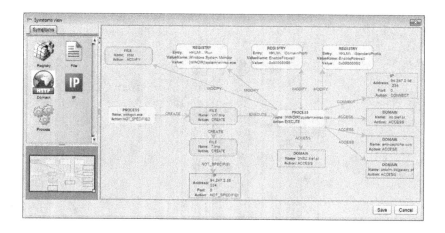

Fig. 7. Editor of malware symptoms

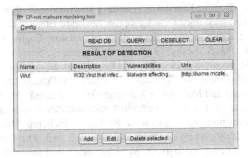

Fig. 8. Result of detection Virut malware

stage, therefore its functions are limited. Transitions are shown, currently, as operations over places. This software will be updated continuously until the end of the ongoing project in this matter at Military Communication Institute. Its results are planned to be demonstrated and tested at the nearest annual edition of NATO CWIX exercises. Nowadays this tool allowed us to detect dozens of malware. One of them is the Virut malware, the detection of which is presented in Fig. 8. A separate article about malware detection and malware modeling tool will be published after advanced tests in the malicious laboratory environment and real exercises with hostile software.

Acknowledgements. This work has been partially supported by the National Centre for Research and Development project no. PBS1/A3/14/2012 "Sensor data correlation module for detection of unauthorized actions and support of decision process", by the European Regional Development Fund the Innovative Economy Operational Programme, under the INSIGMA project no. 01.01.02-00-062/09 and by AGH University of Science and Technology internal project no. 11.11.120.859.

References

1. Aucsmith, D.: Tamper–resistant software: An implementation. In: Anderson, R. (ed.) IH 1996. LNCS, vol. 1174, pp. 317–333. Springer, Heidelberg (1996)
2. Bailey, M., Oberheide, J., Andersen, J., Mao, Z.M., Jahanian, F., Nazario, J.: Automated classification and analysis of internet malware. In: Kruegel, C., Lippmann, R., Clark, A. (eds.) RAID 2007. LNCS, vol. 4637, pp. 178–197. Springer, Heidelberg (2007)
3. Bereziński, P., Szpyrka, M., Jasiul, B., Mazur, M.: Network anomaly detection using parameterized entropy. In: Saeed, K., Snášel, V. (eds.) CISIM 2014. LNCS, vol. 8838, pp. 473–486. Springer, Heidelberg (2014)
4. Bonfante, G., Kaczmarek, M., Marion, J.-Y.: A classification of viruses through recursion theorems. In: Cooper, S.B., Löwe, B., Sorbi, A. (eds.) CiE 2007. LNCS, vol. 4497, pp. 73–82. Springer, Heidelberg (2007)
5. Borello, J.M., Mé, L.: Code obfuscation techniques for metamorphic viruses. Journal in Computer Virology 4(3), 211–220 (2008), doi:10.1007/s11416-008-0084-2
6. Cappaert, J., Preneel, B., Anckaert, B., Madou, M., De Bosschere, K.: Towards tamper resistant code encryption: practice and experience. In: Chen, L., Mu, Y., Susilo, W. (eds.) ISPEC 2008. LNCS, vol. 4991, pp. 86–100. Springer, Heidelberg (2008)

7. Christodorescu, M., Jha, S., Kruegel, C.: Mining specifications of malicious behavior. In: Proc. of the 6th Joint Meeting of the European Software Engineering Conference and the ACM SIGSOFT Int. Symposium on Foundations of Software Engineering, pp. 5–14 (2007)
8. Christodorescu, M., Jha, S., Seshia, S., Song, D., Bryant, R.: Semantics-aware malware detection. In: IEEE Symposium on Security and Privacy, pp. 32–46 (2005)
9. Flake, H.: Structural comparison of executable objects. In: Proc. of the IEEE Conference on Detection of Intrusions and Malware & Vulnerability Assessment, pp. 161–173 (2004)
10. Healy, L.: A model to study cyber attack mechanics and denial-of-service exploits over the internet's router infrastructure using Colored Petri Nets. Tech. rep. Masters Theses and Doctoral Dissertations (2009), http://commons.emich.edu/theses/218
11. Jasiul, B., Śliwa, J., Gleba, K., Szpyrka, M.: Identification of malware activities with rules. In: Proceedings of the Federated Conference on Computer Science and Information Systems, Warsaw, Poland (2014)
12. Jensen, K., Kristensen, L.: Coloured Petri Nets: Modelling and Validation of Concurrent Systems, 1st edn. Springer, Heidelberg (2009)
13. Karim, M., Walenstein, A., Lakhotia, A., Parida, L.: Malware phylogeny generation using permutations of code. Journal in Computer Virology 1, 13–23 (2005)
14. Kirda, E., Kruegel, C., Banks, G., Vigna, G., Kemmerer, R.: Behavior-based spyware detection. In: Usenix Security Symposium (2006)
15. Kolter, J., Maloof, M.: Learning to detect and classify malicious executables in the wild. Journal of Machine Learning Research 7, 2721–2744 (2006)
16. Kruegel, C., Robertson, W., Vigna, G.: Detecting kernel-level rootkits through binary analysis. In: Proceedings of the Annual Computer Security Applications Conference (2004)
17. Kumar, S., Spafford, E.: A Pattern Matching Model for Misuse Intrusion Detection. Tech. rep., Computer Science Technical Reports (1994) http://docs.lib.purdue.edu/cstech/1170
18. Lee, T., Mody, J.: Behavioral classification. In: Proceedings of EICAR Conference (2006)
19. Linn, C., Debray, S.: Obfuscation of executable code to improve resistance to static disassembly. In: Proceedings of the 10th ACM Conf. on Computer and Communications Security, pp. 290–299. ACM (2003)
20. Moser, A., Kruegel, C., Kirda, E.: Limits of static analysis for malware detection. In: Proceedings of the Annual Computer Security Applications Conference (2007)
21. Nalepa, G., Bobek, S.: Rule-based solution for context-aware reasoning on mobile devices. Computer Science and Information Systems 11(1), 171–193 (2014)
22. Nalepa, G., Ligęza, A.: Designing reliable Web security systems using rule-based systems approach. In: Menasalvas, E., Segovia, J., Szczepaniak, P.S. (eds.) AWIC 2003. LNCS (LNAI), vol. 2663, pp. 124–133. Springer, Heidelberg (2003)
23. Rad, B., Masrom, M., Ibrahim, S.: Camouflage in malware: From encryption to metamorphism. Int. Journal of Computer Science and Network Security 12, 74–83 (2012)
24. Rieck, K., Holz, T., Willems, C., Düssel, P., Laskov, P.: Learning and classification of malware behavior. In: Zamboni, D. (ed.) DIMVA 2008. LNCS, vol. 5137, pp. 108–125. Springer, Heidelberg (2008)
25. Sharif, M., Yegneswaran, V., Saidi, H., Porras, P.A., Lee, W.: Eureka: A framework for enabling static malware analysis. In: Jajodia, S., Lopez, J. (eds.) ESORICS 2008. LNCS, vol. 5283, pp. 481–500. Springer, Heidelberg (2008)
26. Sliwa, J., Gleba, K., Chmiel, W., Szwed, P., Glowacz, A.: IOEM – Ontology engineering methodology for large systems. In: Jędrzejowicz, P., Nguyen, N.T., Hoang, K. (eds.) ICCCI 2011, Part I. LNCS, vol. 6922, pp. 602–611. Springer, Heidelberg (2011)
27. Śliwa, J., Jasiul, B.: Efficiency of dynamic content adaptation based on semantic description of web service call context. In: Proceedings - IEEE Military Communications Conference MILCOM 2012, Orlando, USA, pp. 1–6 (2012), doi:10.1109/MILCOM.2012.6415810

28. Szor, P.: The Art of Computer Virus Research and Defense. Addison–Wesley Professional. Symantec Press series (2005)
29. Szpyrka, M., Jasiul, B., Wrona, K., Dziedzic, F.: Telecommunications networks risk assessment with Bayesian networks. In: Saeed, K., Chaki, R., Cortesi, A., Wierzchoń, S. (eds.) CISIM 2013. LNCS, vol. 8104, pp. 277–288. Springer, Heidelberg (2013)
30. Szpyrka, M., Szmuc, T.: Decision tables in Petri net models. In: Kryszkiewicz, M., Peters, J.F., Rybiński, H., Skowron, A. (eds.) RSEISP 2007. LNCS (LNAI), vol. 4585, pp. 648–657. Springer, Heidelberg (2007)
31. Szwed, P., Skrzyński, P.: A new lightweight method for security risk assessment based on fuzzy cognitive maps. International Journal of Applied Mathematics and Computer Science 24(1), 213–225 (2014)
32. Tarapata, Z., Chmielewski, M., Kasprzyk, R.: An algorithmic approach to social knowledge processing and reasoning based on graph representation: A case study. In: Nguyen, N.T., Le, M.T., Świątek, J. (eds.) ACIIDS 2010. Part II. LNCS (LNAI), vol. 5991, pp. 93–104. Springer, Heidelberg (2010)
33. Tokhtabayev, A., Skormin, V., Dolgikh, A.: Dynamic, resilient detection of complex malicious functionalities in the system call domain. In: MILCOM, Military Communications Conference, pp. 1349–1356 (2010), doi:10.1109/MILCOM.2010.5680136

A Proposal of Algorithm
for Web Applications Cyber Attack Detection

Rafał Kozik[1,2], Michał Choraś[1,2], Rafał Renk[1,3], and Witold Hołubowicz[2,3]

[1] ITTI Ltd., Poznań, Poland
mchoras@itti.com.pl
[2] Institute of Telecommunications, UT&LS Bydgoszcz, Poland
rafal.kozik@utp.edu.pl
[3] Adam Mickiewicz University, UAM, Poznan, Poland
renk@amu.edu.pl

Abstract. Injection attacks (e.g. XSS or SQL) are ranked at the first place in world-wide lists (e.g. MITRE and OWASP). These types of attacks can be easily obfuscated. Therefore it is difficult or even impossible to provide a reliable signature for firewalls that will detect such attacks. In this paper, we have proposed an innovative method for modelling the normal behaviour of web applications. The model is based on information obtained from HTTP requests generated by a client to a web server. We have evaluated our method on CSIC 2010 HTTP Dataset achieving satisfactory results.

Keywords: web attacks detection, web applications firewall, machine learning, data mining.

1 Introduction

Currently, providing effective cyber-security solutions for web applications is very challenging. This happens due to the fact that the commonly used IDS (Intrusion Detection System) and IPS (Intrusion Prevention System) systems have problems in recognising new attacks (0-day exploits), since these systems are based on the signature-based approach. In such a mode, when the system does not have an attack signature in its database, such attack is not detected. Therefore, there is a need to develop more sophisticated methods that are both capable of adapting domain expert knowledge [1][2] as well as emerging cyber security solutions (e.g. event correlation [3] and data mining).

The list of top 10 most critical risks related to web applications security, provided by OWASP (Open Web Application Security Project [4]) indicates "Injection" vulnerabilities as the major vulnerability. The Injection flaws, such as SQL, OS, and LDAP injection occur when improperly validated data containing malicious code is sent to an interpreter as part of a command or query.

According to the OWASP ranking, the second on the list are attacks related to Broken Authentication and Session Management. Incorrectly implemented authentication usually allows attackers to compromise passwords, keys, or session

K. Saeed and V. Snášel (Eds.): CISIM 2014, LNCS 8838, pp. 680–687, 2014.

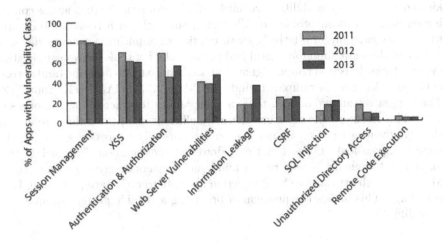

Fig. 1. The 2013 vs. 2012 and 2011 Web Application Vulnerabilities Trends(source [5])

tokens, or to exploit other implementation flaws to assume other users identities. According to Application Vulnerability Trends Report [5] the session management and authorization vulnerabilities are one of the most frequently identified problems during the last three years (2010-2013).

The XSS (Cross Site Scripting) take the third place on the OWASP list. The XSS flaws occur whenever an application takes untrusted data and sends it to a web browser without a proper validation or escaping. XSS allows attackers to execute scripts in the victim's browser which can hijack user sessions, deface web sites, or redirect the user to malicious sites.

Therefore, in order to counter those top ranked problems,in this paper we have proposed an innovative method for modelling the normal behaviour of web application. The model is based on information obtained from HTTP requests generated by client to a web server.

The remainder of this paper is structured as follows. First, we give an overview of methods for we application attacks detection. Next, the detailed method description is presented. The experiments set-ups as well as the results are presented in following section. Conclusions are given thereafter.

2   Overview of Methods for Web Application Attacks Detection

There are several tools and methods for detecting the cyber attacks targeting web applications.

Some of the frequently used tools use static code analysis approaches in order to find the vulnerabilities that may be exploited by any cyber attack. Some examples of such tools include PhpMiner II [6], STRANGER [7], AMNESIA [8]. However, as it is stated in [9], the difficulty relates to the fact that many kinds of security vulnerabilities are hard to find automatically (e.g. access control issues, authentication problems). Therefore, currently such tools are only able to automatically find a relatively small fraction of application security flaws.

One of the most commonly used and popular class of tools for web application cyber attacks detection adapts signature-based approach to describe (and detect) cyber attacks. Some examples include PHP-IDS [10], SCALP [11], Snort [12]. The biggest advantage of such tools is their ability to process huge amounts of data. This is due to the fact that there are efficient algorithms that are able to check a given piece of text against a pattern (usually expressed as PCRE [13] regular expressions) in a short time. However, the common drawback is that an expert knowledge is required to build such patters describing cyber attack. Moreover, such attacks like SQL injection are easy to obfuscate (e.g. using URL encoding). This makes the problem of providing a reliable pattern of an attack very difficult.

3 Proposed Method Overview

The proposed method overview is shown in Fig.2. It adapts a machine-learning paradigm, therefore two distinct phases are presented on the diagram. During the learning phase, the labelled data is required in order to establish the model parameters of normal application behaviour. As mentioned before, only HTTP request headers are used for model training and these need to be labelled as either normal or anomalous.

As it is shown in Fig.2 A, the HTTP requests need to be parsed in order to extract significant parts. In this approach, first the URL (e.g. https://host/users) is extracted and concatenated with the HTTP method name (e.g. GET, POST, PUT, etc.). Those two parameters are used to create a key (address) to entry in hashmap. During the learning phase, the hashmap is populated only with a normal (legitimate) HTTP request. This allows us to build a whitelist of resources that are usually requested by users via HTTP protocol. Whenever the HTTP request has parameters (e.g. parameter1=value1&parameter2=value2), it is encoded using the method described in section 3.1. However, the method produces vectors that are of different length. Therefore, to make it possible to learn a classifier, we transform this vector to histograms of constant length. The final feature vector is extended with information whenever a given request is on the whitelist or not.

During the testing phase (or when the algorithm operates in a production environment), the key is established using the same procedure as before (URL is concatenated with the HTTP method). If the HTTP request contains the parameters, it is encoded in order to produce the feature vector that is extended with information whenever a given request is on the whitelist or not. Such feature vector is recognized as normal or anomalous with the classifier learnt before.

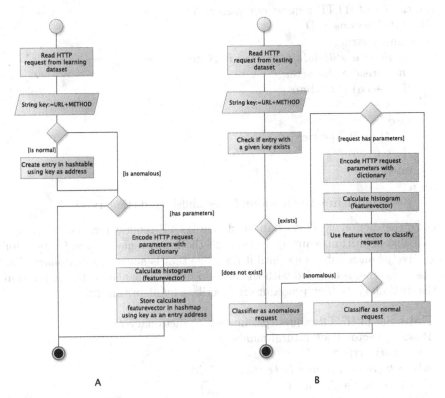

Fig. 2. The proposed algorithm (A indicates learning phase, while B indicates testing/classification phase)

3.1 Encoding HTTP Parameters

In order to encode the HTTP parameters as a feature vector, we use dictionary D that maps parts of text to a set of natural numbers (see equation (1)).

$$D : word \rightarrow \{i : i \in \mathbb{N}\} \tag{1}$$

The dictionary is established on a learning set using the algorithm (1) that adapts a modification of LZW compression method (Lempel-Ziv-Welch [14]). In contrast to the original LZW method we first establish the dictionary D during the learning phase and then encode the text (we do not extend the dictionary further when the method operates in the production environment).

The algorithm scans through the input request parameters S for successively longer substrings until it finds one that is not in the dictionary. If a given substring in not in the dictionary, then it is added and the whole procedure is repeated until the whole learning data set is processed.

Data: Set of HTTP request parameters S
Result: Dictionary D
$s =$ empty string
while *there is still data to be read in S* **do**
  $ch \leftarrow$ read a character;
  if $(s + ch) \in D$ **then**
    $s \leftarrow s+ch$;
  else
    $D \leftarrow D \cup (s + ch)$;
    $s \leftarrow ch$;
  end
end

Algorithm 1. Algorithm for establishing dictionary D

Once the dictionary D is established, the HTTP request parameters are encoded. The algorithm scans again through the input request parameters S for successively longer substrings until it finds one that is not in the dictionary. The longest substring is encoded with the natural number that indicates its position in the dictionary D. The procedure is described by algorithm (2).

Data: Set of HTTP request parameters S, dictionary D
Result: Vector V of natural numbers
$s =$ empty string
while *there is still data to be read in S* **do**
  $ch \leftarrow$ read a character;
  $V \leftarrow 0$;
  if $(s + ch) \in D$ **then**
    $s \leftarrow s+ch$;
  else
    $V \leftarrow V \cup D(s)$;
    $s \leftarrow ch$;
  end
end

Algorithm 2. Algorithm for encoding text with dictionary D

4   Experimental Set-Up

For the experiment the CSIC'10 dataset [15] was used. It contains several thousands of HTTP protocol requests which are organised in a form similar to Apache Access Log. The dataset was developed at the Information Security Institute of CSIC (Spanish Research National Council) and it contains the generated traffic targeted to an e-Commerce web application. For convenience the data was split into anomalous, training, and normal sets. There are over 36000 normal and 25000 anomalous requests. The anomalous requests refer to a wide range of application layer attacks, such as: SQL injection, buffer overflow, information gathering, files disclosure, CRLF injection, XSS, and parameter tampering.

Moreover, the requests targeting hidden (or unavailable) resources are also considered as anomalies. Some examples from this group of anomalies include client requests for: configuration files, default files or session ID in URL (symptoms of HTTP session take over attempt). What is more, the requests not having the appropriate format (e.g. telephone number composed of letters) are also considered anomalous. As the authors of the dataset explained, such requests may not have a malicious intention, but they do not follow the normal behaviour of the web application.

According to the authors knowledge, there is no other publicly available dataset for the web attack detection problem. The datasets like DARPA or KDD'99 are outdated and do not cover many of the current attacks.

5   Results

For evaluation purposes we have adapted the 10-fold cross-validation technique.

For that approach, the data obtained for learning and evaluation purposes is divided randomly into 10 parts (sets). For each part it is intended to preserve the proportions of labels (number of anomalies and normal feature vectors) in the full dataset. One part (10% of full dataset) is used for evaluation while the remaining 90% is used for training (e.g. establishing model parameters).

When the classifier is learnt the evaluation data set is used to calculate the error rates. The whole procedure is repeated 10 times, so each time different part is used for evaluation and different part of data set is used for training.

The result for all 10 runs (10-folds) are averaged to yield an overall error estimate.

In these experiments we have evaluated such classifiers as: J48, PART, AdaBoost, and NaiveBayes.

Table 1. Effectiveness for CSIC 2010 HTTP Dataset

	Detection Rate (True Positives)	False Positive Rate
Nguyen et al. [16]	93.65%	6.9%
NaiveBayes	88.89%	6.26%
AdaBoost	83.23%	15.45%
PART	93.35%	2.79%
J48	**95.97%**	**3.54%**

In Tab.1, a comparison of different classifiers is presented. Moreover, we reported the effectiveness of our method using as a baseline the approach proposed by Nguyen et al. in [16] (the authors of CSIC 2010 HTTP Dataset).

The ROC curve for different classifiers has been presented in Fig.3. It was generated with the WEKA tool [17], which varies the threshold on the class probability estimates. The best results have been observed for J48 tree classifier. It was possible to achieve a better detection rate while having lower false positive

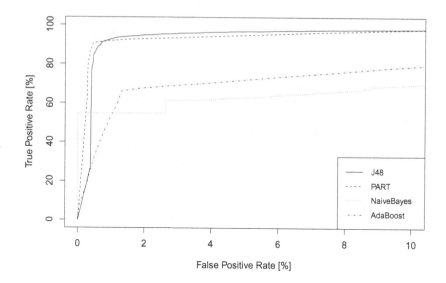

Fig. 3. ROC curve for different classifiers

rate in comparison to the method proposed by Nguyen et al. in [16]. Additional, we have used t-test to evaluate the statistical significance of the obtained results. Test showed that the results are statistically significant at 0.95 level.

6 Conclusions

In this paper we have proposed an innovative method for detecting current cyber attacks targeting web applications.

We have particularly focused on solutions that are using HTTP protocol to communicate clients with the servers. We have shown that recent cyber incidents reports prove that there is an increasing number of attacks targeting these web-based applications.

The analysis show that the attacks exploiting injection vulnerabilities are still one of the most dangerous and frequently reported by institutions gathering statistics about the network incidents.

The proposed algorithm for detecting the cyber attacks targeting the web applications relies on fact that it is more effective to model normal behaviour of an application (observing the HTTP traffic) than to produce the reliable attack signature.

We have evaluated the proposed method using CSIC 2010 HTTP Dataset. The experiments have shown that the proposed method achieves satisfactory results. Moreover, we have compared our method with method proposed by CSIC Dataset authors. We report that our method that it is able to achieve the higher detection rate while having lower false positive rate.

References

1. Choraś, M., Kozik, R., Flizikowski, A., Hołubowicz, W.: Ontology Applied in Decision Support System for Critical Infrastructures Protection. In: García-Pedrajas, N., Herrera, F., Fyfe, C., Benítez, J.M., Ali, M. (eds.) IEA/AIE 2010, Part I. LNCS (LNAI), vol. 6096, pp. 671–680. Springer, Heidelberg (2010)
2. Choraś, M., Kozik, R., Piotrowski, R., Brzostek, J., Hołubowicz, W.: Network Events Correlation for Federated Networks Protection System. In: Abramowicz, W., Llorente, I.M., Surridge, M., Zisman, A., Vayssière, J. (eds.) ServiceWave 2011. LNCS, vol. 6994, pp. 100–111. Springer, Heidelberg (2011)
3. Choraś, M., Kozik, R.: Network Event Correlation and Semantic Reasoning for Federated Networks Protection System. In: Chaki, N., Cortesi, A., et al. (eds.) CISIM 2011. CCIS, vol. 245, pp. 48–54. Springer, Heidelberg (2011)
4. OWASP Top 10 2010, The Ten Most Critical Web Application Security Risks (2010)
5. Application Vulnerability Trends Report,
   http://www.cenzic.com/downloads/Cenzic_Vulnerability_Report_2014.pdf
6. Shar, L., Tan, H.: Predicting common web application vulnerabilities from input validation and sanitization code patterns. In: 2012 Proceedings of the 27th IEEE/ACM International Conference on Automated Software Engineering (ASE), IEEE (2012)
7. Yu, F., Alkhalaf, M., Bultan, T.: Stranger: An automata-based string analysis tool for PHP. In: Esparza, J., Majumdar, R. (eds.) TACAS 2010. LNCS, vol. 6015, pp. 154–157. Springer, Heidelberg (2010)
8. Halfond, W.G.J., Orso, A.: AMNESIA: Analysis and monitoring for NEutralizing SQL-injection attacks. In: Proceedings of the 20th IEEE/ACM International Conference on Automated Software Engineering. ACM (2005)
9. Source Code Analysis Tools,
   https://www.owasp.org/index.php/Source_Code_Analysis_Tools
10. PHP-IDS project homepage, https://phpids.org/
11. Apache Scalp Project homepage, http://code.google.com/p/apache-scalp/
12. Snort project homepage, http://www.snort.org/
13. Perl-compatible regular expressions (pcre), http://www.pcre.org
14. LZW algorithm, http://en.wikipedia.org/wiki/LempelZivWelch
15. CSIC 2010 HTTP Dataset (2010),
    http://users.aber.ac.uk/pds7/csic_dataset/csic2010http.html
16. Nguyen, H.T., Torrano-Gimenez, C., Alvarez, G., Petrović, S., Franke, K.: Application of the Generic Feature Selection Measure in Detection of Web Attacks. In: Herrero, Á., Corchado, E. (eds.) CISIS 2011. LNCS, vol. 6694, pp. 25–32. Springer, Heidelberg (2011)
17. WEKA tool. ROC curve generation, http://weka.wikispaces.com/ROC+curves

Semantic Set Analysis for Malware Detection

Nguyen Van Nhuong[1], Vo Thi Yen Nhi[1], Nguyen Tan Cam[2],
Mai Xuan Phu[1], and Cao Dang Tan[1]

[1]University of Science Ho Chi Minh City,
Vietnam National University – HCMC, Vietnam
[2] University of Information Technology,
Vietnam National University - HCMC, Vietnam
{nvnhcmus,vtynhi2001,camnguyentan}@gmail.com,
mxphu@fit.hcmus.edu.vn, tan@hcmus.edu.com

Abstract. Nowadays, malware is growing rapidly through the last few years and becomes more and more sophisticated as well as dangerous. A striking malware is obfuscation malware that is very difficult to detect. This kind of malware can create new variants that are similar to original malware feature but different about code. In order to deal with such types of malware, many approaches have been proposed, however, some of these approaches are ineffective due to their limited detection range, huge overheads or manual stages. Malware detection based on signature, for example, cannot overcome the obfuscation techniques of malware. Likewise, the behavior-based methods have the natural problems of a monitoring system such as recovery costs and long-lasting detection time. In this paper, we propose a new method (semantic set method) to detect metamorphic malware effectively by using semantic set (a set of changed values of registers or variables allocated in memory when a program is executed). For more details, this semantic set is analyzed by n-gram separator and Naïve Bayes classifier to increase detection accuracy and reduce detection time. This system has been already experimented on different datasets and got the accuracy up to 98% and detection rate almost 100%.

Keywords: Data mining algorithm for classification, x86 instruction set, obfuscation techniques, malware detection, semantic set.

1 Introduction

Today, malware is deployed up faster and faster and has a variety of spreading types. According to the McAfee 2012 statistics [1], *"malware is going unabated, with no sign of slowing down"*, new malware samples in 2012 grew 50% annually over 2011. McAfee catalogs covered 100,000 new malware samples every day in 2012, which means 69 new pieces of malware per minute [1]. Moreover, the obfuscation techniques of malware are being developed more diversely and more complicatedly [2]. New malware samples not only use one obfuscation technique but also combine more techniques, such as metamorphic malware [2], which could make the difficulty to malware detection. Many malware detection methods are widely used nowadays, such

K. Saeed and V. Snášel (Eds.): CISIM 2014, LNCS 8838, pp. 688–700, 2014.
© IFIP International Federation for Information Processing 2014

as: using signature [4], using data mining for classification [4] or using behavior features [5]. Even though signature-based detection can easily classify malwares, the detection's scope is limited around the well-known malware. Data mining-based detection can simply recognize malware with the high accuracy but this system spends more time on both the training process and the detecting process. Moreover, malware detection based on data mining is in static detection type so it cannot categorize metamorphic malwares. Behavior-based detection is effective to defeat the obfuscation techniques; however, its extracting subsystem is too complicated to deploy. In addition, this method belongs to dynamic detection type so it itself has the natural problems of a monitoring system [3]. For instance, the silent malware is used VMM (Virtual Machine Monitor) detection techniques: IDT check, LDT check, MCW check or Virtual PC Special Instruction [3] to detect its executing environment that is whether virtual or not and then automatically changes to the appropriate behavior.

There are many studies of malware detection, but each of them has its advantages and disadvantages. A new detection method by using semantic set as a feature is proposed to recognize malware. Semantic set is a set of values changed on registers and variable allocated memories when program is executing. With the original hypothesis which explains that *"Two programs are similar to each other if and only if their two semantic sets are also similar to"*, therefore, semantic set is an effective behavior for identifying malware. In order to get semantic set, either a monitoring system or a smart tracer tool must be used. In this paper, authors developed an automatic tracer to overcome the limitations of the monitoring system. In the proposed system, semantic set is combined with the n-gram separator and Naïve Bayes classifier to become a more precise malware detection system, which also can detect metamorphic malware. Moreover, this system will give a new perspective on malware detection method: by using the dynamic behavior interpreted by malware's code as an input for the Naïve Bayes classifier [4]. This system will inherit their strong characteristics to be a stronger one.

This paper is organized into sections: Section 2 introduces the related studies in malware detection. Section 3 gives more detail technology about semantic set and its application in malware detection. Section 4 initiates the proposed system and its experimental results. Section 5 gives the conclusions and then introduces some future works.

2   Related Works

From time to time, the malware obfuscation techniques become more and more complicated. Fig. 1 shows the milestone of malware's camouflages [1].

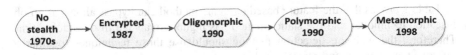

Fig. 1. The milestone of malware's camouflage

There are three general methods in malware detection: static method, dynamic method and hybrid method.

Sachin Jain and *et al.* [4] used n-hex byte as a signature to detect malware. Instead of using a common string matching algorithm, they used data mining for classifying malware. Classwise Document Frequency [4] is proposed to filter the standard n-hex bytes. It not only reduces the space of n-hex bytes but also supplies a good input for the classifier. However, this method requires more time in the training and in the detecting process, especially on big-sized sample files or big datasets. The selected n-hex bytes can help the classifier to detect malware in the ranges: well-known malwares or simple transformable malwares. With the encrypted malware or advanced transformable malware (polymorphic malware or metamorphic malware), this method is not useful.

Without using the static detection method, Mahboobe Ghiasi and *et al.* [5] developed the DyVSoR system which recognizes malware by the set of registers' values. DyVSoR uses a VMware to monitor the values of some registers as EAX, EBX, ECX and EDX when the program called API/function calls. After a monitoring time, the set of register's values is considered as an input of matching-based behavior. By experimenting, this system has the accuracy up to 96%, higher than Kaspersky [5] at that time. However, DyVSoR can be hardly used widely, because the threshold of monitoring time for a sample file is still an open problem. If the monitoring time is too short, malware cannot perform its action; in contrast, if the monitoring time is too long, it could be ineffective. Besides, the restore time after the monitoring will make the system slower. With the smart malwares, they can detect executing environment by VMM detection techniques [3] and easily change to the proper behavior. They is the death weakness (transparent problem) of any monitoring system.

The dynamic method is able to detect the obfuscation techniques of malware, which static method is unable, but the dynamic method could fail in the silent malware. To resolve that problem, Nguyen Anh M. and *et al.* [3] propose the MAVMM (lightweight VMM) system which can detect silent malware. Authors modify the core of VMM and remove unnecessary modules to perform only one objective: to monitor malware behaviors [3]. This system steps over the problems of monitoring systems and reaches some positive results. For example, the monitoring system status is quickly restored after monitoring a sample file, the monitoring time is fixed and the system is transparent to malwares [3]. Even though there are improvements, it is difficult to deploy widely in reality. Besides that, MAVMM's system needs more supports from hardware such as the virtual technology. In addition, there are some troubles when the system removes unnecessary hardware and software modules to make it more lightweight, but some malwares need network card, SD storage or user information such as email, system information, etc., to run.

Table 1 shows the advantages and disadvantages of these analysis methods in malware detection:

Table 1 proves that the feature based dynamic method can bypass almost all of obfuscation techniques and the static method has higher advantage in detection's time. Therefore, the malware detection method should use those techniques together to improve the accuracy and remove problems of the static and dynamic method. Based on the above ideas, authors developed a malware detection system that uses semantic set as a dynamic feature, and segments this semantic set into set of 3-gram values [4] as an input for Naive Bayes algorithm to quickly identify sample files.

Table 1. Comparison of malware detection system

Method	Type	Advantage	Disadvantage
3-gram hex bytes and Naïve Bayes [4]	Static detection	Quickly recognize familiar malware.	- Spend more cost on training or detecting process. - Difficult to detect advanced transformable malware.
DyVSoR [5]	Dynamic detection	Detect malware with high accuracy, including transformable malware.	- Problem of monitoring system. - Cannot overcome MM detection techniques.
MAVMM [3]	Advanced dynamic detection	Overcome the natural problem of monitoring system.	- Need supports from hardware and difficult to deploy in reality.

3   Our Approach

Before introducing to the proposed system, some basic terms are explained:

— Program has a collection of variables which always change their values when is executed. Those variables are loaded into registers or variable allocated memories to execute, then the change of their values are similar to the change of values on registers and variable allocated memories.
— Set of values changed on any register or variable allocated memory is called semantic string. The set of semantic strings is called a semantic set. The semantic set contains all changed values in a program instance. In this way, the semantic set is appreciated as the dynamic feature of the program.
— Semantic set is considered as a form of dynamic feature which can overcome the weaknesses of the traditional methods, such as hex code signature [4] or API/function call signature [6], [7]. As the result, semantic set is used as an n-gram input of Naïve Bayes classification algorithm [6]. So that, the similarity between two semantic sets are decided by Naïve Bayes classifier.

In order to become the input for this classifier, each semantic string is separated into the 3-gram [6] values (a short string contains 3 values) by 3-gram separator [6]. A set of 3-grams is often very large, therefore, it should be reduced by Classwise Document Frequency [6] to only get the 3-gram values, namely:

— The 3-gram values only appear in semantic set of malware or the 3-gram values do not appear in the semantic set of malware.
— The 3-gram values appear in semantic set of malware but their probability of frequencies is very high or very low.

After experiments, 2000 3-gram values is enough to be used as a feature for Naïve Bayes algorithm. Actually, Naïve Bayes algorithm (1) uses all 3-gram value probabilities to identify a sample file:

$$P(X|C_i) = argmaxP(C_i).\prod_{k=1}^{n} P(x_k|C_i) \tag{1}$$

Where X = {x_1, x_2, ..., x_n} and P(X|C_i) is the probability of sample X in class C_i and P(C_i) is the probability of class C_i (class C contains all attributes which needs classifying). Due to the property of multiplication, the total probability will be zero or very near zero if some 3-gram values' probability is zero or very near zero. It will cause the Naïve Bayes classifier become ineffective. In order to deal with this problem, Maximum Likelihood technique is used to increase the accuracy of semantic set system.

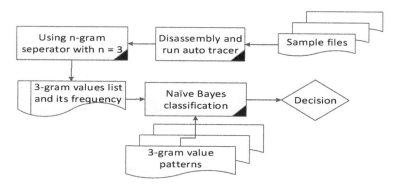

Fig. 2. Diagram of malware detection based on semantic set

The modified Naïve Bayes algorithm classifies a sample file by giving two values: the MALWARE SCORE (the similarity probability between sample file and malware file) and the BENIGN SCORE (the similarity probability between sample file and benign file). The decision function is shown in the following pseudo code:

```
if ( MALWARE SCORE > BENIGN SCORE)
        File is MALWARE.
else if ( BENIGN SCORE > MALWARE SCORE and
BENIGN SCORE - MALWARE SCORE <= WARNING THRESHOLD)
        File is WARNING.
else File is BENIGN.
```

Because semantic set is automatically extracted by a tracer tool, so it can overcome the obfuscation techniques of malware. In the following examples, we will give the examples and sequentially analyze the non-effect obfuscation of malware to the change context of semantic set.

Assuming that, there is the original assembly language code:

(1) e6   XOR ax, 0   ;ax = 0
(2) 2069 6e   XOR bx, 0   ;bx = 0

(3) 206d 6f   ADD ax, 100   ;ax = 100
(4) 2e 0d   SUB bx, 10   ;bx = −10
(5) 64 65 2e   ADD cx, ax, bx   ;cx = ax + bx = 90

The original semantic set is:

$$S_{origin} = [ax = \{0,100\} \ bx = \{0,-10\} \ cx = \{90\}]$$

In turn, the equivalent transform of the semantic set is shown through the following obfuscation techniques (in bold lines):

1 Garbage code insertion.

(1) e6   **XOR ax, 0**   ;ax = 0
(2) 90   **NOP**
(3) 45   **INC ax**   ;ax = ax + 1 = 1
(4) 50   **PUSH ax**   ;Push ax into stack.
(5) 58   **POP ax**   ;Pop ax into stack.
(6) 4f   **DEC ax**   ;ax = ax−1 = 1−1 = 0
(7) e6   **XOR bx, 0**   ;bx = 0
(8) 90   **NOP**
(9) 206d 6f   ADD ax, 100   ;ax = 100
(10) 2e 0d   SUB bx, 10   ;bx = −10
(11) 03c2   ADD cx, ax, bx   ;cx = ax + bx = 90
(12) 83e1 03   **AND dx, 0**   ;dx = 0
(13) 03c2   **ADD dx,dx,0**   ;dx = dx + 0 = 0

Semantic set with garbage code insertion is:
$S_{garbage} = [ax = \{0,1,0,100\} \ bx = \{0,-10\} \ cx = \{90\} \ dx = \{0,0\}]$. As you see, S_{origin} and $S_{garbage}$ are absolutely similar.

2 Garbage function or unused function insertion.

Garbage function or unused function insertion actually uses garbage code insertion but with a larger scale. Thanks to the above definition of semantic set, this obfuscation technique is still not affected to the original semantic set.

(1) e6   XOR ax, 0   ;ax = 0
(2) e6   XOR bx, 0   ;bx = 0
(3) 83e1 03   **AND Reg, 0**   ;Reg = 0
(4) 83e1 03   **ADD Reg, Reg, 100**   ;Reg = 100
(5) Loop:
(6) f9   **BEQ Reg, 0, (9)**   ;if Reg = 0, exit loop.
(7) 2e 0d   **SUB Reg, Reg, 1**   ;Reg = Reg −1
(8) GOTO Loop   ;continue loop.
(9) 83e1 03   ADD ax, 100   ;ax = 100
(10) 2e 0d   SUB bx, 10   ;bx = −10
(11) 83e1 03   **ADD cx, ax, bx**   ;cx = ax + bx = 90
(12) 83e1 03   **ADD Reg, Reg, 100**   ;Reg = 100
(13) e6   **XOR dx, 0**   ;dx = 0

(14) Sum:
(15) f9   **BEQ Reg, 0, (19)**   ;if Reg = 0, exit loop.
(16) 83e1 03   **ADD dx, dx, 0**   ;dx = dx + 0 = dx = 0
(17) 83e1 03   **ADD cx, cx, 1**   ;cx = cx + 1
(18) GOTO Sum   ;exit loop.
(19) 2e 0d   **SUB cx, cx, 100**   ;cx = cx −100 = 90
‿ (20) Exit   ;end

Semantic set with the garbage/unused function insertion is:

$S_{fgarbage}$ = [ax = {**0,100**} bx = {**0, 10**} Reg = {0, 100,99,98,97,...,0,100,99,98,97,...,0} cx = {90, 91, 92, 93, 94, 95,...,190, **90**} dx = {0,0,0,....,0}]

The $S_{fgarbage}$ becomes much larger than S_{origin} but the "shadows" of S_{origin} (bold instruction) still appears in $S_{fgarbage}$. So S_{origin} and $S_{fgarbage}$ are also similar.

3   JUMP insertion and register renaming.

(1) e6   XOR eax, 0   ;eax = 0
(2) eb 05   **JMP (3)**
(3) 2069 6e   XOR ebx, 0   ;ebx = 0
(4) eb 05   **JMP (5)**
(5) 206d 6f   ADD eax, 100   ;eax = 100
(6) 2e 0d   SUB ebx, 10   ;ebx = −10
(7) eb 05   **JMP (10)**
(8) 64 65 2e   ADD ecx, eax, ebx   ;ecx = eax + ebx = 90
(9) 83e1 03   AND edx, 0   ;edx = 0
(10) eb 05   **JMP (11)**
(11) Exit: ;end.

Semantic set with jump insertion is:

S_{jmp} = [eax = {0,100} ebx = {0, −10} ecx = {90} edx = {0}]. Therefore, S_{jump} and S_{origin} are also similar.

4   Equivalent code replacement:

(1) **AND ax, 0**   ;ax = 0
(2) **AND bx, 0**   ;bx = 0
(3) **ADD ax, 1**   ;ax = 100
(4) **MUL ax, ax, 100**   ;ax = ax*100 = 1*100 = 100
(5) **ADD bx,   10**   ;bx = bx −10 = 0–10 = −10
(6) **ADD cx, ax, bx**   ;cx = ax + bx = 100 − 10 = 90

Hence, the semantic set is: S_{equi} = [ax = {0, 100} bx = {0, -10} cx = {90}]

S_{equi} is similar to S_{origin}. Consequently, the equivalent code replacement technique is still not affected to the semantic set. This is a special feature, which traditional method cannot perform.

5   Combine many obfuscation techniques.

(1) XOR dx, 0	;dx = 0
(2) **NOP**	
(3) **JUMP (6)**	
(4) ADD dx, dx, 100	;dx = 100
(5) **JUMP (12)**	
(6) AND ex, 0	;ex = 0
(7) **INC ex**	;ex = ex + 1
(8) **PUSH ex**	;Push ex into stack.
(9) **POP ex**	;Get ex from stack.
(10) **SUB ex, ex, 1**	;ex = ex −1 = 0
(11) **JUMP (5)**	
(12) ADD cx, dx, ex	;cx = dx + ex = 100 − 10 = 90
(13) GOTO Exit	
(14) ADD ex, −10	;ex = −10
(15) Exit	
(16) **JUMP (14)**	

The related semantic set is: $S_{complex}$ = [dx = {0, 100} ex = {0, 1, 0, -10} cx = {90}]

This semantic set will increase the number of its strings and the number of values in each semantic string but the similarity between S_{orign} and $S_{complex}$ is still not changed. In other words, the transformable code techniques are unlikely to be affected to the similarity between two programs if their internal processing is equivalent.

6   Code encryption.

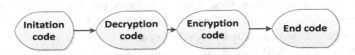

Fig. 3. Diagram of malware encryption

The malware belonging to this group has 4 basic parts as in Fig. 2. When the program is executed, the decryption part will be executed firstly to decrypt the encryption code. After that, the final program will become a normal program. This technique is used by malware to evade detection and loopholes only at runtime. Therefore, the semantic set of this program will increase some semantic strings of decryption part but the semantic set similarity between original program and encrypted program remains unchanged.

7   Malware used another technique.

Some malware opens itself only during its execution. It implements functions and prepares necessary data to execute itself. A sigmoid function is prepared to activate malware's behavior and this behavior is not shown explicitly in the executable code.

One simple example:

(1) **MOV [0x12345]**, locate_0x101;   (5) **JMP [0x1000]**; *executable code*
preparing code.   (6) **JMP [0x12345]**
(2) **MOV [0x22345]**, locate_0x102   (7) **JMP [0x22345]**
(3) **PUSH [0x1233]**, locate_0x103   (8) **JMP [0x1233]**
(4) **POP [0x1000]**

In the above code, the commands (1)→(4) prepare data (started address of the build-in functions) for commands (5)→(8) to be executed by jump commands. The semantic set includes two parts: runtime semantic strings of malware and semantic string of the preparing code. This ensures to detect successfully this malware, otherwise method based on signature such as API/function call or hex bytes cannot do.

In spite of using the same feature as DyVSoR system of Mahboobe Ghiasi [5], the proposed method has some new characteristics:

— Instead of using a VMware system to monitor the changed values of the registers after each API/function call [5], the proposed system identifies malware based on the semantic set. The modified Pyew tool [8] is used for disassembly PE (Portable executable) file. Then, all changed values on registers and variables allocated memory will be extracted automatically into semantic set by our tracer tool. In addition, DyVSor uses VMware thus increases processing time for each sample file, but the proposed system limits it.
— DyVSor only traces the values on basic registers, such as: EAX, EBX, ECX, and EDX [5] when the executed program calls API/function. This API/function call is limited by the set of API collected such as network API system, file system API [5]. Hence DyVSoR is not as general as malware detection system based on semantic set. For that reason, those kinds of malware using the external library with different API/function calls as OpenGL API, OpenCV API or encrypted API, etc., will not be detected correctly by DyVSoR system.
— Besides that, DyVSoR uses string matching algorithm [5] while the semantic set system uses Naïve Bayes algorithm to classify sample files. With the long register's value string, the matching algorithm will not work as effectively as Naïve Bayes algorithm, because Naïve Bayes only uses the features extracted from the training process instead of using all semantic string.
— In addition, the semantic set system uses the tracer (running as an interpreter) to extract the semantic set. Thus, it can control the executing of a program and easily prevent the threat action of malware without recovery time like the DyVSoR system. Moreover, the tracer is independent so it can be integrated into other systems.

In summary, the proposed system used semantic set as an input for Naïve Bayes classifier. Therefore, this system can inherit the advantages of the semantic set and Naïve Bayes filter. The system has already been experimented on common datasets and got the high accuracy.

4   Implement and Experimental Result

4.1   Implementation

In order to compare semantic set method with equivalent malware detection methods, the datasets which have the same ratio in number of files and type of files are used:

Table 2. Experimental dataset

Dataset number	Num. of files	Type of file
Dataset 1 [7]	85 files	10 Benign, 21 Virus, 34 Worm, 20 Trojan.
Dataset 2 [5]	155 files	20Backdoor, 20 P2Pworm, 20 Trojan, 20 Worm, 20 Virus and 55 Begin.
Dataset 3 [4]	107 files	51 Malware, 56 Benign
Dataset 4 [6]	79 files	18 Benign, 61 Malware

Besides, those datasets are chosen because of two other reasons:

— Firstly, the datasets include all common very dangerous and many variant malware's types such as: worm, backdoor, trojan, virus and benign files belonging to Windows32 system files.
— Secondly, the number of samples in the datasets for the semantic set system and these methods such as API Graph [7], DyVSoR [5], n-hex byte Naïve Bayes [4] and Structure and Behavior features [6] are similar in ratio. A list of selected malwares is shown in Table III.

Table 3. Clasification of sample's type in each dataset

No.	Name of sample file	Classification
1	P2P-Worm-Win32.Agent	Worm
2	Backdoor.ASP.Ace	Backdoor
3	Backdoor.PHP.Agent	Backdoor
4	Trojan.Win32.KillFiles	Trojan
5	Virus.Win32.Delf	Virus
6	Virus.Win32.Seppuku	Virus
7	Worm.Win32.Downloader	Worm
8	Worm.Win32.Viking	Worm
9	System32 folder	Benign

4.2   Experimental Result

Table 4. The evaluation parameters table

No.	Parameter	Meaning
1	TP	The amount of malware files are recognized as malware.
2	FP	The amount of benign files are recognized as malware.
3	TN	The amount of benign files are recognized as benign.
4	FN	The amount of malware files are recognized as benign.
5	Accuracy	(TN+TP)/(TN+TP+FN+FP)
6	Detection rate	TP/ (TP + FP)

To evaluate the accuracy of the SSSM system, the above parameters are used (Table IV). After that, the datasets mentioned in Table III has been tested, the accuracy of malware detection system is shown in Table V:

Table 5. Detection result of malware detection system based on semantic set

Dataset	Evaluation	Accuracy	Detection rate
1	TN = 9, FN = 1, TP = 75, FP = 0	98.82%	100%
2	TN = 49, FN = 6, TP = 100, FP = 0	96.12%	100%
3	TN = 50, FN = 6, TP = 51, FP = 0	94.39%	100%
4	TN = 17, FN =1, TP = 61, FP = 0	98.73%	100%

The result proves that our malware detection system has ability to detect most of malware samples in datasets. The detection rate reaches 100% and accuracy is up to approximately 98.82%.Therefore, this new method should be paid more attention to by anti-malware researchers. These precision charts reveal the detection result of our method that compares with API/function Graph, DyVSoR system, n-hex byte Naïve Bayes and Structure and Behavior feature system.

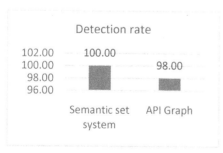

Fig. 4. The detection rate of semantic set system and API Graph system

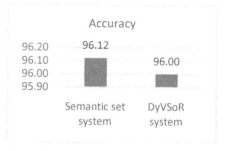

Fig. 5. The accuracy of semantic set system and DyVSor system

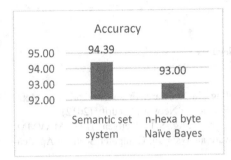

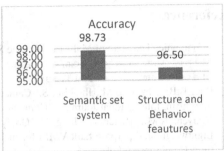

Fig. 6. The accuracy of semantic set system and n-hex byte Naïve Bayes

Fig. 7. The accuracy of semantic set system and Structure and Behavior features system

In addition, the system is able to detect some kinds of malware that are difficult to others. For example, Backdoor.ASP.Agent and Backdoor.PHP.Ace are two malwares that cannot extract API/function call list. As a result, API Graph method [7] cannot be used for them, but semantic set system is able. Moreover, the system can detect the complicated malware as: Worm.Win32.Downloader which has many variations.

5   Conclusion

Today, malwares are deployed faster and faster and their metamorphosis is more and more complicated. Nevertheless, the current detection methods together with some advantages are still limited, so an effective method to classify malware and to be able to overcome the limitations of the current methods becomes more demanded. We propose a new method for malware detection that combines semantic set as a dynamic feature with Naïve Bayes classifier to increase detection accuracy. In addition, the simulating and extracting the malware behavior by our tracer tool help the detection system reduce the detection time and get rid of the effect of malware behavior to system. Further, our system was experimented on different datasets and gained highly accuracy, which provides a new aspect for anti-malware researchers.

In order to improve the accuracy and realize the semantic set system, some future works are listed:

1. Integrate semantic set with other methods to create a new malware detection that can detect malware on a large scale and high precision.
2. Improve system's performance by combining between parallel CPU and GPU programming in order to build a real-time system for malware detection.
3. Develop tracer tool to be a debugger that extracts values on registers and variable allocated memories more and more exactly and therefore increases the reliability and exactness of malware detection system.

References

1. Infographic: The State of Malware, McAfee Security (2013), http://www.mcafee.com/us/security-awareness/articles/state-of-malware-2013.aspx
2. Rad, B.B., Masrom, M., Ibrahim, S.: Camouflage in Malware: From Encryption to Metamorphism. International Journal of Computer Science & Network Security (2012)
3. Nguyen, A.M., Schear, N., Jung, H., Godiyal, A., King, S.T., Nguyen, H.D.: MAVMM: Lightweight and purpose built VMM for malware analysis. In: Computer Security Applications Conference (2009)
4. Jain, S., Meena, Y.K.: Byte Level n–Gram Analysis for Malware Detection. In: Venugopal, K.R., Patnaik, L.M. (eds.) ICIP 2011. CCIS, vol. 157, pp. 51–59. Springer, Heidelberg (2011)
5. Ghiasi, M., Sami, A., Salehi, Z.: DyVSoR: Dynamic Malware Detection Based on Extracting Patterns fromValue Sets of Registers. The ISC International Journal of Information Security (2013)
6. Alazab, M., Layton, R., Venkataraman, S., Watters, P.: Malware detection based on structural and behavioural features of API calls. In: The Proceedings of the 1st International Cyber Resilience Conference (2010)
7. Elhadi, A.A.E., Maarof, M.A., Osman, A.H.: Malware Detection Based on Hybrid Signature Behavior Application Programming Interface Call Graph. American Journal of Applied Sciences (2012)
8. Pyew Python tool, https://code.google.com/p/pyew/
9. Virus heavens Snapshot, https://archive.org/details/vxheavens-2010-05-18

Author Index